MAKING SENSE OF LAW FIRMS

Strategy, Structure and Ownership

MAKING SENSE OF LAW FIRMS
Strategy, Structure and Ownership

Stephen Mayson

Hildebrandt Professor of Legal Practice and Director of the Centre for Law Firm Management, Nottingham Law School

BLACKSTONE
PRESS LIMITED

First published in Great Britain 1997 by Blackstone Press Limited, Aldine Place, London W12 8AA.   Telephone 0181-740 2277

© Stephen Mayson, 1997

ISBN: 1 85431 700 8

British Library Cataloguing in Publication Data
A CIP catalogue record for this book is available from the British Library

Typeset by Style Photosetting Ltd, Mayfield, East Sussex
Printed by Bell & Bain Ltd, Glasgow

CONTENTS

PART II   THE THEORY OF THE LAW FIRM   91

PART III LAW FIRMS AS BUSINESS ORGANISATIONS 171

Preface

I have been trying to make sense of law firms for about 20 years, as a lawyer, as a manager, as a consultant and as an academic. I have (I confess) struggled at times. I was quickly able to see what usually worked and what did not. It took me longer to understand *why*.

Lawyers frequently ask for guidance in running their practices — often, they just want to be told what to do. But if the intended outcome does not follow, they (and their advisers) need to understand why. Indeed, even if the intended outcome *does* follow, I believe that they still need to understand why so that successes can be repeated and passed on to others in the practice.

There have been many books and articles setting out what can be done in managing a law office, but so far little about why it does or does not always work — or about what else might be tried. This book is my attempt to fill that gap. As such, it deals rather more with underlying principles, frameworks and analysis, though the consultant in me will not allow me to ignore practicalities. In this sense, I would hope that it could be read alongside Hildebrandt and Kaufman's *The Successful Law Firm*, and Maister's *Managing the Professional Service Firm* and *True Professionalism*, and that, between us, we provide a full range of theoretical and pragmatic views of law firms.

I am therefore setting out to achieve the following:

(a)   To describe and apply to the special environment of a law firm that part of the wealth of management thinking and theory that I have found particularly enlightening and helpful. Is doing this, I endeavour to put into practice Peter Drucker's injunction to the knowledge worker to 'connect' (*Post-capitalist Society* (1993), pages 174–6), that is, to 'mobilize the multiple knowledges we possess' and to 'use knowledges as part of one toolbox'. Instead of dividing problems into distinct areas that represent, for example, law, economics, management, and finance, and avoiding those with which we are not familiar, we must learn to connect them and so see both the forest and the trees.

(b)   To introduce and explain some theory of my own about the strategy, structure and ownership of law firms. In doing this, I acknowledge that I am building on the work of others, but I am not aware that anyone else has tried to weave the various elements together into a coherent 'theory of the law firm'.

(c)   To provide in a single source the wherewithal to understand the complete range of a law firm's activities. To do this within a manageable scope, I have necessarily not covered some topics in the depth that they might otherwise deserve. And I must stress that the emphasis is firmly on *understanding* more than *doing*: this is not an owners manual that will always contain the answer to a specific issue (though I hope that it will at least identify the right questions). To bring a number of concepts together without too much repetition, I have been generous in cross-references between paragraphs so that, wherever a reader might dip into the text, other supporting material can more easily be located. I hope that these references do not prove too distracting for those trying to work their way through the text.

(d)   To provide a core text for those trying to come to terms with the diversity of issues affecting law firm management, whether as managing partners, employed managers, MBA students, or the merely curious.

Very often, reactions to consultants' suggestions or academics' analyses are, 'That's obvious' or 'It's just common-sense'. I have no problem with these reactions (except to wonder why, if so much is obvious or common-sense, more lawyer's don't *do* it!). This book is my exploration of possibly familiar issues, with my own explanation and interpretation of them. I am reminded of the following lines from 'Little Gidding' in T. S. Eliot's *Four Quartets*:

'We shall not cease from exploration
And the end of all our exploring
Will be to arrive where we started
And know the place for the first time.'

The skilled part of law office strategy, structure and ownership is not having the right answers, but knowing enough to be able to pose the right questions.

There have been a number of influences that have brought me to many of the approaches or conclusions set out in this book. First, two personal debts. Going back more than 25 years, Bill Hurd first awakened my interest in business and entrepreneurialism: he taught me a great deal without him (or even me, at the time) realising. More recently, my former partner Brad Hildebrandt has given enlightenment and support and, in the process, made me a much better consultant. Second, two analytical debts. Charles Handy, in *Understanding Organizations*, opened my eyes to organisational theory and provided some tools that allowed me to make sense of what I could see happening in law firms. And then Karl Erik Sveiby and Tom Lloyd, in *Managing Knowhow*, confirmed for me that my view of law firms as know-how businesses was not misguided. It would be very difficult to live up to the example set by these influences. I have tried, and gratefully acknowledge the personal and intellectual debt that I owe them.

A number of people have contributed to this book — usually without knowing it! Since 1985, I have advised hundreds of law offices, and interviewed thousands of partners, other fee-earners, support staff, and clients of lawyers. I thank them all: they have all in some way shared my thinking and experience of law firms. Their opportunities and problems have been the anvil that has fashioned many of my views. My former partners at Hildebrandt undoubtedly accelerated that process, too.

In 1991, I conceived the idea of an MBA in Legal Practice. Translating that vision into reality took four years and the efforts of many people. The development and delivery of the degree encouraged me both to widen and sharpen my thoughts on many aspects of law office strategy, structure and ownership. I am deeply indebted to Sally Woodward, and to the other tutors (Oonagh Mary Harpur, Simon McCall, Chris Stoakes and Barry Dean), for their tireless support, encouragement, enlightenment, and contribution. Their thoughts have also shaped mine. I also willingly acknowledge the enthusiastic participation and high expectations of our MBA students — 80 in the first three years of the programme, senior practitioners drawn from all areas of legal practice and from all over the world. Their response to the principles of law firm management was the final spur for me to start typing.

Until recently, project management and legal practice would not have been considered natural bedfellows. Now, for some lawyers, project management is a way of life. Stuart Benson was one of the pioneers. Without his foresight and enthusiasm, chapter 21 of this book would not have been written. I thank him particularly for the privilege of working with him on project management in litigation. I also thank my colleagues Peter Jones and Ian McLachlan for their help with the original material from which that chapter is drawn.

I must also thank two others in the Centre for Law Firm Management without whose support this book would not have seen the light of day. Mark Taylor helped trace some of the more obscure materials, and he and Andrea Hines have organised the work of the Centre in such a way that I have been able to devote the necessary time to the final research and writing (as well as carrying on with my consulting work).

Even when the manuscript was finished, much work remained to be done. I should also therefore like to thank Peter Cox for his electronic conversion of the figures and diagrams. Congratulations and gratitude are due to the team at Blackstone Press who have been able to prepare this book for publication within six months of me first setting pen to paper — or at least fingers to keyboard! I should particularly like to thank Alistair MacQueen (who has been a constant supporter and friend throughout my writing and consulting career), Heather Saward and Derek French (whose eagle-eyed editing saved me from many infelicities of explanation and language), and Ray Constant (for the typesetting).

Finally, thanks to my father who, all those years ago, first discouraged me from sloppy thinking, and to both of my parents for their constant and

and continuing support. But the greatest sacrifice has been made by my family — Julie, Chris and Lucy — and the greatest debt is therefore owed to them. Without their love, and their tolerance of my often prolonged absences when consulting, teaching or writing, nothing would have been possible, and what has been achieved would not be worthwhile.

Stephen Mayson
16 June 1997

Introduction

"Books are where things are explained to you; life is where things
aren't. I'm not surprised some people prefer books.
Books make sense of life. The only problem is that the lives
they make sense of are other people's lives, never your own."
(Barnes 1984, page 168)

I am no longer surprised when a partner says of my observations or advice
about a law firm, "That's all very well for big firms, but . . .", or "That
might work in the City, but . . .", or "Surely that's only relevant to a
small, general practice", and so on. My trying to make sense of law firms
is interpreted as making sense of someone else's firm but not the one in
question. This contradiction of seeking help but then denying the relevance or value of the help offered is one that every consultant to law
firms will recognise.

It does us good to be reminded of this scepticism from time to time.
For it reminds us of something that is fundamental: management is a
messy business. There are no immutable rules; there are no guaranteed
formulae; there is not, in short, a *science* of management. But there is an
art, or a craft; and there are some things that seem to be true more often
than not, and that seem to be workable or unworkable more often than
not. We need to know and understand what these are.

Law firms often receive a bad press from commentators and consultants about their management. But I have a simple question: if law firms
and their partners are so bad at management, how have so many law firms
been so successful for so long? Yes, life may have been difficult between
1990 and 1995, and a few firms did go under. But others remained
remarkably successful, and achieved significant growth and development
during the same period. I have a sneaking suspicion (and a vested interest
in suggesting) that firms may have succeeded in spite of themselves, rather
than because of themselves, but I know that that would not be entirely
true. However, I do believe in the need for strong, independent legal
advice, and that this requires a strong business foundation on and through
which to provide it. This book is therefore (I hope) a medium through
which law firms can understand themselves better, become stronger and

better managed, and which can lead to them being successful because of their strengths, rather than incidentally or accidentally.

Law firms *are* a different form of business organisation, and so all the general rules of management do not necessarily apply. But they are not so significantly different in all respects that there are no guiding principles or frameworks. This book is my attempt to make sense of law firms by drawing together the principles and frameworks that I have found applicable and helpful in trying to advise law offices. Some of the selection is necessarily idiosyncratic, and there will probably be far more in here than the average partner (perhaps even managing partner) will ever need. But I am a great believer in tool boxes. Who knows what you might need in the tool box for the next messy problem that arises?

There are four principal themes running through this book. First, there is a fundamental economic and social shift towards knowledge. The Industrial Age is coming to an end, and the Information Age is in its infancy. The legal profession as we know it today, and law firms as we recognise them, are a product of the Industrial Age. I believe that it is not too outrageous to suggest that the solicitor's profession is founded on a particularly strong feature of the Industrial Age — the idea of property rights. Solicitors devote much of their professional energy to creating, transferring, preserving or protecting rights to real, personal, intellectual and reputational property. As the Information Age emerges, the importance of many of these property rights will decline. I do not believe that the legal profession as we know it will survive this transformation. However, I am convinced that legal practice will continue, albeit in a form that many would not today recognise (or accept). For this new form to emerge, the other themes will be crucial.

Second, law firms are know-how businesses. Like much of today's enterprise, the creation, organisation, economics and productivity of knowledge will determine success or failure. The way in which knowledge and experience is combined and used will require more variety and innovation than many lawyers have been used to. This will also challenge law schools and others who train lawyers to provide a broader and more useful process of professional learning.

Third, the ability of lawyers to be entrepreneurial will be a key part of the survival of legal practice. The boundaries of what the Industrial Age has determined as 'legal' are changing. Competition between lawyers, and between lawyers and others, is increasing dramatically. New forms of legal practice are emerging and will become acceptable — incorporated practices, multinational practices, multidisciplinary practices and multi-talented practices. They will need entrepreneurs to create, lead and manage them.

Finally, a secure and sustainable future will be achievable only with a change in attitude and behaviour. Priorities must change. Productivity cannot go on increasing without a cost to personal and organisational stability and sanity. Too many lawyers in practice today mourn a lost world — an age when there was time for clients and for each other, and for a life of their own beyond the office. All they look forward to is retirement. Professionalism and the idea of a 'calling' to professional service is under threat. The law, the legal profession, law firms and individual lawyers are in distress (see Sells 1994). But law firms are not alone in this; many organisations have become soulless places that inspire very few. I share Secretan's view (1997, page 19):

"In its current form, dedicated as it is to the cult of the personality, the modern organization is heading for an evolutionary dead-end. On the other hand, no other sector of society could do as much to bring about the positive changes that would uplift the human spirit. The reinvented modern organization has the global reach, influence, talent, knowledge, assets, and the technology to make the world a better place through service to humanity. More than any other group in society, it has the potential to reclaim higher ground and inspire the soul."

This will no doubt be too 'soft' for some action-oriented, hard-nosed lawyers and business people. But the 'higher ground' to which Secretan refers is "built on trust and integrity" (1997, page 68). Anyone in a business today that is not built on trust and integrity does not deserve to stay in business (and probably will not). There is nothing soft about that. And I dare say that many would recognise and share the message of the senior partner (admittedly a fictional one) who said to his partners: "There is much anger in this room, much hastiness, much fear. And I think that you have forgotten, those of you who ever knew, what it means to be partners. It means that you meet adversity together. A partnership is an institution of great strength, when the partners stand together. But it is weak and pitiful when they war with each other" (Willett 1996, page 89). This book is also, therefore, about understanding how to create a reinvented, modern law firm as a strong institution built on a foundation of trust and integrity.

Not everyone will agree with the messages in this book; and not all of the frameworks, principles and suggestions will immediately appeal. The saying, "You can lead a horse to water . . ." comes to mind. This is my pond: drink as often, and as deeply, as you find life-sustaining and refreshing!

PART I

LAW FIRMS AS A RESPONSE TO THE ENVIRONMENT

Chapter 1

UNDERSTANDING THE ENVIRONMENT

1.1 Introduction

Law firms are not 'closed' organisations, immune from what is happening around them. For the most part, they have to react to the needs of clients. These clients might want to acquire something they did not have before (such as land, a building, goods, a business, employment); they might want to seek compensation or restoration in respect of a wrong they have suffered; they might need protecting from the claims of others; and so on. Law firms have to wait for most such clients to come to them with work to be done. Law firms are fundamentally affected by the activities of their clients: they are truly 'open' organisations — open to the vicissitudes of the environment in which they practise law.

Making sense of law firm strategy and management is therefore dependent on being able to understand the environment in which they operate. And this environment has changed in many significant ways during the last quarter of the twentieth century. As a result, the legal profession has changed, too.

The purpose of this opening chapter is to chart the most important of these developments, to outline and illustrate the transformation that has taken place, and so to suggest those features of the environment that are most likely to influence the practice of law as we approach the next millennium.

1.2 The Social Environment

Since the early 1970s:

(a) The population of the United Kingdom has become larger — up by some 2.5 million people (4.5%) to 58.4 million — and older — 16%

of the population are 65 or more years old (Office for National Statistics 1996, table 2.3).

(b)   The population has become more diverse — there are now more than 3 million people from ethnic minority groups (Office for National Statistics 1996, table 2.4).

(c)   Life expectancy has increased, to 74.3 for a man, and 79.5 for a woman (Office for National Statistics 1996, table 15.1).

(d)   The number of natural deaths has decreased, and the male death rates from heart disease, lung cancer and strokes have declined (Office for National Statistics 1996, tables 2.2 and 15.2).

(e)   People are more affluent — real disposable household income has increased by nearly 90% (Office for National Statistics 1996, table 9.1).

(f)   The number of marriages is declining, and the number of divorces has more than doubled (Office for National Statistics 1996, tables 2.9 and 2.10).

(g)   There are nearly three times as many students enrolled full-time in higher and further education (Office for National Statistics 1996, table 14.7).

(h)   The number of holidays taken abroad has increased by 650% (Office for National Statistics 1996, table 13.12).

(i)   The number of notifiable offences increased by 70% between 1981 and 1994 (Office for National Statistics 1996, table 10.2).

This snapshot of the last quarter-century shows that we now have more people, living longer, doing more, expecting more, and needing more. Age and affluence both affect what people are doing, in terms of health care, investment and leisure activity. The ability to move home more often, to acquire second homes, to take more (and more expensive) holidays in different locations, to spend money on consumer goods, and so on, all affect potential needs for legal services. Better education and a more diverse population both affect the expectations that clients have of the delivery of legal services. People become less tolerant of the 'mystique' with which professional advisers historically sought to cloak their craft.

However, at a time when the population is both more likely to need legal services, and on the face of it better able to afford them, crisis in public-sector funding and dramatic increases in lawyers' fees have combined to remove all but the very rich and the very poor from access to justice. This polarisation in access is reflected in a polarisation in provision which I shall explore in paragraph 1.4.

1.3   The Economic Environment

1.3.1   *General*

The UK economic picture of the past 25 years has been a mixed one. But despite recessionary dips in the early 1980s and the early 1990s, gross domestic product (i.e., the measurement of UK domestic output, including indirect taxes on goods and services) has continued to grow in real terms, and reached £700,890 million at current prices in 1995 (Office for National Statistics 1996, table 4.1). Average earnings are now approaching £17,500 a year (Office for National Statistics 1996, table 9.3). The number of working women has increased by about 30%, although total employment has remained almost constant: figure 1.1 shows the employment trends dramatically — including the recessionary dips.

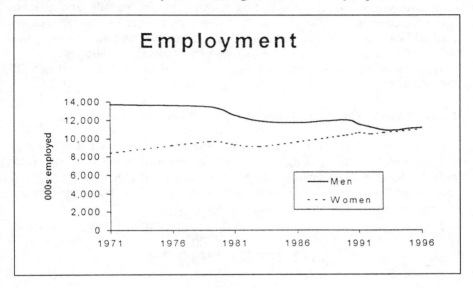

Figure 1.1 (Source: Office for National Statistics)

Overall, unemployment has increased from 500,000 in 1971 to around 2 million (having reached nearly 3 million in 1993), and the proportion of economically active men has declined. It would seem that men have borne the brunt of the shifts in the economy over the last quarter-century (these shifts are explored in paragraph 1.3.2). And the percentage of the population living on less than half the average income has almost doubled from 11% to 21% (Office for National Statistics 1996, table 9.10).

According to Companies House figures, the number of limited liability companies in the UK more than tripled between 1970 and 1995; combined with the increase in the number of unincorporated businesses, this represents almost exponential growth in the size of the business market for legal services.

In the global economy, growth in the industrialised economies is slowing down — halving from about 4% a year in the 1970s to 2% in the 1990s. In the European Union, the Maastricht targets for monetary union are leading to fiscal tightening. Conversely, the Asian economies are growing rapidly (by an average of about 8% a year), as are those in Latin America (at about 4% a year). Financial capital now flows more freely around the world than at any time since 1945. Economic liberalisation, privatisation programmes and changes in technology are also leading to increasing demand for equity capital. Direct corporate investment and acquisitions, as well as portfolio investments in bonds and equities (for example, by pension funds), are resulting in a smaller role for the banks in the transfer of capital.

At the same time, the world economy is being globalised and affected by the extension of free trade and the advance of telecommunications: the world is a much more competitive place than it used to be and many types of businesses are busy substituting technology for people and places. Indeed, according to *The Economist*, "any activity that can be conducted through a screen and a telephone . . . can be carried out anywhere in the world" (*A Survey of the World Economy* (28 September 1996), page 34). Perhaps lawyers should reflect on how much of their work is — and could be — conducted through a screen and a telephone!

1.3.2   *The emergence of the knowledge economy*

For a number of years now, the commentators have agreed that there is a fundamental shift taking place in the economies of the advanced industrialised nations around the world. Superficially, it appears to be a shift away from manufacturing towards services (as the UK employment pattern shown in figure 1.2 clearly shows).

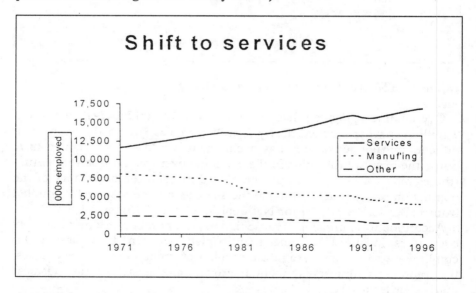

Figure 1.2 (Source: Office for National Statistics)

However, closer analysis shows that manufacturing production is not declining, even if the numbers employed in manufacturing are: manufacturing output per person employed increased by 21% between 1990 and 1996 (Office for National Statistics 1997, table 1.8). What is happening is the introduction of information technology. In manufacturing, new automated production techniques allow the same (or greater) productivity to be achieved with fewer people — the car industry is a prime example of this.

But it is not restricted to manufacturing. There has been a shift to services, but the more fundamental shift has been to knowledge. This shift has been described by management gurus and commentators such as Drucker (1993), Handy (1989 and 1994), Toffler (1994), Peters (1992), Stewart (1977), Davidson and Rees-Mogg (1977), and de Geus (1977). They are all describing the same thing.

At some considerable risk of oversimplifying, let me characterise the traditional approach to management as 'capitalist'. This approach was developed out of the typical business which combined owners' capital with the resources required to create the business product. These resources were property, machinery, and often extensive but relatively cheap labour. To make these resources productive, control of them and their processes was necessary, and management hierarchies were created. Early quality systems also required control at each stage of production. The dominant asset in this type of business was financial capital, which was owned by the investors. The business was therefore controlled by the providers of finance.

Better education and considerable advances in information technology have transformed our business community. Both have been applied to labour-intensive industries such as agriculture and manufacturing, as well as to service industries such as banking and fast food. The fundamental shift that has taken place is that businesses have become much more knowledge-based, relying on fewer, better-educated people, often using technology. Such businesses have to invest heavily in training, motivating and rewarding people.

The structural complexity of many traditional management hierarchies slowed decision-making and reaction to the marketplace to a crawl. This debilitation allowed the emergence of many successful entrepreneurs in the 1980s. Today's problems are not solved by hierarchy and control. Large companies have been bypassing or destroying hierarchy in order to survive: witness the wholesale shake-out of middle management in so many businesses in the 1990s recession. As a result, management theory and practice are now concentrating on flatter management structures, networking, less control and more empowerment, less centralisation and more distribution of responsibility. The dominant asset is no longer financial capital, but knowledge, or intellectual capital. And this dominant asset is not owned or controlled by the providers of financial capital (the traditional owners). We have moved to the 'post-capitalist' era, and owners and managers have to think and behave differently.

Indeed, Drucker (1993), Handy (1989) and Toffler (1994) write not simply of a change in the economics of society, but of a change in society itself. Drucker explains (1993, pages 1–3 and 6–7):

"Every few hundred years in Western history there occurs a sharp *transformation*. . . . Within a few short decades, society rearranges itself — its world view; its basic values; its social and political structure; its arts; its key institutions. Fifty years later there is a new world. . . .

We are currently living in such a transformation. It is creating the post-capitalist society. . . .

We are clearly still in the middle of this transformation — indeed, if history is any guide it will not be completed until 2010 or 2020. But it has already changed the political, economic, social and moral landscape of the world. . . .

The new society — and it is already here — is a post-capitalist society. It surely, to say it again, will use the free market as the one proven mechanism of economic integration. It will not be an 'anti-capitalist society'. It will not even be a 'no-capitalist society'; the institutions of capitalism will survive though some, e.g. banks, may play quite different roles. But the centre of gravity in the post-capitalist society — its structure; its social and economic dynamics; its social classes and its social problems — are different from those that dominated the last 250 years, and defined the issues around which political parties, social groups, social value systems, and personal and political commitments crystallized.

The basic economic resource — 'the means of production' to use the economist's term — is no longer capital, nor natural resources (the economist's 'land'), nor 'labour'. *It is and will be knowledge.* The central wealth-creating activities will be neither the allocation of capital to productive uses nor 'labour' — the two poles of nineteenth- and twentieth-century economic theory, whether Classical, Marxist, Keynesian or Neo-Classical. Value is now created by 'productivity' and 'innovation', both applications of knowledge to work. The leading social groups of the knowledge society will be 'knowledge workers' — knowledge executives who know how to allocate knowledge to productive use — just as the capitalists knew how to allocate capital to productive use; knowledge professionals; knowledge employees. . . .

The *social* challenge of the post-capitalist society will, however, be the dignity of the second class in post-capitalist society: the service workers. Service workers, as a rule, lack the necessary education to be knowledge workers. And in every country, even the most highly advanced ones, they will constitute a majority."

This theme was also emphasised by Reich (1991). He examined the make-up and income distribution of the US workforce. His analysis suggested that knowledge workers (whom he called 'symbolic analysts': pages 177 to 180) accounted for 20% of the total workforce (page 179). Handy labelled this group the 'fortunate fifth' on the basis that the top fifth had a higher after-tax income than all the other four-fifths combined (1994, page 202). Similarly, in the UK in 1994/95, the after-tax income of the top fifth of households was more than twice the national average and more than six times that of the bottom fifth (Office for National Statistics 1996, table 9.6).

Handy also explains the characteristics of intelligence as an economic asset — characteristics that will form part of a continuing theme throughout this book (1994, pages 24–5):

"Intelligence is the new form of property. Unfortunately, it does not behave like any other form of property, and therein lies the paradox. It is, for instance, impossible to give people intelligence by decree, to redistribute it. It is not even possible to leave it to your children when you die. You can only hope that there is some of it in their genes. Of course, there is education — which becomes the crucial key to future wealth — but it is a key which takes a long time to shape and a long time to turn. The situation gets odder. Even if I do manage to share my intelligence or know-how with you, I still keep it all. It is not possible to take this new form of property away from anyone. Intelligence is sticky.

Nor is it possible to own someone else's intelligence. Peter Drucker is right — the means of production can, in practice, no longer be owned by the people who think they own the business. It is hard to prevent the brains walking out of the door if they want to. . . . Intelligence is a leaky form of property.

An added complication is that intelligence is extraordinarily difficult to measure, which is why intellectual property seldom appears on balance sheets. But this also makes it difficult to tax, unlike any other form of property, which makes any form of wealth or property taxation ineffective. Intelligence is tricky, as well as sticky and leaky.''

Considerable economic and social consequences arise from this fundamental shift, which many of today's leading thinkers are addressing. If information and knowledge is so important to today's economies, how do we measure and value it? How do we best develop it? Close to the heart of this book, how do law firms best develop strategies for the selling of intelligence (or 'know-how') and the management of 'knowledge workers'? The message of this section is that lawyers are not alone in these enquiries: perhaps for the first time in many years, the commercial and economic imperatives of legal business are very similar to the commercial and economic imperatives of other businesses.

1.3.3 The world of clients

These economic changes cannot leave the business world of lawyers' clients unchanged. Social changes affect the demand for goods and services, and global competition is altering the structure and competitiveness of many domestic industries, too. The continuing advances in technology are leading to the substitution of technology for people, and creating new services and new demands (such as the Internet). Increasingly, clients compete not only in a physical marketplace, but also in a digital 'marketspace' (see Rayport and Sviokla 1994).

These changes mean that the world of clients is one of an increasingly global market, with increasing competition, combined with a need to respond to advances in technology, cut costs, and improve productivity. It is not surprising that they are reflecting some of these pressures in their dealings with their legal advisers. They are also flattening their management hierarchies, and 'empowering' employees to act at the point of contact with customers and suppliers.

1.4   The Professional Environment

1.4.1   *Background*

The past 20 years have seen significant changes to the legal profession in this country, and to legal professions in other parts of the world. Indeed, there has possibly been more change in the past two decades than in the two centuries before them. Understanding these changes in the professional environment of law firms is therefore as important for strategy and management as understanding general socio-economic changes.

I shall be concentrating my commentary on lawyers in private practice. I am doing this for two reasons: first, most lawyers in this country are in private practice; and secondly, law firms are the principal focus of this book.

1.4.1.1   *Loss of legal skills*

Until relatively recently, lawyers served predominantly private clients. They transferred their property, wrote their wills and administered their estates, litigated personal claims, and defended their liberty, property and reputation. Little did we realise that the sweeping changes of the 1925 property legislation, introduced to "facilitate and cheapen the transfer of land" (according to the terms of reference of the committee charged with the review that led to the 1925 legislation), in fact sowed the seeds of the destruction of parts of the legal profession in the 1980s. Over the years, the transfer of land has been much simplified, proceduralised and computerised. The birth of the post-war property-owning democracy ensured that considerable numbers of properties changed hands regularly. Domestic conveyancing became a cash cow, milked by the legal profession for all it was worth. As the years went by, the legal component of most conveyancing was reduced to negligible levels. The lawyers involved in it were gradually losing their legal skills. It did not matter to them — they were making more than enough money as conveyancing clerks.

Then people began to realise that this monopoly was not in clients' best interests. The scale fees, based on the value of the property, did not reflect the work required to execute the transfer. Clients were paying over the odds for what in most cases had become an administrative service. The abolition of scale fees, and the advent of licensed conveyancers, started a cut-price conveyancing war. Prices were slashed to a point where profit margins were tight, and previously secure and comfortable livings were in jeopardy. Solicitors opened estate agencies, and estate agents and conveyancers started working together under the same roof in the hope of keeping the cash cow producing. The recession changed all that. The property market has all but dried up. Between 1988 and 1989 alone, the value of conveyancing transactions fell by £28 billion (Jenkins 1992, paragraph 6.4) — and that was just the start of the decline. National chains of estate agents have been sold off, and hundreds of offices closed. The work that kept so many conveyancers busy has disappeared. In 1995, the number of residential property transactions was at its lowest level for

10 years, and represented roughly 50% of the number of transactions in 1988 (Lewis 1996, paragraph 6.13). Thousands of deskilled lawyers found themselves with little or nothing to do and nowhere else to go. Many of them will now have left the profession for good. This may also be reflected in the closure of more than 3,200 offices of law firms between 1988 and 1995 (see Jenkins 1994, table 3.5, and Lewis 1996, table 3.6).

At the same time, another stalwart of private practice — probate work — was also suffering. The number of probates issued on personal applications has increased every year since 1989, while the number issued on application by solicitors has declined since 1991 (Jenkins and Lewis 1995, table 6.26, and Lewis 1996, table 6.22).

1.4.1.2 Losing out to others

While all this was going on, two other developments were having an equally profound effect on the future of the profession. In the first place, these private clients that most lawyers were content to confine to domestic conveyancing were becoming better educated, more sophisticated, richer and more mobile. They needed and looked for advice on personal tax, estate planning, investment, pensions and insurance. Too many lawyers were too busy transferring property to realise that this work was going to accountants, banks and other parts of the financial services industry. It was only when new financial services regulation drew attention to these activities, and coincided with more competition for conveyancing work, that lawyers started thinking about regaining lost ground. Not surprisingly, few clients now think of lawyers as their first port of call for general financial advice. Lawyers were simply starting from too far back in a highly competitive market to make much headway. As a consequence, less than 1% of the profession's gross fees are earned from financial advice (Lewis 1996, paragraph 6.25).

In the second place, though, another cash cow was coming along nicely. The 'economic miracle' of the 1980s was turning existing business clients into commercial melting pots, and private clients into entrepreneurs. All over the country, commercial legal practice was growing at a phenomenal rate. The sheer volume of commercial activity and the consequent need for legal advice overshadowed the traditional areas of legal practice — property and litigation. As with conveyancing, much of this new advice often had little to do with law. It involved business deals or financing. Mergers, takeovers and acquisitions, Stock Exchange flotations and company bonds, property developments, and lending secured on business assets like ships and aircraft became common transactions. Certainly, there was an underlying legal and regulatory framework to all of these transactions, and there was a need for increasingly specialised legal advice in competition law, tax, employment law, and the like. But these elements represented a small part of the lawyers' function. Lawyers were spending more and more time with merchant bankers, venture capitalists, accountants and other professionals dealing with aspects of 'legal' practice for which their traditional, academic (and even vocational), training had not prepared them. It is not perhaps surprising that many clients and other professional advisers thought that some lawyers were remote and did not truly understand their businesses or the factors that drove them to make a commercial decision one way or another.

1.4.1.3   Winds of change

In 1989, the government published a Green Paper on *The Work and Organisation of the Legal Profession*. One of the early statements in the Green Paper (paragraph 2.1) was that: "Most services which are 'legal' . . . may also be performed by non-lawyers" — notice "most", not "some". This is an extraordinary conclusion — but true. There are now few monopolies in this country, and law is no exception. Most of the work that lawyers do is not, in truth, legal, and could be done by someone else.

What this all amounts to is considerable potential for competition for the provision of legal services in this country: competition from professionals other than lawyers, and competition between lawyers themselves (this theme is taken up again in paragraph 38.4). Corporate legal departments now handle work that they might once have sent outside; they can even instruct counsel direct without going through a solicitor. Members of the Bar give specialist legal advice that might just as easily be given by a specialist solicitor. Solicitors can apply for rights of audience that will lead them into direct competition with barristers for advocacy work. And, of course, there is now intense competition between law firms for a limited amount of client work that might legitimately go to any one of them.

1.4.2   Growth in size

The need to provide increasingly complex and specialised commercial legal advice, and to invest in training and technology to improve the efficiency and quality of legal services, has led to enormous growth in private law firms. In 1986, there were about 57,000 fee-earners in private practice (of whom almost 39,000 were qualified); 10 years later, this had risen to just over 78,000 (of whom almost 54,000 were qualified) — an increase of nearly 40% (Lewis 1996, paragraph 4.2). In fact, the number of solicitors has more than tripled since 1966, and more than doubled since 1976 (Lewis 1996, paragraph 2.2). In 1986, the largest law firm in this country would have had about 300 lawyers; 10 years later, the largest firm had more than 1,300 (Legal Business 1996).

The total number of people employed in law firms reached an all-time high in 1996 at just under 170,000 people, including qualified lawyers, other fee-earners, and support staff (Lewis 1996, paragraph 4.2). What the Law Society's figures show, however, is that the victims of the recession in the early 1990s were non-qualified fee-earners and support staff. From a previous peak of 168,423 in 1990, the profession had by 1993 shed more than 4,250 people in total; indeed, between 1989 and 1994, law firms lost nearly 8,500 support staff. But throughout this period, the number of qualified lawyers in law firms continued to rise year by year. (An alternative explanation, of course, could be the greater use of desktop technology by lawyers, leading to the substitution of capital for labour: it may be too early yet to know whether this is a better intepretation of the figures.)

Most of the growth in the profession is attributable to the number of women qualifying as lawyers: figure 1.3 shows how the numbers of male solicitors has remained relatively stable, while the proportion of women has increased significantly (see also Skordaki 1996).

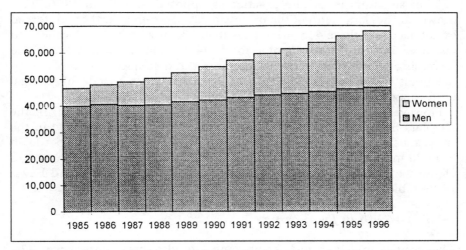

Figure 1.3 (Source: Jenkins and Lewis 1995, paragraph 2.3 and Lewis 1996, paragraph 2.3)

The number of law firms has also continued to increase, from 9,755 in 1992 to 10,119 in 1996 (see Lewis 1996, table 3.6). As well as increasing in number, law firms have also been increasing in size, as figure 1.4 shows.

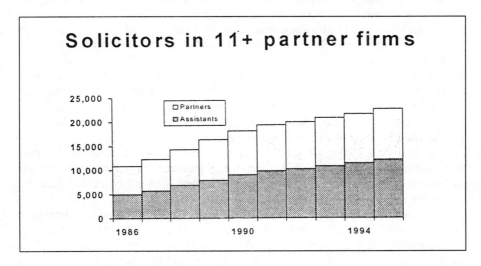

Figure 1.4 (Source: Annual Statistical Reports 1987–1990, and Lewis 1996, table 5.8)

During the 10 years covered by figure 1.4, the number of large firms (for this purpose, meaning those with more than 10 partners) has increased from 321 to 415 (94 more firms), but the number of solicitors in them has more than doubled from 10,836 to 22,574 (Marks 1987, table 7.8 and Lewis 1996, table 5.8). The average size of these firms has therefore increased from 34 solicitors to 54, and they now account for 42% of solicitors in private practice as opposed to 28% in 1986. This growth at the 'large' end of the professional spectrum is further reinforced by the fact that these 415 firms (less than 5% of all law firms) generated just over 56% of the fee income for 1994/95. This growth is leading to increasing polarisation between the largest and smallest law firms — to the point where it probably no longer makes sense to talk of '*a* legal profession'.

However, the 'birth rate' of these large firms is slowing down. In the six years from 1984 to 1990, 102 firms moved into the category; in the six years from 1990 to 1996, the number increased by only 15 (down from 20 in 1994 and 1995 — reflecting the consolidation through merger of some of the largest firms in 1996 (Marks 1987, table 7.4 and Lewis 1996, table 3.14).

1.4.3   *Growth in fee income*

The growth in law firms' fee income has also been impressive. The domestic market for law firms was worth nearly £7 billion in 1994/95 (Lewis 1996, paragraph 5.4): this was three times its volume in 1984/85, and nearly double its volume for 1987/88 (cf. Harwood-Richardson 1991, paragraph 5.4). By any stretch of the imagination, this is considerable growth for a profession that has just been through its worst-ever recession! In addition, the UK legal profession also generated more than £500 million of earnings from overseas (Lewis 1996, paragraph 6.12).

Legal Business (1996) suggested that 50 firms in this country have fee income in excess of £20 million, with six of them at more than £100 million, and the largest (Clifford Chance) at around £280 million (of which one-third is thought to come from its foreign offices: Legal Business 1996, page 6). Many of these firms do not just practise out of one location: they are multinational enterprises with offices in almost every part of the globe where serious business activity takes place. At these levels, the practice of law is big business.

It is also clear from the Law Society's annual figures that large firms not only generate more fee income (as one would expect simply as a result of having more fee-earners), but that the largest also generate significantly more fee income per fee-earner (see figure 1.5).

However, these apparently impressive figures hide a more worrying consequence. The fee income of law firms has gone up, but the number of fee-earners has also increased. As a result, productivity (measured as average fee income generated by each fee-earner) has not kept pace *in real terms*, to the point where the productivity of fee-earners in the largest firms — those with more than 25 partners — is £11,000 less in 1994/95

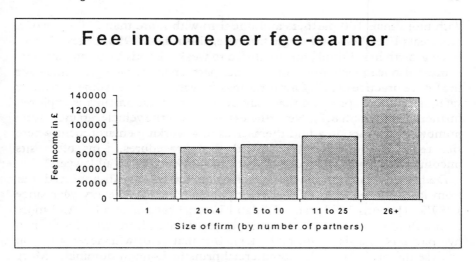

Figure 1.5 (Source: Lewis 1996, table 5.8)

in real terms than in 1990/91 (Lewis 1996, tables 5.6 and 5.8, and taking the retail price index as the measure of inflation: the solicitors' index of inflation gives a £12,000 decline).

Perhaps more worrying for the Lord Chancellor and the public purse, however, is law firms' increasing dependence on legal aid payments. Over five years, these payments have almost doubled to a little over £1 billion. In 1989/90, legal aid payments to law firms accounted for 9.4% of gross fee income; by 1994/95, they accounted for 14.9% (Lewis 1996, paragraph 7.10: as Lewis points out, if one assumes that the firms with more than 25 partners received no legal aid payments, the percentage for the rest of the profession leaps to 25.5%). Further, in 1989/90, 1,126 law offices (7.2% of the total) received legal aid payments of more than £100,000 a year; by 1995/96, this had risen to 2,869 (20.5% of the total) (Lewis 1996, table 7.7 — with the acknowledgement that these figures have not been adjusted for inflation). No wonder the Lord Chancellor's Department is concerned!

1.4.4 New challenges

This growth in the size of the profession, the size of firms, and the volume of the market, has led to lawyers having to treat the practice of law as a business. Unfortunately, lawyers have not traditionally been trained to deal with the consequences of this. They start with no experience of business. Inevitably, the management role has fallen on the partners in law firms, most of whom were not prepared for the mantle or responsibilities of the ownership and management of multi-million-pound businesses. Until 1967, all partnerships were restricted in size to 20 partners. From a management perspective, and from the point of view of collegiality and loyalty between partners, there was a lot of sense in this restriction. But it was removed for law firms, and there are now about a dozen firms with more than 100 partners and one firm with more than 230 — two, if one treats Eversheds as a single firm (Legal Business 1996, pages 12–13). Such growth has, I think, inevitably led to weaker bonds between partners. It must also lead us to question whether partnership is the right vehicle for the future practice of law. Law firms may now incorporate (subject to many safeguards), and for some that may be a better solution (this is explored further in paragraph 8.7). Nevertheless, whatever the vehicle, an increasing number of lawyers now find themselves in a working environment where size requires cooperation, teamwork and procedures. This often sits uncomfortably with the independent, maverick streak in all lawyers.

Do not go away with the idea that small practices have disappeared. Far from it — the number of sole principals has increased every year since 1989/90 (Jenkins 1994, table 5.7, and Lewis 1996, table 5.8). And more than a third of solicitors in private practice work in firms with fewer than five partners (Lewis 1996, table 4.1). But that said, whichever way you analyse the profession, the commercial firms in London dominate. More than a quarter of all law firms are based in London, but they generate a half of the profession's total fee income (Lewis 1996, tables 3.10 and 5.12). The 10 largest firms in London together employ just under 10% of all solicitors in private practice. The profession is undoubtedly polarising with large commercial practices at one end of the spectrum and small, general practices at the other and becoming increasingly vulnerable.

Nevertheless, one of the features of the past 10 years has been the increasing prominence of large regional firms. Whereas almost half of the largest firms (more than 25 partners) are centred in the City of London (49 firms out of 111 in 1996), there are almost as many large firms (with more than 10 partners) in the North West, Yorkshire and Humberside (65 firms) as there are in the City of London (70 firms) (Lewis 1996, table 3.17). Further, the growth in gross fees, and in average fees per fee-earner, of firms in the North and Wales has impressively outstripped that in London (Lewis 1996, table 5.12). These firms are changing the landscape of domestic legal services, although so far they have made little significant impact in international practice.

Competitiveness generally between law firms has noticeably increased in recent years. However, law firms are now facing competitive threats from foreign law firms, and we are seeing the emergence of multinational practices (58 in 1996: see Lewis 1996, table 3.3). At the same time, the largest accounting firms are establishing their own legal practices, adding to the competitive threats coming from non-traditional sources.

With all this change, partnership is also being redefined. Partners are more inclined to move from one firm to another, to join foreign law firms, and to set up alongside the accountants. This mobility, combined with the economic difficulties of the early 1990s, is rewriting the timing and conditions for admission to partnership, and undermining the collegiality on which many firms have historically been built. However, despite this mobility and the increased number of women entering the profession (see paragraph 1.4.2), the partnership prospects for women continue to lag behind those of men, as figure 1.6 shows.

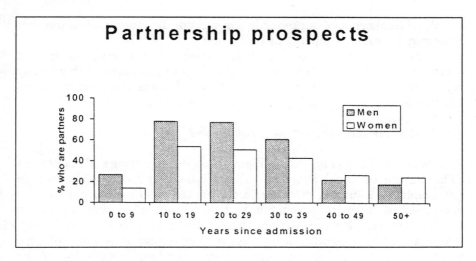

Figure 1.6 (Source: Lewis 1996, table 2.10)

It would seem that women have to spend a very long time in the profession if they want to stand a better chance than men of becoming or remaining partners!

1.4.5 Changing economics

As a result of growth and other developments, law firms have had to invest in more staff, new and more expensive premises, and new technology. All have added considerably to the costs of practising law. This has changed the economic perspective of lawyers. It has been possible for some years now to calculate how much an hour it costs to keep a lawyer behind his or her desk. As a result, lawyers have come to be assessed on how much an hour they can bring into the practice. A variance either way is likely to have financial consequences to the lawyer concerned.

Indeed, the profession took the process a stage further and started charging clients by the hour. In retrospect, a reliance on hourly charging was probably the single largest error of the profession in its recent history. When performance and fees are assessed on this basis, it is inevitable that lawyers will try to create as many chargeable hours as possible. Here is a system that rewards the inefficient, the ignorant, and probably even the downright incompetent. Client satisfaction and service can become secondary issues. In some firms, the evolution of legal practice from profession to business simply went too far. Professional values of putting the client first, maintaining collegiality and loyalty to one's colleagues, and behaving ethically towards other lawyers became less important to some than the pursuit of money. By adopting business techniques and outlook, a law firm does not cease to carry on a professional activity, though some firms seem to have forgotten this. The most consistent and successful firms in the 1990s will be those who remember that the practice of law is both a business *and* a profession, keeping an eye on the economics and supply of legal services but never losing sight of the ethics and values that underpin a strong, independent profession.

At the moment, the cost of legal services is too high. Despite a recession, too many lawyers still expect clients to pay considerable hourly rates, without exploring ways in which their firms can become more efficient in the delivery of legal services. This cannot continue.

1.4.6   A restructuring of the profession?

At this point, I am going to anticipate a little the message of chapter 38 (The Future of Legal Practice). The productivity figures discussed in paragraph 1.4.3 suggest that there are more lawyers than there is work to keep them all busy and profitable. If there is presently excess capacity in the legal marketplace, then there has to be some sort of a shake-out. There has to be a significant increase in the volume of all types of legal work or a reduction in the number of lawyers, and an improvement in the quality of those who remain. There is some anecdotal evidence that in the financial year 1996/97 more law firms are busier than they have been for some years, but this is not yet universal to the profession and we must wait to see whether it is sustained (and whether or not the increased activity improves both productivity and profitability).

The driving force behind future changes will, in my view, be clients — bearing in mind that the Legal Aid Board is also a client for these purposes, albeit monopsonistic. Clients will refuse to pay what they regard as unreasonable fees which bear no relation to the value of the services or benefit they receive. They want value for money. If we start from the premise that the cost of legal services is too high, then either the cost must go down and the income expectations of lawyers must likewise go down, or the client's perception of the quality and value of the services must rise. Not surprisingly, lawyers have been devoting a lot of activity to the quality issue, but for some total quality management is giving way to total quality despair as they realise the enormity of their task and recognise that most clients take quality for granted *and* still expect lower fees. I believe that clients are still willing to pay good money for valuable legal services. But in order to achieve this we must redefine what constitutes 'legal' work to be performed by 'lawyers'.

I have little doubt that those aspects of legal practice that have become simplified and proceduralised will no longer routinely be handled by lawyers in private practice. So, for example, conveyancing, wills and the administration of estates will probably be handled by banks and other financial services institutions. They may decide to employ solicitors, but they will not need to and it will probably be cheaper not to. In addition, there will be more complex personal advice that also will not ordinarily be provided by lawyers in private practice, such as tax advice and estate planning. This will also be provided by accountants, banks and other financial services businesses. In the main, law firms will not be able to compete with the national networks, economies of scale and marketing capabilities of these competitors.

Some specialist private client lawyers may well be able to retain a small following of wealthy individuals who are looking for highly complex advice connected with, for example, landed estates or family businesses. It is also likely that continuing changes in the economics of legal practice will mean that very few of those who continue as private client lawyers will be found within commercial law firms.

Even within private practice, the need for greater efficiency in the provision of legal services will mean that some things presently done by qualified solicitors and legal executives will be performed by so-called 'paralegals' — graduate employees with no formal legal qualifications, but having the ability to deal with the routine and administrative aspects of legal work at lower cost. Once this reallocation of legal work has taken place, many lawyers who are currently handling those activities will be left with nothing to do, unless they are prepared to reallocate themselves to legal executive or paralegal roles at lower rates of pay. Solicitors with expectations of high incomes will not earn them by being conveyancing clerks or mere scribes recording business transactions or personal decisions in over-elaborate language. These activities do not add value — if anything, they are necessary evils for which clients will pay as little as possible.

What will then be left is *real* work for *real* lawyers: work that adds value to clients' activities and can only be performed by lawyers. But let us not misinterpret what this means. Clients will not value only technical expertise in the law. They need that expertise tailored to their particular business or personal circumstances. That requires experience as well as technical ability; it means understanding the client's business operations and industry; it means being able to communicate with the client about practical decisions as well as legal analysis. I am talking about a level and type of seniority and know-how that takes some years to develop, and that adds value in the client's eyes.

Unfortunately, the average age of solicitors has dropped significantly in recent years as more and more graduates have been attracted to the profession by high salaries and the supposed glamour of commercial and international legal work. In 1996, the average age of solicitors was estimated at 40, and more than 50% of all solicitors in private practice were under that age (Lewis 1996, paragraph 2.5). The 'grey-hair factor' is in short supply. With a decline in the sort of work that can keep the less experienced busy, a large proportion of the profession is at risk. However, looking further ahead, time is on the profession's side. Demographic changes in the population will lead to fewer young people entering the job market. Redundancies in the profession in the 1990s, and a consequential lowering in the attractiveness and in the financial rewards of being a lawyer, will reduce the numbers further. Together, these will combine to produce a more experienced profession in 10 years' time that may be better able to cope with the increasingly sophisticated demands being placed on it.

1.4.7 *Anglo-American comparisons*

The picture that I have painted in this chapter of the structure of the legal profession in the UK, and of the changes and pressures to which it has been subject, mirrors almost exactly the picture that would be painted for the US legal profession. Galanter and Palay (1991) consider changes in the structure of the US legal profession between 1960 and 1985. Their research is invaluable, and provides many significant insights into modern legal practice in the United States — even though it covers a period which ended more than 10 years ago.

Galanter and Palay describe a transformation — drastic changes in the US legal profession as part of a dramatic expansion of the scale and scope of the legal world. These changes encompass (1991, pages 37 to 45):

(a)   the amount and complexity of legal regulation,
(b)   the frequency of litigation,
(c)   the amount and tenor of authoritative legal materials,
(d)   the number, coordination and productivity of lawyers,
(e)   the number of clients and the resources they devote to legal activity,
(f)   the amount of information about law and lawyers, and the velocity with which it circulates.

They argue that these changes reflect the surrounding economy and society. For any given law firm, these changes are constituents of the environment — external, given, and not readily influenced. They are part of the ecology of legal practice. But as firms in the aggregate adapt to their surrounding conditions, changes in their number, size and activities then contribute to further changes in the environment for legal services.

Key to this transformation has been the emergence of the 'large law firm', now resulting in a bifurcated or polarised structure to US legal practice organised around different kinds of clients (1991, page 1). Large firms tend to represent large organisations (corporations, unions, government, etc.), and others represent individuals; the divide is rarely crossed (Heinz and Laumann 1982, page 319, referred to by Galanter and Palay 1991, page 1).

Galanter and Palay analyse the emergence of the 'large law firm': what is 'large', they accept, is a variable description that has much to do with the size of the largest firms at any given time relative to others in the marketplace (1991, page 2). They seek to define the characteristics of such a firm, starting from a base in the 1960s (which they describe as "the golden era": 1991, page 20). The large law firm, in their view, emerged with a number of distinctive features (1991, pages 4–9):

(a)   *Its work:* the work of a large firm shifted from contentious to non-contentious (and the lawyer moved from advocate to business adviser), became more specialised, and required new kinds of knowledge; in particular, the proliferation of information (including but not limited to reported cases) meant that specialists were not able to practise without access to the books and research that a large firm was better able to afford, collate, keep up to date and make available.

(b)   *Its clients:* more and larger corporate clients chose the more specialised environment of a large firm, as did other organisations —

specialisation by client as well as by legal area arose. Because of clients' diverse needs for specialists, in a large firm clients came to be regarded as belonging to the firm rather than to an individual lawyer.

(c) *Its partners:* the sharing and common ownership of clients translated itself into an entire practice shared by the partners as opposed to a partnership being a loose association of lawyers sharing premises and facilities (this is a distinction I describe and discuss in detail in chapter 9 between a partnership of 'integrated entrepreneurs' and a partnership of 'individual practitioners').

(d) *Its assistants:* assistants in a large firm were chosen for their excellence and were nurtured; in return, they were expected to make a full commitment to the firm.

(e) *Its support systems:* a large firm's offices became more businesslike, and it made full use of new office technologies (many of which were needed to cope with the proliferation of printed materials that in turn required protracted research, extended advice, and the accumulation of sizeable client files). Curiously, the large firm environment also led to a decrease in meetings with clients, leading to the "destruction of the personal and intimate relation, leaving only that which is purely professional" (Strong 1914, page 385, quoted by Galanter and Palay 1991, page 7).

The credit for combining these features into the concept of the large law firm is usually attributed to Paul Cravath (of New York's blue-chip — or 'white-shoe' — law firm, Cravath Swaine & Moore). The combination resulted in firms in which a large number of highly specialised lawyers were divided into departments or work groups, and were in fact subjected to a hierarchical environment (in the sense that a firm would recruit good, young lawyers and subject them to training, supervision and review before deciding whether to elevate them to partnership).

What Galanter and Palay identify here is the 'up-or-out policy', in which the young lawyers strive to become partners or, if they do not, almost inevitably seek opportunities elsewhere. They rename this process the 'promotion-to-partnership tournament' (1991, page 10): indeed, they regard this tournament as the core of the large firm. The combination of this tournament with the need to maintain leverage (that is, the ratio of non-partner fee-earners to partners) tends to lead to exponential growth, as each new promotion to partnership requires the addition of new recruits to refuel the tournament's combatants. As a result, large firms need either to reorganise themselves to support ever-larger increments of growth, or to reorganise themselves to suppress growth. This part of Galanter and Palay's analysis is discussed in paragraph 3.6.

Growth also changes the character of law firms. Informality recedes as partners and others begin to know each other less well — professionally as well as socially. Collegiality gives way to structure. Notions of public service and professional independence are often marginalised. The "imperative of growth collides with notions of dignified passivity in obtaining business" (1991, page 3). (Many lawyers see the imperative to develop new business as a result of changed economic circumstances — particularly the recession of the early 1990s. Galanter and Palay's thesis might suggest that lawyers have exacerbated that economic imperative by combining into ever-larger firms with so many more mouths to feed. Chicken or egg?)

Some people regarded large firms as 'a factory' — "something at odds with the professional traditions of autonomy and public service. It catches not only the instrumentalism, but the systematization, division of labor, and coordination of effort introduced by the large firm" (1991, page 18). However, say Galanter and Palay, the scope, specialisation, teamwork and continuity that the large firm afforded its clients became the model for what legal representation should be like. It has certainly been borrowed not only by growing law firms in private practice but also by corporate legal departments, government legal departments, boutique or niche firms, and others. In fact, this growth and 'bureaucratisation' of law firms has made many of them begin to resemble other, large, business organisations.

Chapter 2

LAW FIRMS AS ORGANISATIONS

2.1 The Analysis of Businesses

2.1.1 The state of the literature

The literature about business strategy, organisation and management has mushroomed in recent years, as has the attention paid to service businesses as a distinct organisational form. The purpose of this literature is to help us understand the structure, operations and options available. We hope to gain better or deeper insights, to learn from others' analysis and experience, and to avoid reinventing the wheel.

Unfortunately, some of the most popular 'gurus' writing about management have been charged with introducing fads and changing their minds regularly; in other words, they are short-termist, contradict each other, and provide no enduring or underlying theory. But then there are some serious commentators who do not expect a management science to be developed, and do not want one to be, either (see, for example, Sull 1997).

As a result, there is a wealth of academic literature and a wealth of pragmatic literature. Not all of it is relevant to law firms or applicable to their environment, structure or nature. But much of it is, though some requires rather more effort to apply it. Nevertheless, the range of just the relevant and applicable literature remains bewildering. This book is an attempt to identify and apply some of it, and to introduce some new models of my own. Its objective is to remove some of the bewilderment, and to make the available literature more accessible.

I therefore start in this chapter by introducing some of the more enduring and helpful models that can help lawyers and the managers of law firms begin to understand their organisations in the same terms as those who own and manage other types of organisation. These models have been chosen because they can be applied to a law firm, and because they have proved useful in practice.

2.1.2   Dimensions of analysis

There are many different levels, or dimensions, of business analysis. For example, at the broadest level, business organisations operate within a certain environment. This can be analysed according to its political, economic, social, and technological dimensions (the so-called PEST analysis). For law firms, we might add a professional dimension. Next, there is the organisational level, and one can analyse a firm's functions in terms of production, distribution, marketing, finance, people, and so on.

Business organisations exist to carry out various business processes, so that next one can analyse an organisation's operations or processes — the processes by which it turns its resources and raw materials into products and services. In order to do this, it will require individuals to perform certain tasks: at the narrowest level, therefore, one can analyse jobs (or roles) and the people who perform them.

So we have the environment, the organisation, business processes, and individuals and jobs. These different levels are all addressed in this book, together with the points at which each of them interfaces with the others.

2.1.3   The use of models and frameworks

The point of analysis may vary in different circumstances, and the appropriateness of frameworks and models will therefore be contingent on the circumstances. But generally, the purpose of using a model or framework is to provide a better understanding of the situation, organisation or issue to be considered; to identify or provide a checklist of the content or issues in a given set of circumstances; or to lead to better decisions and a better understanding of their likely consequences. Models and frameworks can be used for different purposes, and in assessing and using them it is important to understand what they were designed to achieve. They all have limitations.

There are, then, three purposes for models or frameworks, leading to three categories:

(a)   to provide an aid to understanding: these are *descriptive* models;

(b)   to help the diagnosis of a situation, and to assess options and their implications: these are *analytical* models;

(c)   to determine a decision or course of action: these are *prescriptive* models.

These different purposes lead to different structures of models and frameworks: some are pictures or diagrams; some are charts or tables; some are flowcharts; some are analogies; some are verbal. Different styles and structures appeal to different people; not all will appeal to everyone, and not all will be appropriate. Whichever models or frameworks are used, and whatever the reason, they should not become a substitute for original thought, or for critical evaluation and application, or be interpreted as a blueprint or straitjacket.

In this chapter, the models and frameworks will be grouped under two principal headings: static analysis, and evolution and life-cycle analysis. Static analysis provides a snapshot of an organisation (or part of it) at a particular point in its life; the analysis gives a view of the range, diversity or complexity of the organisation. Evolution shows the organisation (or part of it) at a certain point in its development; the analysis gives a sense of what the organisation has come through, where it is now, and where it might be moving to in the future.

2.2   Static Analysis

When someone is trying to understand an organisation in its entirety, it is often helpful to have a framework which encourages an understanding of the constituent parts. Two will be discussed here: the McKinsey 7-S framework, and Handy's organisational variables.

2.2.1   McKinsey 7-S framework

This framework was devised by McKinsey consultants (including Tom Peters) as a way of thinking about the structure, interdependencies and effectiveness of business organisations (see Peters and Waterman (1982), page 10 and figure 2.1). There are 'hard' S's (strategy, structure and systems — referred to by some as the 'cold triangle') and the 'soft' S's (staff, skills, style and shared values — referred to by some as the 'warm square'). Conflicts arise when there is disagreement between those who favour the cold triangle over the warm square, or vice versa.

The framework shows that an organisation is multi-dimensional, and that all of these dimensions need managing (not just strategy, structure and systems) if it is to remain successful. It also shows that each dimension has a relationship with (and therefore effect on) every other dimension.

2.2.2   Handy's organisational variables

Whereas the 7-S framework looks at the superstructure of the firm, Handy's organisational variables look more at the internal components. His point is that an organisation is made up of many different variables (which can be grouped), and that all of these variables have to work together if the firm is to be fully effective. Figure 2.2 shows these variables (slightly adapted by me to suit a law firm environment).

The structuring of these variables takes account of the environmental, organisational and individual levels of analysis referred to in paragraph 2.1.2. It shows that a law firm (like any other business organisation) is a complex structure of some 50 variables: we should not therefore expect law firm management to be an easy process. Handy also warns against management (or consultants) focusing their attention on only one part of the organisation (1993, page 15). These variables are all interdependent, and affecting some of them will in some way affect the others, or at least

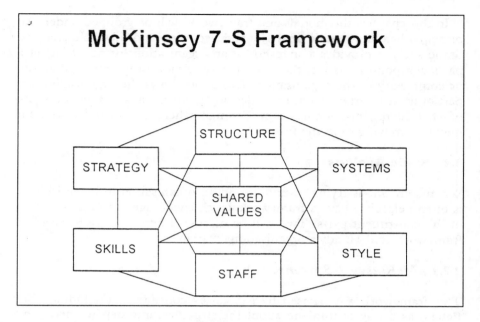

Figure 2.1 (Source: Peters and Waterman 1982, page 10)

distract attention from the things that matter: as Handy puts it, there is no point in "regulating the clocks when the house is burning down" (1993, page 16).

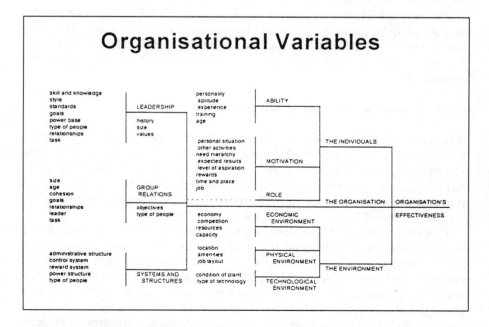

Figure 2.2 (Source: adapted from Handy 1993, page 15)

2.3 Evolution and Life-cycle Analysis

In many contexts, writers on management issues talk about 'life cycles'. These are typically phases of the evolution or development of an environment, an organisation, a service, an individual, and so on. These models can be useful analytical tools to help firms, departments, groups or individuals understand where they might be in their own stages of development. This in turn helps them to understand or explain events that have brought them to where they now are, and to see where others' experience and analysis suggest that the next steps might be. None of them is exhaustive. But in describing trends and common patterns, they have proved remarkably resilient and enlightening.

2.3.1 *Industry life cycle*

The basis of the industry life cycle is the assumption that "industries follow a life cycle that comprises a number of evolutionary characteristics that are common to different industries" (Grant 1995, page 231). It may seem odd to describe the legal profession as an industry, but to the extent that legal services are supplied in an environment of common clients, competitors and suppliers, there is as much an industry of providing legal services as there are industries providing other products and services to common customers, competitors and suppliers.

The four phases of industry evolution are shown in figure 2.3. They are introduction, growth, maturity and decline (Grant 1995, page 231). They can also be applied to the evolution of a particular practice area for legal services (the equivalent of the 'product life cycle').

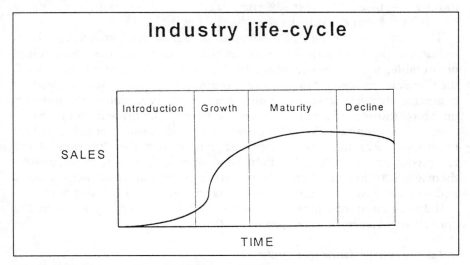

Figure 2.3 (Source: Grant 1995, page 231)

At the introductory stage, there are few suppliers or buyers. Suppliers have to work much harder at creating and selling their products or services, and have to convince buyers that, not only are they the right firm to buy from, but that there is a need for the product or service in the first place. The market is simply not established.

If a market develops, then the industry moves to its growth phase with more buyers being willing to take the product or service, existing suppliers growing to cope with the additional demand, and more suppliers entering the market.

As the market develops, the number of new buyers begins to slow down and the rate of growth starts to slow. The industry enters its mature phase (see also paragraph 4.7.4). The number of suppliers in the market may lead to over-capacity, and competition shifts to issues of quality and cost-efficiency. Profitability across the industry typically falls as a result of this competition. Production and marketing methods have to change to reflect the capacity and competition in the industry. Some suppliers may not be able to sustain their businesses in the competitive environment, and consolidation through 'shake-out' begins (mergers and failures).

Finally, buyers become extremely knowledgeable about the product or service, and about the suppliers. Their sophistication may lead to innovations, specialisation and rationalisation in the industry. As industry sales start to decline, the suppliers with a strong brand name are probably best placed to withstand the effects of over-capacity, intense price competition and rationalisation. Indeed, the industry may not decline into oblivion, but reinvent itself on a new basis, and start the cycle all over again.

There are two driving forces in this process of industry evolution. The first is the growth in demand from buyers. This will be affected by the absolute number of buyers for any given product or service, and by the volume of their buying (they may begin to buy more from the same industry — in our context, different legal services — or become repeat buyers of the same product or service).

The second is the rate of innovation or diffusion of knowledge. If an industry supplies products or services that quickly become standardised or imitable, it will tend to move to the mature phase more quickly. If, therefore, an industry can continue to innovate, it will keep the product or service life cycle replenished and so affect the evolution of the industry on which those products or services are based. The growth and development of the computer industry provides a good example of this constant innovation. Alternatively, if suppliers can protect the diffusion of the knowledge on which their products or services are based, they will protect themselves for longer against the imitation or replication of their business and so slow down the rate of growth (cf. paragraphs 4.6.5 and 5.4).

Industry environment and evolution will be considered again in the context of strategy (see paragraph 4.7.2)

2.3.2 *Organisation life cycle*

Little writing on organisations treats them as entities that are themselves subject to the life cycle of birth, development and death (for an excellent recent example, see de Geus (1997)).

In 1972, Professor Larry Greiner wrote that growing organisations move through five distinguishable phases of development (Greiner 1972). Each phase contains a relatively calm period of growth that ends with a management crisis. Evolutionary phases are periods of growth during which no major upheavals occur in the organisation; revolutions are periods of substantial crisis or turmoil in organisational life. Greiner says that each evolutionary period creates its own revolution, and that the nature of management's response and solution to each revolutionary period will determine whether or not an organisation will move forward to its next stage of evolution (1972, page 38).

2.3.2.1 The forces of organisational development

In explaining the background to his conclusions, Greiner suggests that five factors emerge as being essential to describe an organisation's development (1972, pages 38–40). They are:

(a) *Its age.* The same management structures and practices in an organisation are not maintained for ever, and "the passage of time also contributes to the institutionalization of managerial attitudes. As a result, employee behavior becomes not only more predictable but also more difficult to change when attitudes are outdated" (1972, page 40).

(b) *Its size.* An organisation's problems and solutions tend to change markedly as its turnover and the number of employees increase. Until the 1970s, most law firms were growing slowly, and were still relatively small businesses. It is not perhaps surprising that management issues, structures and attention were not very high on the list of priorities. But as many firms have achieved significant growth, where the size and rate of growth have increased dramatically, organisational issues faced by many other businesses begin to emerge; these include the coordination of increasingly interrelated jobs and communication, as well as the development of management hierarchy. On this basis, Greiner would argue that any current preoccupation with management in law firms perhaps has more to do with growth and the emergence of larger law firms than it does with external factors, such as general economic conditions.

(c) *Stages of evolution.* Greiner's research suggested that once a firm has survived a crisis, it can then expect a period of sustained growth for a number of years without needing to make any significant changes in its structure or approach to management.

(d) *Stages of revolution.* Smooth evolution is not inevitable. As we shall see in paragraph 3.6.2, organisation growth in law firms tends to be exponential rather than linear. At certain times, therefore, businesses "typically exhibit a serious upheaval of management practices. Traditional management practices, which were appropriate for a smaller size and earlier time, are brought under scrutiny by frustrated top managers and disillusioned lower-level managers" (1972, page 40). During these periods of crisis, businesses that cannot adapt will either fail or their rate of growth will level off. During each of these 'revolutions' the firm's management must create the new structure and practices for it that will allow the next period of evolution to take place. However, "these new practices eventually sow their own seeds of decay and lead to another period of revolution" (1972, page 40).

(e) *Growth rate of the industry.* Finally, says Greiner, there is a close link between the speed at which an organisation experiences its phases of evolution and revolution, and the market environment of its industry. For example, evolutionary periods tend to be relatively short in fast-growing industries, while longer evolutionary periods occur in mature or slow-growth industries. It may therefore be that the legal profession will experience a period of relative stability now that the growth rates of the 1980s appear to be behind us. However, Greiner also suggests that evolution can be prolonged — and revolutions delayed — when profits come easily. As he rightly observes, businesses that make serious errors but still make significant profits can still appear successful and so avoid any change in management practices for a longer period. This certainly happened within the legal profession during the late 1980s. Firms were outgrowing their historic management and partnership structures, but many were making so much money that some of them did not see any need for change. The 1990s recession changed their perspective: but as Greiner concludes: "Revolutions seem to be much more severe and difficult to resolve when the market environment is poor" (1972, page 40).

2.3.2.2 Phases of growth
Greiner identified five specific phases of evolution and revolution. Each evolutionary period is associated with a dominant management *style* that achieves growth during that period: creativity, direction, delegation, coordination, and collaboration. Each revolutionary period is associated with a dominant management *problem* that has to be resolved before growth can continue: leadership, autonomy, control, red tape, and (he speculated) psychological saturation. As indicated above, the speed at which these periods of evolution and revolution will occur in a law office will depend on its size and rate of growth, and on the current rate of growth within the legal profession. For commercial legal departments, their occurrence will also depend on the broader organisational phases occurring within the company's business units. In public-sector legal departments, they will reflect current attitudes of (and to) central and local government.

The pattern of growth, and of evolution and revolution (or of growth and crisis), is shown diagrammatically in figure 2.4.

Greiner emphasises that each phase is both an effect of the previous phase and a cause for the next. For example, the management style of delegation is a response to the need for greater autonomy; but increased delegation creates diversity and leads to the need for management to regain control. Further, the principal implication of each phase is that management actions are narrowly prescribed if growth is to occur. A business experiencing a crisis of autonomy cannot return to the directive style of management if it is to move ahead.

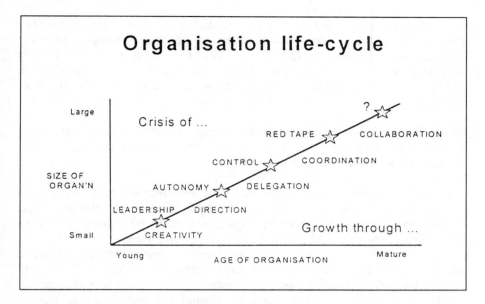

Figure 2.4 (Source: Greiner 1972, page 41)

Phase 1: creativity   The characteristics of the period of creative evolution are:

(a)   The founders of the business are usually technically or entrepreneurially oriented, and they avoid (and often dislike) management activities.

(b)   Communication among staff is frequent and informal.

(c)   Long hours of work are rewarded by modest income and the promise of ownership benefits in the future (e.g., partnership).

(d)   The control of the firm's activities comes from immediate client and market feedback. Founding partners react in line with clients' reactions.

The leadership crisis   All of these activities are necessary to start a new business successfully. But as it grows, organisational issues emerge — increasing turnover requires efficiencies in productivity; a larger number of staff cannot be managed only through informal communication; new staff are not so motivated by the excitement of creating a new business; additional financing may be needed to expand; and new accounting procedures are often needed for better financial control. The founders therefore find themselves facing the management responsibilities they do not want (and may even have left their former firms to avoid): they long for 'the good old days' and perhaps continue to act as they did then. "At this point a crisis of leadership occurs, which is the onset of the first revolution. Who is to lead the company out of confusion and solve the managerial problems confronting it? Quite obviously, a strong manager is needed who has the necessary knowledge and skill to introduce new business techniques. But this is easier said than done. The founders often hate to step aside even though they are probably temperamentally unsuited to be managers" (1972, page 42). This, then, is the first critical choice in the firm's development: to find and put in place effective management, acceptable to the founders and able to pull the firm together.

Phase 2: direction Organisations that survive phase 1 usually experience a period of sustained growth under able and directive leadership. The characteristics of the second phase are:

(a) A structure that separates the different functions of the firm (e.g., fee-earning and support, with increasing distinctions in practice areas and in support operations), and greater specialisation in who does what (e.g., bringing in better qualified or experienced finance staff).

(b) Financial management systems become more sophisticated with, perhaps, greater control over work-in-progress and debtors.

(c) Incentives, budgets and work standards are often introduced.

(d) Communication becomes more formal and impersonal as a 'hierarchy' begins to develop.

(e) The firm's leaders take most of the responsibility for providing direction, and treat 'lower-level' staff more as functional specialists than as autonomous decision-makers.

The autonomy crisis Although the clearer leadership and direction of phase 2 channels people's energies more efficiently into growth, "it eventually becomes inappropriate for controlling a larger, more diverse and complex organization" (1972, page 42). Staff find themselves restricted by increasing bureaucracy and centralisation. They usually have more direct knowledge about the firm's markets, processes and technology than the leaders, and so become torn between following direction from a top perceived to be remote and out of touch, and taking the initiative. The response is usually for the leadership to delegate more work and decisions away from the centre. "Yet it is difficult for top managers who were previously successful at being directive to give up responsibility. Moreover, lower-level managers are not accustomed to making decisions for themselves" (1972, page 42). Consequently, some firms will struggle or even fail as the senior partners inappropriately cling to control, and the frustrated leave or under-perform.

Phase 3: delegation The next period of growth evolves from successful decentralisation. Its characteristics are:

(a) Much greater responsibility being given to those responsible for practice areas or functional activities (such as finance, people, training, technology).

(b) A profit centred approach and the award of bonuses are often used to motivate people.

(c)   The partners responsible for managing the firm rely more on management by exception, based on reports from responsible managers.

(d)   Top management often concentrates on recruiting new 'stars' or looking for merger or other expansion opportunities.

(e)   Communication from the top is infrequent, and usually by correspondence, telephone, or brief visits.

The control crisis   Eventually, the firm's leaders and top managers feel that they are losing control of a diversified organisation. Those who are given responsibility for running a decentralised part of the firm want to do so without having to coordinate their plans, finances, technology and staff with the rest of the firm. But growing, decentralised businesses have a range of activities, and concurrent needs for money, equipment and people, that require some form of coordination.

Phase 4: coordination   The fourth phase is therefore characterised by the use of formal systems to achieve greater coordination:

(a)   Decentralised units are merged into new, larger groups, and each group is treated as an investment centre where performance (usually financial) is an important criterion in allocating further resources or investment.

(b)   Formal planning procedures are established.

(c)   Staff are recruited to initiate centralised, firm-wide programmes to coordinate and review performance.

(d)   Capital expenditure is considered carefully and distributed across the firm.

(e)   Certain functions (e.g., accounting) are centralised, while daily operating decisions remain decentralised.

(f)   Bonus schemes and profit-sharing schemes are used to encourage staff to identify with the firm as a whole.

Red tape crisis   Coordination is useful for achieving growth through the more efficient allocation of limited resources, and encourages managers to look beyond the needs of their own parts of the business. They have to justify their decisions to a firm-wide 'watchdog'. But a lack of confidence gradually builds between the centre and the decentralised managers and staff. The proliferation of systems and programmes begins to exceed its utility, and a crisis of red tape is created — everyone criticises the bureaucratic system that has been created: "Procedures take precedence over problem solving, and innovation is dampened. In short, the organization has become too large and complex to be managed through formal programs and rigid systems. The Phase 4 revolution is under way" (1972, page 43).

Phase 5: collaboration   "The last observable phase in previous studies emphasizes strong interpersonal collaboration in an attempt to overcome the red-tape crisis. Where Phase 4 was managed through formal systems and procedures, Phase 5 emphasizes greater spontaneity in management action through teams and the skillful confrontation of interpersonal differences. Social control and self-discipline take over from formal control. This transition is especially difficult for those experts who created the old systems as well as for those line managers who relied on formal methods for answers. The Phase 5 evolution, then, builds around a more flexible and behavioral approach to management" (1972, page 43). The characteristics of the fifth phase are:

(a)   The focus is on solving problems quickly using a team approach.

(b)   Teams are combined on a multidisciplinary (or at least multi-functional) basis.

(c)   The number of central staff is reduced, and those that remain may well be reassigned to the decentralised teams (to consult rather than to direct).

(d)   A matrix structure is frequently used to assemble the right teams to address the needs in question.

(e)   The previous formal systems are simplified.

(f)   Meetings of key managers are held frequently to focus on major problems or issues.

(g)   Training programmes are used to train managers in behavioural skills for achieving better teamwork and for resolving conflicts.

(h)   Real-time information systems are established and used for daily decision-making.

(i)   Economic rewards are geared more to team performance than to individual achievement.

(j)   Innovation is encouraged across the firm.

The ? crisis   At the time of Greiner's article, the most advanced businesses were in phase 5 of evolution and had therefore not reached their phase 5 revolution. He therefore had to anticipate the nature of the phase 5 crisis: "I imagine that the revolution will center around the 'psychological saturation' of employees who grow emotionally and physically exhausted by the intensity of teamwork and the heavy pressure for innovative solutions. My hunch is that the Phase 5 revolution will be solved through new structures and programs that allow employees to periodically rest, reflect, and revitalize themselves. We may even see companies with dual organization structures: a 'habit' structure for getting the daily work done, and a 'reflective' structure for stimulating perspective and personal enrichment. Employees could then move back and forth between the two structures as their energies are dissipated and refueled" (1972, page 44).

2.3.2.3   Lessons to be learned

Three lessons may be learned from Greiner's analysis:

(a)   *Know where your firm is in the evolutionary phases*   Given the inevitability of the phases and their consequences described (and borne out) by Greiner's research, a firm's leaders should be aware of its current stage of development. If the firm is to survive and grow, they must ensure that it makes the appropriate transition before it is too late.

(b) *Recognise the limited range of solutions* When a firm has been successful, its leaders and managers are tempted to replicate the behaviour that has worked before. One of the messages of Greiner's crises is that a change is required — it is the replication of previous behaviour that is leading to the crisis. Surviving the crises requires different behaviour, and the number of choices is limited because the nature of the preceding period of growth has led to a certain crisis that requires a certain response. It may well be that the leadership and management that have made the firm successful in one era are not appropriate for the next stage of development. This can, of course, be traumatic for everyone. In this sense, partners who push for continued growth may well be *hastening* their own departure from a position of power rather than consolidating their current position.

(c) *Realise that solutions breed new problems* Implicit in Greiner's analysis is that successfully surviving a crisis in the firm will inevitably lead to another one further down the road. It would therefore be tempting, armed with the analysis, to seek to 'skip' some parts of the process by anticipating and managing around the crises that would otherwise lie ahead. Greiner's message, however, is that any period of growth, or any crisis, is a product of what happened before. In other words, if a stage is missed out, the evolution that was hoped for could well not happen because the desired effects are a consequence of a crisis that was avoided.

"Managers often fail to realize that organizational solutions create problems for the future (i.e., a decision to delegate eventually causes a problem of control). Historical actions are very much determinants of what happens to the company at a much later date. An awareness of this effect should help managers to evaluate company problems with greater historical understanding instead of 'pinning the blame' on a current development. Better yet, managers should be in a position to *predict* future problems, and thereby to prepare solutions and coping strategies before a revolution gets out of hand" (1972, pages 45–6).

2.3.2.4 Conclusion
Greiner provides another analytical model which sees a firm's structure from a developmental perspective. Lawyers who are aware from this analysis of the likely problems ahead may well decide that they do not wish their firms or departments to become any larger. They may prefer the informal practices of a small organisation — but recognising now that "this way of life is inherent in the organization's limited size, not in their congenial personalities. If they choose to grow, they may do themselves out of a job and a way of life they enjoy" (1972, page 46). Unfortunately, managing a law firm to *avoid* growth is not easy (cf. paragraph 3.6.5) and requires certain conditions.

2.3.3 Service life cycle

The industry life cycle (paragraph 2.3.1) can also be used to give some idea of a product or service life cycle. A little closer to home for law firms is Maister's notion of the life cycle of a professional firm (Maister 1993a, chapter 2). This model can in fact be applied to the firm, to different practice areas, and to an individual's know-how. It relates to the services provided by professionals, and is based on three key benefits that clients want from professional services: expertise, experience and efficiency (which is why the model is also known as Maister's 3Es). Graphically, this spectrum of service can be represented as shown in figure 2.5.

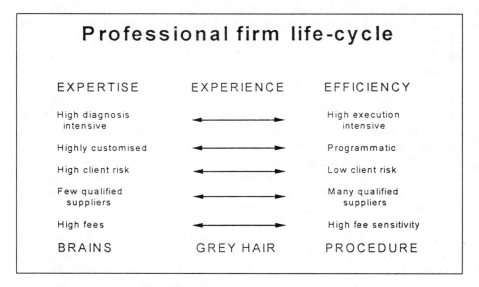

Figure 2.5 (Source: based on Maister 1993a, page 22)

This model is, in my view, one of the most powerful in the analysis of professional services. Maister emphasises that the three categories are not discrete but represent the ends and mid-point of a spectrum; but he does suggest that each category requires a different approach to marketing, recruitment, structure, and economics (1993a, page 22; see also Maister 1997, chapter 13).

Too many lawyers consider their services to fall into the expertise category, forgetting that the important assessment is made by the client. If the client perceives a service to be largely procedural, and capable of being performed by any number of suitably qualified lawyers or firms, then it will be an efficiency service. Competing for that client's work will mean being geared up as an efficiency practice, and being subject to price competition. It would be irrational (and dangerous) to insist that the service requires a high degree of diagnosis and tailoring for which an expensive partner should be retained if the client essentially wants a commodity service provided at the lowest appropriate level of seniority.

The model represents a life cycle because of the tendency for any expertise to become diffused and performed by more people who are developed by the original innovators to handle that sort of work: it becomes experience. And as experience becomes standardised and proceduralised (and possibly even computerised), it evolves into providing efficiency. Over time, therefore, expertise and experience are rationalised and become routine; there is a shift from the left to the right. Indeed, it is possible to imagine the service moving off the model to the right as the clients become self-sufficient or find alternative suppliers (in this case, the fourth E would be the extinction of that type of work for lawyers).

The strategic dilemma for law firms is whether they adapt the structure, marketing and organisation of their practices to reflect the evolution of the services they provide, or whether they try to retain the structural components in place and seek new services that are suited to that structure (which would require frequent innovation in services). The conservative nature of most lawyers does not suit them or their practices for constant innovation. Instead, there is a danger that they keep the same structure and approach which then become inappropriate to the type of service that the client wants. This is one explanation, for example, of why domestic conveyancing became too expensive for clients to want to continue using law firms. Registered title has made the process of transferring property much more routine and 'programmable' than it used to be. Clients perceived an efficiency service; law firms perceived an expertise service, structure and pricing level. The service quickly moved pretty well to extinction (cf. paragraph 1.4.1.1). This trend, however, does not only apply to private client services. There are some commercial clients who already regard 'staightforward' company acquisitions or disposals as a commodity service (that is, an efficiency service) that can be provided by any number of commercial law firms: these have become price-sensitive transactions, regardless of the expertise the lawyers consider themselves to be bringing to bear.

Expertise practices require a high level of technical competence and a lot of attention to individual clients; by definition, there are noᵗ many lawyers who are capable of providing the service. In these practices, then, one would not expect to find large teams of fee-earners (the 'pyramid' would have few partners at the top and very few other fee-earners reporting to them). Conversely, in an efficiency practice, a high level of technical competence is not needed, and the economics of its price-sensitive services do not sustain too many highly paid partners or lawyers. Here, we should expect to find a pyramid structure also with very few partners at the apex, but with many other fee-earners (probably paralegals) reporting to them. In the middle, we should expect a pyramid that is more equilateral in shape. The problem for many law firms is that they fancy themselves to be providers of expertise, but want the perceived higher profitability that comes from a lower, spread pyramid (known as higher 'leverage': see paragraph 28.4). They build such a pyramid, and then find that either they do indeed provide expertise but cannot share the complex work with all the supporting fee-earners they have recruited, or that they have recruited real experts for whom there is not enough expertise work to do or who can demand a significant share of the profit that would otherwise arise. Either way, there is a mismatch of structure and expectations, and the profitability is not derived.

Finally, Maister suggests that the differences in clients' expectations, and the structure and economics of practices in each category, are such that it is "an almost impossible task" to sustain all three types of work in the same firm (1993a, page 22). It may be possible to sustain two adjacent types, but expertise and efficiency practices are fundamentally different.

This model will be used at various points in this book to shed light on the structure and activities of law firms.

2.3.4 Individual life cycle

All life cycles implicitly assume birth, growth and death. Not only will an individual's expertise follow a life-cycle pattern (see paragraph 2.3.3) but the individual will also go through an evolution in his or her professional life. This is articulated by Sveiby and Lloyd (1987), and is shown in figure 2.6.

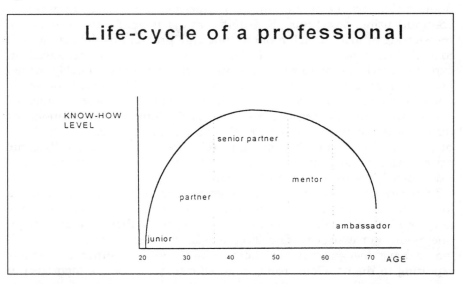

Figure 2.6 (Source: Sveiby and Lloyd 1987, page 109)

The messages in this life-cycle model can, of course, be profoundly disturbing! What it shows is that a professional's know-how increases rapidly in the early years of professional development, reaches a plateau, and then falls off as the professional becomes involved perhaps in other aspects of the firm and then finds it more difficult to keep up with the rate of development in new services and innovations. Firms that are highly geared around personal performance (particularly fees billed) will probably engineer the departure of partners whose measurable contribution begins to tail off with seniority, and consequently deprive the firm of a valuable source of other contributions to the internal and external development of the practice. And of course it does not follow that even if a partner's know-how level begins to drop that his or her fee-earning

Chapter 3

LAW FIRMS AS KNOW-HOW BUSINESSES

3.1 The Importance of Know-how

In the early 1980s, a few law firms began systematically to develop
know-how systems to collect, structure, access and disseminate the
collective recorded knowledge and experience of increasingly specialised
lawyers. The initial rationale for doing so was principally economic
efficiency. It was acknowledged to be a waste to reinvent wheels, to have
expensive and busy lawyers doing again what a colleague next door or down
the corridor had already grappled with. In the mid 1980s, it dawned on me
that law firms were, in fact, know-how businesses. Rather than creating
know-how systems merely to support their practices, law firms needed to
realise that knowledge and experience are the core and rationale of their
very existence. It was some years later that I first heard any law firm describe
know-how systems as one possible element of its competitive advantage.

Lawyers had acknowledged for many years that they were people
businesses (even if they had not fully embraced the consequences). But
this did not go far enough. The key to a successful and sustainable future
is the organisation and development of shared knowledge and experience.
Know-how systems dealt with that part of know-how that was reduced to
writing, but did not embrace the underlying asset. On the other hand, the
thinking of people businesses and human resource management, while
appropriate in parts, did not fully meet the need, either. After all, many
people businesses do not thrive on know-how; and know-how can be
applied to non-people activities.

Like many other lawyers and law firm consultants, I knew that 'traditional' principles of management were not always appropriate to legal
practice — not even to those lawyers who worked in-house in industry or
the public sector, that is, in otherwise structured and hierarchical organisations. The individualism and autonomy of professionals destroyed
structure and systems.

Then — suddenly, it seemed — the world started talking about knowledge-based businesses, organisations or societies. The management writers started talking my language. Developments in the business world and in management generally became more pertinent to legal practice. Understanding these shifts (which are discussed in chapter 1) is therefore an important part of appreciating both the importance and relevance of contemporary management thinking to the world of legal practice. The management challenge is not simply to find a way of managing know-how businesses: it is to place these microcosms of economic and social activity into a macroeconomic and social structure that is itself undergoing a profound transformation.

It is against this background that all know-how businesses must develop. In 1987, Karl Erik Sveiby and Tom Lloyd wrote a book that went largely unnoticed by lawyers. Called *Managing Know-how* (Sveiby and Lloyd 1987), their book examines the whole concept and organisation of knowledge-based businesses, and produced a stimulating analysis of 'know-how companies' — from solicitors to circuses. Ten years and a recession later, their analysis still provides a total framework within which to analyse the structure and delivery of legal services. This chapter begins by considering some of the key messages of the book.

3.2 The Characteristics of Know-how Businesses

Sveiby and Lloyd set out to answer what many law firm managers would recognise as the ultimate question (1987, page 14): How do you manage, control and develop businesses employing talented, egocentric, highly qualified people engaged in complex and creative problem-solving? Their starting point is to identify the characteristics of know-how businesses and draw certain conclusions:

(a) A know-how business produces and sells know-how. While all know-how businesses are service businesses, not all service businesses are know-how businesses. Some businesses may be a mixture of service and know-how (e.g., banks with their 'hole-in-the-wall' services as well as highly tailored financial planning). Table 3.1 seeks to illustrate and apply this thinking, not just to the business as a whole but also to different types of legal service.

Service Business		Know-how Business	
Self-service	Standard package	Service system	Total adaptation
cash points supermarkets petrol stations	credit cards fast food	auditors estate agents car service	lawyers doctors consultants
DIY conveyancing; off-the-shelf wills	cut-price conveyancing; debt collection	precedent-based service; expert systems	personal service and applied know-how

Table 3.1 (Source: adapted from Sveiby and Lloyd 1987, page 18)

The dividing line between some of these services may be very thin. High street banks have been moving generally from right to left, substituting technology and standardisation for a personal service from a bank manager. Accountants have been trying to add value to their core audit service and move to the right. Lawyers have tended to see themselves at the far right, but in reality have not always been there. Further, some have in recent years taken deliberate steps to the left: as they move left, will they face more competition from outside the legal profession?

(b)   Know-how puts individuals at the centre of the stage — knowledgeable people constitute the most important (and sometimes the only) capital (1987, page 15). Recruitment decisions are therefore among the most important decisions that a know-how business makes.

(c)   A know-how business finds it very hard to standardise its business operations: it cannot force its clients to adapt to it, and so must adapt to them. The main distinguishing features of a know-how business are therefore (1987, page 20):

(i)   a high dependence on individuals,
(ii)   creativity and complex problem-solving,
(iii) non-standardisation.

(d)   Financial capital is seldom a significant contributor to profitability in a know-how business (1987, page 21). The problem in valuing a know-how business is its dependence on key people (cf. paragraph 5.5.3). Following a takeover or merger, it may not be able to keep clients or staff (as Barclays Bank found when it created BZW by 'buying' de Zoete & Bevan and Wedd Durlacher Mordaunt for an estimated total of £150 million (1987, pages 149–151).

(e)   Know-how capital grows as people become more experienced (1987, page 22). The rate of growth can be increased by training and other methods of personal development (*successful* know-how businesses "put far more resources than mere maintenance" into training). Know-how capital is lost when people leave or under-perform (usually due to poor leadership or an uncongenial environment). The all-important way to preserve know-how in a professional organisation is to create an environment that encourages, motivates and challenges the professionals.

3.3   The Need for Dual Expertise

According to Sveiby and Lloyd, successful know-how businesses distinguish two types of know-how:

(a)   professional know-how (the 'product'),
(b)   managerial know-how (the production and distribution).

They need to combine a high level of both to achieve a sound business based on creative people. A law firm that is high on professional know-how but low on managerial know-how (as law firms typically have been) is an underdeveloped know-how business (1987, page 25). It is a very creative place, where the lawyers have a high degree of professional know-how and often work well together. They have the freedom to develop their own professionalism — and are under constant competitive pressure to do so. But support staff have low status, and complain that the lawyers take no notice of them. The 'management' is often quite unable to control the firm — even when the top management function is rotated between partners. The professionalism of the rotating (i.e. temporary) managing partner becomes tainted by "menial preoccupations". Sveiby and Lloyd contend that this type of firm is unlikely to survive in the long term: such businesses tend to be broken up by internal rows or to go under because they have failed to develop into a professional organisation (1987, page 26). The longevity of some law firms which clearly fall into the 'under-developed' category perhaps does not fully support Sveiby and Lloyd's thesis. However, it is clear that those firms are not as successful as they would be if they developed into 'the professional know-how business' which combines a high level of both professional and managerial know-how. This, say Sveiby and Lloyd, has long-term stability and value-growth, and an ability to develop both skilled professionals and new leaders. In short, it has learnt to replace key people without a decline in quality (1987, page 26).

To most lawyers, helping to run one's own organisation is a boring activity and lacking in status. The distinction that they draw between 'proper' work, and the menial process of supporting and running the business can cause serious conflicts in know-how businesses between the lawyers on the one hand, and managers and support staff on the other (1987, page 63).

Lawyers — like many other professionals — often show little concern about developing their 'places of work' as organisations; they are usually more interested in developing their own expertise, reputation and client following, and see the firm merely as a convenient place from which to do so. Indeed, it may seem as if they are more loyal to their profession than to the organisations in which they practise (1987, page 64: this point is also made by Handy 1991, pages 178–9). However, it appears that loyalty and commitment to the firm will in fact increase over time (de Oliveira 1996). Legal training, and the prevalent culture of law firms, have produced generations of lawyers for whom management has not been a preoccupation. Because of these attitudes, it is both unusual and perhaps a risk to their notion of professionalism for lawyers to display any interest in or aptitude for management: to do so, they think, makes it likely that fellow professionals will think of them as being somehow 'a failed lawyer'.

Nevertheless, Sveiby and Lloyd believe that the need for a blend of both professional and managerial ability (they call this blend 'dual expertise') is so great that it must be combined in top management — if necessary, by separating functions between partners and professional managers (1987, page 65).

3.4 Ten Success Factors of Know-how Management

Sveiby and Lloyd identify and explain 10 common features that they believe successful know-how organisations have that contribute to their success. In summary, they are (1987, chapter 8):

(a) *Day-to-day leadership*. The leader is almost always an experienced, respected professional whose credibility comes from having been a successful practitioner. Indeed, Sveiby and Lloyd maintain that it is "impossible to lead professionals without being a professional yourself" (1987, page 99). One of the principal roles of the leader is to create an environment which is capable of accommodating a wide variety of personalities. Leadership is discussed in paragraph 23.5.

(b) *Quality and quality control*. In one of their most perceptive comments, Sveiby and Lloyd write (1987, page 100):

"Quality is a fashionable but frequently misused word. No serious management strategy includes among its objectives the deliberate production of poor quality. Everyone wants to be proud of their production and to be praised for its quality. This is important in know-how companies — so important that the successful company may go to extreme lengths to maintain quality. The problem with quality is not the objective itself but the follow-up and control which are the real keys to quality improvement. Successful know-how companies have uncompromising quality control systems but are constantly struggling with the problem of how to measure quality."

Quality is considered at length in paragraph 20.3.

(c) *Respect for know-how*. As anyone who has spent time in a law firm will know, the firm will rank lawyers internally according to the perceived strength of their professional ability (know-how): see further paragraph 24.3.2.2(a). This perceived strength will then determine what each is able to achieve within the firm — professionally and organisationally. A fully developed know-how business, however, will value everyone's contribution, and will take steps both to value and to improve their know-how. There may be formal training programmes, as well as investment in the law firm equivalent of research and development (such as giving people time to write books, or investing in precedent and know-how systems): see paragraph 25.3.

(d) *Combination of professional and managerial know-how*. Consistent with Sveiby and Lloyd's thesis that successful know-how businesses combine both professional and managerial expertise, a success factor is the combination of these two skills into a new one: the dual expertise represented by know-how management (cf. paragraphs 5.2 and 14.2.3).

(e) *A strong, well-defined culture*. For Sveiby and Lloyd, successful know-how businesses start by defining their culture, asking themselves questions like: Who are we? What do we want? What is our core know-how? and What are our distinguishing features? The principal benefit of culture as a management tool is that it can be used as a framework (cf. Bhide 1996, page 128): this allows a degree of independence so valued by professionals, while keeping them attuned to the firm's overall objectives and values. Organisational culture is dealt with in paragraphs 23.1 to 23.3.

(f) *Focus on core know-how.* In a statement that many proponents of large and multidisciplinary practices would find hard to swallow, Sveiby and Lloyd assert: "The professional conglomerate is an impossibility" (1987, page 102). Nevertheless, the experience in the world of advertising, for instance, would support their conclusion since Saatchi & Saatchi and WPP have both found diversification an expensive and difficult process. Sveiby and Lloyd's justification is that managing a number of different know-how areas is very difficult — so difficult, in fact, that quality cannot be maintained, let alone improved. The strategic conclusion from this is to 'stick to the knitting' and focus on core know-how (assuming that the firm knows what this is!): see paragraphs 4.5.2 and 4.6.3.1.

(g) *Know-how preservation.* Given that know-how is what resides in people's heads, the principal objective of know-how preservation must be to discourage professionals from leaving the firm. This is an issue partly of structure and partly of motivation (see chapters 19 and 26). Many modern know-how businesses have some form of employee ownership and profit-sharing structure: however, the culture and structure of most law offices do not reflect this 'modern' approach.

(h) *Developing the people.* The only way to develop a know-how business is to develop the know-how that its people have. On this view, the success of the business becomes dependent on recruiting and developing people (see paragraph 22.4.2 and chapter 25).

(i) *Changing key people.* Most know-how businesses are formed and sustained around the leadership and reputation of one or more key people (usually founders or senior partners). Sveiby and Lloyd therefore suggest that a successful know-how business must learn how to make the transition from one set of key people to another to demonstrate that it has the resilience to survive as a business rather than being the reflection of one individual (or of a few individuals). There seem to be two components of a successful changeover: the leader must become dispensable, and the rest of the organisation must learn that a leadership change is an opportunity rather than a threat (see paragraph 2.3.2.2 and chapter 27).

More generally, a know-how business's ability to survive is, to a large extent, equivalent to an ability to transfer know-how from the more experienced to the less experienced. The sudden death or departure of a key partner can throw a know-how business into turmoil — unless his or her core know-how has been transferred to others. A successful know-how business therefore takes steps to share this know-how with others so that the firm can withstand a change in professionals (see paragraphs 5.4, 25.3.4 and 25.3.6.5).

(j) *Stable structures.* Know-how businesses often appear to lack any tangible structure and substance. But what they lack in the concrete

substance normally associated with traditional companies, they compensate for in terms of the breadth, depth and value of their know-how. The
challenge for a law firm is to 'embed' this intangible asset into other
structures to give the firm some coherence and stability. The 'corporate'
culture (see success factor (e) and chapter 22) is part of the informal
structure (and the ways of creating it are specific to a particular firm). The
more formal structures are the legal structure (partnership, incorporation,
service companies, etc.) and the accounting system.

3.5 The Business and Personnel Ideas

The role played by know-how is such a strong component of Sveiby and
Lloyd's notion of a successful professional firm that they link two key
concepts — the business idea and the personnel idea. A know-how
business exists to exploit know-how. The strategy for the exploitation of
the know-how is the business idea — in short, how to make a successful
and profitable business out of know-how by combining professional and
managerial ability (1987, page 129). Sveiby and Lloyd suggest four
generic business ideas (which I shall explore later in the context of
strategy: see paragraph 4.8.3). In most know-how businesses, the business
idea belongs to one or more key people: they are the people with the most
exploitable know-how and the networks to do so.

The personnel idea is "a general opinion about what kind of people
should be employed, how old they should be, how well educated and
what attitudes they should have if they are to fit in with the organisation"
(1987, page 51: see paragraph 22.4 for a fuller articulation of the
personnel idea). The importance of people and know-how in the overall
success of a know-how business means that the business and personnel
ideas are intimately connected and may be almost indistinguishable.

For the purposes of this chapter, the business idea of legal practice is
the exploitation by a lawyer of contacts, reputation and know-how in
solving clients' legal problems. A successful lawyer could practise on his
or her own. But if a sole practitioner is successful, it is likely that there
will be more client work on offer than he or she can handle: if the solution
is to 'share' some of that 'surplus work' with others, then a law firm will
emerge. The sharing could take place with other self-employed lawyers
(lawyers who become partners), or with other employed lawyers (lawyers
who become assistants). This idea of shareable surpluses is fundamental
to the theory of the law firm which I develop in part II.

3.6 The Promotion-to-Partner Tournament

The expression 'promotion-to-partner tournament' is taken from the
work of Galanter and Palay (1991). They explore the reasons why law
firms grow and why, given the conditions that often prevail in legal
practice, they will tend to grow exponentially. Their arguments all
surround the particular circumstances of a know-how business.

3.6.1   The growth of law firms

Firms begin to evolve when an established lawyer (a 'partner', for the sake of exposition) begins to share surplus work with another. When this sharing takes place, the established lawyer will want to monitor the performance of that shared work. Law firms, therefore, use a complex monitoring system. Partners supervise the work of assistants, and in so doing maximise the returns on the investments that they have made. These investments are made in relationships with clients, in their reputation, and in the assistants they develop. If the partner is to earn a full return on them, it is important that those with whom the sharing of surpluses takes place do not take advantage — for example, by not working effectively, by 'stealing' the client, or by leaving before the investment in an assistant's new skills has been 'amortised' through profits on productive client work. This implies that assistants need some incentive not to behave opportunistically. Traditionally, this incentive has been provided by 'deferring' some part of the assistant's remuneration, dependent on continuing good behaviour. The deferral took the form of improved status through promotion to partnership, or of improved income through performance bonuses (or the higher income associated with partners' profit-shares rather than assistants' salaries).

Thus, the deferral encourages assistants not to leave so that they stay long enough to recover their full return on the investment they have made in the development of their own skills and know-how. It is also supposed to provide some motivation to stay by participating in the promotion tournament. The message of the tournament is that those assistants who perform their side of the sharing bargain by not shirking, by not stealing clients, and by not leaving, will be rewarded with promotion to partnership. To 'win' in the tournament, therefore, the assistants must work hard to develop their skills and to maintain their productivity.

Part of the economic logic of law firms is that the pyramid structure contributes to profitability by allowing equity partners to take the profit generated by assistant solicitors. The ratio (or leverage) of assistants to equity partners is therefore part of the profit structure of the firm. To maintain profitability, the firm will need to maintain its pyramid ratio. A law firm will tend to grow because, as it promotes 'winners' in the tournament to equity partnership, it must recruit more assistants in order to maintain its leverage ratio. For example, if a law firm has two equity partners and four assistants, its leverage is 4 : 2 (or, more properly, 2 : 1). If one of the assistants becomes an equity partner, the firm will still need two assistants for each partner if it is to maintain its leverage ratio, and so will need to recruit *three* new assistants.

I must emphasise (as I shall on a number of occasions, principally in paragraph 28.4) that this mathematical logic only works if the three partners can generate enough surplus work to share with six assistants, and can effectively monitor the performance of that work. If they cannot, then their leverage structure will not produce enough profit to maintain previous levels of profitability. Similarly, if they do not recruit new assistants when they promote someone to partnership, there will now be more partners sharing in the same amount of profit as before. (This ignores the possibility that, other things being equal, profitability will inevitably go up as the former assistant's employment costs cease to be overheads, and that profits may also rise simply because the new partner is able to charge higher fees than before; it also assumes that the three partners share in profits equally whereas in fact differential profit-sharing may ensure that individual partners' incomes are not affected by sharing in the same amount of net income as before.)

3.6.2 *Exponential growth*

Galanter and Palay's notion of a 'tournament' not only provides incentives for associates to work hard, but in their view usually guarantees that a firm will grow at least exponentially — that is, by more than the number of newly promoted partners. A firm's growth rate will depend on (1991, page 103):

(a)   the ratio of assistants to partners in the 'base year',
(b)   the percentage of assistants promoted to partnership,
(c)   the number of assistants that the firm must recruit to replace the newly promoted partners *and* to maintain the assistant-to-partner ratio.

Their theory of exponential growth only holds good, of course, if the number (or proportion) of assistants promoted to partnership remains reasonably constant, and if the ratio of assistants to partners also remains constant (or increases). In fact, their analysis of large US firms supports the theory — at least for the period covered by their review. The theory also holds true for the large English law firms.

If a law firm, formed with two lawyers in 1925, grows at a sustained rate of 10% a year, its growth curve will look like that in figure 3.1. For the first 30 years, the growth is barely noticeable, rising to 35 lawyers by 1955. In the next 30 years, however, the growth is dramatic — to just over 600 lawyers. This is the effect of compound growth: the same rate of growth applied to small numbers gives a very different result when applied to larger ones. In the five years from 1985 to 1990, the firm would add almost 300 lawyers, and by the year 2000 it would have more than 2,500 lawyers.

This graph probably looks fanciful to some. Interestingly, the growth of many of the large US firms until 1990 in fact mirrors this curve almost exactly (comparable data are not available for English law firms, but anecdotal evidence suggests that their growth has followed the same pattern). However, if firms continued to grow larger, unconstrained exponential growth would lead to law firms of unimaginable (and, I think, unmanageable!) size. Part of Galanter and Palay's exposition is that, every so often, there is a 'shock' that changes the rate of growth. The principal 'shock' to which they direct their attention is an apparent increase in the

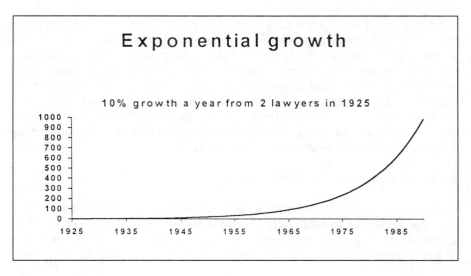

Figure 3.1

rate in about 1970. However, there was a shock in about 1990 that resulted in a decrease both in the rate and in absolute numbers: this shock was clearly the recession that affected the industrialised Western economies and resulted in law firms making lawyers redundant. The seemingly inexorable growth of the large law firms was over. Galanter and Palay therefore describe their 'complete story' as one in which (1991, page 105):

> "firms grow exponentially for a considerable period, then something shocks the system to make them grow at a different rate, but that new percentage growth-rate remains stable for a considerable period of time. We have focused our discussion on why the law firm's tournament produces this stability. But we acknowledge that periodically something might shock the entire industry so as to permit one-time changes in promotion (or growth rates). So long as there is a return to stable growth at these new rates our story is consistent with the known facts. Promotion rates will be stable, but kinked, and the pattern of firm growth will be exponential, but kinked. Exactly how the changed promotion rate will impact on the kinked growth rates depends on the changes in a number of additional variables as well, including changes in promotion rates, associate-to-partner ratios, attrition rates, and the length of the tournament."

In other words, there will be factors arising within the environment of law firms which can affect the rate of growth across the profession; and there will be factors arising because of the internal structure of law firms (the promotion-to-partner tournament) that will also affect the rate of growth for a particular firm. Although firms grew exponentially both before and after 1970, the *rates* of increase were different for the two periods:

something changed the rate of growth around 1970. They therefore emerge from their analysis with a 'kinked' exponential theory (1991, page 88):

> "A theory that seeks to account for kinked exponential law-firm growth, as ours does, must explain not only the "kink" but the underlying non-linear growth pattern as well. In the kinked exponential model the change in growth rates after 1970 accounts for no more than 50 per cent of the growth in recent years. Fully half of the post-1970 growth would remain even if the percentage growth rate had remained unchanged. . . .
>
> Thus, the rapid growth of the large law firm has two components: one exogenous to the structure of the firm, accounting for the kink in the curves; the other endogenous, explaining the underlying shape of the curves . . . created by what we term the 'promotion-to-partner tournament'."

3.6.3 The 1970 shock

A number of possibilities are advanced for the 'exogenous component' that led to the 1970s kink (Galanter and Palay 1991, page 110):

(a) *The supply of lawyers.* Between 1960 and 1970, the number of lawyers in the US increased by 26%, but between 1970 and 1980 it almost doubled. The growth in the supply of English lawyers has also been dramatic (see paragraph 1.4.2).

(b) *Increased merger activity.* This may be plausible, but none of the possible reasons for mergers (increasing market share, diversifying risk by developing a broader range of services, growing to take advantage of cross-selling opportunities and to provide 'one-stop shops', or mimicking client activity) explains why the exponential growth of law firms began in the early 1970s before law firms accelerated their merger activity. In the UK, it was probably due in part to the removal in 1967 of the restriction on law firms of a maximum of 20 partners.

(c) *Increased demand for legal services.* It is true that the demand for legal services increased after 1970, but the large firms grew at a significantly faster rate than the rest of the profession, suggesting that more than a general increase in demand was at play. The view that the additional demand was for the corporate legal services provided by large firms has some credence: between 1967 and 1982, spending by US business clients grew from $5 billion of law firms' revenue to $34 billion (and from 39% of the total income of law firm to 48.6%). However, Galanter and Palay argue that this fails to distinguish between the need for more corporate lawyers and the demand for larger law firms, and conclude that there was insufficient objective evidence that the size of work teams or the complexity of the work done within firms has grown. England has also seen growth in the size of its largest law firms (see paragraph 1.4.2).

(d) *The rise of in-house lawyers.* Increased reliance by businesses on their own internal legal departments does not suggest a need for larger law firms. If anything, sophisticated buying of legal services by in-house lawyers would suggest fewer opportunities for cross-selling and 'one-stop shopping'.

(e)   *Changes in the business use of law.* The business world of today is more complex than ever before, with more competition, more regulation, greater risk, and more uncertainty about the rewards of taking risks. There have been profound changes in domestic and world economies, including increasingly competitive global markets, floating exchange rates, liberalisation of capital markets, and increased economic importance of service industries — particularly finance (see paragraph 1.3). This complexity has changed the amount and character of legal work: handling any particular matter (whether contentious or non-contentious) may now require teams of lawyers working to shorter timescales, with a greater need for specialisation, and with considerable amounts of money at risk. Changes in the methods of delivering legal services might therefore suggest a need for larger law firms.

Galanter and Palay suspect that each of these explanations may well have contributed in some way to the increased rate of growth since 1970: how (and in what proportion) they left to future research, but they feel intuitively that changes in the business use of law and working methods will provide the most fertile ground. Unfortunately, as Galanter and Palay acknowledge, there are no data to test whether or not the *demand* for legal services (particularly the services of large firms) increased exponentially. This is important: Galanter and Palay's thesis is that, whatever external reasons there may have been for the 1970s kink, there was nevertheless in addition a built-in 'growth engine' responsible for a significant share of the growth in law firms witnessed after 1970. They suggest that about half of the growth is a by-product of the promotion-to-partner tournament. Indeed, they argue that this tournament leads *inevitably* to a pattern of exponential growth. For them, the internal (endogenous) factors are more influential in exponential growth than the environmental (exogenous) factors. While the external environment — demand by clients and the supply of legal expertise — supports this internal growth, that conclusion may appear to hold good.

3.6.4   The 1990 shock

In about 1990, the growth rates of the large US law firms (and many English ones, too) slowed — or even went into reverse as lawyers and support staff were laid off (see paragraph 1.4.2). The theory of exponential growth takes account of the possibility of shocks that might change the rate of growth, but appears to assume that there will still be exponential growth, albeit at different rates, either side of the shock. Whether the post-recessionary upturn in business leads to a restoration of exponential growth remains to be seen.

The 1990 shock is evidenced by the closure of law offices (see paragraph 1.4.1.1), a slowing in the 'birth rate' of new large firms (see paragraph 1.4.2), a slowdown in the rate of growth of the large firms (see paragraph 1.4.2.2), and a slowdown in the rate of growth in the profession's fee income (see paragraph 1.4.3). Another indicator is the rate of partnership promotions: in the late 1980s, the rate of increase in the number of principals in English law firms was around 4%, but for five of the six years since 1990 it has been less than 1% — falling as low as 0.36% in 1992 (based on Lewis 1996, table 4.2).

3.6.5 Firms that do not grow

Finally, Galanter and Palay have to face the reality that some firms do not grow in accordance with their theory. They acknowledge three types of small firms (1991, page 108):

(a) *The incipient large firm* — that is, a firm at the earlier stages of exponential growth. Although it is structured so that over a period of time it will grow exponentially (because of the promotion-to-partner tournament), at the moment the effects of that growth are not noticeable.

(b) *Firms that have made a conscious decision to remain small*. These firms usually do not engage in a promotion tournament, making up partners only occasionally (and often unpredictably). Indeed, some firms will only promote an assistant when a partner dies, leaves or retires — a zero-growth promotion policy. Niche and founder-led firms often fall into this second category. Such firms have limited success in using the incentive of partnership as a mechanism for protecting their investments: as assistants develop their own know-how, reputation and client relationships, the likelihood of them leaving the firm increases.

(c) *Firms that have no surplus, shareable work*. Many small firms have partners who have enough client work and client following to keep themselves (and perhaps a paralegal) busy. There is no surplus work to be shared, and so no opportunity to build a pyramid. Similarly, one often finds lawyers who have more work than they can cope with it, but because their surplus is not shareable they cannot build a larger firm on the basis of their reputation and skills. Some expertise is so arcane, or the client following so personal or idiosyncratic, that the lawyer concerned cannot pass on the expertise required by clients or cannot 'lend' charisma to assistants.

3.7 Limits to Growth

It is clear that law firms do not and will not grow exponentially forever. Galanter and Palay accept this — in fact, the distinction between a firm's *need* to grow and its *ability* to do so is at the root of their broader argument. As firms grow, they must come to terms with one or more of three constraints on their growth.

3.7.1 Generating sufficient fee income to cover costs

When a firm grows too quickly, or new business is not developed commensurate with a firm's size, there is a danger that a 'revenue gap' develops. This can, of course, happen to a business of any size and is not therefore a constraint to be associated only with large firms. However, the development of specialisation associated with large firms will encourage clients to 'shop around' more. Added growth might therefore increase the risk to the law firm that clients will take their work to other firms. Clients can also use their additional bargaining power to exert pressure on the fees of firms they do engage.

When a revenue gap develops, survival means that a firm must change in one of three ways:

(a)   *Stretch existing income to cover more lawyers,* by requiring assistants to work more (chargeable) hours without any increase in their remuneration or by partners accepting lower profits. In the US, it seems that while the fee income of large firms increased considerably, partners have not necessarily benefited proportionately. For example, while profits-per-partner remained relatively flat between 1965 and 1985 (a real increase of 1% a year), associates' incomes increased at three times that rate. This implies a significant redistribution of income from partners to associates. The productivity figures for English law firms (see paragraph 1.4.3) suggest that this 'stretching' of fee income has been happening here in recent years.

(b)   *Reduce the rate of growth,* by aligning growth more closely to the demand for services. Changing any one of four variables will result in a different rate of growth:

(i)   the ratio of assistants to partners,
(ii)   the percentage of assistants becoming partners,
(iii) the length of time it takes to become a partner,
(iv)   the number of partners leaving the firm.

Adjusting any of the first three variables also implies a change in the underlying structure of the firm. Many of these changes were beginning to happen in the late 1980s and were therefore marking a transformation even before recession took hold. Indeed, because these adjustments could have created difficulties in the morale, retention and recruitment of assistants, it is more than arguable that the recession *helped* some of the large firms through what could have been a very painful transformation. Nevertheless, since the tournament is a necessary feature of creating leverage (or a pyramid structure) that maintains or improves profit per partner, the medium to long term picture may not look so favourable.

(c)   *Increase the demand for services.* Before the recession, this was inevitably the preferred strategy of most large firms. It created greater competition for clients, more marketing activities, and even moving into non-law businesses (such as financial services and estate agency). For some of the largest firms, increasing the demand for their services internationally saved them from the worst effects of the domestic economic downturn in the early 1990s.

3.7.2 Finding a sufficient number of new assistants

As the output of the top law schools failed to meet the demand of the large US law firms, those firms began to encourage experienced assistants who were already with another law firm to join them, so creating the 'lateral' movement of lawyers. In addition, if a firm with surplus work or excess capacity (underemployed assistants) can find a 'mate' with the opposite problem, a merger can make sense to balance out the respective surpluses. If a number of firms simultaneously find themselves with surplus labour and insufficient work to keep them busy (as happened at the beginning of the recession), mergers become less attractive.

3.7.3 Maintaining quality

As a firm grows and diversifies its services, its ability to control and maintain quality diminishes. The methods of ensuring the required standard of performance must change along with the scale of operation: indeed, it may be that the inability of a firm effectively to monitor the output of its fee-earners will be the ultimate constraint on the growth and diversification of law firms (see further chapter 8).

3.8 Conclusions

Understanding the nature of law firms as know-how businesses, and the influences of both the exogenous and endogenous components of growth, are important not just in making sense of law firms as business organisations but also in beginning to see and assess strategic opportunities.

Chapter 4

STRATEGY: THE MATCHING PROCESS

4.1 Introduction

One of the initial sources of confusion about strategy is the absence of a common language and framework. Business planning was all the rage in the legal profession during the late 1980s. Much of it was seeking to predict the likely environment for legal services in the coming years. These planning exercises tended to be either historical financial analysis used for extrapolation of continuing financial trends, or partners' and others' unsubstantiated assertions of what would happen without any systematic analysis of client base, finances, or economic trends. In both cases, the resulting document was usually little better than the partners' 'wish lists' for new clients, adding new areas of work to become 'all things to all clients', and increasing profitability. Many regarded the plans as futile, prescriptive blueprints that were inappropriate for a fast-changing world, and most business plans lay on shelves gathering dust. The economic circumstances of the early 1990s rendered worthless many of the optimistic assumptions made during the planning process. The 'traditional' idea that strategy determined a structure that was then supported by systems is challenged and refuted by Bartlett and Ghoshal (1994–95): the strategy-structure-systems philosophy needs to be replaced with purpose, process and people.

The notion of planning therefore gave way to the expressed need for flexibility, and so for strategic thinking rather than strategic planning. Understanding the legal environment and clients' views of lawyers became more important than analysis and prediction. This was undoubtedly correct, but the thinking often resulted in no concrete, identifiable actions to be taken to respond to the strategic environment. The pendulum had swung completely the other way.

It is against this background that we must now try to make sense of the concept of strategy in legal practice, and to assess what at a practical level its uses are. Can lawyers create a strategy, or must they merely react to the changing needs of their clients? Are the strategies of law offices the result of what their leaders plan, or a reflection of what their lawyers actually do? Is a business strategy in fact any different to a marketing strategy? Is a merger a strategy, or is it part of the implementation of a strategy? Learning about strategy is a journey of exploration. It involves looking at different ways of viewing the business world, and any given organisation's interaction with it. You will find models, tools and ideas along the way. Some will appeal to your way of thinking and working; some will not. Making sense of where your organisation fits *is* the essence of strategy. How you make sense of it, and what you do with the understanding you develop, is up to you.

4.2   The Essence of Strategy

Grant describes strategy as a matching operation — matching or linking a firm's resources and capabilities with its environment, and the opportunities that that environment presents (1995, pages 30 and 114). In this sense, the essence of strategy is this matching process. A crucial question still remains, however: should a business gear up its resources to meet the needs and opportunities of the environment it sees; or should it attempt only to meet the needs and opportunities for which it has the appropriate resources? Both could be correct approaches. The one chosen will depend on the degree of entrepreneurialism within the business (see chapter 7), and the degree of risk that the entrepreneurs and those who finance the business are prepared to accept. Particularly for the smaller firm (and perhaps an in-house legal department), strategy may have to be dictated by available resources. But the important point is that, whether the emphasis is placed on the environment or the resources, there should be a match.

This approach is consistent with Drucker's theory of the business (see paragraph 2.4), and is one reason why Drucker's apparently simple approach can be so compelling in law firms.

In conversations about strategy, mission statements (and 'the vision thing') are often dismissed as worthless or referred to in derisory terms. This is usually because vision or mission are perceived not to be based on hard data, that they are perhaps more intuitive than analytical and, therefore, not to be taken seriously. First, let me suggest a distinction between vision and mission. To my mind, vision is about *where* you are trying to get to whereas mission is more a sense of *what* you want to achieve. Of course, there are senses in which vision and mission can be stated in the same terms. But vision is more about creative thinking, mission about actions and results. In organisations like law firms that are characterised by a number of individuals with a degree of autonomy and authority to commit it to certain actions, it is quite possible for it to appear to have no strategy at all, no sense of direction, no apparent purpose. A mission statement may be an effective way of providing a *framework* for the exercise of this autonomy and authority. Indeed, Payne thinks that "an effective mission statement is especially important in services because of the need for focus and differentiation in service sector businesses" (1993, page 42).

4.3   The Concept of Strategy

4.3.1   *Corporate and business strategies*

Grant (1995, pages 41–3) distinguishes between corporate strategy (which industry or industries you should be in) and business strategy (how to compete within your chosen industry or industries). It might be tempting to think that a law firm is 'stuck' with the legal industry and that corporate strategy is irrelevant consideration. This issue is further clouded in law firms because, as yet, few law firms have incorporated the delivery of their legal services (as opposed to their support functions), and the label 'corporate' usually creates an adverse reaction in lawyers when talking about their own businesses. In fact, the ability of law firms to engage in financial services and estate agency shows that multidisciplinary practice has already raised questions about 'corporate' strategy. The broader development of multidisciplinary practices is a significant strategic issue for law firms (see further paragraphs 17.1 and 38.4), and we should not therefore assume that 'corporate' strategy is a given. We should not let a label blind us to the reality of our business environment.

4.3.2   *Strategic fit*

Building on the 'matching' idea, Grant (1995, pages 31–3) also introduces the notions of strategic fit, and consistency. Not only must a successful strategy ensure a match (consistency) between the firm's environment and its resources, but it must also be consistent with its goals and values and its structure and systems. His concept of strategy therefore goes beyond industry environment and internal resources (staff, skills, and style) to embrace the firm's shared values, structure and systems: there are strong echoes of McKinsey's 7-S framework (see paragraph 2.2.1), emphasising the need for an all-inclusive approach to formulating strategy. Drucker's theory of the business (see paragraph 2.4) also requires 'fit' between environment, mission and competencies, and with reality.

4.3.3   *Deliberate and emergent strategies*

There are a number of distinct approaches to strategy. One is the idea that strategy can be created at the top of an organisation, based on analysis of the firm's environment and resources, and then 'handed down' for implementation. This is often called the deliberate, rationalist or planned approach. This one-sided philosophy has been strongly criticised by Mintzberg (1987 and 1994). For those lawyers who are uncertain about (or dissatisfied with) the process of strategic planning in their organisations, the following extract from Mintzberg (1994, pages 404–6) may provide some reassurance:

". . . the field of planning, in its literature and its manifestations in practice, has generally taken the machine form [meaning the classic bureaucracy, highly formalised, specialised, and centralised, and dependent largely on the standardisation of work processes for coordination] for granted, and promoted formal planning as the 'one best way' for all organizations. Such thinking has therefore spilled over to professional organizations, often with most unfortunate consequences. . . . Almost all rely on the conventional assumptions of planning, namely that strategies should emanate from the top of the organization fullblown, that goals can be clearly stated, that the central formulation of strategies must be followed by their pervasive implementation, that the [professionals] will (or must) respond to these centrally imposed strategies, and so on. It is almost as if the whole structure were supposed to be shifted to accommodate the needs of planning. . . .

In fact, these assumptions are wrong, stemming from a misunderstanding of (or an unwillingness to understand) how nonmachine forms of organization must function. The result has been a great deal of waste, trying to fit the square pegs of planning into the round holes of organization. At best, the pegs were damaged — the planners failed, they merely wasted their time. . . . But at worst, the holes were damaged — the planners succeeded, and the *organization* wasted its time, possibly becoming dysfunctional in the process. . . .

The reason for these problems are [sic] not difficult to understand, so long as one remains open to forms of organization other than the traditional machine. [Professional organizations are] driven by operating work that is highly complex if rather stable in execution. As a result of this one major difference, many of the basic cornerstones of the machine organization . . . collapse, notably those of top-down control and centralized strategy making.

The result is a strategy making process almost diametrically opposed to that of the machine organization — and the conventional wisdom. . . . Many actors get involved in the process, including operating professionals, who create many of the key product-market strategies individually by deciding how they will service their own clients. The direct influence of administrators is often restricted to strategies of support; and together with the operating professionals, they tend to enter into complex, interactive processes of collective choice that take on collegial as well as political colorings. The result is a rather fragmented process of strategy formation, with the organization's strategies typically being the aggregation of all kinds of individual and collective ones. . . . Ironically, the overall strategic orientation of professional organizations seems to remain remarkably stable while individual strategies seem to be in a state of almost continual change.

The stability of the overall strategy may suggest a role for action planning [meaning before-the-act specification of behaviour: strategies are supposed to evoke programmes that are supposed to prescribe the execution of tangible actions], but the complexity of professional work and its decentralization to the professional operating employees largely precludes this, or at least restricts it to the nonprofessional work of the support staff or to very broad or peripheral areas of organizational activity (such as the construction of new facilities, or the scheduling of space utilization).

But . . . strategic analysis has a major role to play in the professional organization, but not in the usual way. That is because much of the analysis is conducted, not by [employed] planners, but by the professionals themselves, and it is used, not so much for central control and coordination, as in the debate and interplay that make up the collective process of decision making."

Mintzberg (1987) contends that strategies do not need to be deliberate, they can emerge; they can form as well as be formulated; they can be crafted as well as planned. I confess that I have a sneaking preference in the context of law firms for Mintzberg's notion of crafting. The following extract will help to explain (1987, page 69):

"Smart strategists appreciate that they cannot always be smart enough to think through everything in advance. No craftsman thinks some days and works others. The craftsman's mind is going constantly, in tandem with her hands. Yet large organizations try to separate the work of minds and hands. In so doing, they often sever the vital feedback link between the two. . . .

In practice, of course, all strategy making walks on two feet, one deliberate, the other emergent. For just as purely deliberate strategy making precludes learning, so purely emergent strategy making precludes control. Pushed to the limit, neither approach makes much sense. . . . No organization . . . knows enough to work everything out in advance, to ignore learning en route. And no one . . . can be flexible enough to leave everything to happenstance, to give up all control. . . . Thus deliberate and emergent strategy form the end points of a continuum along which the strategies that are crafted in the real world may be found. Some strategies may approach either end, but many more fall at intermediate points."

Mintzberg also advocates the use of 'deliberately emergent' strategies in businesses that require great expertise and creativity (1987, pages 70–1):

"Consider first what we call the *umbrella strategy*. Here senior management sets out broad guidelines . . . and leaves the specifics . . . to others lower down in the organization. This strategy is not only deliberate (in its guidelines) and emergent (in its specifics), but it is also deliberately emergent in that the process is consciously managed to allow strategies to emerge en route. . . . [Businesses] that require great expertise and creativity . . . can be effective only if their implementors are allowed to be formulators because it is people way down in the hierarchy who are in touch with the situation in hand and have the required technical expertise. In a sense, these are organizations peopled with craftsmen, all of whom must be strategists."

If Mintzberg's reference to 'way down in the hierarchy' was replaced with 'in proximity to clients' (which would not, in my view, destroy the sense or validity of his message), his conclusion provides a powerful message to law firm strategists. Mintzberg also reinforces the point that partners cannot abdicate the strategic process to others in the firm — they are craftsmen who must also themselves be strategists.

For those lawyers who are concerned that strategists are creative or inventive, who believe that strategic thinking means finding something new or different, the idea of emergent strategy can come as a relief. Nor is strategy necessarily about advocating change — "not so much to promote change as to know *when* to do so . . . obsession with change is dysfunctional" (Mintzberg 1987, page 73).

Although strategy does not need to promote change, strategists must be able to detect discontinuities. Some discontinuities are obvious. We are going through a discontinuity at the moment as we shift from the capitalist world to a post-capitalist one, from the dominance of financial capital to the dominance of intellectual capital (see paragraph 1.3.2). Handy writes (1989, pages 19 and 22):

"Discontinuous change requires discontinuous thinking. If the new way of things is going to be different from the old, not just an improvement on it, then we shall need to look at everything in a new way. . . . It is a time of new imaginings, of windows opening even if some doors close. We need not stumble backwards into the future, casting longing glances at what used to be; we can turn round and face a changed reality. It is, after all, a safer posture if you want to keep moving."

In a similar vein, Davidson and Rees-Mogg write (1997, page 26):

"It will therefore be crucial that you see the world anew. That means looking from the outside in to reanalyze much that you have probably taken for granted. This will enable you to come to a new understanding. If you fail to transcend conventional thinking at a time when conventional thinking is losing touch with reality, then you will be more likely to fall prey to an epidemic of disorientation that lies ahead. Disorientation breeds mistakes that could threaten your business, your investments, and your way of life."

But it is not just Drucker's social transformation, or Handy's age of unreason, or Davidson and Rees-Mogg's epidemic of disorientation, that creates a discontinuity: "The real challenge in crafting strategy lies in detecting the subtle discontinuities that may undermine a business in the future. . . . They can be dealt with only by minds that are attuned to existing patterns yet able to perceive important breaks in them" (Mintzberg 1987, page 74). To be able to this, the strategist must have a deep understanding of his or her business — not just facts and analysis, but an intimate knowledge and wisdom that allows patterns to be detected and changes in them to be apparent. Lawyers who keep their heads firmly fixed on the files on their desks may miss the most important clues about their practice.

Part of the difficulty of strategy is that people often carry on business without expressing their knowledge of it, perhaps even without being aware of the assumptions they are making in doing so. One of the great benefits of Drucker's theory of the business (see paragraph 2.4) is that it shifts the focus of strategic thinking towards a conscious articulation of the assumptions on which a business has been built. Drucker looks to the environment and to resources (competencies); he also talks about the need for these strategic assumptions to 'fit' — in his case, to fit reality and to fit each other. Drucker offers an effective framework for testing an organisation's concept of its strategy: a successful strategy would embody a coherent theory of the organisation's business, consistent with the reality of its environment, mission and competencies.

If this discussion has led you to prefer the emergent, crafting approach to strategy, remember that it still needs to be based on some analysis — if by 'analysis' we mean understanding the environment and the business, and the issues that surround them. Strategic analysis is one of the building blocks for *any* approach to strategy and strategic thinking. Analysts must justify the utility of their analysis; crafters must justify the basis of their assumptions. "The purpose of strategy analysis is not to provide the answers but to help us to understand the issues" (Grant 1995, page 25).

4.4   The External Environment

4.4.1   *The five forces of competition*

A key part of strategy, therefore, is understanding the external environment. One of the most popular models for doing this is Porter's five forces of competition (Porter 1980, page 4), reproduced as figure 4.1.

The five competitive forces identified by Porter apply to all industries, but not with equal or equivalent strength. For example, until the 1980s, the bargaining power of buyers and the threat of substitutes were not forces of competition that particularly worried lawyers in private practice. In fact, to a large extent, it could have been argued that, for most of the history of the modern legal profession, the five forces were kept almost in perpetual balance by the protection afforded to the legal profession by restrictions on the right to practise, and by the existence of scale fees. New entrants to the profession, and rivalry among existing firms might, from time to time, shift the balance a little, but very little happened to cause any fundamental shifts. My review of the changes in the legal profession in recent years (see paragraph 1.4) shows how much has changed in a short space of time. All of the five forces are now exerting their influence.

These forces will also determine the profitability of the industry as they shift the balance between competition among different suppliers, the

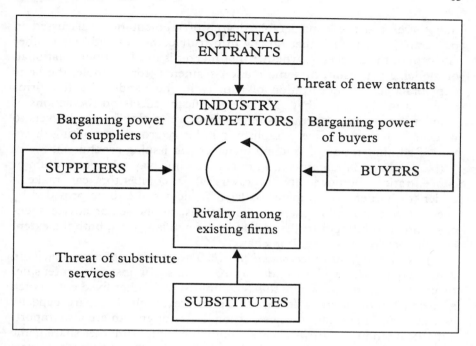

Figure 4.1 (Source: Porter 1980, page 4)

relative bargaining positions of all those involved in the 'chain' that results in the supply of the service to the client, and the value of the service to the client.

Porter elaborates on each of the forces. The following discussion highlights those elements that are particularly relevant to legal practice.

4.4.2 *Rivalry among existing firms*

There is a great tendency for law firms to follow a lead — once one firm does something, its competitors tend to follow. We can call this 'the herd instinct' or 'mimetic behaviour'. In this sense, as Porter points out, firms are mutually dependent (1980, page 17). Price cuts (like those that we saw in the domestic conveyancing market with the advent of licensed conveyancers in the mid 1980s) "are highly unstable and quite likely to leave the entire industry worse off from the standpoint of profitability. Price cuts are quickly and easily matched by rivals, and once matched they lower revenues for all firms" (Porter 1980, page 17).

Rivalry is caused by a number of structural factors affecting the profession:

(a) *The fragmentation of the legal profession* (see paragraph 4.7.3). Generally, a fragmented marketplace will allow firms to do things without being noticed readily or quickly. On the face of it, the legal marketplace has a high degree of fragmentation. It is important to remember, however, that there is also a considerable degree of segmentation (discussed in paragraph 4.5.2), such that no law firm truly competes with every other law firm in the market — whether that market is local, regional, national, or global. As a result, in some market segments (for example, the large City practices), concentration of activity in the hands of a few firms creates a market force that can have significant effects on the actions of competitors (such as opening foreign offices, recruiting foreign lawyers to work in a domestic office, establishing industry groups, recruiting directors of administration or training managers, or issuing brochures).

(b)   *Diversity of competition.* In much the same way as fragmentation or concentration, homogeneity (or diversity) in competitors can make it easier (or harder) to compete. As legal services come to be provided by licensed conveyancers, financial institutions, public-sector advice agencies, and accounting firms, as well as by foreign law firms, both the extent and the nature of competition change.

(c)   *Capacity, cost structure and growth.* The presence of overcapacity in a marketplace (as will exist during recessions, for instance) intensifies rivalry between firms. Where this is combined with other fixed costs (such as being bound in to a lease), the pressure to fill the spare capacity escalates, and may lead to price-cutting. Rates of growth are also important: "Slow industry growth turns competition into a market share game for firms seeking expansion. Market share competition is a great deal more volatile than is the situation in which rapid industry growth insures that firms can improve results just by keeping up with the industry, and where all their financial and managerial resources may be consumed by expanding with the industry" (Porter 1980, page 18, in a perfect description of the legal profession of the 1980s).

(d)   *High strategic stakes.* Firms can affect the market (and more so where competition is concentrated) by investing a lot of their future in a certain strategy. The danger for them is that they might fail; the danger for their competitors is that they might not follow suit (or not follow quickly enough) and miss out. As Porter says, ". . . the goals of these firms may not only be diverse but even more destabilizing because they are expansionary and involve potential willingness to sacrifice profitability" (1980, page 20). The globalisation of Clifford Chance's practice may be seen as having 'destabilised' some of the other large City firms, but its investment is now paying off while others seek to catch up (see Legal Business 1996, page 6).

(e)   *High exit barriers.* If firms cannot readily leave a highly competitive market, or diversify into other activities, they will remain and intensify the rivalry. Exit barriers will prevent them moving out. The legal market tends to be characterised by such high exit barriers: law firms invest a great deal in specialised assets (client base and fee-earners) which are difficult to shift into other activities; there are few other business activities open to law firms (and perhaps even for individual lawyers); there is often a strong emotional and professional attachment to the legal profession, and to a firm and its clients. These barriers will fuel rivalry and fragmentation (hence the increase in the number of sole practitioners during an economic downturn: see paragraph 1.4.4).

The transition of the industry through introduction, growth, maturity and decline (see paragraph 2.3.1) will also bring about changes in the structure of the market that will affect interfirm rivalry (see further paragraph 4.7.4).

4.4.3 *Threat of new entrants*

If exit barriers from the legal marketplace are high (see paragraph 4.4.2), it could be argued that the entry barriers are really quite low. Of course, a new entrant needs to have qualified as a lawyer, and will need sufficient capital to provide the minimum resource base. But, in the overall scheme of starting new businesses, a new law office does not face significant barriers.

However, there may be significant barriers to entering certain segments of the legal market (usually called barriers to mobility rather than barriers to entry, because they refer to existing law firms already within the industry entering a segment as opposed to competitors coming in from outside it: see further paragraph 4.5.2.3). For example, the large City firms are not likely to enter the legal aid market — not because they could not afford the costs of doing so, but because their resource base is different. A legal aid practice is sufficiently differentiated from large commercial practice for that differentiation to be a barrier: the 'switching' costs would be too great; the infrastructure costs of a large commercial firm would not 'match' the needs of the legal aid environment; and the commercial firm would lack access to the 'distribution channels' (that is, the network of contacts) that provide legal aid work. The issue is whether the new entrant can imitate or replicate the success factors. Similarly, it is not sufficient simply for a law firm to be large if it wants to compete with the top City law firms for the best corporate clients and work. Size alone is not the success factor. There are significant capital requirements, the need for an appropriate infrastructure (technology, support staff and procedures), as well as appropriate know-how, access to the 'distribution channels', and credibility. I shall return to the important issue of imitation or replicability in paragraphs 4.6.5 and 5.4.

These issues may help to explain why the assumed threat of large foreign law firms, or of accounting firms forming multidisciplinary practices, entering established legal territory need not cause discomfiture to all law firms. Whether or not these multinational or multidisciplinary forays are successful will depend on their ability to replicate the success factors that are critical in the market segment or segments in which they choose to compete. Equally, however, we should not assume that *none* of these new entrants will find the success factors they need (cf. paragraph 38.4.2).

4.4.4 *Threat of substitutes*

Whether we regard multidisciplinary practices as new entrants to the legal marketplace, or as substitutes for legal services, may well depend on precisely how these practices choose to compete. Much may depend on how widely or narrowly one defines the 'industry' (cf. paragraph 17.1). But on a broad interpretation, substitution is now rife within the marketplace for legal services. Licensed conveyancers can compete with solicitors for conveyancing work; do-it-yourself wills and conveyancing products compete with a traditional legal service; advice agencies may compete for matrimonial work; arbitrators and mediators are competing with litigators; solicitors may compete with barristers for advocacy in the higher courts; in-house lawyers are substituted for external law firms; technology (expert systems, litigation support systems, etc.) may be substituted for lawyers or paralegals; accountants and lawyers compete for tax work; and so the list goes on.

Not only will substitution affect the availability and flow of work within an industry, but it will also tend to limit the profits that can be derived from substitutable services.

4.4.5 Bargaining power of buyers

Whether or not substitutions are made will depend on the propensity of buyers to switch from 'traditional' sources of legal services to the substitutes. But even within the marketplace, buyers can, in certain circumstances, exert a lot of pressure. This may be largely a matter of the economics of supply and demand. However, the various factors can be broken down into (Porter 1980, pages 24-6):

(a) the size and concentration of buyers relative to the number of service providers;

(b) the profitability of the buyers (that is, their likely ability and willingness to pay fees, the cost of legal services relative to their total costs, and the importance of the legal service to the quality of the buyers' own products or services);

(c) the costs to buyers of finding out about alternative providers, negotiating with them, and monitoring their performance (these are 'transaction costs', which we shall come across again when we explore why firms exist at all: see paragraph 6.3), and the costs of switching from one provider to another;

(d) the threat of 'backward integration', that is, of potential clients providing the service for themselves: this means either 'do-it-yourself' for private clients, or setting up an in-house legal department for public sector and commercial clients.

The Legal Aid Board is an example of a powerful buyer. As the only buyer of legal aid services, it is a monopsony; firms dependent on legal aid work for their business are dependent on the Legal Aid Board, and must largely do as the Legal Aid Board wishes. Further, through franchising, the Board can reduce both its transaction costs and switching costs by ensuring greater commonality in procedure and structure within firms that provide legal aid services.

Other large providers of legal work (such as insurance companies, and in-house legal departments) can also exert pressure on providers of legal services; the individual private client or small business will find it all but impossible.

4.4.6 Bargaining power of suppliers

In theory, the factors affecting supply are similar to those affecting purchase (paragraph 4.4.5), except that in this instance the firm is the buyer. Wage costs represent the largest single cost of any law firm (see paragraph 28.5), and so employees represent the most important suppliers. As Porter puts it (1980, page 28): "There is substantial empirical evidence that scarce, highly skilled employees and/or tightly unionized labor can bargain away a significant fraction of potential profits in an industry". The increasing salaries of qualified lawyers in the 1980s, as well as the costs of mandatory training, added significantly to the cost structure of law firms (cf. paragraph 3.7.1(a)). At the same time, investments were being made in more expensive premises, in office technology, and in the process of promoting a practice; professional indemnity insurance costs escalated too. These various suppliers have demonstrated the influence that this competitive force can have on the behaviour and profitability of the legal profession.

4.5 Market Analysis

4.5.1 Thinking about the market

In a profession and marketplace that is, in its totality, as fragmented as the market for legal services, strategic thinking becomes impossible at a market-wide level. Even the largest firms in any jurisdiction do not seek to compete against every other firm for every type of legal work available. All firms seek to provide certain types of services, for certain types of clients, in certain places, and in certain ways. In other words, the whole market is subdivided into segments. These segments each have their own characteristics, a different group of competitors, and different success factors. Understanding these components is a critical part of strategic thinking. Deciding which segments to compete in is the function or outcome of strategic thinking. This cannot be done effectively unless the strategists know what the characteristics are, who the competitors are and how they behave, and what the firm must do in order to be successful in a market segment.

4.5.2 Segmentation

Dividing a marketplace into different segments is largely a matter of opinion. Essentially, the choices for law firms reduce to:

(a)   what is offered (services),
(b)   who wants it (clients),
(c)   where it is wanted and delivered (geography),
(d)   how it is delivered (process, culture, and style).

Grant (1995, pages 90–8) suggests five stages in analysing market segmentation.

4.5.2.1 Identify the strategically significant variables
For the most part, in legal services the strategically significant variables will be either the type (characteristics) of the legal service, or the type (characteristics) of the clients. Characteristics of the service will relate to such issues as legal content, procedural know-how, the necessary degree of lawyer-client contact and interaction, the support services required (particularly the ability to use technology), and price. Characteristics of the client might include private client or business client, wealth or size, job or industry, location, lifestyle, owner or manager, repeat client or transactional, and so on. The particular nature of services may also lead to consideration of the tangible and intangible elements of the service (see paragraph 20.3.3), the degree of customisation and exercise of independent judgment by those who have contact with clients, and how peaks and troughs in the level of demand for the service can best be met (Lovelock 1983).

Each firm must make its own decisions about what the most important strategic variables are for its actual or potential market segments. It is important in this process not to be constrained by the firm's existing thinking or approach: identifying these variables is not an exercise in rationalising what the firm (or a practice area) already does, but to identify what *can* be done.

4.5.2.2 Construct a segmentation matrix
The next stage is to create a matrix of the identified variables. For a commercial practice, for instance, a matrix might look something like figure 4.2 (the principle and pattern is more important for illustration than the likely accuracy).

Again, the matrix should not only plot what *is* done by the practice, but also what *could* be done. This allows the strategists to identify both existing coverage and further possibilities.

4.5.2.3 Analyse segment attractiveness
The matrix analysis should show the opportunities that exist in a market segment, and highlight opportunities that are presently unexploited, under-exploited, or over-exploited. This should allow the firm to analyse how attractive it is to maintain or expand its activities in that segment, or to enter a new segment. The analysis for this purpose can use Porter's five forces of competition model, suitably adapted (see paragraph 4.4.1). In this context, barriers to entry are replaced by barriers to mobility (the threat of new competitors is not from outside the industry or profession, but of rivals switching into the market segment being analysed: see paragraph 4.4.3).

4.5.2.4 Identify the segment's key success factors
The different possible combinations of variables suggest that the keys to success in one segment will differ to those in another — and, depending

CLIENTS	SERVICES: CORPORATE/COMMERCIAL								PROPERTY					LITIGATION						PRIVATE CLIENT				
	coy sec	m&a	finance	contracts	compet'n	employ	IP	tax	acq/disp	construct	L&T	plan & de	environ	prop lit	comm	employ	licensing	IP	debt	will & pro	trusts	tax & EP	finan serv	matrim
PROPERTY																								
developers	•	•	•	•		•		•	•			•	•	•										
construction	•							•		•			•	•	•	•			•					
estate agents		•				•									•	•			•					
housing trust			•	•		•			•	•	•	•	•	•		•								
AGRICULTURE																								
farming			•	•		•		•	•		•	•	•	•	•	•			•	•	•	•		
garden centres	•	•	•	•		•	•	•	•	•		•	•		•	•	•	•	•					
landed estates			•	•		•	•	•	•	•	•	•	•	•	•	•	•	•	•	•	•	•		
LEISURE																								
brewers	•	•	•	•	•	•	•	•	•	•	•	•	•	•	•	•	•	•	•					
gaming, etc	•	•	•	•	•	•	•	•	•	•	•	•		•	•	•	•	•	•					
leisure centres			•	•		•		•	•	•	•	•		•	•	•	•							
golf clubs				•		•			•			•				•	•							
PROFESSIONALS																								
lawyers															•							•		•
doctors				•		•			•		•				•	•				•	•	•	•	•
accountants				•		•			•		•				•	•				•	•			•
professional ass'ns			•	•		•		•	•		•				•	•								
PUBLIC SECTOR																								
local government			•	•		•		•	•	•	•	•	•	•	•	•			•					
charities			•	•		•		•	•		•			•	•	•			•					
PRIVATE																								
entrepreneurs		•	•	•		•	•		•		•				•	•		•	•	•	•	•		•
personal									•		•					•				•	•	•	•	•

Figure 4.2

on the segment, could differ significantly. Deciding whether or not to compete in a particular market segment should therefore be based on an understanding of the factors that contribute to sustainable competitive advantage. This is discussed more fully in paragraph 4.5.4.

4.5.2.5 *Consider specialisation or diversification*
A final part of the strategic issue for a firm is how many market segments to compete in — whether to focus or diversify. As Grant puts it (1995, page 96): "If different strategies need to be adopted for different segments, then not only does this pose organizational difficulties for the firm but the credibility of the firm in one segment may be adversely affected by its strategy in another". The idea of diversification of legal services is discussed in paragraph 8.5. Although it is not possible to state definitively whether or not diversification makes sense, it is clear that the general business trend in the US and the UK in recent years has been away from diversification (Grant 1995, pages 368–70). Grant suggests that diversification becomes more achievable if the key success factors of the diverse segments are similar and if there can be shared costs (1995, page 96). He also refers to Davidow and Uttal (1989), who argue that, in service industries, economies from specialisation and differences in the key success factors in different market segments militate *against* diversification (Grant 1995, page 97).

4.5.3 *Competitors*

Competitors form a key component of any firm's marketplace and external environment. They cannot be ignored in considering future strategy, since what they do (or do not do), and how they do it, may have a significant effect on clients' choices and expectations. However, the extent of competitor analysis that is necessary in formulating strategy may differ. For firms that operate in a 'mass market' where it is difficult to differentiate clients' needs and expectations, the service offered, or the method of delivery, competition will be fragmented, and the most influential competitors will probably be those that are the most proximate. This is likely to be true of the legal aid and personal injury markets, for example, but may not be true of 'disaster' and class action litigation. In the global marketplace, for heavyweight commercial work, and for some niche specialisations, on the other hand, the competition will be more concentrated and may be regional, national or even international.

Grant (1995, page 101) identifies three major purposes to competitor analysis: forecasting competitors' strategies; predicting their likely reaction to your own strategy; and considering how competitors' behaviour can be influenced in your own favour. Achieving any one of these purposes effectively requires good market intelligence, and the idea of sophisticated competitor analysis may seem far-fetched in an industry like the law where reliable information about competitors' behaviour and performance can be difficult to come by. But a combination of published information (for example, the Law Society's annual statistical reports, as well as interfirm comparisons, *The Legal 500, Chambers & Partners Directory* and other commercial sources) and local intelligence can take you a long way.

4.5.4 Success factors

The final stage in understanding the market in which the firm operates is to establish what the key success factors are (these are also often referred to as KSFs, or as the 'critical' success factors, CSFs). In broad terms, the success factors relate to providing what clients want, and doing what is necessary to be better than competitors. The analysis of client demand is therefore important: a firm must pose some fundamental questions and seek answers and insight. Who are the clients? Where are they? What do they do? How many of them are there? What legal issues arise for them? When and how often? In what form? What are their expectations of law firms? How do they choose lawyers? How much will they pay? And so on. The analysis of competitors (discussed in paragraph 4.5.3) will raise other questions. Who are the competitors? Where are they? How intense is the competition? To what extent are (and can) competitors be different? Is competition based on reputation, expertise, price, quality and service, proximity, size of operation? And so on.

Putting the needs and demands of clients in balance with the existence and behaviour of competitors should help a firm determine what the key success factors are in helping it attract and keep clients in the face of competition. These factors may relate to location, size, flexibility, low costs, better or more consistent service and quality, known expertise or client following, or the blending of a number of these (or other) factors into a distinctive market position.

The point of identifying key success factors is not to generate a blueprint for a successful strategy, but to make the firm aware of what its strategy must achieve.

4.6 Resources and Competencies

4.6.1 Introduction

Having considered the external environment and the marketplace, strategic analysis next shifts to the internal resources and competencies the firm or department has (or should have) available to it in order to meet the needs and opportunities presented by that environment. A good match (or one that is better than the competitors') will create a competitive advantage.

Grant makes the point (1995, pages 114–16) that strategic analysis historically focused rather more on external analysis than on internal analysis. He suggests that when the external environment is changing or in a state of flux, the firm itself (meaning its resources and capabilities) may be a much more stable basis on which to define its identity. A word of caution here: Grant does not suggest that resources and capabilities can be the *only* basis for formulating strategy, or that external conditions (such as economic environment, clients' needs and preferences, activities of competitors, and so on) can be ignored or glossed over. Unfortunately, this has too often been true in the legal profession. There has been a tendency to fix strategy on the basis of what partners have *wanted* to do, often irrespective of — or even in defiance of — external conditions, and then try to persuade clients to take whatever it is the firm has set out to provide. This is not strategic thinking, but wishful thinking. Nor is it the client-driven approach that is necessary for survival *in legal practice* in the 1990s. A firm must accordingly *balance and match* internal resources with external conditions: resource analysis is therefore a necessary part of understanding the capacity and requirements of the resources at a firm's disposal (see also Hamel and Heene 1994). Equally, however, achieving operational effectiveness is not a strategy (see Porter 1996).

4.6.2   The nature of the resources

A firm's resource base clearly includes its physical or tangible resources, such as premises, furniture, equipment and technology, library, and other 'fixed assets' that will typically appear on the balance sheet — along, the cynics would say, with partners' cars! Money may also be regarded as a tangible resource. In relation to other resources, Grant (1995, pages 123–6) distinguishes intangible resources (software and intellectual property rights, reputation, and culture) from human resources (specialised skills and knowledge, communicative and interactive abilities, and motivation). This distinction reflects the deepening importance of knowledge workers in all industries (see paragraph 1.3.2). Economists refer to this productive capacity of people as 'human capital', and the literature on how to measure, value, manage and develop this asset is increasing all the time (see, for example, Schultz 1971, Itami 1987, Sveiby and Lloyd 1987, Badaracco 1991, Crawford 1991, Quinn 1992, Becker 1993, Nonaka and Takeuchi 1995, Scarbrough 1996, Wilson 1996, Stewart 1997 and de Geus 1997).

Few of the intangible assets appear on the balance sheet (goodwill was often one of the exceptions for law firms, but is only rarely included these days). The nature of human capital in law firms is explored in more detail in chapter 5. In addressing strategic opportunities, a firm must have the tangible, intangible, human, and financial resources in place to allow it to achieve them. Being able to identify and, so far as possible, quantify them is an important part of the assessment required for strategic thinking.

4.6.3   Resources and capabilities

It is not sufficient merely to have resources at the firm's disposal: the firm must be able to turn them to productive capacity. The difficulty is not that the resources need to be individually productive, but that they need to be *combined* into productivity. Given the danger that lawyers will each act as an individual unit, their calls on other resources may be difficult to predict, fluctuating and in frequent conflict. They may also miss opportunities to combine their own capabilities and to provide a service that is different or better than anything they could achieve individually. Indeed, it may be the collective reputation of the individuals that attracts clients and creates a competitive advantage (as is often the case with the larger law firms with a 'brand name'): see paragraph 5.2.2.

There is a suggestion that businesses learn from their prior experience, and that the cost of production declines as experience increases. This is known as the 'experience curve'. In principle, its effect seems logical, and given the experience-dependent nature of much of legal practice, its application appears attractive. The idea that costs of production decline relative to output suggests that firms should chase market share as a way of 'leveraging' existing experience into profit. However, these apparent economies of scale (or economies of learning or of experience) do not inevitably follow, and using the experience curve in strategic analysis can be misleading. Grant writes (1995, page 250): "High-quality, low-volume production with lack of competition encourages craft-based production that is vertically integrated, makes intensive use of highly skilled labor, and places little emphasis on attaining economies of scale or experience. Typically, the experience curve for these industries is shallow, and, in the absence of volume gains and process innovation, annual reductions in real unit costs are usually less than 2 percent." The need to tailor services to the needs of clients, and to maintain close client contact, makes the reality of leveraging experience a difficult one to achieve in legal practice. A strategy of chasing market share in the fragmented, competitive marketplace of today may therefore be both expensive and unprofitable.

A firm therefore needs to understand and analyse its ability to turn its resources into productive capacity, and to assess whether it has any capabilities that are individually or collectively distinctive.

4.6.3.1 Core competence

Hamel and Prahalad (1990 and 1994) have articulated the concept of 'core competence' . The terms 'capability' and 'competence' are used interchangeably in the strategy literature. Hamel and Prahalad use the expression 'core competences' to distinguish those capabilities that are fundamental to a firm's performance and strategy from those that are more peripheral: "A competence is a bundle of skills and technologies rather than a single discrete skill or technology. . . . A core competence represents the sum of learning across individual skill sets and individual organizational units. Thus, a core competence is very unlikely to reside in its entirety in a single individual or small team" (1994, pages 202–3). In this sense, therefore, a competence is a core competence if one or more of the following applies:

(a) It will "make a disproportionate contribution to customer-perceived value" (page 204); this is not to imply that the competence "will be visible to, or easily understood by, the customer" (page 204), though the customer/client is "the ultimate judge of whether something is or is not a core competence" (page 205). The firm's analysis of client demand (see paragraph 4.5.4) should enable it to assess whether, for example, some aspect of expertise, the combination of individual talent into a particular service, or part of the process of delivery, will be perceived as a core competence of the firm.

(b)   It is "competitively unique. This does not mean that to qualify as core, a competence must be uniquely held by a single firm, but it does mean that any capability that is ubiquitous across an industry should not be defined as core unless, of course, the company's level of competence is substantially superior to others. . . . In any industry there will be a number of skills and capabilities that are prerequisites for participation in the industry, but do not provide any significant competitor differentiation. . . . In short, there is a difference between 'necessary' competencies and 'differentiating' competencies. It makes little sense to define a competence as core if it is omnipresent or easily imitated by competitors" (pages 205–6).

(c)   It "forms the basis for entry into new product markets" (page 207) or, in the context of law firms, for providing new services (or possibly existing services in new or different ways or locations).

4.6.3.2   Benchmarking

In recent years, benchmarking has been used to provide a degree of objectivity in the comparative assessment of capabilities or performance. Grant (1995, page 133) identifies four stages to benchmarking which, with some adaptation, are:

(a)   identifying the activities or functions of the business that need measuring, comparing or improving;

(b)   identifying businesses that are leaders in each of these activities or functions;

(c)   contacting those businesses, visiting them, talking to the managers and staff, and analysing first hand how they do so well;

(d)   using the new learning to redefine goals, redesign processes, and change expectations regarding the firm's functions and activities.

As with competitor analysis, this process may prove difficult in the legal profession. Perhaps we should stop to consider why such benchmarking information is not generally (and reliably) available within the profession. What is it in the mindset of lawyers that generally hinders the process of sharing comparative information? Such information is quite often available in other industries, where even fierce competitors openly benchmark against each others' performance. And even within the legal profession, there is some (albeit self-selecting) benchmarking being done — for example, through networks, select meetings of managing partners, and interfirm comparisons.

4.6.4   *The value chain*

Whereas the external environment will be the same for all competitors in an industry, the internal resources provide a source of difference (or differentiation) and so of competitive advantage. It is in this sense that the way in which the firm harnesses its resources and moulds them into a total offering to the marketplace creates its strategy. But while it is this totality that might *create* a strategic advantage, Porter contends that competitive advantage cannot be *understood* by looking at the firm as a whole (1985, page 33). He therefore introduces the 'value chain' as a tool for systematically examining the many discrete activities which a firm performs. Its purpose is to disaggregate a firm "into its strategically relevant activities in order to understand the behaviour of costs and the existing and potential sources of differentiation" (1985, page 33).

The value chain can therefore provide a starting point for resource analysis, though it should soon become clear that not all resources are uniformly important or valuable. Indeed, if done properly — and if it were possible to compare them — value chain analysis should show both similarities and differences between rival firms (1985, page 34):

"The value chains of firms in an industry differ, reflecting their histories, strategies, and success at implementation. One important difference is that a firm's value chain may differ in *competitive scope* from that of its competitors, representing a potential source of competitive advantage. Serving only a particular industry segment may allow a firm to tailor its value chain to that segment and result in lower costs or differentiation in serving that segment compared to competitors. Widening or narrowing the geographic markets served can also affect competitive advantage."

Porter's generic value chain is shown in figure 4.3, and shows a combination of primary and support 'value activities'.

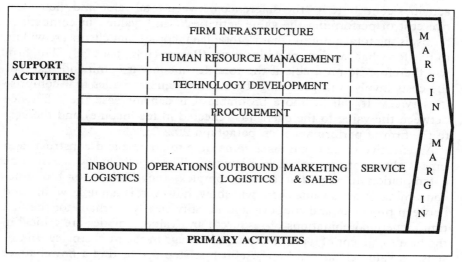

Figure 4.3 (Source: Porter (1985), page 37)

In the context of legal services, the generic value chain is not immediately appealing. However, by using its concepts and tailoring its components, a meaningful value chain can be created (see figure 4.4 for an example).

The value activities are the building blocks by which a firm creates a service that is valuable to its clients. In fact, suppliers and clients of the firm (if they are businesses) will have their own value chains, too: the firm therefore occupies a position in a series of other value chains, and it will be clients' own value chains that determine their needs for legal services. According to Porter (1985, pages 39, 45 and 48):

> "Identifying value activities requires the isolation of activities that are technologically and strategically distinct. Value activities and accounting classifications are rarely the same. . . . The appropriate degree of disaggregation depends on the economics of the activities and the purposes for which the value chain is being analyzed. . . . the basic principle is that activities should be isolated and separated that (1) have different economics, (2) have a high potential impact of differentiation, or (3) represent a significant or growing proportion of cost. . . . *Everything* a firm does should be captured in a primary or support activity. Value activity labels are arbitrary and should be chosen to provide the best insight into the business. . . . Ordering of activities should broadly follow process flow, but ordering is judgmental as well."

The value chain is therefore designed to show the total range of the firm's activities. For strategic thinking purposes, it may be necessary for a firm to prepare a value chain for each of its practice areas, rather than for the whole firm (particularly where the practice areas can be distinguished by different client needs — and therefore different client value — different economics, or different processes). The 'margin' to which all of the value activities contribute is "the difference between total value and the collective cost of performing the value activities", and 'value', in competitive terms, is the total amount (that is, total fee income) that clients are willing to pay for what the firm provides them (Porter 1985, page 38). The firm will therefore be profitable if the total fee income it commands exceeds the costs involved in providing the various value activities that comprise its services. It will be more profitable if it can increase the difference between the value to the client (as reflected in fee income) and the cost to the firm of performance (cf. paragraph 20.2.2).

An effective value chain takes some time to analyse and construct, and time is always at a premium in a law firm. There will always therefore be a temptation to regard it as too complex, too difficult, or too time-consuming. What a value chain will show, however, is the links within and between processes and support, and identify clearly (perhaps for the first time) where combinations of resources and value activities are critical in the firm's concept of its competitive advantage in the marketplace. In this sense, a value chain can be a useful first step to creating a flowchart or blueprint of the firm's services (see further paragraph 20.2.2).

SUPPORT ACTIVITIES

INFRASTRUCTURE
Departmental structure; administrative support; filing systems; quality management procedures; library and know-how systems

PEOPLE
Recruitment and induction; training and development; job design: appraisal and career structure; pay structure and review: grievance and discipline procedures

FINANCE
Budgets; time-recording and financial reporting; WIP management; cost and disbursement control; billing and collection procedures; cash flow management

TECHNOLOGY
Word processing; financial systems; telecommunications; practice support systems (e.g. know-how, case management, conflict checks); marketing and other databases

PROFILE AND MARKETING
Networking; brochures, newsletters, articles; client seminars

SELLING	TAKING INSTRUCTIONS	CASE PLANNING	EXECUTION	POST-COMPLETION
Targeting	Client interviews	Case analysis	Teamwork	Billing and collection
Beauty parades	Case acceptance	Case strategy	Meetings	File storage, etc.
Persuasion	Conflict checks	Project/case plan/management	Negotiations	Internal review
	Scoping the matter	Work allocation	Drafting	Client review
	Matter budget	Delegation	Choice/use of counsel	Ongoing client care
			Supervision	
			Financial monitoring	
			Reporting and communication	

MARGIN

PRIMARY ACTIVITIES

Figure 4.4

4.6.5 *Imitation and replication*

To the extent that a firm has resources and capabilities that are part of its value chain and contribute to its competitive advantage, the firm will be able to sustain its competitive advantage if those resources and capabilities cannot be imitated or replicated. Thus, a competitive advantage will be difficult to sustain if it is founded on homogeneous tangible (or even intangible) assets such as technology and proprietary software, or even know-how that is freely available in the marketplace because it is widely dispersed. On the other hand, if the advantage lies in arcane know-how, or information that is specific to certain of its clients (or an industry in which its clients are predominantly based), or in the particular combination of resources or processes used within the firm, imitation and replication will be much more difficult.

Similarly, if the firm wants to move into a market that requires certain resources and capabilities, it will be easier to achieve if the resources and capabilities are themselves easy to acquire, imitate or replicate. This may be demonstrated by considering markets where would-be competitors saw that the competitive advantage of established firms lay wholly or partly in size (or 'critical mass', as it is sometimes put). The strategy of the new entrants was to acquire lawyers and staff by merger and lateral recruitment to grow their firms over a short period of time to the same sort of size as the established players. But this is not just a numbers game: the lawyers and staff have to have the sort of legal, practical and client experience that the clients of large firms need — if you like, a compatibility in their respective value chains. Very often, the distinguishing feature of the larger, established firms was not just their size, but their internal culture (which is a product of history and personalities). Not having this history can effectively create barriers to entry or mobility: the strategy of the large, established firms "cannot be duplicated by other firms, for firms without that particular path through history cannot obtain the resources necessary to implement the strategy" (Barney 1991, page 108). This may also suggest reasons why the establishment of law offices within or alongside accounting firms may not always pose the competitive threat that many lawyers fear.

The imitability of professional know-how and processes may therefore be *the* key to competitive advantage in legal services. Whether and how this might be achieved is considered in paragraph 5.4.

4.7 Competitive Advantage

4.7.1 *The nature of competitive advantage*

Now we get to what many regard as the real heart of strategic analysis — the quest to match the external environment and internal resources and capabilities in such a way that the firm is competitively and economically successful. Each firm, however, may have its own definition of 'competitive advantage'. It might be maximising profits or market share; or establishing, maintaining or improving the firm's reputation in a certain field; or attracting high-quality work or certain clients; the possibilities are many and varied. Some of these possible advantages may, indeed, be traded off against each other — for example, by seeking to maintain fee-earners' satisfaction with their work at the expense of maximising profitability.

For competitive advantages to emerge, there must be differences between firms. Establishing a competitive advantage will then depend on the extent of the differences, the extent to which the environment is changing, and the ability of firms to respond to those changes (cf. Grant 1995, page 151, and Hamel and Heene 1994). Responding to change in turn depends on entrepreneurialism (see chapter 7), the availability of information and the ability to process it, and organisational flexibility.

4.7.2 Competitive advantage and the state of the industry

4.7.2.1 Industry evolution

We should not assume that a firm's choice of competitive advantage is an open book. We have already seen that every industry has its own structure and competitive forces (paragraph 4.4), and that industries tend to develop through certain stages or cycles (paragraph 2.3.1). Just as an industry's structure will affect competition, so increasing competition within an industry will cause the industry's shift to another stage in its evolution or life cycle. Strategic analysis must therefore also consider the effects of this evolution on the opportunities for competitive advantage. As Grant explains (1995, pages 244–5):

"Critical to sustaining competitive advantage is not simply protecting one's competitive position against competitive imitation but also ensuring that one's competitive advantage is not rendered obsolete by changes in the industry environment. IBM did not *lose* its competitive advantage in the world computer industry; the problem was that changes in the market meant that its enormous investments in internal resources and capabilities, such as its research labs, its sales and marketing organization, and its customer support capabilities, no longer matched industry key success factors as well as they did during the early 1980s.

The evolution of industries, and with it the changing requirements for success, creates a dilemma for the firm. The firms that are successful at one stage of the life cycle are unlikely to be successful at a subsequent stage because the resources and capabilities that provided the foundation for their success at one stage are not appropriate to the subsequent stage. . . . The solution . . . is for firms to pursue *dual strategies*: they must manage to maximize performance under today's circumstances, but strategy must also be involved with *change* in order to meet the circumstances of the future."

Drucker's theory of the business (see paragraph 2.4), with its emphasis on 'fit' between environment, mission and competencies, also suggests that the theory must change to reflect evolution.

4.7.2.2   *Competitive advantage in a fragmented profession*

Despite the emergence of much larger law firms in recent years, the professional polarisation that they have created, and their dominance of the legal marketplace (see paragraphs 1.4.2 and 1.4.4), the legal profession still remains very broadly dispersed in its number of firms, its geography, and the variety of services that it provides to a variety of clients. I believe that industry fragmentation is a fundamental issue in understanding strategy for law firms. Porter identifies the following as some of the underlying economic causes of fragmentation (1980, pages 196–200):

(a)   low entry barriers;

(b)   absence of economies of scale or experience;

(c)   high transportation costs: "they are effectively high in many service industries because the service is 'produced' at the customer's premises or the customer must come to where the service is produced" (page 197);

(d)   no advantages of size in dealing with buyers or suppliers;

(e)   diseconomies of scale stemming from, for example, diverse services, high creative content, personal service, or local control, image or contacts;

(f)   diverse market needs;

(g)   exit barriers: what else are lawyers equipped to do?!

Many of these factors affect the legal profession, and create — and, indeed, perpetuate — fragmentation. The regulation of prices that is common in many professions (through the use of scale fees) often helps to insulate them from the effects of fragmentation. Once the insulation is removed, however, the full forces of competition can wreak havoc.

Porter's first approach is to suggest ways in which the fragmentation can be overcome (1980, pages 200–6). Essentially, these involve trying to change the fragmented nature of the industry by seeking forms of concentration. This includes creating economies of scale or an experience curve, seeking to standardise diverse market needs, or making acquisitions to achieve a critical mass. But all of these approaches are difficult in legal practice given the *extent* of the fragmentation: even Clifford Chance, as the largest law firm in England and Wales, has a relatively small percentage share of the total market for legal services (about 3% of the domestic market). It is unlikely, however, that Clifford Chance (or any other law firm) would see itself as competing within the *total* market. Most firms, strategically, will define a narrower market (segmentation: see paragraph 4.5.2), and on this basis the extent of fragmentation may be reduced to more manageable levels. After all, what was the merger of Clifford-Turner and Coward Chance about if not to achieve some greater critical mass within the marketplace of City law firms?

Where a firm feels that it cannot overcome the fragmentation of its industry, Porter identifies some possible strategic responses that may allow it at least to compete within the industry (1980, pages 206–10). His suggestions include: 'formula' facilities (i.e. efficient, low-cost, volume processes at multiple locations); a 'bare bones/no frills' service or, alternatively, increasing the value added; specialising by type of service or client (both of which might "limit growth prospects for the firm in return for offering higher profitability"); tightly managed decentralisation; or a focused geographic area to achieve a higher market share within that area ("having bits and pieces of business in a number of areas . . . accentuates the problems of competing in a fragmented industry" (1980, page 210)).

Porter also identifies some interesting strategic traps "which should serve as red flags in the analysis of strategic alternatives in any particular fragmented industry" (1980, page 210):

(a) *Seeking dominance.* "The underlying structure of a fragmented industry makes seeking dominance futile unless that structure can be fundamentally changed. Barring this, a [firm] trying to gain a dominant share of a fragmented industry is usually doomed to failure. . . . Trying to be all things to all people generally maximizes vulnerability to the competitive forces in a fragmented industry, although it may be an extremely successful strategy in other industries in which there are cost advantages to volume production and other economies" (pages 210–11).

(b) *Lack of strategic discipline.* "The competitive structure of fragmented industries generally requires focus or specialization on some tight strategic concept. . . . Implementing these may well require the courage to turn away some business, as well as to go against the conventional wisdom of how things are done in the business generally. An undisciplined or opportunistic strategy may work in the short run, but it usually maximizes the exposure of the firm to the intense competitive forces common in fragmented industries in the longer run" (page 211): in my experience, encouraging partners in law firms to turn away business can be a very difficult process!

(c) *Over-centralisation.* "The essence of competition in many fragmented industries is personal service, local contacts, close control of operations, ability to react to fluctuations or style changes, and so on. A centralized organizational structure is counterproductive in most cases, because it slows response time, lowers the incentives of those at the local level, and can drive away skilled individuals necessary to perform many personal services. Whereas centralized control is often useful and even essential in managing a multiunit enterprise in a fragmented industry, centralized structure can be a disaster" (pages 211–12).

(d) *Assumption that competitors have the same overhead and objectives.* "The peculiar nature of fragmented industries often means that there are many small, privately held firms. Also, owner-managers may have noneconomic reasons for being in the business. Under these circumstances, the assumption that these competitors will have [the same overhead structure or objectives] is a serious error. . . . Similarly, such competitors may be satisfied with much different (and lower) levels of profitability . . ., and they may be much more interested in keeping up volume and providing work for their employees than profitability per se" (page 212).

(e)   *Over-reactions to new products.* "In a fragmented industry, the large number of competitors almost always insures that the buyer will exercise a great deal of power and be able to play one competitor against the other. In such a setting, products early in their life can often appear as salvations to an otherwise intense competitive situation. With rapidly growing demand and buyers generally unfamiliar with the new product, price competition may be modest and buyers may be clamoring for education and service from the firm. This is such a welcomed relief in the fragmented industry that firms make major investments in gearing up to respond. At the first signs of maturity, however, the fragmented structure catches up with demand and the margins that were there to support these investments disappear. Thus there is a risk of overreacting to new products in ways that will raise costs and overhead and put the firm at a competitive disadvantage in the price competition that is a fact of life in many fragmented industries" (page 212).

Are any of these red flags waving in your practices?!

4.7.2.3   Competitive advantage in a mature marketplace
In terms of industry evolution (see paragraph 2.3.1), there is a strong argument that the law is now emerging as a mature marketplace. As such, it is probably too fragmented, too competitive, and too specialised for any firm to seek to provide too many (let alone all) services to all clients. The transition of any business activity to maturity (and law is no exception) will result in (Porter 1980, pages 238–40):

(a)   a slow-down in growth,
(b)   the emergence of more sophisticated and experienced repeat buyers (whose decision is not *whether* to buy but *where from*),
(c)   competition may shift towards greater emphasis on cost and service,
(d)   overcapacity, which accentuates price-competition,
(e)   changes in the methods of marketing and selling,
(f)   a fall in profits across the business activity (often combined with reduced cash flow and difficulty in raising debt finance).

These are the characteristics of *any* industry in its transition to maturity: they are certainly the characteristics of the legal professions in most of the industrialised economies in the 1990s.

Using Porter's advice (1980, pages 241–7), the strategic response to this transition should be as follows:

(a)   *Decide on the firm's focus.* Unfortunately, 'focus' is not in itself a clear word. It should not be taken to mean either a single focus or a straitjacket. However, the more focuses the firm chooses, the harder it is to maintain quality at the same level across often diverse areas and styles of practice, the harder it is to market consistently and effectively, and the more expensive it is to resource them and meet the key success factors.

Focus means defining the way in which a firm or practice area can compete more effectively to strengthen its market share. It means making choices about *how* to compete. It means being prepared to turn some types of business away. An unwillingness to make these choices usually results in a firm that finds it difficult to define itself (in its own eyes, as well as in clients' minds).

The firm's client base and fee-earning activities are a complex mix of type of client and their business activity, the legal services provided, and the geography involved (see paragraph 4.5.2). It may also be defined or identified by its culture or style of practising law. Deciding on focus will therefore be a complex process.

(b) *Increase business from existing clients.* When a marketplace is expanding and economic confidence is buoyant, new work will flow in, virtually without effort. When that marketplace matures, there will be more competition for work, and increased market share means taking business from competitors: while concentrating on being a predator, a firm may lose some of its own flock to other raiders. Therefore, it should identify its good clients, and find ways of locking them into the firm — personal, technological, financial, or whatever it takes.

(c) *Raise financial consciousness.* In the growth phase of a business, its owners focus on bringing in new clients, in the knowledge that revenue follows. In maturity, it is necessary to focus on profit rather than revenue. Therefore, a firm should consider pruning historically or chronically unprofitable services (or at least making a fully informed decision about the extent to which it is prepared to support them); it should be sure to charge in a way and at a level that is consistent with clients' expectations; and it should never lose sight of the billing and collection imperative (a significant amount of potential profit can be wasted in financing unbilled work-in-progress and uncollected fees and disbursements).

(d) *Innovate the delivery of legal services.* This is perhaps one of the most difficult strategic issues. Firms should look for lower-cost options; consider replacing permanent labour (with all the space, overhead and remuneration costs that that implies) with temporary or special project help; consider replacing expensive, highly qualified lawyers with paralegals to handle transactions (or those parts of them) that do not require highly qualified attention; consider replacing labour with capital (i.e. finding ways of using technology to reduce costs). It is very easy to cling to the notion of quality as a necessary feature of legal services. However, it is not a necessary feature of *every aspect* of legal services — clients do not always want, and will not always pay for, the Rolls-Royce. In any event, again, as a market matures, quality differentials are eroded. Equally, we should not forget that the sophisticated and experienced clients *are* often more willing to trade some 'quality' for lower fees.

Many people confuse innovation with invention: they are, in fact, very different. The following extract from *The Economist* (18 June 1994, page 111) might help:

"In rich countries, innovation is the principal engine of economic growth. Understanding innovation is one of the most important tasks in economics. It has also been one of the most neglected. Research on

economies in the aggregate (macroeconomics) has concerned itself
overwhelmingly with short-term fluctuations in output, employment
and prices. Economics still lacks a persuasive theory of long-term
growth — a theory that puts innovation at the centre, where it belongs
. . . .

It is a commonplace that technologies move only slowly from first
invention to widespread use. What is striking in the history of technological innovation, however, is that the dispersion of a new technology
is not just slow but extraordinarily uncertain even after its first commercial applications have been realised. . . . Consider the laser — a
comparatively young technology with more development in store. . . .
Together with fibre optics, the laser has revolutionised the telephone
business — yet lawyers at Bell Labs were initially unwilling even to
apply for a patent on their invention, believing it had no possible
relevance to the telephone industry. . . . In 1949 the boss of IBM said
the firm should have nothing to do with computers, because world
demand could be satisfied by 10 or 15 machines. . . .

What can economists learn from all this? Many things, but principally
that the first invention is but a fraction of innovation. One reason is
obvious: the first invention is, by later standards, primitive. . . . *So
innovation is in practice more about improvement than invention* [emphasis
added]. The fact that the bulk of rich-country R and D spending goes
on developing existing technologies does not point to any lack of
creativity or imagination: mankind's most spectacular and unexpected
advances have come from 'mere' improvement of that kind.

Just as important, however, is that few of the potential uses for any
invention, however much improved in due course, may at first be
apparent. In other words, the subsequent invention of uses (which may
be long delayed) matters just as much as the first invention of the
means."

Competitive advantage in legal practice, therefore, may come from
improving service delivery through innovation — that is, from the *application* of existing knowledge and technologies. Innovation may be the key
to rejuvenating legal practice if you take the view that law is a mature
industry.

(e) *Be more accountable to each other.* A mature market allows much
less room for slack — in economics, performance and communication.
Better coordination, budgeting, cost control, and communication are
required. This implies greater mutual support, and so *some* loss of
personal autonomy.

(f) *Pay more attention to the human dimension.* A business that is
dependent on the know-how of individual intelligent, egotistic — and
mobile — fee-earners requires a different and far more subtle approach to
human resource management. In a mature marketplace, expectations of
advancement and remuneration need to be scaled down; some lawyers
may need to be re-educated about the nature of legal practice and then
re-motivated. In this sort of environment, leadership has a premium.

Porter's approach is very much to look at the effects of maturity across the industry as a whole, and then to suggest generic responses to a generic environment. Baden-Fuller and Stopford are at pains to point out that simply *being* in a mature business should not lead one to assume that the strategic options are limited. They agree that strategic innovation is still the primary basis for securing competitive advantage, but they shift the emphasis (1992, pages 13 and 15):

"It is the firm which matters, not the industry. Firms can be successful in the most unpromising and tough environments. . . . Our first and central theme is that the industry is not to blame for any shortcomings in firm performance. Successful businesses ride the waves of industry misfortunes; less successful businesses are sunk by them. This view contrasts sharply with the popular, but misguided, school of thought which believes that the fortune of a business is closely tied to its industry."

Later, they suggest (1992, pages 35 and 38–9):

"The ability to create new strategies which alter the competitive rules of the game in its industry is the hallmark of the successful organisation. McDonald's did not invent the American hamburger nor the French fry. It did not invent the idea of take-away service, but it did bring these together with many other small and large inventions to achieve the principle of the mass merchandising of hamburgers. . . . All these together allowed McDonald's to develop the concept of fast food and innovate a new method of competing. . . . Whilst competition takes on many forms, one of the most powerful challenges which organisations can offer is strategic innovation. A strategic innovation is *the creation of combinations of actions which were hitherto thought to be impossible.* . . . Strategic innovations may provide a more lasting benefit to the organisation and they tend to complement rather than be a substitute for new products and services [and] require new combinations of actions, functions and firms. Understanding how to make strategic innovations work requires significant investments, and also requires a change in the mental models used by managers. . . . We also point out that organisations do not seek to create just one new combination: they also look for multiple advantages."

Porter also observes the following 'pitfalls' as businesses seek to come to terms with changes in their marketplace (1980, pages 247–9):

(a)   self-delusion: perceptions become inaccurate as clients' priorities change and competitors respond in different ways — indeed, all assumptions about the marketplace, clients, competitors and suppliers are invalidated by the transition (hence the need for Drucker's theory of the business: see paragraph 2.4);

(b)   being stuck in the middle: firms without focus suffer most (or disappear) because the transition squeezes out the slack that has made an 'all-things-to-all-men' strategy viable in the past;

(c)   focusing on revenue instead of on profitability;

(d)   being unwilling to accept lower profits during the transition: the tendency to maintain short-term profitability by cutting down on marketing, training and other investments can be seriously short-sighted;

(e)   refusing to compete on price: thinking that price competition is unseemly or beneath one's dignity can be a dangerous and irrational reaction to the transition (particularly when others are willing to price aggressively and so take clients in the short term and long term);

(f)   resenting changes in practice can put a firm seriously behind in adapting to a new, competitive environment (e.g., changes in marketing and selling techniques, new ways of working);

(g)   over-emphasising new services rather than improving and aggressively selling existing ones: new services are harder to generate in a mature industry;

(h)   clinging to 'high quality' in order to resist aggressive pricing and competitors' marketing: quality differentials erode as an industry matures, and it is often difficult for some firms to accept either that they do not have the highest quality or that their quality is unnecessarily high;

(i)   failing to deal with excess capacity (e.g., people, space): this creates both subtle and unsubtle pressures to use it, and may undermine the firm's strategic focus; it is often desirable to scrap excess capacity rather than have it pull the business into a cash trap (i.e., tying up much-needed capital).

4.8   Generic Strategies

Of course, life and strategic thinking would be so much easier if there were some 'ready-made' strategies for competitive advantage that a firm could simply adopt as its own. Not surprisingly, the academic and consulting communities have examined the competitive strategies of different industries, and they suggest that there are, indeed, such things as generic approaches.

4.8.1   *Porter's generic strategies*

Porter identifies three generic strategies (1980, page 35):

(a)   cost leadership (i.e., being the cheapest in the marketplace);

(b)   differentiation (i.e., being different to all competitors);

(c)   focus on a market segment (expertise or clients), competing if necessary on the basis of cost leadership or differentiation.

Few law firms wish to adopt cost leadership as their overall strategy. Differentiation is also very difficult in a market which is as fragmented as the law. What most law firms are therefore looking for in the 1990s is *focus*. Without it, Porter's analysis suggests that they will remain undefined, stuck in the middle, and struggling to maintain their client base in an increasingly differentiated and competitive world. In the context of legal services, focus usually implies some degree of segmentation (see paragraph 4.5.2) combined with some differentiation. This combination will define the firm's market 'position' (this is explored in more depth by Payne (1993), pages 101–20).

Porter's generic strategies are a useful framework for strategic thinking, but should not be taken to represent absolutes: for example, in many industries these days, it is important to be both cost-effective *and* qualitatively different.

Lawyers are not the only people grappling with differentiation and the value of 'branding' a product or service as being in some way different, as the following extract from a lead article in *The Economist* (2 July 1994, page 11) shows:

"If you are in the business of making something that has become indistinguishable from its rivals, it has in effect turned into a commodity and will therefore sell chiefly on price. . . . It is an axiom of capitalism that if you make a better mousetrap the world will beat a path to your door. The oddity of modern times is that it has become so much harder to make a product that is genuinely different from or better than a competitor's. And if you do make one, it is harder than ever to stay ahead. One reason is that technical expertise is more widely held by a bigger universe of companies, and is disseminated at ever faster speeds. Make a better mousetrap and the probability is that, within a few weeks, a cheaper version will appear next to yours. . . .

You might think that this was always the way of capitalism. But in the past the better mousetrapper could expect a breathing space before a competitor made a rival product. This interval, plus advertising, allowed brands to establish themselves. . . .

In other brand businesses, companies have been slower to innovate, clinging in some cases to the hope that what ails brands is merely cyclical; that consumers buy on price when times are hard, but return to brands once they feel richer again. Yet . . . there is some evidence that it is the better-off and better-educated who are the most likely to forsake a brand for a cheaper alternative. The horrible truth may be that education makes consumers buy more rationally, and that if there is little or no difference in the perceived qualities of a range of products the rational buyer will go for the cheapest.

Yet that argument also offers the beginning of an explanation for why brands will survive — perhaps in different forms, perhaps with less extravagant price premiums, but survive nevertheless. The point of brands is, and always has been, to provide information. . . . In some ways, commoditisation has made this information more important, not less. When prices vary greatly, it is worth a buyer's while to investigate which . . . offers the best value; when they converge, buying a well-known name is an easier solution."

4.8.2 *Boston Consulting Group's growth-share matrix*

Another popular model, the BCG growth-share matrix, focuses on two variables: the rate of growth in the industry, and the firm's market share relative to its largest competitor (see Grant 1995, pages 412–15). Given that each variable needs only to be expressed as 'high' or 'low', the matrix is easy to use, and so provides a good starting point for considering strategic options; it can also be used for different practice areas. The combination of two variables on a measure of high or low leads to four possibilities (each of which has a description and a recommended strategy):

(a)   low rate of market growth and low relative market share tends to give high, stable earnings and high, stable cash flow: the strategy should be to *milk the 'cash cows'* (the cows);

(b)   high rate of market growth and low relative market share tends to give high, stable or growing earnings and neutral cash flow: the strategy should be to *invest for growth* (the stars);

(c)   low rate of market growth and high relative market share tends to give low, unstable earnings and neutral or negative cash flow: the strategy should be to *divest* (the dogs);

(d)   high rate of market growth and high relative market share tends to give low, unstable, or growing earnings and negative cash flow: the strategy should be to *analyse* to see if the business can be grown into a star or will degenerate into a dog (the question marks).

It may be that this matrix is too simple, concentrating as it does on only two variables which are open to different interpretations and different measurement. But certainly the cows strategy would seem to be an accurate description of many domestic conveyancing practices until the mid 1980s, and the stars strategy a good description of commercial practices in the late 1980s.

4.8.3   Sveiby and Lloyd's generic business ideas

The theme of Sveiby and Lloyd (1987) is that a successful know-how business will combine technical and managerial expertise, and that this combination must take place in the context of a sound business idea. Like the BCG growth-share matrix, Sveiby and Lloyd's four generic business ideas are the result of combining two variables.

For know-how businesses to be successful, they have to rely on people with know-how. The strategic challenge is therefore being able to use the know-how of individuals within a business organisation. If the most important know-how in the business belongs to one or a few individuals, the opportunities to grow the business will be limited by the constraints on any of those individuals significantly to add value to their know-how. The possible business ideas will therefore depend on being able to multiply know-how to allow others to use it, or to combine it with financial capital. The two variables are therefore dependence on key individuals, and dependence on financial capital and, again, each can be measured as 'high' or 'low'.

The four strategic possibilities are then:

(a) high dependence on key individuals and low dependence on financial capital ('the consultant'): this represents the most common business idea for English law firms because they are prevented from seeking capital from external sources, and tend to rely on the business-generating abilities and expertise of a few key partners (these firms would be providing expertise and experience in terms of Maister's service life cycle: see paragraph 2.3.3);

(b) low dependence on key individuals and low dependence on financial capital ('the know-how multiplier'): the multiplication is usually achieved by embedding know-how in the firm's routines and procedures (increasingly in databases and software); some of the more procedural aspects of legal practice can begin to achieve this, but they also tend to be in price-sensitive areas such as debt collection (the efficiency end of the service life cycle: see paragraph 2.3.3);

(c) high dependence on key individuals and high dependence on financial capital ('the asset manager'): merchant banks and venture capital houses would be good examples of asset managers, combining, as they do, a high level of specialised know-how with access to finance; it is difficult to envisage this idea being implemented in legal practice — except perhaps in the context of a multidisciplinary finance business;

(d) low dependence on key individuals and high dependence on financial capital ('the high-tech company'): this business idea rests on investment in technology and in 'proceduralising' technical know-how so that the service can effectively be delivered as a product; the transform-ation of legal practice from an advisory service into an information service, and of the lawyer into a 'legal information engineer' is part of Susskind's vision of the future (1996, pages 286, 287 and 291).

4.8.4 The dangers of generic strategies

Grant sounds a warning note (rightly, I think) against the possible 'absolutism' of Porter's generic strategies, saying that "few firms are faced by such stark alternatives" (1995, page 169). This view is also expressed — more forcefully — by Baden-Fuller and Stopford (1992, page 29):

"The advocates of generic strategy make an (implicit or explicit) assertion: that the opposites cannot be reconciled. According to the generic strategists, it is not possible to be both low cost and high quality, or low cost and fashionable, or low cost and speedy. Trying to reconcile the opposites means *being stuck in the middle*. This, it is suggested, is the worst of both worlds.

Generic strategies are a fallacy. The best firms are striving all the time to reconcile the opposites. . . . At any point in time, there are some combinations which have not yet been resolved, but firms strive to resolve them. . . . Given the enormous rewards which accrue to those which can resolve the dilemmas of the opposites, it is not surprising that there are *no lasting or enduring generic strategies*."

4.9 Conclusion

Strategy is a complex issue that involves understanding and trying to match a number of varied dimensions of a firm, its performance and potential, and its environment. To be successful, a strategy cannot be entirely intuitive; but equally, a firm does not want to suffer 'paralysis by analysis'.

I provide in chapter 11 some guidance about the process of strategic thinking and strategy making. However, first I want to develop a more robust framework for the analysis of law offices and to examine some of the strategic possibilities both from a different perspective and in more detail. For those readers who are content to skip over the theory, the journey can be picked up at chapter 11 (perhaps pausing at chapter 10 for a summary of the next five chapters!).

PART II

THE THEORY OF THE LAW FIRM

Chapter 5

KNOW-HOW: THE UNDERLYING ASSET

5.1 The Fundamental Role of Know-how

The emergence of the knowledge economy (discussed in paragraph 1.3.2), and the central role of knowledge and skills in know-how businesses (see paragraphs 3.1 to 3.5, and 4.6.3, 4.6.5, and 4.8.3), highlights the strategic importance of know-how. It is the principal asset of a knowledge-based business. Its acquisition or creation, development, management, productivity and economics are the keys to success. Without it, there is no business.

Economists call this asset 'human capital'. There are many conceivable ways in which human capital can be described or defined because it is multi-faceted: "human capital takes many forms, including skills and abilities, personality, appearance, reputation, and appropriate credentials" (Becker 1993, page 262); "Intellectual capital is intellectual material — knowledge, information, intellectual property, experience — that can be put to use to create wealth. It is collective brainpower" (Stewart 1997, page x and elaborated in chapters 4 to 9). Our first difficulty therefore lies in finding an acceptable working definition of what this important business asset is.

Many people use the expressions 'know-how', 'knowledge', 'expertise', 'skills', 'experience', and so on, interchangeably. For no better reason than personal habit I shall predominantly use 'know-how' as a suitable portmanteau word in the context of law firms. But they are different concepts. For instance, know-how represents applied knowledge — the difference between *knowing* something and being able to *do* something with that knowledge. And yet the doing of something with the knowledge — assuming that the know-how exists to know what to do — still requires the skills actually to do it: knowing how to do something and being able to do it are different. So expertise might be said to represent the ability to know something and to know how to do something with that knowledge, as well as the ability actually to do it. As the doing is repeated, one develops experience — we might call it the repetition of expertise. However, for some people, expertise might imply a qualitatively higher or more specialised ability to do something — which would suggest that expertise is more valuable than mere experience (this is so in Maister's characterisation of the shift of services from expertise to experience: see paragraph 2.3.3).

This underlying asset is therefore difficult to define, and the varied terminology may confuse or obfuscate its nature. For the purposes of this book, it is thankfully not necessary to define know-how, but we do need to understand its components.

5.2 Components of Know-how

A full analysis of the know-how used by lawyers and law firms would require a book in itself. This paragraph therefore represents more of a summary of current thinking than a complete analysis. In the context of organisations generally, human capital comprises both individual human capital or know-how, and firm-specific human capital or know-how. For my purposes, 'human capital' and 'know-how' are interchangeable expressions.

5.2.1 Individual capital or know-how

Since human capital is necessarily based on human beings, its core must be individual know-how. Galanter and Palay provide a useful starting point for the description of this individual capital in lawyers (1991, pages 89–90). It includes (a) pre-law-school endowment of intelligence, skills and general education; (b) legal education and experience-dependent skills; (c) professional reputation; and (d) personal relationships with clients. As lawyers develop their professional skills and reputation, part of their individual capital will also include client-specific know-how (a result of the personal relationships in (d)), and transaction-specific know-how (part of the experience-dependent skills developed under (b)).

It is important not to underestimate the importance or value of the personal relationships with clients (d). In fact, Nelson goes so far as to suggest that the ability to 'control' client relationships, to use knowledge of and contacts with clients, is *the* source of power for partners in law firms: ". . . power in the firm remains inextricably tied to 'control of clients'. . . . Managerial authority in the law firm can never achieve autonomy from those partners with client responsibility. . . . the organizational rationalization of the firm will be controlled by the partners with power" (1988, page 5).

In Sveiby and Lloyd's terms, categories (a) to (d) above may be thought of as professional know-how (see paragraph 3.3). Part of their thesis of know-how businesses is that managerial know-how is also required for such businesses to reach their full potential. In addition to categories (a) to (d), therefore, it seems that we should extend the notion of individual capital to include the managerial know-how of individuals.

This gives us the following components of individual know-how:

(a)   general education, intelligence and skills;

(b)   legal education;

(c)   the skills developed from experience in a law office, including the know-how relating to specific types of transactions;

(d)   personal and professional reputation and credibility;

(e)   client following, client relationships, and specific knowledge about clients;

(f)   knowledge, experience and skills of management, including management of oneself, of others, of transactions and matters, and of the whole or parts of businesses.

5.2.2   *Firm-specific capital or know-how*

When individuals combine together for business purposes, they will begin to combine their respective individual human capital. As a result, they start to create firm-specific capital. For law firms, this firm-specific capital (according to Gilson and Mnookin 1985, pages 356–68) comprises clients — client-specific information and predictable flows of work — and a reputation for quality — perhaps through specialisation and quality assurance procedures. As suggested above, the ability to control client relationships will represent a significant source of power within the firm, and will in turn affect the ability to determine how firm-specific capital can be exploited.

To Gilson and Mnookin's categories of firm-specific capital, I would add 'situational know-how', that is, the knowledge and experience of a firm's personalities, culture, and working practices and procedures that arise both formally or informally: this know-how can make one firm more productive and efficient than another with an otherwise similar combination of individual and firm-specific capital. (It is arguable that situational know-how is a contributor to a reputation for quality, and is therefore already encompassed in Gilson and Mnookin's description. I think there is some merit in treating situational know-how separately.)

Equally, any group of homogeneous people will also demonstrate common attitudes and values. These may encompass attitudes to client service and the practice of law, or respect for professional autonomy. I believe that these attitudes, values and beliefs (whatever they are) also form part of the firm-specific capital where they are sufficiently common and instrumental to the way people in the firm act. Collectively, we might call this the firm's 'culture' (this is explored in chapter 23).

It is also arguable that, although Gilson and Mnookin talk only of a reputation for *quality*, the combination of client following, quality work, situational know-how, and values results in a wider reputation. This reputation should also, in my view, be considered as part of the firm-specific capital. The general reputation and standing of an established, successful firm may be decisive, for example, in the ability to attract new clients or lawyers, or to raise funds from banks. This is the value of 'branding' (cf. paragraphs 4.8.1 and 8.5.6).

This, then, gives us the following components of firm-specific capital:

(a)   the client base;

(b)   information about clients;

(c)   client following, manifested in predictable flows of work;

(d)   access to the collective individual know-how of people in the firm (and, through appropriate systems, to the retained know-how of those who are no longer with the firm);

(e)   the combination of individual know-how into greater depth or breadth of legal or practical specialisation;

(f)   the ability to assure quality in the delivery of legal and support services, particularly through supervision and monitoring, training and development, precedents and know-how systems, and quality management;

(g)   common culture, values, attitudes and beliefs;

(h)   situational know-how: knowledge of the personalities, culture, and working practices and procedures ('organisational routines': see Grant 1995, page 134, and Nelson and Winter 1982) that allows delivery to be achieved more effectively and efficiently;

(i)   the managerial know-how that leads to the creation of a structure and ways of working within which much of the situational know-how becomes productive;

(j)   the firm's reputation and credibility in the marketplace.

Is firm-specific capital just an academic expression for 'goodwill'? It could be argued that goodwill is the firm's reputation (j) supported by a client following (c), and that the other components listed are simply necessary elements without which reputation and client following would not result. This is probably true. But normal conceptions of goodwill do not incorporate culture or situational know-how, for example. Indeed, goodwill is normally considered to be an accountant's concept designed to place a fair value on a business whose market worth cannot entirely be accounted for by its tangible assets. As such, it tends to value the *fact* of client following and pays no attention to its *reasons*. Even then accountants are usually valuing goodwill that has been bought rather than self-generated.

For all these reasons, I believe that there are differences between firm-specific capital and goodwill, but confess that drawing watertight distinctions is very difficult.

5.2.3   *Relationship between individual and firm-specific capital*

Although firm-specific capital will not begin to emerge until people start sharing their individual human capital, firm-specific capital is more than the sum of the constituent individual capital. The combination leads to the creation of a new, interdependent, asset.

Where a lawyer is a sole practitioner, individual capital and firm-specific capital will be inextricably linked because the sole practitioner *is* the firm. The distinction may begin to emerge if the sole practitioner takes in other lawyers as assistants (that is, becomes a sole principal), because it is possible for those others to help in the development of client relationships and work flow, as well as contribute to the development of a common culture, situational know-how, and a collective reputation. Even here, though, the fundamental value of the firm-specific capital may well continue to attach to its association with the sole principal. So it is perhaps only when individual lawyers combine their individual capital in partnership that the true significance of firm-specific capital starts to emerge.

There is, however, one crucial distinction between individual capital and firm-specific capital: when individuals leave a firm, they can take their individual capital with them, but they cannot take the firm-specific capital. Admittedly, it is possible that their departure will affect the value of the firm-specific capital (either negatively or positively). It is also possible that an identifiable group within a firm might, if they leave together and re-establish themselves as (say) a niche practice, be able to 'take' with them some of the reputational firm-specific capital of the firm they leave. In my view, however, this is not so much a removal of part of the capital as the depreciation of the original firm-specific capital (by their departure) combined with their ability effectively to recreate part of the capital in different circumstances (their new practice): see, further, paragraph 5.4.

To the extent that firm-specific capital can therefore be devalued, and recreated, by others and because it will cease to exist at all when the firm itself no longer exists, and because (as we shall see in chapter 8) it depends on sharing and teamwork for its full exploitation, it is in my view very difficult to say that firm-specific capital is an asset capable of ownership.

5.3 Other Classifications of Know-how

The distinction between individual and firm-specific know-how, though important for the analysis in succeeding chapters, is not the only one. In understanding the nature of this underlying asset, it might help to be aware of some of the other distinctions (see also Blackler (1995) and Morris and Empson (1996)).

5.3.1 Explicit and tacit knowledge

This first distinction flows from the oft-quoted statement by Polanyi that "we can know more than we can tell" (1966, page 4). What we know, but do not tell, he called tacit knowledge. It is very difficult to formalise and communicate tacit knowledge, whereas we are easily able to articulate and share explicit knowledge. Explicit knowledge is therefore typically knowledge that has been codified by analysis and study, and is often referred to as objective. Tacit knowledge is personal and subjective. In fact, our tacit knowledge may be the result of internalising and using explicit knowledge over a period of time; it will be the product of experience; equally, it may be the result of socialising (working) with others whose tacit knowledge we absorb osmotically. Tacit knowledge will become explicit to the extent that ways are found to articulate it. These concepts are further developed by Nonaka and Takeuchi (1995, chapter 3).

5.3.2 Embedded and migratory knowledge

The nature of explicit knowledge means that it can 'migrate' from person to person, or from firm to firm. Tacit knowledge, on the other hand, is firmly 'embedded' in an individual. For these reasons, embedded and tacit knowledge are often used as interchangeable concepts, as are migratory and explicit knowledge. However, from a firm's point of view the tacit, embedded knowledge of an individual (as well as his or her explicit knowledge) will be lost to the firm if he or she leaves: in this sense, tacit knowledge becomes migratory and the concepts are not interchangeable.

The challenge for a firm is therefore to 'embed' as much as possible of the explicit and tacit knowledge of its people. In organisations, "embedded knowledge resides primarily in specialized relationships among individuals and groups and in the particular norms, attitudes, information flows, and ways of making decisions that shape their dealings with each other" (Badaracco 1991, page 79). Firms that encourage teamwork, common training, regular meetings, and the creation of know-how systems are therefore investing in embedding know-how, and so making themselves less vulnerable to the departure or loss of any one of their practitioners. It could therefore be argued that the creation of firm-specific capital is dependent on the firm's ability and success in embedding the know-how of its people.

5.3.3 Static and dynamic knowledge

The great facility of human beings, as living organisms, is their tendency to change constantly. This applies to their know-how, too. The principal benefit of working with people, therefore, is that others always have access to the most up-to-date know-how that those people possess. The migration of explicit knowledge from its source to an individual is the dynamic transfer of what then becomes static knowledge. For example, if a fee-earner submits a letter of advice or a precedent to a library or know-how collection, that person's know-how becomes available to more fee-earners (it becomes embedded). But it has also become fixed in time: other people then have access to the explicit (codified and static) know-how of the fee-earner if he or she leaves the firm, but not to the tacit (personal and dynamic) know-how of the same person.

This is one of the practical difficulties of know-how systems in law firms. Not to capture work product because it is static, and might become out-of-date, and only reflects the circumstances of a particular client-matter, increases the firm's risk that valuable know-how will be completely unavailable if a respected fee-earner defects, dies or retires. Such a system has to decide whether its only function is to collect static know-how, or whether it is also to provide pointers — particularly in larger firms — to individuals who can be approached for help (so giving access to their dynamic as well as static know-how).

5.4 Imitation and Replication of Know-how

The variety in the components of know-how (see paragraph 5.2) suggests that different components may be created in different ways. Some are created by formal learning and communication (the transfer of explicit knowledge); some are developed through training, support and less formal communication (the development of tacit knowledge); some are the result of systems and procedures; and so on.

I have already suggested that competitive advantage can be derived from know-how, provided that it is not too easy to imitate or replicate (see paragraph 4.6.5). The know-how can be individual or firm-specific, though it may be that individual know-how needs to be combined with firm-specific know-how for it to be fully productive and that, again, individual capital may be worth less in a different firm unless the firm-specific capital can also be imitated or replicated (see paragraph 5.2.3). Even within the same firm, though, competitive advantage may still be lost or eroded if know-how is not transferred (replicated) to other fee-earners.

In assessing the extent to which knowledge can be imitated or replicated, von Krogh and Roos identify six facets (1996, pages 35–44):

(a) how closely the knowledge to be imitated or replicated can be observed: in the legal profession, the exchanged work product (letters, agreements, etc.) of lawyers can be observed, as can the work of lawyers through supervision or by moving from one firm to another;

(b) whether the knowledge is explicit or tacit (see paragraph 5.3.1), how complex it is, how transaction-specific it is (see paragraph 5.2.1), and how easy it is for the imitator or replicator to know the extent to which this knowledge contributes to competitive success; if it is difficult to know whether or not something contributes to competitive success, this will create 'causal ambiguity' (see Grant 1995, pages 159–160, and Reed and DeFillippi 1990);

(c) the social complexity of the firm and its history — the creation of firm-specific capital, and its effect on individual know-how — are dependent on the interaction of people in the firm; because the group of people in any given firm will always be unique, and their interactions incapable of replication, where these factors are an important part of the competitive advantage of the know-how in question, it may effectively be impossible for that competitive knowledge to be recreated by the imitating firm;

(d)   the extent to which the knowledge can be internalised: facet (c) concerned the extent to which knowledge could be 'externalised', that is, meaningfully brought outside the originating firm; even where this is possible, the imitating firm may not be able to 'internalise' the new know-how — because its absorption is dependent on the knowledge foundations to which it is added (which may not be equivalent to the originating firm's);

(e)   the ability of the imitating or replicating firm to communicate the explicit and tacit knowledge that forms the new know-how; and

(f)   the ability of the imitating firm to 'legitimise' the new know-how: where the new know-how takes the imitating firm into areas of practice it has not tackled before, there may be some difficulty in establishing a common language and acceptance of the new area and in creating the appropriate attitudes, structures, and procedures to make it productive.

Firms that attempt to copy or follow market leaders or other competitors simply by creating identical or similar external appearances (such as merging or recruiting to achieve the same size, opening new offices in the same locations as competitors, or structuring the firm's fee-earning or support departments in the same way) are missing the point. These 'aping' strategies are not sufficient. Until the firm has in place the right type and combination of underlying know-how, and the appropriate abilities, attitudes, and processes to make it productive, its competitive dream cannot be turned into a sustainable and profitable reality — no matter how similar it looks from the outside.

Where the costs or practicalities of imitation or replication are high, where there is significant causal ambiguity, or where the risks of trying (or of failing) are too high, a firm may not embark on imitation or replication. Instead, an imitator may seek access to the know-how by forming an affiliation with another firm that already has it, or is prepared to join in spreading the risk of imitation. For this to work, there will have to be a mutual competitive advantage and commitment to the relationship. (These affiliations are considered further in the context of international legal practice in paragraph 13.3.2.)

5.5   Measurement and Valuation of Know-how

5.5.1   *Nature of the problem*

Having laboured the importance and complexity of know-how as a law firm's underlying asset, I want to finish this chapter by touching on perhaps the most difficult issue of all. If it is so important, this know-how capital ought to be carefully measured, and a firm should have some sense of its value. But the difficulties here reflect the diversity and complexity of the asset itself. So much of it is individual, personal, subjective, tacit and embedded that it may not manifest itself in such a way that it can be measured. And its productive capacity may be affected by so many unpredictable and non-business issues (such as health, enthusiasm, chemistry with the client), that the idea of giving it an objective value perhaps seems ridiculous. However, other business assets are quantified, assessed, valued and managed. We cannot deny that there is a market in legal talent.

It is true that more work needs to be done in this area (and as the knowledge economy develops, this issue of measuring and valuing the intangible is receiving a lot of attention). So for now, I shall outline the issues and offer some tentative conclusions.

My first suggestion is that the purpose of measuring is both to be better able to manage know-how, and to be able to value it. However, valuation tends to be a composite figure: know-how is only worth something when, in its entirety, it can be turned to productive and profitable use. But its management requires an understanding of the component parts, which in turn allows a better understanding of how to improve the asset and then how to make it more productive. Measurement addresses the process of composition, and valuation is concerned with the effects of that composition.

5.5.2 *Measurement*

This is the area that causes me most difficulty. When know-how has been broken down into its component parts (as in paragraph 5.2), one might be encouraged to think that measurements should readily be available. This is only partly true. Measurements are often available, but some are necessarily subjective assessments, and others may only be proxies.

For example, in relation to individual know-how, general and legal education can be objectively measured by the fact (and grades) of formal qualifications awarded to individuals. Experience can be measured by the total number of years of professional experience (suggested by Sveiby and Lloyd 1987, page 75), but some professionals have 25 years' experience and others have one year's experience repeated 24 times! Reputation can be assessed through a proxy of results from client surveys, and client following through the number (or percentage) of clients each year that have brought repeat business to a fee-earner.

Even this superficial treatment suggests that there is unlikely to be a single measure of individual know-how (which is not surprising given the diversity of its components). But how does one then compare one individual's know-how with another's? What relative weight would one give to formal qualifications as against years of experience? Who would make an assessment about the relative substance of two practitioners each with 25 years' experience (and on what basis)?

Some of the individual measures could be aggregated or averaged to provide some measures of firm-specific capital. For example, a firm could track the total number of years of professional experience available to it year on year; for comparative purposes, it might be better to track the average number of years of experience. These numbers could also be kept by different categories of people in the firm (partners, fee-earners, support staff, and so on). Situational know-how could perhaps be measured by the total and average number of years staff have been with the firm: a higher number and an increasing average would indicate a good level of such know-how (though it might also indicate the possibility of increased resistance to innovation and change). But how does one begin to measure culture?

To be sure, this is a complex area. However, that should not prevent a firm from taking a look at components for which some form of measurement is possible. Over time, it will refine its approach, learn what is most appropriate for its own circumstances, and see which measurements help in the management of this important asset.

5.5.3 Valuation

5.5.3.1 Need for valuation
The tangible assets of a business are valued and entered on its balance sheet. In a knowledge-based business, the contribution of these assets to its performance, profitability and market value is often negligible. Where a company is quoted on a stock exchange and has a market value based on its share price, we could deduce that the market's assessment of the value of its intangible assets is the difference between market value and the balance sheet value of the tangible assets. With law firms, we are not able to make that calculation, because there is no public market.

We must therefore look for an alternative approach. Valuations are usually relevant either on the sale of a business, or when its owners want to make a comparative assessment of their business (and then either to compare current worth with previous valuations, or to compare its worth as against the valuation of another business). If a business is sold for more than the balance sheet value of its tangible assets, the difference will usually be described as a payment for goodwill: it is an estimate of the value of the firm's intangible assets. But how is such a figure arrived at? Are there any principles which suggest an objective approach to the valuation of firm-specific capital?

5.5.3.2 Profitability as a base for valuation
Goodwill is usually based on the present value of expected future client following. As such, business valuations are usually founded on some valuation of the expected volume of future cash flow in the business. In other words, the valuation is not based on capital assets at all, but on the continuing ability of the business to be productive — in our context, for the firm to continue to earn fees and generate a profit. What the acquirers of a law firm will want for their investment is a share of the firm's future profits. This suggests that to increase a law firm's value, its present partners should maximise its profits.

However, the statement 'maximise profit' itself needs clarification. Does it mean gross profit or net profit? Does profit include or exclude notional salaries for equity partners? Is it absolute profit or the rate of return that is to be maximised? If it is the rate of return, is the return (profit) to be return on total income (profit margin), on fee income (operating profit), on net assets (RONA), or on equity — capital employed or invested (ROCE or ROI)? When those decisions have been made, is what is to be maximised total profit, or profit per equity partner, or profit per fee-earner, or profit per member of staff?

As if this does not seem complicated enough, is the profit to be measured as the accounting profit or as the 'pure' profit? Accounting profit is the profit that results from the application by accountants of the appropriate accounting principles. Pure profit (which is also known as economic profit, economic rent, and economic value added) is the economist's notion of the surplus income that is left when the costs of all the inputs are taken into account. Pure profit is therefore operating profit less notional salaries for equity partners, tax (the income tax liabilities of the equity partners), the cost of debt (interest on borrowings), and the cost of equity (the opportunity cost to the equity partners of having financial capital tied up in the firm).

Tax and interest are usually relatively easy to identify, but in the context of a law firm the cost of equity is difficult to measure. For business generally, the cost of equity is the opportunity cost of capital — that is, what the owners (or investors) could have earned on their capital by putting it to some alternative use. The data on rates of return in different industries are often collected and published, making available an industry beta for calculating the cost of equity. The beta (β) is the measure of market sensitivity and is therefore a reflection of market risk. To this extent, it allows an assessment of the degree of risk to which capital invested in an industry will be subjected.

For in-house legal departments, their companies may well have measures of alternative uses of capital which could be used as a benchmark cost of equity in assessing the pure profit of an in-house legal department. This will require a notional value to be placed on in-house legal services. The 'natural' alternative use for the partners in one law firm would be to invest in another firm — but where are the data to identify what the return on capital would be in that other firm (there is no known beta for the legal profession)? So, in the absence of comparable data, what would be the *appropriate* alternative use of the capital to give a cost of equity? Partners could put the money on deposit with a bank or building society and earn (relatively low) risk-free interest; they could invest it in high-risk equity shares on the stock market; they could invest it in a personal pension plan, or in property; and so on. Each alternative is likely to give a different rate of return, rather than a standard cost of equity.

Being pragmatic, either partners should agree on an appropriate alternative measure of the cost of equity, or perhaps we should accept that the notion of pure profit is too problematic for our purposes.

5.5.3.3 *The idea of 'shareholder value'*
Another approach to valuation is not to think so much of maximising profits as maximising 'shareholder value'. In other businesses, maximising profit and maximising shareholder value are often regarded as much the same thing. The value will be the market value of the shares, and the market value will in essence be the discounted value of the returns

(profits, or dividends). But by focusing on value, the tendency is to think about longer-term development. As Grant puts it (1995, page 36):

> "While the notion of economic profit avoids many of the problems inherent in accounting profit, it does not address the problem of the time period over which profits are to be maximized. Resolution of this problem requires that future profits are capitalized and that the firm maximizes its present value. The principles of discounted cash flow (DCF) analysis that firms apply to their individual investment projects can also be applied to the firm as a whole. Strategies can then be selected that maximize the net present value of the firm.
>
> The appeal of maximizing the net present value of the firm's cash flows is that such maximization corresponds to the firm's maximization of its stock market valuation and hence maximizes the wealth of its shareholders. By maximizing profits, the firm can thereby simultaneously *maximize shareholder value*. Maximization of shareholder value has received wide support as the appropriate goal of the firm and the primary yardstick for measuring performance."

However, de Geus asserts that "the emphasis on profits and the maximization of shareholder value ignores the two most significant forces acting on companies today: the shift to knowledge as the critical production factor and the changing world environment" (1997, page 27).

Grant's interest in net present values as part of the strategy process is to assess the anticipated effects on the net present value (NPV) of a business of adopting different strategies: the strategy that leads to the highest NPV would be the one to choose (assuming, that is, that value maximisation is the key factor in choosing between strategies). In all of this, however, Grant is assuming that there is an open market for the ownership interests which are being valued. In such a market, the cost of equity can again be found by using a beta value (1995, page 47). The difficulties of such a calculation in the context of the legal profession were referred to in paragraph 5.5.3.2.

All methods of valuation based on future cash flow are, in a sense, subject to similar issues as in assessing profits. What does 'cash flow' mean? Over what future period are the anticipated cash flows to be taken before they are discounted? What is an appropriate discount rate? Grant's definition of cash flow (1995, page 38) is as follows:

(a)   He starts with *net cash flow* which is net income *plus* depreciation and other non-cash expenses *minus* the increase in working capital *minus* capital expenditure. This definition looks strictly at the inflows and outflows of cash on both the revenue and capital sides of the business (depreciation, for example, is an accounting entry that reduces net profit but does not involve parting with any cash — that is the capital expenditure).

(b)   *Operating cash flow* is operating profit *plus* interest and tax *plus* depreciation. This is more appropriate as an indicator of the maximum potential cash flow yield, on the assumption that a firm's managers can adjust interest, tax and capital expenditure in order to maximise the net cash flow generated by any given operating cash flow. Operating cash flow is therefore a more generous measure of cash flow.

(c)   *Free cash flow* is net income *plus* depreciation and other non-cash expenses *minus* the increase in working capital *minus* replacement capital expenditure. The significant difference here between net cash flow and free cash flow is that free cash flow calculations restrict the deduction of capital expenditure to *replacement* cost rather than total investment (additions and replacements). Grant also subtracts dividends, which of course would reduce corporate cash flow: however, in a partnership the balance of net profit will be allocated to equity partners' current accounts, which would reduce free cash flow to zero every year. It would be more realistic to take drawings rather than total distributions, since the partners must have some cash to live on, and the balance could be treated as 'free' (try selling that to them!): this would also assume that there had been no allowance for notional partners' salaries in computing net profit in the first place. It seems to me, therefore, that free cash flow only works in our context if notional salaries have been deducted in computing net profit, and where the notional salary used is in fact a realistic drawing (if it is not realistic, drawings up to a realistic level should perhaps be deducted, but not total distributions). On this view, the 'free' cash flow then represents the undrawn 'super-profit' of the firm.

These measures of cash flow demonstrate the inherent tension between shareholders and managers. The managers will want to reduce surplus cash by retaining funds to invest in the future so that they can preserve future profitability and value. Shareholders, on the other hand, usually prefer to have cash in their pockets now and will want to maximise cash flow to themselves and thus reduce the 'surplus' available for retention or investment. Equity partners, of course, are usually managers *and* shareholders, but given that the tax system charges tax on all profit whether distributed or not, preference and personal cash flow requirements will normally dictate a bias in favour of distribution rather than retention.

5.5.3.4   *Valuation of a law firm*
In the context of a law firm, my view is that the net, free, or 'surplus' income should be something of a combination of Grant's three methods. Given the structure of professional partnerships, the ownership interests of equity partners, and the method of taxation, the most realistic assessment of surplus cash flow in a law firm is:

Operating profit *plus* depreciation and other non-cash expenses *minus* the increase in working capital *minus* capital expenditure *minus* 'living' drawings (or the balance of them over notional salaries for equity partners if they have been deducted in computing operating profit) and tax on drawings.

Operating profit is based on fee income rather than income from all sources. Year on year, this will provide a more accurate assessment of what the *business* of the law firm can generate, as opposed to what it might expect to derive from, for example, property lettings and interest on client deposits.

For law firms, the definition of 'surplus' cash flow and the fixing of the multiple are therefore complex and problematic issues. Even when multiplication has been done an appropriate discount factor must be applied to achieve a net present value for the firm, and I have already identified the difficulties in establishing the appropriate discount rate (cost of equity).

5.5.3.5 *Valuation of individual and firm-specific capital*

By focusing on the valuation of a law firm as a continuing business, the discussion so far has avoided the distinction drawn earlier in this chapter between individual and firm-specific capital. It has suggested that the value of know-how is, in essence, the net present value of its future profit-earning ability. This approach can be applied to the valuation of both individual and firm-specific know-how. To the extent that the value of the business is based on the value of both individual and firm-specific capital, the value of firm-specific capital would be the difference between the sum of the values of individual know-how and the total valuation.

This appears to be broadly consistent with Gilson and Mnookin's view when they describe the value of individual human capital as "the capitalized value of the amount of money that the lawyer would expect to earn by leaving the firm and taking alternative employment — either by joining a different law firm or by forming a new law firm" (1985, page 354). The "amount of money" is effectively the surplus cash flow from individual practice, and the "capitalized value" is the multiple of the discounted value of that amount. On the other hand, "the value of firm-specific capital is the capitalized value of the difference between a firm's earnings as an ongoing institution and the combined value of the human capital of its individual partners, if this human capital were deployed outside the firm in its next most productive use. Because firm-specific capital can be neither easily removed from the firm nor duplicated outside the firm, the return on this capital is available to lawyers *within* the firm but is lost to lawyers who leave the firm" (1985, page 354).

5.5.3.6 *Investing in the invisible balance sheet*

Valuation of a law firm based on its financial standing and performance is therefore possible — even if difficult. While this may be necessary (and indeed) sufficient for a sale, I do not believe that it represents the complete picture. For example, valuations that are based in any way on tangible assets would encourage a law firm to over-invest in property and equipment, or to increase its balance sheet value by not distributing profits to partners (even though the additional cash would still represent distributions-in-waiting). Valuations by reference to profits can be increased by maximising profits, which can be achieved by *not* investing in know-how (training, know-how systems, reputation, and so on). And increased profitability may in any event be attributable to a buoyant economy generally or the market specifically, rather than any inherent value in the underlying ability or quality of the firm's fee-earners.

Where I would depart from the usual approaches to valuation, therefore, is in not confining the assessment of value to items in the profit and loss account or on the balance sheet — that it is not, in other words, simply a financial issue. I agree with Sveiby and Lloyd's notion of an 'invisible balance sheet', and the need to manage this invisible asset (1987, page 148):

> "One of the greatest errors the leader of a knowhow company can make is to accept the methods, objectives and yardsticks of the conventional industrial company.
>
> While it may be quite acceptable for the industrial company to strive to maximise the growth of financial assets, to apply the same objective to a knowhow company would be to court disaster. For the knowhow company it is the expansion of the knowhow capital which is the measure of growth.
>
> Knowhow capital growth normally involves growth in the number of professionals but the company's clients are not interested in whether it is the biggest in the world in terms of numbers of people or turnover. Clients do appreciate, however, a company that can show it has more knowhow than its competitors. The contemporary focus on growth of turnover or capital as evidence of success is *a leftover from the industrial age*. For members of the knowhow society volume measured in that way has no meaning. Whether an organisation is large or small is likewise a matter of indifference to the professionals. All they care about is whether the work and their colleagues are interesting and stimulating and whether their clients appreciate them."

Perhaps Sveiby and Lloyd overstate or overgeneralise the views of clients and professionals about the size of law firms, but there is more than a grain of truth in what they write.

For those who continue in a law firm (as opposed to those who sell it and walk away), there will be a realisation that whether or not the firm produces the future income flows on which the valuation was based will depend entirely on how it manages, develops and sells its know-how. Professional and managerial know-how will increase with continuing education and training, work experience, personal development; know-how underperforms because of lack of resources, lack of situational familiarity, and lack of motivation. It will increase as people join the firm, and decrease as people leave.

Other measures of performance should therefore be tracked, some of which could be financial (such as fee income per fee-earner, net profit per partner, and the profitability index: these and other indicators are described in chapter 30). Investments in know-how should also be tracked; these can be measured, for example, as hours and money devoted to training and development (preferably on an averaged per employee basis), or the time and money devoted to the creation of standardised know-how and precedents, or a know-how system. Maister has a useful discussion of many of the dimensions involved here (1993a, chapters 13 and 14). Given the importance of dual expertise to a know-how business (see paragraph 3.3), a law firm should not only track investments in its legal expertise, but also in its managerial know-how. As de Geus puts it: "we need a new way of thinking about the measurement of success in our companies. By outsiders, we are judged and measured in economic terms: return on investment and capital assets. But within the company, our success depends on our skill with human beings: building and developing the consistent knowledge base of our enterprise" (1997, page 28).

5.6 Conclusion

I hope that this chapter has given a sense of the nature of the principal business asset on which law firms are founded. Its central role, and the issues implicit in its development, management, productivity and economics, are often ignored or underestimated in many firms. Without it, though, they would fail. The way in which it is acquired, combined and presented to the marketplace is the essence of legal practice. The following chapters will build on this theme.

Chapter 6

THE ALLOCATION OF ECONOMIC RESOURCES

6.1 The Nature of Resource Allocation

The exploitation of a commercial opportunity requires someone:

   (a)   identify the opportunity;
   (b)   to establish what resources (the economist's factors of production — typically, land, labour, raw materials, and financial capital — but also, in our context, individual and firm-specific capital: see chapter 5) are required to exploit the opportunity;
   (c)   to acquire those resources;
   (d)   combine the resources into productive use to create the product or service that meets the opportunity;
   (e)   to monitor the standards and efficiency of the creative or production process;
   (f)   to sell the product or service to those who wish to buy or use it.

These activities can be described as inquisitive, acquisitive, managerial, and marketing. They are all required to lead to the effective and profitable exploitation of the opportunity, and the activities need coordinating. This process of total coordination usually falls to 'the entrepreneur', though of course an entrepreneur may also decide that exploiting the opportunity effectively also requires the acquisition of a 'resource' (a manager) to carry out some of the combining and monitoring activities. The issue for this chapter is why an entrepreneur should choose to combine and coordinate the required resources and activities within a firm. It might also be expressed as a decision about what to 'internalise' within a firm. The nature of entrepreneurship will be discussed in chapter 7.

   Economic resources can be allocated through three principal governance structures: (a) markets (where the exchange of resources is achieved through individually negotiated spot contracts); (b) hierarchies (also called institutions or firms, where the resources are brought within an organisation under a contract and traditionally allocated and coordinated through the command and control of those resources by an entrepreneur or manager); or (c) networks (where independent contractors allocate resources on a basis that is more structured and permanent than spot contracts, but less structured than employment, and where relationships are built on trust and cooperation).

In the context of legal services, there seem to me to be four types of interaction or allocation involved in the delivery of the services: between the lawyer and the client; between the lawyer and suppliers (e.g., landlords, stationers, equipment and technology businesses, couriers, accountants); between the lawyer and support staff; and between the lawyer and other lawyers. Any one of these relationships (resource allocations) can take place through a market, an institution, or a network. For example, if the lawyer–client interaction takes place in a market, the client will negotiate with a lawyer (or law firm) for the delivery of the required service. Alternatively, the client may decide to internalise the legal service and create an in-house legal department, thus moving the lawyer–client relationship from the market to an institution. Equally, the client might set up a network (such as a panel of preferred suppliers), which reduces dependence on the total market, but stops short of internalising legal services.

Some of the identified interactions may change, or be combined. For example, a law firm may initially use only external recruitment agencies (the lawyer–suppliers relationship operating in a market). Later, it may create its own personnel function and recruit a personnel manager: the market allocation of recruitment services is replaced by a lawyer–support-staff relationship operating within the institution of the firm. The personnel manager may, of course, continue to use the recruitment agencies (the market) for certain purposes, thus leading the lawyer to combine both market and institution allocations for personnel needs.

6.2 The Theory of the Firm

Economists have been considering for many years why firms are created. Why do entrepreneurs choose to conduct some of their economic transactions and the allocation of the resources they can direct or control through a firm rather than through independent contracts in the market? The founding father of this line of enquiry is generally acknowledged to be Ronald Coase in a 1937 article, 'The nature of the firm' (Coase 1937).

So what are the economic, social, or psychological imperatives that make firms desirable or necessary as a form of business organisation? Let us try to track the evolution of the firm as a form of economic organisation (I have relied on Dietrich 1994, chapter 4 and Ricketts 1994 for the bones of this exposition). In doing so we can explore what economists call 'the theory of the firm'.

Setting aside illegal or antisocial forms of economic resource allocation such as theft and trickery, the earliest form of allocation must have been bartering. This will hardly sustain a sophisticated exchange of resources: the odds of finding someone with a supply of goods or services that I might want, and whose needs for other goods and services I can satisfy from my own resources or efforts, are considerable (economists call this 'double coincidence'). It may take some time for me to find such a person, and yet more time to agree a suitable 'rate of exchange'. Bilateral trade through bartering is thus time-consuming and difficult; multilateral trade through bartering is all but impossible. This method of exchange becomes very much easier if the exchange is not the direct bartering of goods or services, but indirect bartering of those resources through the introduction of a third, distinct, freely exchangeable commodity — money.

6.3 Transaction Costs Theory of the Firm

The development of money as a common medium of valuation and exchange eases the way for smoother trading relationships, and markets are then better able to develop. Classical economic theory holds that the economic system is coordinated by the price mechanism, that is, that the exchanges of resources in a market are governed by price equilibrium (meaning a price that balances supply and demand). Coase then asserts: "The main reason why it is profitable to establish a firm would seem to be that there is a cost of using the price mechanism" (1937, page 391). These costs have become known as 'transaction costs', and include (Dietrich 1994, page 33):

(a) the costs of discovering suppliers and prices (search and information);
(b) the costs of negotiating and concluding contracts (bargaining and decision); and
(c) the costs of monitoring and correcting performance (policing and enforcement).

If a transaction depends on a number of independent people or resources (factors of production) for its completion, multilateral contracts (all carrying the transaction costs set out above) between them will probably be needed. If one person (an entrepreneur) could act as a coordinator by bringing the various people or resources into a firm, and also acquire the right to direct their performance or use at the appropriate time, the transaction costs can usually be reduced. As Coase (1937, pages 391–2) puts it:

"It is true that contracts are not eliminated when there is a firm but they are greatly reduced. A factor of production (or the owner thereof) does not have to make a series of contracts with the factors with whom he is co-operating within the firm, as would be necessary, of course, if this co-operation were as a direct result of the working of the price mechanism. For this series of contracts is substituted one. At this stage, it is important to note the character of the contract into which a factor enters that is employed within a firm. The contract is one whereby the factor, for a certain remuneration (which may be fixed or fluctuating), agrees to obey the directions of an entrepreneur *within certain limits*. [*Footnote in original*: It would be possible for no limits to the powers of the entrepreneur to be fixed. This would be voluntary slavery [and] such a contract would be void and unenforceable.]. . . .

When the direction of resources (within the limits of the contract) becomes dependent on the buyer in this way, that relationship which I term a 'firm' may be obtained."

Thus, whereas the price mechanism coordinates the allocation of economic resources in the market, the entrepreneur coordinates the allocation of resources within a firm. Indeed, says Coase, "the distinguishing mark of the firm is the supersession of the price mechanism" (1937, page 389).

Transaction costs are all largely dependent on access to information, which has led one commentator (Brian Loasby) to say: "In conditions of perfect knowledge, the theory of the firm is very simple: there are no firms". In other words, if we could find out everything we wanted to know in order to make a decision, process that information, and act on it, *without any cost to ourselves*, there would be no need for firms. Such a state is not possible, for we live in a world of bounded rationality where we cannot know everything we need to know (informational uncertainty), where we cannot perfectly process all the information we do have (informational complexity), and where information is not evenly or fairly distributed among economic actors (informational asymmetry): see Dietrich 1994, pages 19 and 20.

One of the theories of the firm, therefore, is that institutions (firms) develop as a response to the transaction costs associated with resource allocations through markets. Coase (1937) is attributed with having 'invented' transaction costs (although he did not use that term); but transaction cost theory has subsequently been developed most notably by Oliver Williamson (see Williamson 1975, 1985). There appear to be three dimensions that determine whether or not a firm will emerge to counter the effects of transaction costs (Dietrich 1994, chapters 2 and 3):

(a)   *Bounded rationality.* As stated above, if information were freely and fairly available, firms would not necessarily develop, because there would be no costs of using the market.

(b)   *Frequency of use.* Unless someone uses a particular resource frequently, there may be no (or insufficient) savings from bringing that resource into a firm. For example, if a lawyer does not need tax expertise other than sporadically, there is no benefit from bringing a tax lawyer into a firm, since the expertise can probably be sought from a market (sole tax practitioner or counsel). Although there would still be transaction costs associated with doing this, they would be lower than the costs of bringing the resource permanently into the firm.

(c) *Asset specificity.* Where two people regularly conduct business together, they acquire useful information about each other, their personality, circumstances, preferences, and so on. Where this 'inside knowledge' is important to the continuing trading relationship, there is a danger that the supplier will use this asset-specific knowledge to hold the buyer to ransom. He can use the existence of this knowledge to exert pressure on the buyer to continue using the supplier — and, in the market, to push the price up because of the costs and consequent loss of familiarity involved in changing suppliers. The buyer may be able to remove this threat of being 'held to ransom' by internalising the relationship and bringing the supplier into his firm.

The search and information costs, and the bargaining and decision costs, all arise before the trading contract is performed (economists call these *ex ante* costs). By bringing suppliers into a firm, these *ex ante* costs are only incurred once (for example, in finding and recruiting people and establishing a working relationship: in other words, by effectively creating an 'internal labour market'). But the costs of policing and enforcement, being *ex post* costs (that is, arising after the trading relationship is established) will arise whether the relationship is external (market) or internal (firm). The question for the entrepreneur is then whether the required monitoring is more easily, or cost-effectively, performed internally or externally.

The traditional transaction costs theory of the firm therefore suggests that firms will be created where the costs of organising the allocation of resources within an institution (call them 'organisation costs') are lower than the costs of organising the allocation of resources through a market ('transaction costs'). In other words, in these circumstances, the resources in question (goods, services, labour, property, financial capital) will be 'internalised' within a firm rather than being left to be acquired or exchanged in the external market. More recently, however, economists have sought to shift the ground of transaction costs theory away from a purely cost-based analysis to one of cost-benefit (see Dietrich 1994, chapter 3), suggesting that firms will form when the cost-benefit of organisations is higher than the cost-benefit of markets. This shift is necessary because, on the face of it, transaction *cost* analysis is not consistent with maximising *profits*. Traditional transaction cost theory would be satisfied if, as the result of a firm being created, the organisation costs were lower than the transaction costs of performing the same exchanges in the market. But, having done this, the firm might find that its overall revenues (or other benefits) are lower within the firm than they would have been in the market. Thus, although transaction cost theorists would have been satisfied, the entrepreneurs would not! The saving in transaction costs has not preserved or enhanced profitability, but rather reduced it. A cost-benefit analysis would therefore take account of the net effect of the revenue and cost implications of the market and a firm. Indeed, the organisation costs of a firm may be higher than the transaction costs of the market: provided the net benefit to the organisation is worth more to it than that from the market, a firm will still result.

One final observation: transaction cost theory assumes that resource allocation through the market is always an alternative to resource allocation within a firm. This must mean that 'economic actors' are always willing to operate in the uncertain conditions of a market, that is, to be entrepreneurs. However, there is no doubt that some people do not want to be risk-takers and prefer the 'security' of employed relationships.

6.4 Agency Theory of the Firm

Agency theory requires that we look at a trading relationship in terms of a principal (buyer) and agent (supplier) operating in a market. For economists, the terms 'principal' and 'agent' do not have the strict meanings that lawyers would ascribe to them.

Because transactions and relationships are subject to bounded rationality, both the principal and agent might be tempted to renege on their market agreement to the detriment of the other. This gives rise to two problems: opportunism (grabbing or leaving), and moral hazard (shirking). For example, if one lawyer (the agent) agrees to perform legal services on behalf of another (the principal) for a client of the principal at a fixed rate or amount, both of them will enter into this transaction (resource allocation) on the basis that, prospectively, the agreed services and fee seem reasonably fair to both sides. As the work progresses, or when it is finished, the agent may decide that the fee is too low and then seek to 'grab' more of the principal's money by renegotiating the fee. Alternatively, in the belief that the fee is too low and that the principal will not pay more, the agent may withdraw from ('leave') the relationship before the work is completed (since I am seeking to explore the economics of the firm at the moment, I am ignoring the professional ethics point in this!).

Equally, the nature of the agent's service is such that it is very difficult for the principal to know whether or not the agent has actually spent the agreed (or requisite) amount of time on his client's affairs, or that all of the time spent has been as productive as it should have been. In other words, the agent might have been 'shirking'. Economists call this problem of verifying *ex post* whether someone's actions have been consistent with the agreed contract terms the problem of 'moral hazard'.

To the extent that the problems of opportunism and moral hazard arise from bounded rationality, they are equally relevant to a transaction costs theory of the firm. However, the notions of grabbing, leaving and shirking are seen as particular problems of economic cooperation and thus of agency relationships.

The agency theory of the firm therefore sees institutions as an attempt to reduce the costs of self-seeking behaviour by either party (or at least to reduce the potential for it). The principal will seek to reduce the risks of the agent's opportunistic behaviour and of moral hazard by bringing the agent into a firm. Accordingly, there will be governance mechanisms built into the firm, such as monitoring and control relationships, and incentives (such as pay and benefits, and promotion), which are designed to encourage the realisation of mutual benefits that might not be (or so easily be) realised in the market.

6.5 Property Rights Theory of the Firm

If monitoring and control, or incentives, are required to overcome the possibility of opportunism and moral hazard, then whoever carries out the monitoring must have some authority over those monitored (to impose sanctions or deliver incentives), and it must be worth the monitor's effort to do so. This authority must be derived from the contractual agreement between the entrepreneur (or principal or employer), and another. It is the right of the entrepreneur under the contract to direct and control the other (or his resources) which gives rise to the notion of a 'property right'. Indeed, the whole field of economic exchanges, whether in goods or services, may be rationalised not as the exchange of the goods or services themselves but as the exchange of *rights* in the goods or over the output of people. As a result: "An owner of property rights possesses the consent of fellow men to allow him to act in particular ways" (Demsetz 1967, page 31).

This theory therefore suggests that a firm is a mechanism for the exploitation of property rights. It requires the existence of a monitor with rights to direct and control others, and this establishes a hierarchy (which is why institutions or firms are called hierarchies by economists). To the property rights theorists, it is the exploitation of these rights that gives rise to a profit in the firm. The monitor therefore plays a key role in realising the full gains from this exploitation, and the monitor is for this reason usually given a share of the profit.

Of course, unlike some rights, the property rights which exist within a firm are not freely tradeable, and will in any event lapse on death, retirement, or leaving the firm.

6.6 Behavioural Theory of the Firm

The emphasis of agency theories is on the (self-seeking) behaviour of individuals, and that of the property rights theories on the monitoring, control or adjustment of behaviour. The behavioural theories (associated particularly with Cyert and March 1963) see an organisation as coalitions of individuals whose responses to change are made in the context of internal behavioural norms: to some extent, therefore, behavioural theory is concerned with economic decision-making. Early thinking seemed to restrict the decision-making behaviour to short-term reactions to external changes, and assumed that search and information activity allowed all problems (and therefore organisational goals) to be specified *ex ante*. More recent developments recognise that change can be internally generated, and that decision-making can be an iterative process of search, learning and refining (see Dietrich 1994, pages 137–41).

For present purposes, behavioural theories need not be further explored because they focus more on *how* firms function than *why* they exist.

However, it is important to recognise that some theorists will use behavioural arguments to challenge the economic theories of the firm. For example, economic theory assumes that the relative cost-benefits of market transactions and organisational allocation will determine whether or not firms are created — that there is a mixture of transaction cost analysis, profit maximisation, and property rights responses to agency risks that will, in certain circumstances, predetermine the creation of a firm. But in the context of professionals, there are (as we all know!) strong professional and social norms and behaviours that can lead them to *assume*, without analysis, that firms are inevitable. The drive for partnership status as a career goal, or for professional recognition, the 'socialisation' of lawyers into similar and largely predictable patterns of behaviour, and the tendency for certain types of clients and work to gravitate towards larger, corporate law firms and therefore to attract certain types of lawyer, could all be cited as *other* reasons for the creation of law firms. It seems to me, though, that while these factors undoubtedly *perpetuate* law firms (or certain types of law firm), they do not explain the underlying drivers that led to their *creation* in the first place.

Chapter 7

THE NEED FOR ENTREPRENEURS

7.1 Origins and Meaning of Entrepreneurship

I have so far assumed that some people are able to spot opportunities for
the exchange of economic resources at the end of which exchange they
will be in a better position than before. As suggested at the beginning of
chapter 6, there are several requirements for a successful outcome: the
identification of an opportunity; the acquisition of appropriate resources
(which also usually implies a need for financial capital); identifying
potential customers or clients and suppliers; negotiating the terms of the
exchange of resources with suppliers; organising and coordinating the
exchange (either in the market, within a firm, or through a network); the
monitoring of those exchanges to ensure that they are properly carried
out; selling the product or service; and a resulting profit. These activities
were described as inquisitive, acquisitive, managerial, and marketing. The
process of identifying an opportunity and of coordinating a response to it
was assumed to be the role of the entrepreneur.

English classical economists did not recognise the role of the entrepreneur. They tended to assume the existence of opportunity, and further
assume that the provider of capital and the organiser of resources were
the same person. On this view, 'profit' became the return to the provider
of financial capital. However, this confuses the different requirements.
Profit (on the classical view) has to cover not only the 'wages' of financial
capital but also the wages of marketing and development, and of organising economic exchanges. Such a view might be acceptable where the
originator, marketer, financier and organiser are the same person or
group, but not where they are functionally separate.

It therefore fell to French classical economists to point out the logic of
functional separation. Where financial capital is provided by 'outsiders',
the 'wages' or cost of money is usually contractually defined (as the rate
of interest). It is also possible that the task of carrying out the necessary
exchanges will fall to 'managers', and they will expect to receive a reward

for their labour — and usually even if the sum total of the exchanges does *not* yield any surplus. Accordingly, 'profit' is not a contractually defined sum (rate of interest, or wages for employment), but a residual — what is left after all of these other exchanges have been paid for. To the French, profit is thus the reward for the assumption of risk (usually an uninsurable risk) and for bearing uncertainty. This reward does not belong to a third-party financier or manager, since such persons will already have been rewarded for the function they have performed. It belongs to the 'entrepreneur' (and there is no equivalent English word, so we have kept the French description).

7.2   Nature of Entrepreneurship

This might tell us *who* an entrepreneur is, and *how* he or she is rewarded, but it does not explain *what* an entrepreneur does (see also Bhide 1996). This is more problematic, but seems to boil down to three possibilities. Across all three, the role clearly involves identifying opportunities that have not otherwise been exploited (or at least not *fully* exploited): entrepreneurs are therefore inquisitive. It also involves arranging the exchange of resources: entrepreneurs therefore need access to resources and so also tend to be acquisitive. But then the gains will derive from one or more of:

- the use of new knowledge — invention;
- the new use of existing knowledge — innovation;
- the new combination of resources — combination.

There is also a final requirement: to ensure that the gains are actually derived (achievement). For the distinction between invention and innovation, see paragraph 4.7.4.

Entrepreneurship can therefore be described as bringing about change for gain. The longer it takes to do so, the greater the risk. Indeed, since time and a myriad of other changes constantly alter our environment, individual entrepreneurs may become obsolete as their original ideas are superseded. As Bhide puts it: "Entrepreneurs must continually ask themselves what business they *want* to be in and what capabilities they would *like* to develop" (1996, page 120). It is also clear that it is not necessary for the entrepreneur to *own* any of the resources he is exchanging — provided that he can 'engineer' the requisite exchange and appropriate some of the resulting gains for himself. In this sense, an entrepreneur's profit will not necessarily represent a return on ownership (this is an important point in the context of legal practice, to which I shall return in chapter 8).

Within the legal environment, therefore, I would suggest that entrepreneurial activities comprise:

(a)   developing client work or the firm's practice as a result of identifying opportunities for:

(i) introducing a new service to existing or new clients (invention);
(ii) selling different (existing) services to existing clients (innovation);
(iii) selling existing services to new clients (innovation);
(iv) opening a new office (innovation);
(v) introducing new methods of working — often by substituting capital (technology) for labour, by substituting part-time for full-time staff, or by substituting less well qualified and expensive labour (paralegals) for fully qualified staff (innovation);
(vi) selling more of the same services to existing clients (combination) — by keeping the client relationship going and securing a flow of similar work;
(vii) combining resources in different ways (combination) — either vertically (e.g., recruiting more assistants or paralegals, or bringing in more support staff, services or technology) or horizontally (by bringing in lateral partners or by merging);

(b) exploiting the opportunities identified, principally by organising appropriate resources, and by distributing the opportunities and work derived from them among others in the firm (that is, achievement by sharing); and

(c) managing and monitoring the use of resources to ensure that the expected allocations and exchanges of those resources actually take place and do so effectively (achievement by managing and monitoring).

Some people might believe that activity (a)(vi) should be expected of all practising fee-earners, and is not therefore truly entrepreneurial. If a fee-earner simply sits and waits to be fed work by others, I would agree. But the situation that I have in mind in (a)(vi) is that someone is actively seeking to *exploit* an existing relationship, not merely reacting to a current need. The process of exploitation involves spotting and developing opportunities for more work of the same type (different types would fall within (a)(ii); it is about securing future transactions and not just responding to the current one. Given that, typically, 75% or more of a firm's current year's business will come from existing clients and contacts, it would also seem vacuous to suggest that securing more of the same work from existing clients is *not* entrepreneurial!

My definition of entrepreneurial behaviour in law firms is therefore a broad one — certainly broader than developing business from new clients ('rainmaking': (a)(i) and (iii)). There may be a sense in which the definition appears to cover the activities of most people who are partners in law firms. So be it: the point made above about the difference in business philosophy between the active exploitation of opportunities and the reactive acceptance of work originated by others is, to me, the crucial distinction. But I accept that there is also a difference in the *degree* of entrepreneurial behaviour exhibited in the nine categories and, correspondingly, a difference in the degree of risk undertaken. Most of the internal stature in law firms seems to be derived from activities (a)(iii);

followed by (a)(i) — which is rare; (a)(ii) — which is usually described as 'cross-selling'; and with (a)(vi) being expected rather than respected. Activities (a)(iv), (v) and (vii) are not particularly prized; nor are activities (b) and (c).

One preliminary conclusion, therefore, could be that, if profit is the residual gains or return to entrepreneurs and in a law firm profit is payable to partners, then profit-sharing partners should each be engaged in entrepreneurial activities. In other words, partners should be doing one or more of the nine activities in (a), (b) or (c) above, and should not receive shares in 'profit' simply for providing financial capital (for which an agreed rate of interest is an adequate return), or for simply effecting the exchange of legal services (that is, fee-earning, for which an agreed 'wage' is the appropriate return). Financiers and fee-earners are available in the open market, or could (if appropriate) be brought within the firm, though not necessarily as partners. Whether this conclusion holds up, we shall see (in paragraph 8.9).

It could further be argued that managers and monitors (those who carry out activity (c)) could also be available through the market or brought into the firm other than as partners — that is, that managing and monitoring achievement is not an entrepreneurial activity. I shall suggest later (see paragraph 8.4.4; and cf. paragraph 6.5) that monitoring carries a risk that is probably best avoided by giving the monitor a share in the residual gains: in other words, ensuring that a profit in fact results from the opportunities identified for exchanging resources is as important as identifying the opportunities and organising the resources needed to address them, and is therefore part of the risk and uncertainty appropriately borne by an entrepreneur and rewarded accordingly.

In fact, entrepreneurialism is a necessary, but not sufficient, condition for an effective and successful firm. If entrepreneurs are free within an organisation to do exactly as they please, they may develop business that is harmful to the reputation of other parts of the firm, which is not within its areas of expertise, which it does not have the resources to deal with effectively, or which has unwanted consequences for the firm's rate of growth (cf. paragraph 3.6.2). The firm's entrepreneurs therefore need to act within and consistently with its strategy (see chapter 4) and values (see chapter 23), and in a way which allows growth to be properly managed.

7.3 Making Money as a Strategic Objective

The thrust of this chapter has so far been that firms exist to exploit opportunities, and therefore implicitly to pursue strategies that allow them to do this. Grant's key assumption is that the purpose of strategy is "to pursue profit over the long term" (1995, page 34). On this view, "the purpose and the content of a firm's strategy is defined by the answer to a single question: How can the firm make money?" (1995, page 42). This strikes me as a somewhat narrow view. I would be the first to agree that law firms are in business, and that lawyers are not therefore *merely* engaged in a professional calling which they can pursue without regard to the requirements of running a business. But is not the pursuit of money as *the* single business objective at odds with professionalism (and with a lawyer's position as an officer of the court) and a fuller notion of entrepreneurialism?

Many partners in law firms assert that their strategic objective is "making money" or "maximising profit". Now, I accept that no one in business is likely to set out with the objective of *losing* money. But a stated objective of 'making money' raises more questions than it answers: Does it mean making as much money as possible? Doing what? For whom? How? Over what period of time? With what degree of investment? With what degree of risk? With what regard to legality, professionalism, ethics or values involved in the activity? The answers to *these* questions will provide the strategic objectives, and will define the entrepreneurialism involved. Remember that Grant draws the distinction between corporate strategy and business strategy (see paragraph 4.3.1). For a company with a choice of industries to enter, corporate strategy (choice of industry) may be a fundamental decision. The profit potential offered by different industries — the ability to make money — will therefore be a necessary enquiry. For law firms, this is still a valid enquiry, since they may decide to enter 'non-legal' markets. In the minds of many lawyers, however, the industry is a given, though there may be choices about which practice areas to enter (which, in their context, may be as fundamental as choice of industry and could well depend on likely profitability).

I have already considered the difficulties of maximising profits as a basis for increasing the value of a law firm (see paragraph 5.5.3, and the nature of profitability will be explored in chapter 28). Suffice to repeat at this point that increasing profits, and managing the firm's underlying asset (its know-how) to increase its productivity and so sustain the long-term profitability of the firm, may not be consistent. A choice has to be made between short-term and long-term profitability. Both are about maximising profits, but require other strategic decisions to be made. In this sense, maximising profits is a strategic contradiction and cannot therefore be a strategy.

In the context of know-how businesses generally, and of law offices in particular, notions of making money, maximising profits, and increasing the value of ownership interests are fraught with conceptual and practical difficulties and inconsistencies. Making money (however that is to be defined and quantified by a firm) will be the *result* of the choice and successful implementation of a corporate strategy about *which* business or businesses to be in (or practice areas to pursue), and of a business strategy which ensures a competitive advantage and success *within* the chosen business and practice areas. But if professional success and reputation, job satisfaction, respect for clients and colleagues, and professionalism are to have any meaning in legal practice, then it seems to me that, in and of itself, making money will for most professionals be a sterile and deceptive strategic objective — though not an undesirable result!

Chapter 8

A THEORY OF THE LAW FIRM

8.1 Combining Lawyers' Talent

It would be possible to apply the generic 'theories of the firm' discussed in chapter 6 to all of the lawyer–client, lawyer–supplier, lawyer–support-staff, and lawyer–lawyer relationships that can arise in the delivery of legal services. In applying these generic theories in the hope of developing the 'theory of the law firm', however, I am going to confine the following exposition principally to the lawyer–lawyer aspect.

It is important to recognise that there are many instances of lawyers buying legal services from other lawyers in a market. The relationship between solicitor and counsel, the use of High Court agency solicitors and locums, and the existence of 'special projects lawyers', all fall into this category. It is not the case, therefore, that all lawyer–lawyer needs and relationships can only (or best) be satisfied by internalising them. Further, the creation of networks for the delivery of legal services shows that the 'raw market' and a law firm are not the only appropriate responses to lawyer–lawyer resource allocation: the issues around networks are considered more fully in the context of international practice (see paragraph 13.3.2).

8.1.1 A diversified portfolio

The question we need to address is, first, why an actual or potential sole practitioner would choose to combine with one or more other lawyers and, if so, second, whether to choose to do so in a horizontal (partnership) or vertical (employment) relationship. Economically, the decision may be seen to represent a choice by an entrepreneur of whether or not to diversify. Gilson and Mnookin examine this choice in the context of portfolio theory, the principles of which they explain as follows (1985, page 322):

"The modern development of portfolio theory rests on the insight that risk averse investors will always hold a diversified 'portfolio' of capital assets. This observation follows from two premises: (1) that investors prefer more return to less given the same level of risk, and (2) that investors prefer less risk to more given the same level of return. By combining assets in a portfolio, the investor can reduce the level of risk without reducing expected return. A rational investor will then select the portfolio of assets that offers the most desirable combination of risk and return."

Gilson and Mnookin distinguish between systematic risk (risk associated with holding any asset because of changes in general economic conditions) and unsystematic risk (risk associated with holding a particular asset). Portfolio theory assumes that investors *choose* unsystematic risks, and therefore will choose a portfolio of assets in such a way that the unsystematic risks associated with each of them can be combined to cancel each other out (1985, page 323):

"A fully diversified portfolio is thus simply not subject to unsystematic risk. The only risk that remains in a diversified portfolio, then, is systematic risk — the risk of events that will alter the value of all assets. The final point in the development of portfolio theory for our purposes involves the recognition that the market pays no premium to investors who bear avoidable risk. The return on, and therefore the price of, a capital asset will depend on how much *systematic* risk is associated with it. If the asset carries a great deal of systematic risk — if it is quite responsive to general economic conditions — an investor will require a higher return, and the asset will warrant a lower price, than would an asset that is less sensitive."

8.1.2 *Diversifying lawyers' know-how*

So much for the theory: now comes the problem for law firms. The capital asset in question is human capital (know-how: see chapter 5). Diversified individual capital would imply being a general practitioner. The range of legal services today, however, is such that no one lawyer can be fully diversified: he or she thus has to choose one or more areas of practice (specialisation to one degree or another). This very act of choosing limits diversification, and therefore introduces unsystematic risk. In other words, it is impossible for an individual lawyer to avoid unsystematic risk, that is, "the variation in earnings from law practice resulting from the individual characteristics of a particular lawyer" (Gilson and Mnookin 1985, pages 324–5).

Some of the unsystematic risk (e.g., from death, illness, or disability) can be insured against, and thus diversified from the legal market to the insurance market. But some of it — such as shirking and other forms of underperforming — cannot. Imagine being able to seek through insurance the difference between an expected income and actual income where that difference is paid because the insured has been shirking. The people who stand to gain most from such insurance would be those with a predisposition to underperform and then claim the benefits of the insurance for their reduced income. No insurer would realistically want to take on this risk: it is a foregone conclusion that someone who insures against shirking will in fact shirk in order to claim the benefits! This is what economists call the principle of 'adverse selection', that is, self-selection by people whose choice would always benefit themselves at the expense of another party to the arrangement in question. It is compounded by the relevant information being controlled by only one of the parties — the one who would benefit: how could an insurer counter the insured's assertion that loss of income was the result of shirking? This informational asymmetry also creates moral hazard, too (see paragraphs 6.3 and 6.4).

This discussion of shirking has assumed that the underperformance is deliberate. A lawyer may, however, underperform because of the loss of an important client, a fall-off in demand for the lawyer's specialist expertise, the death of a close relative, divorce, a child's illness or abduction, or a crisis of confidence. These are not instances of deliberate underperformance, but nor are they realistically insurable risks. They deserve compassion, but for a sole practitioner there would be no relief from such unsystematic risk. To Gilson and Mnookin, therefore, the creation of a law firm allows the development of a diversified portfolio of legal services that collectively, in theory, should allow the unsystematic risk associated with any one lawyer or service to be set against the continuing gains of others.

8.2   Towards a Theory of the Law Firm

Now we can begin to consider why law firms are created in the way they are; similar issues arise in considering the further growth of a firm that already exists. If the question was put to lawyers, most would probably give one or more of the following reasons: to improve the service to existing clients (that is, to improve efficiency or reliability), to broaden the service to clients (that is, to diversify or achieve a minimum scale), to add to the depth of the service (that is, to add resource or to specialise), or to spread the costs — and risk — of practice (that is, to seek economies of scale or scope). These possibilities obviously overlap: none is 'pure', nor are they necessarily mutually exclusive. For analytical purposes, I shall resolve them into three categories: addressing surplus costs, addressing surplus client needs, and addressing surplus opportunities.

There is, as we have seen (in paragraph 8.1.2), a further possibility which seems rarely these days to be articulated by lawyers: to help each other out in good times and — particularly — not so good times (that is, to diversify unsystematic risk). Because it is rarely identified separately, I shall not treat it separately in this analysis, though I shall allude to it as the analysis proceeds.

I shall follow the example set by Galanter and Palay (1991) and refer to partners/principals as 'she' and employed fee-earner/agents as 'he' as a method of avoiding cumbersome configurations of gender.

8.3 Addressing Surplus Costs

There are two points here. First, for a lawyer practising alone, there is a possibility that she could acquire all the necessary supporting services in the marketplace. This may not be a very efficient use of time and energy because of the transaction costs associated with each independent arrangement (see paragraph 6.3). From this standpoint, therefore, the creation of a firm may be able to reduce the market costs (transaction costs) by replacing them with lower internal costs (organisation costs). This makes economic sense when the cost-benefit of internal organisation exceeds the cost-benefit of market transactions. It also represents the diversification of some of the unsystematic risk that a sole practitioner would otherwise have to bear in setting up in practice.

Second, however, is the possibility that the cost-benefit may *not* be higher for internal organisation. This is the economy of scale point. It presupposes that a lawyer (or existing firm) has more office resources than are needed to service existing clients: "A single lawyer or small firm, for example, may be unable to utilize optimal amounts of such things as staff support (like secretaries, paralegals, and even associate lawyers) or hard assets (like word processing machinery, duplicating equipment, and library resources)" (Gilson and Mnookin 1985, page 316, note 9). Rather than seeking to expand to meet a strategic need (surplus client needs, or surplus opportunities), the lawyer or firm is simply looking for other practitioners to absorb some of those surplus costs. Indeed, on this view, there is no reason why the additional 'sharers' should in fact be other lawyers.

While not disputing that such surplus costs can, and do, arise, the concept of economies of scale in legal practice remains a difficult one. Certainly, some overhead costs can be spread across a number of lawyers. But after a short while, the additional resource or capacity needed to service added lawyers means that the relative unit cost (usually the hourly cost) of the production of legal services remains much the same: indeed, to the extent that larger firms are expected to have bigger and better resources, and employ more expensive lawyers, the unit cost may well rise rather than fall. In these events, there are no economies of scale. Gilson and Mnookin concentrate in their article on the existence of large law firms, and they do not accept that the existence of these firms can be attributed to economies of scale (1985, page 317 and note 13):

"Nearly all of the returns to scale appear to be achievable by a firm much smaller than today's large law firms. . . . The most striking characteristic of the economies of scale explanation — that firms grow to exhaust scale economies — is not that it is wrong, but that it does not seem sufficient to justify the increase in the number and size of very large firms. While capital expenditures may be "lumpy," it certainly does not take a very large organisation to achieve the necessary scale for many of them. . . . One lawyer may not be able to use a secretary full time, but surely two or three can. Moreover, technology seems to be changing in a way that reduces substantially the size at which firms exhaust scale economies with respect to certain assets. . . . Furthermore, it would seem that sole practitioners can achieve a number of these gains by contracting among themselves as opposed to by creating or joining a firm. . . . Indeed, office sharing — by which sole practitioners share a considerable portion of their overhead, but *not* income — has long been a familiar phenomenon among sole practitioners. . . . All of this is not to say that economies do not exist. Instead, we simply mean to suggest that they do not seem very difficult to achieve, can in fact be achieved by contract rather than through formation of a firm, and in any event, would hardly explain a cost advantage for a firm of 50 lawyers over a firm of 20 lawyers.''

The existence of surplus costs may therefore suggest a mistaken or premature decision to create an organisation, such that the resources that have been internalised should perhaps still be acquired through the market, or could be resourced through sharing in a network (as in barristers' chambers or through groupings of law firms). Alternatively, surplus costs may be a short-term issue that further (anticipated, but not necessarily significant) growth will absorb. But this growth — if it is to be sustained — will need to be pursued for a *strategic* reason rather than as an end in itself. As such, surplus costs do not explain the creation of a law firm and, in the absence of surplus client need or surplus opportunities, cannot in my view truly be incorporated into a theory of the law firm.

8.4   Addressing Surplus Client Needs

8.4.1   *Responding to transaction costs*

From the perspective of an individual lawyer, a surplus client need will arise when that lawyer can generate more client work than she can handle, or when client work requires the input of specialist expertise that she does not have. In these circumstances, the lawyer can 'contract out' that surplus to another lawyer. In either case, the lawyer will incur transaction costs — finding a suitable additional resource or specialist, negotiating with them, and monitoring the satisfactory completion of the work. In other words, there are issues of bounded rationality (see paragraph 6.3). If there is a sufficient surplus and that surplus is shareable (in the sense that the client is happy to have the work carried out by another lawyer of the principal lawyer's choice), the 'frequency of use' condition can be met to warrant bringing the additional resource within a firm. Further, the additional lawyer will acquire client-specific and transaction-specific knowledge, giving rise to 'asset specificity'. Transaction cost theory (see paragraph 6.3) can therefore show that bringing an additional lawyer into a firm is a reasonable response to surplus client needs. This reflects Galanter and Palay's (1991) description of surplus, shareable human capital (pages 91 and 109): see paragraph 3.6.1.

8.4.2 Responding to agency costs

As soon as the principal lawyer shares this surplus with an additional lawyer, she is lending or sharing part of her individual capital, that is, making an effort to diversify her human capital portfolio by investing in the creation of firm-specific capital, the net benefits from which she hopes to appropriate. This investment, however, carries risks — the agency problems of opportunism and moral hazard that arise from the lending transaction (see paragraph 6.4). The additional lawyer might demand or 'grab' a greater share of the fee (or, indeed, the client relationship), or 'leave' the sharing relationship before the principal lawyer realises the full benefit of the other's involvement. Further, the additional lawyer might simply 'shirk', by putting in less than the required effort or by producing less than the required quality of output. There is, of course, an equivalent danger that the principal will not fulfil her side of the bargain, by corresponding forms of grabbing (paying less than agreed), 'leaving' the relationship (by asking the additional lawyer to stop working but keeping the benefits of surplus work or relationships developed by him), or shirking (overestimating the principal's effort in carrying out the work or contribution to the quality of the output, or by not delivering promised rewards).

To counter these risks, processes of monitoring and control, as well as incentives, will be needed. The principal will want to ensure that the additional lawyer performs effectively and does not jeopardise her client-specific and firm-specific capital. This will usually be achieved through supervision and the ability to increase or reduce remuneration. The additional lawyer will probably also be looking for a future share of the property rights and benefits that accrue from promotion to partnership and participation in firm-specific capital and profits. This is analysed by Galanter and Palay (1991, see pages 93–8). In other words, agency and property rights theories (discussed in paragraphs 6.4 and 6.5) can show that a law firm can equally provide a governance structure suitable to the needs of lawyers who share work arising from surplus client needs.

The incentives to the principal of this arrangement are the ability to maximise her entrepreneurial gains (profit) from the exploitation of her human capital, and to increase that capital by increasing the level of client satisfaction — in both cases, by achieving more together with the additional lawyer than she could have on her own. The protection for the principal arises from the actual performance of the additional lawyer, her ability to monitor his actions, and the right to dismiss him if the expected benefits do not accrue. Dismissal is usually a costly option because of the nature of the investments that the principal has to make in transferring and developing the asset-specific skills (usually relating to clients and transactions) in the additional lawyer which, by definition, are not readily available in the market and are therefore difficult to substitute. At a personal level, this raises all the issues of the imitability and replicability of know-how discussed in paragraph 5.4.

For the additional lawyer, the incentives are the opportunity to develop further his individual capital (particularly experience-dependent and transaction-specific skills, and client relationships), and the possibility of promotion. Protection arises from the actual performance by the principal of her obligations, the reality of promotions, and the ability to leave if the expected benefits do not accrue. As with dismissal by the principal, departure by the additional lawyer can also be costly because of the asset-specific nature of his investments in her practice which he may not be able to capitalise on in the market or with another law firm. In other words, his individual capital may need to be combined with another individual's human capital or with a certain type of firm-specific capital before its full potential and value can be realised.

8.4.3 Limits to the response

For a sole proprietor, the incentive to monitor is to maximise client satisfaction and profit. Her ability to expand her business will thus, in part, be restricted by her capacity and ability to monitor. If she employs someone to carry out this monitoring for her, at a contractual wage rather than a share of the profits, there is as much a possibility that the monitor will shirk (i.e., a risk to the sole proprietor of moral hazard) as there is that the lawyer being monitored will shirk. Of course, in appropriate circumstances, the proprietor could give the monitor a share of the profits, thus making the monitor a partner. However, in legal practice, it is extremely unlikely that the proprietor would bring someone else into the firm as a partner simply to act as a monitor. In the context of the present discussion, it would also be pointless. We are assuming the existence of a sole lawyer who needs help to deal with work that she cannot handle. The extra person is therefore needed to carry out client work, and the problems of moral hazard would suggest that the proprietor would not allow that additional lawyer to be his own supervisor.

This suggests, therefore, that a sole practitioner or sole principal would respond to surplus client needs by bringing in one or more employed assistants or paralegals, provided that she could effectively carry out the monitoring that these additional fee-earners would require. From there, it is entirely possible that the practice would evolve organically as one or more of the assistants succeed in the 'promotion-to-partner tournament' (see paragraph 3.6).

I have so far assumed that the surplus client need arises to a sole practitioner or sole principal. It is possible, of course, that there could be a collection of surplus (but sufficiently similar) client needs arising to a number of partners in the same firm. Taking on additional lawyers may help each of them (over and above their association with each other) diversify the unsystematic risks associated with their own practices. The analysis otherwise remains the same, except that the existing partners should now have combined monitoring capacity and a collective reputation. Both are part of the firm-specific capital. Indeed, the existence of a reputation (part of the firm-specific capital) may be part of what attracts the additional lawyer to the firm in the first place. As long as the monitoring activities of the partners are verifiable (a big assumption!) —

meaning that there is no incentive for a partner to shirk her monitoring obligations — this will allow the business to grow to the limits of the combined monitoring capacity of the partners (Galanter and Palay 1991, pages 105 and 108–9): see paragraph 5.2.2.

As the number of partners increases, however, their individual monitoring activities become harder to verify and there is an incentive for them to shirk: assigning responsibility for the poor performance of the firm to any one partner will be difficult (if not impossible). This may suggest practical limits to the effective size of a law firm. Economists regard it as significant that the maximum legal limit for partnerships is 20 partners (section 716 of the Companies Act 1985, though of course professional partnerships have been excluded from this limit): they believe that the commingling of partners' resources and the existence of unlimited, joint and several liability creates risks that almost predetermine small partnerships between individuals who trust each other and who are susceptible to peer pressure to moderate their behaviour (see Ricketts 1994, pages 95–9, and Galanter and Palay 1991, pages 107–8 and 120).

8.4.4 Vertical or horizontal responses

This discussion has so far sought to show that there is no immediate *economic* reason why an incoming lawyer brought in to a firm to service a surplus client need should come in as a partner. In other words, it assumes that the incoming lawyer will come in as an employed lawyer (vertical recruitment) rather than as a partner (horizontal or lateral recruitment). It is implicit that the incoming lawyer is dependent on the principal lawyer or lawyers for the additional work — he is, in short, dependent on her or their human capital. In this sense, it is only the principal lawyer or lawyers who can be said to be entrepreneurial and therefore it is only she or they who should be sharing in any residual gain (profit) accruing to that human capital. It is also in this sense that the principal lawyer is not, generally speaking, diversifying the unsystematic risk associated with her practice by bringing in an assistant because that person is also dependent on her individual capital for the generation of work. There might conceivably be some diversification if the principal's clients generate specialist work that the assistant can handle: this would provide some compensation for a downturn of work in areas handled by the principal. If such a situation were prolonged, however, it is likely that opportunism would surface through the assistant either 'holding up' the principal for partnership — grabbing — or moving to another firm (or setting up on his own) with the client in tow — leaving (see paragraph 6.4).

In practice, however, the entrepreneurial emphasis may not lie so clearly with the principal. The principal lawyer (or lawyers) and the incoming lawyer might both be looking to circumstances in which the latter can make other contributions. If these contributions expand the human capital of the firm (that is, begin to add to *firm-specific* capital) then it seems to me that the possibility of the incoming lawyer sharing in profits — becoming a partner — can arise. For example, the incoming lawyer may be able to help address the surplus client need, but may not otherwise be sitting around idle — he may have an existing or embryonic sole practice of his own (as either a generalist or a specialist). By integrating it with the practice of the principal lawyer or lawyers, he will add to the firm-specific capital by bringing in his own client relationships and work flow, and reputation for quality. The incoming lawyer will still have to be monitored in the process of satisfying the surplus client need (to reduce the risks of opportunism and moral hazard faced by the principal). Although this will be horizontal (partner–partner) rather than vertical (partner–assistant) monitoring, it would be naive to pretend that all partners are equal: partnerships tend to evolve hierarchical relations between partners in such a way that monitoring, incentives and sanctions are just as effective at partner level as they are elsewhere in the firm.

The determining factor here may not be the *fact* of dependence on the principal's human capital but the *degree* of that dependence. So, if the incoming lawyer is more dependent on his own human capital for a continuing flow of work than on the practice he joins, a partnership should probably follow because it is arguable that he is adding value to the firm-specific capital by joining (but cf. paragraph 35.1.2).

It is also possible, of course, that in addition to addressing surplus client needs, the incoming lawyer will recognise or present surplus opportunities. Addressing these opportunities is considered in paragraph 8.5. But in this event, it is much more likely that the incoming lawyer will be able to add to firm-specific capital and so more likely that he could justify entry as a partner.

The choice of vertical or horizontal recruitment may, in practice, depend on the bargaining ability of the incoming lawyer and the desperation of the recruiting lawyer. But this simply poses the same question in a different way: what factors give rise to respective bargaining ability? It is, as we shall see, all about power (see particularly paragraph 24.3.4).

In addition to the degree of dependence on human capital, one way of resolving this would be to return to the premise that a partner should be an entrepreneur (see chapter 7). So, any lawyer whose individual activities have been sustained in a market would qualify as an entrepreneur, since he will have demonstrated those attributes and skills that mark him out as such. This would mean that another sole practitioner or partner in an existing firm who demonstrates the abilities of an entrepreneur as defined above should in principle be brought in horizontally.

A lawyer who is an assistant with another firm, some senior lawyers who are specialists in a narrow field of law, and some partners who have been simply fee-earners in another firm, would not qualify as entrepreneurs on my definition — and therefore should not be brought into the firm as partners (see paragraph 7.2). It may be argued that such a view pays no attention to the *potential* of these people. I would respond that whereas scope may be allowed within a firm for the demonstration of potential by existing lawyers, bringing someone into the firm as a partner who has not demonstrated *actual* entrepreneurial ability exposes that firm to undue

risk. Sharing part of the profit from entrepreneurial activities with someone who has no track record of being able to make a net contribution to
that profit is to succumb to the likelihood of opportunism (the incoming
partner 'grabbing' a larger share of the residual than he should be entitled
to): see also paragraph 36.5.4.

8.5 Addressing Surplus Opportunities

8.5.1 *Nature of the opportunities*

The discussion of surplus client needs has assumed that a lawyer is
responding to a known need of an existing client. The response gives rise
to strategic considerations for the lawyer, and will still usually require the
exercise of entrepreneurial ability to realise gains from the opportunity
that the surplus need presents. There may also be circumstances, however, where the lawyer *anticipates* that existing or potential clients have
unfulfilled needs. This anticipation also gives rise to strategic considerations and the need for some different entrepreneurial activities. I have
separated them because responding to needs tends, I believe, more often
to give rise to organic development of law firms, whereas anticipating
needs usually involves greater risk and uncertainty, and may require
non-organic development. Organic growth seems to depend principally
on monitoring capacity (see paragraph 8.4.3); non-organic growth also
often depends on greater (human and financial) capital investment. The
distinction may not be this black and white in practice, though.
  So, although surplus client needs might also have been classified as
surplus opportunities, on the basis that attending to those needs of
existing clients has already been dealt with (see paragraph 8.4), surplus
opportunities for present purposes seem to fall into four categories of
diversification:

(a) diversification of *services*, that is, providing a new or different
service to existing clients;
(b) diversification of *clients*, that is, providing the same services to
more (or different) clients;
(c) diversification of *location*, that is, opening a new office in a
different geographical area from the existing office or offices; and
(d) *multiple* diversification, that is, any combination of (a), (b) and (c).

It may be thought that diversification by location should not be a
separate category because it must necessarily presuppose some extension
of the client base or some additional services (category (a) or (b)).
Nevertheless, a firm may grow by adding offices comprising different
lawyers who provide the same *range* of services to the same *type* of clients
— though clearly these different lawyers would not be providing the *same*
services to the *same* clients. The method of growth could involve reloca-
ting an existing partner (and some other existing staff) but would usually
also entail lateral recruitment, or merger or acquisition. The merit of

keeping diversification of location separate is that a firm's geography is a strategically different consideration (see paragraph 4.5.2), and that the human capital requirements are different (the ability to manage separate offices — the need for managerial know-how — is an additional requirement over above the know-how needed to manage the clients and the services).

All forms of diversification discussed here should, in principle, represent the diversification of the unsystematic risk associated with any individual lawyer's practice.

8.5.2 Diversification of services

For diversification of services to be successful, a firm will have either to develop or to acquire the new services. Development will require existing lawyers to make further investment in their individual capital, and they will need reassurance that their performance in the meantime will not be assessed on the basis that they are as fully competent and productive as they were immediately before the further investment began. Usually, for an individual lawyer to diversify his or her own expertise successfully and to be able to continue to work in the same firm, that lawyer is relying on the firm's reputation for quality (part of the firm-specific capital). Acquisition of lawyers with expertise in the new services poses the same issues as the acquisition of specialists to service surplus client needs as discussed in paragraph 8.4. Both courses of action assume that client-specific information (as part of the firm-specific capital) can be used to discover which of the existing clients might need and want the new services. In other words, diversification of services is crucially dependent on the *sharing of firm-specific capital*.

8.5.3 Diversification of clients

Diversification of clients will mean attracting new clients to the firm. It is, of course, possible that clients may be attracted by the strength of an individual's reputation (the quality of his or her individual capital). In principle, therefore, there is no reason for that lawyer to rely on a firm. But if this lawyer in fact does not need the firm, then it is hard to see why he or she stays. If the lawyer is a partner, she will necessarily be bearing a part of the organisation costs which will be diluting or eroding the profit arising from her activities. If the lawyer is an assistant, he is having all of the profit arising from his activity appropriated by the firm. The answer may be that both the partner and the assistant value the reputation or infrastructure (or both) of the firm and are willing to forgo all or part of the profit that they could otherwise generate. The infrastructure of the firm is made up partly of tangible resources, partly of property rights to direct and control resources, and partly of working practices and procedures that are part of situational know-how. If the partner or assistant values the use or benefit of these rights, then again they are *sharing in or benefiting from firm-specific capital*.

Further, as the lawyer succeeds in attracting more clients, he or she will face exactly the same issue of coping with surplus client needs discussed in paragraph 8.4. In these circumstances, the lawyer can benefit from an existing monitoring framework and possibly the greater ease with which an established firm might be able to attract additional lawyers. Again, therefore, the lawyer is *benefiting from firm-specific capital*.

It is also possible, however, that diversification will arise from new clients being attracted to the firm by the strength of *collective* reputation. This will derive from the nature of the existing client base and the firm's reputation for quality. In this sense, diversification of clients is the result of *exploiting firm-specific capital*. Teamwork will be needed to identify and work on prospective clients, which will presume a decision to invest time and money both to improve total returns to the firm from its firm-specific capital and to improve the capital itself by adding to the breadth or depth (or both) of the client base.

All or part of this form of diversification may be achieved by attracting a lawyer to the firm who has an established client following — improving firm-specific capital by adding new individual capital. This requires both that the lawyer should be attracted to the firm and that his clients should also remain loyal to him. The firm's reputation will be relevant to the decisions of both the new lawyer and his clients, in other words, this method of diversification will be *influenced by the firm-specific capital*. It is possible, however, that the lawyer and the client may each be influenced by different dimensions of that capital.

There is therefore a message embedded in this analysis concerning the lateral movement of partners. Clients or client work do not inevitably follow a partner who leaves a firm, and one of the reasons is that the firm-specific capital of the firm that the partner leaves may contain dimensions that are important to the client. The departing partner necessarily leaves this behind (although his or her departure may affect its value). For the client to follow, these dimensions must exist, or be replicated, in the firm that the partner joins. Depending on personalities, reputation, client-specific or transaction-specific knowledge, culture, or working practices and procedures, this may not be the case or be possible (see paragraph 5.4).

8.5.4 *Diversification of location*

Diversification of location is usually based on the belief that the firm's reputation is such that work or clients can be attracted in an area beyond the firm's previous geographical reach. By basing the diversification on the firm's reputation, it is particularly *reliant on firm-specific capital*. The diversification may, of course, also be *effected* in much the same way as diversification of services (see paragraph 8.5.2) or diversification of clients (see paragraph 8.5.3) and, as such, is further reliant on firm-specific capital in the ways discussed in those paragraphs. In addition, the management of a geographically diverse firm leads to a need for more sophisticated managerial know-how and internal procedures (situational know-how), and so again is drawing on firm-specific capital.

8.5.5 Multiple diversification

Analytically, multiple diversification does not pose separate issues, and requires little further consideration. However, by combining types of diversification, it clearly poses additional risks, and therefore requires higher levels of human and financial capital. To the extent that all forms of diversification rely on firm-specific capital, multiple diversification will make even greater claims. It will also increase the need for a greater breadth and depth of managerial know-how. Arguably, therefore, the more extensive or combined the diversification, the more extensive and stronger the firm-specific capital will need to be.

8.5.6 Common features of diversification

Addressing surplus opportunities thus appears to be based on the ability to exploit firm-specific capital. As a result, this form of exploitation is less accessible to sole practitioners and sole principals (see paragraph 5.2.3). Addressing surplus client needs is founded more closely on individual capital (personal client relationships) with perhaps some need for firm-specific capital (in the form of monitoring capacity leading to a reputation for quality). As such, it is based principally on a surplus of individual capital which the principal is willing and able to share with others who can be effectively monitored. It can also be based on a collection of surpluses arising within an existing firm and one could argue that these surpluses are part of firm-specific capital (see paragraph 8.4).

On the other hand, addressing surplus opportunities is based principally on the existence of firm-specific capital. Individual capital is exploited by choosing to share it *with* others, and can be protected by monitoring and incentives. Firm-specific capital is exploited by sharing its constituent attributes (client relationships, work flow, reputation for quality, monitoring capacity, etc.) *among*, or allowing *access* to it by, others. The scope for the abuse of firm-specific capital by any individual or group of partners is reduced partly by the horizontal monitoring of its exploitation by other partners, and partly by the inability of any individual to transfer his share in it (it is, in fact, valueless to an individual except in the context of the firm).

In all of this, there is an issue of the firm's credibility. Clients gain knowledge of firms, the individual capital and the firm-specific capital (although they may not look at it in those terms!). The firm becomes a familiar institution and a signal of quality. This knowledge reduces the client's search and information costs in its quest for the effective handling of its legal affairs. In short, the firm reduces the client's transaction costs. For as long as the firm does not, in the client's eyes, overstretch its firm-specific (or financial) capital, the development of the firm through organic growth and diversification will be both possible and acceptable. Thus, the more a firm wants to do, the larger or more diverse it wishes to become, the larger must be its firm-specific capital and the better able the firm must be to exploit it. This is the economy of scope point — larger firms are in principle able to do some things (e.g., open other offices, enter emerging markets, invest in larger infrastructure) that smaller firms cannot (or find more difficult or risky), because their larger size allows them both to reduce and spread the risks associated with certain types of development. Similarly, one might see these developments as consequences of the diversification of unsystematic risk.

To respond to a prospective client's search costs, a firm must send out 'signals' that will satisfy the client's needs for information about the service and the supplier — in other words, the firm must engage in marketing. A firm's reputation and credibility — part of its firm-specific capital — is part of this signalling process. As a result, the existence of firm-specific capital reduces the signalling costs that any individual lawyer in that firm would otherwise have to bear to attract certain types of work or client. (It might be worth reflecting on a firm's approach to marketing in the light of this conclusion.)

8.6   A Theory of Optimum Size?

The question of whether there is an optimum size for a law firm is one that has vexed lawyers for many years. I have already looked at Galanter and Palay's assertion that there is an inbuilt growth engine leading to the exponential growth of law firms (see paragraph 3.6.2). In practice, there are constraints on growth (see paragraph 3.7), including the availability and flow of work, the supply of additional lawyers, and maintaining quality. If a firm can manage its growth, it might also be able to engineer an optimum size.

The question of size also needs to be considered in the context of clients' needs and expectations. For example, corporate law firms wishing to serve the largest clients, or to be engaged in the largest or most complex transactions or litigation, certainly appear to need to have achieved a minimum scale. This implies that they need to be able to maximise their exploitation of an already sizeable firm-specific capital. This exploitation arises from sharing by and among partners, and this in turn usually develops from the experience and trust that come from working together. While it is therefore possible, from both a theoretical and practical standpoint, to create a large firm-specific capital by joining a number of partners together in one firm in a short space of time, their ability to exploit this joint asset to its full potential may not develop so quickly. The likelihood that such a firm would then reach a credible minimum scale (not in terms of sheer size, but from the perception of the clients who form part of its firm-specific capital) is also then compromised. In this sense, imitating size without also being able to imitate a corresponding history and culture will not of itself lead to market credibility (see Barney 1991, and paragraphs 4.6.5 and 5.4). This explains why some law firms that have achieved rapid growth have not been able, despite equivalent size, to challenge and compete on equivalent terms with established firms: the quality and credibility of their respective firm-specific capital (and of the underlying individual capital) is simply different, and — in the circumstances — less attractive to the clients for whom firms of that size are possible suppliers of legal services.

Members of niche practices may be wondering at this point whether these theories are applicable to them. Part of their rationale is to achieve at least the same depth of specialisation in a certain area as larger, more diversified firms. They do not therefore take on the risks of substantial growth and diversification; they normally seek to maintain themselves at a relatively modest size. Unfortunately, niche practices suffer from one major drawback: they compound the unsystematic risk of their individual lawyers. Not only will they suffer through a general economic downturn (unless their niche is counter-cyclical (such as insolvency) — in which case they will suffer in an upturn), the whole practice is at risk if the area of practice becomes unnecessary or unfashionable. Gilson and Mnookin (1985) refer to a niche practice as a 'boutique', and say:

". . . our analysis reveals an important disadvantage to the boutique: its lack of diversification. The individual lawyer in a boutique law firm faces the ever present risk that the specialty will somehow fall out of fashion. Because of this disadvantage, we think a large, more diversified firm will have important competitive advantages. While the increased sophistication of purchasers should decrease reliance on the brand name of the large 'department store' firms, the 'cost savings' of diversification remain. . . . Absent such diversification, we predict that most boutiques will not have long-term institutional lives beyond the retirement of their founding partners. In addition, we would predict that those boutiques that do survive longer will be in areas of practice where there is a reasonably stable long-term demand — tax and labor may be good examples" (page 386).

The conclusion seems to be that there is not *an* optimum size appropriate to all law firms, but that, given a particular combination of human and financial capital in a firm, there will be an optimum size for that firm. In these circumstances, any further increase in size would lead to economic or production difficulties *unless the elements of human or financial capital could also be changed* to support further growth. Such a view does, admittedly, accept unlimited growth — in theory. However, the practical difficulties of achieving unlimited growth in the real world (the cost or availability of resources, flows of work, the challenges of teamwork, the need for managerial know-how, and limits on the span of control, coordination and communication — to name but a few) are such that it is unlikely.

Coase dealt with this issue as follows (1937, pages 393–7):

"A firm becomes larger as additional transactions (which could be exchange transactions coordinated through the price mechanism) are organised by the entrepreneur and becomes smaller as he abandons the organisation of such transactions. The question which arises is whether it is possible to study the forces which determine the size of the firm.

Why does the entrepreneur not organise one less transaction or one more?. . .

A pertinent question to ask would appear to be (quite apart from the monopoly considerations . . .), why, if by organising one can eliminate certain costs and in fact reduce the cost of production, are there any market transactions at all? Why is not all production carried on by one big firm? There would appear to be certain possible explanations.

First, as a firm gets larger, there may be decreasing returns to the entrepreneur function, that is, the costs of organising additional transactions within the firm may rise. Naturally, a point must be reached where the costs of organising an extra transaction within the firm are equal to the costs involved in carrying out the transaction in the open market, or, to the costs of organising by another entrepreneur. Secondly, it may be that as the transactions which are organised increase, the entrepreneur fails to place the factors of production in the uses where their value is greatest, that is, fails to make the best use of the factors of production. Again, a point must be reached where the loss through the waste of resources is equal to the marketing costs of the exchange transaction in the open market or to the loss if the transaction was organised by another entrepreneur. Finally, the supply price of one or more of the factors of production may rise, because the 'other advantages' of a small firm are greater than those of a large firm. [*Footnote in original*: It is sometimes said that the supply price of organising ability increases as the size of the firm increases because men [sic] prefer to be the heads of small independent businesses rather than the heads of departments in a large business. . . .] Of course, the actual point where the expansion of the firm ceases might be determined by a combination of the factors mentioned above. The first two reasons given most probably correspond to the economists' phrase of 'diminishing returns to management'. . . .

Other things being equal, therefore, a firm will tend to be larger:

(a)   the less the costs of organising and the slower these costs rise with an increase in the transactions organised.

(b)   the less likely the entrepreneur is to make mistakes and the smaller the increase in mistakes with an increase in the transactions organised.

(c)   the greater the lowering (or the less the rise) in the supply price of factors of production to firms of large size.

Apart from variations in the supply price of factors of production to firms of different sizes, it would appear that the costs of organising and the losses through mistakes will increase with an increase in the spatial distribution of the transactions organised, in the dissimilarity of the transactions, and in the probability of changes in the relevant prices. As more transactions are organised by an entrepreneur, it would appear that the transactions would tend to be either different in kind or in different places. This furnishes an additional reason why efficiency will tend to decrease as the firm gets larger."

Thus, diversification of services, clients or location is likely to reduce efficiency. Unless a growing firm can properly manage the resources and their costs, the potential for waste, and spatial distribution (geography), its success will be jeopardised. In short, growth and diversity put a premium on teamwork and managerial know-how: law firms are not especially noted for either, but they are perhaps more likely to be found in a firm that values and invests in its firm-specific capital.

8.7   Size and Structure

For most businesses, size will also determine structure. There will be a progression from sole proprietor to partnership and then (beyond 20 partners) to incorporation. We have already seen that the monitoring ability of entrepreneurs is required to protect against the risks of opportunism and moral hazard, that that ability in any one person will be limited, that new risks (of monitoring the monitors) arise as the number of partners increases, and that because fully effective partnerships must be built on trust and susceptibility to peer pressure there may be a natural limit on their size (see paragraph 8.4.3).

Accordingly, for businesses to grow beyond this size, an alternative structure is required. The normal rationale for a company is to decrease the risks that entrepreneurs need to bear by separating the necessary connection between the ownership and management of the property rights of the firm. With this separation comes the possibility of transferable ownership (shares — a new form of property right — carrying the right to claim the profit) and liability limited to the investment in ownership. For public companies, of course, there is also a market in their shares, making ownership freely transferable. It does not follow from the separation of ownership and management that owners cannot become managers (or vice versa).

Within the legal profession, the development of ever larger law firms is undoubtedly leading to increasing 'bureaucratisation' and 'stratification' in these firms. Nelson writes (1988, page 4):

> "The turmoil generated by the changes taking place in the large law
> firm suggests that this organization is trapped in a conflict between
> bureaucracy and professionalism. . . . The structural changes that mark
> the bureaucratization of firms — specialization, departmentalization,
> and increasing stratification in the earnings and authority of partners —
> run counter to traditional conceptions of the professional partnership
> in which all partners are in some sense peers. . . . These conflicting
> tendencies produce a collegial hierarchy in which processes of organiza-
> tional rationalization are modified or cloaked in traditional professional
> terms and in which the dynamics of hierarchical relationships between
> lawyers are denied or left unstated."

Given an environment of decreasing homogeneity, trust and institutional loyalty (see paragraph 1.4), it will not be surprising to see the conflict created by this 'false' behaviour leading to the breakdown of the traditional partnership structure.

Thus, the conditions which, in general business, would give rise to incorporation probably exist in the legal profession, too. Despite the possibility of incorporation of a law firm (see the Solicitors' Incorporated Practice Rules 1988), the principal benefits of incorporation from an economists' point of view are still denied. All the shareholders and directors must be lawyers (rules 3 and 4), and although liability may be limited additional indemnity insurance must be maintained (rule 13). Transferability of ownership is thus constrained within the profession (significantly limiting the value of transferability, since transfer outside existing shareholders would necessarily be to actual or potential competitors). It would be possible to transfer shares to a lawyer outside the firm (unless prohibited by the articles of association), effectively foisting a potentially unwanted owner on the other shareholders; however, in large professional partnerships, it is equally possible that a new partner can be foisted on others who in practice are unable to object. The directors of an incorporated practice must also be lawyers, thus depriving an incorporated legal practice of the division of labour that would allow experienced people with substantial managerial know-how to run the business.

This denial of some of the normal benefits of incorporation is not surprising, given a professional culture that values the independence and autonomy of lawyers. And I am certainly not suggesting that the mere fact of incorporation will magically transform the attitudes, behaviour or expectations of practitioners. But the partnership structure as we know it may simply not be able to sustain itself economically or socially beyond a certain size. The fact of incorporation may bring home the need for some of those changes in attitudes, behaviour or expectations that are required if legal practice as we know it (let alone any given law firm) is to survive. So, despite my instinctive feeling that partnership is the best form and structure of organisation for a law firm, I think I now have to accept the economic and social reality that *large* practices of the future will be incorporated. I cannot then see any remaining justification for anything short of fully limited liability. That said, I also suspect that the largest, highest-quality firms may not *need* to incorporate because their branded reputation, their (sometimes) more collegiate behaviour, and their (usually) more developed sense of management maturity reduces most of the tensions that would otherwise lead to incorporation.

As the Law Society's *Annual Statistical Report 1996* shows, there are only 160 incorporated practices in England and Wales (Lewis 1996, paragraph 3.5) — fewer than 2% of all practices. Although a number of large firms have formed incorporated service companies, there is no evidence that they are incorporating their fee-earning activities.

8.8 The Role of Financial Capital

My exposition so far has concentrated almost exclusively on human capital. However, a business could not survive on this form of capital alone, even though historically law firms have required little financial capital (see paragraph 29.1). Except in the limited circumstances in which law firms can grow to exhaust economies of scale (see paragraph 8.3), any growth is now more than likely to require further financing. The amount needed will obviously depend on the firm's strategy or business idea (cf. paragraph 4.8.3). The ability to raise this finance may also present constraints on the achievement of growth. The capital investment will either have to come from partners or third parties (see paragraph 29.7). Given that law firms face monitoring requirements (see paragraph 8.4.2), the contribution of capital can act as part of the monitoring solution: if partners have to risk individual financial capital as well as individual human capital, their behaviour may well be less individually opportunistic (cf. Galanter and Palay 1991, page 120). This commingling of financial assets should perhaps therefore be encouraged rather than discouraged.

Raising money from banks may be a lot easier if the firm has a strong reputation, that is, valuable firm-specific capital. This will also be true if incorporation ever leads to the reality of external investment (i.e., the true separation in law firms of investment through shareholding and participation through management). Nevertheless, given the nature of the productive asset in law firms (human capital), its ownership, its inherent fragility, its mobility, and the risks of opportunism and moral hazard to which it is subject, I still wonder (even if I can live with incorporation) whether an investor who is not a lawyer, and who does not actively participate in the management of the firm, would accept the unsystematic risk of this investment (see, further, paragraph 38.5.2). True, portfolio theory would suggest that the investor could cancel out this risk in a diversified portfolio; but does the initial choice to invest in a law firm even satisfy the premises of preferring 'more return to less given the same level of risk' and 'less risk to more given the same level of return' (see paragraph 8.1.1)?

8.9 Returns, Rewards and Residuals

The final piece of the theoretical jigsaw is splitting the profits derived from the exploitation of the human and financial capital in law firms. In the course of the preceding exposition, three distinct roles can be seen to emerge: those who take risks and bear the uncertainty of the business (entrepreneurs); those who work in the firm (workers); and those who provide finance (financiers). The position in law firms is often complicated because partners might perform one, two, or all three, of these roles. But because the roles *are* different, we might expect to find that the reward for each role would be different, too.

For the purposes of this paragraph, 'residual gains' (or simply 'residual') refers to net profit after all other financial obligations in running the firm have been met. I shall examine the claims of financiers, workers, and entrepreneurs to share in this residual. For the moment, try not to presuppose that only equity partners are entitled to share in the residual.

8.9.1   *Returns to financiers*

Economic analysis suggests that a contractually defined sum is not part of the residual (see paragraph 7.1). The normally accepted return for the use of capital is a contractually defined rate of interest. Thus, bankers do not — and cannot expect to — share in the residual of a law firm. Of course, the rate of interest may depend on the perceived degree of risk to the money lent or invested. If bankers are not entitled to share in residual because their return is an agreed rate of interest, money lent or contributed by *all* others (including partners) ought to be analysed in the same light. Thus, if a firm's partners contribute capital and net profit is calculated on the basis that interest is not payable to them, the 'residual' is to that extent distorted. In measuring the true residual, therefore, a market rate of interest on all capital and borrowings should be deducted (whether actually paid or not). For partners, this may be considered the 'cost of equity' (the opportunity cost of capital that is also explored in paragraph 5.5.3.2). The exchange transactions here are, first, the supply of money by banks and others outside the firm in return for interest (a market exchange carrying a market rate of interest), and, second — at least analytically — the supply of money by partners in return for an agreed rate of interest (an internalised exchange that should attract a rate of interest comparable to a market rate for an equivalent use of that money).

8.9.2   *Rewards to workers*

The people who supply their time and effort to a business are rewarded for their labour. This reward may well be based on their marketability, which in turn will be dependent on the productivity of their individual capital. In this sense, therefore, all lawyers (including partners) who work in the firm should be treated in the same way as other employees. They should receive a market wage in return for their supply of human capital. The exchange transaction here is a market wage for the supply of individual know-how. As with interest, there may be an apparently disproportionately high return because of the scarcity or value of that know-how in the marketplace. The point, however, is that this reward has no intrinsic or necessary connection with being a *partner*. Someone appointed as a partner may well have more (or more valuable) know-how than someone who is not, and therefore attract a higher market rate (wage). But it is entirely possible for an assistant in one firm to be worth more in the marketplace for legal services than a partner in another firm (or even, for that matter, in the same firm).

The rewards issue is complicated because any given lawyer may choose to take part of his or her rewards in a non-monetary form. Benefits in kind (pensions, cars, insurance, etc.) fall into this category. But the rewards may be more subtle than this. A commitment to public service (pro bono work, for example), or postponing earning potential at assistant level in the belief that a balance will be restored on promotion to partnership (economists call this 'deferred compensation': see, for example, Ricketts 1994, page 150), are also examples. This level of sophistication may be unnecessary for most practical purposes, but I shall return to its significance in paragraph 8.9.4.

8.9.3 *Residual gains to entrepreneurs*

When suppliers, financiers and workers have been paid, there may or may not be any money left over (the residual). This is part of the risk that entrepreneurs take. The residual is therefore the entrepreneur's return for bearing the risk and uncertainty. On this basis, the proper calculation of the residual is important to quantify the precise return for the risk taken. It is also necessary to ensure that only true entrepreneurs receive a share of the residual because only true entrepreneurs are taking any risk (see paragraph 7.2).

In some businesses, the financiers may feel that the degree of risk they are assuming is such that any rate of interest is not adequate compensation. They might alternatively feel that the extent of their financing increases their risk, too. In these circumstances, they are assuming a risk above and beyond that of a normal financier who can be rewarded by interest, and they will also take a share of the profits. This additional risk makes them entrepreneurs (we usually call them venture capitalists) and justifies the participation in the residual. External venture capital investment is not (yet) likely in law firms, although there may be many partners who feel that this description otherwise adequately defines their position!

8.9.4 *Sharing the spoils*

It would follow from the foregoing analysis that the 'profits' of a law firm should be split (at least analytically) as follows:

(a)   A contractual or otherwise pre-agreed market rate of interest should be paid to all internal financiers.

(b)   A contractual or otherwise agreed market 'wage' should be paid to all lawyers (including partners), as well as taking account of the value of other non-monetary benefits, as they are in the case of other employees. This is one reason why many calculations and comparisons of law firm profitability take account of notional salaries for equity partners; but unless these are fixed at the appropriate (and full) market rate for each individual and include benefits, for my purposes they will distort the calculation of the residual.

(c)   Any balance then represents the true 'residual' (i.e., return to business risk) that should be shared among the entrepreneurs: for this purpose, entrepreneurs would be defined as in paragraph 7.2, and therefore would not necessarily include all equity partners.

If interest and wages (a) and (b) are the market returns to individual financial and human capital, the residual (c) represents the return for risking individual and firm-specific capital — the returns to the risk of sharing that capital with others in its competitive exploitation. In theory, one should distinguish between the returns to individual and firm-specific capital in allocating the residual among the entrepreneurs. How this might be done will be explored in the context of profit-sharing arrangements (see paragraph 37.6).

On the basis of this analysis, partners who are only entitled to a return under (b) should not be equity partners at all. If the status of partner is conferred on them, they appear to be, literally, a salaried partner. It further seems to me that if partners are also entitled to a return under (a), that combination alone should not automatically make them equity partners: the agreed interest should be an adequate return for their investment. Of course, at the moment (unless he or she is the holder of a share in an incorporated legal practice), such a person would be a partner — on the basis that non-partners do not contribute financial capital. Although the point remains analytically valid, the emotional point is perhaps more problematic: why should a lawyer who invests capital in a law firm partnership forgo any right to be involved in the direction and control of that firm? In fact, it may well be the case as a practical matter in an incorporated legal practice that there is no such involvement; it is also effectively the case in many large law firm partnerships, too, where equity partners who have contributed capital are often in practice excluded from participating in management.

This reasoning changes where the degree of investment of capital effectively makes the investor a venture capitalist (even though the person might not otherwise be an entrepreneur on my paragraph 7.2 definition). In this case, and where a lawyer is an entrepreneur on that definition, there is a justifiable claim to share in the residual, that is, to be an equity partner.

There is one final twist. On my definition of an entrepreneur in the legal environment, there is no requirement that the person identifying and exploiting the opportunities mentioned should be a partner at all — indeed, for some of them, there is no reason why that person should even be a lawyer. An entrepreneur who is not a partner, or a lawyer, has (analytically) a legitimate claim to share in the residual. This — for support staff, at least — cannot be done by making the entrepreneur a partner (or even a shareholder in an incorporated legal practice). It would have to be done by adding a 'bonus' to the person's wage for labour, thus reducing the residual available to the entrepreneurs who are partners. This inability of the legal structure of law firms (whether unincorporated or incorporated) to recognise true entrepreneurs may well limit their potential — their ability fully to exploit their firm-specific capital.

If such an analysis of the residual is carried out, better and more reliable comparisons can be made. The year-on-year return to risk accruing to the same firm can be accurately compared; the true residuals earned by different firms could also be more accurately compared because variations due to differences in financing policies, wages and benefits, and partnership promotion and retirement policies are extracted. If a lawyer knows that he or she, in any firm, will receive a market return for whatever capital is contributed, and for the individual capital used in supplying his or her labour, a realistic assessment can then be made of the return to the risk of being an entrepreneur in any particular firm. The analysis might also show that those who happen to be called equity partners in a firm are unreasonably appropriating (i.e., 'grabbing') residual that should properly be distributed to others who are more entrepreneurial than they are!

Chapter 9

A CLASSIFICATION OF LAW OFFICES

Having developed various facets to a theory of the law firm in chapter 8, it is now necessary to see what conclusions can be drawn. The theoretical conclusions are drawn in this chapter; the practical consequences are explored in parts III to VII. I shall attempt to do this by applying the theory to different classifications of law firms: the sole practitioner, the sole principal, a partnership of 'individual practitioners', a partnership of 'integrated entrepreneurs', a mixed partnership (comprising both 'intergrationist' partners and others), and an incorporated law firm. In each case, I shall try to set out the principal asset which is being traded (individual or firm-specific capital, or both), the circumstances in which they can exploit surplus client needs or surplus client opportunities, the role of internalisation of fee-earning and support services in the development of the firm, the relative importance of individual and firm-specific capital to the firm, and the distribution of the profit. I conclude this chapter with some thoughts about in-house legal departments, and some comments about 'property rights'.

The extent to which a firm grows into any of the categories I describe will depend on a variety of factors, including inclination, resources and client's expectations. Any strategic conclusions that are drawn in this chapter are, in a sense, incidental: I am not seeking to describe what law firms might (or should) do, but to classify the *results* of what they do and how they behave.

The concepts and terminology used in this chapter are those developed in chapters 5 to 8.

9.1 The Sole Practitioner

By definition, the sole practitioner practises without combining with any other lawyers in a firm, and can therefore only trade on her own individual capital. As such, a sole practitioner bears both systematic and unsystematic risk (see paragraph 8.1): there is no portfolio of services to diversify the unsystematic risk — except to the limited extent that a sole practitioner might attempt diversification by being a general practitioner.

Surplus client needs — assuming no spare capacity or lack of relevant expertise — can only be addressed either through the market (counsel, agent, locum, etc.) with the associated transaction costs of search, negotiation and enforcement, or by affiliation. If the needs are such that these costs are greater than those of organising fee-earners in a firm, the sole practitioner may well evolve into a sole principal (see paragraph 9.2) or a partnership (see paragraphs 9.3 to 9.5).

A sole practitioner may prefer to share office and space costs with others (or buy them in the market, for example, from a business centre), and therefore have nothing that could be described as a 'firm'. Perhaps more likely, the sole practitioner will internalise core support services and staff (secretarial, switchboard, reception, general office, etc.) into a firm. The particular needs of clients and the sole practitioner's preferred ways of working provide a sufficient degree of asset specificity: provided there is also a sufficient volume of work to satisfy the frequency of use criterion, and an adequate cost-benefit reward, internalising these support functions into a firm is a justifiable development.

Addressing surplus opportunities through diversification is unlikely for a sole practitioner. New services would require additional investment in her individual capital, which would require compromising existing work flow or income in order to develop the new expertise (acquiring the expertise by recruitment would again turn the sole practitioner into a sole principal or a partnership). An additional (as opposed to a replacement) office location would seem unnecessary for a sole practitioner. Diversification of clients is possible, and would involve the exploitation of the individual's client base: again, in the absence of spare capacity, this form of diversification is structurally no different from addressing surplus client needs.

Accordingly, there are very limited responses that a sole practitioner can make to both surplus client needs and surplus opportunities.

Although with a sole practitioner it is very difficult to distinguish between individual capital and firm-specific capital (because the sole practitioner *is* the firm), it may be possible. For example, a lawyer running an efficiency practice (using the service life-cycle classification: see paragraph 2.3.3) will be relying heavily on the procedural support and working practices of the support staff. To this extent, her reputation is as dependent on the productivity, reliability and quality of the support staff as it is on her personal reputation and productivity — in other words, it is at least partly dependent on the firm-specific capital created by the collaboration of the lawyer and the support staff. (Whether the support staff are allowed to share in the residual gains (profits) of this collaborative exploitation of firm-specific capital is a different question!) Even here, though, the flow of client work is likely to be more dependent on the personal reputation of the lawyer to attract and process the work than on the reputation of the support staff. For most practical purposes, therefore, the firm-specific capital of a sole practitioner is almost entirely incidental to the practice.

In this type of practice, there will probably be a complete coincidence (if not confusion) of the entrepreneurial, working and financing roles of the sole practitioner. Apart from the possibility raised above of there being some incidental firm-specific capital, the 'profit' will in practice all be attributable to the lawyer's individual capital; there is, perhaps, little incentive to separate the different elements. However, if the sole practitioner wanted truly to compare her position with practice in another law firm (perhaps in order to consider whether to expand, merge or move laterally), this analysis should be done. There seems little doubt that a sole practitioner is an entrepreneur (in at least activities (a)(iii) and (vi) in paragraph 7.2), and should receive some return to risk. Given the dominance of individual capital, though, it is highly likely that the profit will correlate quite closely with the market 'wage' that the sole practitioner could otherwise command. The true residual returned to the entrepreneurial function may therefore be quite low. Indeed, as a sole practitioner, there is a risk that the profit will not be high enough to return even a market wage let alone a residual over above that and the interest on capital. This *is* the entrepreneurial risk that a sole practitioner takes, and demonstrates the reality of unsystematic risk and why some lawyers prefer employment and a wage: they are happy for the risks of legal practice to be borne by others. If this is their attitude, it is important that they do not become partners sharing in returns to risk since they are not, by definition, risk-takers.

9.2 The Sole Principal

A sole principal will also be trading principally on individual capital. However, the existence of at least one other fee-earner (although not a partner) in the firm gives rise to some sharing of individual capital, and so raises the greater likelihood of more firm-specific capital than for a sole practitioner.

The existence of one or more other, employed, fee-earners in the firm assumes that previous surpluses of client needs have given rise to frequency of use and asset specificity in the principal's surplus capital sufficient to justify employing them within the firm. We therefore presuppose that there is some surplus, shareable individual capital that the principal chooses to share in a *vertical* relationship with another fee-earner. Any surplus client needs that arise beyond the capacity of the principal and existing fee-earners in the firm can either be met through the market, or through the appointment of one or more additional fee-earners in the firm. (Lateral recruitment would create horizontal sharing between partners, and so result in a partnership: for which see paragraphs 9.3 to 9.5.) The ability of the sole principal to appoint additional employed fee-earners will be limited by her capacity to monitor their performance (and their willingness to be and remain in a vertical relationship): see paragraph 8.4.3.

As well as internalising additional legal expertise, it is also more likely than not that the sole principal will have internalised core support functions. Indeed, an increase in the number of fee-earners to be serviced is almost certain to lead to the necessary frequency of use of many support services.

Surplus opportunities give rise to much the same issues for a sole principal as they do for a sole practitioner (see paragraph 9.1), in that the firm is still principally exploiting the individual capital of the principal. Diversification of clients may be easier, however, if the employed fee-earners have some capacity to absorb the additional work (that is, if the principal can develop a *shareable* surplus). Diversification of services would also be possible if the principal could develop new areas of practice after sharing existing work with the employed fee-earners, or if an employed fee-earner has the spare capacity and ability to develop a new area while the principal and any other employed fee-earners maintain the existing services. The principal might also consider recruiting an additional fee-earner to provide capacity or expertise for this diversification but, as with surplus client needs, only to the limit of the principal's capacity to monitor the performance of *all* fee-earners and support staff. Diversification of location and multiple diversification will usually appear to be too risky (and perhaps even unnecessary) for a sole principal, and will certainly stretch her monitoring capacity to the limits.

Although a sole principal's practice is primarily dependent on the principal's individual capital, the contributions of other fee-earners over time will create firm-specific capital. This will particularly be the case if diversification of services or clients is achieved through the direct involvement of employed fee-earners or support staff. In this event, the sole principal is probably beginning the move towards admitting partners. However, initially at least, the diversification of the practice will be founded on the principal's individual capital; and even where additional fee-earners are recruited to help with the diversification (or to make it possible), it is most likely that it will be the principal's reputation (individual capital) that attracts them rather than the firm's reputation (firm-specific capital). As with a sole practitioner, therefore, the firm-specific capital will be incidental to the practice, unless it is used for the development of the firm into a partnership. In terms of portfolio theory (see paragraph 8.1.1), then, there might be some diversification of unsystematic risk, but not full diversification (the principal probably could not afford to be away from the practice for too long).

In fact, it is likely that, where the employed fee-earners are qualified lawyers (rather than legal executives or paralegals), the sole principal will face pressure over time to meet their expectations to be admitted into partnership — the pressure of the 'promotion-to-partnership tournament' discussed in paragraph 3.6. Such a move would clearly change the practice and its internal dynamics (see paragraphs 9.3 to 9.5).

In this type of practice, too, there will probably be a complete coincidence of the entrepreneurial, working and financing roles of the sole principal. Apart from the possibility raised above of there being some incidental firm-specific capital, the 'profit' will all be attributable to the principal's individual capital, and so perhaps there will be little incentive to separate the different elements. Nevertheless, there are now other fee-earners in the practice receiving a wage for their services as fee-earners, and in this respect, the principal is no different. Indeed, as with the sole practitioner, if the sole principal wanted truly to compare her position with practice in another law firm (perhaps in order to consider whether to expand, admit one of the employed lawyers into partnership, merge or move laterally), this analysis should be done. Although there may be less absolute dependence on a sole principal's individual capital than there is on a sole practitioner's, the residual returns to risk *should* be greater simply because the sole principal takes greater risks than the sole practitioner by choosing to share her individual capital and its surpluses with other fee-earners, and has to invest in a larger support infrastructure so that this sharing can be better exploited. There is again no doubt that the sole principal is taking entrepreneurial risks and there should, accordingly, be *some* return to the firm-specific capital if the human capital assets are properly exploited. In practice, however, it may be very difficult to distinguish between the part of the gain attributable to the principal's individual capital and the part attributable to the firm-specific capital.

9.3 A Partnership of 'Individual Practitioners'

This description of a partnership is intended to refer to a firm which legally exists as a partnership, but where the partners continue to practise law as individuals, serving exclusively their own clients and not sharing any surpluses (of client need or opportunity) with their fellow partners. In this sense, they are each trading on their individual capital. Assuming, for the moment, that there are only partners as fee-earners in the firm, a partnership of individual practitioners is in reality nothing more than an office-sharing arrangement — a form of 'solicitors' chambers'. The benefit would seem to be the sharing within an organisation (firm) of the transaction costs (relating to premises, support staff, office services, etc.) that would otherwise be borne by each practitioner. However, although there has been an internalisation of these office costs, there is a significant difference between this type of partnership and other forms of organisation. A typical office-sharing arrangement among sole practitioners does not involve profit-sharing (Gilson and Mnookin (1985): see extract at paragraph 8.3 above); and, for barristers' chambers, professional rules prevent the formation of partnerships. It seems improbable, therefore, that a partnership of individual practitioners would share its profits other than in the proportion in which individuals have generated fees for the 'firm'.

A partnership of individual practitioners is predicated on no sharing of surpluses with other partners. At first sight, therefore, any individual practitioner's surplus client needs would be addressed through the market. However, it would be wrong to suggest that there might *never* be any internal sharing between partners. The structure of the partnership arrangement may well enable the 'purchase' of time or know-how from other partners, effectively using an internal market transaction under which fees are shared according to the input provided (meaning that it is, at heart, a fee-sharing relationship rather than a profit-sharing one). It is, however, possible to envisage circumstances where, at any given time, this collection of individual practitioners has a need for a certain type of help to deal with their collective surpluses (frequency of use). Depending on the nature of their respective practices, the need may be for general fee-earning support or for specialist expertise. Accordingly, just as they share premises and office services, it might make sense for them to internalise this fee-earning support by bringing in one or more additional fee-earners whose time — and wages — they also share. As with the sole principal (see paragraph 9.2), this will be a vertical sharing of surplus individual capital. And since it is her individual capital that each partner will want to protect from opportunism and moral hazard, she will monitor that aspect of an additional fee-earner's activity that relates to her capital (i.e., client work), but not that which relates to another partner's individual capital. Because of this, the firm's growth through the addition of employed fee-earners is not likely to be substantial.

I have assumed that this type of practice will have internalised its office and support functions in a firm. They may be exactly the same functions as those for barristers' chambers, but barristers may not organise into a firm: nor do these functions operate in the market. On my analysis, therefore, chambers would constitute a network — see paragraph 6.1. Given the nature of this type of partnership, there may be some difficulty in the monitoring of support staff: the partners will not derive the full benefit of internalising support services if staff are able to 'shirk' (the risks of opportunism seem much less with support staff, but moral hazard remains). The opportunity cost of monitoring versus fee-earning may be such, however, that the partners are willing to take the risk of moral hazard, but on the basis that the activities of support staff that relate specifically to the client base and work (individual capital) of each partner will be closely monitored by that partner. Nevertheless, the absence of monitoring, supervision and guidance for support staff, and the apparent indifference of the partners to their needs and development, may well lead to relatively high turnover of support staff (cf. paragraph 22.3): this, in turn, will stultify the development of any firm-specific capital based on situational know-how — particularly in relation to the client-specific and partner-specific knowledge that a stable support staff gain, as well as common and efficient office working practices (see paragraph 5.2.2).

The recruitment of employed fee-earners may also give rise to some internal difficulties. Whereas the partners will probably make relatively equal use of office and support facilities (at least to the extent that the 'transaction costs' of negotiating internally any alternative cost-sharing arrangements would not be worth bearing), the use of employed fee-earners is much less likely to be equal. Unless the partnership is of a size where the average of large numbers begins to approximate to a point where again the transaction costs of negotiating any other basis of cost-sharing become marginal, one of two consequences is likely to follow. First, partners may well negotiate differential cost-sharing. Second, any partner whose practice cannot sustain (or does not need to sustain) the additional organisational costs of the employed fee-earners will leave the partnership. This latter situation is simply indicative that the cost-benefit to her of the organisation costs of the firm is less than the cost-benefit of the transaction or organisation costs of an alternative arrangement (the market, another firm or sole practice, or a network).

Responses to surplus opportunities could also be limited. Since each partner is essentially a sole practitioner, opportunities are most likely to accrue to individual capital and suggest an individual response (see paragraph 9.1). Diversification of clients is possible, and would involve the exploitation of the individual's client base: again, in the absence of spare capacity, this form of diversification is structurally no different from addressing surplus client needs.

New services would need additional investment in individual capital, which would require compromising existing work flow or income in order to develop the new expertise. It is conceivable that all or a significant number of the partners might together identify the same opportunity to diversify into new services from their individual client bases. In these circumstances, they might consider recruiting an additional fee-earner. They could do so horizontally by bringing in another specialist practitioner as a partner: in the absence of surplus costs or scale economies (cf. paragraph 8.3), this might require an increased office infrastructure. Or they could do so vertically by recruiting an appropriately experienced employed fee-earner: this gives rise to the same issues as recruiting an employed fee-earner to meet surplus client needs. In the case of both horizontal and vertical recruitment, the aggregate effect of the individual reputations of the partners may attract the recruit and offer some credibility to introducing the new service. In this sense, it may be that even a partnership of individual practitioners begins to develop some firm-specific capital.

Diversification of location in itself would not appear to offer any advantages to this type of partnership. However, if other offices are acquired to respond to the inadequacy of existing space as the partnership expands, and an individual partner can practise 'peripatetically', there may be some advantage. This assumes, of course, that within each office there would be adequate space for visiting partners to conduct their practice, and this may impose higher organisation costs than some partners are prepared to bear (leading again to the likelihood of differential cost-sharing or departures). It is also possible that, if an additional partner or fee-earner is brought into the firm to provide or develop a new service, that person might be better located in a new office: again, however, the financing costs of such a move might make it a non-starter with a group of individual practitioners, or lead to differential cost-sharing or departures.

This discussion has identified the dependence on individual capital that is inherent with any practice built by sole practitioners. However, it has also identified that there might be circumstances for the development of firm-specific capital. This will result from the aggregate reputations of the individuals (though this would seem to be fortuitous), or possibly from the contribution that the support functions make to the reputation for quality. As identified earlier, the attitude of the partners to the support function perhaps makes this development problematic. As with the sole practitioner (see paragraph 9.1 above), therefore, firm-specific capital is almost entirely incidental to the individual capital of the partners. It is certainly the result of reactive rather than deliberate development, and so will remain relatively unexploited. Each partner continues to bear the unsystematic risk of her practice: this type of firm does not in fact seem to represent a serious attempt to diversify that risk.

Given the individualistic nature of these partnerships, the vast majority of profits will be attributable to the individual capital of the partners. Once expenses and returns to financial capital (interest) have been paid, individual profit-shares are likely to be computed either on the basis of making these apportioned deductions from individual fee income generated (with adjustments for fee-sharing transactions), or by sharing the residual profit according to the proportion of total fee income generated by each partner. As individual practitioners, the partners are entrepreneurs, but what they are risking is mainly their individual capital so most of the return will be to individual capital (and then mainly as a 'wage'). Any residual over and above expenses, financing costs and wages will therefore principally be a return to the risk to individual capital; but, to the extent that there is any firm-specific capital, it may also be regarded as in part a return to that capital, too.

9.4 A Partnership of 'Integrated Entrepreneurs'

Businesses do not have to grow — or even survive. Bhide writes: "lifestyle entrepreneurs, who are interested only in generating enough of a cash flow to maintain a certain way of life, do not need to build businesses that could survive without them" (1996, page 122). These are my individual practitioners — entrepreneurs, but not business-builders. Bhide continues: "But sustainability — or the perception thereof — matters greatly to entrepreneurs who hope to sell their businesses eventually. Sustainability is even more important for entrepreneurs who want to build an institution that is capable of renewing itself through changing generations of technology, employees, and customers" (1996, page 122).

A partnership of individual practitioners is a partnership of entrepreneurs — but of individual entrepreneurs who seek no gains from sharing their individual capital or from the development and exploitation of firm-specific capital. Taking the classification of entrepreneurial activities in paragraph 7.2, a partnership of integrated entrepreneurs would seek to exploit not just their own individual capital but also the opportunities for those activities presented by the full and joint exploitation of the combined individual and firm-specific capital — in other words, building a sustainable business. Indeed, success for this type of partnership is perhaps particularly founded on this exploitation of firm-specific capital. In fact, much of the writing on partnership seems to encourage the development of all partnerships to a structure, attitude and behaviour that will result in this full exploitation of joint opportunity and endeavour (see, for example, Maister 1993a, chapters 27, 28 ('farmers') and 30, Hildebrandt and Kaufman 1988, chapter 4, and Gilson and Mnookin 1985). Thus, Hildebrandt and Kaufman write about the development of the law firm as an 'institution', and say (at page 102, note 1):

"An institutional firm does not necessarily mean a firm that services banking, corporate, or other institutional clients. Rather, it is directed at the basic underlying relationship that exists between partners and sets the tone for the structure of the firm. A firm having partners with an institutional mentality is one in which all recognize that the entity is more important than the individual and in which certain reasonable agreements exist that stress the continuity of the entity over the interest of any one member. Accountants have developed more stable, larger and, in many cases, more profitable organizations because they have learned the value of such an organization. Lawyers, on the other hand, are trained from law school on as single practitioners and generally have little understanding of the value of a well-organized firm. Furthermore, they tend to look at clients as personal property and foster this type of relationship rather than educating the client in the benefits of firm practice."

There is no doubt in my mind that there are many gains (financial and otherwise) to be derived from the full exploitation of firm-specific capital. There is also no doubt that that exploitation (and its consequent gains) is only possible through sharing, collaboration and teamwork. But the development and exploitation of firm-specific capital involves far greater sharing — integration — of individual capital than other forms of legal practice, and therefore carries different risks as well as opportunities. From a certain standpoint, it may seem the obvious way to reap the most gains from practising law. But it is not true that partners in these collegial, integrated partnerships are the happiest, the most professionally satisfied, or the most highly rewarded (taking both 'wages' and 'residual' into account). And it is not the case that all lawyers want to be entrepreneurs.

For me, then, rather than trying to coax all partnerships into this integrated entrepreneurial paradigm, the task is to help lawyers recognise sharing and common values where they exist and to understand the costs, benefits and consequences of different forms of legal practice so that they make an informed decision about which is best for them given their expertise, inclination and resources, and their clients' expectations (cf. Maister 1997, chapter 13). If I were still in private practice, I would probably want to be part of a firm that shared, collaborated, and used teamwork to integrate and exploit its collective expertise, and being an entrepreneurial partner would be my choice. I cannot say that there is no other acceptable structure or method, for to do so would be to seek to impose my preferences and philosophy on others. But if partners do not recognise or understand the sort of structure and behaviour that is appropriate to the environment they wish to work in, it is likely that there will be a mismatch of expectations, values or attitudes, leading to the sort of 'mixed partnership' that is discussed in paragraph 9.5. To adopt a lawyer's formulation, the structure which it is best to adopt depends on all the circumstances of the case.

Partnerships of integrated entrepreneurs therefore trade on both individual and firm-specific capital. To address surplus client needs arising from the client base of any one partner, they can of course still use the market, but are more likely to share that surplus either horizontally with other partners who have the appropriate expertise and capacity, or vertically with employed fee-earners who have the appropriate expertise and capacity. There is still the risk from bounded rationality of opportunism and moral hazard associated with the sharing of individual capital, but a firm that encourages and is used to such sharing will tend to have a culture that minimises those risks and an effective protection and incentive structure (discussed in paragraph 8.4.2) — and this culture will, itself, be part of the firm-specific capital.

The larger the practice, the greater the likelihood of surpluses and the greater the opportunity to share. This is likely to lead to the satisfaction of the asset specificity and frequency of use criteria for the development of a firm (see paragraph 6.3), and so provide circumstances in which the firm can grow by adding employed fee-earners. This in turn will be based on some sort of 'promotion-to-partner tournament' and could lead to the possibility of exponential growth (Galanter and Palay 1991: see paragraph 3.6.2) unless this exploitation of firm-specific capital is properly managed within the constraints of organic development (see paragraph 3.7). As with other types of practice, therefore, the partnership of integrated entrepreneurs will benefit from sharing surplus, shareable human capital. Unlike other types of practice, however, the sharing is consistently both vertical and horizontal, and the firm-specific capital (the contribution of shared values, or culture) provides more effective, shared monitoring of performance.

As well as internalising employed lawyers, these partnerships internalise more support functions, too. Their culture of sharing and developing firm-specific capital places greater emphasis than in other practices on maintaining effective procedures and quality: as such, it may invest in this capital in the form of more extensive infrastructure (e.g., know-how systems), as well as internalise some of the 'supplier' functions (e.g., personnel, training). These higher infrastructure costs (i.e., organisation costs) are justified by greater residual returns to firm-specific capital: the cost-benefit of the organisation costs (internalisation) is greater than the cost-benefit of transactions costs (the market). It is important to recognise, however, that these tendencies to internalise are presently inconsistent with the moves to outsourcing that one sees in the general business world.

It is in addressing surplus opportunities that partnerships of integrated entrepreneurs should come into their own. The diversification of services requires the use of client-specific information (which is both individual and firm-specific capital) and investment either in developing fee-earners in the new service or in recruiting new fee-earners to 'buy in' the expertise to provide the new service. In both cases, firm-specific capital is being used to support or attract the required talent (see paragraph 8.5.2). Equally, the successful diversification of clients, and of location, will also derive from exploiting firm-specific capital (see paragraphs 8.5.3 and 8.5.4). In short, an integrated entrepreneurial partnership which succeeds in sharing and exploiting its firm-specific capital will be better placed than any other practice to reap the rewards of diversification. For this reason, it may also be better placed to achieve quicker, more cohesive growth and so achieve multiple diversification (see paragraphs 8.5.5 and 8.5.6), and any benefits accruing to minimum scale will be more readily in reach and sustainable (see paragraph 8.6).

For a partnership of integrated entrepreneurs, the existence of firm-specific capital is not merely incidental or even coincidental — it is crucial. Such a firm will invest in developing its collective capital, it will encourage the further development of individual capital in the belief that this will lead to further increases in firm-specific capital, and it will work hard to exploit both individual and firm-specific capital to the full. Here, more than in other types of practice, the scope for employed fee-earners and support staff to contribute directly to the development of firm-specific capital is greatest. Here, more than elsewhere, they can make a contribution to adding value to the firm. This type of firm exists to reap the most benefits from the diversification of the unsystematic risks attaching to each lawyer's practice: its whole ethos is about sharing rather than individual performance.

Compared to the previous types of firm discussed, the partnership of integrated entrepreneurs also raises some clearer distinctions in the distribution of profit. If the opportunities for growth and diversification are greater for this type of partnership, then its needs for financial capital will probably be greater. It is therefore important that, where the partners have contributed capital, an amount of interest at an agreed rate is taken into account in computing the true residual. As in other circumstances, the partners should be 'paid' a 'wage' for their individual labour. Any balance is then the true residual and represents the return to the risk undertaken in the exploitation of collective individual and firm-specific capital. This is the return to all the entrepreneurs. It is possible, of course, that not all of the people who have acted entrepreneurially will be partners, and some of the residual could be shared with them in the form of contractual or extra-contractual bonuses.

There may be some drawbacks with partnerships of integrated entrepreneurs. The application of the theory of the law firm has suggested that they are probably best placed to grow and to diversify because of the sharing principles on which they are founded. But there are, as we have seen (in paragraphs 8.6 and 8.7), some natural and other limits on growth. Size makes monitoring more difficult. The consistency and quality associated with this type of firm may be compromised by too much growth and diversification. There may be internal pressure to create a stronger departmental structure or to establish parallel partnerships in order to maintain the feeling that lawyers and staff are part of a 'small' organisation (either of these moves might threaten the benefits of diversification by setting up conflicting loyalties). There may be internal and external pressure to incorporate or to enter a network.

9.5   A Mixed Partnership

Partnerships made up entirely of individual practitioners or of integrated entrepreneurs would be 'pure', and could be said to represent two ends of a spectrum. As in most things, it is unlikely that any partnership will in reality be totally pure. The result will be a mixed partnership of some kind.

I have three types of possible 'mixture' in mind — integrated entrepreneurs with, respectively, individualist practitioners, 'employee-minded' partners, and unintegrated laterals.

9.5.1   *Integrated entrepreneurs and individualist practitioners*

In the first mix, partners whose preference would be for a practice which fully exploits firm-specific capital (entrepreneurial partners) find themselves in partnership with those who are at heart and in reality sole practitioners. This mixture of sharing and non-sharing partners can be problematic. The individualist practitioners will resist 'contributing' to the additional organisation costs that go with integrated, entrepreneurial practices (increased infrastructure, investment in the development of individual and firm-specific capital, the costs of diversification, and so on), and will probably want to see profit-shares more closely geared to personal productivity measured by fees billed. The entrepreneurial partners may also resist sharing the (true) residual from the mutual exploitation of individual and firm-specific capital with those who have resisted its development and exploitation and possibly played little or no part in the achievement of that development and exploitation. This type of partnership would be truly mixed. The division of profit that I have suggested, involving separating out the return to financial capital, the wage for labour, and the true residual return to risk, would allow the latter to be restricted to the entrepreneurial partners. But this restriction goes against the ethos of partnership and may be difficult to achieve in practice. The philosophical and emotional differences are such that, perhaps, such disparate people should not be in partnership together at all.

9.5.2   *Integrated entrepreneurs and 'employee-minded' partners*

The second mixture is perhaps more of a variation than a mixture. Assuming the existence of a partnership of integrated entrepreneurs, it is possible that while a majority of the partners are entrepreneurial, willing to take risks, and to engage in entrepreneurial activities (as described in paragraph 7.2), others are more risk-averse, or prefer to service clients rather than be 'entrepreneurial'. This does not make them individualist practitioners (necessarily), since they are comfortable in the integrated, sharing environment and may well benefit from the horizontal sharing of surplus client needs. However, their input would be adequately compensated by the payment of interest on any contributed capital, and a 'wage' for their labour. They are, in fact, more properly regarded as 'employee-minded'.

There may also be some partners who have been promoted to partnership but who, in the event, have been elevated beyond their level of competence. Tongue-in-cheek, we might describe them as 'Peter principals'!

Not being entrepreneurs in the sense I have described in paragraph 7.2, such partners ought not to share in the residual gains of the practice since there has been little risk undertaken that would not also be undertaken by a senior employed fee-earner in the same practice. Such a partner is, in the literal sense, a 'salaried' partner (since the principal return to the exchange that takes place should be a 'wage' for labour). Of course, a senior employed fee-earner (or a salaried partner in the more usually accepted sense) would not have contributed financial capital. But the partner's return to financial capital, on my analysis, would be an interest payment. Unless the partner has invested such an amount of financial capital that the risk to that capital is disproportionate and the partner has become a 'venture capitalist' (which seems highly unlikely in a discussion based on a risk-averse individual), a share in the residual seems indefensible. Again, there will be the philosophical and emotional issues to be dealt with. The solution might be formally and structurally to call such partners salaried partners, and to require no contributions of financial capital. Alternatively, the shares of profit might be calculated in such a way that the division effectively takes account of the distinction between returns to financial capital, wages for labour and returns to entrepreneurial risk. But unless these tensions are addressed, it is likely that the practice will be split.

There is a sense in which this analysis could prove unfair to the individualist practitioner or employee-minded partners. I have suggested that the residual (profit) may be regarded in most partnerships as the 'surplus' returns to both individual and firm-specific capital. The *market return* to individual capital is the 'wage'. But the act of sharing within a partnership gives rise to *some* risk over and above that which would be incurred by a truly sole practitioner. Accordingly, it is possible that there might be some return above the market wage, reflecting the return to this narrow, entrepreneurial risk. In a partnership comprised entirely of integrated, sharing entrepreneurs (see paragraph 9.4), it may be unnecessary to separate out the returns to individual and firm-specific capital before allocating shares in the residual profits — because all partners are undertaking broadly equivalent risks, and the profit-sharing scheme will reflect this.

But where some partners (whether the individualist practitioners or the employee-minded) are not taking equivalent entrepreneurial risks, it could be necessary to distinguish residual gains to individual capital and those to firm-specific capital. Such a distinction presents many difficulties for the operation of a profit-sharing system (see paragraph 37.6), but would be perceived by the individualist practitioner and employee-minded partners to ensure an absolutely 'fair' total compensation for them; it would, unfortunately, probably be totally contrary to the ethos of profit-sharing in the partnership generally.

This conclusion suggests that individualist practitioner and employee-minded partners should not be admitted to partnership where the philosophy is one of integration and sharing or, if admitted, should later be excluded. This begs some difficult questions. Can these partners be identified before they are admitted, or do they develop into such partners after admission? If before admission, should they actually be excluded from promotion to the partnership? If they are the first to be considered for admission, and can be identified, the answer might well be positive, since to admit them would necessarily compromise an existing partnership of integrated entrepreneurs. If they are not admitted, can the firm deal with the issues of motivation, status and professional recognition that such lawyers will still be seeking, or do they have to leave the firm? And perhaps the biggest problem of all in this is dealing with an individualist who is a 'heavy-hitter', running up considerable chargeable hours, bringing in large fees, and making a significant contribution to profit. There are few integrated entrepreneurs with the stomach to throw such an individualist out!

9.5.3   *Integrated entrepreneurs and unintegrated laterals*

The third type of mixture arises from mergers and the recruitment of lateral partners. It is, of course, possible that partners admitted in either of these ways will be individualist practitioners or employee-minded. If so, the issues are the same as those already discussed. However, they may not be. The fact that they have not previously been imbued with the attitudes, values and beliefs of the firm may mean that, although they are inherently sharing entrepreneurs, they are nevertheless *different*. If they become fully integrated into the partnership, this issue will go away; if they do not, a mixed partnership of a slightly different kind results. Whether this jeopardises the sharing relationship and integration to a point where the analysis in paragraph 9.4 cannot apply will probably depend on the extent of the mismatch.

9.5.4   *Conclusions*

Mixed partnerships, by not concentrating on the full integration and exploitation of *everyone's* individual capital and maximising the collective efforts of all partners in the development of firm-specific capital, may find it more difficult to capitalise fully on investments in diversification, to undertake multiple diversification, or to achieve minimum scale. These firms do not achieve the full diversification of the unsystematic risks associated with the practices of individualist practitioner, employee-minded, or unintegrated partners.

Given that there are few 'pure' partnerships, the vast majority of law firm partnerships are, to some greater or lesser extent, mixed. If there is a preponderance of individualists or integrated entrepreneurs, then a dominant culture and style will emerge, and it will be much easier for the firm to deal with the minority. In fact, it is unlikely that partners with a leaning for integrated entrepreneurialism would stay for long in a partnership of individual practitioners (unless they converted to individualism themselves). Partnerships of tolerant integrated entrepreneurs are able to coexist with a few individual practitioners — particularly those who have high billings and contributions to profitability! However, the culture may make life uncomfortable for the individualists, who may feel that they are not receiving their proportionate reward — especially if the firm is in the process of making investments for the future which are presently diluting profitability.

The more difficult situation is where there is no clear preponderance of individualists or integrationists, and where there are a significant number of the employee-minded or mismatched laterals. Such firms are often characterised by open conflict and tensions, turf wars between partners, no clear strategy or direction, confused leadership, and profit-sharing squabbles. I am inclined to believe that such hybrid arrangements are not sustainable over the long term — at least for individuals who want to feel that they are part of a firm that is going somewhere, is successful, and is a pleasant place to work. My assertion in this paragraph, therefore, is that the culture of the integrated entrepreneurs is more likely to be 'polluted' or diluted by the admission of other types of partners than is the culture of the individual practitioners. My reasoning is that integrated entrepreneurs will want to work together and will tolerate some others in the interests of trying to build an institution. Individual practitioners, by definition, are more concerned with self-interest and will therefore be both less interested in the behaviour of others and less inclined to build a sustainable business beyond their own personal careers. The most difficult environment is a firm that is trying to build something that will outlast the present partners, where the integration efforts of some are thwarted or disrupted by the individualism of others who believe that they are more important than the firm and that they can therefore behave (and be rewarded) individualistically.

9.6 The Incorporated Law Firm

An incorporated legal practice is, in principle, simply an incorporated version of those types of practice already discussed in paragraphs 9.1 to 9.5. However, the requirement to distinguish structurally between investors (shareholders), managers (directors and senior support staff), workers (fee-earners and support staff at all levels of seniority), and financiers (bankers or shareholders), means that there is perhaps more incentive to distinguish the different types of return in the way suggested in paragraph

8.9. Incorporation would certainly allow assistant solicitors in the firm (though unfortunately not legal executives, paralegals or support staff) to acquire an entrepreneurial interest (shares).

The degree of entrepreneurial risk or uncertainty taken by any given shareholder would depend on the number of shares owned. In theory, it would be possible for an incorporated firm to be controlled by its employed lawyers, but in practice this seems improbable. However, the ownership interest might well encourage those who are entrepreneurially minded to set about improving the value of their shares by increasing the value of the collective individual and firm-specific capital in the ways considered above. Were this to happen on any significant scale, law firms might then be controlled by true entrepreneurs rewarded by a share in residual gains for the risk undertaken (dividends on shares owned), and by 'wage' for the value of any labour exchanged. (Shareholders do not receive interest on their contributed capital — though they should on loans — but, for the same reasons as in a partnership, the true return to risk can only be calculated by deducting from the dividend the notional interest return for an alternative, risk-free investment of the same amount.) The notion of 'partner' might then disappear altogether. Different lawyers could find their own level of comfort, reflecting their preferences for investment, risk-taking, and fee-earning without being subject to a limited hallmark of success — being 'a partner'.

Finally, I suggested in paragraphs 8.7 and 8.8 that the largest law firms might benefit most from incorporation. The preceding application of the theory of the law firm has also suggested that the firms most likely to grow and most likely to diversify successfully are the partnerships of integrated entrepreneurs (see paragraph 9.4). The conclusion must therefore be that incorporation should be considered most seriously by partnerships comprising at least 20 integrated, sharing entrepreneurs. Time will tell!

9.7 In-house Legal Departments

Although this chapter is principally directed towards an analytical framework for examining private practice, I believe that the theory of the law firm can be adapted for analysis of in-house legal departments.

The existence of in-house legal departments can be explained as a response to transaction costs by the company, public body, or agency concerned. The alternative is to seek an exchange in the market involving the supply of legal services for reward. The existence of bounded rationality, frequency of use, and asset specificity could combine to make the cost-benefit of internal organisation greater than the cost-benefit of market transactions (see paragraph 6.3).

We can then regard the in-house legal department (lawyers, support staff, tangible assets) as an analytically separate 'firm' for the purposes of applying the theory of the law firm. It is possible to envisage both the individual human capital of the lawyers and support staff, and the creation of 'firm-specific' capital from their combined efforts: knowledge about the employer that arises is, for these purposes, as much 'client-specific' knowledge and part of the firm-specific capital as it would be in private practice, as is the situational know-how arising from knowledge of personalities, culture and working practices.

Individual and firm-specific capital can be exploited in the same way as in private practice. Surplus client needs (responses to overwork or the need for specialisation) can be met in the market or by the recruitment of additional staff where the organisational cost-benefit outweighs the transactional cost-benefit. Diversification of services, clients and location can also be addressed in much the same way.

The structure and behaviour of in-house departments, depending on the number and authority (corporate hierarchy) of the people involved, may also reflect individualist practitioner, employee-minded, or entrepreneurial approaches.

The significant difference between in-house departments and private legal practice perhaps arises in relation to rewards — although 'employee share schemes' are probably better established in industry than they are in private practice. There is unlikely to be any capital contribution (except in the acquisition of shares), and there should be a market wage for labour supplied. The difficulty in in-house practice is that there is no residual gain attributable to the in-house 'firm' — unless there is a system of internal charging or transfer pricing between different parts of the company, public body or agency that provides a quantifiable fee income. If this quantification exists, it would be possible to identify the surplus return to individual or firm-specific capital (and to argue for the distribution of this residual among the people who created it!).

Alternatively, the in-house department might be able to quantify the market (i.e., private practice) cost of the services it has provided, together with a valuation of the intrinsic added value from having in-house lawyers on-site. The difference between market cost (and added value) and total internal costs could represent a notional residual gain to the employer. However, it is roughly this cost-benefit analysis that leads the employer to decide whether to bear the transaction costs of the market or the organisation costs of the in-house legal department. It would therefore be unrealistic to expect the employer, on this calculation of residual gain, to share a significant part of it with the members of the in-house 'firm', since to do so would result in the in-house department actually costing almost as much as the market and thus erode the rationale for the in-house department! I say 'roughly' this cost-benefit analysis because the costs of private practice would here refer to the fees actually paid by the company: this, of course, ignores the additional transaction costs that would be borne by the company if it opted for a market exchange (search, negotiating and monitoring).

9.8 The Notion of Property Rights

I want to conclude this application of the theory of law firms with a word about property rights. As we have seen, generic theories of the firm can be developed on the basis that exchanges of economic resources are built on exchanges of property rights in goods and services (see paragraph 6.5). This is very much the product of the mercantile, capitalist thinking of the Industrial Age. Certainly the application of property rights to determine the right to human capital under contracts for services in post-industrial society (or the Information Age) may not be appropriate.

Success in law firms comes from the exploitation of individual and firm-specific capital. An individual may, of course, correctly say that she 'owns' her individual capital. To the extent that that capital includes personal knowledge and experience, that is true; to the extent that it includes client-specific information and client relationships, it is not. Exchange transactions between individuals based on sharing their respective individual capital may give rise to 'property rights' in or over part of each other's capital; but those rights do not give rise to any property rights in or over the *individual*. Further, the right to exploit collective individual, or firm-specific, capital, can only derive from rights to share in it, but not to own it.

My conclusion, therefore, is that notions of law firms or of partnership based on ownership are misguided. True, shareholders or partners can claim ownership of contributed financial capital, and of a share in tangible assets acquired by the firm. But in the assets that matter most — individual and firm-specific capital — there can only be ownership of one's own individual capital. To treat other people in the firm as though they are human assets to be directed, controlled, moved, misused or abused in the same way as owned tangible assets might be to act in a fundamentally short-termist, flawed and dangerous way.

Chapter 10

SUMMARY OF THE THEORY: THE BOUNDARIES OF THE FIRM

10.1 Why Boundaries are Important

To bring this rather more academic treatment of law firms to a conclusion (and to provide a short-cut for those readers who preferred to skip chapters 5 to 9!), I shall now restate my theory of the law firm as a series of propositions, with cross-references to the preceding chapters for those who wish to track them back.

The theory of the law firm attempts to set out why law firms exist in the way that they do; in so doing, it examines why they do what they do. In other words, the theory tries to explain the basis on which firms decide to do something for themselves, that is, to 'internalise' something that could be supplied to them by independent contractors or by affiliates. What a firm chooses to internalise or not will then define the boundaries of the firm (see Coase (1937), quoted in paragraph 8.6). For example, if a firm chooses to recruit more employed lawyers rather than going to counsel or engaging agency solicitors, it will extend the boundaries of the firm. If it decides to outsource accounting, word-processing, cleaning and maintenance, recruiting, or training services, it will be limiting the boundaries of the firm. If it chooses to form an affiliation with a foreign law firm rather than open its own office abroad, it is likewise limiting the boundaries of the firm. A firm therefore sets its boundaries by deciding whether to do everything for itself by bringing all its possible suppliers into the organisation; to do virtually nothing for itself by outsourcing as much as possible, and using independent support and networked affiliates for legal as well as support services; or (more usually) doing some things internally but not others.

The theory of the law firm seeks to explain the *basis and rationale* for these decisions to internalise. It should therefore help a firm to explain what it has already decided to internalise (or not), and therefore to review decisions already made; it should also help when future decisions have to be made about whether or not to internalise other resources.

10.2 The Propositions

Proposition 1: A law firm exists to exploit the know-how of its partners and staff — both individual and firm-specific — in the service of its clients (see paragraphs 5.1 and 5.2).

Proposition 2: The exploitation of market opportunities depends on the activities of entrepreneurs to identify opportunities, acquire and organise the resources needed to satisfy the market, sell the service to a buyer, make those resources productive, and monitor their performance (see paragraphs 6.1 and 7.2)

Proposition 3: The know-how and other resources that a law firm needs can be organised externally through independent spot contracts (the market) or through a network of affiliated suppliers (a network), or acquired and managed internally within an institution (a firm) (see paragraph 6.1).

Proposition 4: All interactions in the legal marketplace can be organised in accordance with one or more of the forms of resource allocation in Proposition 3, whether they are lawyer–client, lawyer–supplier (including support services), or lawyer–lawyer (see paragraph 6.1).

Proposition 5: The use of the market gives rise to 'transaction costs', that is, in relation to each spot contract, the buyer has to incur the costs of searching for an appropriate supplier, negotiating a contract, and monitoring its performance (see paragraph 6.3).

Proposition 6: To the extent that the buyer has to rely on a supplier, the buyer runs the risk that the supplier will not perform to the required standard (shirking), might steal the market opportunity that the buyer is trying to address (leaving the supplier–buyer relationship to supplant the buyer), or seek to appropriate more of the buyer's profit by holding out for higher-than-contracted payment (grabbing). These are the 'agency costs' of moral hazard (shirking) and opportunism (leaving or grabbing) (see paragraph 6.4).

Proposition 7: Where the search costs of spot contracts are high, the transactions are repeated sufficiently often, the supplier is acquiring valuable inside knowledge about the buyer and his transactions, or the agency costs are high, it will usually pay the buyer to 'internalise' the supplier: this replaces many different spot contracts with one, continuing contract for supply or employment (see paragraph 6.3). This internalisation creates an organisation, and so leads to organisation costs.

Proposition 8: Whether or not a buyer internalises a supplier relationship as suggested in Proposition 7 will normally be decided on the basis of whether the cost-benefit of the organisation costs exceeds the cost-benefit of the transaction costs (see paragraph 6.3).

Proposition 9: Propositions 2 to 8 also apply to one lawyer seeking the help of another: the services of the 'supplying lawyer' can be organised through the market (as, for example, with counsel), through a network (as, for example, with an affiliated firm), or through a firm. The 'buying lawyer' faces transaction costs in finding a suitable supplying lawyer, negotiating an arrangement and fee, and ensuring that the work is properly carried out. He or she also carries the agency costs of the supplying lawyer shirking, taking the client, or grabbing a disproportionate share of the fee. If the supplying lawyer is a regular supplier, and has acquired client-specific or transaction-specific knowledge (see paragraph 5.2.1) of the buying lawyer's business, then the buying lawyer may wish to internalise the supplier if the cost-benefit of doing so outweighs the cost-benefit of independent contracting. There may, of course, be some professional constraints (such as the movement of barristers into firms of solicitors); nevertheless, the principles hold good.

Proposition 10: Every individual lawyer bears the risk that the exploitation of his or her know-how will be subject to personal and market conditions that will affect its productivity: for example, the lawyer might be ill, undergo marital or emotional difficulties, lose clients, or find that his or her specialisation is no longer needed by clients (see paragraph 8.1.2).

Proposition 11: Proposition 9 assumes that the buying lawyer has a 'surplus' client need that he or she cannot meet without help. However, one lawyer might choose to combine with another in the hope of reducing through mutual support (sharing or diversifying) the individual risks identified in proposition 10 (paragraph 8.1.2).

Proposition 12: The diversification envisaged by proposition 11 might embrace sharing the costs of office space and services (surplus costs: see paragraph 8.3), sharing work from existing clients that one of them does not have the time or appropriate know-how to deal with (surplus client needs: see paragraph 8.4), or sharing market opportunities that one of them cannot exploit effectively alone (surplus opportunities: see paragraph 8.5). On any of these bases, the rationale of a law firm is sharing.

Proposition 13: Law firms do not sustain growth by absorbing surplus costs, because economies of scale do not explain the growth of law firms (see paragraph 8.3).

Proposition 14: The ability of a firm to grow in response to surplus client needs will be limited by the capacity of the lawyer or lawyers with surplus client needs to monitor the effective performance of the work shared (that is, to manage the agency costs) (see paragraph 8.4.3).

Proposition 15: Whether an incoming lawyer will be a partner (horizontal sharing of the surplus client need) or employed (vertical sharing of the surplus) will probably depend on the extent to which the incoming lawyer is dependent for productivity on the individual know-how of the sharing lawyer or on firm-specific know-how (which would suggest employment) or on his or her own individual know-how (which could support partnership) (see paragraph 8.4.4).

Proposition 16: Responding to surplus opportunities may be based on the diversification of one or more of legal services, clients, or location; all appear to be founded on the exploitation of firm-specific know-how more than individual know-how (see paragraph 8.5).

Proposition 17: The optimum size of a law firm is dependent on the availability of client work, the market's assessment of the firm's credibility, the entrepreneurial ability of partners to identify and bring in new work, the availability of other partners and employed fee-earners, the willingness and ability of partners to share (delegate) client work with others, the willingness and ability of those who share surplus work with others to monitor its effective performance, and the extent and effectiveness of the firm's managerial know-how (see paragraph 8.6): in other words, size is constrained by the individual and firm-specific know-how on which the firm is built.

Proposition 18: Partnerships are built on trust and the susceptibility of partners to peer pressure. These both decline with increasing size, and in practice hierarchy and bureaucracy increase. In these circumstances, the economic and social reality of legal practice increases the pressure and justification for incorporation as a firm grows (see paragraph 8.7).

Proposition 19: A law firm's net profit should be seen as a combination of a return on invested financial capital (actual or notional interest at market rates), a reward for providing professional expertise (the equivalent of a market wage), and a residual amount that represents the entrepreneurs' reward for bearing the risks and uncertainty of the business. There is no theoretical justification for mere financiers or workers to be given a share of profit when interest or wages is adequate recompense, and therefore all equity partners should be entrepreneurial (as defined in paragraph 7.2), and entrepreneurs should be equity partners (see paragraph 8.9).

Proposition 20: Law offices can be classified as belonging to one of seven types: sole practitioner, sole principal, partnership of individual practitioners, partnership of integrated entrepreneurs, mixed partnership, incorporated law firm, or an in-house legal department (see chapter 9).

Proposition 21: A sole practitioner necessarily has to bear all of the risks associated with the exploitation of his or her individual know-how. Surplus client needs have to be addressed through independent arrangements or through an affiliation, or the sole practitioner has to become a sole principal or enter into partnership. Surplus opportunities identified by a sole practitioner are likely to remain unexploited. There is likely to be a complete coincidence of individual and firm-specific know-how, and of the entrepreneurial, fee-earning, and financing roles (see paragraph 9.1).

Proposition 22: A sole principal also bears the risks of exploiting his or her individual know-how, although the existence of one or more employed fee-earners will mean that the sole principal is better able to address surplus client needs (and possibly even surplus opportunities), and will therefore be starting the development of firm-specific know-how. As with the sole practitioner, however, there is likely to be a complete coincidence of the entrepreneurial, working and financing roles of the sole principal (see paragraph 9.2).

Proposition 23: Where a partnership legally exists, but the partners do not share surplus client needs or surplus opportunities with each other (except, perhaps, by 'internal' contracts for the supply and reward of fee-earning expertise), there is a 'partnership of individual practitioners'. Such a partnership is trading on the individual know-how of the partners, and any firm-specific know-how is limited and incidental. In fact, it may be that increased organisation costs derived from the internalisation of certain support services (or even some employed fee-earners) may be higher than the transaction costs that certain partners would need to bear in the exploitation of their own know-how: this will tend to lead to differential cost-sharing between partners or the departure of those who do not need (or cannot afford) to bear a share of the additional costs. Internal responses to surplus client needs, and more so to surplus opportunities, will be limited. Although the partners are entrepreneurial, the partnership is not predicated on sharing and integration: as with sole practitioners, there is likely to be a coincidence of the entrepreneurial, working and financing roles of partners. There may be cost-sharing, but not necessarily revenue-sharing; even where there is, profits are likely to be allocated on an individual fee-related basis after the deduction of the appropriate share of overheads (see paragraph 9.3).

Proposition 24: At the other end of the spectrum, where a partnership is founded on the sharing of surplus client needs and surplus opportunities, and the creation of an infrastructure and culture to facilitate the maximum exploitation of both, there will be a 'partnership of integrated entrepreneurs'. The rationale of the firm is the creation, exploitation and maximisation of firm-specific capital, and it trades on both individual and firm-specific know-how. The sharing of surpluses is consistently both horizontal (with other partners) and vertical (with employed fee-earners); the infrastructure that such extensive sharing and teamwork requires is also more likely to lead to the internalisation of more support services. Partnerships of integrated entrepreneurs should be the best placed of any form of legal practice to respond to surplus opportunities through the diversification of services, clients, location, or even some combination of them. The efforts of partners in contributing to the development and exploitation of firm-specific know-how, and its diversification, are also more likely to be better articulated and more sophisticated in this type of partnership; this will lead to differentiation between the entrepreneurial, working and financing roles of the partners (see paragraph 9.4).

Proposition 25: Partnerships of individual practitioners and of integrated entrepreneurs represent the ends of a spectrum. Few firms will fall entirely at one end or the other; some will display more of the characteristics of one than the other, but a large number of firms will also fall at a point in between which does not allow them to be characterised as either. I call these 'mixed partnerships' (see paragraph 9.5). They have a substantial number of partners who are (or who wish to be) sharing entrepreneurs, but who are in partnership with a significant number of individual practitioners (who at least are still entrepreneurial but who are not sharing, team-players), or 'employee-minded', risk-averse partners (who are not entrepreneurial), or unintegrated partners (usually brought in through merger or lateral recruitment, who may eventually become sharing entrepreneurs, individual practitioners, or employee-minded but who for the time being are just different). Such mixed partnerships will veer towards integration or individualism depending on the balance of power in the firm (or they will remain hopelessly confused and in conflict in the middle). In any event, the firm-specific know-how of the practice will remain underdeveloped, and the partners will not be able to exploit fully that which exists. Responding to surplus client needs, and to surplus opportunities through diversification, is likely to lead to greater risks and tensions than in either the partnership of individual practitioners or the partnership of integrated entrepreneurs. The disparity of attitudes, expectations and performance in a mixed partnership is likely to lead to an implicit (if not explicit) distinction between the entrepreneurial, working and financing roles of partners, but usually without any common or accepted framework for doing so, leading as a result to some serious profit-sharing disputes.

Proposition 26: An incorporated law firm is simply an incorporated version of the types of practice described in propositions 21 to 25, though the distinction between owners, managers, workers and financiers will be more apparent. In these circumstances, it might be easier for a law firm to create an environment where fee-earners can find an appropriate level and role for themselves which reflects their preferences for investment, risk-taking, and fee-earning without being branded a failure if they do not achieve the status of 'partner' (see paragraph 9.6).

Proposition 27: These propositions can be adapted to apply to an in-house legal department (see paragraph 9.7). The existence of the department can be seen as an organisation's response to the transaction costs of engaging external legal advisers on a transactional basis. The legal department can therefore be regarded as an analytically separate 'law firm' for the purposes of the theory of the law firm. It can be assessed on the extent to which it develops and exploits individual and 'firm-specific' capital, and whether the organisation's 'surplus client needs' or 'surplus opportunities' are met by the legal department by internalisation or otherwise.

PART III

LAW FIRMS AS BUSINESS ORGANISATIONS

Chapter 11

THE STRATEGY PROCESS

11.1 Business Planning

Do not regard business planning as a quest for the right answers, since there may not be any. The key is not so much to end up with the right plan as to engage in strategic thinking. In today's changing legal and economic climate, any type of practice raises some fundamental issues that require strategic thought. Planning is a process; but it is not a question of adopting the *right process* so much as thinking strategically about the *right issues*. This requires the partners to articulate and understand their assumptions about the environment for legal services, about what they are setting out to achieve within that environment, and about the skills and competencies that the firm needs to bring those achievements to fruition. Do not let the reactive nature of legal practice prevent necessary forward thinking.

Thinking strategically requires you to acknowledge that what has worked before may not be successful in the future. Do not stifle new ideas with judgmental comments. Challenge your assumptions. Do not expect the marketplace to buy what you want to deliver. Instead, find out what your current and prospective clients want, and then recreate the firm to deliver it. The practice of law is not what you want it to be, but what your clients want it to be.

This chapter describes a process for thinking strategically: *what* you should think about, and why, is the subject of chapter 4. See also Boutall and Blackburn 1996.

11.2 Look Outside

Too many firms that have been in practice for some time begin their strategic thinking by looking internally — indeed, some never look beyond internal issues. The starting point, whether the firm is established or a start-up, is to look outside the firm, at the environment for legal practice, and at the trends and conditions that will affect future practice.

(a)   Identify your clients (or potential clients), their type, their location, the types of work you do for them (or would like to do), the amounts they spend with you on various matters (or would be likely to spend, given the market): look for trends or patterns that will help your future thinking. How did they (or would they) choose the firm (e.g., the reputation of the firm, of a practice area, or of a particular lawyer; personal association; referrals from current or former clients or professional agencies)? What are they looking for? What do they think of the service they receive from you (or their present lawyers)? The best way of answering many of these questions, and others that follow, is to ask a cross-section of your actual or prospective clients and referral sources (see paragraph 11.8).

(b)   Analyse your existing or likely referral sources (e.g., other lawyers, professionals, accountants, banks, etc.), their background, actual or likely effectiveness and future potential.

(c)   Identify existing and potential markets or niches that offer opportunities to you. Examine relevant key success factors affecting those markets (see paragraph 4.5.4). The opportunities will usually arise in some way from your existing client base or contacts, so make sure you do enough homework. It is not sufficient merely to wish, or to hope, that you can create a new practice or diversify into a new area; you need to understand the market in depth.

(d)   Outline the services and expertise needed by each market.

(e)   Assess your significant competitors for the different types of work you undertake (or would like to undertake), their distinctive features, their market representation and legal specialisation.

11.3   Look Inside

Having established from an external examination what your best business opportunities are likely to be, you can now look at your ability and resources available to capitalise on them. This part of the process should be carried out simultaneously with the external assessment described in paragraph 11.2.

(a)   Assess your strongest and weakest areas of legal and market expertise. Identify how you can build on the strengths and eliminate or improve the weaknesses.

(b)   Study the profitability of your practice over both the short term and long term. Look at different lawyers, types of work, and types of clients. If you are starting a new practice, look *critically* at these issues as best you can.

(c)   Consider types of work currently undertaken by the firm (or which might, without proper control, be undertaken in a start-up) that should not be — perhaps because of limited expertise, inadequate experience, or cost; consider individuals who are doing work (or might take work) that they should not; and consider types of work you are not currently undertaking that you should be.

The firm should also look at the 'balance' of its client base. For example, how many active clients has it had in each of the last three to five years, and how many active matters? What is the trend? What proportion of fee income in each of those years has been produced by the top 10, 50 and 100 (in other words, what degree of client dependence is the firm sustaining)? What is the firm's dependence on high fees for a few clients (plotted as shown, for instance, in figure 11.1)? Do any clients falling in the top 100 (by fees billed) share any common features — being from a certain location; belonging to the same or a similar industry; are they, for example, unincorporated entrepreneurs or private clients? Looking for these clues may suggest a basis for segmentation (see paragraph 4.5.2) and differentiation (see paragraph 4.7.1).

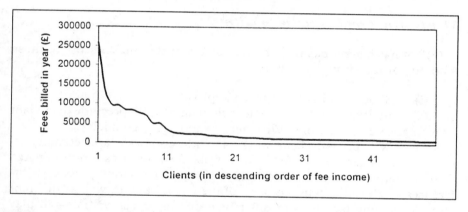

Figure 11.1 This shows the fees billed in a year for the top 50 clients of a firm which has a mixed commercial and private client practice (a total of more than 4,600 active clients in the year), and a total fee income of around £2.6 million. About 1% of the clients were responsible for nearly 60% of the total fee income, and the top client alone for almost 10%! This degree of dependence is considerable: the remaining 4,550 clients are averaging fees of less than £250. The strategic challenge for this firm would be managing the considerable differences between the services required by the few heavyweight commercial clients who generate a large proportion of the firm's revenue, and the 'volume' business conducted for the vast majority of clients.

In line with the 80–20 rule, almost every law firm that I have studied has a dependence on about 20% of its clients in any one year producing about 80% of its income: this means that the firm has two distinct types of client base, and each category cannot be treated in the same way. Each category, in my view, represents a *strategically distinct* group. The top 20% are very important to the firm's continued success and those clients need the best treatment and nurturing its lawyers and staff can offer. The firm has to work very hard on the other 80% (which may represent thousands of clients) to produce a smaller proportion of its income: it is impossible to provide the same degree of attention to each of them, and the trick is to identify those who may one day move into the top 20% category.

11.4 Intended Market Position

With information from the external and internal assessments, you are now able to identify the strategic issues that require debate among partners. Force yourselves to address them: they will not go away, and they do not become any easier with the passage of time.

As you discuss strategy and competitive advantage, address two dimensions:

(a) What makes sense to clients?
(b) What makes sense to partners?

11.4.1 *What makes sense to clients?*

(a) What market position should you adopt that makes sense to those who buy or may buy your services?

(i) Should you adopt a niche approach?
(ii) In litigation, for example, will plaintiff work preclude defendant or insurance defence work? Will there be too many conflicts?
(iii) Will private client work preclude corporate and commercial business? It is generally difficult for private client or litigation-dominated firms (whether plaintiff or defendant) to build corporate practices: differences of attitudes between parts of the client base, as well as different attitudes among lawyers and different economic considerations, all play their part. Many litigation firms also suffer from the 'transactional' nature of their practice, and find it difficult to build institutional, long-term relationships with clients — particularly where the practice is dependent on referrals from agencies where staff changes make relationships difficult to build and maintain.

(b) Will conflicts restrict you? There are three types of conflict:

(i) Conflicts of client interest (the traditional conflicts): in many firms with mixed practices, the partners' interest in maintaining work from corporate clients or insurers nearly always takes precedence over their interest in private clients.
(ii) Business conflicts: if you represent too many clients of one type (e.g., plaintiffs, insurers) or in one industry (e.g., airlines, retailers), you may find increasingly that other clients are reluctant to use you.
(iii) Position conflicts: the position you take in one piece of litigation may be at odds with the position you want to take in a subsequent action (for example, in advancing the cause of a plaintiff you may adopt a position that puts you in difficulty with some defence clients who are

less than impressed with the vigour with which you espouse the plaintiff's cause).

To the extent that conflicts exist, choices have to be made. They should be decided in the context of the firm's overall strategic thinking, and not left to be resolved ad hoc. Future growth may well be constrained more by conflicts than by any other factor.

(c) Will there be cultural differences between clients? The needs of private clients may be very different to those of corporate clients and insurers. They think differently, have different economic needs and sources of finance, have different expectations of lawyers, and may even dress differently. Can you accommodate both cultures without offending the other, and without giving private clients (particularly) the feeling that they are paying for things that they do not want (e.g., plush meeting rooms)? If you cannot accommodate them, stop talking about or expecting cross-selling — it simply cannot happen.

11.4.2 *What makes sense to partners?*

(a) Will there be cultural differences between lawyers in a mixed practice? Plaintiff lawyers tend to be more of the 'lone ranger' types who focus on getting a result for their client. Insurance defence lawyers tend to concentrate more on the legal process and procedure. Does each think that the real money is on the other side? Do defence lawyers resent the media promotion of plaintiffs more than of defendants? Do corporate and commercial lawyers understand litigators — particularly personal injury litigators? Do they understand the desire to help private clients? Again, differences of internal culture can destroy all prospects of cross-selling.

(b) Are there economic differences? Emphasising profit-centre accounting, charge-out rates and chargeable hour comparisons will create problems for firms that try to integrate (say) private client or 'tripping' or whiplash personal injury work with other practice areas. Increasing financial pressures also require private client and personal injury practices to refine their economic assumptions. This will usually mean encouraging greater leverage to allow the work to be performed profitably. Leverage will come in the form of additional assistants and paralegals (with consequent training and partnership expectations that must be dealt with) and through better use of technology. Profit-sharing systems may need to be changed to reflect differences, though if a firm is committed to a practice area it should not penalise those lawyers who pursue it.

11.5 Improvements in Delivery

Whatever market position you decide to adopt, you should always be looking for new or improved ways to deliver legal services. In a competitive and cost-conscious marketplace, this aspect to your strategic thinking is vital. One of the most challenging issues here is the staffing of work. The economics and efficiency of legal practice in the future will be

determined by the people doing the work. The work required to implement recommendations under this heading may take longer than the
overall planning process. Timetables for implementation should be established, setting out specific goals and actions that allow responsibility to be
allocated and achievement monitored. In addition, the firm should
address:

(a)   practice area organisation (specialisation, structure, work allocation, etc.),
(b)   communication and responsiveness,
(c)   timeliness and billing,
(d)   procedures (e.g., for case acceptance, conflict checking, initial
client interviews, file opening, limitation dates, reminder systems, case
management, instructing counsel, retaining experts, locating and dealing
with witnesses, starting and defending actions, discovery, pre-trial procedures, and trial preparation),
(e)   training, precedents and know-how,
(f)   quality management.

Always try to view your structure and procedures from the clients'
perspectives. For instance, does your procedure for dealing with enquiries
make the prospective clients feel wanted, well-treated, and leave them
with an impression of an efficient, sympathetic firm capable of providing
an expeditious service?

11.6   Bringing it all Together

Strategic thinking should focus a practice area on the needs of its clients,
what it does best (and why), and the flexibility it will need to respond to
new opportunities. It should result in a clear statement of that practice
area's intended position in the marketplace and how it can differentiate
itself from its competitors. Its lawyers should also understand *how* to
compete before they decide *where* to compete. It should define the market
segments to be targeted, by defining the services offered, the clients to be
served, the locations involved, and the process, culture and style required
to be successful (cf. paragraph 4.5.2).

The planning process should be based on fact and analysis rather than
partners' assumptions and personal agendas. In larger firms, strategy
should be addressed on a departmental or practice area basis, though each
area's strategy should be consistent with the firm's overall strategy. The
strategy should guide the allocation of resources, the recruitment of
lawyers, and investment in technology and other capital items (cf. Barwise
et al. 1989). Implementation should focus on clear goals, specific timetables, the allocation of responsibility, and the expectation of accountability. Depending on the size of the firm and its commitment, the entire
process should take between three and six months.

Achievement of the strategy should be monitored against goals, timetables, and the discharge of allocated responsibilities: perhaps, indeed, a

partner's profit-share should reflect his or her contribution to achieving the firm's strategy as much as (or even more than) contribution to personal chargeable hours and fees billed.

11.7 The Challenge of a New Practice

Lawyers who are starting a new practice are faced with many challenges. They may be confronted with a range of administrative issues such as choosing office space, arranging insurance and buying equipment as well as the strategic business issues facing any start-up. It is perhaps not surprising that a significant number of start-up businesses fail within five years. But it is not usually the administrative overload that causes the unsuccessful firms to fold. It is their failure to address some of the most fundamental issues and philosophies which will guide the practice's operations.

Like any law firm, a new practice should have considered its strategic rationale. The strategic thinking and planning process is described above. But in addition, other issues need to be considered:

(a) Partners should have compatible, but not necessarily identical, personalities. A common mistake in small firms is to assume that all partners should be alike. Diverse lawyers can still share common priorities and philosophies about running and developing the practice. Match philosophies, not personalities, and capitalise on complementary strengths and weaknesses.

(b) Be clear about the admission of future partners: when will you consider assistants for partnership, and on what basis? Under what circumstances will the practice admit partners from other firms? How will profits be shared as the number of partners increases? If you contemplate recruiting partners from other firms, be very clear about the volume and value of business they anticipate bringing with them: most overestimate! Think carefully about the nature of their initial relationship with the firm, and allow yourself flexibility if things do not work out within a 'probationary' period (see paragraph 36.5.4).

(c) Discuss how the practice is to be managed, identify the decisions that are reserved to all partners, and how the day-to-day activities of the practice are to be run.

(d) Set a realistic budget for the practice's operations. Focus partners' attention on the amount of fee income that needs to be generated to achieve their expected levels of profit; what expenses will be incurred and when; the cash flow needs of the practice and the consequent questions about how best to provide fixed and working capital; how much of their own money they need to invest, how much to borrow, and so on.

(e) In a new firm, embody the fundamental elements of the relationship (including those discussed above) into a partnership agreement. The agreement should also address partners' departures through retirement, ill-health, death and expulsion.

11.8   Client Surveys

11.8.1   *Reasons for client surveys*

Much of the investigation relating to market demand and the feasibility of competitive advantage will depend on the views of clients. The best way to find out what the firm's clients think about it and its future is to ask them. Client surveys are now much more popular than they were and, for their part, clients usually respond positively.

In this paragraph, I am addressing client surveys in the context of approaching clients and referrers of a single firm in order to seek their views about the market position, image or performance of that firm. I am therefore distinguishing this activity from generic or generalised surveys designed to elicit clients' views about the profession, or aspects of it.

In essence, there are two reasons for a firm to conduct a client survey:

(a)   to undertake market research in order to discover what its clients are doing, what they want, where they might want it, and who they might want to buy it from; such a survey can also supplement a firm's knowledge of the volume and value of its marketplace and the trends within it (or within different parts of it);

(b)   to test client satisfaction, and thus to discover the extent to which clients are currently happy with the way the firm performs: unfortunately, too many lawyers think that this is the *only* reason for surveys.

With fragmentation both of the marketplace and of the profession, and structural changes being brought about as the market for legal services approaches maturity (see paragraphs 4.7.3 and 4.7.4), a greater depth of understanding is required which only talking to clients can bring about. There is a tendency to believe (or hope) that clients make rational decisions when they choose their lawyers. In truth, there are many 'soft' and irrational factors that go into their choices (of which even apathy is one). The only way forward is to be truly client-driven, and that requires a greater understanding of clients.

One final hurdle for some firms is persuading partners to go through with a survey. Resistance usually arises from:

(a)   a belief that they already know their clients well, or well enough: it is true that lawyers normally know what clients want in relation to the particular transactions or matters for which they are engaged, but there are few clients who feel that their professional advisers understand as much as they would like them to about the broader picture (of course, if the client buys legal services on a transactional or 'commodity' basis, there will be little encouragement or opportunity to seek to build a deeper relationship);

(b)   a misguided notion that they should protect their clients from exposure to others (usually for fear of another partner 'stealing' the client, or that the person who is conducting the survey will discover how ineffective they are);

(c)   a fear of hearing bad news: clients who are still with the firm rarely have very bad news to deliver through client surveys — they will find other ways or move their business elsewhere.

Partners may need to have some of these things pointed out to them before they will acquiesce in the process.

There is also usually a direct marketing benefit to conducting client surveys. The clients who are invited to participate can be described as 'important' and will therefore be flattered to be included in the process. The mere act of conducting a survey may also be sufficient to demonstrate that the firm is open in its professional relationships and is sufficiently different to care enough about those relationships to try to improve them.

11.8.2   *Conducting client surveys*

The mechanics of conducting a client survey will depend on a variety of factors, including:

(a)   *The purpose of the survey.* There are three principal reasons, each giving rise to a different focus to clients' input:

(i)   *to help formulate a strategy:* such a survey will concentrate on the clients' views of the firm's business focus (clients and services), the location of its offices, and their perception of its size (and possible changes to that size);

(ii)   *to assist with business development:* this type of survey will look at clients' views of the different methods of developing new business and will seek their opinion of relative effectiveness;

(iii)   *to assess quality and client satisfaction:* clients will be asked about the firm's performance in the delivery of its legal services.

Of course, any particular survey may combine two or even all three of these reasons. However, the more ground a survey tries to cover the less focused it will be and (usually) less effective in gathering meaningful facts and opinions.

(b)   *Choosing participants:* The clients who should be approached will depend on the nature of the firm's practice and the purpose of the survey. Other factors include:

(i)   whether the clients should be *specially selected or chosen at random*: if the purpose of the survey is to help with the formulation of strategy, clients should be chosen on the basis of their perceived importance to the future of the firm, the likelihood of them offering constructive views, and their willingness to help the firm in such a process;

(ii)   whether clients who are known (or suspected) to be *critical (or supportive)* of the firm should be included: the fear of bias is understandable, but in my experience most clients are open in their comments and are more likely to be positive than critical; again, if help with strategy is sought, supportive clients should be used;

(iii)   depending on the nature of the firm's client base, a choice between *commercial clients or private clients* (or a mixture of the two) will be required; in addition, given the importance of recommendations for all professional firms, *referral sources* should also be included.

(c)   *Number of participants.* The issue of how many clients to include in the survey is another variable depending on:

(i)   *quantity v. quality* of clients: given a choice, go for quality every time;

(ii)   *quantitative v. qualitative* research: quantitative research would suggest involving as great a number of clients as possible; however, help with qualitative issues such as strategy or effective business development normally suggests seeking better-informed opinions rather than sheer numbers of views;

(iii)   the *purpose of the survey*, the focus of the questions, and what the firm would like to be able to do with the results: there are no golden numbers but, for example, for a qualitative survey involving a small or niche firm, or a department, 15 to 20 clients would be my suggested target; for a larger, multi-office firm, somewhere around 50 will be required; for a quantitative survey, 100 to 200 clients will probably be needed.

Take-up rates for qualitative surveys can be as high as 100%, and are not likely to fall below 70%. For quantitative surveys, responses are rarely less than 40% or more than 85%.

(d)   *Frequency of surveys.* Most surveys are conceived as one-off processes, and if they are intended to help with *one-off* or irregular issues (such as a strategy review) that makes sense. But in these days of being client-driven, of continuous improvement in quality and client satisfaction, and of constant reviews of strategic thinking, there is a lot to be said for instituting a *regular* process of seeking client feedback. Frequency is not therefore an isolated question subject to an ideal response, but will depend on the nature and purpose of the survey or surveys being conducted.

(e)   *Third-party involvement.* Whether a survey should be carried out by someone within the firm or outside it is an open question, and there are arguments both ways. In my view, there are four circumstances or reasons that would favour an outsider:

(i)   *independence and objectivity:* clearly, this cannot be brought by someone from inside the firm, and there are some clients (perhaps a majority, though not a large one) who will be more frank with a third party — which will also make it easier for a third party to ask 'difficult' questions;

(ii)   *confidentiality and attributions:* some clients prefer their responses to remain confidential and unattributable and, again, feel more comfortable with a third party;

(iii) *frequency:* if the survey is an important, one-off event, or internal resource is stretched, a third party with previous experience of knowing what to ask (and how best to ask) can be invaluable;

(iv) *comparative responses and trends:* a third party can also judge the responses given by the clients of a particular firm against responses and trends arising from similar surveys conducted for other firms.

Allowing a third party to visit the firm's clients inevitably carries some risk, not least because the firm is holding that person out as a credible representative. It is therefore vital that the firm should choose a third party with a good track record in client interviewing, and preferably someone who is familiar with the nature of the solicitor–client relationship.

(f) *Form of survey.* The form that the survey takes should depend entirely on the issues to be canvassed and the number of clients involved:

(i) *questionnaires* are popular, but are not always effective: designing them to pose unambiguous questions and so elicit the information required by the firm is very difficult, and response rates are generally low; however, questionnaires are probably the best option for quantitative research;

(ii) *face-to-face interviews* are undoubtedly the most effective method for qualitative surveys: nuances and supplementary questions can be asked, and the relative value of responses judged; they require a commitment from the client to be available at an appointed time, and busy clients may not feel that the process is worth their effort; given that time might be short, the interviewer should also know which are the 'priority' questions so that best use is made of the time and maximum value derived from it;

(iii) *telephone interviews* are the second-best option for qualitative research, and are often used for quantitative surveys; they may also require clients to make a commitment to an appointed time.

Face-to-face and telephone interviews will take an average of about 45 minutes, with a likely range of 30 to 90 minutes. In arranging interviews, it is best to indicate that 45 to 60 minutes will probably be required. Shorter or longer interviews are usually dictated by the availability of the client or referrer, or his or her willingness to talk.

There are few differences apparent in the approaches to client surveys that need to be adopted by large firms or small ones. The reasons for conducting a survey, and the methodology employed, are usually very similar (though the scale may be different). It is worth pointing out that larger firms often do not achieve better qualitative or quantitative results from surveys by throwing money or people at the process. Indeed, as clients increasingly emphasise the importance of the personal relationship between lawyer and client, it may be that the bigger firms are in danger of losing a competitive advantage.

11.8.3 *Analysis and report*

Once the interviews have been completed, the responses must be analysed and written up. The nature of the analysis will clearly be different for quantitative and qualitative reports (though even the latter will normally include some quantitative elements). A report should set out at least:

(a)   a list of participating clients;
(b)   a description of the methodology and timescale of the data collection or interviewing;
(c)   a statement of the results of the analysis (perhaps best organised according to the issues being explored by the survey — for example, basis of choice, use of other lawyers, quality, value, reactions to marketing efforts, opportunities for further work); and
(d)   conclusions and recommendations for action.

The author of the report will need to know at the outset of the project the intended readership and distribution of the report so that he or she can match the form and style of the report to the needs of its readers. The presentation of results can be done in narrative form, tables, graphs, and so on, and the readers may have preferences. In a qualitative survey, the interviewer will also need to check with clients (preferably at the interview) whether they will allow their views and comments to be attributed to them in the report. Finally, the author may have to bear in mind any internal sensitivities to issues raised or comments made by clients.

11.8.4 *Follow-up*

Whatever the reason for the survey, the firm should write to thank clients who took part. It is often difficult to circulate the report to clients because the confidentiality of client relationships might be compromised if the names (let alone the comments and views) of other clients were disclosed. This will clearly depend on the final format and content of the survey report. If it cannot be circulated, it is well worth preparing a summary of its findings for circulation to the participants — and perhaps the broader client base, too.

Wider distribution of the report (or a summary) within the firm should also be considered to keep everyone informed of clients' views on the issues canvassed by the survey.

The firm must decide what it is going to *do* as a result of the report. Clients' confidence in the firm will be eroded if they take the time to express their views and the firm appears to ignore them.

A sense of the sort of responses that might emerge from client surveys, and some indicators that will allow comparisons to be made, is given in paragraph 18.2.2.

Chapter 12

MERGERS

Law firm mergers are complex processes, and the subject is worth a book in its own right. I am grateful to two of my former partners for sparing me (see Malone and Mudrick 1992)! Given the importance and frequency of law firm mergers, however, it is worth devoting a chapter to the principal issues. My purpose is to give a sense and flavour of the issues and process involved but not to provide a detailed how-to guide.

12.1 The Logic of Mergers

People often think of mergers as putting two different businesses together. I prefer to think of them as putting two groups of *people* together. Merger analysis based on whether two law firms' client bases, service offerings, and finances are compatible ignores the factors that will actually determine whether or not the merger will be successful. It is not that these issues do not matter or are not important: they are. But what will be more important in determining success or failure of the merger of know-how businesses is personalities, values, culture and effort. Even if everything makes sense, a merger will still have significant consequences for the culture and morale of a know-how business, and low morale can have a dramatic effect on a firm's profitability and success.

Sveiby and Lloyd go so far as to suggest that, in the context of know-how businesses, mergers are an idea borrowed from 'industry', and the "problem with mergers is not that they are morally wrong but that they do not work" (1987, page 155). Indeed, they also express the view that a know-how business "that grows only through mergers and acquisitions cannot demonstrate the soundness of its core business idea" (1987, page 148: see paragraphs 3.5 and 4.8.3 for the discussion of business ideas).

12.2 Strategic Reasons for Merging

Merger is not a strategy in its own right, but is one (or perhaps one of the principal) steps in the implementation or achievement of certain strategies. On the basis that strategy is concerned with matching the firm's resources and competencies with its external environment (cf. paragraph 4.2), a firm's strategy represents an appropriate mix of clients, services, geography, and process, culture and style (cf. paragraph 4.5.2) designed to achieve that match. In this sense, merger can help a firm to add new clients or meet the needs of a more diversified client base, add or strengthen services, or add or develop new offices (see also Maister 1997, chapter 15). It may help the firm address surplus client needs or achieve diversification (see paragraphs 8.4 and 8.5), or it may simply make the firm larger to give it greater critical mass (cf. paragraph 8.6). Although the constituent firms in a merger will inevitably become part of a larger organisation, the *boundaries* of the merged firm will only have spread if new professional or support services, or new offices, are added as a result — that is, if the new firm 'internalises' people or resources that were previously external, or did not exist at all (cf. paragraph 10.1).

12.2.1   *Increased breadth of services*

A merger may allow a firm to address increases in the demands from clients or to cope with the range of demands being made by clients. As such, it may enable the firm to consolidate its position with existing clients, or to diversify its existing practice, by adding expertise and specialisation (whether technical or industry-related) not previously within the firm.

12.2.2   *Increased depth of expertise*

As legal services become more complex and sophisticated, a firm may need to be able to offer a greater depth of specialisation. A merger may or may not immediately bring greater depth of expertise, but the achievement of critical mass will better allow it to be developed and sustained. Such a move may be necessary if the firm's clients are not to 'outgrow' its legal advisers, and if the firm wishes to attract and retain excellent professional talent.

12.2.3   *Correcting internal weaknesses*

At some time, or over a period of time, a law firm is likely to have developed some internal weaknesses. These may be caused by recruitment policies or by departures that have left gaps in age, experience, business development skills, or leadership. The firm may have developed the 'spare tyre' effect (cf. paragraph 21.4.2). While in my view it is difficult to recruit 'leaders' or 'rainmakers' (because of their lack of internal credibility or — usually — large egos), if potential gaps are identified early enough, it may be possible to bring in people who will develop into those roles. Similarly, if done before the need is dire, a merger may also allow people to acclimatise to each other and encourage the development of these skills. Mergers of firms with complementary practice areas, client bases, and age profiles can also create a stronger merged firm.

Although often floated as an idea, a merger is not likely to be successful in helping a firm solve its people problems — such as underperforming partners or fee-earners, hard-working but unprofitable partners or fee-earners, or ineffective leaders or managers. Nor is it likely to help in dealing with unprofitable offices or practice areas, high levels of debt, or unfunded obligations to actual or prospective former partners. If a merger prospect does its homework, or is properly advised, it will require the other firm to address these issues itself before any merger takes place. Of course, it may just happen that the merger prospect is strong enough financially or dominant enough culturally to be able to absorb these problems and deal with them. However, this presupposes that the prospect has a strong strategic need of its own for the merger sufficient to outweigh these difficulties; and it is most likely that the prospect will be in a much stronger position in the merger negotiations and implementation.

12.2.4 *Economies of risk*

I have explored elsewhere the difficulties of achieving economies of scale in legal practice (see paragraph 8.3). Indeed, firms often find that expenses per fee-earner increase as they grow, and profit margins fall (cf. paragraphs 30.2.3 and 30.2.4). With greater sustained leverage, however, profits per partner can still continue to rise (cf. paragraph 28.4). The result is that the unit costs of the firm, measured as cost per hour of production, increase — a diseconomy of scale. It might be that there will be some duplicated costs in the two merging firms that can be stripped out following a merger. But these are usually one-off savings that are often absorbed by the additional costs that any merger will bring (cf. paragraph 12.5.1.1), and are rarely a long-term strategic basis for a merger.

However, the increasing need for investments and the escalating costs and risks of expansion may well be shared as a result of a merger, and so allow the merged firm to achieve something that neither constituent firm could have achieved on its own. These are economies of risk or scope — sharing the costs and risks of further development or diversification. Although there should be a principal strategic reason for the development or diversification, one of the other subsidiary strategic reasons for a merger may well be to broaden the capital base available to the combined practices that would not be available to them individually. This will allow investment in new practice areas, people, offices, premises, or technology. It may also help to diversify the financial risk associated with the dependence of one or both of the constituent firms on a small number of clients, a type of work, an industry, or on one or more key partners.

12.3 Contemplating a Merger

A firm that seeks to initiate a merger should first of all have established its strategic reasons for doing so. It should then develop a reasonably detailed profile of its own firm looking principally at its know-how profile and its financial profile. The purpose of these profiles is to portray the firm in a *realistic* light. If the merger negotiations are successful, partners will have to work together in a new firm: there is no point — and much danger — in being 'economical with the truth'. Of course, the full picture may not emerge until later in the negotiations through the selective release of increasingly sensitive information. If the merger does not go ahead, the two firms may well remain competitors, so the innermost secrets are unlikely to be divulged until it is clear that a merger is possible in principle. However, selective release, on the one hand, and deception or distortion on the other, are not the same thing.

12.3.1 The know-how profile

This could also be described as a practice and people profile. It should describe:

(a) the firm's history and current position in the marketplace;
(b) its principal clients;
(c) its expertise by practice area;
(d) the number, experience and degree of competence of its people (professional, managerial, and support);
(e) a description of the work actually done (as opposed to the descriptions in brochures and other marketing materials!);
(f) a description of the firm's fee-earning and management structure;
(g) a statement of the firm's culture and values — including the firm's work ethic, the degree of autonomy allowed, and approaches to training and development and to remuneration; and
(h) a statement of the firm's strategic reasons for seeking a merger.

12.3.2 The financial profile

Using financial indicators (see chapter 30), a firm should develop a detailed financial profile, showing the current position and recent trends. Depending on the availability of information and the ease of processing it, as well as giving a picture of the firm as a whole, the profile might also show indicators and trends for different departments and practice areas, offices, and types of work (or client base served).

12.3.3 The target profile

Having put together its own profile, a firm should also create an outline profile of the attributes and make-up of the sort of firm it would like to merge with in order to realise its strategic ambitions. This profile can become a useful tool for weeding out merger prospects and a checklist that can be used as the investigations and negotiations progress.

12.4 Negotiating and Evaluating a Potential Merger

12.4.1 The merger team

In small firms, it may be necessary (or at least desirable) to involve all partners in merger meetings, and possibly the negotiations. In medium-sized and larger firms, the partners (or management) should appoint a special merger group or committee. Their function is to investigate, coordinate, negotiate and recommend.

At an early stage, the group or committee should establish and agree with the merger prospect a plan or process for the exchange and evaluation of information, and a timetable for meetings. Depending on the size of the constituent firms, and the complexity and time involved in the investigation and negotiations, it may even be necessary to appoint subgroups or subcommittees. These are common for investigating and considering separately economics and finance, management structure, partnership issues, practice areas, administration and technology, and business development and marketing.

In addition to discussing the issues listed above that might be considered by a subgroup, the principal functions of the merger team are:

(a)   to set (and keep) the merger in a strategic context;
(b)   to look carefully at people issues (such as values, personalities, work ethic, resistance, loss of autonomy, reactions to changes in the size, structure or operations of the firm)
(c)   to consider the best legal structure for the merged firm;
(d)   to ensure that the benefits of the merger outweigh the disadvantages; and
(e)   to think how to 'sell' the merger to the other partners.

The merger team must also decide what to tell whom, how and when — including who in each firm will deal with media enquiries and how. It is important for both firms to give consistent messages, both internally and externally.

12.4.2 Seeing the wood for the trees

It can be easy to be carried away with the idea of a merger and so to overlook some of the principles and detail which will determine success or failure; it can also be easy to become bogged down in the minutiae of merger negotiations and lose track of what it is all about.

Negotiating and evaluating a merger is a time-consuming and often difficult process. It should not be rushed; but, equally, both firms need to maintain their enthusiasm for the idea and the momentum of the process.

It is pointless to be didactic about a process. Merger negotiators and consultants often have their own preferences, but there is no right or wrong method — except that it is always wrong to analyse the merger to stagnation and despondency or to press ahead without any due diligence. But these are unlikely extremes.

Any merger assessment will entail agreeing on the strategic objectives of the merged firm (that is, why the firms consider merging at all), the principles on which the constituent firms will come together (that is, the basis on which the merged firm will be built), and the details of implementation (that is, how the merged firm will happen).

As such, there is an element of investigation and verification required in order to establish the compatibility of the two firms — in terms of clients, practice areas, people, finances, and values. Compatibility does not necessarily mean being identical or even comparable (cf. paragraph 11.7). In some areas — such as clients and practice areas — the firms may need to be different in order to create strategic 'fit'; in others — such as people, values and finance — they may well need to be comparable. Once these issues are dealt with, and there is a basis of compatibility on which to move forward, the merger process shifts from examining two constituent firms to establishing one new one.

At this point, a number of potential 'deal-breakers' may be apparent. Typically, these include: differences in the firm's economic performance or capitalisation; differences in profits or profit-sharing (sometimes this is about the philosophy of profit-sharing — seniority or merit (see paragraphs 37.3 and 37.4) — but usually it is about the relative amounts of profit-shares!); client conflicts; the name of the merged firm; unfunded retirement liabilities to partners; or personality differences or conflicts. Some people prefer to address these deal-breakers as soon as possible, on the basis that if they cannot be resolved the merger will not happen and it is therefore pointless to waste time negotiating other details. Others take the view that, if the rest of the merger deal can be put together, partners in the constituent firms can see the prospective benefits and are then more likely to be amenable to resolving some of the more fundamental issues.

Again, there is no right or wrong advice. My own preference is to deal with these points as soon as possible: my objective is to encourage the firms to think about the creation and reality of the new firm as quickly as possible, and to move away from two-firm thinking. But this is a judgment that has to be made in the circumstances of each prospective merger. If there are fundamental differences in values and lifestyle, there may be no sensible or realistic basis for a successful merger. It is better to realise this sooner than later. And I agree with Malone and Mudrick (1992, page 26): "Nothing neutralizes egos"!

12.4.3 *Taking stock of the trees*

Details do have to be investigated and negotiated. The following issues frequently arise for discussion and resolution.

12.4.3.1 *Client and practice area fit*
The evaluation of practice areas should be conducted in accordance with the principles outlined in paragraph 11.3. It is in every sense a strategic evaluation. Often the most difficult issues to handle and resolve are those that concern a range of client conflicts (cf. paragraph 11.4.1(b)).

12.4.3.2   *People fit*

Assessing the compatibility of people in two firms is a difficult but essential process. The following are likely to be the main concerns:

(a)   Fear of the unknown and of change: this is an inevitable human reaction to merger (as it is to any fundamental change in an organisation: for further discussion, see chapter 27). People will feel insecure about their roles in the merged firm, and will have concerns about their future prospects — either to retain their jobs or to advance in the new firm. Fee-earners may worry that the clients on whom much of their work is dependent may decide to instruct other firms as a result of the merger (because of conflicts or the dislike of being a client of a larger practice). And people at all levels (including partners) may well be concerned that people they do not presently know will have control or authority over them in the future.

(b)   Personality clashes: these manifest themselves most acutely where some partners in the constituent firms know each other and declare that they will not work with so-and-so, do not respect them, do not rate the quality of their work, do not like their style, would not admit them as a partner in the present firm, and so on. Depending on the relative importance (power and influence: see paragraph 24.3) of these individuals, and their degree of open-mindedness — or forgiveness! — this issue may become a deal-breaker (see paragraph 12.4.2).

(c)   Different approaches to human resource issues: if one firm treats its people as assets to be nurtured and developed, and the other as expendable commodities to be exploited and controlled, the difference may be unbridgeable. If one firm carefully plans its human resource requirements and development, and values and respects its personnel management, and the other does not (and will not), the firms are incompatible. If one firm has successful and harmonious staff relations and low staff turnover, and the other does not, the warning signs are there to be heeded. Similarly, there may be differences in approach to recruitment, induction, training, supervision, appraisal, and promotion, as well as in the comparability of pay and benefits.

(d)   Differences in work ethic: the constituent firms must compare their standard working days for professional and support staff: significant differences in average chargeable, and non-chargeable, hours may represent incompatible priorities and approaches to work ethic and quality-of-life issues — provided, of course, that lower average chargeable hours in one firm are due to work ethic rather than the absence of sufficient chargeable work (a market, or marketing and selling, problem) or the hoarding of work by certain people (a delegation and management problem).

(e)   Different approaches to underperformance: some firms are aggressive and some passive in dealing with this issue; some are supportive and some are ruthless. Again, differences of approach in similar circumstances could indicate the potential for problems further down the line.

(f)   Different attitudes to accountability: these are usually differences of degree rather than of fundamental importance. However, staff who are used to individual accountability can find a transition to a team or firm-wide approach difficult to come to terms with. Equally, staff who have not really been held accountable for their actions or performance at all, or to any significant degree, may find any form of accountability problematic!

12.4.3.3   Financial fit

Financial analysis must clearly be a vital part of the merger process. Assessing financial compatibility will be important, as will preparing financial projections for the merged firm (see paragraph 12.5.1). The use and comparison of indicators and an examination of the trends in these indicators in both firms (see chapter 30) can be particularly instructive.

One of the important initial considerations must be to compare like with like. For example, adjustments may need to be made for different accounting periods, the use of different bases of accounting (cash, bills delivered, accrual), different billing and collection policies, and different policies for depreciation, tax reserves, the inclusion and valuation of work-in-progress, and drawings and distributions. In these days of incorporation, there may also be differences caused by one firm being incorporated, or using a service company for its support functions.

Beyond this, there may also need to be an investigation and discussion of off-balance-sheet items (particularly payments to former partners and retirement arrangements for current partners), and of professional indemnity issues (the firms should exchange details of their claims histories, and of any actual or potential claims). Approaches to capitalisation should also be discussed: differences of approach can create difficulties if, for example, one firm relies on partners' contributions and the other relies more on overdraft or debt.

Merging two financially weak firms does not create a strong merged firm, and may in fact simply double the size of the problems. The merger of two financially strong firms is more likely to be successful, particularly where the strengths are comparable. Merging a strong firm and a weak one may or may not work, depending on the strategic reasons for the merger and the attitudes of each of the constituent firms in moving forward.

12.5   The Shape of the Merged Firm

The creation of a merged firm raises all the issues of strategy, structure and ownership considered in this book. Many of the messages in other chapters therefore need to be taken on board at the time of a merger. A number of issues will need to be addressed in anticipation of the integration of the two firms.

12.5.1   Financial projections

In order to make an informed decision about whether a merger is likely to be successful financially, realistic projections for the combined firm will need to be prepared. Unfortunately, it is difficult to project sensibly more than 12 months into a merger, although many of the intended benefits and effects of integration may well not be felt until the second year. However, reasonable assumptions will have to be made, and it could make sense to prepare alternative projections based on both conservative and aggressive assumptions.

12.5.1.1 Budget

The starting point for a budget for the merged firm is to take 'standstill' budgets from each of the constituent firms assuming that the merger was not going to take place. These figures can then be combined and adjusted to take account of the merger. The adjustments would strip out duplicated costs (for example, in relation to premises that can be offloaded, or positions that are no longer needed), as well as the costs of the merger itself (including the lost fee income of partners involved in the merger negotiations and its implementation, the costs of accountants and other advisers, etc.). There may be other costs arising from the merger, such as:

(a)   Equalisation costs: in multi-office, or multi-location, firms there may be salary differences between people of equal position or seniority. If the salaries are to be equalised, there will be an additional cost (there rarely seems to be a reduction!) of doing so. Similarly, the constituent firms may have operated different benefits packages — either in the range of benefits provided, or in the extent to which they are supported (for example, free lunch facilities or only subsidised facilities; different contribution levels for pensions; different values of cars that can be acquired at the same level in the firm).

(b)   Consequential costs: as a result of any merger, there will be additional costs created by the need for new stationery, new brochures and other new or replacement marketing materials, publicity costs, accounting and consulting fees, and additional travel costs where the new firm has more offices than either of the two previous ones.

(c)   Integration costs: these may be costs associated with office moves or refurbishment, replacement or upgraded technology, and the direct and opportunity costs of meetings and social events that will be required to ensure integration (see paragraph 12.7.1).

12.5.1.2 Cash flow projection

The subject of cash flow projection is dealt with in paragraph 29.2.2. For a merger, the projection should be based on the income and expense budget (see paragraph 12.5.1.1), adjusted for depreciation (an expense, but does not involve the payment of cash), the acquisition of fixed assets (a cash outgoing, but not a deductible expense), the proceeds or repayment of borrowings, and contributions or withdrawals of partners' capital.

12.5.1.3 Balance sheet projection

As with the budget, the balance sheet projection should be based on the combined 'standstill' balance sheets of the constituent firms. Adjustments will be needed to reflect the consequences of new borrowing or the repayment of previous debt, the equalisation of partners' capital accounts, the introduction of capital from new partners as at the merger date, and the effects of the departure of former partners who do not continue with the merged firm.

12.5.2 *Other issues*

In addition to projections, a number of other issues will also need to be discussed and resolved. Typically, these will include:

(a) *Duplicated positions.* This more usually arises in relation to managerial or support functions. If the constituent firms each have a practice manager, a librarian, a cashier, or head of a certain department, and the like, and only one will be needed in the merged firm, then clearly decisions have to be made. However, most mergers create extra work, and it may not always follow that two *jobs* are not available. Expansion of the firm following the merger may also create a need for more staff in the future. It does not inevitably follow, therefore, that duplicated staff have to leave, even if duplicated posts can only be filled by one of them.

(b) *Post-merger invoices and fees received.* Once the merger takes place, the firms must decide what happens in respect of invoices issued after the merger for work carried out by one of the constituent firms before it, and in respect of money received after the merger date for invoices issued before it. There may be unanticipated premiums payable in respect of work valued at cost, and special arrangements may be needed for conditional fee work (either resulting in a write-off or a premium on standard value). In some cases, firms will pool these post-merger invoices and receipts, and in others they will not; or they may pool subject to the exclusion of fees on certain matters.

(c) *Billing and collection policies.* If the constituent firms operate different billing and collection policies and procedures (cf. paragraph 29.2.1), they must agree what their approach will be after the merger, since there will need to be uniformity. The decision may result in the need for transitional arrangements.

(d) *Leases.* The constituent firms must determine their space requirements for the merged firm. This may mean moving people around in the short term, or seeking a new office that is large enough for the combined practices. A move will depend on the availability of suitable accommodation and financial resources; if one of the firms vacates existing space, there will also be issues of subletting, assignment, continuing obligations or liabilities, and so on.

(e) *Professional indemnity insurance.* Responsibility for pre-merger acts resulting in later claims will need to be agreed, and the new firm may wish to establish a contingency reserve.

(f) *Technology.* The merger teams should have examined the range and use of technology in each firm, and its compatibility. Part of the discussions leading up to merger should also assess the need for integration, upgrading or replacement.

(g) *Profit-sharing*. A new profit-sharing system will need to be agreed. If it is anything other than a pure equality or seniority system (see paragraph 37.3), there may be some difficulty in establishing confidence in those who make the performance or merit assessments and profit allocations. In smaller firms, it may be that the respective leaders from the constituent firms will be able to work together sufficiently well to alleviate any difficulties. In larger firms, though, it may be necessary *for the first year only* to maintain separate assessment and allocation of profit-shares. In any event, it often makes sense to keep a bonus pool of profit (even if there is not normally one) to allow the new leadership and management to compensate for any anomalies that arise during the transition from two firms to one.

(h) *Capitalisation*. Any differences in approach to financing the firms will need to be resolved, and again transitional arrangements may be required. As part of this debate, the merger teams will need to establish the merged firm's requirements for fixed and working capital (cf. paragraphs 29.4 and 29.5), and agree how it will raise the required amounts. The new firm must ensure that it has the proper mix of debt and partners' funds to be able to implement the strategy on which the merger is predicated: this may well depend on the current capital structure of the constituent firms, and on the availability of additional funds from partners and from third-party lenders.

(i) *Decision-making*. Another important issue is to determine the basis on which partners in the merged firm will make its decisions at partner level. The issues of voting participation, proportion of votes required to reach decisions (simple, special majority, weighted votes, unanimity, etc.) are discussed in the context of partnership in paragraph 33.5.

12.6 Reaching a Decision

Although at the end of the negotiations and deliberations there may be a single vote in each constituent firm to determine whether or not it proceeds with the merger, the process of getting there is likely to be the result of a series of decisions, perhaps made by different people at different times but all of which affect the outcome.

12.6.1 Keeping partners informed

The extent to which partners need to be kept informed will, in the first place, depend on the extent to which all partners have or have not been involved in the discussions and negotiations (see paragraph 12.4.1). Second, the flow of information to partners during the merger discussions will also depend on the firm's normal process and culture of communication. In large firms, there will simply be too many issues for all partners to be involved in the process and consulted at every stage. However, the merger team will need to be holding meetings to inform partners, to gain feedback, to test reactions on certain issues and approaches, and to build a consensus. Irrespective of the method, the merger team need to communicate along the way to allow an informed, final decision to be made by partners.

In some mergers, the whole process is kept a secret from the majority of partners until the deal is negotiated and ready to be put before them. In very large firms, this may be necessary, given the scale of the exercise and the market sensitivity involved. In other firms, there needs to be a very good reason for not informing partners of the process and progress.

12.6.2   A merger notebook

When the deal is negotiated and partners are required to consider and vote on it, Malone and Mudrick suggest the creation of a merger notebook (1992, pages 70–2). I have always found this a good idea in principle. The purpose of the notebook is to gather in one place all the relevant comparative information and projections, including (Malone and Mudrick 1992, page 71 and exhibit 22):

(a)   profiles of the constituent firms,
(b)   detailed comparative financial analysis of the two firms and projections for the merged firm,
(c)   details of client base, principal clients and possible conflicts,
(e)   practice area descriptions,
(f)   business development and marketing opportunities,
(g)   the terms of the proposed merger.

In smaller firms, a detailed notebook may be a counsel of perfection, but some statement of the complete package is still sensible. It is likely that the partners in a smaller firm will have been more involved and informed: the contents of the notebook may therefore be dependent on how much has been previously communicated to partners. Nevertheless, it is still helpful to gather in one place the fundamental information on which the merger decision should be made. The partners then know that they are all making the decision on certain common information.

The notebook should be distributed to partners about a week before they vote on the merger. Depending on the previous process, it may be necessary or desirable to hold one or more follow-up meetings with partners to allow any outstanding questions to be addressed. Attendance at such meetings should be optional, and their purpose is to inform and explain, not to relive the negotiations or to reopen negotiated issues.

12.6.3   Voting

The voting requirements to approve a merger in each partnership will be a matter for the existing partnership agreements of the constituent firms. If the merger team's investigation, negotiation and communication during the merger process have been effective, the vote will be a formality. If there is any need for a debate, or there is a close vote on the approval, this can be divisive and is usually an indication that the merger team has moved too far ahead of the partners, has not been sensitive enough to partners' concerns, or has not involved partners enough in the merger process (Malone and Mudrick 1992, page 72).

The vote at both firms should be scheduled to take place on the same day at the same time (or as close together as possible). This will mean that one firm will not be influenced in its own deliberations by the known reactions of the other.

Once the vote has been taken and a merger agreed, the merger teams must draw up a separate merger agreement to give effect to the new firm. Sometimes, the constituent firms amend their existing partnership agreements to give effect to their decision. Usually, there will be a new partnership agreement for the merged firm. But then the hard work really begins.

12.7 Post-merger Implementation

12.7.1 Cultural integration and communication

If a merger is about putting two groups of people together (cf. paragraph 12.1), then implementing a merger is about integrating those two groups of people. This process should begin as soon as possible — and often before the merger itself takes place. So, once any deal-breakers have been resolved (see paragraph 12.4.2), the firms can start socialising, building trust, and so developing a new culture. In fact, it is impossible to become one firm unless there is only one dominant culture. This is a major challenge that will take some time — possibly years. The most difficult mergers to integrate are those involving firms of similar size (where the merged firm will have no dominant existing culture), firms in different towns or cities (where it is difficult to get people together), and firms in different offices in the same town or city.

Partners must be committed to making the merger work (the use of 'negative power' can be particularly insidious and destructive: cf. paragraph 24.3.2.2(c)). Partners should be careful not to push 'old firm' thinking and not to develop an 'us and them' attitude: if they do not do it, it is more difficult for others in the firm to do so. Partners and management should therefore set an example and lead from the top.

The integration should be carefully planned. It should cover structural, physical, procedural, and social integration. Partners need to encourage fee-earners and support staff from the original firms to work together; and to encourage both work-related and social meetings involving professional and support staff. They must also give people time to adapt to the change in structure, procedures, values, etc. (cf. chapter 27).

Part of this process is for partners, and especially the leaders and managers, to spend a lot of time communicating. Successful integration takes enormous time and energy, and the management team needs to be visible and available: it is easy to become absorbed in the detail of implementation, but the needs of others should not be overlooked. Many more people will not have been involved in the merger process, and will not have made the decision to merge. As Malone and Mudrick write (1992, pages 79–80): "A good rule during the transition period is to give people more information rather than less. If management is open with information, people will feel more secure. In addition, management should actively seek ideas and provide an easy way for people to express their concerns."

12.7.2 Practice integration

The key to a successful merger is being able to practise law together: this means integrating the practice areas and fee-earners into distinct groups, sharing clients with each other, and developing new business together. Part of the difficulty, of course, is that the new firm will need to continue serving clients with minimal disruption.

The new firm will have to work together to create a new departmental or practice group structure, and to decide on the degree of centralisation in practice area management, and whether the firm needs to relocate any fee-earners. It will also have to agree or confirm work acceptance procedures, as well as policies for the allocation of work, managing workloads, quality control, delegation and supervision, departmental meetings and training. These issues are discussed in chapters 19, 20 and 21.

12.7.3 Management and administrative integration

Often one of the principal issues here is the need for a transitional structure. The establishment of a new structure is rarely a merger-breaker, but can certainly be a source of low morale, confusion, misinformation, and staff turnover (Malone and Mudrick (1992), page 97). In general, firms would be better advised to avoid a transitional structure if they can, though one may be necessary in a larger merger. It is therefore important for the firm to consider the issues carefully: they are addressed in chapters 14, 15 and 16.

A review of systems, procedures and administrative staffing will be needed, as well as of the capacity, integration, compatibility, new purchase, and upgrading of technology, and its inter-office use.

Where the merged firm practises out of more than one office (either temporarily or permanently), it should accept the logistics and costs of its geography. Integration will not happen unless people in the firm are moved around and start working together.

12.7.4 Marketing and publicity

One of the major challenges in a merger is communication with clients. A distinction will probably need to be drawn between key clients and other clients: indeed, the key clients may well be consulted as part of the merger deliberations to determine whether or not they find it acceptable. After the event, at least the key clients should receive personal visits from the appropriate client partners — perhaps even with the managing partner and a partner from the 'other' firm. Certainly, every client and referral source should receive either a visit, a personal letter, or a brochure.

Internally, partners should also ensure that fee-earners are kept up to date with success stories, client introductions, and new targets for the merged firms. It is important to educate the fee-earners about the combined capabilities of the new firm, and to inculcate good feelings about the success of the merger.

The new firm must also have a plan for dealing with the media — whether general, legal, business, or trade media. For firms practising out of different offices, different approaches to the media may need to be taken in each location. Partners and staff should be given instructions about how to deal with media enquiries, usually by being told clearly to whom the enquiries should be referred in any office. When the firm is ready, it should also issue an information package to its media contacts, including a press release, fact sheets about the constituent firms and the merged firm, a brochure if there is one, articles about the constituent firms and any advance publicity about the merger, and so on (see Malone and Mudrick 1992, exhibits 24, 25 and 26).

12.7.5 *Partners*

The management of the merged firm should not assume that all of the partners are happy and comfortable with the merger simply because they voted for it. They need care and attention just as much as employed fee-earners and staff.

Chapter 13

STRATEGIES FOR INTERNATIONAL LEGAL PRACTICE

13.1 Introduction

For many firms, the reality or prospect of international work is increasingly appealing. For most, it will represent a major strategic step which may well change the boundaries of the firm (cf. paragraph 10.1) and will usually involve a considerable financial commitment. This chapter sets out to present a framework for the analysis and discussion of international legal practice, particularising many of the issues discussed in chapters 4 and 11. In so doing, it raises the questions that any law firm embarking on internationalisation should ask itself and answer. Although I shall often use 'international' in a generic sense, there will be some occasions when I use it only to denote the practice by a firm of its own domestic (or 'home') law — though it may do that both on its home territory and on foreign soil. When firms practise both their home law and foreign (or 'local') law — and again whether at home or abroad — I shall use the expression 'multinational practice'. Of course, the development of multinational partnerships will make it increasingly difficult to say what a firm's 'home' law is.

Academic writing in this area is rare (but see Flood 1996).

13.1.1 Many strategies for international legal practice

Many law firms have some international element to their practice: this does not necessarily make them 'international law firms'. For some firms, there will be no foreign offices or alliances, but there will be a commitment to developing international work from the home office. In fact, for many firms, strengthening their home base will be the most successful strategy for international legal practice. For others, the strategy may encompass a number of foreign offices, either alone or in cooperation with other firms. The choice of strategy will usually involve considering the boundaries of the firm (cf. paragraph 10.1), since the choices normally come down to independent contracting with foreign lawyers, internalising through the establishment of a foreign office, or networking through the creation of an affiliation or alliance (cf. paragraph 6.1).

Table 13.1 shows that there are a variety of ways of practising law internationally. In essence, international practice strategies are either competitive or cooperative. The competitive approach means that a firm will build its own practice (in whichever is the best way for that firm — internalisation) without entering into affiliations or similar arrangements. The cooperative approach (networking or independent contracting) implies working with lawyers in other countries to achieve the strategic objective. For most firms, one of these strategies will predominate; but they are not mutually exclusive. In penetrating a new market, a firm may decide for ease of access (or because of local professional restrictions) to enter into an affiliation or joint venture arrangement.

The race for domination of the international legal market is really between the larger English and American law firms. The review of law firms in the October 1996 issue of the *International Financial Law Review* (page 16) shows that 31 of the 50 largest law firms in the world are American, and 12 are English. Those US firms have a total of 167 offices abroad (an average of 5.4 per firm), whereas the English firms together have 100 offices abroad (an average of 8.3 per firm). If Baker & McKenzie is excluded from the US figures, there are 120 overseas offices (an average of 4 per firm). Further, of the 10 largest law firms in the world, six are English and four are American, and in all there are nine English firms with more than 10% of their lawyers abroad compared with six US firms. However, the American firms are stronger in Europe than the English firms are in the US. As the IFLR survey shows, there are more large US firms than English ones, which should also suggest a greater potential for international expansion. The US firms are also being more aggressive in London by recruiting English lawyers; very few English firms have sought to recruit US lawyers in America. The battle is truly joined!

13.1.2 All are profitable . . . and all are unprofitable

In choosing between the various strategic approaches to international legal practice, economics must play a part. Unfortunately, although there appear to be some emerging trends, and guidance can be given, there are no absolutes. For each strategy, or combination that you care to devise, there is almost certainly a law firm somewhere that is making that strategy or combination work profitably, and another that is not. Perhaps the only sure advice is that a one-lawyer office in Tokyo is not likely to be profitable!

It would also appear that the increasing gulf between the largest London and US firms and the rest of the profession is being emphasised by their international practices, which in turn reflects their ability to respond to the globalisation of business (cf. paragraph 1.3.1).

	COMPETITIVE, INTEGRATED STRATEGY	COOPERATIVE STRATEGY
DOMESTIC LAW FIRM	INTERNATIONAL practice from HOME OFFICE Home law only	INTERNATIONAL practice from home office through NETWORK OR AFFILIATION Home law only; mutual referrals
INTERNATIONAL LAW FIRM	OPEN OWN FOREIGN OFFICE A. INTERNATIONAL practice Home law only B. MULTINATIONAL practice Home law and local law	ALLIANCE with joint venture FOREIGN OFFICE A. INTERNATIONAL practice Home laws of alliance firms only B. MULTINATIONAL practice Home laws of alliance firms and local law
MULTINATIONAL LAW FIRM	MULTINATIONAL PARTNERSHIP Home law = local law	PARALLEL PARTNERSHIPS Home laws of partner firms and local law

Table 13.1 International practice strategies

13.1.3 *Economic success depends on business soundness*

Inevitably, the financial success of any strategy will depend on whether the adoption of that strategy was in itself a sensible business decision. Simply following clients may not be sufficiently sound. Clients can be very good at hinting that there might be work for a firm in another country if it had an office there; they can be equally oblique in delivering work to that office when a firm has incurred the expenses of opening and moving lawyers there.

Detailed analysis of business opportunities, their value and cost, is therefore an essential step in making money out of the strategy a firm decides to adopt. There are no short-cuts to this process (see chapters 4 and 11). Unfortunately, too few lawyers are able to provide any sound analysis of their client base, sources of work, volume and profitability of different types of work, and so on. In short, they simply do not understand their underlying or core business — even domestically, let alone internationally. There is no point in asking 'What should we do?' without having first obtained basic information that allows informed decisions to be made.

13.1.4 *Invest in underlying business and execution of strategy*

Ultimately, therefore, profitability will depend on understanding and developing the underlying international business of the firm, and in the proper execution of the strategy it chooses. Both are necessary: one without the other will run the risk of jeopardising the firm's success.

Some of the benefits that a firm might expect from international practice are:

(a)   guarding against the loss of domestic clients to other domestic competitors with international practices who could service those clients abroad;

(b)   attracting other domestic (and foreign) clients for whom the firm's ability to service their needs abroad is attractive;

(c)   the possibility of cross-border referrals for all of the firm's offices and practice areas;

(d)   the prestige of being perceived as an international firm by clients, competitors and potential recruits; and

(e)   providing opportunities for continued growth and development despite mature, competitive domestic markets (that is, to diversify some of the risks of the domestic practice: see paragraph 8.1).

Against these benefits must be considered the additional demands for management expertise and time, the possibility of increasing the incidence of conflicts of interest, the difficulty of maintaining quality and consistency in a geographically diverse practice, and increased demands on the firm's financial capital (cf. paragraph 8.6).

13.1.5 *Long-term profit based on serving the interests of clients, not lawyers*

As with all aspects of legal practice, long-term success as we approach the millennium will be based on serving the interests of clients. The days when a law firm could be organised, run and financed for the convenience of its lawyers (and particularly of its partners) have disappeared. The legal 'global village' is nearly complete. Competing in the international marketplace will mean meeting the expectations of clients who are themselves sophisticated operators in various parts of the world. But this does not mean opening offices everywhere. For example, it is on the basis of meeting client expectations that Slaughter and May claims to have been able to maintain its client base without opening offices in as many locations as its immediate English and American competitors (Chambers 1996, page 24).

13.2 Underlying Business

In order for a firm to understand its underlying international business, it needs to address certain aspects of both the globalisation of business generally, and the globalisation of its own practice specifically (cf. chapter 11). This will mean asking some searching questions, and only being satisfied with analytical rather than intuitive responses: too much is at stake to do otherwise.

13.2.1 *Inbound or outbound work*

Is the firm advising foreign clients on the home law implications of their activities in the firm's home country (inbound work), or do its home clients want advice on the home (or foreign) legal issues arising from their ventures abroad (outbound work)? Perhaps it is doing both, but the most appropriate strategic responses to inbound and outbound work are not necessarily the same. For example, an office may be appropriate for dealing with outbound work, though alliances might be needed for foreign local law issues.

13.2.2 *Volume of work*

For inbound and outbound work, a firm should understand what volume of work in each category it has been handling. This should be measured by volume of new matters and fees generated for as long a period as the information is available. In many firms, this information is purely anecdotal, coming from partners who fancy themselves as international advisers and who deliberately or inadvertently 'talk up' the possible volume and value of opportunities. Look for hard data and trends that will give some guidance about the way in which the firm's international work is moving.

13.2.3 Sources of work

Look at where the international work comes from, and see which sources are the most fruitful. Is work coming from existing clients increasing their international activities and using the firm because it is their law firm? Is work being referred by foreign lawyers, other home lawyers, banks and accountants, or other bodies? Are new clients being brought in by partners making foreign trips, attending conferences, and the like?

Look at the geographical origin and destination of clients' activities: in which parts of the world are they most active? Which countries are producing most volume of work, the highest level of fee income, or the greatest potential for growth and profit?

Much international work is transactional, which makes it difficult for a firm to secure a flow of continuing work — especially without a local presence or practice. If referrals from foreign lawyers are a principal source of overseas work, a firm must also consider carefully the balance of referrals: will they still exist if the firm opens an office abroad, or if it enters into a closer relationship (such as an alliance) with one of the referral sources?

13.2.4 Markets

Based on a geographical analysis, a firm can begin to consider which international markets it should devote attention to, and what their order of priority should be. It can also begin to assess what level of commitment or involvement it should be contemplating. The firm should investigate the costs of doing business in those countries, as well as the professional rules there which govern the activities of foreign lawyers (e.g., whether a firm can open an office to practise even its home law, whether it can recruit local lawyers, whether there are immigration rules or local capital requirements that it must comply with). The firm should also consider whether any country in which it might intend to set up is a net importer or exporter of legal services: this often affects the ease with which lawyers can establish themselves and practise successfully, as well as giving some indication of the size and volume of the market.

The firm should also analyse its client base to see if it is serving any particular type or types of business or industry (e.g., capital markets, automotive, pharmaceutical, distribution, construction). If it is, it should examine the international trends for these industries and their levels of activity (e.g., emerging capital markets in South America, construction work in Central Europe).

Some industries are now almost by definition global (e.g., shipping and air transport, information technology and telecommunications, pharmaceuticals), and some are not; some industries may have global competitors, and some (even though the industry is active globally — construction, for example) may not; some may be more or less active in the future.

The development of free trade areas, and the liberalisation of world trade that followed the successful conclusion of the GATT negotiations, are leading to the emergence of more common standards for goods and services, further deregulation and open government procurement, greater fiscal harmony and reforms in taxation and tariffs. The integration of economies in Central and Eastern Europe into those of the West (particularly the European Union) is accelerating these processes in Europe. Interestingly, the demise of the 'superstate', such as the European Union and even the United States, is foreseen by some (see, for example, Davidson and Rees-Mogg 1997).

A great deal of international legal practice is founded on banking and finance. Accordingly, the leading international law firms have offices in the major financial centres — London, New York, and Tokyo. They also tend to establish presences in the secondary capital markets (e.g., Hong Kong, Singapore, Paris; Frankfurt has not been successful for many firms). The development of the whole banking and financial services industry is therefore likely to be of critical importance in the continued evolution and success of international legal practice. The greatest challenge facing the financial services industry is operating in an increasingly borderless environment.

13.2.5 *Legal work*

Next, the firm should examine the types of legal work that it is engaged in internationally (e.g., banking and finance, joint ventures, competition, intellectual property, environmental). Again, it should examine the hard data, trends and expectations for these practice areas in the parts of the world in which the firm's clients are active.

The international practice of the leading law firms is based primarily on corporate work, mergers and acquisitions, cross-border transactions, and global financial products. For some firms, there may also be other specialist activities (e.g., shipping work in Hong Kong, construction work in the Middle East and Eastern Europe). Environmental law, entertainment and intellectual property work are expected to increase both in Europe and Asia. There is virtually no litigation being handled abroad (although there is certainly litigation which has cross-border elements and implications): one reason for this is that just about every jurisdiction in the world reserves to local lawyers the right to conduct litigation and to appear in court. This does, of course, increase the need for multinational cooperation between lawyers in cross-border litigation

Many of the leading English firms believe that because, for historical reasons, English law is the governing law of many overseas transactions, this gives them a competitive advantage as against US and mainland European firms (except in transactions where there is otherwise no compelling reason for one law rather than another to be the governing law of the transaction). Some US firms believe this, too, and part of their international strategy is that, on the basis that English law is most likely to prevail in Europe and Asia, they should be developing an English component to their practices, either by recruiting English lawyers or through a merger with an English firm.

For most law firms practising overseas, there is a heavy emphasis on finance (including international finance and banking, capital markets, project financing, privatisation, insurance and tax). Certainly in countries with mature economies, a finance practice is regarded as a must. The most successful international law firms have strong financial practices at least in New York and London. In emerging economies, such as those in Central and Eastern Europe and in South America, the emphasis may well be more on project financing as they build (or rebuild) their infrastructure.

The question of whether or not to practise local law in another jurisdiction will probably have as much to do with the type of law covered as with the local regulations governing the ability to practise. Some areas of the activity of law firms, although they may involve acting abroad for home clients or for foreign clients, may not entail practising local law. For example, in some transactions, lawyers may be invited to undertake a coordinating role even though the transaction is effected in one or more jurisdictions in which those lawyers are not (and cannot become) entitled to practise (see Chambers 1996, page 24).

13.2.6 *Conflicts*

As a firm grows and extends its client base, domestically as well as internationally, the likelihood of conflicts of interest arising increases significantly. Equally important, however, are not legal conflicts but business conflicts between clients (see paragraph 11.4.1(b)). Paradoxically, if a firm increases its expertise and experience of serving clients in certain industries, there is an increased risk that clients in that industry will choose other lawyers. Conflicts of all kinds may represent the greatest constraint on international growth.

13.2.7 *Resources*

Having analysed the underlying business with an essentially external perspective, the firm can finally turn its attention to trying to match its resources to the likely needs of its clients or the perceived opportunities in new markets (cf. paragraphs 4.5 and 4.6).

Does the firm have lawyers with the necessary legal, industry and geographical know-how? If not, are there any who are willing to develop that know-how, or can the firm credibly attract people who have it (cf. paragraph 9.4)? Does the firm have the financial strength and culture to see its strategy through? Recessions have shown how quickly financial priorities need to change, and how transient partner support can be. Any successful international strategy will demand significant amounts of management and other partner time. Is the firm willing to devote what is necessary? Are all partners prepared to support the development or extension of its international practice in the way suggested by the analysis and strategy (cf. paragraphs 9.3, 9.4 and 9.5)? If not, the firm should not even start.

13.3 Execution

13.3.1 *Own office*

Currently it is unlikely that a law firm can match in a foreign office the range or sophistication of work handled out of its main office. In other words, firms cannot internalise the same services or create the same degree of credible firm-specific know-how in a foreign office as it can in its main office. This may change in the future: for example, Cleary Gottlieb's Brussels and Paris offices are major practices in their own right (as are the Paris offices of a number of the leading English and American firms); and Baker & McKenzie has built its foreign structure on the basis of substantial local firms (its London office would certainly regard itself as a major English practice in its own right). But for most firms, clear choices have to be made about geography, practice areas and people.

13.3.1.1 *Home law*
Most overseas offices of law firms were originally opened to practise home law in a foreign location, either for home clients with overseas activities or for foreign clients investing into or trading within the home market. For many firms (Slaughter and May is perhaps a prime example), this has remained their international strategy. The strategic reasons for this approach seem to boil down to:

(a) Achieving greater proximity to clients — actual or prospective: some firms have opened foreign offices in order to retain clients in the home market as well as internationally. All firms find it difficult or impossible to measure the volume of inbound work generated by their foreign offices (and often ignore it in assessing the success of a foreign office or the profit-shares of partners based there).

(b) Representing expatriates abroad.

(c) Reducing the impact of significant cultural or language gaps, where home clients would prefer to deal locally abroad with home lawyers (if only as a means of communicating with local lawyers): this is true for many Asian offices of Anglo-Saxon and European firms.

(d) Seizing a market opportunity, where clients are exploring emerging new markets — as is currently the case in Central and Eastern Europe, South America and some parts of South-East Asia.

On this basis, firms have followed their clients abroad, and practised only home law using expatriate lawyers (usually on rotation). They therefore tend to advise mainly home clients, though they pick up some foreign clients with business dealings and interests in the home market; as such, they are often restricted to transactional work.

Firms who stick to this strategic approach are often considered to be part of the 'elite' in a jurisdiction; they see themselves as experts in their home law, and may appear to be concerned to preserve the purity of their non-competitive approach to international practice (and thus to maintain the flow of referral business from foreign lawyers). Indeed, it is usually a characteristic of this strategy that the firms involved seek very good relations with the local legal professions and hope to enjoy productive referral relationships. In fact, with the top names, the loss of referral work that would follow from competing by practising the local law could be significant. For the same reasons, these firms usually try not to be seen to be too close to any particular local law firm. The increasing number of alliances and affiliations is making referral relationships harder to maintain and is reducing their effectiveness.

Although some firms have adopted a home-law-only approach, a number of them have effectively strayed from it in Paris where the change in the Paris Bar rules that converted all established lawyers there into French *avocats* able to practise local law if they wish encouraged most of them (including Slaughter and May) to become local, full-service, firms. The same was often true for English firms in Hong Kong, where local law was very similar to English law.

Some firms open offices only as representative, marketing, or 'embassy' presences, not to practise law (even home law) locally but to find and feed work back to the home office. This approach to international practice is less common than it used to be and, by most firms' reckoning, is not particularly effective in the modern conditions of legal practice.

13.3.1.2 Home law and local law

Most firms that practise only home law abroad find it difficult to make money. The cost of maintaining expatriate lawyers in foreign locations through subsidised housing, cost-of-living increments and other expenses frequently exceeds an office's ability to generate work. As a result, more firms have been turning to practising local law and recruiting local lawyers wherever that is allowed. The addition of a local practice tends to improve the prospects of profitability for an office, and foreign lawyers are generally cheaper than American or English lawyers who are seconded or rotated. It is now emerging as a successful strategy. Indeed, the firms that are generally acknowledged to be successful internationally (e.g., Baker & McKenzie, Cleary Gottlieb, Clifford Chance, Coudert Brothers, Freshfields, Shearman & Sterling, White & Case) seem to have in common that they started opening foreign offices more than 20 years ago and have learned from that experience; they practise local law wherever possible; and they take great pains to integrate their overseas offices closely into the firm (often by rotating lawyers).

One of the results of this type of strategy is to shift perceptions (and the behaviour) of the firms concerned increasingly away from being an English (or American) firm with foreign offices to being an international firm with offices in many countries (see, for example, Chambers 1996, pages 26 and 30). For some firms, local offices are developed out of initial relationships with local lawyers: Baker & McKenzie has shown that a network of foreign offices can be built on this basis.

Practising local law and recruiting local lawyers raises many questions of internal culture. Some firms, such as Cleary Gottlieb, Clifford Chance, and Shearman & Sterling, guard their culture jealously and work methodically to foster and preserve it. This usually entails continuing to rotate lawyers around offices, encouraging all offices and partners to participate in the firm's management, and developing practice groups and cooperation on client matters across offices. There is a cost in doing this, but these firms have achieved a degree of integration that produces few client transition difficulties as lawyers move around. Other firms do not emphasise the integrated approach to the same degree (e.g., Baker & McKenzie), and some are looking to reduce rotation and move towards longer-term assignments of at least five years. Permanent postings are even on the agenda for those partners prepared to contemplate them.

13.3.1.3   General issues

For all sorts of reasons, the costs of practising law abroad are higher and the opportunities to generate fees lower. There is thus an immediate difficulty with the profit equation. Further, if a firm only takes account of fees billed and costs incurred in relation to a particular office, it will be taking too narrow a view, and almost certainly ending up with an 'unprofitable' office. How should the firm account for work generated by a foreign office but handled and billed out of the home office (or another foreign office)? How should it account for increased domestic business generated by the firm's perceived stature as an international law firm because it has foreign offices? How should it account for additional communication and integration costs created by foreign offices but paid for out of the home office? Once partners start talking about profitability in relation to international practice, they need to be very clear about how the firm will choose to account for international fees and expenses, and how profit is determined.

In summary, if a firm opens its own office, it should bear in mind the following points:

(a)   It is the most expensive international strategy, and therefore needs considerable support. A firm is not likely to achieve the necessary level of support if the partners feel that they are not being kept informed or are not being involved in the development of the offices. Three years is normally the minimum period over which a firm should probably assess whether the expectations of an office's performance have been achieved.

(b)   It is very difficult for a small office to be profitable: a few lawyers may not be able to cover the fixed overhead costs, and the level of work will vary from too busy to not busy enough. Staffing with the right number and type of lawyers will be problematic.

(c)   The emerging trend seems to be that foreign offices that practise both home law and local law are more likely to be profitable (or more profitable) than those that practise only home law. The successful offices also tend to have been established for a number of years and to have become an integral part of the local legal scene. Such offices pose challenges in their need to produce high quality and a seamless service. The nature of the work done and the future for that work must also be such as to require a presence by way of an office (which may not yet be the case for many firms, for example, in Central Europe). And some work can be won in sophisticated jurisdictions without an office at all: for example, when Singapore Telecom was privatised, the US law firms Cleary Gottlieb and Sullivan & Cromwell (which did not have local offices) were preferred over the English firms Allen & Overy, Clifford Chance, and Linklaters & Paines (all of whom did).

(d) Lawyers based in foreign offices tend to feel neglected, uninformed, insecure and paranoid! Serious international firms therefore take great pains to integrate their foreign offices into the firm: they go to great lengths to involve them in the firm, to communicate with them, and to make sure that home lawyers visit on a regular basis.

The cost of space should be considered carefully: a firm may be locked into lease commitments that make it difficult for it to close a disappointing foreign office or to move a successful and expanding office into new premises. The start-up costs may be reduced by using serviced office centres, or entering into a joint venture.

One of the most difficult decisions will relate to the lawyers in a foreign office. If the office is practising home law, the firm will need to persuade lawyers with an existing home practice (and possibly a client following) to move abroad for a limited period. There will be an opportunity cost that it will need to measure (it was this cost, for example, that led Slaughter and May to conclude that its Frankfurt office was not sustainable: see Chambers 1996, page 25). Lawyers moving abroad on the basis that they will be replaced in two, three or five years' time have to develop a new practice abroad; just as they have established their contacts and become productive, they are sent home and replaced by lawyers who have to start the process again. The returning lawyers have to pick up whatever is left of their home practice (often very little). This is an expensive and possibly disheartening process for all involved, and a number of firms are now looking for permanent — or at least longer-term — postings to overseas offices.

Lawyers moving abroad often expect attractive packages to reward them for the upheaval: differential profit-shares (to reflect the higher or lower costs of living abroad), tax liability adjustments (to reflect higher or lower liabilities abroad), cost-of-living supplements (which might be affected by status, income levels, family size, and might be capped), subsidised housing (and should the firm require lawyers who move abroad to rent out their home property?), school fees or other educational allowances, paid return flights for the lawyer and family members, car and telephone allowances, and the like. These expectations must all be addressed.

Local professional rules may prevent a firm from recruiting local lawyers to practise local law. Even if it can recruit them, it may be prevented from taking them into partnership. A local office may therefore be faced with a turnover of legal staff, which brings additional costs, although local lawyers have tended to be more cost-effective than rotated or seconded home lawyers. Increasingly, however, a firm which sees itself as an international firm with a number of offices may find it difficult to differentiate remuneration levels — for employed lawyers and partners — on the basis of which of the firm's many offices they happen to be in.

Local rules may also restrict a firm's opportunities or ability to market its presence in another country. In any event, there will be an additional cost of developing business for the office.

13.3.2 *Affiliation*

Both American and English firms have historically been active in forming networks or affiliations of varying degrees of closeness. Some of them have developed out of the old 'club' relationships, which are generally thought to have had their day. Referrals were never great, and have fallen off even more after closer affiliations were developed. Most clubs were loosely organised, had too many members, and were expected to work without communication or commitment.

Closer affiliations or alliances between smaller numbers of firms have been developed to overcome some of the looseness inherent in clubs and networks. Such relationships also tend to be predicated on referral work and introductions, but because they usually involve fewer firms than clubs they can be better developed and so more productive. The best of them involve assigning lawyers from each firm to spend time working in the offices of other members, and also the sharing of practice management experience as well as other information and resources.

The principal difficulties of alliances are:

(a) finding the time and money to make the relationship part of the firms' culture, especially for those lawyers whose daily practice is not affected by international factors;

(b) addressing cultural differences between the member firms, which can be particularly acute if an American or English firm adopts an 'imperial' attitude;

(c) the patience required to allow the relationship to develop, flourish and bear fruit, which is even harder to achieve if there is no business plan or clearly defined objective for the relationship;

(d) an increasing number of legal or business conflicts between clients of the firms in the alliance;

(e) difficulties created by actual or perceived exclusivity in the relationship, which is not attractive to some clients, and certainly leads to a tailing off in referrals from other lawyers; and

(f) partners in one firm being unable to control the lawyers in other firms (and therefore the quality of work or a client relationship): this is an increasing concern to professional indemnity insurers.

A number of alliances are termed 'strategic' because the members get together to achieve an objective that perhaps none of them would attempt on their own — especially opening a joint foreign office or developing a new practice area. There have been several such alliances between US and UK firms, for example, involving O'Melveny & Myers with Macfarlanes, Sidley & Austin with Ashurst Morris Crisp, Weil Gotshal with Nabarro Nathanson, Donovan Leisure with Alsop Wilkinson, and Dewey Ballantine with Theodore Goddard: interestingly, none of these relationships still exists, even though each of them used the relationship as the basis for opening one or more foreign offices.

The largest London law firms have so far steered clear of alliances, usually because they have more to lose in referrals than they stand to gain. The major exception is Allen & Overy which formed an association with Gide Loyrette in Paris and Loeff Claeys Verbeke in Belgium and the Netherlands. Linklaters & Paines also has a joint operation in Frankfurt (Linklaters & Schön). Another is Denton Hall with Heuking Kühn in Germany, and the larger group of Denton International firms. However, some American and English lawyers believe that strategic alliances (or multinational partnerships) will become their only option for international practice because they will be the only way of developing a critical mass sufficient to challenge the integrated or organic global practices of firms such as Cleary Gottlieb, Clifford Chance, Freshfields, Shearman & Sterling, Skadden Arps, and White & Case.

Affiliations and alliances are often seen as lower-cost alternatives to opening offices. They do often reduce the direct costs, but bring unforeseen indirect costs. Necessarily, one is dealing not with one firm, where partners are used to each other and (should) share a common view of legal practice and willingness to help each other, but with two or more firms that need to get used to dealing with each other. If they remain essentially separate, the assimilation of a joint-venture international practice will be almost impossible.

Exchanges of lawyers and of written know-how are a very good way of encouraging lawyers to share and develop together. So, too, is the promotion of joint training sessions (which can also be turned into joint marketing sessions by inviting other professionals or clients along). Interaction between lawyers is vital for success: social gatherings are important, but it is even more important to get lawyers working together. They need to understand each other's client base and practice, methods of working, and therefore opportunities to share both clients and experience. Do not underestimate the costs of doing these things properly, and do not be tempted to cut corners.

Marketing a joint practice, office or relationship poses many new challenges, irrespective of local publicity rules. Agreeing objectives and targets needs to be carefully done, so that joint marketing efforts can be undertaken that make best use of limited resources. Again, analysing each firm's client base and practice activity is a necessary precondition to developing new business effectively.

In most affiliations, there is an inevitable lack of common history or style; there may also be geographical, time, language and cultural differences. These things add to the burden of being satisfied that an affiliate's approach to the competence of its lawyers and quality of its legal work and service is compatible. Without this level of confidence, however, it will be difficult to persuade partners to introduce their clients to affiliates.

So far as money is concerned, it is of course vital for the alliance members to agree the financial arrangements between them. How are fees to be shared when work is referred or handled in a joint-venture office? How will costs be borne? Most jurisdictions presently forbid profit-sharing, but with the advent of multinational partnerships, how and when will profits be allocated and distributed?

The key to successful international affiliations or alliances is to find areas of joint development for people in the firm to work on together, and then to institutionalise the relationships rather than leaving them to the interest and inclination of just a few lawyers in each firm.

13.3.3 *Multinational partnerships*

At one level, a multinational partnership (MNP) is not a distinct strategy for international strategy but is merely a form of ownership of a law firm pursuing one or more of the strategies already discussed. However, because MNPs make possible the merger of two or more firms originating from different jurisdictions, they potentially allow a degree of integration that was previously much more difficult to achieve. There will be a spectrum of MNPs, ranging from firms (large or small) who admit into partnership a small proportion of overseas lawyers, to a full-blown merger between two or more firms of comparable size. In terms of their effect on the marketplace, the latter will be considered far more significant. Nevertheless, the development of MNPs by accretion rather than merger may still, over time, lead to some significant, truly global, practices.

13.4 Conclusion

There is no sure way to make a profit out of international practice. All strategies have the potential to succeed . . . and to fail. A good understanding of the factors involved, clear and agreed expectations, investment, commitment and patience will pay off. The direct and indirect costs should not be underestimated: both will be substantial. Equally, the returns from international practice should also not be overestimated: most failures in international practice are not so much failures to perform as failures to meet unrealistic expectations.

Chapter 14

MANAGEMENT STRUCTURE

14.1 The Difference between Management and Administration

Many firms confuse management with administration. Management concerns itself with 'big picture' issues and those related to the delivery of legal services to clients. This will encompass strategic thinking, business development and marketing, and partner-related decisions (such as new partners, new offices, mergers); it will also extend to ensuring the quality, quantity and economic soundness of client work, and the development of know-how and skills (for partners, fee-earners, leaders, managers and support staff). Almost everything else is administration. Unfortunately, partners often focus too much time on administration and not enough on management. This misunderstanding can encourage them to recruit too many administrative and support staff. Without a management framework and management support, the administrative staff cannot perform effectively. Nor can they perform effectively if they are subjected to constant review, second-guessing or undermining by partners. It is certainly necessary to set the administrator's parameters and to require him or her to be accountable for actions taken. But it is not necessary to review every decision or action to see whether it was right, or made on the correct assumptions.

14.2 The Dimensions and Levels of Management

14.2.1 The background

I have already discussed and emphasised the importance of looking at law firms as know-how businesses (chapters 3 and 5), and particularly their need for dual expertise — that is, both professional and managerial know-how (see paragraph 3.3). We shall also explore later how the culture, values and leadership of the firm may determine or constrain the firm's activities (see chapter 23). It is against this background that a firm must be managed, and its management structure created (see Howard 1991).

We have also seen how law firms have been growing in size (paragraph 1.4.2), and how this contributes to the 'bureaucratisation' of firms (see paragraph 8.7). Sveiby and Lloyd suggest that successful know-how businesses have an ethos that militates against size: the need for dual expertise and hands-on management favours small groupings of professionals (1987, page 193: these small groupings could, of course, be achieved by effective departmentalisation). All professional people value their autonomy (which is often derived from insecurity and self-questioning). Self-management is therefore important to them: they do not expect (or usually want) to manage their peers (1987, pages 59–60). However, they may well see others as 'subordinate' and adopt classic styles of command and control management.

14.2.2 The management challenges

This background gives law firm managers a set of problems which are by no means easy to work with: there is confusion of management and administration, with a tendency to emphasise administration (but not necessarily to value either); there is a culture of autonomy and self-management, with a consequential reluctance to manage (or be managed by) peers; there is an outdated view of the process of managing others, with a tendency to adopt the command and control style with 'subordinates'; and there is a reluctance to understand the need for dual expertise, and to develop the skills required by its managerial dimension.

There are no 'magic wands' to be waved here, or infallible management structures to be implemented. These challenges have to be understood and faced. This requires an analysis of the different dimensions and levels of management, and of the management of autonomy. The creation of an effective management structure will require the balancing of these dimensions and levels.

14.2.3 The dimensions of management

Taking Sveiby and Lloyd's imperative, the need for dual expertise (paragraph 3.3) will mean that the firm will want to ensure that it has the appropriate levels and mix of both professional and managerial know-how. The nature of these was explored in chapter 5. For present purposes, the managerial side will have to cover strategy (chapters 4 and 11), the management of the firm itself (chapters 14 to 16), the management of departments and practice areas (chapters 17 to 20), the management of cases and projects (chapter 21), the management of people (chapters 22 to 26), the management of change (chapter 27), the management of the firm's economic position (chapters 28 to 31), and the management of inter-partner relations (chapters 32 to 37).

14.2.4 The levels of management

Without wishing to portray law firms as necessarily hierarchical organisations, there are nevertheless different levels within any organisation. Each of these levels must be properly designed if the firm is to be fully effective. The levels move from the smallest component (an individual) to the largest (the firm). Individuals come to the firm with their own stock of human capital (knowledge, skills, experience, etc.): appropriate jobs need to be designed for them to do. Most firms organise jobs on some basis of division of labour — usually into departments or other operating units; and the firm must assemble and coordinate these units in some way. The four levels are, therefore, the individual, the job, the department or unit, and the firm.

14.2.4.1 The individual

At the individual level, the firm must manage and monitor the development and utilisation of a person's productive capacity (see, respectively, chapters 5, 19 and 25), as well as encourage appropriate behaviour and motivation (see, respectively, chapters 23, 24 and 26).

14.2.4.2 The job

In essence, the design of individual positions looks at the management of inputs, processes and outputs (see Mintzberg 1993, chapter 2). Input refers to the knowledge and skills required of the individual who holds the position in question. Once these are identified, the firm can seek to acquire and maintain them through recruitment, induction (also referred to as socialisation and indoctrination), and training (see paragraphs 22.4.2 and 25.3).

Once people are in post, firms then often seek to prescribe the way in which they should work — to design work processes or to formalise or regulate their behaviour. This is usually achieved through job descriptions, work-flow specifications, or procedural rules and operating manuals. This formalisation can help to maintain consistency and quality of work by standardising the process of its production, and is most likely in areas of activity that are repetitive. Fee-earners' needs for professional autonomy make this type of control difficult to achieve in law firms. A great deal of management theory and research has been dedicated to this part of organisations, and much of lawyers' antipathy towards management generally may well stem from thinking that 'management' necessarily entails control of their productivity and loss of autonomy. This is considered further in paragraph 14.2.5.

Standardisation and quality in professional practice are not typically achieved by formalisation of processes, but by training the professionals to common standards. This leads Mintzberg to suggest that "formalization and training are basically substitutes . . . [and so] the professional organization surrenders a good deal of control over its choice of workers as well as their methods of work to the outside institutions that train and certify them and thereafter set standards that guide them in the conduct of their work" (1993, pages 42 and 43). Interestingly, however, as legal practice becomes more specialised and the legal profession more polarised, it appears that individual firms are having to assume greater control over the training of their professionals and, through quality systems like ISO 9000, resort more often to control of processes as well as training. The imposition of post-qualification mandatory continuing professional development is also an acknowledgement that practising lawyers cannot be 'certified' as fully prepared professionals and be assumed to remain so (see, further, paragraph 38.4).

Firms may also seek to control outputs (the results of the job, rather than its processes — ends, rather than means). This is usually achieved through some form of specialisation, or division of labour. The specialisation may be horizontal — relating to the 'breadth' of the job — or vertical — relating to its 'depth'. The purpose of specialisation is to increase productivity, and it might again (as with processes) be seen to be a product of repetition: the more someone performs a task, the more 'expert' and reliable he or she becomes. The increasing specialisation seen in law firms has been horizontal specialisation, for the most part: the scope of legal practice has been reduced for most lawyers. However, an increasing degree of horizontal specialisation is balanced by very little vertical specialisation, because fee-earners control most of the processes of handling client work: usually short of bringing the work in, and typing and delivering the work product, the whole process can be handled by an employed fee-earner — though business pressures and the spread of technology are blurring even these distinctions. This combination of specialisation (high horizontally, but low vertically) may well be the hallmark of professional work (Mintzberg 1993, page 32).

These design issues are just as pertinent to the work of professional managers and support staff as they are to fee-earners, and to lawyers who occupy management positions.

14.2.4.3   The department or operating unit
Having defined the roles and positions of individuals, the next step is to think about how best to group the individual positions together. At this stage, it will also be necessary to start bearing in mind more specifically the firm's strategy or mission (see chapter 4), since the basis on which people and jobs are grouped may well determine the firm's effectiveness in realising its strategy.

14.2.4.3.1   Basis of grouping jobs   Mintzberg proposes two principal bases for grouping jobs: the first relates to the market (the firm's 'ends'); and the second relates to the firm's functions (its 'means'). Within each category, there are three subcategories (1993, pages 48–54), although as with all classifications there may be room for ambiguity or 'double counting':

(a)   Market grouping (ends):

(i)   by output — in our context, the services offered to clients, such as corporate, property, litigation, matrimonial, tax, etc.;

(ii) by type of client — commercial, high-net-worth private client, agricultural, retail, etc.;

(iii) by place — location of offices, within a town, or in different towns, regions, or countries.

(b) Functional grouping (means):

(i) by knowledge and skill, or specialisation — content (corporate, property, litigation, etc., where there is no real difference between market grouping by services), type of skill (contentious or non-contentious, drafting, advocacy, etc.), or level of skill (partner, senior fee-earner, junior or recently qualified fee-earner, paralegal, trainee, etc.): there seems to be little merit in these groupings in law firms, except in relation to the work of administrative and support staff who may well be grouped, for example, into a word processing pool, photocopying and reproduction unit, accounts office, personnel staff, etc.;

(ii) by work processes and function — fee-earning, secretarial, general office services, financial, personnel and training, marketing, etc.: to some extent, this type of functional grouping takes place in law firms (and may be a useful classification for different types of internal communication as well as for management structure);

(iii) time — which would usually relate to departmental distinctions caused by shift work (perhaps only relevant to very large firms that maintain 24-hour support services operated in shifts).

On balance, therefore, it would seem that the reality in most law firms favours structure by market groupings — at least for fee-earning jobs — with some element of functional grouping by knowledge or process for support staff (although even here, secretarial staff are more likely to be grouped with fee-earners on a market basis than on a functional basis).

14.2.4.3.2 Interdependencies between jobs Having proposed different bases for grouping jobs, Mintzberg also suggests the criteria on which the structural design decisions should be taken. The criteria are based, not surprisingly, on the interdependencies between jobs (1993, pages 54–8):

(a) *Work flow.* The 'natural' flow of fee-earning work between partners and fee-earners working together on a matter (reciprocal interdependence — the most complex), and between fee-earner and secretary (sequential interdependence), suggests that this interdependence of work flow should support market grouping by services offered or by type of client. Pooled interdependence (the least complex) can also exist where a group of people share resources, for example, in a dedicated photocopying facility in which operators who share the same equipment must manage their work flow to maximise the productivity of the equipment.

(b) *Processes.* Interdependencies between different specialists might favour grouping by functional knowledge and skill. For example, the skills of using copying equipment and binding machines for the production of reports may be functionally very different; but the need to prepare a finished product might suggest the functional grouping of copying and binding in one reproduction department.

(c) *Scale*. Many or all departments of the firm might need the same support services, but not be able to justify a full-time appointment in their own unit — at which point, the creation of a single, centralised facility would make sense. This is what many law firms do, for example, with their library and know-how staff. Interestingly, grouping people for scale may also encourage process specialisation.

(d) *Social*. This type of grouping "relates not to the work done but to the social relationships that accompany it" (Mintzberg 1993, page 58), and amounts to grouping people on the basis of 'getting along' together. This can be important, for example, where strong personalities are involved, where the firm needs to develop or reinforce specialisation, where people have to work under pressure and need to be able to rely on each other, or where the work might be boring.

14.2.4.3.3 Coordinating the work In addition to market and functional issues in grouping jobs, says Mintzberg, an organisation must also consider how it proposes to coordinate the work of people within those groups. The coordinating mechanism chosen might also determine the optimum size of any given group (1993, pages 66–70). He identifies five basic mechanisms to coordinate work (1993, pages 4–7):

(a) mutual adjustment (informal communication between workers),
(b) direct supervision (instructing and monitoring a 'subordinate'),
(c) standardisation of work processes (methods of working are pre-scribed),
(d) standardisation of outputs (of service or performance by specification of results or service measures),
(e) standardisation of inputs (requirement of specified skills or training).

Mintzberg also suggests that these five mechanisms fall into a 'rough order' (1993, page 7):

"As organizational work becomes more complicated, the favored means of coordination seems to shift from mutual adjustment to direct supervision to standardization, preferably of work processes, otherwise of outputs, or else of skills, finally reverting back to mutual adjustment."

Most firms are, in fact, likely to use all five mechanisms at one time or another, or in one way or another.

In relation to the size of groups, it would appear that a group can be larger to the extent that it is able to rely on some type of standardisation as a coordinating mechanism (1993, page 66). Reliance on mutual adjustment or direct supervision is likely to result in smaller units —

particularly where complex tasks are interdependent (1993, page 68). However, Mintzberg makes the point that professional work can be either independent or interdependent, and each requires a very different structure (1993, page 69):

"In one case, the standardization of skills handles most of the interdependencies, so there is little need for mutual adjustment and the professionals can work independently, in large units. . . . In the other case, interdependencies remain that cannot be handled by the standardization of skills, so there must be considerable mutual adjustment. The professionals must work cooperatively in small, informal units."

This discussion is also tied in to leverage and the shape of the fee-earning pyramid that a partner can support, because the type and extent of coordination required for the work being done will determine how many fee-earners and staff she can coordinate and monitor (see paragraphs 2.3.3, 3.6.1, and 8.4.3).

14.2.4.4   The firm

Finally, the firm must create a structure to bring together its different operating units in such a way that its strategic objectives are achieved. This involves balancing the need to divide the firm into operating units (Mintzberg's groupings, discussed in paragraph 14.2.4.3; Hunt calls this 'differentiation' (1992, page 157)) with the need to ensure appropriate liaison between them (which Hunt calls 'integration' (1992, page 157)). This balancing of differentiation and integration is the subject of paragraph 14.3.

14.2.5   The management of autonomy

Before looking at the ways in which the various features of organisational design can be pulled together, it is necessary to take a slight detour to consider an issue of considerable importance in the structure and management of law offices. Autonomy has long been thought to be one of the 'hallmarks' of a profession. Unfortunately, it is also often advanced by professionals as a reason for resisting management.

An excellent analysis of the issues of autonomy and management in professional environments is provided by Raelin (1989), and is also considered by Maister (1997, chapter 6). The core problem is the supposed conflict between autonomy and management control: if the lawyers want autonomy and freedom from control, and managers want to command and control these lawyers' activities, then there will inevitably be no common ground. But is it, in fact, correct to assume that autonomy and management are the antithesis of each other?

Raelin identifies three components of autonomy (1989, page 216):

(a)   strategic or institutional autonomy, which is the freedom to choose the goals and policies that guide the firm;

(b)   administrative autonomy, which is the responsibility for managing part of the firm and coordinating its activities with other parts of the firm (in light of the distinction drawn above between management and administration, 'managerial autonomy' might be a better expression for our purposes); and

(c)   operational autonomy, which is the freedom to achieve the firm's goals or solve its problems within the strategic and administrative (managerial) framework.

Raelin refers to executive management, middle management, and professionals: for my purposes, I shall interpret this in the law firm setting to mean respectively senior equity partners, senior managers (who may be partners appointed to management positions, or senior professional managers), and professionals (who, depending on the context, may be fee-earners involved in client work, or other professional managers engaged in support services).

Raelin describes a 'standard view' (1989, pages 218–21) under which strategic and managerial autonomy reside in the firm's management (and we might further suggest that strategic autonomy resides with senior equity partners, and managerial autonomy with senior managers); operational autonomy resides with the professionals. In broad terms, management (senior equity partners and senior managers) sets and controls the achievement of the firm's 'ends', while the professionals control the 'means' of achievement. Raelin accepts that the boundaries between the three components can be blurred.

However, he then goes on to suggest an 'alternative view' (1989, pages 221–7). On this view, the professionals should be given strategic or managerial autonomy (the control of 'ends') in different circumstances that in fact reflect the four levels of management considered in paragraph 14.2.4:

(a)   when the *firm* relies on the fee-earners to achieve its mission and the mission is still emerging, or where the firm is open, innovative and growth-oriented: this can apply to many professional service firms, which have to rely on their professionals in achieving their strategic goals (their involvement is the essence of the business);

(b)   where the *department* or practice area is strategically vital;

(c)   when the professional's *job* requires client involvement or is high level: client involvement is the essence of a law firm's services, and the involvement in strategy of those who have direct contact with them is vital; similarly, managers may play a key role in managing the firm in such a way that strategic and managerial goals are met; and

(d)   when the *individual* professional is a highly trained, high performer or proven contributor, someone whose expertise is broadly based, or someone who is known to share the firm's goals: in these cases, the professional will need greater strategic and managerial autonomy in order to perform effectively — and, in some cases of key individuals, what they do and how they do it may in fact determine the firm's overall strategy.

These will all be circumstances that those who have worked in law firms will recognise. Raelin's point is that the structural purity of autonomy for strategy and management only residing in senior equity partners, or senior managers, cannot always be maintained when the success of a firm, a department (or practice area), a job, or a key individual depends on the broader involvement of a professional who may not be a partner or senior manager. The tendency for all partners (and sometimes all fee-earners) to feel that they can and should involve themselves in strategy and management is therefore supported — in certain conditions — by Raelin's analysis.

However, Raelin's analysis also supports the involvement of senior equity partners or senior managers in the professionals' domain. This managerial control of the means, suggests Raelin, is legitimate at the same four levels:

(a) when the *firm* requires greater teamwork and coordination of professional activities;

(b) when the *department* or practice area needs new professionals to be brought in, a broader perspective, or an improvement in interpersonal skills and teamwork: these interventions are most likely to be made by the senior manager (probably a head of department or practice area manager), and in this sense have a strategic or managerial dimension rather than a purely operational view;

(c) when time limits are approaching for the performance of a *job*, or the task is not clear and needs to be clarified (or new skills introduced): again, it is most likely that this intervention will come from a senior manager; and

(d) when the *individual* professional is performing poorly, demotivated, insecure, over-specialised, a new recruit, or taking on tasks that are outside the firm's mission, or beyond his or her range of experience.

The involvement or intervention of partners and senior managers who are lawyers will often be accepted by professionals as part of normal fee-earning supervision. But Raelin's view goes further, because the intervention is not as a fee-earner but as executive or senior management — not, in a sense, on behalf of the client, but on behalf of the firm or department. Raelin concludes (1989, page 227):

"The management of autonomy may be the most essential skill in managing professionals in organizations. As I have shown, it is not a simple matter of letting the professional alone, nor is it a matter of having the manager maintain constant oversight. Balance is required."

14.3 Designing a Structure

14.3.1 *Influences on design*

Mintzberg makes the point that firms do not design their management structures in a vacuum (1993, page 46: see also Maister 1997, chapter

13). Structure is subject to many influences, which he calls 'situational' or 'contingency' factors. These factors can be described as evolution, power, environment, and culture or fashion.

14.3.1.1 Evolution
We have already seen from Greiner's organisational life cycle (see paragraph 2.3.1) that a firm can expect to go through various stages as it ages and grows. Mintzberg concludes (1993, pages 123 and 126) that as a firm grows older and larger it will formalise its behaviour more (because repetition of work and situations allows greater predictability, and therefore more standardisation of processes). Further, as it grows in size, it will have more specialisation, more differentiated (and larger) operating units, and a more developed administrative component (1993, pages 124–6). This supports the view that larger firms will inevitably become more 'bureaucratic' (see Nelson 1988, quoted in paragraph 8.7, and paragraph 14.3.3).

14.3.1.2 Power
The use of power and influence in a firm will be discussed in depth in paragraph 24.3. The drive for people (particularly, perhaps, professionals) to control the decisions that affect their work — in other words, to exercise power in and over their environment — tends to lead to structures that are excessively centralised (Mintzberg 1993, page 147). In the context of law firms, this tends to mean 'centralisation' in the equity partners. Also, in the light of the developing trend for multinational and multidisciplinary practices, it might be worth noting that Mintzberg's research also suggests that "the greater the external control of the organization, the more centralized and formalized its structure" (1993, page 146).

14.3.1.3 Environment
The influence of the external environment was considered at length in chapter 4. Designing an appropriate structure for the firm is part of the strategic matching of the external environment with internal resources and competencies. Mintzberg characterises the environment along four dimensions (1993, page 136):

(a) *Stable to dynamic.* This refers to the degree of predictability in the environment.

(b) *Simple to complex.* This refers to the degree of complexity in understanding and performing the work of the organisation.

(c) *Diverse to integrated.* Diversity (as exists in the legal marketplace) can result from the range of clients served, the services offered, or the locations in which the clients are served or the services marketed.

(d) *Hostile to munificent.* Hostile environments are typically dynamic, too, and may be the result of competition, intervention by government or the public sector (for example, the Lord Chancellor's Department, or the Legal Aid Board) or by professional bodies (such as the Law Society), or a lack of resources (skills shortage or competition for staff).

Mintzberg then draws various conclusions about the structure of a firm reflecting its environment (1993, pages 137–43). First, the more dynamic the environment, the less formalised the structure: if the firm cannot predict its environment, it needs to maintain its flexibility, whereas a stable environment will encourage standardisation. Dynamic environments also have more influence on structure.

Second, the more complex the environment, the more decentralised the structure. A complex environment cannot resort to standardisation, but needs greater facility to collect and process information (this is the issue of bounded rationality considered in paragraph 6.3), as well as mutual adjustment in its operations. These forces will tend to push management away from the centre. In Raelin's terms, the professionals need strategic or managerial autonomy (see paragraph 14.2.5).

Third, the more diversified the firm's markets, the more likely it is that it will be split into market-based groups (cf. paragraph 14.2.4.3.1(a)). Again, the need for professionals to have access to market information, to be able to understand and process it, and to be able to react appropriately and quickly to it, all suggest that they need greater autonomy. This certainly seemed to happen in many law firms in the late 1980s as they tried to diversify into 'full service' practices in the hope of meeting a broad range of legal needs for a broad range of clients.

Extreme hostility will drive a firm to centralise its structure temporarily. When a firm is under threat — and perhaps its very survival threatened — its leaders need to be able to act quickly and decisively. This is not consistent with any significant degree of differentiation, even in a complex environment that would otherwise suggest decentralisation. Centralisation was often a response by law firms to the hostile environment of recession.

Finally, different parts of the firm may be subject to different types of environment. In this case, decentralisation to different groupings is necessary. For example, the firm's financial and support functions may well operate in a stable environment, even if its fee-earners do not. There would then be centralisation and formalisation in some or all support services, and differentiation and decentralisation in fee-earning activities. In this sense, a firm can be both centralised and decentralised at the same time. If partners do not understand the environmental and structural need for the difference, it will lead to inappropriate management (usually of support services) and serious misunderstandings.

14.3.1.4 *Culture and fashion*

Organisational culture is important to a firm and will be considered in chapter 23. Law firms (like other organisations) may also be influenced by what other similar (or even dissimilar) firms are doing. A firm's structure may therefore simply reflect the 'fashion' of the time, even though the structure may be inappropriate for the firm's situation (Mintzberg 1993, pages 147–9). For example, moves to appoint managing partners, personnel or training managers, or non-lawyer chief executives, or to move to industry-based departments (rather than law-based departments) would all be instances of fashion affecting the structure of law firms.

14.3.2   Characteristics of management structure

The two principal characteristics of organisational design are differentiation and integration (Hunt 1992, page 157):

> "How managers balance these two forces will partly determine the effectiveness of the organization. Too much differentiation can lead to anarchy and organizational collapse. Too much integration stifles the creativity and innovation through which individuals adapt to changes in the environment. When creativity is stifled the dynamic processes that let organizations grow and develop begin to die."

14.3.2.1   Differentiation in structure

The degree of differentiation in the firm will depend on the extent to which different groupings of jobs are created (see paragraph 14.2.4.3). Along with this differentiation, there will also be various degrees of decentralisation (or delegation) of power and decision-making. Centralisation and decentralisation should not be seen as two distinct concepts, but as the ends of a continuum (Mintzberg 1993, page 98).

All organisations are faced with reasons and pressures to decentralise (1993, pages 95–7). Often, these relate to the need for professionals and others to respond quickly to local conditions (whether they are 'local' geographically, or in terms of client understanding or expertise, does not matter for these purposes). They can also reflect a concern that not all information can be understood, or appropriate decisions taken, by central management (who might also be unable to process the information quickly or accurately enough, or out of touch: this is the issue of bounded rationality again (paragraph 6.3)). Finally, it may be easier for smaller, more homogeneous groups to provide a motivating environment and satisfy professionals' needs for autonomy.

Normally, power is delegated either to the manager of an operating unit, to those who design the systems of the unit, to those who have the appropriate knowledge, or to everyone (though I have never come across a law firm that is perfectly democratic!). These are instances of horizontal decentralisation, because power is dispersed across the firm. Power can also be decentralised vertically, depending how far 'down' the organisation the delegated power goes. In law firms, power related to the operational autonomy of fee-earners can go some way down, but usually little power is given to support staff — even in areas where they ought to be allowed operational autonomy, let alone managerial autonomy. In this sense, too, the firm can be centralised and decentralised at the same time. And the firm does not have to adopt the same breadth or depth of delegation for every operating unit; it can 'selectively decentralise' by using different approaches to grouping and delegation.

14.3.2.2 Integration

Differentiation without integration would lead to a loss of management control, perhaps even organisational anarchy and destruction (cf. paragraph 2.3.2.2). To achieve this integration, Mintzberg identifies four 'liaison devices' that can be incorporated into the firm's formal structure (1993, pages 81–93):

(a) *Liaison positions.* These positions do not usually carry any formal authority (which normally goes with the exercise of power down a hierarchy, whereas the liaison position works across the firm). Whatever status the position has is derived not from the role (compare with the integrating manager described at (c) below), but from the knowledge that its occupant possesses: see the discussion at paragraph 24.3.2 for the difference between role power and expert power.

(b) *Task forces and standing committees.* Task forces are usually formed to consider or achieve a particular task — often (but not necessarily) within an operating unit. Standing committees are more permanent, and may be drawn from across the firm's operating units and have an existence independent of their members at any given time. These groups are, in effect, institutionalised meetings — with delegated authority, formal participants, and scheduled meeting times: they are part of the formal structure of the firm.

(c) *Integrating managers.* This is effectively a liaison position (see (a) above) but with formal authority. However, the authority is only for liaison or coordination, not for staff. The position is appropriate when people who would normally coordinate their interaction through mutual adjustment need more control over their actions and behaviour (cf. paragraph 14.2.4.3.3). As we shall see (paragraph 24.3.2), exercising authority in a law firm simply as the holder of a position can be very difficult; unless the formal authority is backed up by some credible expertise or charisma, the position may not be successful.

(d) *Matrix structures.* The existence of multiple roles and functions in law firms — particularly responsibility for clients as well as specific matters, or for a department as well as clients — makes the matrix structure attractive. Lawyers do not like hierarchies and the 'unity of command' that goes with them. Mintzberg writes (1993, page 87):

"Two kinds of matrix structures can be distinguished: a permanent form, where the interdependencies remain more-or-less stable and so, as a result, do the units and the people in them; and a shifting form, geared to project work, where the interdependencies, the market units, and the people in them shift around frequently."

Project-based structures are considered in chapter 21.

Matrix structures therefore seek to balance the formal power of equivalent parts of the firm (for example, to cope with the autonomy and decentralisation of different fee-earning departments for commercial, property, litigation, and private client work). The absence of unity of command can mean that these 'equivalent' parts of the firm are often engaged in a power struggle for scarce resources (people, marketing funds, new technology, and so on — even client work). This type of structure can be disconcerting for people who need security and stability; managing people in such an environment becomes both more important and possibly more problematic because of the increased likelihood of conflicts, confusion and stress. Indeed, the use of a matrix structure might lead to the need for *more* managers (and perhaps a more highly developed personnel function).

Because a highly differentiated structure is more likely in firms handling work that is complex, highly specialised, and interdependent, the use of these liaison devices is also more likely and more necessary in those firms.

14.3.3   Mintzberg's structure in fives

One of the most influential works on designing effective organisations is Mintzberg (1993), to which extensive reference has already been made. His view is that there are five basic organisational configurations:

(a)   the *simple structure* (for young, small, unsophisticated, or possibly founder-led firms),

(b)   the *machine bureaucracy* (for carrying out specialised, routine tasks using formalised procedures),

(c)   the *professional bureaucracy* (for carrying out specialised, complex, professional work independently),

(d)   the *divisionalised form* (for quasi-autonomous market-based divisions producing standardised outputs and controlled by top management), and

(e)   the *adhocracy* (for specialised, complex project work based around ad hoc teams).

In labelling two of his configurations 'bureaucracies', Mintzberg is not using the term in its now pejorative meaning but in its technical sense, that is, that an organisation's behaviour "is predetermined or predictable, in effect standardized (whether by work processes, outputs, or skills, and whether or not centralized)" (1993, page 36).

Each of these configurations in turn has five parts:

(a)   the *operating core* (the people who perform the basic work of producing products or rendering services — in our case, fee-earners and, because they provide *direct* support to the fee-earners, paralegals and secretaries),

(b)   the *strategic apex* (those who have *overall* responsibility for the organisation — in our context, a management committee, senior partner, managing partner, or similar),

(c)   the *middle line* (meaning managers with formal authority who join the strategic apex and operating core together — in law firms, usually heads of department, but perhaps senior professional managers as well),

(d) the *technostructure* (work-study analysts who standardise work processes, planning and control analysts who standardise outputs, and personnel analysts who standardise skills — in most law firms, the technostructure is underdeveloped and tends to focus on personnel recruitment, induction, training and know-how), and

(e) the *support staff* (specialists who are not part of the operating core, but who exist to provide indirect support, such as telephonists, receptionists, mailroom, cleaning, finance, payroll, etc.).

In many organisations, the middle line and the technostructure are 'lumped' together and called middle management; or the technostructure and the support staff are grouped together and called support.

We have already met Mintzberg's five coordinating devices (see paragraph 14.2.4.3.3).

For Mintzberg, therefore, the design of a firm's structure will be based around a configuration that employs a prime coordinating mechanism, where one part of the firm is predominant, and where a certain type of decentralisation (see paragraph 14.2.4.2) is appropriate. These combinations are set out in table 14.1.

Structural configuration	Prime coordinating mechanism	Key part of organisation	Type of decentralisation
Simple structure	Direct supervision	Strategic apex	Vertical and horizontal centralisation
Machine bureaucracy	Standardisation of work processes	Technostructure	Limited horizontal decentralisation
Professional bureaucracy	Standardisation of skills	Operating core	Vertical and horizontal decentralisation
Divisionalised form	Standardisation of outputs	Middle line	Limited vertical decentralisation
Operating adhocracy	Mutual adjustment	Operating core	Selective decentralisation

Table 14.1 (Source: Mintzberg 1993, pages 153 and 257)

14.3.4 Fives in law firms

Adopting Mintzberg's analysis, in law firms the operating core dominates, and firms tend to be either professional bureaucracies or operating adhocracies; they normally rely on the standardisation of skills and mutual adjustment for their coordinating mechanisms. This is not to suggest that there are *no* law firms that might be considered simple structures, machine bureaucracies, or divisionalised forms, but that there are preponderances.

The essence of a professional bureaucracy is the ability of the professionals (the operating core) to use their professional training and skills to 'diagnose' clients' problems and then apply the appropriate solutions or processes to them. It is most relevant, perhaps, to the traditional private client services such as conveyancing, wills and probate, divorce, small claims litigation, and so on (what Maister would call the 'experience' service: see paragraph 2.3.3). In other words, it is more of a 'performance' structure than a problem-solving one. As such, it needs the support of a technostructure and of support staff to design and implement the relevant performance processes. The highly proceduralised practice area (Maister's 'efficiency' service) will be dominated by standard processes — often supported by technology — and would represent Mintzberg's machine bureaucracy. Examples might be computerised debt collection and uninsured loss recovery practices.

On the other hand, the operating adhocracy is more concerned with problem-solving (and often innovation). It looks more to teamwork and cross-disciplinary efforts. As Mintzberg puts it (1993, pages 255, 257):

". . . whereas each professional of the Professional Bureaucracy can operate on his own, in the Adhocracy the professionals must amalgamate their efforts. . . . In fact, for every Operating Adhocracy, there is a corresponding Professional Bureaucracy, one that does similar work but with a narrower orientation. Faced with a client problem, the Operating Adhocracy engages in creative effort to find a novel solution; the Professional Bureaucracy pigeonholes it into a known contingency to which it can apply a standard program. One engages in divergent thinking aimed at innovation; the other, in convergent thinking aimed at perfection."

14.3.4.1 *The professional bureaucracy*

As table 14.1 shows, the professional bureaucracy relies on the standardisation of skills to coordinate the efforts of the professionals in its operating core. This is achieved largely through training and socialisation. The professional bureaucracy is the archetypal professional practice. The professionals are specialised, and work autonomously within the firm but yet closely with their clients. Common training, on-the-job development and socialisation mean that they know what to expect from their colleagues. The professionals apply the accepted standards of their profession: in a machine bureaucracy, the people in the operating core apply the standard of the *system* or *process* they are required to adopt (Mintzberg 1993, pages 191–2).

An important aspect of the professional bureaucracy is what Mintzberg describes as 'the pigeonholing process' (1993, pages 192–3):

". . . the professional has two basic tasks: (1) to categorize the client's need in terms of a contingency, which indicates which standard program to use, a task known as diagnosis; and (2) to apply, or execute, that program. . . . It is this pigeonholing process that enables the Professional Bureaucracy to decouple its various operating tasks and assign them to individual, relatively autonomous professionals. Each can, instead of giving a great deal of attention to coordinating his work with his peers, focus on perfecting his skills."

The reference to a 'standard program' is not to something which is as structured as the process of a machine bureaucracy, but refers to the application of an accepted professional approach to the diagnosed need.

Diagnosis is therefore fundamental to this process, but it is geared towards seeking a solution that has already been encountered in professional experience (which is why the firm is bureaucratic rather than an adhocracy — which would require a creative solution). Nevertheless, it is not an infallible process, and conflicts over professional or specialist territory can arise (1993, page 207):

"But that process can never be so good that client needs do not fall in the cracks between the standard programs. The world is a continuous intertwined system. Slicing it up, although necessary to comprehend it, inevitably distorts it. . . . Needs that fall at the margin or that overlap two categories tend to get forced — artificially — into one category or another. . . . The pigeonholing process, in fact, emerges as the source of a great deal of the conflict of the Professional Bureaucracy."

In addition, the proper exercise of the pigeonholing process assumes that the professional making the diagnosis is both knowledgeable and responsible. The professional bureaucracy's lack of direct supervision means that it "cannot easily deal with professionals who are either incompetent or unconscientious" (1993, page 207).

Although the operating core is the key part of the professional bureaucracy, there is also usually a developed support staff. The professionals in the operating core are an expensive resource, and the purpose of support staff is take away from them as much of the routine work as possible (1993, page 194). Unfortunately, the coordination of the support staff can also give rise to conflict. The professionals feel that they are entitled to direct ('command and control') the support staff, even though they are not their hierarchical or 'line' managers. The support staff can therefore be caught in the middle of a power struggle between their formal managers up the hierarchy, and their professional 'managers'.

The professional bureaucracy is a democratic structure and the professionals are necessarily given considerable autonomy to serve their clients and perfect their skills. However, control through standardisation of skills may in reality mean little control at all. Co-ordination through supervision or mutual adjustment may be seen as interference with professional autonomy, and standardisation of result or process is rarely appropriate for professional work where the needs and expectations of individual clients may be difficult or impossible to specify.

Thus, the professional bureaucracy is:

"a flat structure with a thin middle line, a tiny technostructure, and a fully elaborated support staff . . . [in which] the technology of the organization — its knowledge base — is sophisticated, but its technical system — the set of instruments it uses to apply that knowledge base — is not. Thus, the prime example of the Professional Bureaucracy is the *personal-service organization*, at least the one with complex stable work . . . . [L]aw . . . offices . . . rely on this configuration as long as they concentrate not on innovating in the solution of new problems, but on applying standard programs to well-defined problems" (1993, pages 195 and 203).

This means, of course, that the professional bureaucracy may not be well equipped to deal with the unusual or the unexpected; it is better suited to individualism than to teamwork and integration. These changed conditions call for a different structure — the operating adhocracy.

14.3.4.2 The operating adhocracy

Mintzberg distinguishes two types of adhocracy — operating and administrative. I will not consider the administrative adhocracy here because I am more concerned with the management structure surrounding an operating core of lawyers. The operating adhocracy is an innovative and creative organisation which, by definition, cannot rely on any form of standardisation for coordination — indeed:

". . . it must avoid all the trappings of bureaucratic structure, notably sharp divisions of labor, extensive unit differentiation, highly formalized behaviors, and an emphasis on planning and control systems. Above all, it must remain flexible. . . . Of all the configurations, Adhocracy shows the least reverence for the classical principles of management, especially unity of command" (Mintzberg 1993, pages 254–5).

With innovation as a base, the operating adhocracy cannot formalise its knowledge and skills and use them as a base for repetition and standardisation, but must instead use existing know-how as a base on which to build new knowledge and skills. In doing this, it must therefore cut across the boundaries of existing specialisation and rely on the professionals to collaborate in the development of new approaches and solutions. This means that coordination through mutual adjustment (see paragraph 14.2.4.3.3) and the use of liaison devices (see paragraph 14.3.2.2) become key components of the firm's structure. The skills of project management are also required (see chapter 21).

Those familiar with law firms will see a structural description here that may be thought to be emerging from the more traditional, archetypal structure of the professional bureaucracy — in other words, familiarity with the legal profession suggests that law firms are seeking to move from professional bureaucracy to operating adhocracy. In fact, Mintzberg's research suggests that firms will move in the *opposite* direction (1993, page 272):

"Adhocracy is not a very stable configuration. It is difficult to keep any structure in that state for long periods of time — to keep behaviors from formalizing and to ensure a steady flow of truly innovative, ad hoc projects. All kinds of forces drive the Adhocracy to bureaucratize itself as it ages. . . . Success — and aging — encourage a metamorphosis in the Operating Adhocracy, driving it to more stable conditions and more bureaucratic structure. Over time, the successful organization develops a reputation for what it does best. That encourages it to repeat certain projects, in effect to focus its attention on specific contingencies and programs. And this tends to suit its employees, who, growing older themselves, welcome more stability in their work. So the Operating Adhocracy is driven over time toward the Professional Bureaucracy to concentrate on the programs it does best. . . . The organization survives, but the configuration dies."

There are strong overtones here of Greiner's transition from the creative phase (see paragraph 2.3.1); and also of Maister's drift from expertise to experience (see paragraph 2.3.3 — and then perhaps to efficiency — Mintzberg's machine bureaucracy). This transition can therefore be a very trying time for the firm — and may not, in fact, be appropriate for it at all: resisting the trend could be difficult but vital for survival, and will depend on a flow of creative work rather than repeated problems that are susceptible to standardisation (1993, pages 278–9).

An operating adhocracy is a very fluid place to work, and those people who have a low tolerance for ambiguity in their working lives will find it difficult (see the discussion of role stress in paragraphs 24.2.2 and 24.2.3). Mintzberg also believes that:

"Adhocracy emerges as the most politicized of the five configurations. No structure can be more Darwinian than the Adhocracy — more supportive of the fit, as long as they remain fit, and more destructive of the weak. Structures this fluid tend to be highly competitive and at times ruthless" (1993, page 276).

Instinctively, just as many lawyers would describe their service as 'expertise' rather than 'experience' or 'efficiency', they will also describe their firms as operating adhocracies rather than professional bureaucracies. It is likely to be the environment they would *prefer*, because it values independence and autonomy. But by focusing on the complex, unusual and different, the operating adhocracy is well suited to the extraordinary and the one-off project. Because of this, it can also be a very inefficient organisation:

"The root of its inefficiency is the Adhocracy's high cost of communication. People talk a lot in these structures; that is how they combine their knowledge to develop new ideas. But that takes time, a great deal. . . . A further source of inefficiency in the Adhocracy is the unbalanced workloads. . . . It is almost impossible to keep the personnel of a project structure — high-priced personnel, it should be noted — busy on a steady basis" (1993, pages 277–8).

14.3.4.3 Hybrid structures

Mintzberg acknowledges that his five configurations may not be 'pure types', that there may in fact be structural hybrids manifesting elements of more than one configuration. This will be the result of different forces affecting the firm at any one time, or affecting parts of it in different ways. There are three hybrid possibilities:

(a)   the genuine hybrid, that is, the considered result of the various forces and design parameters at play leading to the conclusion that the organisation needs a blend of more than one 'pure' configuration in its structure;

(b)   the transitional hybrid, that is, a firm which is in the process of moving from one configuration to another and which has lost some of the characteristics of one 'pure' configuration but has not yet acquired all of the characteristics of the next; and

(c)   the differentiated hybrid, that is, a firm that has different operating units in it that require 'pure' (but different) configurations in each part — for example, a corporate finance department that is an operating adhocracy, a property department that is a professional bureaucracy, and a debt collection department that is a machine bureaucracy.

14.3.5 Conclusion

The question of what is the best management structure will ultimately depend on the work of the firm, its culture, and the abilities of its partners. Mintzberg's analysis suggests that one of the fundamental questions is whether the firm is, in essence, a collection of individuals (the professional bureaucracy) or a team (the adhocracy). In my terms, it is the distinction between a partnership of individual practitioners (see paragraph 9.3) and a partnership of integrated entrepreneurs (see paragraph 9.4, although I am not suggesting that a firm of integrated entrepreneurs must be an adhocracy and cannot be a professional bureaucracy). If the former, the management structure will probably be limited, with decentralised decision-making reserved to partners at (perhaps infrequent and poorly attended) partners' meetings. If the latter, there may be a more integrated, communicative structure in which professional managers and administrators are intermingled. If there is an individual who has the respect and support of the other partners, and management talent, then it may well make sense to have a managing partner with delegated powers to run the business (see chapter 15).

Without such an individual (and even in some cases with one), it may be sensible to have specific partners or committees with stated responsibilities and accountability. Such roles should have a defined need and a real purpose, and should not be created to salve the egos of one or two partners who feel that their ownership of the business should give them a say in its running on a daily basis. In a mature (in attitude rather than age) environment, the role of professional managers can also be developed successfully (see chapter 16).

14.4   The Evolution of Law Firms and their Management Structures

14.4.1   The process of evolution

Trying to take account of Mintzberg's configurations and design parameters might leave one with a feeling that the task is just too complicated. A law firm is, in fact, a complex organisation, so we should not be surprised that its analysis and design are complex, too. Thankfully, though, as a law firm grows and develops, it will tend to go through a fairly predictable pattern of management evolution. Like Greiner's life cycles (see paragraph 2.3.1), which the following description closely mirrors, the pattern is a necessary generalisation. It is not a given that *every* firm will go through *every* stage; nor is it inevitable that a firm will go through the evolutionary process in exactly the order set out. Nevertheless, looking at the evolutionary stages, and their benefits and disadvantages, can help a firm decide where it is at the moment, how it might have got there, and where it might move to in the future.

The following description is based on Hildebrandt and Kaufman (1988, chapters 1 and 3).

14.4.2   Stage 1: founder-led

All firms begin with one or more founders (usually entrepreneurial types) who carry out pretty well all of the entrepreneurial functions: see paragraph 7.2.

Characteristics:	founder-led firms tend to be run by one or more dominant senior partners who dictate the management policies; this is an implicit assumption of management power, since there will usually not be any formal management structure.
Potential advantages:	strong, consistent leadership; there is little doubt about the firm's leadership or the decision-making processes.
Potential disadvantages:	lack of communication with other partners; failure of the founder(s) to adopt policies that meet the realities of their developing firm; failure of the founders to groom other partners for leadership; waiting too long to replace the founder(s).

Comments:	an essential part of a firm's development, but if succession is delayed, it can result in a power struggle.

14.4.3   Stage 2: democracy

Once the founders have died, retired, or been pushed aside, those who have been excluded from management often feel a burning desire to be involved in the running of their firm.

Characteristics:	a committee structure.
Potential advantages:	involvement for a number of partners.
Potential disadvantages:	indecision; lack of direction; partners more involved in administration than substantive management; 'pass the buck' mentality, or power struggles between committee members.
Comments:	an inevitable part of the evolutionary process, and often works initially; after a period of strong leadership (and often the exclusion of some partners from the firm's management), a founder or leader stepping aside results in partners feeling that they should be 'involved'; however, "involvement in meaningless areas is not involvement at all" (1988, page 17); this stage often diverts partners from practising law (for which they have been trained) to business administration (for which few have been trained); it can therefore be a costly error and "the worst of all forms of management" (1988, page 16), but often has to be endured to show how ineffective and destructive it can be!

14.4.4   Stage 3: managing partner and professional managers

14.4.4.1   Managing partner by natural selection
Sometimes, the founder (or one of the founders) explicitly and formally 'assumes' the management mantle.

Characteristics:	a founder or rainmaker assumes the role of managing partner (possibly as well as that of senior partner); or where there are two strong founders or leaders, they may split the roles of senior partner and managing partner between them.

Potential advantages:	lawyers spend their time practising law; decisions are made on a timely basis; action is taken when it is necessary.

Potential disadvantages:	lack of communication with other partners; failure of the managing partner to groom other partners for the role (or other management roles); waiting too long to replace the managing partner; the managing partner is distracted by fee-earning work.

Comments:	often extremely effective in the less complicated environments of young or smaller firms, where a lead partner can have an unquestioned position of authority; power is not granted, and so cannot 'peaceably' be taken away; the managing partner will not necessarily have any inherent ability to manage.

14.4.4.2 *Managing partner by appointment*

There will come a point where a founder (or managing partner by natural selection) steps aside, or realises that the management function needs to be formalised and handled by someone else.

Characteristics:	a partner is appointed (or anointed) by the founder, senior partner or the first managing partner.
Potential advantages:	lawyers spend their time practising law; the firm's administration is tightened up and better supervised; the culture of management is preserved; it is a less authoritarian environment.

Potential disadvantages:	management is not as firm; decisions are delayed, undermined or second-guessed; there is less control; the managing partner is distracted by fee-earning work.

Comments:	the appointed managing partner nearly always has less natural authority than his or her predecessor, and therefore tends to concentrate on administrative matters which other partners cannot be bothered with; as a result, strategy and management are usually neglected (often

at a time when the firm has grown into a significant business): the other partners become disillusioned with both the role and the incumbent, who is not devoted to fee-earning work and does not, in the eyes of his or her peers, appear to be 'managing' either.

14.4.4.3 *Practice manager*

As the founders, or senior or managing partners, tire of administrative detail, they usually appoint an office or practice manager (or partnership secretary) to take away some of the day-to-day routine.

Characteristics:	often an accounting or military background, brought in to sharpen up and take control of the firm's administration.
Potential advantages:	relieves partners of administrative matters; professionalises the firm's administration and infrastructure.
Potential disadvantages:	the practice manager does not understand the culture of a law firm, and thinks partners should be controlled; the firm outgrows the practice manager; the practice manager wants to run the firm (cf. paragraph 16.4).
Comments:	the first appointment of a practice manager in a firm is usually a short one, as the firm adjusts to the idea of a non-partner manager; most firms find the adjustment difficult and take it out on the practice manager.

14.4.4.4 *Managing partner by election*

A founder or managing partner by natural selection almost by definition does not require a mandate to manage the firm: circumstances dictate that it is a logical thing for him or her to do. However, an appointed (or anointed) managing partner will probably suffer from lack of a clear mandate from the rest of the partnership. The next development is to give the mandate by election rather than appointment.

Characteristics:	a partner elected for ability and respect; often a split role with an elected senior partner/ chairman.
Potential advantages:	election provides a mandate from partners to manage the firm rather than merely control the administration;

the managing partner manages by consent, but the election usually ensures that an individual with stature and natural authority is appointed.

Potential disadvantages: partners still undermine or second-guess decisions;

'management by seniority or rotation' in disguise (cf. paragraph 15.6.1);

the managing partner is distracted by fee-earning work.

Comments: after an appointed managing partner, an elected post gives other partners a sense of involvement and control: the power is given, but it can also be removed; a common difficulty is a firm with no one who is willing or has the ability to take the job on, or who enjoys the respect and support of the partners.

14.4.4.5 *Director(s) of finance and administration*

A practice manager may suffer from many of the same problems as an appointed managing partner — the lack of a clear role with specific authority. As the firm grows, its operations also become more complex and specialised, often requiring more sophisticated and specialised administrative support. Depending on background, aptitude and inclination, the practice manager may not be able to provide it and is replaced by a more senior position.

Characteristics: someone with experience of a similar role in a law firm or professional services environment.

Potential advantages: the director relieves partners of administrative matters;

the director further professionalises the firm's administration and infrastructure;

provides support to the managing partner in wider strategic and management issues;

the director introduces specialised management support.

Potential disadvantages: the director does not understand the firm's culture;

the firm outgrows the director;

the director wants to be the managing partner;

the director becomes too closely associated with a particular partner or group of partners (cf. paragraph 16.4).

Comments: with the right person who fully understands the
                                   firm, and his or her role in it, who can build the
                                   support staff, and not alienate either partners or
                                   staff, this stage of a firm's management evol-
                                   ution can be the most beneficial.

14.4.5 Stage 4: elected management or executive committee

There may well be a 'management committee' at stage 2 (or at stage 3
instead of an appointed managing partner), but its role will normally be
purely administrative and — like the appointed managing partner — it
may lack any real mandate to manage the firm. By stage 4, the need for
serious management is acknowledged in the firm: a committee is elected
with a mandate. Despite good intentions, the reality may be different.

14.4.5.1 Instead of a managing partner

Characteristics: the major players in the partnership collectively
                                   act to run the firm because none of them is
                                   willing to become the managing partner or is
                                   not willing to allow another to take the role on.

Potential advantages: spreading of the management load;
                                   a forum for, and for the control of, the direc-
                                   tor(s) of finance and administration, and sup-
                                   port staff.

Potential disadvantages: indecision;
                                   lack of direction;
                                   partners more involved in administration than
                                   substantive management;
                                   a splitting of functional responsibilities among
                                   committee members, with consequent lack of
                                   coordination and communication;
                                   'pass the buck' mentality, or power struggles
                                   between committee members.

Comments: this situation still reflects a lack of management
                                   maturity, despite previous experience during
                                   the evolution; there is a very narrow dividing
                                   line between this and stage 2, with the danger
                                   that an experienced director of finance and
                                   administration may leave in frustration because
                                   the lines of communication and control are
                                   blurred or conflicting; this situation is probably
                                   only sustainable in a medium-sized firm.

14.4.5.2 As support for the managing partner

Characteristics: the major players in the partnership collectively act as a sounding board and as support for an elected managing partner; often the heads of departments.

Potential advantages: provides the managing partner with the ability to consult senior colleagues, and ensures support in implementation;
helps with communication around the firm.

Potential disadvantages: committee members second-guess the managing partner or usurp his or her executive power; the managing partner defers too much to the committee, with consequently slower decision-making.

Comments: as a firm grows, even a good, elected managing partner will feel the need for a close group of confidants; in a sense, the group will serve a better purpose as a policy board looking at and advising on strategy and policy.

14.4.5.3 Non-executive member(s) of committee

Characteristics: an external, experienced non-lawyer or non-practising lawyer is invited to sit on a policy-making, strategic or senior management committee to bring an external, independent (and often business) perspective to the firm's thinking.

Potential advantages: exposes the firm to different points of view and experience;
challenges the assumptions of partners about clients' needs and business practice;
adds specialised knowledge;
possibly creates an ambassador for the firm in the marketplace.

Potential disadvantages: a non-executive who does not understand the culture of a law firm;
a non-executive who does not take his or her duties seriously enough;
the firm does not use or value the non-executive properly.

Comments: still a relatively underused and untested option, showing mixed results in UK and US law firms.

14.4.6 Stage 5: a chief executive

This possibility is being actively canvassed in a number of firms and, like the non-executive committee members, is so far showing mixed results.

14.4.6.1 As a development from the elected managing partner

An effective and respected managing partner may become the chief executive with greater powers and management autonomy than is normally allowed to an elected managing partner. As such, the characteristics and advantages are the same as for an elected managing partner, but the disadvantages have usually by now been overcome (see paragraph 14.4.4.4).

14.4.6.2 As a replacement for a managing partner

Characteristics: a full-time appointment, usually of a non-lawyer, to run the firm in place of an elected managing partner, and with or without an executive committee (if the person appointed is a lawyer, the role is really that of an elected managing partner as described in paragraph 14.4.6.1).

Comments: relatively untested in the UK because there are few people with the requisite experience or authority; the US experience has not been entirely successful over the medium to long term (see, for example, Orey 1991).

The dilemma is expressed by Mintzberg as follows (1993, pages 199–200). He uses the word 'administration' not in its narrow — and often pejorative — sense, but to mean the higher levels of management carried out by people other than the fee-earners:

"The professional faces a fundamental dilemma. Frequently, he abhors administration, desiring only to be left alone to practice his profession. But that freedom is gained only at the price of administrative effort. . . . This leaves the professional two choices: to do the administrative work himself, in which case he has less time to practice his profession, or to leave it to administrators, in which case he must surrender some of his power over decision making. And that power must be surrendered, it should be added, to administrators who, by virtue of the fact that they do not wish to practice the profession, probably favor a different set of goals. Damned if he does and damned if he doesn't."

Chapter 15

MANAGING PARTNERS

15.1 The Role of Partners in Management

The previous discussion of the evolution of law firm management (see paragraph 14.4) has shown that, at different stages in a firm's development, partners may be involved collectively (full partners' meetings and decision-making), individually (senior partner, managing partner, finance partner, etc.), or representatively (as a Committee member). The success of any of these approaches will depend very much on the firm's evolution, the prevailing circumstances within the firm, the ability and commitment of partners to the roles they have, and the attitude (management maturity) of those who are not directly involved at any given time. Suffice to say that any roles should be as clearly defined as possible, the nature and degree of authority carried by that role should be agreed, and any necessary training to fulfil the role offered (see further paragraph 24.2).

This chapter is concerned principally with the role and responsibilities of those partners who assume the position of 'managing partner' (whether that label is used or not). The role of a partner as a head of department is discussed in paragraph 19.3, and that of project or case manager (team leader) in paragraph 21.5.2. Although the specific roles are not discussed, the range of responsibilities for a marketing partner is addressed by the discussion in chapter 18, for personnel and training partners in chapters 22 to 26, and for finance partners in chapters 28 to 31. For all of them, the issues of leadership (paragraphs 23.5 and 23.6), understanding the role (paragraph 24.2), the use of power and influence (paragraph 24.3), and managing change (chapter 27) are dealt with in other chapters. However, to the extent that the following discussion is concerned with 'a partner in a management position', it will also be of value to partners occupying these other roles.

15.2 The Need for a Managing Partner

There is a common assumption that firms must achieve a certain size before they need a managing partner. This is a myth. It is not a question of size, but of need and the availability of someone with the necessary qualities to undertake the task. Even very small firms (say up to six partners) can work very effectively with a managing partner if the circumstances allow; if there is no managing partner, firms have to 'manage' through the consensual or democratic involvement of all partners. The question is not whether the firm has reached the 'right size', but whether it has achieved a level of management maturity that makes a managing partner the correct choice at that point in its development.

The existence, role, status and functions of a managing partner will depend on a wealth of factors. Whether there is a single managing partner, or a number of partners engaged in management functions, is for my purposes irrelevant. The work needs to be done by someone: whether and how that work is split between partners will be the result of many issues (see chapter 14). To ease exposition, I shall assume that there is a single managing partner, but the underlying premises remain valid if the work is split.

Chapter 14 introduced two types of management structures — the professional bureaucracy and the operating adhocracy — as the two most likely structures in law firms. This chapter considers the position of the managing partner in each, before going on to look more practically at the role of a managing partner and the particular difficulties associated with making the transition from one managing partner to another.

15.3 Managing Partners in the Professional Bureaucracy

There is no doubt that management and administration are difficult in the professional bureaucracy. Indeed, Mintzberg (1993) seems to assume that the only 'administrators' are professionals who have become administrators (in our case, lawyers). He calls them 'professional administrators' — not to be confused with administrators who are professional in their own right (for example, as chartered accountants or personnel directors) but not lawyers, and who I would prefer to describe as professional managers.

The first managing partners in law firms tend to spend their time on routine administrative matters, and may be seen as little better than a glorified member of the support staff. The credibility of the position can be low, and the respect for an individual who is prepared to take the job on reduced as a result. But as the firm grows and develops, and partners begin to realise that a multimillion-pound business cannot run itself, perceptions of the role begin to change, and its credibility increases.

Managing partners may be regarded as part of Mintzberg's strategic apex or middle line of the organisation (see paragraph 14.3.3); they are certainly part of the hierarchy of authority or interface between the partners as the owners of the business and the fee-earners and support staff who make up the operating core. Indeed, Mintzberg suggests that professionals need to control not only their own professional work, but also the administrative decisions that affect it (cf. paragraph 14.2.4.2): this requires that the middle line must also be controlled and therefore "staffed with 'their own'" (1993, page 197) — in our context, a lawyer.

However, although the managing partner may be 'one of our own', he or she is still not always regarded as an equal: to the extent that the managing partner gives up fee-earning work, there is a danger that other fee-earners will regard the manager as being 'beneath them'. Although this might leave the managing partner in a vulnerable position, it is not necessarily a weak one: "*Individually*, they are usually more powerful than individual professionals . . . even if that power can easily be overwhelmed by the *collective* power of the professionals" (Mintzberg 1993, page 200).

The distinction between the 'real' work of the lawyers and the work of the support staff (see paragraphs 3.3 and 24.3.2.2(a)) is a difficult one to shake. This leads to a bifurcated structure, with the possibility for confusion and conflict (Mintzberg 1993, page 198):

"What frequently emerge in the Professional Bureaucracy are parallel administrative hierarchies, one democratic and bottom-up for the professionals, and a second machine bureaucratic and top-down for the support staff. In the professional hierarchy, power resides in expertise; one has influence by virtue of one's knowledge and skills. In other words, a good deal of power remains . . . with the professional operators themselves. That does not, of course, preclude a pecking order among them. But it does require their pecking order to mirror the professionals' experience and expertise. . . . In the nonprofession hierarchy, in contrast, power and status reside in administrative office. . . . Unlike the case in the professional structure, here one must practice administration, not a specialized function of the organization, to attain status. But 'research indicates that a professional orientation toward service and a bureaucratic orientation toward disciplined compliance with procedures are opposite approaches toward work and often create conflict in organizations' (Blau 1967–68, page 456). Hence, these two parallel hierarchies are kept quite independent of each other."

One of the responsibilities of the managing partner, therefore, may well be to resolve conflicts between the parallel hierarchies of the fee-earners and the support staff. Given the fallibility of the pigeonholing process, and the potential conflict it can cause (see paragraph 14.3.4.1), another role of the managing partner could be to mediate in the "jurisdictional disputes between the professionals" (Mintzberg 1993, page 199).

One of the benefits of having a managing partner is that the existence of the role allows the fee-earners to concentrate on serving clients without being 'distracted' by other aspects of the business. Depending on the role of 'senior partner' in a firm, this can also extend the managing partner's functions to external issues as well as internal ones:

"On the one hand, the administrators are expected to protect the professionals' autonomy, to 'buffer' them from external pressures. On the other hand, the administrators are expected to woo these outsiders to support the organization. Thus, the external roles of the manager — maintaining liaison contacts, acting as figurehead and spokesman in a public relations capacity, negotiating with outside agencies — emerge as primary ones" (Mintzberg 1993, page 199).

To a large extent, the business strategy of the professional bureaucracy will reflect the individual initiatives of its partners and senior fee-earners (cf. paragraph 4.3.3). For this reason, the managing partner is often excluded from strategic activity. The managing partner's role is seen as being to support the professionals and to provide the necessary resources and infrastructure. However, as we have seen from chapter 14, the creation of an appropriate structure for the firm is also an important 'strategic' development and critical to the overall success of the organisation. It is here that the managing partner's strategic influence may be particularly felt. Even so, this is not always done overtly:

"Instead, he must rely on his informal power, and apply it subtly. Knowing that the professionals want nothing more than to be left alone, the administrator moves carefully — in incremental steps, each one hardly discernible. In this way, he may achieve over time changes that the professionals would have rejected out of hand had they been proposed all at once" (Mintzberg 1993, page 202; cf. paragraph 24.3.2).

15.4   Managing Partners in the Operating Adhocracy

The operating adhocracy is a much more fluid and uncertain environment than the professional bureaucracy. As a result, the role of the managing partner becomes much more strategic and related to human interaction. Indeed, given the diversity and fluidity of the organisation, it may be difficult for a single managing partner to cope. The project-based work of the firm, and the emphasis on teamwork, means that its managers "must be masters of human relations, able to use persuasion, negotiation, coalition, reputation, rapport, or whatever to fuse the individualistic experts into smoothly functioning multidisciplinary teams" (Mintzberg 1993, page 266). They must also be effective project managers (see chapter 21).

The emphasis on projects also means that the firm's work is more transactional. The role of partners in entrepreneurial business development then comes to the fore and, if there is a single managing partner, increases his or her role in strategy and marketing. The job is not simply about providing resources and infrastructure, but encompasses more direct participation in ensuring a steady flow of work. The external role of the managing partner is therefore more important to the operating adhocracy than it is to the professional bureaucracy. In a description that many a law firm that wishes to become more transactional and entrepreneurial might find difficult to take to heart, Mintzberg writes (1993, pages 266–7):

"Nowhere is this more clearly illustrated than in the consulting business, particularly where the approach is innovative and the structure therefore Adhocracy in nature. An executive once commented to this author that 'every consulting firm is three months away from bank-ruptcy'. In other words, three dry months could use up all the surplus funds, leaving none to pay the high professional salaries. And so when a consultant becomes a partner in one of these firms — in effect, moves into the strategic apex — he normally hangs up his calculator and becomes virtually a full-time salesperson. It is a distinguishing charac-teristic of many an Operating Adhocracy that the selling function literally takes place at the strategic apex."

The idea that partners stop practising law and devote all of their time to project management and marketing is more than most can cope with!

Mintzberg therefore envisages a structure in which all partners play some strategic and management role, thus putting the emphasis of a managing partner's role on coordination, monitoring and (it seems to me) the sort of strategic cajoling and stealth envisaged for the managing partner in the professional bureaucracy.

Although the managing partner's involvement in strategy is more pronounced in the operating adhocracy, it is still not one of direction and control (Mintzberg 1993, pages 262–3):

". . . control of the strategy formulation process in the Adhocracy is not clearly placed, at the strategic apex or elsewhere. Moreover, the process is best thought of as strategy *formation*, because strategy in these structures is not so much formulated consciously by individuals as formed implicitly by the decisions they make, one at a time. . . . Now if strategy evolves continuously according to the projects being done, it stands to reason that strategy formation is controlled by whoever decides what projects are done and how. And in the Operating Adhocracy, that includes . . . potentially everyone in the organization."

This is consistent with Mintzberg's notion of emergent, crafted strategies (see paragraph 4.3.3).

15.5 The Roles of a Managing Partner

Against this background, it is of course dangerous to generalise about the role of a managing partner. As suggested in chapter 14, there can also be other structures in law firms, and some of them can be hybrids of other configurations (see paragraph 14.3.4.3). Nevertheless, experience sug-gests that there are a number of common issues, even if they are resolved differently. Where a managing partner is appointed, the correct balance must be found between fee-earning and management responsibilities. Every firm should resist the suggestion that it might need a full-time managing partner — the vast majority of firms will never need that (although I accept that for some large or disparate firms a full-time role, though it should still be resisted, may in practice, or politically, be inevitable and necessary).

In my view, managing partners should try to divide their time into the following areas.

15.5.1 Spend time with clients

If a managing partner is appointed, it is normally preferable for him or her to retain some client-related responsibilities. In larger firms, this may not amount to very much direct involvement in fee-earning, but in any firm part of the role of the managing partner should be to spend time with the firm's clients, finding out more about what they need from the firm, and what they think of the service they are receiving. In this way, the managing partner could still be spending about half of his or her time on 'client work'. It is not necessary for the managing partner to be engaged in the detail of matters; he or she can, for example, adopt a client partner, or coordinating or project management, function. In small firms with a higher caseload of smaller matters, where there are few (if any) opportunities for teamwork and delegation and the client relationship is more personal, it is inevitable that any managing partner would spend most of this time in a direct fee-earning role.

15.5.2 Spend time on the firm

The managing partner will also need to spend time directing and coordinating the administrative and support services of the firm. With the right administrative staff in place, however, it will be neither necessary nor appropriate for the managing partner to be involved in the firm's administration. This should accordingly take as little time as possible (target a maximum of 20%), though in smaller firms it will tend to take up more of a managing partner's time.

Personnel and finance issues may take up a significant part of this time (as may managing the firm's reputation through marketing and public relations). The following administrative areas will also need to be addressed:

(a) secretarial services,
(b) office equipment and technology,
(c) communications (telephones, fax machines, etc.),
(d) word processing,
(e) library and information services,
(f) photocopying,
(g) messenger, mail and courier services,
(h) premises, office facilities, cleaning and furnishings,
(i) filing and storage,
(j) reception,
(k) office security,
(l) stationery and supplies,
(m) conference or meeting rooms.

15.5.3   Spend time with partners

The balance of a managing partner's time should be spent with other partners — communicating, helping them manage their practices (particularly if they are heads of department or otherwise responsible for a practice area), dealing with partners' problems and with 'problem' partners, being involved in partner performance reviews (and possibly profit-sharing assessments), and so on. The range of partnership issues is considered in chapters 32 to 37. This may well prove to be the most valuable part of a managing partner's efforts, and yet is in too many firms the most often neglected area of responsibility.

15.5.4   Define the role and communicate

Many partners in law firms of all sizes find it difficult to comprehend how a managing partner spends his or her time, and tend to assume that most of the time is wasted or unnecessary. Such a situation indicates a lack of understanding of the true role of a managing partner, resulting in a wide variety of views and expectations that cannot all be met. Chapter 14 and the earlier part of this chapter should help the managing partner and other partners begin to appreciate the magnitude of the job!

There is also often a failure on the part of a managing partner to communicate enough about the job for the partners at large to appreciate what they are being spared in terms of running their business. One can understand the reluctance: one rationale for the role is to spare the partners from involvement, and it may not appear to make sense then to burden them with details of what they are intended to be spared from. However, it seems to me that particular credibility for a managing partner will come from maximising the time he or she spends with clients or on client work, and with partners. If the partnership at large thinks that the job is all about counting paper clips and maintaining photocopiers, taking the time to communicate with them will help them understand the range of responsibilities and the effectiveness of their chosen manager.

15.6   Replacing a Managing Partner

There does come a time when one managing partner steps aside, and someone else takes over. In England, the success of this transition does not have a good history. A number of managing partners have left the firms they managed — often to try something unrelated to law. I therefore want to examine the process to see if any lessons can be learnt.

15.6.1   The need for replacement

We are assuming that it is necessary to replace the current managing partner. I want to assume further that he or she is willing to move on. In many firms, managing partners serve limited terms, sometimes with the option to serve a second term. There is, though, something perverse in appointing someone because of his or her seniority, or in requiring a good managing partner to step aside simply because 'the rules say so' (this is management by seniority or rotation, and has no inherent logic — or, indeed, history of success). It takes a lot of time and effort to become an effective manager: the individual and the firm both make an enormous investment in that development of managerial know-how. When a managing partner moves on, most firms lose that investment, and then put their faith and future in the hands of someone who has to go through the same extended learning process, and runs the risk of repeating mistakes. There should be a very good reason for doing this!

When a change in management is required, most firms spend far too much time arguing (and politicking) about who the successor should be. All firms are in a state of evolution. They should therefore spend their time analysing where they are in the business and management cycle and discussing what kind of management they need, how much of it, and the qualities required to provide it (cf. paragraph 2.3 and chapter 14).

15.6.2 *Appointing a replacement*

The appointment of a replacement managing partner is a vital part of the firm's succession planning. Like anything else, its success will be in direct proportion to the preparation that goes into it. Defining the firm's management needs, and the role of the managing partner, as well as identifying early on who the successor should be, and grooming that person for the role, will increase the chances of a successful transition. Managing a law firm is now a complex and sophisticated activity for which any managing partner will require training and development. In some of the larger firms, a prospective managing partner is sent on an intensive management programme. In others, the formal training period is shorter and sporadic. In some, there is a transitional period where the outgoing and incoming managing partners work together. In any event, early identification allows everyone to come to terms with the new appointment.

A new managing partner will also need to reflect on how the role has changed. Originally, managing partners tended to be responsible for supervising support staff, introducing new administrative systems, and organising office moves, and so on. It was rarely a credible or respected activity for a lawyer to undertake. The persistent confusion in lawyers' minds between management and administration, and the equation of administration with bureaucracy, made the role very difficult (cf. paragraph 14.4.4.2). Today, managing partners are more likely to spend their time on strategy, managing the delivery of legal services, and dealing with inter-partner issues (particularly promotion, productivity and rewards). They have more responsibility and authority, and the distinction between their role and that of the senior partner has become blurred. During the 1990s recession, the need for strong management and some tough decisions has increased the profile and importance of the job (cf. paragraph 14.3.1.3): management has become respectable. These changes necessarily redefine the qualities required of the person doing the job. What you looked for last time is not likely to be what you should be looking for now.

A managing partner is also a leader, someone who can lead by example, take decisions and see them through, and who regards the firm as his or her most important client during the period of stewardship. The managing partner should also be a good communicator, discreet but not secretive, who gets on well with people and who can deal with people problems both firmly and compassionately. This description is not definitive but, in short, the managing partner is a paragon of virtue! More seriously, the issue is not so much a question of finding a person who has all the right qualities as *not* appointing someone who is lacking in one or more critical areas.

A final question in the process of appointing a successor is the effect that the new role will have on that person's practice, and then on the firm's finances. It is crucial that the firm's managing partner should be a respected fee-earner — to give credibility with the professionals he or she will have to manage (see paragraph 3.4(a)). The managing partner will therefore have a substantial (and often personal) client following. There is an opportunity cost to every appointment. This will probably be the hardest part of the decision. Depending on the size and needs of the firm, the new managing partner may not need (and perhaps should not be encouraged) to give up client work entirely. But a significant commitment to client work can only be maintained at the expense of the management activity. Both the new managing partner and the firm need to be clear about the extent of the commitments to client work and management. With forethought and good support, there is much that he or she can do to service clients without detailed involvement. At the end of the day, deciding whether the opportunity cost is justified will be as much an act of faith as of analysis, resulting in a belief that the needs and continuing success of the firm require a controlled degree of sacrifice. Again, planning and support will ease the transition of the managing partner from full-time fee-earning. The transition should not be happening overnight, and so there will be opportunities to balance these changing priorities.

15.6.3 Re-entry problems

As the new managing partner assumes the mantle and grapples with the current issues, so the former managing partner has to come to terms with a new existence. Many of the difficulties of re-entry and re-integration begin back in the mists of time. When the former managing partner was originally appointed, the future issue of re-entry was probably not considered. Sometimes, no one thought about how long the appointment was for, and on what basis it was made, so no one foresaw the timing or potential difficulties of reverting to practice.

A key factor in the success of the transition will be the extent to which the former managing partner maintained any continuing commitment to clients and client work during his or her period of office. Without any, the period of transition will be longer and more difficult. As with the new managing partner, the continuing relationship need not have been daily contact or involvement, and certainly should not have entailed any detailed drafting or preparation. But maintaining the client relationship, project managing, and being consulted on matter strategy can keep valuable contacts current.

The former managing partner and the firm should together agree a transition plan. This should cover the length of the intended transition period, new objectives for chargeable and non-chargeable time, how the transition will be made, whether the partner's profit-share will be affected in any way during this period, whether any continuing management involvement is envisaged, and ways in which the firm can help.

The transition period is usually one of great personal difficulty for former managing partners, and few other people in the firm will realise what he or she is going through. Partners generally do not understand what collective demands they used to make on the managing partner's time, and how they made him or her the centre of their management attention. Suddenly to be removed from this core position, no longer to be informed or consulted, can create a devastating void. There is a question of ego, of being valued; and there is a great danger of instantaneous devaluation ('role underload': see paragraphs 24.2.2.5 and 24.2.3).

The pace of management activity and of legal practice are often different, too. Along with all the other changes, a former managing partner faces a change in lifestyle, a shift in pace and horizons, and changed performance standards. These will require considerable personal readjustment. It is therefore very important for both parties to be clear about the expectations that each should have of the other. And in firms where partners are not rewarded by previously determined points allocations or lock-step profit-shares (see chapter 37), the former managing partner will need to know how long he or she has to readjust before contribution is assessed again on exactly the same basis as any other practising partner. Without some short-term guarantees, a former managing partner may well give up practice altogether.

To ease the succession, it often makes sense to allow a former managing partner a short sabbatical. This allows the new managing partner to settle in without feeling that someone is looking over his or her shoulder. It also allows the former managing partner time to step back and start the process of readjustment without the immediate pressures of client work and time sheets.

Firms should also assess the management experience that now resides in former managing partners, and consider whether they should play any continuing role in the firm's management. Often, they will be happy enough to step right back and let someone else get on with it. But they may also be offended not to be asked and feel 'dumped' if not at least asked. In most law firms, managerial know-how is still in short supply: it is important not to waste what exists.

15.6.4   Conclusion

The key to a successful transition between managing partners is to eliminate the element of surprise and abrupt changes for both the new and former incumbents. In both cases, planning, preparation, support and consideration are required. The ability to identify, develop and change leaders is a sign of management maturity in any organisation. When it is achieved, partners can rest assured of a more secure future (see paragraph 3.4(i)).

Chapter 16

PROFESSIONAL MANAGERS AND SUPPORT STAFF

16.1 Introduction

The potential difficulties of managers and support staff will be put into a human resource context in paragraph 22.3. Suffice to say at the moment that managers and support staff are often looked down on by professionals. Their work is rarely regarded as being either as 'proper' or as important as fee-earning activities (see paragraphs 3.3 and 24.3.2.2(a)). From the start, therefore, professional management and administrative support are difficult activities to perform in a law firm.

The evolution of professional managers is closely tied to the evolution of a firm (see paragraph 14.4). Because many law firms are concurrently developing in similar ways (to reflect their business and professional environment), there are also discernible trends within the profession over a period of time (such as the appointment of managing partners, directors of finance and administration, directors of personnel, training, marketing, information technology, and so on). What is right for a firm at any given time in its development will therefore depend on a variety of (constantly changing) factors. And if the herd instinct comes into play (cf. paragraphs 4.4.2 and 14.3.1.4), it might be helpful to know which herd one is choosing to follow.

In very general terms, the role of a professional manager can be described as being to help the firm's managing partner (or other partners with management responsibilities) in the structuring, resourcing and management of those areas of support set out in paragraph 15.5.2; the role of the support staff is to carry out the functions of those areas.

Mintzberg's distinctions between various types of organisational configuration (see paragraph 14.3.3) show that different types of administrative infrastructure may be required for any given configuration to be successful. As in chapter 15, therefore, I shall begin by looking at the role of professional managers and support staff in the two configurations considered in detail in chapter 14 — the professional bureaucracy and the operating adhocracy.

16.2 Professional Support in the Professional Bureaucracy

Although fee-earners tend to be expensive people, and part of the rationale for having professional managers and support staff is to 'spare' them from more routine tasks, many lawyers still insist on performing administrative activities for themselves. This derives from their need to control as much of their work as possible (vertical decentralisation: see paragraph 14.2.4.2). This is perverse, given the low standing which is normally attributed by professionals to managers and administrative staff.

In addition, the desire for autonomy and self-management which is so strong in fee-earners (see paragraph 14.2.5) results in a largely 'democratic' organisation. But, as Mintzberg points out (1993, page 197): "For the support staff . . . there is no democracy in the Professional Bureaucracy, only the oligarchy of the professionals. Support units . . . are as likely as not to be managed tightly from the top. They exist, in effect, as machine bureaucratic constellations within the Professional Bureaucracy." This leads to the bifurcated structure — and its problems — described in paragraph 15.3. In particular, managers and support staff may be the victims of power struggles between partners, and of the lack of coordination between fee-earners (identified by Mintzberg: see paragraph 14.3.4.1).

16.3 Professional Support in the Operating Adhocracy

The fluid and project-based environment of the operating adhocracy leads to a political environment with a distinct lack of any stable organisational structure (see paragraph 14.3.4.2). And yet the support staff may still need to operate as a 'machine bureaucratic constellation' (cf. paragraph 16.2). This can cause significant confusion and stress for the support staff — "confusion of members as to who their boss is, whom to impress to get promoted; . . . a lack of clarity in job definitions, authority relationships, and lines of communication; random and unplanned personal development" (Mintzberg 1993, page 276). It also exacerbates the bifurcation between the fee-earning structure and the support structure (cf. paragraph 15.3).

Adhocracy also encourages or tolerates inefficiency (see paragraph 14.3.4.2). Again, for administrators and support staff — whose *raison d'être* is often efficiency and order — this can also be a particularly trying environment.

However, where operating adhocracies can operate in the fully innovative, creative and productive way envisaged by Mintzberg, the position of managers and support staff can be the most exciting and secure of any of his structures, since (1993, page 258) "members of what in other organizations would be called the support staff — typically a highly trained and important group in the Operating Adhocracy — may take their place right alongside the operating specialists on the project teams. And even when distinctions are made, a close rapport must develop between the administrative and operating levels."

16.4   Pitfalls for Professional Managers

Given the risks to which professional managers are potentially subject in a law firm (see paragraph 16.1), it may be helpful to elaborate the circumstances in which they or the firm may create difficulties.

16.4.1   *Trying to control the fee-earners*

Managers generally are appointed to bring structure, order and efficiency to organisations. Professional service firms, however, have to cope with a principal resource made up of autonomous, largely self-managing, professionals. The most common mistake made by professional managers is to try to control or to impose structure and order on the activities of these people.

The professional manager in a law firm has the same range of possible coordinating mechanisms as any other manager (see paragraph 14.2.4.3). But the complexity of professional services, and the vague nature of their output, means that what the manager normally engages in is "bothersome exercises", because the use of these mechanisms assumes "that professional work can be controlled, like any other, in a top-down manner, an assumption that has proven false again and again" (Mintzberg 1993, page 211).

Managers may seek to justify intervention on quality grounds — that it is necessary to ensure the competence of the fee-earners. This is partly consistent with the idea that management can interfere with professional autonomy (see paragraph 14.2.5). However, no structure or system created by a professional manager will make an incompetent lawyer into a competent one, but the "plans, rules, and orders can impede the competent professional from providing his service effectively" (Mintzberg 1993, page 212).

16.4.2   *Failures caused by the manager*

Mintzberg was writing generically (but nevertheless correctly). In the context of law firms, Hildebrandt and Kaufman (1988) offer an analysis of 'administrator failures'. They distinguish between failures caused by the manager or administrator, and failures caused by the firm. In the first category, they identify the following examples (1988, pages 94–7). They suggest (1988, page 97): "If you see your administrator in one or more of these six examples, discussion should take place before it is too late. A little timely communication on both sides can do wonderful things for the management, the administrator and, most importantly, the law firm."

16.4.2.1 *Trying to build the perfect law firm*

Being a professional manager in a law firm can be a lonely existence. Talking to others outside the firm, attending management conferences and reading management articles can all be sources of information and ideas. Unfortunately, it is not sufficient simply for the manager to know all the latest developments and theories. They are only worthwhile if they are relevant to the firm in which he or she works, and can be made to work in it. Failing to recognise this can significantly damage the firm's perception of the manager: "By the time he has learned to deal with the firm he works for rather than trying to turn it into the great law firm in the sky, he has failed so often that his credibility is gone. He may succeed once in a while, but lawyers seem to keep better scorecards on administrators' failures than on their successes" (Hildebrandt and Kaufman 1988, pages 94–5).

A variation on this theme is simply copying what other firms are doing (cf. paragraphs 4.4.2 and 14.3.1.4): again, unless what is done is appropriate for the administrator's firm, this approach will also lead to difficulties.

16.4.2.2 *Failing to find the middle ground*

This usually means being too closely identified as 'management' by the support staff, putting across and justifying the partners' (or managing partner's) position to them, but not representing them to management. Alternatively, the manager may be so busy representing the views of support staff that in the eyes of the lawyers he becomes merely a senior member of the support staff rather than a manager . Both amount to being caught in the middle, rather than finding the right balance.

16.4.2.3 *Playing the politics*

All organisations have a political dimension to them, resulting from the balance and use of power (see paragraph 24.3). A manager who is keen to be 'on the side' of the current power brokers often provides different levels of support and service to others in the firm. Such a manager usually becomes a victim when there is a change in the firm as a result of which "some of the former 'second-class citizens' now run the firm" (Hildebrandt and Kaufman 1988, page 96).

16.4.2.4 *Not understanding the politics*

There is a difference between playing politics and not understanding them, but their effect on the manager may be the same. Again, it is a question of balance. Just as building the perfect law firm is a mistake, so is not recognising the effects of power and influence. Firms have their own culture, as well as people who are better able to get things done. Treating the firm as 'machine' devoid of history, culture and power is another sure way of losing credibility. If avoiding the politics means not pandering to political 'favourites', it does not follow that everyone in the firm then has to be treated in exactly the same way irrespective of their status, reputation, or ability.

16.4.2.5   *Forgetting who pays the salary*
Managers who feel that lawyers should be controlled (see paragraph 16.4.1) often also react misguidedly in other situations, for example, to "lawyers who 'unreasonably' request overtime secretarial help, messenger service, a file cabinet, or use of a conference room" (Hildebrandt and Kaufman 1988, page 96). No manager can afford to forget that the job exists only for as long as he or she is serving the fee-earners (although this equally does not justify constant reminders of the fact from the fee-earners!).

16.4.2.6   *Not understanding the numbers*
Hildebrandt and Kaufman's final suggestion is that a manager cannot survive without a knowledge of the firm's finances, and of how to interpret and use financial information.

16.4.3   Failures caused by the firm

We should not assume, however, that law firms are entirely free from blame in the failures of their professional managers to survive. Hildebrandt and Kaufman identify five possibilities (1988, pages 91–4).

16.4.3.1   *Unwillingness or inability to accept a 'non-lawyer' manager*
The almost constant refrain from lawyers is, 'Leave me alone to practise law'. The idea of appointing a professional manager to take responsibility for some (or all) of the administrative and support services is therefore attractive. Until, that is, the manager does something that the lawyers do not like. Even if the manager is not otherwise guilty of a 'manager pitfall' (in paragraphs 16.4.1 or 16.4.2), the position can still result in failure.

16.4.3.2   *Recruiting the wrong person, or changing the rules*
It is not unknown for a firm to appoint the wrong person — meaning someone who is underqualified or (more usually) overqualified for the job that actually needs doing or that the firm will allow to be done. Even when they appoint a person who is admirably and suitably qualified, it is quite common for the firm to change the reporting structure, or subsequently interpose committees or levels of management between the manager and partners.

16.4.3.3   *Undermining the manager's authority*
Professional managers are often appointed to head up the whole or part of the support services, and are then nominally given responsibility for the corresponding support staff. However, very often the manager's decisions will be ignored or overturned by partners (particularly the powerful, high-billing, 'heavy hitters'). This may be a particular problem with employment matters, for while the partners may be content for the manager to engage new staff, he or she is not an owner (partner) and not therefore in a technical sense an employer (cf. paragraph 16.3). All too frequently, the partners will be seen to have "clearly communicated to the

staff that although [the manager] was to be considered their 'boss', he was not the final word" (Hildebrandt and Kaufman 1988, page 93).

16.4.3.4 Boredom

Law firms that try to restrict their professional managers to a purely administrative role will usually face a difficulty of bored or demotivated managers — particularly where they recruit people for their broader experience. The managers' self-concept has them in a more involved role, and the failure of the firm to use them fully can create role underload and role stress (see paragraphs 22.5.1 and 24.2). "While administrators do not make the policy, their involvement in almost everything other than the direct practice of law will keep them challenged and stimulated" (Hildebrandt and Kaufman 1988, page 93).

16.4.3.5 Under-utilisation

This is very similar to the previous point, in that "the skills for which he or she was hired must be utilized or he or she will leave. . . . There is no promotional ladder to climb, and advancement comes to him only through salary increases or more challenge and stimulation. Administrators leaving a position seldom complain that they were expected to do more than they were able to, or that they were overworked or challenged beyond their capabilities" (Hildebrandt and Kaufman 1988, pages 93–4).

16.5 Conclusion

One of the themes of this book is Sveiby and Lloyd's notion of dual expertise (see paragraph 3.3). Of the four groups of people in know-how businesses, two are the manager and the clerical (or support) staff: see paragraph 22.3. Professional managers and support staff necessarily play a key role in providing managerial expertise. I shall examine later the difficulties faced by these managers in gaining and maintaining internal credibility in an environment where fee-earning is paramount (see paragraphs 24.3.2.2(a) and 24.3.3.2), as well as possible differences in motivation (see paragraphs 26.2.2 and 26.3.2). There may also be a tendency to describe such staff as 'non' people (e.g., non-lawyers, non-partners, non-fee-earners, non-qualified), or perhaps to regard them as peripheral (see paragraph 22.2). These tendencies are all reflected in Mintzberg's analyses, and show that the legal profession perhaps still has some way to go towards the acceptance and integration of a key element in the management structure of its businesses.

PART IV

LAW FIRMS AS CLIENT-DRIVEN ORGANISATIONS

Chapter 17

DELIVERY OF LEGAL SERVICES

17.1 Meaning of 'Legal Services'

17.1.1 Shifting boundaries

It would once have been relatively easy to define 'legal services', and it might have been possible to do so by reference to activities carried out by lawyers and law firms. Indeed, traditionally, a profession has been defined in relation to a body of knowledge and experience: the unifying, socialising and legitimising effect of this common professional knowledge can be said to create 'know-how communities' (I have taken the idea of a know-how community from Holzner's concept of an 'epistemic community' (1972, pages 69–71); see also Salter 1994). These communities develop their own norms of behaviour, methods of working, and approaches to developing and sharing new knowledge: in other words, their own culture. The boundaries and legitimate spheres of influence between the different communities (professions) are then founded on their own distinct body of common knowledge, and regulated by a professional body.

Increasing specialisation, while leading to greater differentiation of knowledge *within* a profession, is in some ways leading to greater integration of knowledge *across* professions. In many different areas, the boundaries between different bodies of knowledge are breaking down — to a point where it is much more difficult to identify the exact parameters of each. A quarter of a century ago, Esland wrote: "It may be possible to detect in the alliances and segmentation occurring within professional associations the generation and growth of new organizing frameworks for knowledge. The intra-professional negotiations which are already occurring indicate [that the] boundaries are only human constructs and can, therefore, be broken" (1971, page 97). This leads him to the conclusion that "Professional knowledge is negotiable currency" (1971, page 105).

That there should be a crisis in professional epistemology is not surprising (see Schön 1991, chapter 1); that some professionals foresee the destruction of their professions is also not surprising: the 'know-how communities' that have so far sustained them are experiencing fundamental changes (see, further, paragraph 38.4).

Looked at in this way, it is easy to see why the national borders of professions are being eroded, why accountants and financial institutions are offering services once the preserve of lawyers, why some law firms are diversifying into estate agency and financial services, why licensed conveyancers can undertake property transactions, and why the government can say that most legal services may also be performed by non-lawyers (see paragraph 1.4.1.3). The advent of multinational and multidisciplinary practices is not surprising. Of course, there is a dimension of competition and survival in this; but there is also an element of challenge and (dare I say it) inevitability as the knowledge boundaries continue to fall. If others will provide 'legal' services, then perhaps law firms need to consider what 'non-legal' services they should be offering.

I shall continue to use the expression 'legal services' to mean that combination of services that any given law firm chooses to offer — and ignore the objections that law firms may offer 'non-legal' services, that 'legal' services may be offered by businesses other than law firms, and that even the term 'law firm' may now be open to ambiguity!

17.1.2 Nature of services

Whatever the scope or nature of the services offered, they will display the same characteristics as any other professional services. Payne identifies four characteristics of services, and suggests that each of them represents part of a continuum (1993, pages 7–8; and see figure 17.1): intangibility; heterogeneity (non-standard and highly variable); inseparability (typically 'produced and consumed' at the same time, often with client participation in the process); and perishability (they cannot be pre-prepared and stored for later use). All services, therefore, have tendencies to these characteristics, although the precise combination of them (and their point on the continuum of each) will differ from service to service. Legal services have typically been highly intangible, extremely varied, often created and delivered with the client present (for example, advice given in a consultation or over the telephone), and highly perishable. The increasing tendency to standardise some aspects of legal service — for instance, in 'do-it-yourself' wills or conveyancing — is perhaps moving some services to different points on the continuum. However, most legal services fall at the most challenging points.

17.1.3 Consequences

If the boundaries between the different bodies of professional knowledge and services are changing, and the boundaries between the professions that might supply the services are changing, and the services themselves

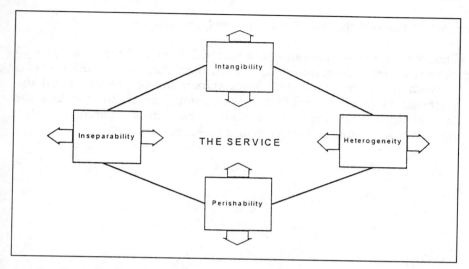

Figure 17.1 (Source: Payne 1993, page 9)

are subject to variables, law firms will face difficulties in describing, 'packaging' and selling their services. Clients will have a potential multitude of expectations about the services they want from their lawyers. But the intangibility and perishability of professional services will make it very difficult for clients to know in advance what they will receive or experience. As Maister points out (1993a, page 71): ". . . while goods are consumed, services are *experienced*". The result is that clients 'buy an expectation' — the expectation that they will get what they need or want. At this point, client satisfaction can be defined as the difference between delivery and expectation: if what is actually delivered to them by way of results and service exceeds their expectations, they will be satisfied.

The delivery of legal services, therefore, is not just a matter of 'doing the job', or 'providing the service'. Clients' expectations have to be met — which means that they have to be understood and, to the extent that they are unrealistic or unreasonable, managed.

17.2 Components of Delivery

It might be tempting to think about managing the delivery of legal services as part of the process of running a law firm. Delivery is, however, the very *essence* of the firm. It is here, in what Mintzberg would call the operating core of the practice (see paragraph 14.3.3), that the entrepreneurialism of the firm needs to be brought to bear. It is here where the real matching of the external environment with internal resources and competencies — the achievement of strategy (see chapter 4) — actually takes place. The nature of this entrepreneurialism (see paragraph 7.2) is:

(a)   to identify and bring in new client work;
(b)   to organise and use resources in such a way that the needs of those clients and their work can be met; and

(c)   to ensure that the work is properly carried out.

This, then, provides the framework for the following chapters: chapter 18 looks at business development and marketing; chapter 19 considers ways in which the expertise and skills of fee-earners can best be structured and organised to meet the needs of clients; and chapter 20 examines the productivity and quality of fee-earning work, with a separate consideration of case, matter or project management in chapter 21.

Chapter 18

OPPORTUNITIES, MARKETING AND SELLING

18.1 Securing a Flow of New Business

18.1.1 Exploitation of know-how

Law firms exist to exploit their know-how (see paragraphs 3.1, 3.6, 4.6.2, and 4.6.3, and chapters 5 to 9). This know-how usually relates to solving clients' problems; acquiring or disposing of assets or rights to property; facilitating other personal or commercial activities; protecting their assets, rights, reputation or freedom; or resolving disputes. In order to do this, entrepreneurial partners must first recognise unexploited or under-exploited opportunities in the marketplace (see paragraph 7.2), and then persuade potential clients to engage them.

Clients must therefore have a need for legal services (this is an opportunity); the client must know of the lawyer's existence, which the lawyer will do by raising his or her profile in the marketplace (this is marketing); and the lawyer must be able to persuade the client that he or she is the right person to be engaged to address the client's need (this is selling).

If the client comes straight to the lawyer as a result of a referral from an existing client or a referral source, the marketing effort on that occasion will be minimal, and the selling may be easier. But in one way or another, these three elements are always present in the search for new work.

18.1.2 The importance of credibility

The nature of professional services (see paragraph 17.1.2) means that there are few aspects of the service that can be demonstrated before the service provider is engaged. Because of this, prospective clients will be looking for comfort from other sources. The likelihood of a client's needs and expectations being met increases if the lawyer he engages has a reputation for satisfying the needs and expectations of previous clients — this is the lawyer's reputation. In these circumstances, the lawyer becomes a more credible supplier of legal services than another lawyer whose track record is not known or is known to be poor.

The nature of some legal services may be such that an individual lawyer has few opportunities to develop a personal reputation; or it may be that the client's needs (on a large or complex transaction such as a Stock Exchange flotation) are such that one lawyer alone could not satisfy them; or it may be that the lawyer has not been in practice long enough to have established a reputation. In these circumstances, although not able to verify the track record of an individual lawyer, the client may draw comfort from the market reputation of the law firm in which a lawyer or group of lawyers practises. The firm's credibility is then transferred to a lawyer, or supplements an individual's reputation. This is all part of a 'signalling' process which transmits information needed by clients who are looking for legal advice (see paragraphs 6.3 and 8.5.6).

The process of marketing and selling must therefore address how best to develop and present the personal and institutional credibility that may be required in order to persuade clients that a fee-earner (or group of fee-earners) in the firm represents a sound choice. In chapter 5, I described these dimensions of reputation and credibility in terms of individual and firm-specific capital (see paragraph 5.2).

18.2   Market Research and Client Surveys

18.2.1   *The need for information*

Gaining new business in part depends on being able to identify clients' needs for legal services, as well as understanding a prospective client's perception of the lawyer's or firm's ability to meet those needs. Information is therefore required about the sort of client needs that could arise, their frequency, their reasons and their consequences. The firm will also want to know how it can determine which prospective clients are likely to have those needs, and how they react to them. It is also important to appreciate how those clients would go about seeking legal services in relation to those needs, where from, and on what basis, and to know how the firm stands in the perception of the marketplace.

Research about the marketplace for legal services can be conducted simply by *being* in practice, talking to other lawyers, and reading the legal journals to pick up information and comment about trends and developments in legal practice.

Information about what is happening in clients' marketplaces can be found by reading the informed general and business press, specific trade or industry press, and perhaps by commissioning generic market research. The best source of this information, however, comes from talking to the clients themselves. This does not need to come across as blatant touting. Showing a genuine interest in what is happening to clients, their families, or their businesses, is part of being a good lawyer — using information about the client to present the legal service in the most effective and helpful way. This is what good lawyers have always done: it is not a consequence of changes in the legal profession's publicity rules. Talking to clients also provides an opportunity to explore with them ways of improving the delivery of the service to them as well as making sure they receive the right sort of advice. This market and client information also needs to be *shared* within the firm (which is more likely in a partnership of integrated entrepreneurs: cf. paragraphs 9.3 to 9.5, and 18.8).

18.2.2   Guidance from client surveys

I have already described the process of conducting a client survey in the context of looking at the firm's business strategy (see paragraph 11.8). It might be useful in the context of marketing and selling to describe some of the general conclusions that have emerged from client surveys that I have conducted on behalf of law firms. These are the results of talking to nearly 1,000 clients of law firms. The conclusions given here are necessary rationalisations of ultimately idiosyncratic views. In any collection of survey results, a wide variety of views, spanning both ends of a spectrum and all shades in between, will emerge: in short, there will be exceptions to every statement that follows. These conclusions are offered as a *preponderance* of client views rather than absolute statements of client behaviour (see also Maister 1993a, chapter 10).

18.2.2.1   Basis of choice
When asked to disclose on what basis they chose their legal advisers, the top five responses (and the percentage of clients giving them) were:

- a previous connection with the lawyer or firm chosen   34%
- recommendation from another professional (e.g., accountant, bank)   17%
- the lawyer's or firm's reputation for a certain expertise   12%
- *dissatisfaction with existing lawyers*   *10%*
- inheriting an existing relationship from a predecessor   9%

These results clearly show the marketing benefit of what might be called 'networking'. When prospective clients cannot be too certain about the nature of the service quality and experience on which they are about to spend money (cf. paragraphs 17.1.2 and 17.1.3), it is clear that 'proxies' for this in the form of their own prior experience or the views of other respected people will count for more than brochures and other marketing tools.

The fourth most popular response is in fact a reason for seeking another lawyer rather than a basis on which the new lawyer was chosen — but then clients do not have to be rational! However, in a separate question about what prompted clients to change their lawyers, the possible reasons for dissatisfaction and change were:

- a declining quality of service   28%
- cost   15%
- mistakes   14%
- the client's need for more specialised advice (or outgrowing the firm)   8%
- people issues (lack of chemistry or continuity of fee-earners)   8%

This shows that quality of service (dealt with in paragraph 20.3) is roughly twice as important as cost and making mistakes.

Clients were also asked what qualities they looked for when they were about to engage a lawyer. The top five responses were:

- business understanding   60%
- technical (legal) ability   57%
- speed   39%
- chemistry/communication/empathy   32%
- reasonable cost/value for money   26%

The margin of difference between the top two is not perhaps statistically significant, and they should be regarded as equally important: the relative ranking of business understanding and competence in these results is entirely consistent with other, slightly different, investigations (see paragraph 20.3.3). Lawyers are often surprised that cost and value issues are not higher up the list, but the message from clients is that they are quite capable of making a sophisticated assessment and will not normally be totally influenced by cost (except where other factors which are important to them are perceived to be equal between competing firms).

Interestingly, as law firms are increasingly allowed through the relaxation of professional rules to 'institutionalise' their images (through marketing brochures, newsletters, client seminars, etc.), it is clear that some clients still 'personalise' their buying pattern (relying more on personal contact, recommendation or referral, personal chemistry, trust and integrity, and so on). In addition, increasing personalisation in buying legal services is also a reflection of clients choosing specialists: this 'horses for courses' approach does, however, make cross-selling (see paragraph 18.8) much more difficult — the question is how many horses a firm is perceived to have in its stable.

It may be tempting to believe that, because many clients now rarely use a single firm to meet all their legal needs (as, perhaps, they used to), there has been a decline in client loyalty. However, this is only superficially true. There is no doubt that clients are less inclined than previously to use one law firm for all their legal services: but, having chosen the horse for each of their various courses, they are usually very loyal to that horse. To the extent that shopping around takes place, it is perhaps more for specific transactions rather than for firms.

18.2.2.2 *Image, profile, reputation, and differentiation*
By and large, clients perceive very little difference between *firms* (except as expressed in generalisations relating to size, geography or niche areas

of practice). For most clients, differentiation relates to the individuals with whom they deal. This has important lessons for marketing and selling, in the sense that differentiation through marketing is very difficult (because it could only normally be achieved at an organisational level), and that individuals must concentrate much more on how to differentiate themselves in the quest for new work rather than trying to distinguish their firm from a rival firm (see, further, paragraph 18.6.3.2).

18.2.2.3   Quality and value for money

Quality is obviously important to clients, but they acknowledge that their assessment is highly subjective, and for most of them is not influenced by formal quality management systems. Most commercial clients who themselves have ISO 9000 accreditation or the like know that it is not a guarantee of quality, that it costs money, time and effort to maintain, and that quality management may focus too much on process rather than result. Increasingly, sophisticated clients are showing a willingness to trade some aspects of quality for lower fees (as in moving routine matters to smaller, local practices).

In client surveys, the following factors arise as the five most important to clients in assessing quality of advice and service:

* getting the result   38%
* speed of response   36%
* reasonable cost/value for money   22%
* smoothing the transaction/helping it along   18%
* good communication   16%

Quality in legal services is considered in more detail in paragraph 20.3.

18.3   Marketing and the Firm's Profile

18.3.1   Managing the profile

The firm's profile is more or less equivalent to its reputation: it is how the firm is seen in the marketplace. To some extent, this can be managed by the firm through its marketing activities. Reputation is also governed by what others say about it in the marketplace: this cannot be managed, but can be influenced by the way the firm handles both its marketing and its day-to-day client work.

The way in which the firm manages its profile through marketing is therefore dependent on three factors, only two of which it can control. First, the firm must decide what it wants to be known for. This is part of its strategic thinking and positioning (see chapter 4 and paragraph 11.4). Second, profile will depend on the marketing and other activities in which the firm engages. These profile-raising activities will usually include (and see further Maister 1993a, chapters 11 and 12):

(a)   *firm publicity and promotion:* brochures, newsletters and seminars which demonstrate and reinforce the firm's expertise;

(b) *individual promotion:* lawyers giving speeches and presentations, writing articles and books, and joining professional and trade organisations, and so being seen as 'an insider' by clients and other professionals who are associated with the firm's areas of activity; and

(c) *networking:* personal entertainment and invitations to sporting and social events.

However much is invested in developing and raising a firm's profile, more will always be required — not more of the same, but something additional. Just *being* with clients and contacts may result in further work (and surveys show that it very often does). But even with existing clients more may be needed, and profile-raising activities are very unlikely to lead directly to instructions from people the firm has never acted for before. This form of marketing is not, therefore, the end of the marketing responsibility. Gaining new business also requires the *selling* of legal services (see paragraph 18.5).

Third, profile will ultimately depend on how credible and effective the firm's chosen market position and its marketing activities are seen to be by clients, prospective clients and other 'influencers' (such as professional referral sources and the media). Sound investigation of the market and of client needs should reduce the firm's risk of its choice of market position or of marketing activities being misdirected.

18.3.2 Effective promotion

Although marketing covers a range of activities, publicity and promotion are perhaps the most difficult to gauge. For example, most clients now regard brochures as a more expensive form of business card: they make potential clients aware of the firm and its services, but they do not actually sell legal services. They should be designed to raise interest and prompt enquiries.

The most effective promotion provides opportunities for the firm's fee-earners to demonstrate their knowledge of the market and clients' needs (which may or may not mean displaying *legal* knowledge). Certain activities have shown themselves from client surveys to be popular:

(a) Departments or practice groups should consider running targeted client seminars. In some situations, it may be beneficial to run them jointly with other departments: the choice will depend on the area or clients to be targeted. Similarly, professional intermediaries or other third-party contacts and experts can also be brought in. The presenters should also think about 'dry running' these seminars on other fee-earners in the firm who should have an interest in the subject matter, both to test the seminar itself, and to increase the internal exposure to help cross-selling and to encourage lawyers to spot opportunities in other clients.

(b) Promotional material should be focused. Newsletters or updates should be designed to update in a concise, easy-to-read manner, and should therefore be as short as possible and as frequent as the news requires. Whatever the length of the firm's publicity materials, clients will give them about 10 seconds in which to make their impact. In order to do so, they must be well-targeted, well-designed and well-written. This activity should not prevent partners from thinking individually about their principal or target clients' needs and preparing a letter or short document drawing their attention to something in a focused, personal way.

(c) It is absolutely vital that the firm should take every possible step to ensure that seminar invitations, and updates are targeted to those clients and other recipients who are likely to have a real need for them. In this way, they will have far greater impact. It will also reinforce the view that the firm is close to its clients and really understands their needs (or conversely will avoid giving the impression that they are just fodder for any material that the firm wants to send out on the off-chance).

18.3.3 An act of faith

To a large extent, marketing is an act of faith. It is almost impossible to prove which specific cases or matters come into a firm as a result of which particular profile-raising activity. A law firm is not a uni-dimensional organisation, and so its marketing cannot be uni-dimensional either. Clients are looking for a complex package of credibility, the whole of which needs to be presented to them. It is probably true, however, that if a firm does not engage in any form of profile-raising, then the flow of new business will not be as great. In today's competitive market, relying entirely on vicarious marketing through satisfied clients and referral sources to bring in new work is a high-risk strategy.

This process of 'reputation management' and sending marketing messages into the marketplace represents the firm's 'signalling costs', which are the firm's attempt to reduce prospective clients' 'search and information costs' (see paragraphs 6.3 and 8.5.6). The need for personal and institutional credibility (referred to in paragraph 18.1.2) means that both individual fee-earners and the firm have to bear these signalling costs. If a law firm has a good reputation (a 'brand name' in effect, part of the firm-specific capital: see paragraph 5.2.2), then the signalling costs of an individual fee-earner may be reduced — but not eliminated entirely — since he or she can bask in some reflected glory. Although larger firms may be better resourced and so better able to bear the direct costs of raising the firm's profile through publicity and promotion, all lawyers have to invest in the indirect costs of personal promotion and networking. The evidence from client surveys is that publicity and promotion are most effective in *reinforcing* a reputation, but not so successful in *creating* one.

18.4 Client Care and New Business

Despite the message of paragraph 18.3.3 that a firm needs to engage in some active reputation management and signalling, there is also little doubt that the vast majority of new business for any law firm will come from existing clients and contacts (see paragraph 11.3). In many firms, this can be as high as 80%. Unfortunately, too many firms devote 80% of their marketing time and budget to chasing the smaller number of new clients instead of taking additional steps to retain and nurture their core clients. Some of this has to do with the status attributed in law firms to 'rainmakers' (those who are able to bring in large amounts of new business). But there is at least equivalent value in my mind in 'mist-makers' (who may not be able to bring about a heavy downpour, but can at least secure a steady drizzle!).

The first stage in any 'marketing plan' should therefore be to concentrate on caring for existing clients and providing the speed and quality of advice and service that they need (see Maister 1993a, chapter 9; and cf. Jones and Sasser 1995). Although in one sense client care requires that fee-earners 'do a good job', it means more than that. Of course client care presupposes that the client's expectations for quality are met (see paragraph 20.3). But it also suggests that partners in particular should take steps to strengthen and deepen the relationship with clients, spending time learning about the client's personality, and their business or other activities. This form of 'market intelligence' will never be wasted because it becomes part of the individual or firm-specific capital (or both): see paragraph 5.2. And as we shall see later in relation to power and influence (see paragraph 24.3.4), the more dimensions there are to a relationship, the easier it is to influence someone and the harder it is to sever the relationship.

It is in this context that entertaining and socialising come into their own. These are not really marketing activities; they should be seen as opportunities to improve personal relationships and to get to know clients and referrers better. Given the right circumstances, they may well lead to immediate new business, but that should be regarded as a bonus rather than an inevitability.

Bear in mind that your most important 'clients' might well be referral agencies. Treat them as you would 'real' clients: make sure you develop good personal relationships with their staff (which is even more important where the staff are transient).

An important part of 'caring' for clients is not assuming that you always know what they want and how they want it delivered. Clients' personal and business needs may be changing all the time, and their needs in relation to a particular transaction or matter may not be the same as a previous (or even concurrent) issue on which you have advised or are acting. Talking to clients about *how* they would like you to do something for them is as important as discussing *what* you are going to do. In fact, you may find that clients who know little of the law and its working will judge your performance much more on how you worked than on what you did (see paragraph 20.3.3): being technically brilliant may count for nothing in the client's eyes if your manner or method of delivery puts them off.

18.5 Targeting

18.5.1 *Nature of targeting*

Profile-raising is normally geared towards influencing a large number of people, or at least a group of people with common needs or outlook. But it is extremely rare for clients to buy legal services 'en masse'. Gaining new work presupposes a client with a need. Targeting is the process of identifying a prospective client who is likely to have a need that the firm thinks it can address, and setting out to persuade that client to engage it. The client may not even be aware that a need for legal services currently exists, and the selling job is twofold — the client must be convinced that there is a need, and persuaded that the firm has the credibility to meet it. Targeting is therefore taking active steps to gain the clients and business that the firm wants rather than waiting for a knock on the door. As the following description will show, it is an intensive process, and cannot therefore be done for many potential clients.

Each firm, department or practice group should therefore begin by deciding where its best opportunities are among its existing client base as well as among potential new clients, and then 'target' these opportunities. If the firm's strategy is to be fulfilled, these targets will be consistent with it. This is why segmentation is such an important part of the strategy process (see paragraph 4.5.2): targeting and credibility are much easier to achieve when lawyers can focus their efforts.

As part of its targeting activities, each department, practice group and fee-earner should consider sources of referral, assessing which are most valuable and productive, and which are in need of greater attention. The possibility of new relationships should also be canvassed. Given expectations of reciprocity, and limited opportunities for many lawyers to introduce business to other professionals, the proper management of these existing and potential relationships is important if they are to be continued and to remain productive. The firm may therefore need to review its spread of reciprocal business.

In the same way, departments, groups and individuals should review memberships or possibilities for membership of associations and other bodies (e.g., the local law society, the IBA, chambers of commerce, trade organisations, and so on): the firm's investment of time and money should be measured relative to the quantitative and qualitative outcomes.

The firm's marketing partner and marketing staff or advisers (if any) should be actively involved in the targeting and research of potential clients. With firm-wide involvement, they can begin to see (and coordinate) all the promotional activities of the firm, and thus capitalise on opportunities that others may miss. This allows the development of publicity and promotion activities (see paragraph 18.3) that reflect and support the firm's targeting of new business.

Targeting includes a number of activities, described in the following paragraphs. I am using the expression 'client' to include both an existing client from whom the firm is trying to develop new or further work, and a prospective client who has never engaged the firm before.

18.5.2 Identification of client and needs

It is not sufficient just to identify a client who is bound to have a need of some kind and seek a meeting in order to explore the possibilities (this is pure networking, and may well be successful in leading to more work, but it can also draw heavily on time and costs without producing any benefits simply because it is a 'scatter-gun' approach). The fee-earners involved must identify the nature of the potential need, and be satisfied that the firm has the ability and resources to meet that need.

18.5.3   *Information gathering*

The more a partner or fee-earner knows about an existing or prospective client's background, business structure and activity, future plans, and current use of lawyers the better. For existing clients of the firm, much of this information should be available internally, but in any event with many commercial clients and prospects much can now be gained from electronic searches of public databases and news reports cheaply available on the Internet, or by subscription.

18.5.4   *Identifying the appropriate individuals*

Most lawyers hate the idea of 'cold calling' — and with good reason. To be successful in attracting new work, it is important to speak to someone who has the authority to engage lawyers. In most commercial organisations, this could be one or more of several people at different levels and places within the organisation. A targeted approach is more likely to be successful if the partner or fee-earner making it does so at the right level.

The use of internal knowledge, or contacts with others, should help find the right individual to approach. This should also be seen as a matching exercise so that the firm can make the best assessment of who is the best person inside the firm to make the approach; this is as much a question of personality as it is of expertise and experience.

18.5.5   *Arrange a meeting*

Knowing whom to approach is only a first step: they must then be persuaded that a meeting with you is worth their time. If necessary, use other people inside the firm to make an initial approach, use professional intermediaries and other contacts to effect an introduction if that is needed, or use other known contacts in the client's organisation to open doors at the right level.

Whether or not someone will agree to meet you comes back in part to credibility again. Using a respected intermediary may well be sufficient to gain a hearing (this is 'transferred credibility', or credibility by association: Miller and Heiman 1987, page 226). But in most situations credibility can be improved by treating the approach as a business issue and offering the potential client a *business* reason for meeting: too many lawyers offer only a social reason such as lunch, dinner, or some form of entertainment.

18.5.6   *Have a business reason for meeting*

Think about giving a potential client a reason for spending time with you (the idea of a valid business reason is taken from Miller and Heiman

1987, chapter 12). The reason you offer should be one that makes sense from the client's perspective. Try to emphasise the client's priorities rather than yours:

(a) you should give the client *information* that he or she needs to understand who you are (if that is necessary) and why you want to meet; and

(b) you should also establish a *foundation* for the meeting so that, when you meet the client, you will be able to spend your time in a focused, effective way.

A valid business reason is therefore very precise. It does not focus on the client in general, or on your firm in general, but on a specific issue that you believe affects the client. The *primary purpose* of any valid business reason is to make the client want to see you because it makes sense from his or her business perspective to do so. There are *other purposes*, too:

(a) to give a reason for the meeting: there should be no deception or sleight of hand here — both of you should know what you have in mind;

(b) to show that you have done some thinking and preparation — that you want to help the client and that you are interested enough to think about it beforehand;

(c) to minimise the time needed — you can get straight down to business;

(d) to set mutual expectations; and

(e) to allow the client to prepare.

Lawyers often express concerns about looking for a valid business reason to meet as part of the marketing process:

(a) *It can't be necessary with every meeting.* There are some meetings where socialising is the principal purpose. This is acceptable, but do not equate socialising with selling. Of course, socialising can also be a very good way of gaining background information about client concerns and preferences, current problems, or industry developments. But in a selling situation, both people are giving up professional or business time, and both need to benefit.

(b) *Not wanting to appear hard-nosed.* No one should neglect the personal side of a relationship, but do not confuse the personal and professional sides of a business relationship. If you are entertaining someone, relax and develop the personal relationship. When it comes to selling, focus on mutual business needs.

(c) *Not wanting to be direct.* If you feel uncomfortable about stating the reason for seeing someone, it is probably because you do not have a valid reason for taking up his or her time.

You need to be able to determine what a valid business reason might be. There are five possible criteria:

(a) The client must perceive you to be helping solve his or her problems — that you are part of the solution. Your business reason must therefore be acceptable to the client, and be seen as a major thrust of your concern (and not merely as incidental to your principal objective of winning more business).

(b) Focus on current, pressing issues — you are competing with other priorities.

(c) Your reason must help the client make a decision about engaging a legal adviser, reinforce a decision that has already been made, or give information that will help with future decisions. Most potential clients are constantly being asked to make decisions — usually without sufficient information. If you put your target in a better position to decide something, he or she will probably want to spend the time talking to you.

(d) Show the client what the benefits might be in talking to you — he or she will know what you hope to gain (or can guess): explain how the client will benefit, too.

(e) Make it clear that the business reason relates to the client's business or activity, not just yours.

18.5.7 *Plan*

There is no point in carefully targeting a client and setting up a meeting, and then only thinking about what you want to say or achieve as you step into the car or taxi to go to the meeting. Review what you know about the client or prospect, and what needs adding or clarifying; be clear about what the firm wants to offer, the degree of expertise and similar experience it can offer, and the results or benefits that it envisages. In other words, prepare to sell your services.

18.6 Selling Legal Services

18.6.1 *The preconditions*

At some point, either as a result of networking or targeting, a lawyer can sit down with a client to discuss specific needs. If it is the result of networking, the discussions may be preliminary, unstructured and un-focused: in this case, it is less likely that the discussions will result in much more than a further opportunity to meet other people or talk more specifically later (to be fair, this may also be the result of 'targeted' conversations; such a result is not failure, since generating new business often proceeds incrementally over a period of time).

But however much (or little) profile-raising or targeting has been done, a client will only engage a lawyer for a specific case at a specific time if the client has a current need for legal services and is convinced that the lawyer is a credible, competent and willing provider of the service. The only way to achieve this is to spend time with the client talking the issues through, identifying needs and expectations, and drawing on past experience to convince the client that he or she will not be taking an unwarranted risk.

In this sense, therefore, the best networking, targeting and selling may still not result in new work — not because the individual or the firm is not credible, but because the client does not have a current, pressing need for legal services.

18.6.2 *Beauty parades*

It is also possible that you will be talking to a prospective client as part of a 'beauty parade' or competitive tendering exercise. In these circumstances, the client should have a clearly articulated need for legal services, and should have provided sufficient background information. The preparatory process should still be thorough, and should cover many of the issues discussed in paragraph 18.5.

Be prepared to ask for further background information: if the client is reluctant to help you respond to a request to help them, consider seriously whether or not you really want to do business with them. There is no doubt that some clients who hold beauty parades do not fully understand the requirements and nuances of a fully effective and productive lawyer–client relationship.

The selling process involved in a beauty parade may also be more formal, and so less flexible than that described below. If a presentation is required, be sure to practise it beforehand.

18.6.3 *Components of selling*

Successfully selling legal services is a complex activity that cannot follow any predetermined, universally applicable, process. The client must have a need, the lawyer and law firm must be credible suppliers of legal services able to meet the client's need, there must be a good reason for the client engaging your firm rather than a competitor, and there must be some overriding imperative or cost-benefit to the client that justifies engaging a legal adviser.

18.6.3.1 *Asking the right questions*
However well prepared you are, you need to be sure that there is something for you to achieve and that you are approaching it on the right lines. So rather than immediately breaking out into your prepared standard description of what you do and how you do it, ask some background questions to encourage the client to talk. The more you know about them, how they think, what their problems or thoughts are, the easier it is for you to tailor what you say to meet their current needs. Remember: no one buys legal services unless they have a current need, sufficient urgency to require legal advice, and a belief that you can help them. You do not persuade anyone of these things by overwhelming them with lengthy and detailed descriptions of all the possible ways in which you could ever conceivably help them.

Effective selling therefore begins with the ability to ask good questions, and being able really to listen to the answers. Good reasons for asking questions are:

(a)   to help you understand the client's current situation;
(b)   to help establish rapport, credibility and comfort;
(c)   to help you understand the client's decision-making process;
(d)   to help you uncover competitors' strengths and weaknesses;
(e)   to help motivate and sustain the client's interest, to stimulate his
or her thinking, and to modify his or her opinion of you or the firm.

18.6.3.2   *Differentiation*

When you have confirmed through responses to questions that your
preliminary information about the client and his or her likely needs was
correct (or gathered additional information that can help you), you can
then begin to explain how you can help. This should be founded on your
understanding of the business or other background involved, your previous
(or acquired) knowledge of the client and the surrounding circumstances,
and the importance of these issues, as well as on your technical knowledge
and prior experience of helping similar clients in similar circumstances.

In this sense, differentiation means drawing on your unique previous
experience and the expertise derived from it to convince a prospective
client that you have the ability to help them deal with their current
concerns. These differences may be drawn from the lawyers' or the firm's
previous legal, market or client experience; from the firm's ability to put
together a different combination of expertise; from the firm's resources or
geography; from price or cost-effectiveness. It comes, in other words,
from individual and firm-specific capital (see paragraph 5.2). Finding
unique strengths cannot be achieved generically, which is why differentiation at the firm-wide level is so difficult. Unique strengths apply to this
client, for this need, at this time, and in the current circumstances. If they
can be identified, they reduce price-sensitivity; if they cannot be identified, then price may be the only difference on which you can compete.

18.6.3.3   *'Closing' the sale*

When people are ready to buy something, they start to give off 'commitment signals' (which lawyers often miss). These are messages from the
buyer that he or she is ready to move the buying process forward (see
Miller and Heiman 1987, pages 154–6). These signals are often misinter-
preted as just another question. But commitment signals are almost
always phrased in the form of a question or statement about *implementation*. Examples are:

(a)   questions about timing (how soon you can start, how long you
think the work might take);
(b)   requests for references;
(c)   questions about who would handle the work;
(d)   specific questions about fees (billing frequency, payment terms,
invoice information).

These are not questions about *whether* you can help (i.e., questions
about credibility), but *how* and under what *conditions*. Except in a beauty

parade or competitive tender where a process and set questions are being used for every potential adviser, recognise this shift in emphasis and respond positively (beauty parades are different because the one-off nature of the meeting means that all participants are usually asked the same complete range of questions irrespective of the likely outcome).

Selling legal services is not a 'blanket' process that can be applied by anyone in all circumstances. It requires time, thought and effort. Do not worry if you cannot find the time or money for brochures and entertaining. Marketing is less about these things than it is about carefully targeting your unique and specific experience to the needs of actual or prospective clients.

18.6.4 *Possible outcomes*

With adequate preparation, one of three results will emerge:

(a) *New work.* If the targeting was accurate, and the assumptions about needs well-researched, a client who has a current, pressing need for legal advice on an issue, *and who is convinced that the lawyer he or she is talking to is a credible person who can deliver to the client's expectation,* may well return you to the office with a piece of new business.

(b) *Prospective work.* The need identified may not be pressing enough for the client or prospect to engage a lawyer at the moment. However, if you have struck the client or prospect as a credible provider, the opportunity for work may arise in the future. In many cases, this situation is combined with the offer for you to meet other people in the client's organisation.

(c) *No work.* The client may not have the need you identified, or any other immediate needs for which he or she believes that the firm is a credible provider. The client may well have the need, but not be convinced that you or the firm is a credible provider (lacking expertise or experience of similar situations or clients, insufficient strength in depth, not cost-effective, etc.). You need to develop your antennae sufficiently to be able to identify when the situation is leading nowhere and to leave it on the most positive footing without alienating a prospective client.

18.7 Measuring Success

The targeting and development effort described above may well be seen as a counsel of perfection. But in a fragmented and competitive market, unstructured marketing can waste significant resources simply by not thinking through who is most likely to need the firm's services given its strengths and reputation, the current state of business and the market-place, and the discoverable needs of existing or potential clients. Too many lawyers see the occasional, unplanned lunch as the key to business development. Certainly, such opportunities (as well as other forms of entertainment and networking) can be invaluable in learning about clients and their needs, but they need to be seen as part of research and assessment rather than as the selling process itself: in this way, there will not be an expectation of immediate new business, and therefore expectations of 'success' will be more realistic.

In a competitive marketplace, a significant volume of work rarely walks in simply as the result of raising the firm's profile and doing a good job. While it is necessary to spend a lot of time behind one's desk doing a good job, therefore, it is also necessary to be out of the office, being with clients and contacts, building networks, and making sure that while other firms have lawyers behind their desks doing a good job you are out talking to their clients! To do this properly requires research, targeting and preparation. But how do we measure its success?

In so many ways, measuring the success of marketing efforts is very difficult. But that is no excuse for not doing anything. The variables that can be tracked reduce to: the time it takes, the monetary investment required, the number of new clients or matters generated, the volume of fees generated, and the profit created. The following are therefore some of the possibilities:

(a)   Record the time taken in, respectively, profile-raising, market research, targeting, selling, networking, and socialising: these are all different processes, and some people will otherwise appear to record a lot of 'business development' time when in fact they are socialising extensively at the firm's expense and not bringing in much new work.

(b)   Establish timetables for the targeting of new business and for bringing that process to a successful conclusion: measure individual, practice group, departmental and firm performance against these timetables (this will also help in future timetabling and in bringing a degree of realism to how long it can take to develop new business).

(c)   Measure the cost (both the direct costs and the opportunity costs (the cost of partners' and fee-earners' time)) of bringing in each targeted new matter: use the data to discover departmental or practice group ranges or averages that can be used in allocating future resources, and to understand the differences in bringing in different sorts of work or targeting various types of clients.

(d)   Measure the fee income generated by a targeted new matter, and compare it with the cost of winning the work (this will begin to show over a period of time how much fee income is likely to be generated for every pound of direct and indirect marketing cost).

(e)   Measure the *profit* generated by a targeted new matter (see paragraph 28.8.2), and compare it with the cost of winning it.

These measurements will allow the firm to make more informed decisions about where or how best to use its marketing time and budget, and who the most successful developers of new business are — not just in terms of the number or value of new matters brought in, but in relation to the cost-effectiveness of development, and the contribution to the firm's strategic and financial success. These measures can, in fact, be incorporated into a 'balanced scorecard' (see paragraph 20.2.4).

However, these measurements should not be seen in isolation (see, for example, Maister 1997, chapter 20). There are other, qualitative, measures that the firm should be encouraged to examine: does the new work involve other departments, the development of fee-earners' ability, the development of new areas of law or practice, or a contribution to the firm's reputation or profile, and so on? Such assessments will be more subjective, but no less important. Most of the suggested measures should be used more to improve everyone's understanding of the effort and process required than to attribute blame for any lack of work generation or to allocate 'bonuses' for successful business development.

18.8   Cross-selling

Securing new business can also be achieved through cross-selling. As we saw in chapter 9, the firm may have been built on the notion that its lawyers would share their surplus client work and expertise with others in the firm. This can lead to active or reactive cross-selling. Active cross-selling means incurring 'signalling costs', while reactive cross-selling means responding to a potential client who is incurring search and information costs (see paragraph 18.3.3).

Reactive cross-selling means introducing an existing client with a current problem to a specific lawyer who has the expertise to help with that problem. Fee-earners who do this should make sure that they do not just 'bow out' of the client relationship. The client will probably expect them to be available, and to be abreast of developments. This may be described as the 'client partner' role. Think less in terms of selling the client on to another fee-earner (or 'handing over'), and more in terms of 'project managing' the client's various interests in the firm.

Active cross-selling means introducing existing clients or referral agencies to other lawyers in the firm so that when, at some indeterminate time in the future, a client has a problem, the client immediately thinks of the range of services the firm can offer.

Cross-selling is problematic in nearly every law firm — usually because lawyers look at it from their point of view rather than the client's (see Maister 1997, chapter 19). Effective cross-selling is not possible unless the firm's lawyers understand what they each do, which clients they act for, and what sort of issues they have experience of handling. Without good internal communication (see paragraph 18.9), cross-selling is impossible. A culture of individualism and setting personal billing targets will also discourage cross-selling and client-sharing. For these reasons, cross-selling (or 'integrated' selling) tends to be better handled and more successful in partnerships of integrated entrepreneurs (cf. paragraph 9.4).

18.9   Marketing Communication

In order to coordinate the implementation of the firm's strategy and positioning, the heads of departments or practice groups should meet regularly (at least every month) with each other to discuss the clients and potential clients they wish to target, successful and unsuccessful business development meetings with clients and prospects, how they might improve cross-departmental cooperation on specific matters and the servicing of clients, and how to coordinate newsletters, articles and seminar contributions.

Communication among heads of departments and practice groups will not be sufficient to keep other fee-earners informed about the firm's activities and successes. Accordingly:

(a)   Departments and groups could hold meetings (perhaps monthly), and involving all fee-earners, to review new business and how it was won, to discuss possible new targets and the progress being made on existing ones, and to discuss new initiatives (such as newsletters and seminars, speaking engagements and articles). In this way, everyone has the opportunity not only to share relevant information and to feel that they are making a contribution, but also to learn from everyone's experience of marketing and targeting about what works and what does not. It is not necessary for the group to discuss every new matter or target, but it will be necessary for the head of department or practice group to select those that are, or are likely to be, important to the firm in terms of fee income, profile, opportunity or new developments. I am aware that such meetings are not necessarily popular. However, given the right lead from senior partners, their importance will be appreciated, and everyone will begin to get the message that business development cannot be left to a few self-selecting individuals, but is in fact the responsibility of every fee-earner who comes into contact with clients.

(b)   Copies of newsletters, articles and conference speeches or presentations should be distributed to all practitioners in the firm having an interest in their subject-matter. It is amazing, given the effort that goes into the preparation and production of these promotional activities, that the firm's own fee-earners are often the last people to be aware of them!

(c)   In much the same way, information about clients should be collected from fee-earners and incorporated into a database which can record business information (activity, structure, key personnel, activities, other advisers) as well as preferences for newsletters, seminars, types of entertainment, contact, etc. To ease the collection burden on fee-earners, the marketing partner or other marketing staff (if appointed) could also attend the departmental or group meetings recommended above. Indeed, the real (but often ignored or under-rated) value of a marketing 'department' lies in coordination, connection and support of the partners' and fee-earners' targeting and selling activities. Marketing partners and other marketing staff should not be expected to *sell*, that is, to bring in new business.

18.10   Conclusions

Marketing and selling are therefore combined activities which, at different times and in different ways, involve the firm, departments or groups, and individuals (and see Stoakes 1994). The firm should define its strategy and put central resources in place to support it (for example, funds or contacts for client meetings and entertainment, a marketing department to help in maintaining a sophisticated database of client information and preferences, in preparing brochures and newsletters, in running seminars, and in researching clients or prospects). The department or practice group should be specific in identifying targets that will attract resources for the development of new business, and in providing information and support. Individuals should prepare specific target plans for a manageable number of clients or prospects, and implement them against a budget for doing so.

The most successful lawyers are those characterised by their clients as people who "clearly understand me", who "complement my own strengths and weaknesses", and for whom "nothing is too much trouble". The most effective marketers are lawyers who translate the attitudes and understanding implicit in this description into all their meetings with clients and prospective clients. These lawyers 'bat' for their clients, keeping in touch to let them know of *specific* developments that affect them. They listen, take a keen and informed interest in the client's activities, are available when clients really need them, return calls promptly, treat deadlines as though their livelihoods depended on them, and provide progress reports without being prompted. They differentiate mountains from molehills. They talk to their clients about fees, and avoid any surprises. This all translates into stronger working relationships, and in turn more success in being involved in and resolving clients' problems.

This all amounts to good client understanding and good client care. It is not touting, but it is effective selling. It amounts to convincing clients that, if they are considering engaging you to help them with a transaction, a problem, or some litigation, you are credible, interested and capable.

Chapter 19

STRUCTURE AND ORGANISATION OF DEPARTMENTS

19.1 Why have Departments?

Many firms now divide their fee-earners into different groups. It does not matter for these purposes whether the groups are called departments, teams, units or groups. For simplicity, I shall refer to them as departments or practice groups.

As a matter of exposition, it may seem that I am assuming that a firm has created a business strategy (see chapter 4), has generated client work consistent with that strategy (see chapter 18), and is now considering how best to structure and organise its fee-earners to handle that work. In reality, of course, the strategy and marketing of the firm — and therefore the development of new business — may be a product of its existing structure and performance (the idea of emergent strategy discussed in paragraph 4.3.3). In law firms, the process is more of a circle (or spiral) than a straight line.

The issue of choosing and establishing fee-earning departments follows exactly the principles discussed in relation to structuring the firm generally: see paragraphs 14.1 to 14.3. The dimensions and levels of management are the same and, in particular, the bases of grouping (paragraph 14.2.4.3) apply. The purpose of departments, therefore, is to combine a number of individuals carrying out certain jobs — that is, to achieve the appropriate division of labour and, in so doing, to improve one or more of reputation, marketing, selling, productivity, quality, effectiveness, efficiency, and profitability.

More specifically, in the context of delivering legal services, the creation of appropriate departments can contribute towards:

(a) improving case management,
(b) improving work allocation and work distribution,
(c) improving lawyer training and development,
(d) the development of specialisation,

    (e)   marketing and cross-selling,

    (f)   strategic thinking.

19.2   Basis of Departmentalisation

Adopting Mintzberg's principles, departments or practice groups can be established as either market or functional groupings (see paragraph 14.2.4.3). In most firms, they are formed on the basis of legal expertise, that is, market groupings by output (or service). The usual structure follows a commercial, property, litigation and private client framework. Sometimes, these groups are further subdivided: for example, commercial might be split into corporate finance, commercial contracts, and tax; and private client could be split into estate planning, wills and probate, and matrimonial. In some firms, specialist areas are added as departments in their own right — for example, intellectual property, competition law.

Increasingly, however, firms are also establishing industry or market groups, that is, market groupings by type of client. This may be true of technology, travel, retail, sports and leisure, agriculture, and so on.

In a few instances, the area of law applies to a particular industry and it may be difficult to tell whether the firm is divided by type of law or by industry: examples could be shipping, banking, insurance, media, oil and gas. Further investigation often reveals that the firm only acts for one 'side' of these industries, so that there may be an element of combined legal and industry specialisation (for example, acting for shipowners rather than cargo owners, lenders rather than borrowers, music producers rather than entertainers, etc.).

In other instances, firms might create 'matrix structures' (see paragraph 14.3.2.2(d)) which, for example, combine formal departments organised by expertise and informal groups created by industry or type of client. And of course, some firms may concentrate their entire fee-earning activity on either a narrow area of practice or a particular industry or client group (or a combination of both). These firms are usually called 'niche' or 'boutique' practices (cf. paragraph 8.6): those that are based on a particular industry are more likely to maintain the typical departments based on expertise — the expertise is, by definition, focused on the needs of an industry.

The choices that a firm makes should reflect its business strategy (and particularly its decisions about segmentation: see paragraph 4.5.2), as well as market versus functional grouping , and the interdependencies between jobs (work flow, processes, scale, and social: see paragraph 14.2.4.3). Just as the whole firm has to balance the combination of clients, services, geography, and culture across the entirety of its practice (cf. paragraph 4.5.2), so a department should do so for its part of the practice.

19.3   The Function of Departmental Management

19.3.1 *Essential elements*

A head of department or practice group manager occupies a management position somewhere between the managing partner of the firm (see chapter 15) and a matter partner or project team leader (see paragraph 21.5) — part of Mintzberg's middle line (see paragraph 14.3.3). Because of this, it is closer to day-to-day client work than the managing partner, but more of a coordinating role than the matter partner.

There are therefore three essential elements to departmental or practice group management:

(a)   managing the development and flow of new work;

(b)   coordinating the practice area, and particularly the allocations and distribution of client work; and

(c)   managing performance.

These elements reflect the three strands of entrepreneurialism (see paragraphs 7.2 and 17.2).

19.3.2   *Managing the flow of new work*

The successful development of new client work is the result of departmental or practice group strategic thinking (see chapter 4), and of effective marketing at firm-wide, departmental or practice area, and individual levels (see chapter 18). It is the result of entrepreneurialism (see chapter 7). It also requires attention to client service and satisfaction, and quality management. The head of department or practice group may need to take steps to encourage other partners and fee-earners to prepare and follow through on the practice's business development plans. To keep an eye on this, the head of department or practice group will need frequent reports on marketing activities that have been undertaken (or are planned), and on new clients and matters coming in.

However, effective departmental or practice group management does not mean accepting *all and any* new work. Unchecked entrepreneurialism and business development is not necessarily in the firm's strategic or operational best interests (see paragraph 7.2). All departments should establish client and matter acceptance procedures and guidelines. These guidelines must require compliance, and not merely suggest, and partners should be held accountable for complying (or not complying) with them. Work acceptance guidelines typically require that:

(a)   the new work is within an area of expertise (legal and industry) in which the department or group works (the firm should also be specific in outlining the types of work it will *not* do);

(b)   the work is within the matter partner's personal expertise;

(c)   the work will be charged at standard charge-out rates (or higher), and billing procedures will be followed;

(d)   the client does not currently have an overdue account with the firm and (if appropriate) credit checks are conducted;

(e)   there is an engagement letter on the file, and money on account has been requested where appropriate;

(f)   there are no sensitive issues involved.

The head of department should also be mindful of (and may have to adjudicate on) conflicts of interest (see further paragraph 11.4.1(b)).

Work within the guidelines may usually be accepted by partners without any type of approval. Any exceptions should be approved by the head of department or practice group (or, in very sensitive cases, by the firm's managing partner). Further, files that are opened without a letter of engagement should be referred to the head of department or practice group: these files will usually be the ones that cause problems further down the road.

19.3.3 *Coordinating the practice area*

It is not sufficient simply for the firm to organise fee-earners into departments or practice groups, and then hope for the best. It is becoming increasingly important for those departments and practice groups to be managed. As with any other management role for a partner, the role of a head of department or practice group should be defined and taken by someone with the aptitude to manage, not simply by the most senior lawyer or highest biller.

As the occupant of a management role, the head of department or practice group is not there simply to represent the views of other lawyers in the department, but to ensure that certain things happen. These are:

(a) coordinating the lawyers' practices and ensuring the appropriate degree of cross-selling;

(b) being ultimately responsible for work acceptance and allocation;

(c) ensuring the billing and collecting of fees in respect of the work done, on a timely basis to minimise the amount of unbilled work-in-progress and to maximise the firm's cash flow;

(d) overseeing the development of the required specialisations (implicit in this is the recruitment and training of lawyers);

(e) monitoring delegation and supervision, productivity and profitability (by department or group, individual fee-earner, and client);

(f) formulating strategic and marketing plans for the department or group; and

(g) setting policies and guidelines for the effective implementation of plans, and for the performance of the group (including the performance of other partners in it).

Work allocation is often a difficult issue for practitioners who do not want to feel that their professional autonomy or responsibility is being interfered with. However, if larger firms and departmental structures are to make any strategic, marketing and economic sense, the ultimate responsibility for work allocation must rest with the head of department or practice group (cf. paragraph 14.2.5). Other partners in the department or group should be able to assign work directly to fee-earners, provided that the assigned lawyer has sufficient expertise to handle the issue or matter. Otherwise, allocation should be made through the head of department. In any event, he or she must be able to reassign matters to equalise workloads within the department or group: this should not be seen as an explicit or implicit criticism of a fee-earner's case management, but as a necessary process to maintain client satisfaction and service quality.

19.3.4   *Managing performance*

This is a complex area involving many aspects of law firm management, including the recruitment and training of suitable fee-earners (see paragraphs 22.4.2 and 25.3), the management of their productivity and quality of work and service (see chapter 20), and being responsible for the economic viability of the work done (see paragraph 21.6, chapter 28 (particularly paragraph 28.8), and paragraph 29.2).

Controlling the firm's work and improving the quality of its output can be further enhanced through the use of:

(a)   Matter lists for the department or practice group, and by:

    (i)   client;
    (ii)   matter partner;
    (iii)   fee-earner;
    (iv)   matters where no time has been recorded for 60 days (an exception report to suggest problems or a need for billing).

(b)   Matter status (progress) reporting and communication between:

    (i)   fee-earner(s) and matter partner;
    (ii)   matter partner and client partner.

(c)   Office and personal reminder systems (see Mayson 1992, pages 33–7).

(d)   Approval of letters of advice, draft agreements, and other work product.

(e)   Precedent and know-how systems.

Of course, not all of these need to be the responsibility of the head of department.

Particular case management problems that arise are:

(a)   incompetent, unconscientious or unconcerned lawyers (cf. paragraph 16.4.1);
(b)   the hoarding of work;
(c)   failure to delegate to lowest competent level;
(d)   unrealistic or uninformed commitments to clients;
(e)   lawyers working outside their area of expertise;
(f)   staffing shortages;
(g)   inadequate training, delegation or supervision;
(h)   failure to develop systems to ensure that work is done on time.

Heads of department or practice groups should be alive to these issues and take appropriate steps to improve performance before the quality of work, client perception, or the firm's reputation are adversely affected.

19.4 Departmental Meetings

Groupings can be based entirely on social interdependencies — particularly if the firm or department wants to develop or maintain a specialisation or to ensure that members will be able to rely on each other when the pressure is on (see paragraph 14.2.4.3). Whether or not this is one of the criteria for putting a department or practice group together, it is always a good idea to bring its members together on a regular basis. Within departments or practice groups, therefore:

(a) The partners should meet monthly to discuss:

    (i)   new matters;
    (ii)   workloads and work distribution;
    (iii) staffing needs;
    (iv) work-in-progress, billings and aged debts;
    (v)   business development and marketing;
    (vi) departmental or practice group management.

(b) The partners and fee-earners should meet weekly to discuss:

    (i)   new matters;
    (ii)   workloads and work distribution;
    (iii) other important developments.

(c) The partners and fee-earners should also meet at least every two months to discuss:

    (i)   important new matters;
    (ii)   departmental or practice group performance;
    (iii) recent interesting matters;
    (iv) new developments in law or practice;
    (v)   new precedents or know-how.

While it might seem that this is adding to the non-chargeable activities of the fee-earners (and therefore potentially setting up conflicts with client work), firms that hold regular meetings find that they are better able to capitalise on the contacts, expertise and experience of fee-earners. Partners and fee-earners should remember that they have an obligation to the firm as well as to their clients, and that the full exploitation of firm-specific know-how requires sharing, integration and teamwork (see paragraphs 5.2, 8.4, 8.5, and 9.4).

Chapter 20

PRODUCTIVITY AND QUALITY

20.1 Introduction

Productivity and quality are perhaps the two most critical areas of the delivery of legal services in the 1990s. This is consistent with the increasing maturity of the marketplace, since one of the features of maturity is the presence of more sophisticated clients whose decisions to engage lawyers will shift to service issues (see paragraph 4.7.4).

Productivity and quality are both dependent on the existence and management of many different factors that will be discussed in this chapter; together, these different factors are combined and used in a *process* of service delivery. But they are also dependent on work to be done (see chapter 18), and a structure being in place for doing it (see chapter 19).

20.2 Productivity

20.2.1 *Key assumptions*

Productivity is concerned with the effective use of resources. In any business, these resources can be many and varied, depending on what is needed by the entrepreneur to meet the market opportunities identified, and whether these resources are acquired in the market or through a network, or brought within a firm (see chapters 6 and 7).

We therefore have to assume that there are some resources ('raw materials') that need to be turned to productive use. In a law firm, the most important of these resources will be the know-how of the fee-earners. Productivity does not therefore become an issue until there are fee-earners with the ability and capacity to work, work available for them to do, and an infrastructure of other resources within which they are expected to work. The essence of productivity in a law firm is blending these factors into effective performance.

Productivity can also assume that there is a process involved for the effective and efficient use of these resources. A law firm may therefore establish case management procedures and encourage good time management as part of its attempt to manage productivity (considered separately in chapter 21).

In short, maximising productivity depends on a range of factors and assumptions. Poor productivity may be the result of fee-earners wasting their time, or not following the work processes that exist — in other words, it may be their fault. But poor productivity might also be the result of them not having enough work to do because the partners do not share available work with them, or because effective processes, supervision and support services are not provided (or do not achieve their purpose). Indeed, in law firms, it could be argued that effective delegation and supervision are the principal keys to fee-earner productivity, and these skills are often underdeveloped (see Mayson 1992, pages 5–10).

20.2.2 *Nature of productivity*

Like quality, productivity is a difficult issue in law offices (as it is in all professional services). The management idea of productivity is that it is the result of four elements (Mill 1989, page 278):

(a) *inputs* — resources (people, space, equipment);
(b) *intermediate output* — the organisation of the resources to create the capacity to provide the service (capacity management);
(c) *outputs* — the actual output achieved (performance, its identification and measurement);
(d) *outcomes* — the effect that the service has on the client (identification, utility and value).

It can often be very difficult for a firm to conceptualise and analyse the different processes and steps involved in its productivity. Useful techniques are creating a flowchart (see Lovelock 1992), and blueprinting (see Shostack 1992); and cf. paragraph 4.6.4.

Performance improvement is achieved by improving the efficiency of the relationship between the inputs and outputs, for example, by:

(a) reducing inputs;
(b) increasing outputs;
(c) reducing inputs and increasing outputs;
(d) increasing inputs, and increasing outputs by a greater margin;
(e) reducing inputs, and reducing outputs by a smaller margin.

Two of these improvements do not involve reducing inputs (fee-earners, support staff, tangible resources, or other costs of the business). Performance improvement or productivity need not always therefore start from a cost-cutting perspective.

In the context of law firms, productivity improvements would usually amount to maintaining the same level of services with fewer fee-earners;

requiring fee-earners to work harder or charge more (or both); or adding more fee-earners and increasing the overall level of work on a headcount basis (per fee-earner) of all of them. These choices will probably be determined by the availability of work and the ability of the firm's partners to capture and share it (cf. paragraph 7.2).

There is a danger in professional services, however, that striving to do more with less will result in declining quality of advice and service. Increased productivity bought at the expense of quality is not an attractive option to lawyers. There is no doubt that this is a difficult issue; when it is combined with a culture of autonomy and self-management (see paragraphs 14.2.2 and 14.2.5) it becomes even more problematic.

The productivity issue is not unique to law firms: nor is it simply a question of investing in information technology (see Roach 1991 and 1996, and Susskind 1996). Drucker describes raising the productivity of knowledge and service workers as the "single greatest challenge facing managers in the developed countries of the world" (1991, page 69). His answer is 'working smarter' by which he means asking:

> "'What is the task? What are we trying to accomplish? Why do it at all?' The easiest, but perhaps also the greatest, productive gains in [knowledge and service] work will come from defining the task and especially from eliminating what does not need to be done" (1991, page 72).

It is important, however, in this client-driven era, to focus the answers to these questions on the needs and expectations of clients, and this may suggest further questions such as, 'What is the client paying for?' and 'What value is this task or process supposed to add?'. Finally, productivity can be achieved by making knowledge workers responsible for their own productivity and holding them accountable for it, including their own continuous learning (1991, pages 77 and 78).

20.2.3 *Strategic determinants of productivity*

Managing productivity in service operations creates strategic challenges because of the following variables (Mill 1989, pages 279–81):

(a) *The volume of demand.* Rising volume gives the ability to spread costs, develop areas of specialisation, and achieve economy of experience.

(b) *The variety of services offered.* The greater the variety of services, the greater the dilution of the resources available to provide them.

(c) *The variation in volume and demand over time.* For any given service, the demand for it is likely to vary from time to time, and so the volume of take-up (and need for resources) will similarly vary. This leads to chase-demand, or demand-led, strategies (where a law firm will seek to gear up to meet changes in demand) and level capacity, or resource-led, strategies (where a firm will resource itself for an average expected level of demand and outsource any excess demand).

(d) *The variability of demand for the range of services.* Across a range of services, collective demand will vary depending on the variation in demand for any given services. This creates the need for flexibility in the use of resources, and raises the danger of overspecialisation.

As strategic and structural issues, they should be considered in the context of strategic thinking (see chapter 4) and of how best to structure the firm and its fee-earning departments (see chapter 19). They also raise issues about the extent to which a firm 'internalises' what it needs, and so affects the boundaries of the firm (cf. paragraph 10.1).

20.2.4 *Measuring productivity*

This is perhaps the most difficult aspect of productivity, and is compounded by a number of factors:

(a) Any measurement is a process of quantifying: the difficulty with productivity in legal services is putting a quantitative measure to something that is qualitative and intangible.

(b) Although productivity can be measured in some dimensions (such as hours worked, number of cases handled), these give no indication of whether increases in productivity are achieved at the expense of the quality of the work done. A fee-earner may also be dependent on partners to bring work in and to delegate it, so that his or her productivity figures based on volume may be distorted by the unavailability of work, or the failure of partners to share available work, rather than lack of effectiveness in doing it.

(c) A fee-earner's productivity (both quantitatively and qualitatively) may be affected by dependence on others or interference by others. For example, a client may keep telephoning for updates or may not supply relevant information on time; the supervising partner may not be available for a consultation with a fee-earner for hours or days; the 'other side' may be deliberately obstructive and unhelpful; secretarial or other support services may not be available or overstretched.

(d) Financial measures of output (e.g., fees billed or fees collected) may be the result of fluctuations in the market value — up or down — of the service in question (for example, in the competition for debt collection work, or as a result of a property recession).

Although it may be difficult to measure aspects of the delivery of legal services accurately, that should not prevent a firm from measuring something. The firm must decide, however, for what *purpose* it is seeking measures of productivity. It may be to compare actual performance with expected or budgeted performance. It may be to compare actual performance over a period of time. It may be to compare the performance of some parts of the business with other parts, or to compare its performance with that of other firms. For some processes, quantitative measures could be used (e.g., the time taken to draft a document, the number of files being opened, handled or closed). Obviously, where a firm can standardise its work processes, the easier it will be to find standard measures of input (which can be costed) or output.

It may be important to include qualitative as well as quantitative measures, to ensure that, for example, client satisfaction with the service is put alongside hard data to encourage individuals not to cut corners in striving to meet quantitative criteria of performance. In fact, to the extent that the productivity of the firm's fee-earners will determine whether or not its overall business objectives are met, there is a good case to be made for seeking a range of measures of productivity and performance (see McCall et al. 1996 and Heskett et al. 1994). This is the thrust of the concept of the 'balanced scorecard' suggested by Kaplan and Norton (1996). Such a scorecard would be designed to provide "a comprehensive framework that translates . . . vision and strategy into a coherent set of performance measures" (1996, page 24). Indeed, these measures can be used "to articulate the strategy of the business, to communicate the strategy of the business, and to help align individual, organizational, and cross-departmental initiatives to achieve a common goal" (1996, page 25). In this sense, it is less about performance measurement and more about strategic management.

A balanced scorecard, suggest Kaplan and Norton, should look at the firm's strategy from four perspectives: client, financial, internal business process, and learning and growth (1996, chapters 3 to 6). For each of these perspectives, there should be "a linked series of objectives and measures that are both consistent and mutually reinforcing" (1996, pages 29–30). Generically, they might be client satisfaction, client retention, market share; profitability, return on capital employed, and economic value added; quality, response times, costs, rate of service innovations; staff satisfaction, expertise and skills inventory (1996, page 44).

It may, of course, be necessary to develop distinct scorecards for strategically distinct departments, practice areas or offices.

The idea of the balanced scorecard is relatively recent, and although some law firms are experimenting with the concept it is still too early to know whether it will provide a genuinely more balanced approach to productivity assessment.

20.3 Quality

20.3.1 Introduction

A lot of ink has been wasted on the quality issue in recent years, and I hope that I am not about to add to the waste (see also the quotation from Sveiby and Lloyd (1987) in paragraph 3.4(b)). The difficulty in legal services, it seems to me, is the tendency of lawyers to equate quality with excellence and, in particular, with a choice between providing correct or incorrect legal advice. Properly understood, quality has many different dimensions, of which technical accuracy is one. Clients' perceptions of quality incorporate all or most of these dimensions, and it is a fundamental error for lawyers to focus only on one. If lawyers and clients are not using a common perception of what quality is, then it is inevitable that dissatisfaction and tension will arise.

20.3.2 Definitions of quality

According to the International Organization for Standardization (ISO), quality is "the totality of features and characteristics of a product or service that bear on its ability to satisfy stated and implied needs" (1990, page 6). This can be further classified in the context of legal services from four possible standpoints (see Gummesson (1992), pages 183–4):

(a) *transcendent quality* — a matter of craftsmanship, professionalism and a feeling for excellence;

(b) *specification-based quality* — a technical view of performance, based on complying with specified requirements (for example, the use of standard documentation turned around within predetermined time limits): this is a process-based, measurable, and usually internal, view of quality;

(c) *user-based quality* — this means that quality is whatever the client says it is; it is a sort of 'fitness for purpose' measure of quality, and can be measured by asking the client for an assessment of whether or not the legal services achieved the client's objectives and purposes: in this sense, it is a measurable, but external, view of quality;

(d) *value-based quality* — this dimension represents the client's assessment of the value of the legal services they have experienced compared with the fees paid; this can be seen as a 'value-for-money' assessment which is, again, made by the client externally.

Most law firms focus on transcendent quality, and 'good quality' is the assessment of one's professional peers — usually based on the technical competence displayed. Law firms are instinctively uneasy with user-based and value-based quality because the quality assessment is left entirely to the client — who may not understand or appreciate the legal complexities involved. Quality management systems may shift some emphasis to specification-based quality, but is usually only considered appropriate for those legal services that can be 'routinised' in some way that makes them susceptible to standardisation and therefore specification. There are some aspects of legal practice where such proceduralisation is possible and appropriate (in England, for example, much work has been done on this in debt collection and the conveyancing of domestic registered land). Offices that apply for accreditation under the international quality standard ISO 9000 are also required to document their procedures and so create internal specifications for performance and maintenance of quality.

20.3.3 Dimensions of quality

The quality of a service is a composite concept, comprising what is done (technical quality) and how it is done and whether it achieves its purpose (functional quality). For many clients who are not in a position to make an informed judgement about the technical quality of legal services, functional quality then becomes the focus for their attention and assessment of whether or not the firm has produced a 'quality service'.

Functional quality can also be further broken down into its tangible and intangible dimensions, giving us three dimensions for discussion: technical quality, service quality, and tangible quality.

20.3.3.1 Technical quality
The quality of a fee-earner's 'legal product' can be assessed by other lawyers, and ultimately by the courts. Technical quality is therefore a matter for the exercise of professional assessment and judgment. A firm can take a number of steps to assure its technical quality, for example:

(a) recruiting fee-earners with minimum and advanced qualifications,

(b) ensuring that legal knowledge and skills are maintained and developed through appropriate training,

(c) creating and maintaining standard-form know-how and investing in libraries, and precedent and know-how systems,

(d) organising fee-earners to improve their level of expertise through specialisation,

(e) ensuring competence through effective supervision and appraisal.

The best law firms now recognise that, while recruiting good people is clearly necessary, it is only the starting point in the delivery of a quality service, and that further development and support need to be offered.

20.3.3.2 Service quality
Research by Parasuraman, Zeithaml and Berry showed that the criteria on which service quality is judged by 'consumers' are consistent across service businesses. In order of their relative importance to consumers, the 10 determinants of service quality are (1985, table 1, page 47):

(a) reliability (consistency of performance and dependability),

(b) responsiveness (willingness and readiness to provide the service, and timeliness),

(c) competence (the required skills and knowledge to perform the service),

(d) access (approachability and ease of contact),

(e) courtesy (politeness, respect, consideration and friendliness),

(f) communication (keeping clients informed, using language they understand, listening),

(g) credibility/integrity (trustworthiness, believability, honesty, having the client's best interests at heart, the firm's reputation),

(h) security/confidentiality (the freedom from personal or financial risk or doubt),

(i) understanding/knowing the client (making the effort to understand the client's needs, learning their specific requirements, providing individualised attention),

(j)   tangibles (physical evidence of the service).

Two of these dimensions are dealt with separately (competence, or technical quality, in paragraph 20.3.3.1, and tangibles in paragraph 20.3.3.3). The other criteria show how broadly service quality is likely to be assessed by clients, and provides some guidance about which aspects of the firm's approach to the delivery of legal services should be addressed.

Using these 10 characteristics, my own (unpublished) research of the clients of law firms shows a different order of relative importance:

(a)   competence,
(b)   understanding/knowing the client,
(c)   reliability,
(d)   responsiveness,
(e)   credibility/integrity,
(f)   access,
(g)   communication,
(h)   security/confidentiality,
(i)   courtesy,
(j)   tangibles.

The higher rankings for competence and understanding the client are consistent with the basis on which clients choose lawyers (see paragraph 18.2.2.1).

20.3.3.3   *Tangible quality*
In both lists, tangibles are the least important aspect of service quality. This does not mean that they are not important — the lists are about relativities, not absolutes. Tangible quality will encompass:

(a)   the physical environment (e.g., reception area, meeting rooms, offices), the ambience (temperature, light, noise, scent, cleanliness), and the design of space (aesthetic and functional design),
(b)   equipment (its features, reliability, durability),
(c)   physical manifestations of the service (such as letters and documents, brochures, business cards),
(d)   appearance (the dress and behaviour of partners and staff).

As one of the tangibles of a law office, information technology and other equipment is increasingly important. The following checklist of the determinants of technology quality could be adopted in choosing and assessing information technology hardware and software (adapted from Gummesson 1992, pages 191–6):

(a)   ability to perform to requirements,
(b)   reliability,
(c)   ability to adapt to changes in specifications,

(d)   compatibility,
(e)   efficiency in the use of hardware,
(f)   portability to different hardware,
(g)   verifiability of acceptance or failures,
(h)   integrity against unauthorised access, amendments, theft, viruses,
(i)   ease of use — operation, training.

20.3.3.4 Evaluation of service quality

The nature of professional services (see paragraph 17.1.2) makes them very difficult to assess before their delivery. Of the service quality criteria, only credibility (through reputation) and some of the tangibles can be judged in advance: this is why law firms must still set such store by their reputations and profile-raising activities (see paragraph 18.3). These are the 'search properties' of services (Parasuraman, Zeithaml and Berry 1985, page 48), and are correspondingly part of the firm's 'signalling' costs (see paragraph 18.3.3). Two other criteria — competence and security — may be impossible for the client to judge, even after the service has been delivered and paid for: these are the 'credence properties' of the services (1985, page 48). The remaining criteria are then factors of the experience of using the firm, and we can conclude that "because few search properties exist with services and because credence properties are too difficult to evaluate, [clients] typically rely on experience properties when evaluating service quality" (1985, page 48). The experience properties are: understanding/knowing the client, reliability, responsiveness, access, communication, and courtesy. These are the areas which therefore require at least equal attention in law firms along with maintaining and demonstrating technical competence, and providing impressive office space and marketing materials. Lawyers should also not forget how important it is to achieve the client's objectives and to provide value for money (cf. paragraph 18.2.2.3).

20.3.4 Quality gaps

The research of Parasuraman, Zeithaml and Berry also resulted in the 'quality gap model' shown in figure 20.1.

The model shows that a client's expectation of legal services will be influenced by the client's past experience of the firm and its competitors (including the determinants of service quality discussed in paragraph 20.3.3), by the firm's reputation, and by the client's needs at the time. It also shows that a law firm, in order to deliver a quality service, must manage a number of activities and processes, including understanding the client's needs and expectations, creating a service delivery process that meets those needs and expectations, actually delivering the service to the client, and managing a series of external communications to the client and to others. The model also illustrates the points at which discrepancies or 'gaps' can exist:

(a)   a difference between what the client expects, and what the firm thinks is expected (gap 1);

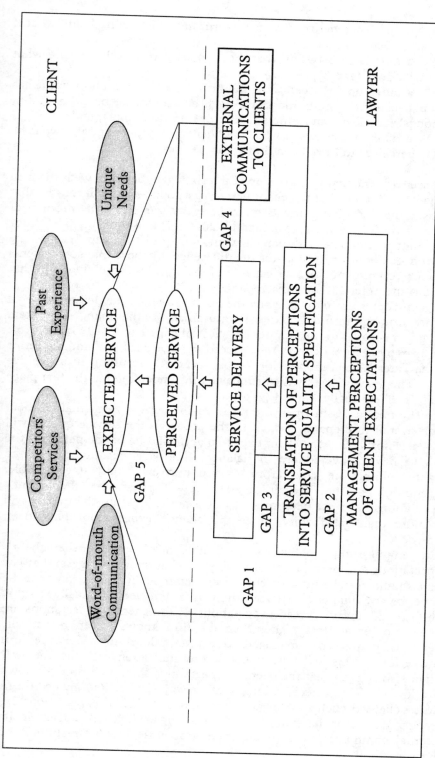

Figure 20.1 (Source: adapted from Parasuraman, Zeithaml & Berry (1985), page 44)

(b)   a difference between what the firm thinks is required, and what it sets out to achieve (gap 2);

(c)   a difference between what the firm sets out to achieve, and what it actually does (gap 3);

(d)   a difference between what the firm actually does, and what it has (through external communications, such as brochures, beauty parades, meetings) led clients and others to expect it to do (gap 4); and

(e)   a difference between what the client was expecting, and what he or she perceives to have been done (gap 5).

It seems to me that there is scope for a sixth gap, between what the firm actually does, and what the client perceives it to have done. It may be that Parasuraman, Zeithaml and Berry believe this gap to be the product of the credence properties (see paragraph 20.3.3.4) and thus too difficult for the client to evaluate. As such, it would not lead to a gap because the client does not attempt to assess the difference. I believe that some clients (though certainly not all) are capable of making this evaluation, and that there is the potential for a discrepancy here.

The model is useful in showing the points at which the delivery of legal services can run into difficulties. Parasuraman, Zeithaml and Berry state that gap 5 is equal to the cumulative effect of gaps 1 to 4 (1985, page 46). For example, actual delivery may exceed the 'specification' and the terms of the external communication (gaps 3 and 4), resulting in a positive 'gap'. This may be lost by the firm having misunderstood in the first place what the client really wanted (gap 1).

In the final assessment, if the result of the gaps is zero (that is, there is no overall discrepancy or gap in the process), the service quality will be satisfactory; what the client expected and what he or she perceives the firm to have delivered are in balance. If it is a negative result, the quality will not be satisfactory — and may be totally unacceptable, depending on the magnitude of the discrepancies; the client's expectations have not been met. If it is a positive result, the quality will be more than satisfactory, since the client's expectations have been exceeded.

In emphasising quality as the difference between the client's expectations and perceptions of quality, the gap model suggests that law firms should seek to manage clients' expectations in such a way that the scope for any difference between the two is removed or (ideally) so that the firm will always exceed expectations. If the client's expectations are unrealistic (or at least higher than the firm knows it can realistically meet), they must be 'managed' down to a level to which the firm can perform. This will require good communication with the client. It might also suggest that the clients' expectations should be brought down to a low level that the firm knows can always exceed (so giving rise to more delighted clients). However, the danger is that if expectations are brought down too far before the firm is engaged, it will appear in its external communications to be offering so little that it might not be engaged at all!

20.3.5 An approach to quality in legal services

Although clients will assess retrospectively whether they feel they have received a quality service from their lawyers (cf. paragraph 18.2.2.3), very few of them can define or describe in advance what they expect a quality service to be (except in very general terms). This is consistent with the distinction between the search, credence and experience properties of legal services (cf. paragraph 20.3.3.4). Collectively, they have no common approach to quality, which makes it very difficult for law firms to determine what their approach should be.

Although it is not possible to identify a definitive and infallible approach to providing a consistent quality of legal services that will satisfy all clients, nevertheless, client surveys show that a number of common factors or features emerge (cf. paragraph 18.2.2):

(a) Legal expertise is usually taken for granted, but clients do want to deal with lawyers who understand their personal circumstances, industry or their own business specifically. Much of this is demonstrated by previous experience of similar situations (part of individual and firm-specific capital: see paragraph 5.2), and showing a genuine interest in the clients' activities.

(b) Lawyers need to be accessible and responsive: difficulties in getting through on the telephone to talk to a lawyer, dealing with difficult or obstructive secretaries, and messages that are not attended to are all indicators of poor quality.

(c) Advice needs to be concise and well-expressed, and lawyers should avoid 'sitting on the fence'.

(d) While nearly all lawyers meet deadlines when matters are urgent, clients are irritated that other issues are allowed to slide until they become urgent or the client complains.

(e) Charges should relate to the value of the work (however calculated).

These are necessary generalisations, and clients will express many other personal indicators of quality. But these five represent the core of quality legal services, and are all underpinned by good communication.

A firm's ability to deliver consistent, quality legal services is also underpinned by many other internal factors. It is these factors that quality management systems seek to identify or define, each in its own way. Most generic quality management systems place a heavy emphasis on internal issues, and therefore tend to emphasise internal systems. I believe that quality should be put into a slightly wider context.

I believe that there are three elements to the delivery of quality legal services: expectations, effectiveness and economics. These elements can be phrased as three corresponding questions:

(a) What do clients expect from the firm?

(b) How can the firm best deliver legal services to meet clients' expectations?

(c)   How should the firm run itself to provide the legal services clients expect, at a price clients are prepared to pay and that will yield a profit to the partners?

These issues are expanded on in table 20.1, which shows that quality is a 'holistic' issue which encompasses every aspect of the firm's operations.

EXPECTATIONS	EFFECTIVENESS	ECONOMICS
What do clients want from the firm?	How can the firm deliver?	How does the firm provide value for money and make a profit?
SOLICITOR-CLIENT RELATIONSHIP Client partner Business understanding Complaints procedure Entertainment Newsletters, seminars	**PRACTICE AREA ORGANISATION** Departments; practice groups Heads of department; practice group leaders Development of specialisation Training and professional development Information and know-how	**PARTNER RELATIONS** Admission and retirement Salaried and equity tiers Profit-sharing Capitalisation
CLIENT MANAGEMENT Terms of business Pricing, basis of charging, likely cost, billing Reporting relationship Cross-selling	**MATTER MANAGEMENT** Case acceptance Matter allocation Matter team Matter strategy Delegation and supervision Case processing; project management File and document management Matter completion	**BUSINESS MANAGEMENT** Management structure Financial management Administration and support Personnel management Premises management

Table 20.1 Elements of quality

Not surprisingly, the quality factors that clients most often focus on relate to the delivery of legal services, and most specifically to matter management (see the middle column of table 20.1). It is these factors that, in my view, should receive the most attention in a quality review. They are elaborated on in table 20.2, and the issues raised are the subject of chapter 21.

1. **Case Acceptance**	6. **Case Processing and Project Management**
Guidelines: authority; conditions. Competence; resource. Instructions: record; confirmation. Conflicts; sensitivities. Economics; matter budget.	Critical path. Identify and record key dates. Use of internal and client rescources. Choice and use of counsel, foreign lawyers, experts, etc.: instructions, checking opinion and reports, fees. Progress tracking and reporting. Response to client enquiries. Reviewing matter strategy and resources. Monitoring matter budget.
2. **Matter Allocation**	
Responsibility for conduct; matter partner. Staffing needs. Priority of matters. Work distribution; overloading superstars; sidelining.	7. **File and Document Management**
3. **Matter Team**	File and filing. Document identity and tracing. Case plan; action checklists. Record of advice given; attendance notes; correspondence. Agreements and precedents; travelling drafts. Record of undertakings given and received; authority and monitoring. Financial transactions. Security and confidentiality.
Selection: expertise, seniority, cost, availability, personality. Roles and responsibilities. Expertise: business and legal. Communication: meetings and reporting.	
4. **Matter Strategy**	8. **Matter Completion**
Client involvement. Formulation; brainstorming. Risk analysis. Contingency planning. Case plan: timetables and resource implications.	Client review: report outcome; explain further action; account for outstanding money; return original documents and other client property; advise on storage and retrieval of retained documents and property; advise on need for future review. Team review: report outcome; determine post-completion action. Billing and collection. Payment of outside fees and accounts. Matter profitability. File closing and storage.
5. **Delegation and Supervision**	
Work allocation: assignment and expectations. Supervision; review meetings; feedback. Quality control; incoming and outgoing post.	

Table 20.2 Matter management

For quality to be a reality in any law firm, there will be a recognition that:

(a) Quality is judged by the client on a basis that may differ from a fee-earner's assessment (see paragraph 20.3.3).

(b) Partners will need to demonstrate clear quality values and ensure that they form part of the firm's way of working (see paragraph 23.1).

(c) Quality does require well-designed and well-executed processes for the delivery of legal services.

(d) Looking for new and better ways of providing services must become part of the firm's philosophy of client work and the management of its business (cf. paragraph 7.2(a)(v) and (vii), and (c)).

(e) Supervision and quality assurance are significant elements of effective quality in legal services.

(f) Decisions need to be based on facts rather than the unsubstantiated assertions of partners, professional managers or consultants.

(g) All partners, lawyers and staff must be suitably trained, not just in the technical substance of what they are expected to do but also in those activities on which clients' evaluation of service quality will be based.

In other words, the *attitude and approach* of partners, fee-earners and support staff to quality issues are as important as the *systems and procedures* through which they seek to assure or control quality.

It is often difficult to address quality issues in a firm — especially one that is already perceived to be a high-quality law firm. But delivering high-quality legal services is not, by itself, sufficient. Quality is no longer a competitive advantage; it is simply a precondition to staying in practice. There may well need to be improvements in a firm. However, quality is not a separate issue that can be isolated and dealt with. It is an intrinsic part of the delivery of legal services and of value for money. It is therefore essential that the quality debate engages lawyers' attention (and particularly partners' attention). If not, they will all agree with the principles and approach, and go back to practising law as they always have.

The management of quality legal services is not about perfection or 'zero defects': such an approach is not always consistent with clients' needs, and achieving perfection normally involves a disproportionate effort that is rarely consistent with clients' perceptions of value. Nor is it necessarily about efficiency: many firms are efficient without being effective in the minds of clients. A quality approach is not about perfection, systems to remove defects, or efficiency. It should principally be about people:

(a) clients, and what they want; and

(b) the firm's lawyers and staff, and creating an environment where they can give their best.

Only then can any firm decide which *system* is appropriate to its environment and needs. At this point, one might expect the discussion to lead on to a consideration of ISO 9000, Investors in People, total quality management, the Law Society's Practice Management Standards, and other quality management systems. To do so would, in my view, take up a disproportionate amount of space. The choice of a system must depend on business strategy, the firm's structure and culture, the attitudes and aptitude of partners and staff, and preference. In some types of work, the choice might be constrained or inevitable. Whichever it is, there is a wealth of publications about the specific systems.

If your practice needs to achieve a quality accreditation in order to compete for business, go into it with your eyes open. It will require a major investment of time, effort and money. Be sure that it is necessary before you embark on the process. Also, be careful that you are not lulled into thinking that when you are accredited you have already achieved quality and that all you need to do is follow the procedures. Taking care of clients is far more sophisticated than such a mechanistic approach would suggest.

There is a close correlation between quality and marketing. Quality is all about meeting (or preferably exceeding) clients' expectations. These are almost infinitely variable, and the service provided by a firm or individual fee-earner must be specifically tailored to the needs of a particular client, in relation to a particular piece of work, at a particular time. Marketing is partly a process of discerning and managing clients' expectations. Unfortunately, the expectations of the same client might well be different on a new matter or at another time. Quality is such a difficult issue precisely because clients may not always articulate (or even know) their expectations about service quality — until it is too late to do anything about it — and because their expectations will vary and change (both individually and collectively). The only response is informed and open communication between lawyers and clients about these expectations.

Chapter 21

PROJECT MANAGEMENT IN LEGAL PRACTICE

21.1 Introduction

The interface between delivery to clients and the management of people is the day-to-day management of cases. This chapter is therefore 'sandwiched' in its appropriate place. Increasing pressure on lawyers, as well as the increasing size of many matters and transactions (and of the financial value and consequences attached to them) has led to a recent interest in the process of case management. In particular, attention has focused on whether the principles of project management can be applied to the delivery of legal services. My answer is that they can. I gratefully acknowledge the help and insights provided by Briner, Geddes and Hastings (1993) and Reiss (1992) in leading me to this conclusion.

The principal objective of this chapter is therefore to provide a framework for analysis and action for project management in legal practice. Rather than to provide definitive answers, its purpose is to articulate and make explicit some things which may happen instinctively. Although there are some specific suggestions, the chapter is designed more as a checklist, and some of the statements may therefore be a necessary reflection of the simple and self-evident. It is clear from the views of clients, the Legal Aid Board and the Office for the Supervision of Solicitors, however, that the self-evident is not inevitable!

The increasing tendency for clients to perceive some legal services as a 'commodity' (cf. paragraph 2.3.3) means that the service has to be delivered efficiently as well as effectively. This gives rise to variable notions of 'quality' — and these do not always equate with 'excellence', 'zero defects' and other qualities that might be associated by lawyers with the technical quality of what they offer (as discussed in paragraph 20.3). We have to remember that legal services are (see paragraph 17.1.2):

(a) intangible,

(b) heterogeneous (there are different expectations from different clients),

(c) inseparable (production often cannot be separated from delivery),

(d) perishable (the services cannot be produced and stored for later use).

Individuals, departments or firms should also consider whether the services they provide are perceived by the client to be expertise, experience or efficiency (see paragraph 2.3.3), since this will also determine structural and productivity issues.

With all these changes in attitudes and sophistication, the need for the more effective delivery of legal services is crucial — both in terms of the internal workings of a law firm and in its dealings with clients and others outside the firm. It is for this reason that lawyers are turning to the techniques of project management. So far, most work has been done in relation to litigation, but is not confined to it.

Increasingly, those clients who might be described as 'professional' buyers of legal services — which, for the most part, means the insurance companies and in-house lawyers — are taking a harder line with lawyers, and are requiring more planning, thought and accountability. Indeed, some of them are already using technology to access lawyers' case files as and when they please (whether the lawyers involved know about it or not): it makes a difference to the way you run a file!

In addition, there are signs of increasing judicial 'management' in the process of litigation. Written arguments in the Court of Appeal, streamlined processes and judges assigned early to actions in the Commercial Court and the Official Referees' Court, are examples of judges intervening to manage and control the conduct of litigation. The implementation of Lord Woolf's access to justice reforms will lay even more emphasis on the need for greater judicial involvement in the process through case management conferences, assisted by the wider use of information technology to enable the progress of actions to be more easily monitored.

It is, therefore, no longer sufficient to point to the actions or behaviour of 'the other side' to justify playing along with delays, prevarications and the document explosion. All lawyers need to reconsider the way in which they manage cases and transactions if they are not to find their clients seeking alternatives that do not involve lawyers (see also Maister 1997, chapter 14).

In short, clients now expect their matters to be properly managed as well as to achieve the intended result or outcome. In terms of addressing client needs and expectations, and the need for *appropriate* and cost-effective results in legal practice, project management represents a significant contribution to the way ahead. You may be tempted to think that it is a good idea in theory, but too difficult or, indeed, impossible or even unnecessary in practice. You are not alone! Working in teams brought together for specific cases has not in fact been unusual in the law (though the sophistication required is increasing in leaps and bounds). But in the business world generally, project working is becoming more commonplace and important, as the following extract from Peters (1992, pages 154 and 156) shows:

> "Most of tomorrow's work will be done in project teams. Project teams will neither quash individualism nor blunt specialization. To the contrary, individual contributions will be more important than ever. . . . Though expertise and specialization are more important than ever, developing 'peripheral vision', a feel for the whole task, is essential. . . . The 'project manager' and 'network manager' are the star players of tomorrow! Everyone will routinely fill project management/network management roles, directly or indirectly. Attention to these skills, and training in these skills, will be vital. Promotion will go to those who are particularly adept at exercising such skills."

This does not mean that we should embrace the process uncritically, or not be prepared to acknowledge some difficulties. By focusing solely on 'the project', is there a danger that the lawyer will compromise his professional responsibilities to his clients, his fellow professionals and to the court? If the lawyer is entirely client-focused, may other compromises have to be made? Does a lawyer qualify in order to be a lawyer and not a manager? I do not on this occasion suggest ways to resolve these issues, but they have to be faced and overcome. Lawyers who wish their firms to be successful must respond to the client-driven and judge-driven changes that are already on us, and learn new skills.

21.2   A Question of Focus

Lawyers tend to approach a transaction or matter with one of four focuses:

(a)   procedural focus: they follow the rules of court (White Book, Green Book, etc.), a conveyancing protocol, or other procedural method, and are driven reactively by procedure: they may reach an outcome which is not in line with the client's needs, expectations or pocket;

(b)   case or matter focus: they become absorbed in the case, in its merits or demerits, in the technicalities, in its interesting points, in the justice of the claim, in the pursuit of the highest possible quality, and again may reach an outcome which is not in line with the client's needs, expectations or pocket;

(c)   firm focus: the case or transaction is seen as a way of making money, reaching hours or fees targets, of being a cash cow, at the end of which the firm may have made a lot of money (but lost the client?);

(d)   client focus: the client's objectives and concerns are kept at the forefront, and the case or transaction is handled with proper regard for economics and cost-benefit.

Good project management, in fact, emphasises client focus, but has regard to a proper balance between all four, avoiding the worst excesses of any of them and adding benefit by incorporating the best of each. For this reason, I am using the expression 'project management', rather than 'client management', 'case management' or 'matter management', in order to emphasise this holistic approach. Case or matter management tends to concentrate on internal issues of process, procedure or systems. Client management works to keep the clients happy and provide a positive experience during and after their contact with the firm. Project management seeks to balance all the internal and external issues of people involvement, resources, process, procedure, systems, timing, economics and meeting clients' and others' expectations.

21.3 Nature of Project Management

Most approaches to project management, having originated in the construction and engineering industries, tend to focus on 'the project' and on the planning and control of the project. But good project management — even in those usually well-defined, timed and costed projects — is also about managing people and their performance. Most legal work does not have the definition of a construction project. But it does have the same two principal elements which need to be reflected in project management:

(a)   the project,
(b)   teamwork.

A project may be defined as any task which:

(a)   has a beginning and an end;
(b)   is made up of a series of separate activities, each of which absorbs time and money, but which can occur in parallel or sequentially.

The project will also have objectives for quality or specification (meaning substantive objectives or outcomes), cost, and time, one of which will usually be dominant and will therefore affect decision-making throughout the project (Reiss 1992, pages 39–41).

The nature of the project management required will depend on the nature and variables of the project (case or transaction) involved. Some cases may well be tightly defined, run according to a known process, and involve fixed budgets (e.g., domestic conveyancing, straightforward wills, whiplash or uninsured loss claims, debt recovery): in these circumstances, the applicability of some project management is not difficult to envisage. Indeed, in any well-run firm, there will probably be lawyers conducting 'routine' matters and who may be described as 'unconsciously competent' project managers. Many lawyers would claim that such cases are so uniform and repetitive in their process that project management is *not* required. This is untrue, but the project management expertise necessary may be of a lower level. Other matters may be nowhere near so straightforward. The need for project management is not therefore solely a question of the size of the matter, although perhaps it is easier to appreciate the need in relation to 'larger or more complex cases and transactions.

21.4 The Project

21.4.1 *Nature of the project*

Two of the primary variables in a project will be (cf. Briner, Geddes and Hastings 1993, page 34):

(a)   the degree of specificity or ambiguity of the outcome; and
(b)   the degree of formality or informality of the process involved.

These variables can be plotted simplistically to show the effect of their combination (see figure 21.1).

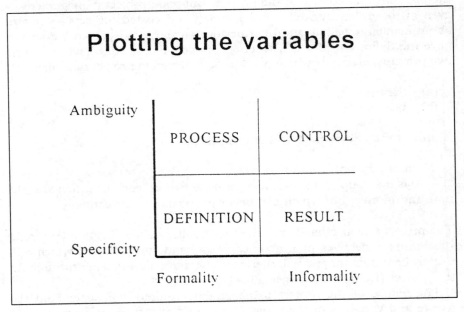

Figure 21.1

With a specific result required (for example, an interlocutory injunction), and a formal process to follow (for example, Rules of the Supreme Court, Order 29, r. 1), the project is capable of a high degree of definition. The areas of it that need to be managed towards the desired result often become self-evident and make the job of project management much easier: a process and a goal give the project a much-needed focus. That said, this is a short-term goal. Any good lawyer will acknowledge the dangers of adopting a short-term strategy without having regard to the position in the longer term — inevitably a good deal less certain. This is one reason why a theory of the matter can be a powerful tool (see paragraph 21.4.3).

If the desired outcome is unclear, a *process* can at least provide a path to follow: unfortunately, the process can take over. A litigator's emphasis on the procedure of litigation, or a property lawyer's use of registered conveyancing, provides some comfort to the lawyer, but not necessarily a truly beneficial result for the client. Even when the result is specific, and the process should be driven by the result, all too often the procedure still dominates. And then there are the other parties. Clients often report that when they enquire of their lawyers why a matter has become so complex and long-winded, the response is to blame 'the system' or 'the other side' for blocking progress.

Of course, when the result is ambiguous, and the procedure is inappropriate or unclear (e.g., multi-party actions), figure 21.1 suggests that chaos — and a costs 'black hole' — is most likely. The message is that, with any ambiguity in the intended result, or any doubts about the degree of formality in the process that is to be (or can be) adopted, project management *is even more important*, to ensure that the best result is achieved.

21.4.2 The client as stakeholder

Any project has a number of 'stakeholders', that is, people who have an interest in its outcome. In legal practice, the client tends to be the principal stakeholder (others may include the client partner, the head of department, or other partners; in high-profile cases, there may be a public interest at stake).

The client as stakeholder is therefore a major influence (and possibly constraint) on the conduct of the case. Is the client a private client, in business, in the public sector, an insurer, the Legal Aid Board? What sort of activity or industry is the client engaged in? What is the client's perspective — someone who pays your fees (e.g., private client, chief executive), someone who is affected by your involvement (e.g., an in-house lawyer), or someone whose behaviour is at the core of the matter (e.g., a fraudster, party to divorce)? What are the client's objectives; do the goalposts keep moving? Does the client see your involvement as putting them in a better position, as restoring them to where they should have been, or as a necessary evil with no positive or negative connotations? What is the client's personality, and how do you get on? How is the action being financed, and who is ultimately paying for it? There may be conflict between more than one 'client': there may, for instance, be conflicts between the interests of the insurer and (real) client; there may be conflicts between individual plaintiffs; between the interests of a company and those of its managing director; between trustees and beneficiaries; between one family member and another. All of these factors will affect the running of a matter, including the desired outcome, the resources available, and (in litigation) the appetite for a fight. You cannot afford to be so objective or legalistic in your assessment of the case, and in your approach to it, that you forget about these 'soft' issues.

Many of these issues arise (and should be addressed) at the outset of the lawyer–client relationship. The thoroughness (and open-mindedness) with which the client's instructions are taken, and the basis on which the relationship is established, will be key to being given the right sort of information in the first place, and to establishing the clients' expectations. The use of checklists, and acceptance or engagement letters, is also an important part of the process. Indeed, there is a 'risk assessment' for the firm to conduct in deciding whether to accept the instructions — ethical, professional, or resourcing risks, as well as financial risk.

21.4.3   *The theory of the matter*

In any endeavour, it is always helpful to have some idea of the destination, objective or goal. A matter theory is therefore a concise statement summarising the position or objective of your client in the matter on which you are acting. It may change or need refining as more facts are obtained or the legal issues become clearer or are researched more thoroughly. Everything done during a matter should then be consistent with the positions or objectives contained in the matter theory.

A matter theory (also known as the theory of the case) can be particularly important in litigation. It should be constructed by selecting the most effective and persuasive legal and factual positions; it should provide the decision-maker with the reasons why your client is entitled to judgment. An effective matter theory is therefore understandable, persuasive, comprehensive and compelling, and should motivate the decision-maker to want to decide a case favourably. In this sense, the matter theory should be repeated often during the development of the case: it should provide the basis on which all decisions relating to the litigation are taken — in other words, a basis for asking, "Is what we propose to do going to advance in a positive way our theory of the case?"

21.4.4   *Planning the project*

Having decided on the objective — the matter theory — it is important then to develop a plan for achieving it. Most clients are intolerant of an open-ended, open-chequebook approach to legal work. Legal problems rarely take place in a vacuum — either for the client or for the lawyers. Other things have to be done at the same time, and therefore there is a requirement for some definition to the project. Planning is the opposite to merely reacting to the other side, or being driven by the procedure to reach a result — any result. Of course in litigation, if you are acting for a defendant, you will to an extent be driven by the plaintiff. But even this does not mean that you should be entirely reactive. By considering the people and variables involved (that is, the factors already considered above), a defendant is just as capable of developing a case plan as any plaintiff: it may not drive the overall action, but it will provide a framework for driving the nature and timing of the defendant's responses.

The key features of the planning process will be to determine (cf. Briner, Geddes and Hastings 1993, pages 81–6):

(a)   the principal steps in the matter (key dates, events, etc.), and which of them you or your client can control or influence;

(b)   a breakdown or schedule of the work involved and the sequential relationship between them (see figure 21.2 for an example);

(c)   the critical interdependencies between the principal steps (i.e., those which cannot proceed until another has been addressed): it is possible, but not essential, to develop this into a 'critical path analysis'; and

(d)   the resources required.

Be prepared to acknowledge that you may be able to exercise much greater control over events than you may have thought possible. This is the very essence of project management.

Work breakdown schedules (or project plans) may need to be prepared at different levels of detail, from a 'macro-plan' for the whole case or matter, to 'micro-plans' for specific activities (e.g., discovery). These days computerised project management is possible. However, in my experience, it is important to understand the principles of project management before attempting to use (or rely on) a computer-generated project plan.

The resources will be:

(a)   Skills — what do you need, who has them, are they internal or external, when do you need them?

(b)   Technology and equipment — what do you need, is it available internally or do you need to acquire or hire?

(c)   Finance — how much is needed, when, and where from?

(d)   Time — for how long will you need the various resources and when?

Thinking about resources is very important for a number of reasons: if they are not in place at the right time, opportunities may be lost, costs incurred or delays suffered. Some resources, like money and time, are consumable and once gone cannot be retrieved. Others, such as people and equipment, are non-consumable. However, if there are insufficient of these resources (people, skills, technology) or they are subject to conflicting priorities, you may experience considerable aggravation in the running of the matter. In larger firms, or with bigger matters, you may be able to consider subcontracting (e.g., special projects lawyers) or outsourcing (e.g., litigation support systems); you may be able to bring some activities forward and do them when they *can* be done as opposed to when they *must* be done. If a case is handled reactively, resourcing will also be dealt with reactively. At the last minute, there may simply be too little time to organise everything effectively. As the *Guide for Use in Group Actions* says (at page 8, in a comment that I believe applies generally to all legal practice):

"Even though specialist advice from the Bar is always available, it is the plain duty of every solicitor not to take on work which that solicitor

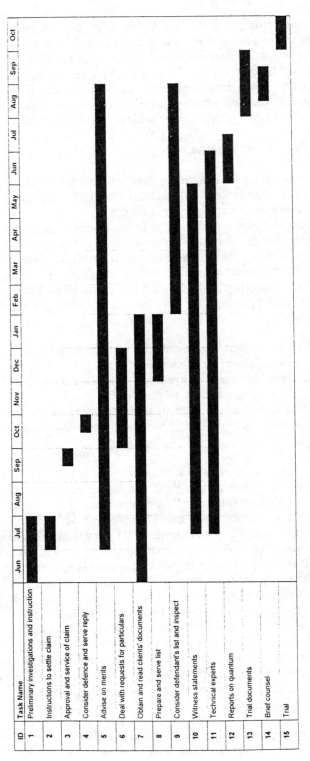

Figure 21.2 (based, with thanks, on Benson 1991, page 8)

does not have the experience or the resources to handle. There comes a point when even the best-equipped firms have to say that the firm has as much work as it can efficiently handle."

The project plan, and the allocation and timing of resources will also allow a budget and cash-flow forecast to be prepared (this is considered separately in paragraph 21.6).

21.4.5 Setting targets

With some idea of how the matter is expected to unfold, you can begin to prepare a budget and set targets. Planning in legal practice is not a question of exercising strict control over what happens and when. But it is necessary to have an overview, and to set some intermediate targets and then long-term targets. Clients are likely to set short deadlines, and other targets may be imposed by constraints of time or cash, or the availability of people or other resources to devote to the project. In litigation, it may well be that we will see a greater tendency for courts to fix dates for trial at the outset of (or at least earlier in) proceedings. In many instances, therefore, the 'long-term' target date will be prescribed and, by working back, a series of intermediate targets can be set. These intermediate targets could relate, for example, to:

(a)   critical dates and possible bottlenecks (for example, those things that must be achieved before other activities scheduled for later in the project can begin);

(b)   the costs that may be incurred without further authorisation from the client, or the resources that may be available, used or needed.

21.4.6 Maintaining commitment

It is one thing to embark on a new matter; it is quite another to be sure that the client has the same approach to it in one, two or three months' (or years') time. You may be proceeding on a long-term basis, only to find that the client's priorities, business conditions, ownership or pocket have changed. Even without these things, the issue may well recede in importance as time goes by.

Clients' commitment can be maintained through involving them in the matter and through progress reports. Progress-reporting is not possible without some form of monitoring: indeed, without monitoring, a case will not in fact be managed, and nothing will be learned from the experience of planning; nor would you be able to prepare accurate progress reports. Monitoring should therefore:

(a)   Keep track of events and costs: *who* is going to tell you, and *when?*

(b)   Concentrate not on everything, but on the critical areas or activities that need to be monitored: *what* are they?

(c) Be appropriate to the situation or objective, giving positive reports (for the need to know), exception reports (to provide warning signals), or sign-off reports (for approval to go ahead to the next stage): *how* should you be monitoring effectively in different situations, for different people, and for different purposes?

Many of these factors are, of course, reflections of the firm's approach to quality assurance and control and of the procedures it has put in place.

In relation to progress-reporting to clients, consider:

(a)   form (written; oral: meeting, telephone);
(b)   regularity (to be chosen by or agreed with the client, rather than imposed);
(c)   nature (task-by-task, remaining activities and duration, expected completion and outcome).

The most important factor is not to spring any surprises on the client.

Information technology can play a useful role in relation to monitoring, for example, by providing electronic reminders, or generating work-in-progress reports (see further paragraph 21.6.2).

21.4.7 *Project completion*

Jumping forward a little, it is all too commonplace that the lure and excitement of the next, new piece of work makes the process of properly completing a current matter less attractive. However, the following need to be considered to round off successfully:

(a)   billing and collection, including the payment of outside fees and accounts (e.g., counsel, expert witnesses), taxation (in litigation), and a review of matter profitability; and
(b)   file closing and storage.

Think also about holding an internal review: how many law firms conduct a review with the project team to consider how the case or transaction was handled; how the team worked; what was successful (and why); what needs to be improved (and why); the lessons learnt? A well-constructed and planned review need not take very long, but the proven benefits to the management of future matters will be considerable (they become part of firm-specific capital and then part of the firm's competitive advantage: see paragraphs 4.6 and 5.2.2).

You might also ask, whether the client would appreciate a review. This would provide an opportunity to report or discuss the outcome of the matter, and explain any further action that may be required; account for any outstanding money; return original documents and other client property; advise on the storage and retrieval of materials that are retained; and advise on the need for any further review of the matter, its outcome, or any expected subsequent activity. Not all clients will take you up on the offer — but at least an offer will have been made. Such reviews provide an ideal opportunity to gauge the temperature of the client's feelings about the likely costs (and therefore level of fee you should seek), as well as giving an opportunity to explore the prospect of any further work.

21.4.8 Summary

Successful coordination of the project will therefore require someone to (cf. Briner, Geddes and Hastings 1993, pages 6–7):

Manage *performance*	look *outwards*	clients, experts, counsel, etc.
	look *upwards*	client partner, head of department.
Manage *the case*	look *forwards*	planning, resources, targets, timetable
	look *backwards*	monitoring and reporting.
Manage *performance*	look *downwards*	teamwork
	look *inwards*	self-management.

21.5 Teamwork

21.5.1 Who is in the team?

All legal matters involve a team — the larger the matter or action, the more obvious this fact becomes, but it is true for *every* case. From the lawyer's perspective, this team usually comprises:

(a) The client.
(b) The internal team:

   (i) the matter partner;
   (ii) core lawyers — those who are regularly involved in the matter and are formally associated with it;
   (iii) irregular specialists (who are not necessarily formally associated with the matter);
   (iv) support staff;
   (v) supporters who may not be — and usually are not — involved on a regular basis (for example, the client partner or head of department).

(c) The external team:

   (i) specialists (e.g., experts, health care professionals, consultants);
   (ii) counsel or foreign lawyers;

    (iii)   advisers (e.g., banks, accountants, economists, insurers, archi-
tects, surveyors, engineers, actuaries);

    (iv)   perhaps even the media.

Some parts of the team are *visible* by being directly involved in the
matter (e.g., the matter partner, core lawyers, counsel); other parts are
invisible because they are not directly involved (e.g., irregular specialists,
support staff, supporters, advisers): Briner, Geddes and Hastings 1993,
pages xvii and xviii. It is clearly important to make sure that the visible
team members are kept up to date with developments; however, it is also
very important to make sure that the invisible team members are not left
out, disregarded or missed out of communications (as they often feel).

The characteristics of such a team (unlike many teams in other business
environments) is that:

    (a)   its members usually participate on a 'part-time' basis (and are
often therefore members of other teams);

    (b)   there are often no clear roles or relationships between the mem-
bers (especially internally, where lawyers from different departments are
involved, and between internal and external members);

    (c)   expectations of and about the team members emerge and change,
rather than being fixed from the outset and remaining constant;

    (d)   there is usually little planning or control (internally, let alone
externally) simply because the team members are often independent,
drawn from inside and outside the firm, or from different parts of the firm.

Matter teams (even within the firm) will form, act, dissolve, and then
re-form to start another case (cf. paragraph 2.3.4). The process is also
unlikely to be sequential, with new actions starting — and new teams
being formed — during the currency of others. Matter teams are therefore
complex and shifting groups of people.

It is, in fact, quite possible for no one to be in overall charge of a
transaction or case, if the client believes that the lawyers are handling it
and does not take control, and the lawyers are too busy wrapped up in
the procedural requirements without thinking about managing the project
in its entirety. Increasingly, therefore, clients with in-house legal departments will take control and will then dictate the way in which a case is to
be handled.

21.5.2 The team leader's performance

Ultimately, the way a team performs will depend on the sum of the
activities of the individual team members and of the organisation(s) to
which they belong. The team leader's job is to link the various individual
contributions together in order to achieve the client's objectives, that is,
to manage the collaboration of team members.

It may be difficult to determine who is the overall team leader for any given action. For the purposes of this chapter, I am assuming that the team leader is the matter partner, and will therefore address predominantly those issues which relate to law firms. Even so, the matter partner should not forget that there are external and invisible members of the team whose needs and performance should be taken into account: the matter partner may not be able to control, or even influence, their behaviour or accountability, but he or she cannot afford to ignore them.

The matter partner's role is:

(a)   to form the matter team (at least internally — both visible and invisible), which should include working out who should be part of the formal, visible team, as well as the need for and timing of contributions from other specialists and supporters inside and outside the firm, reserving their time in advance, if necessary;

(b)   to make demands for resources (people, skills, time, technology and equipment, cash, etc.): the ability of clients to provide resources in kind as well as in cash should never be overlooked — in commercial matters, for example, clients may have better technology, people with a greater understanding of the client or how to get things done, or a more cost-effective process, than their lawyers;

(c)   brief the team thoroughly before work starts, and on a continuing basis: many irregular specialists and members of the invisible team (particularly support staff) often complain that they do not understand enough of the 'big picture' to be able to focus their contributions to the right framework or on the right priorities; this is wasteful, and may be missing the opportunity to perform an outstanding job rather than a merely satisfactory one;

(d)   to allocate work to team members, and ensure that it remains properly and effectively distributed;

(e)   to decide who is to attend meetings, and what function they are to perform: clients do not like to think that they are paying for people to sit in on meetings unnecessarily, particularly if the contribution is restricted in time, importance or consequence, or if they feel that people are learning at their expense;

(f)   to establish lines of contact and communication, to ensure that all team members know what they need to and ought to (including how the 'big picture' is changing or progressing), and that people are aware of what others are doing (so that work is not unnecessarily duplicated or may be overlooked).

21.5.3 *Team understanding*

It may be worth reflecting at this point on the various issues that the team must understand — not in terms of the detail, but of the characteristics. Without this understanding, the team will be less effective. There must therefore be understanding and agreement on:

(a)   *What are the closed issues?* Closed issues are those on which the client has a definite view or objective. Does the team know what these are?

(b)   *What are the open issues, and what approach should be taken towards them?* Open issues are those on which the client does not have a definite view or objective — the client may have no view at all, and yet it might be an issue which is important to lawyers in terms of moving the action forward. Much of a lawyer's credibility can derive from the way he or she handles these open issues. If the lawyer's view is that 'Clients must know what they want, so why don't they just tell me?', or 'If clients don't know what they want, they must be incompetent or stupid', then there is great potential for a breakdown in the solicitor-client relationship, and a dissatisfied client.

On the other hand, a lawyer who demonstrates an understanding of how the client might see the issue — of why it is more (or less) important than it might seem, of the business, technical, financial and staff (as well as the legal) factors and consequences that go into the client's decision-making process — will have gone a significant way towards establishing credibility with the client. Credibility is the all-important foundation on which an effective client relationship is built and maintained. It is also a basis for helping the client reach a conclusion on open issues, or of providing a basis on which to negotiate their outcome.

(c)   *What are the criteria for success?* Litigators all too often assume that the only measure of success is winning the action; other practitioners may think in terms only of completing a transaction at all costs. But there are two categories of success criteria — hard and soft (Briner, Geddes and Hastings 1993, pages 63–7). The hard criteria relate to what is to be done (e.g., outcome, deadlines, cost): even these can often be unarticulated, leading to confusion or differences about what the objectives really are. In some cases, it can help simply to know what is *not* to be done. The soft criteria relate to *how* things are to be done (e.g., attitude, cooperation, progress-reporting, interpersonal relationships): these are often overlooked, but are the ones which clients experience most immediately, and which can give them a sense of comfort if the action does not lead to the result they wanted. The soft criteria are often the most neglected but are probably the more important; unfortunately, they are less easily measured. The lawyer needs to understand how far the client will really go, and the matter partner must then be prepared to establish a team that will fit in with all the objectives and success criteria.

21.5.4   *Team meetings*

No team will have any sense of identity, cohesion or involvement unless it meets together: to be effective, it must go through the 'forming, storming, norming, and performing' cycle. Many failings of team effort (both internally, and as between internal and external team members) are due to failures to get the team together. This is not to suggest that meetings should become social occasions, and should be held for the sake of it. Far from it: meetings must still have a purpose. Project team meetings are necessary (Briner, Geddes and Hastings 1993, page 116):

(a)   to communicate information,
(b)   to solve problems,
(c)   to make decisions.

Of course, meetings are not the only way to carry out these activities; but if a meeting is not doing one of these things, it will be a waste of time unless everyone is there with only a social expectation.

Depending on the purpose, the matter partner (team leader) also needs to consider carefully which team members should be present — internal and external, visible and invisible. It may be necessary to have different meetings to communicate much the same information to different types of people. However, meetings are a fundamental part of team performance, and should not be underrated or overlooked.

21.5.5   Team members' performance

The individual contributions of each team member are an inevitable part of the team's overall success. The matter partner should therefore consider (Briner, Geddes and Hastings 1993, pages 118–19):

(a)   which team member should be doing what, and when;
(b)   the appropriate degree of delegation and supervision, aiming for trust and minimum interference without abdication;
(c)   how to protect team members from distractions and conflicting priorities which may take their attention away from the matter in hand (the trouble is, of course, there are other, equally valid and important, matters to be worked on simultaneously): liaison with other matter partners and the heads of department is a necessary part of making continuing bids for the human resource;
(d)   how to maintain the momentum and commitment of team members: as the first flush of excitement of a new matter fades, and an action drags on, motivation may become a significant role for the team leader; 'management by walking about' is an effective (but not sufficient) way of doing this;
(e)   setting and monitoring standards to exercise quality control across the team.

21.5.6   Thoughts about group theory

A project team is, ultimately, just another group, and its effectiveness will depend on a variety of factors that influence the successful working of groups. The role preferences of the group's members will be important (see Belbin 1981). Handy (1993, chapter 6) examines the determinants of group effectiveness. He divides those determinants as follows:

The givens:
The group   *The task*   *The environment*

Size   Nature of the task   Norms and
Member characteristics   Criteria for   expectations
Individual objectives   effectiveness   Position of the leader
Stage of development   Salience of the task   Inter-group relations
                           Clarity of the task   Physical location

The intervening factors:
                           Leadership style

                           Processes and procedures
                           Tasks functions
                           Maintenance functions
                           Interaction pattern

                           Motivation

The outcomes:
                           Productivity

                           Member satisfaction

21.6   Economics and Budgeting

21.6.1   *Matter economics*

The economics of legal services is becoming increasingly important. These days, clients expect a more helpful response than, 'It all depends . . .', and 'So much is difficult to foresee, and there are so many variables, that . . .'. Understanding the economic and financial structure of legal practice is consequently very important. Clients approach lawyers because they are experts — because they have 'been there before'. They therefore expect an expert and professional response to their concerns about cost. They recognise the uncertainties, but want as good an idea as possible of what they are letting themselves in for.

Matter economics has to be based on the anatomy of each given matter, which it is not appropriate to explore here (see paragraph 28.8.2). The idea of the work schedule (see paragraph 21.4.4) is to allow a lawyer to see the 'bones' of a matter, to explore interrelationships and key dependencies. On this basis, the matter partner can also plan to put the most effective team and resources together. By breaking a case or transaction into its constituent parts (which is necessary to put a work schedule together and a team in place), it is also possible to begin to budget (see figure 21.3: although shown as a single number, it would also be legitimate to use a range of likely expenditure in each instance).

Costs schedule

	Solicitor	Counsel	Technical experts	Financial experts	Arbitrator's costs (50%)
Preliminary investigation and instruction	£5,000				
Points of claim	£3,500	£1,000	£1,750		
Points of reply and defence to counterclaim	£4,000	£1,000			
Discovery and inspection	£8,000				
Preliminary hearing before arbitrators	£1,500	£1,250			£2,500
Witness statements	£7,500	£1,500			
Technical experts	£3,500	£2,000	£7,500		
Reports on quantum	£2,500	£1,250		£6,000	
Brief to counsel	£5,000	£20,000			
Trial documents	£1,500	£1,250			£3,000
Hearing	£12,000	£9,000	£2,500	£1,750	£18,000

Figure 21.3 (based, with thanks, on Benson 1991, page 4)

Matter economics then involves:

(a) *planning and budgeting:* predicting what will be spent, how, by whom, and when, and using that information to create not only a budget but also a cash flow forecast;

(b) *financial reporting and monitoring:* being aware of how costs are actually being incurred and discharged, and comparing actual performance against the budget and cash flow forecast, revising both as necessary; and

(c) *controlling:* using the results of the monitoring to take steps to control the financial consequences and requirements of the action.

Clients are rarely content to allow their lawyers an 'open-chequebook' approach to their work. They will assess the risks and potential benefits involved, and may even determine in their own minds what the 'value' of the matter is. Thus, for most matters, there will also be an 'optimum' cost (although it will often be very difficult to determine what it is). Nevertheless, as a way of thinking about the economics of litigation, for example, it can be a useful concept. If cost could be plotted against time (see figure 21.4), it would usually demonstrate that, by throwing resources at a problem in the early days, it might be possible to resolve the matter quickly — but at a significant cost. By matching resources and time, costs can be reduced to an 'optimum' level (see Reiss 1992, page 90). However, if the transaction or case takes too long, elements of repetition, forgetfulness or boredom, difficulties of tracing evidence or witnesses, or staff turnover, will begin to increase the costs again as time goes by. This is obviously a generalisation: some actions, for example, if settled quickly, can be dispatched at a fraction of the cost of prolonged litigation. Nevertheless, the concept of an optimum cost may encourage lawyers to explore the best balance of time, resource and cost.

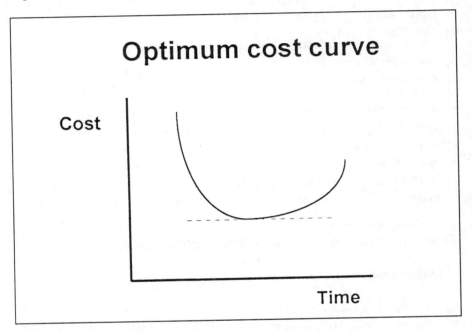

Figure 21.4 (Source: Reiss 1992, page 90)

Cash flow forecasts can also be explored. This is perhaps best done as a range (for example, by month 6 of the action, it is likely to have cost between £X and £Y). This range can also be plotted (see figure 21.5). Such a range (or 'cash flow envelope': see Reiss 1992, page 97) will give clients and the firm a better sense of the likely financial consequences, and may also allow the transaction or case to be planned or controlled to coincide with other financial imperatives. By monitoring and plotting the actual cost over time, the matter partner can also see whether that cost falls within the cash flow envelope: if it does, the project can be said to be on target. With appropriate technology, these calculations, tables and graphs can be produced (and updated) with relative ease.

21.6.2 *Financial reports*

Just as financial monitoring and control are impossible without budgets, so it is impossible without financial reports which track performance. The following should be regarded as minimum requirements:

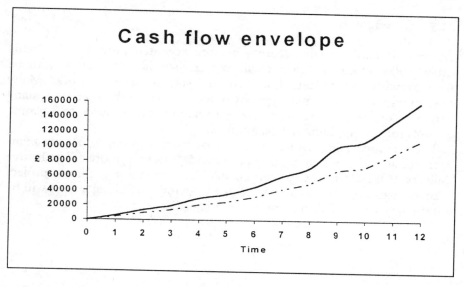

Cash flow envelope

Figure 21.5

(a) work-in-progress reports showing hours recorded (and their value) both for the matter as a whole and by individual, together with unbilled disbursements: these reports are required to assess whether the action is on target in its use of human and financial resources, whether the right people are working on it, whether the work is properly distributed, and to measure part of the firm's risk in unbilled work;

(b) outstanding invoices and billed disbursements: this will show the degree of risk the firm is exposed to in continuing to act; the client or matter partner may consider it appropriate to set 'credit' limits for work-in-progress, outstanding invoices, and billed and unbilled disbursements;

(c) budget variances, including:

(i)   planned costs to date against actual costs to date;
(ii)   estimated total costs against actual costs to date + estimated costs to completion;
(iii) comparison with cash flow forecast.

These reports not only provide a basis for financial assessment, but should also form part of the progress reporting to the client. Together, they can help eliminate any of the financial or timing surprises that clients dislike. They provide a basis for reviewing (and revising) the client's assessment of the value of the case or transaction. Where the client can control or influence whether the action should be progressed, settled or dropped, these continual reviews allow a much more informed assessment to be made. For lawyers who prefer to have happy (or at least not unhappy) clients, they are vital.

21.7 Conclusion

As project management becomes a more accepted procedure in many other walks of life, so clients will expect their lawyers not only to be familiar with the process but also to *apply* it to their work. Many businesses use project management precisely *because* there are too many variables or people involved: lawyers cannot allow these to become excuses for not applying the techniques.

There is increasing evidence that lawyers are turning to project management as a way of helping them to provide a tighter, more cost-effective delivery of legal services to their clients. As with so many things, project management may not be a competitive edge for much longer — it will be a necessary precondition to being on a shortlist.

PART V

LAW FIRMS AS SOCIAL ORGANISATIONS

Chapter 22

MANAGING PEOPLE

22.1 Introduction

Is human resource management (HRM) different from personnel management? In 1963, the Institute of Personnel Management adopted the following definition of personnel management (cited in Hendry 1995, page 10):

> "Personnel management aims to achieve both efficiency and justice, neither of which can be pursued successfully without the other. It seeks to bring together and develop into an effective organization the men and women who make up an enterprise, enabling each to make his own best contribution to its success both as an individual and as a member of a working group. It seeks to provide fair terms and conditions of employment, and satisfying work for those employed."

This 'balancing' view of personnel management was symptomatic of those days in the post-war years when personnel professionals tried to balance the interests of employers and employees. The industrial strife that characterised the 1970s, however, forced them to abandon the neutral stance. Personnel management had more to do with representing the interests of employers in collective negotiations to 'balance' the power wielded by trade unions. In this sense, personnel management was often concerned with fire-fighting, though the importance of it (or at least its potentially disrupting effect) led many businesses for the first time to appoint personnel directors at board level.

However, when the crises of the 1970s subsided, personnel staff were not then typically shifted from a fire-fighting role to a strategic one, and the consistent failure in earlier decades of businesses to take a strategic view of their human resources was perpetuated.

For the most part, personnel management has been confined to introducing and maintaining *systems* relating to employment, and to providing the administrative support required for recruitment, training, promotion, appraisal, pay and benefits, grievance and dismissal. These systems have often been introduced in isolation from the rest of the business because personnel professionals have been excluded from the highest levels of business decision-making.

22.2 Themes of Human Resource Management

Human resource management appears to have three themes (which are not necessarily consistent with each other). These themes are drawn from Hendry (1995, chapter 1):

(a) *People are a business's most important asset.* Human resources are sometimes described as 'assets with feet' or 'assets with hearts'. The asset value of human beings is being increasingly recognised (see the discussion of human capital in chapter 5). Some commentators draw telling distinctions between 'human resources' and 'resourceful humans', and this seems to reflect McGregor's (1960) notion of Theory X people, who are inherently indolent assets who need to be controlled, managed and motivated, and Theory Y people, who are inherently self-motivated and who are looking for an environment that will allow them to develop. HRM therefore picks up on the Theory Y approach and seeks to recognise that personal growth is entirely compatible with achieving business objectives and should be encouraged by the organisation.

(b) *The need to match employment practices to business strategy.* This theme assumes that a business will not meet its objectives (or will meet them less efficiently) if its human resource systems are not aligned with other aspects of the business systems. Human resource systems have the potential to encourage human behaviour towards specific performance goals: for the strategic performance to be achieved, all these behaviours must be channelled in the right direction. Further, human resource practices (either explicitly or implicitly) create organisational values and thus a 'culture' (see chapter 23). Indeed, culture may be a crucial intervening variable in the achievement of strategic goals. This theme therefore assumes that human resource systems are contingent on strategic need.

(c) *HRM is a philosophy of management.* The second theme puts the emphasis on *systems*. Another school of HRM thought (referred to as the Harvard group) puts more stress on *people*. This third theme therefore emphasises the importance of mutual goals, mutual respect, mutual rewards and mutual responsibility. On this view, people are not assets or tools who can be manipulated (i.e., motivated). Mutuality will create commitment, and people will then direct themselves towards the achievement of the mutual goals.

The difference is broadly between the organisation as a control mechanism with systems (the second theme advocated by the strategy theorists), and the organisation as an enabling environment with a set of values (the values theory of the third theme advocated by the Harvard group). The key *systems* of the strategy theorists are selection, appraisal, development (including training), and rewards. The key *values* of the values theorists are congruence (of organisational and individual goals), competence, cost-effectiveness, and commitment.

There are, therefore, some similarities between personnel management and HRM, and some differences. However, there is a difference between the systems and values approaches to HRM. Writing recently, Hendry has sought to reconcile these differences (1995, pages 15–18):

"It is evident that personnel management has been stronger in providing an integrative framework for employment decisions and management actions by means of employment policies than in structuring employment systems to implement particular business strategies. . . .

The theory of HRM thus has the potential to sharpen up the discipline of personnel management. HRM is more explicit in both areas — in the exposition of a philosophy underlying employment strategy, and in its analysis of business strategy and associated employment strategies.

Personnel management and HRM, nevertheless, share the same ambivalence about the relationship between these, with the fault lines strongly reflected in the differences of approach taken by [the strategy theorists] and the Harvard school. This ambivalence is not surprising, of course. It reflects a tension between corporate needs for control and individual needs for freedom and fulfilment which to some degree are always likely to be with us. At another level, it reflects also the economic, social and political struggle for control of organizations between shareholders, top managers, employees, and community. The resolution of this struggle is open to considerable flux and ingenuity, from generation to generation, and country to country. . . .

It may, indeed, be the case that modern conditions make [the values approach] widely appropriate. Because economic circumstances demand high quality and innovativeness in products, firms need also to be innovative in their work practices. Modern technology demands high skills, adaptive behaviour, and the exercise of discretion. Independent of such factors, people also demand and expect to be given responsibility and discretion, as a result of higher levels of education. Finally, governments support such expectations through laws and infrastructure investment in education and training.

On the other hand, these conditions may apply only to certain kinds of business or to certain groups of employees. It is matter of common observation, after all, that employees in the same organization get treated in different ways. Indeed, it has been suggested that there is a trend for firms to develop employment structures which differentiate between 'core' employees and those who are 'peripheral' (that is, less permanent or less critical to operations). The 'high commitment' HRM strategy is likely to be especially applicable to the 'core' group, to bind them to the organization, but less so to 'peripheral' employees. . . .

However, the value-specific version may be of general relevance in the light of two trends that affect modern organizations. One is the changing character of markets in which firms operate and the rate of change that needs to be managed; the other is the degree of complexity and the need to manage this complexity in an integrated way.

When organizations operated in mass-markets and were dominated by large production/service functions, the primary task of personnel management and industrial relations was the maintenance of organizational stability. Job evaluation, gradings, contracts, disputes and grievance procedures, apprenticeship schemes, routine training programmes — these were the stuff of personnel management. As technological change has reduced the size of the production function, and as firms have had to adjust to rapid and continuing change in their markets, a different style of personnel management is required. This is more concerned with managing change, adjusting personnel systems to organizational needs, and adapting the structures and cultures of work systems and of the organization as a whole to strategic shifts. . . .

This provides a broad justification for the systems model of HRM. But it also implies more individualized organizations, operating with higher levels of trust and commitment to allow such flexibility to be practised. Similar requirements apply to the growing market-oriented service sector. The limiting factor is, of course, how prevalent 'flexible specialization' has actually become, something which is disputed.

Managing change and maintaining flexibility is one imperative, therefore. A second imperative is coping with increased complexity in the external environment and the structural elaboration of the organization in the face of this. . . . This demands new approaches to training, career moves across traditional boundaries, perhaps forms of job rotation, information flowing more freely, team working, and attention to culture and management style. Personnel management cannot then also remain compartmentalized in its thinking, managing selection, training, and so forth in isolation. Again, while this provides a justification for the systems model of HRM, it also raises the importance of trust and commitment."

22.3 People in Know-how Businesses

Continuing the theme of this book, the challenge in a know-how business is how to "manage, control and develop . . . talented, egocentric, highly qualified people engaged in complex and creative problem-solving" (Sveiby and Lloyd 1987, page 14). All know-how professionals earn a living by exploiting their know-how. As such, many of them have larger networks *outside* their firm than within it. Their talent is heterogeneous, and not owned by the organisation. Know-how professionals are therefore inherently mobile, and know-how organisations are prone to fission or breakaways.

Sveiby and Lloyd identify four different groups in know-how businesses (1987, pages 59–63):

(a) *The professionals.* These people typically think of themselves as the most important resource and confer on themselves the highest internal status. They are also typically unable and unwilling to manage others, preferring to retain the freedom to manage themselves and to develop their own careers (cf. paragraphs 14.2.1 and 14.2.2). As such, they have a high level of professional know-how, but a low level of management know-how.

(b) *The clerical staff.* In my view, this group would be better described as 'support staff', since their prime function is to support the professionals by providing secretarial, accounting, office and other services. Support staff are often thought by the professionals to be relatively easy to find, and to be worth a 'going rate' for the job they do. However, if the support staff feel that a sense of inferiority is being imposed on them by the professionals, they can become "a dangerous source of discontent". Without support staff, most businesses will become inefficient. Poor morale and a lower of quality of work from support staff will also become noticeable to clients.

(c) *The manager.* This is someone often with a low level of 'professional' know-how — meaning legal knowledge and experience in our context — but with a high level of managerial know-how. Because of this, a manager typically lacks internal status and is denied promotion to the top of the firm (as a partner). Indeed, in many know-how businesses, the manager is confined to lower-level managerial tasks, which he or she finds frustrating, and may even be considered a luxury in smaller firms. The position of professional managers was considered in chapter 16.

(d) *The leader.* In underdeveloped know-how businesses, the leader is usually someone with a high level of professional know-how but without any knowledge or experience of management. In the early days of a business, the leader will be the driving force (often the founder) and the source of motivation for others. As the business grows and develops, the leadership role may be split, with a professional taking over some of the more 'managerial' aspects of leadership — and hence the emergence of both senior and managing partners. The managing partner, however, rarely develops the same high level of managerial know-how as 'the manager'. The leader may not even be formally appointed, but receives his or her mandate to lead from credibility as a professional.

Sveiby and Lloyd refer to the need for dual expertise, that is, the blend of professional and managerial ability (1987, page 64; and see paragraph 3.3). As a know-how business itself becomes more professional, however, there is an increasing tendency (cf. paragraph 14.4):

(a) to elect leaders who are appointed for their ability to fulfil the leadership function rather than their mere credibility or seniority;

(b) for the leadership function to be split between professional (senior partner) and managerial (managing partner);

(c) for the managerial function to be split between the professional (managing partner, heads of department) and the managerial (directors of finance and administration, marketing, personnel, training, etc.).

22.4 The Personnel Idea

22.4.1 *A broad concept*

The personnel idea is a broad concept comprising the arrival, development, motivation and departure of people (Sveiby and Lloyd 1987, page 52). If people are the repository of know-how, the personnel idea becomes an integral part of a firm's business strategy (see also Schneider 1994): indeed, the notion and success of the firm's 'business idea' may be very closely related to the know-how of key individuals (see paragraph 4.8.3). People are a constituent part of the firm's 'invisible' balance sheet (cf. paragraph 5.5.3.6). They are assets — but not constant or 'fixed' assets. Like fixed assets they are subject to investment and depreciation. The firm's personnel idea must therefore allow for change through training, development, experience and maturity.

22.4.2 *Arrival*

The relationship between people, know-how and competitive advantage means that recruitment is a powerful strategic weapon in a know-how business. It presents an opportunity to change the firm's market position, alter its know-how level (up or down), and adapt its business strategy. On one view, therefore, like-for-like recruitment is a recipe for stagnation (Sveiby and Lloyd 1987, page 111).

The key arrival issues are therefore (Sveiby and Lloyd 1987, page 51):

(a) What kind of people should be employed?

(b) How old should they be? Firms need to be mindful of the life cycle of a professional (see paragraph 3.2.2), and avoid the 'spare tyre effect' (the tendency of professionals to work with and recruit people of their own age, so creating a 'bulge' of professionals at the same stages of their careers (1987, page 108)).

(c) How well educated should they be?

(d) What attitudes or values should they have?

Once the successful applicant arrives at the firm, a transformation must begin. First, the individual must change his or her behaviour to reflect the norms of the firm. This may relate to issues as diverse as hours of work, standards of appearance, modes of address, as well as broader aspects of interpersonal relationships. Second, the individual will need to transfer his or her loyalties and commitment from a previous organisation. To do this, the individual needs to understand precisely what sort of firm he or she has joined, and where the position fits. This process of socialisation or induction is therefore very important, and needs to cover:

(a) *Expected behaviour:* e.g., hours of work, dress and appearance, modes of address.

(b) *A sense of belonging:* information about the firm, its size, location, business, clients, structure, successes, goals, history, heroes, pecking order.

(c) *The job:* its relationship with others in the firm, other team members, issues of teamwork, accountability, support functions available and procedures for using them.

(d) *Reviews:* appraisal, training and development, salary and benefits, career expectations.

22.4.3 Development

If the objective of dual expertise is to be fulfilled, all types of personnel need developing (professionals, support staff, managers and leaders). Managers and support staff should be encouraged to develop careers so that they do not become "imprisoned in boring jobs" (Sveiby and Lloyd 1987, page 115). To recognise individual differences, preferences, skills and aspirations, flexibility will be required. Emphasising the importance or supremacy of professional know-how can inhibit the development of managerial know-how — in professionals, managers and leaders.

Development is considered in chapter 25.

22.4.4 Motivation

Recruiting and developing people merely gives them the *potential* to become productive contributors to the firm. The one factor that will turn this potential into productivity is motivation. Since most professionals are self-motivated, the need for effective feedback is an important stimulus for self-improvement. It is also important not to create an environment that *demotivates* people.

Motivation is the subject of chapter 26.

22.4.5 Departure

It is inevitable that people will leave an organisation. When they do, part of the firm's accumulated know-how (whether professional or managerial) is lost: this form of know-how 'leakage' is inevitable. Steps can be taken to 'codify' and 'embed' their know-how into the firm (see paragraph 5.3), but the active know-how will always go with them.

People who leave can become ambassadors for the firm and advertisements for its quality and culture. If departures are handled gracefully and professionally, this can happen; if they are handled ungraciously or unprofessionally, it is not likely. Some of the better firms, therefore, are keen to maintain an 'alumni association' with their former partners and staff.

As stated in paragraph 22.4.2 in relation to arrivals, someone's departure presents an opportunity to reassess what the business needs and whether it is time to change the know-how mix.

22.5 The Self-concept and Psychological Contract

There are two aspects of organisational psychology that might be helpful at this point, and to which reference will be made in later chapters.

22.5.1 The self-concept

Our self-concept (or ego-ideal) is a picture that we have ourselves and of our relationship with the world and people around us. As Hunt explains, this picture is often an idealised vision of what we would like to be in an ideal world (1992, pages 45–6):

> "This idealized version is most imaginative as a teenager when any fantasy is possible. As we get older reality requires that the ideal and the self are reconciled; ambitions are relaxed; unrealistic goals are abandoned as time and opportunity compel us to change the idealized concept we have for ourselves. We call this maturing. For the mature individual, reality and the self-concept are reconciled. . . .
>
> If you want me to change my behaviour then I need to perceive some advantage in doing so. That is, I need to change my self-concept, which is not always easy, especially if the change means forgoing one of my most treasured dreams about myself."

The self-concept is formed as the result of our interaction with others, and may be influenced from our early years by our parents and teachers. Later, it will be affected by those with whom we live and work. Forming and settling on a self-concept may be a difficult and painful process, as we come to terms with the reality of our own position, ability and potential. Finally, Handy points out (1993, pages 55–6):

> "As we grow older we tend to fix on a self-concept. We then tend to find ways of protecting that selection by surrounding ourselves with people whose self-concept is roughly the same and who confirm ours as being sensible. So we go to live amongst similar kinds of people, select newspapers which reflect our values, join clubs and go on holidays where our self-concepts will not be challenged. Criticism of our chosen self-concept can be ignored, either by rejecting the source of it ('he's only an old fool') or by physically avoiding the chance of incurring it, e.g. by not mixing out of one's chosen group. But a different and/or traumatic experience can often cause us to revise our ideal self-concept, our ego-ideal."

My experience suggests that law firms can be particularly brutal places for seeking to change the self-concepts of people. The 'young Turks' are dismissive of the 'old guard' who are thought no longer to be pulling their weight; the partnership aspirations of some are tossed ignominiously to one side; a partner's comments about our work and ability in front of clients or colleagues can be especially hurtful. These are all assaults on a self-concept — the very ideal to which we live.

22.5.2 *The psychological contract*

Most of us (whether as lawyers, employers or employees) will be familiar with the notion of employment contracts that seek to define the relationships within the workplace. What we usually fail to realise is that there is also a psychological contract between an individual and an organisation. The psychological contract takes one of three forms (Handy 1993, pages 45-9):

(a) *coercive:* as the name implies, the contract here is not entered into voluntarily, and is therefore found in organisations in which people feel they have no choice — where failure to comply will result in punishment (such as prisons or schools);

(b) *calculative:* the contract is voluntary, and is based on an exchange (of services for money, promotion, opportunities, better work, etc.): it is the dominant contract for most employees in most organisations; however, if the firm tries to 'encourage' further effort or productivity for no further reward or under the 'threat' of reduced benefits or opportunities, the contract may then appear to be coercive;

(c) *cooperative:* this is the contract that most firms aspire to, since under it individuals are assumed to identify with the firm's overall goals and are then given a good degree of freedom in the way in which they contribute to achieving those goals.

The only psychological contract that management can impose is a coercive contract: the others have to be encouraged and nurtured through the office environment and partners' responses to that environment. Although most people prefer a cooperative contract, partners often fail to realise that their goals may not mean anything to people 'lower down', who then do not cooperate in achieving them. In addition, freedom to achieve under a cooperative contract necessarily brings responsibility: not all people want responsibility and again they may reject the opportunity to cooperate in the way desired by management.

Different psychological contracts, like different roles, bring differing expectations. The mistake most make is to assume that everyone's psychological contract is the same (or at least, based on stereotypes, assume that certain types of people in certain parts of the firm, will prefer a particular approach). This is not the case.

Chapter 23

CULTURE, VALUES AND LEADERSHIP

23.1 The Importance of Culture

Culture has perhaps been most famously (and succinctly) described by Marvin Bower of the consulting firm McKinsey as "the way we do things around here". This definition incorporates a 'here' (an environment), a 'we' (that is, a group of people), and a 'way of doing things' (behaviour and processes). In this sense, organisational culture is a way of influencing behaviour. It is therefore the result of, and affected by, history, ownership, size (perhaps the most important variable), technology, goals and objectives, the environment (national, geographic, societal, economic and competitive), and people (Handy 1993, pages 191–200).

People also talk about national cultures — the difference, for example, between common law and civil law traditions and the effect that this has on legal practice, or between 'Western' and 'Eastern' philosophies, and approaches to people and management. They would clearly form part of the history, environmental and people factors listed above, but are not further considered for the purposes of this chapter (see Handy 1991, chapter 4).

Using the McKinsey definition, it is also possible to see that different offices, departments, and groups may have a different 'here' (for example, contentious and non-contentious; commercial and private client; lawyers and support staff). Firms should not therefore be afraid to differentiate their cultures and structures according to the dominant kind of activity in each part of its business. It should never try to force a single organisational culture on every part of the business. However, managing cultural diversity brings its own challenges.

The culture may be visible or tangible (e.g., the size, location or furnishings of partners' offices, separate dining facilities, or work ethic), or abstract (e.g., sets of values, beliefs or norms, the exercise of authority

— the use of power and influence, the 'us and them' syndrome), and may be part of the firm's 'rituals' (e.g., opening or signing the post).

Culture is constantly changing, and this change will give rise to (and result from) internal politics. Every so often, the change may be significant and lead people to suggest that 'the place is not how it used to be' (cf. Schein 1983, page 24).

Strong cultures can lead to the creation of strong organisations, and they can be successful in law firms in providing an intangible framework within which relatively autonomous professionals can work together without the need for too much control. Culture can establish acceptable boundaries. But organisational cultures can also be dysfunctional: they may reflect an earlier environment or set of personalities and so no longer be appropriate, or they may act as a constraint on necessary development of the firm to reflect changed circumstances. They may also lead to conflicts of values, motivation, leadership style, and control (for example, in a difference between greater centralisation of the business versus decentralisation).

Discussions about organisational culture often fail to distinguish culture from style (for example, people might suggest that a firm is 'aggressive', 'modern', 'friendly'). There may be some overlaps but, as paragraph 23.2 will show, organisational culture has a distinct meaning. It is also important to distinguish culture from internal politics (see paragraph 27.6), which is the result of the *interaction* of different cultures, personalities or methods of influence.

Lawyers considering merger or changing from one firm to another rarely examine or take account of culture. They know it is there, but perhaps lack the analytical tools or insights to pursue the topic.

23.2 Types of Organisational Culture

Cultural analysis suggests four types of organisational culture (Handy 1993, pages 181–91, and 1991). Each cultural type is usually associated with an image, and a structure:

- power or club   THE WHEEL   autocracy/oligarchy
- role   THE PYRAMID   democracy
- task   THE MATRIX   meritocracy
- person or existential   THE GALAXY   autonomy

No individual or organisation is 'culturally pure', that is, entirely within one cultural description. However, individuals do tend to have a preference for a certain culture, and may well be out of place in a different culture. Every organisation needs a mix of cultures — a different one for each of its major activities or processes; but *within* an activity or section of the firm, the culture should be internally consistent (i.e., cultural purity should prevail for maximum effectiveness).

There are, it would seem, only two ways to run any organisation without much time being spent on management — autocracy or autonomy. Both can work (with the right people), but tend to require small environments to be effective. However, if the necessary relationships are neglected, autocracy can become dictatorship, and autonomy can become anarchy.

23.3   Cultural Types and Law Firms

At the risk of some generalisation, I shall now seek to apply the four types of organisational culture to law firms, using Handy's structure (and Handy 1991).

23.3.1   Power and founders

(a)   *Characteristics.* Built around a strong character or controlling group (typical of founder-led or small firms); self-sufficient, and learn by trial and error; strong on networking with others outside the firm; tend to grow by the centre attracting people it likes and approves of.

(b)   *Atmosphere.* Competitive, power-orientated, risk-taking — the most political of cultures; uncertainty is valued as providing freedom for manoeuvre; assistants and support staff are treated as though they were at the disposal of partners, and may suffer low morale or high turnover — people are dispensable in this culture; there is a distrust of outsiders, and the admission of a need to learn is the admission of deficiency; may be regarded as crude, irrational, unpredictable, or perhaps even frightening by 'institutional' people.

(c)   *Structure and control.* Control is exercised by the strong centre — the hub of the wheel; little administrative structure, few rules and procedures; judged by results rather than means; more faith in individuals than committees (and the centre — the hub, again — selects the key individuals).

(d)   *Decision-making and power.* Political, impressionistic and intuitive (based on the balance of influence — who you know rather than what you know), unequal, clear (with the ability to move quickly), effective; power is personal power/charisma and resource power — personal credibility is all (see paragraph 24.3.2).

(e)   *Communication.* Personal conversations (or telepathy!) — if those in control decide to share any information at all.

(f)   *Partnership.* Offered to the 'founder's favourites' — after an extended apprenticeship of learning at the master's feet; a reward for long service, loyalty and good client service, based on trust and empathy; unequal, often difficult to withdraw (question of loyalty) and difficult for laterals to integrate.

(g)   *Rewards.* Unequal, based on personal power, longevity and investment; may be negotiated, or lock step after a time (see chapter 37).

(h)   *Appropriateness.* For founder-led, small, or entrepreneurial firms, aggressive and independent firms; not for people who rate security highly; good for dealing with crises and the unexpected, and for setting policy and direction, priorities, and standards; size and succession are usually a problem (because of the influence of or dependence on the centre), despite the often frequent identification of protégés or heirs apparent: succession is crucial to continued success (many firms fail or stagnate at this point).

23.3.2 Roles and institutions

(a) *Characteristics.* Everyone has their place, which everyone else knows and understands; the firm is more important than any individual; a sense of history; often pejoratively described as a 'bureaucracy'; a culture often found in the most prestigious law firms (which are not necessarily the largest); tend to grow organically.

(b) *Atmosphere.* Respect for age and status; security and predictability; adherence to the customary standards of personal behaviour; the role is more important than the person who fills it, so strong on training people to perform their role; performance beyond the role is not required (and can be disruptive); populated by people with a low tolerance for ambiguity in their jobs, or a need for security (and therefore frustrating for someone who wants power, more control over their work, is ambitious or more interested in results than method — unless they are already in senior management!); preference for compromise rather than conflict.

(c) *Structure and control.* Built on interlocking functions or specialisations (including support activities, particularly finance, personnel and planning), each of which is usually considered to be strong in its own right; procedures are developed for roles (e.g., organisation charts, job descriptions, training, appraisal) and for communication; control is coordinated at the top by senior management; change derives from changing the structure or systems, not individuals.

(d) *Decision-making and power.* Usually structured and equal; decisions are taken on the basis of authority, logic, analysis and rationality (and often precedent); often committee-based; efficiency depends on the rationality of job allocation and responsibility (i.e., the structure); power is position power, and rules and procedures are major methods of influence (see paragraphs 24.3.2 and 24.3.3: personal power is frowned on and expert power is tolerated only in its proper place).

(e) *Communication.* Formal, through procedures (e.g., committees and briefings, circulation lists, copies of internal memoranda, minutes and papers), and tending to flow down and up rather than across functions.

(f) *Partnership.* Long track to partnership; ownership seen more as custodianship; may or may not be salaried partners; often difficult to withdraw (loyalty of 'institutionalised' people), but easier for 'institutional' laterals to integrate.

(g) *Rewards.* Based on status and seniority and so often a lock-step system, or rewards for total contribution through a subjective performance-related system (see chapter 37).

(h) *Appropriateness.* Succeeds only in a stable, predictable environment; slow to perceive the need for change and slow to change even when the need is seen (usually leading to the collapse or replacement of senior management); more appropriate to a seller's market; usually found where economies of scale are more important than flexibility, or where technical expertise and depth of specialisation are more important than innovation or cost (though may be appropriate to parts of a firm — such as administration or routine, steady-state, operations); in general, size pushes firms towards a role culture — they are more formalised and tend to develop specialised groups or functions which need systematic coordination.

23.3.3 *Tasks and flexibility*

(a) *Characteristics.* Emphasis on getting a task completed; extremely adaptable, seeking to bring together the right people at the right level, with the appropriate resources, and let them get on with the job; groups, teams, etc. are formed for a specific purpose, and can be re-formed, abandoned or continued; there is a project management approach to practice (see chapter 21); tend to grow by laterals, bolt-ons and merger.

(b) *Atmosphere.* Job or project orientated — the 'product' is all-important, and the client is always right; easy working relationships within a group, with mutual respect based on ability and capacity rather than age or status; a team or collegiate culture, thriving on self-motivation and learning-by-doing.

(c) *Structure and control.* Although a structure exists, the firm is pragmatic rather than structural — it uses the unifying power of the group or teamwork to improve efficiency and to identify the individual with the objectives of the organisation; control is difficult and retained by top management through the allocation of work, people and resources; the firm exercises little day-to-day control over the methods of working, giving individuals a high degree of control over their work and judging them by results (formal appraisal is either embraced as a way of recognising achievement or rejected as an interference with getting the job done; but self-appraisal is constant).

(d) *Decision-making and power.* Usually made by the person with the most knowledge, expertise or experience of the problem, in a distributed or delegated management structure, which works quickly since each group ideally contains all the decision-making powers that are required; resources are usually available or made available for all who can justify them; power is more widely dispersed than in other cultures (and each individual tends to think that he or she has more of it!); power and influence often lie at the intersections of the firm's activities and are based more on expert power than on position power or personal power (see paragraph 24.3).

(e) *Communication.* Flows in all directions, and tends to be ad hoc, based on the need to get the job done; people may feel left out of the loop because it is ad hoc rather than structured.

(f) *Partnership.* Usually a tiered partnership (equity and salaried), with ownership offered as a reward for achievement; easier to move in or out (people accept the need to go to the best environment for getting the job done and believe in the transferability of expertise).

(g)   *Rewards*. Lock step with bonus, negotiated on the basis of excellence of contribution or achievement, or subjective performance-related system (see chapter 37).

(h)   *Appropriateness*. Thrives where speed of reaction, creativity, integration, flexibility or sensitivity to the market or environment are more important than specialisation (and therefore most suited to dealing with changes in the market, competitiveness, non-routine operations); the form of management that most people accept and aspire to, but an expensive and luxurious way of running a firm.

23.3.4   *Existentialism and transience*

(a)   *Characteristics*. Idiosyncratic individualists, entrepreneurial; the individual is more important than the firm; self-motivated individuals looking for stimulating work and opportunities; loners who gather together in partnership for their own convenience (cf. paragraph 9.3).

(b)   *Atmosphere*. People often feel little or no allegiance to the firm (and may display greater allegiance to their 'profession'); a place to 'do your own thing' (but with some perceived consequential benefit to the firm); either predominant selfishness or a respect for others' values and personal needs (that is, either tolerance or intolerance of others); individuals do not believe that they can learn from anyone else, and can therefore seem arrogant or rude; only the most talented survive.

(c)   *Structure and control*. Structure is minimal and exists only to serve and assist the individuals in the firm; control mechanisms and management structures are possible only by mutual consent, and the psychological contract states that the firm is subordinate to the individual and, indeed, depends on the individual for its existence; appraisal is impossible, conflict is constant.

(d)   *Decision-making and power*. No effective structure; influence is shared and expert power is used (when power is needed); however, little influence can really be brought to bear on the individuals, so decision-making tends to be ad hoc and individual, made by the people most personally involved and affected by the outcome; agreement is often difficult to reach, and then subject to interference and second-guessing; coercive power is not usually available, the individuals are not easily impressed by personal power/charisma, and position power not backed up by resource power achieves nothing (see paragraph 24.3).

(e)   *Communication*. Very little, and nothing formal; based on personal relationships between individuals formed through work, shared values or friendship; meetings are disliked and avoided.

(f)   *Partnership*. Often a reward for client following or business development; easy to move in or out — but although an individual can leave, the firm rarely has the power to evict.

(g)   *Rewards*. Characterised by self-sufficiency, often an 'eat-what-you-kill' environment, negotiated based on achievement, or an objective performance-related system (see chapter 37).

(h)   *Appropriateness.* In general, only the founders achieve any real success in this culture: soon the firm achieves its own identity and begins to impose that on its individuals (a task culture?); it is rare to find firms where the existential culture predominates for any length of time (cf. barristers' chambers), although one often comes across *individuals* who have a preference for this type of culture!

23.4   Values and Beliefs

As individuals, we all have our own attitudes, values, beliefs and opinions (this is explored further in paragraph 24.4.2). As we combine together in organisations, these affect — and are affected by — the people around us. Over time, the organisation comes to have a set of values and beliefs that are common or predominant (and become part of the firm-specific capital: see paragraph 5.2.2). Like culture, they define ways of behaviour and of reaching decisions on various issues.

The issues here are more fundamental than complying with the requirements of professional ethics or canons of behaviour — they go to the heart of moral and ethical behaviour generally. If an individual is required or expected to act in a way that is inconsistent with their values or beliefs, that is, contrary to their standards of ethical behaviour, he or she will suffer some sort of 'dissonance' which may cause stress or resignation. The organisational challenge is balancing client satisfaction, partner satisfaction, lawyer satisfaction, and staff satisfaction, while remaining true to everyone's values and beliefs (see, further, Paine (1994) and Maister 1997, chapter 8).

To be able to achieve this balancing act, it may help to understand better the ethical foundations on which different people make ethical choices. The following very short summary serves merely to outline the subject at its most basic level, and is drawn from Chryssides and Kaler 1993, chapter 3.

At the most fundamental level, people have different views about cognitivism (that is, that there are objective moral truths which it is possible for everyone to know) and non-cognitivism (that there are no objective moral truths, and ethics is a matter of subjective opinion and attitude). However, even for the cognitivists, there is a further division between consequentialism and non-consequentialism. Consequentialists believe that if one's actions result in a good outcome then one must by definition have done the right thing. Jeremy Bentham's notion of utilitarianism (an ethic of welfare or the common good) is perhaps the best-known theory of consequentialism. Non-consequentialists believe that if one does something for the right reasons then one must have done the right thing whatever the outcome. This finds expression in Immanuel Kant's deontological approach (an ethic of duty — the 'right reason' being that some imperative requires one to act in a certain way irrespective of one's own wishes). It also finds expression in John Locke's doctrine of natural law (an ethic of rights — the 'right reason' here being that there are fundamental human rights that require certain types of behaviour in given circumstances).

Faced with an ethical dilemma, individuals, groups or the firm must determine the exact nature of that dilemma and generate solutions to it. The solutions and their choice between them will then be determined in broad terms by the strength of their preferences for the non-cognitivist approach or the ethics of welfare, duty or rights. None of these will guide the firm to a universally acceptable solution; but if individuals and firms understand the basis on which they are making their decisions, they are in a better position to explain them, and if there is knowledge and consensus about the way in which decisions are made, it is more likely that the decisions will be acceptable and upheld.

23.5 Leadership

23.5.1 *The need for leadership*

Leadership is a difficult concept — much like culture, we know it when we see it manifested or feel its effects. Leadership is certainly influential in creating an organisational culture and in setting the tone for the values and beliefs of the firm (see Schein 1983 and Maister 1997, chapter 7).

Handy suggests that there is a need in all organisations for individual linking pins (1993, page 96):

(a) to bind a group together, and
(b) to represent the group in its dealings with others.

This is the role of the leader. In addition, most people prefer to be led rather than to be managed (if management is assumed to mean control).

23.5.2 *Theories of leadership*

There have been different theories of leadership put forward over the years, and there is probably some truth in each of them, though none provides the 'right' answer.

23.5.2.1 *Trait theories*
The basis of the trait theories is that the individual is more important than the situation. Further, if it is not possible to *make* leaders then, provided the traits can be identified, at least the right people can be selected.

The most frequently identified of the traits come down to the following (Handy 1993, pages 97–9):

(a) above average intelligence, and good at solving complex and abstract problems;
(b) initiative, independence and inventiveness — the capacity to see a need for action and the urge to do it;
(c) self-assurance and self-confidence;
(d) the ability to rise above the particulars of a situation and see the big picture (so-called 'helicopter vision').

Other characteristics are also often identified, such as good health, of above average height (or well below it), and coming from the upper socio-economic levels in society.

There are a number of difficulties with the trait theories:

(a)   few people possess all of the traits, leading to the notion of an impossible ideal,

(b)   those who possess the major traits do not necessarily make good leaders,

(c)   there are some acknowledged leaders who do not possess the major traits,

(d)   the traits are often so ill-defined as to be useless as a management tool or guide.

23.5.2.2   Style theories

The foundation of the style theories is that people will work harder for leaders who employ certain styles of leadership. These styles are usually characterised as being somewhere on a spectrum between the authoritarian and the democratic, between the structuring and the supportive (cf. Tannenbaum and Schmidt 1973). At the authoritarian end, power stays with the leader; at the democratic end, the leader shares power and responsibilities with the group.

Other things being equal, people tend to produce more under democratic conditions (though research suggests that the differential may be no more than 15%). However, some people prefer to be directed and structured — particularly individuals who have low needs for independence (which probably rules out lawyers!), and in cultures where participation with the leader is not possible (which probably rules out partnerships!). Nevertheless, repetitive and routine work — the standardised or commoditised areas of practice — tends to produce better productivity from structured, authoritarian leadership, though it may also be accompanied by low morale.

Style alone is not, therefore, the answer. Even so, where the psychological contract encourages a supportive style (see paragraph 22.5.2), the level of involvement and contentment usually improves because of the opportunities for greater variety and stimulation leading to higher esteem and self-actualisation.

23.5.2.3   Contingency theories

Here, as the name suggests, the style and method of leadership are contingent on the circumstances. Thus, the variables in the *situation* will influence leadership, particularly the task to be achieved, the group, and the leader's position within the group (Handy 1993, pages 103–5):

(a)   when the task is clearly defined, and the leader is strong and respected, the leadership style can be structured or directive;

(b)   when the task is ambiguous, and the leader is in a weak position, the style can again be structured or directive;

(c) when the task is ambiguous, and the leader is respected, the style should be supportive (allowing the group to work its own way to a solution).

This formulation is perhaps a little too simplistic in suggesting that leadership style can be the result of a calculation. Nevertheless, it does begin to show how firms can help individual leaders by structuring or defining a task more clearly, improving the 'formal' power within a group, and changing the composition of a group. But even then, the contingency theories suggest that surrounding circumstances should be changed to suit the leader: if only life were like that!

23.5.2.4 Best-fit theories

An extension of the contingency theories allows more flexibility of thinking all round, and gives rise to the 'best-fit' theories. These theories hold that leadership has to be exercised within an *environmental* (meaning organisational) setting: this will affect the power or position of the leader, the relationship with the group, the variety of tasks to be performed, and the variety of people available to perform them; it will also provide the organisational culture or norms, and the structure and technology for performance. The best-fit theories suggest that there is no right style of leadership, but that leadership is most effective when the requirements of the task, the leader and the group (subordinates) fit together within the environmental setting.

According to these theories, then, there are four sets of factors which influence leadership: the environment, the task, the leader, and the group (see Handy 1993, page 107).

The *task* will vary in its nature, importance, objectives, complexity, and timescale. Unimportant tasks, for example, will not merit much time or attention, and a structured style of leadership may be most effective in completing them. On the other hand, tasks involving creative decision-making or issues of technical or conceptual complexity will need a more flexible, open-ended approach.

The *leader* will most probably have his or her own perceptions of the leader's role, and may have a preferred style (for instance, older people tend to prefer to exercise structured leadership). These will be affected by the confidence that he or she has in the group members. In turn, they will affect the leader's assessment of the need for certainty (flexibility will reduce predictability) as well as for his or her own contribution to the task.

The *group* may have their own past experience of working together to build on, and may have expectations or preferences for the style of leadership that works best for them. Like the leader, they will have an estimation of their ability and competence, as well as understanding how much ambiguity in the task they can work with. Their interest in the task, their assessment of its importance, and the psychological contract will all influence the degree of direction and structuring that will be acceptable and effective.

By balancing these factors, the leader should determine whether his or her style needs to be tight or flexible. If there is a mismatch between that style and the requirements of the situation, the leader must also be able to judge which factor to adjust.

The variety of needs, circumstances and approaches shows why successful leaders spend so much time getting to know those whom they must lead: the better they know them, the better able they are to achieve results.

23.5.3 *Handy's new synthesis*

Handy, having reviewed the theories, offers a new approach, which reduces to (1993, pages 115–17):

(a) Leaders are needed at all levels of an organisation and in all situations: in short, leadership is too important to be left only to those at the top!

(b) A leader is someone who can develop and share a vision which gives meaning to the work of others through whom the leader wants to get something done. This requires:

(i)   a vision or objective,
(ii)   communication to be able to share that vision (be that communication verbal, visual, or by example),
(iii) trust (consistency, integrity, and reliability),
(iv)   self-knowledge (meaning knowing one's own worth and weaknesses, as well as making others feel good about what they are doing).

The less than comforting conclusion that Handy draws is that, in terms of role theory (see paragraph 24.2), "the role of leader is a complex one, riddled with ambiguity, incompatibility and conflict" (1993, page 118). This may or may not provide comfort for partners!

23.5.4 *Requirements for leadership*

From this analysis, the following conclusions can be drawn about leadership in law firms (cf. Handy 1993, pages 118–19):

(a) Partners should understand the complexity of leadership roles (otherwise they run the risk of stereotyping leaders on the basis of narrow trait definitions): a better understanding is needed of the relationship between situations and leadership requirements.

(b) Partners should help others reduce the complexity of their leadership roles by:

(i)   providing clearer role definitions,

(ii)   allowing people the freedom to pursue different leadership styles: one of the hardest management tasks is to allow someone to behave differently,

(iii)   judging effectiveness by the ends, not the means (that is, by performance and results rather than style),

(iv)   giving people time to produce results.

(c)   Individual leaders should learn:

(i)   to develop and communicate a clear vision of the task (to provide a sense of common purpose or objective for the group),

(ii)   to allow others within the group to influence the vision (so that they are committed to achieving it),

(iii)   to build the trust and respect of their group (these are essential conditions to being able to adapt leadership style to the contingencies of the environment and situation),

(iv)   to represent the firm to the group (and therefore practise its precepts).

23.6 Leadership in Know-how Businesses

Sveiby and Lloyd (1987) identify the need for day-to-day leadership as one of the success factors of know-how management (see paragraph 3.4). They also describe a number of role models that can be used to classify leadership in know-how businesses (1987, chapter 7). It is worth reflecting on them in the context of legal practice.

23.6.1 *The leader as patriarch*

The leader is "intimately involved" in the life of the firm — usually the result of "life-long companionship and involvement with everyone" in it. This is perhaps a declining role, but Sveiby and Lloyd think that there might still be something to be learnt from the style of patriarchs.

23.6.2 *The leader as creator of the environment*

Such leaders often appear to be "low-key players with few overt symbols of power" — indeed, they may not be immediately identifiable as leaders by visitors to the firm. These leaders create an internal environment, and are often interested in the physical characteristics of the office: how lawyers are grouped together, who sits with whom, and where practice area groups (and support staff) are located in relation to each other. Leadership in law firms has a lot to do with creating environments, establishing frameworks, delineating boundaries, encouraging lawyers to ever greater efforts, and transferring culture and know-how to new arrivals (Sveiby and Lloyd 1987, page 89).

This facet of leadership is part of the process of creating a culture and a set of values and beliefs for the firm, as discussed in paragraph 23.4.

23.6.3   *The leader as tutor*

This leader tries to "stretch people by exposing them to challenging opportunities", for example, by (Sveiby and Lloyd 1987, page 89):

(a)   taking someone along to visit a client,
(b)   allowing someone else to make presentations to a client,
(c)   testing various combinations of lawyers in client or matter teams,
(d)   giving lawyers their own clients and matters as soon as possible.

Able lawyers want to control their own development, exploit their talent, take their own decisions and be confronted by challenges. Leadership is therefore not so much a matter of decision-taking, as creating structures, frameworks, cultures and environments (1987, page 90; and see Schein 1983). The leader does not tell others what to do but creates opportunities for lawyers to find their own way. A law firm is full of highly educated people looking for an opportunity to prove themselves to clients, colleagues, and others. It is part of the leader's task to create circumstances in which they are able to do so.

23.6.4   *The leader as guarantor of continuity*

Some lawyers act spontaneously, and may always seem to be one step ahead of the firm — and often on the point of leaving. They are constantly seeking new know-how, new experiences, and new contacts. Wilfulness in lawyers is natural. Leaders must try to "complement and channel" this intellectual energy, without suppressing or crushing the creativity. They must therefore keep a clear sense of direction in their own minds and in the minds of others, and maintain continuity. Leaders must also moderate impractical business ideas, without disillusioning the dreamers (the best way to do this is to ask the dreamer to implement the idea — they soon lose interest!).

23.6.5   *The leader as a symbol of security*

Law firms, like all professional service organisations, lack the visible security of factories and tangible products. The leader must therefore try to create a substitute by undertaking other tasks that yield security. This will include things like dealing with difficult clients, ensuring that the support services are working, or helping with personal problems. This is a common goal for good leaders in all organisations: ". . . it is crucial in the professional organisation" (Sveiby and Lloyd 1987, page 91). Lawyers can be unhappy souls, often working alone (and perhaps even away from the office). They "need a fixed point of reference", and the "leader must provide it because no one else can" (1987, page 91).

Schein also refers to the role of a founder/leader in "containing and absorbing anxiety and risk" (1983, page 25).

23.6.6 The leader as coach

This leadership approach requires the leader to formulate strategy, define the areas of professional activity and select the players. Recruitment is a very important task here, finding people who are both technically proficient and who fit into the team. This leader often takes no active part in the delivery of the service — which is why the role of the senior or managing partner can be so frustrating.

23.6.7 The leader as manager

As a law firm grows, either organically, by lateral acquisitions, or by merger, the role of the leader will begin to focus more on strategic issues — particularly matters which have to do with the balance of the firm's business in its marketplace and practice areas. But success during this phase is still dependent on the approaches and qualities considered above. The strategic role is, in fact, an addition to the role rather than a replacement for those other approaches.

23.6.8 The leader as know-how tycoon

Some parts of law firm activities (and, indeed, some law firms) are beginning to assume the characteristics of traditional companies. Their leaders often embark on "development strategies that force them to become more and more remote from the day-to-day professional operations" (Sveiby and Lloyd 1987, page 94). In this role, they become know-how tycoons, indistinguishable in a sense from the tycoons of traditional industries. But a price has to be paid for the industrialisation of a law firm: the firm's culture may be diluted by growth and polluted by lateral acquisitions; managerial problems can increase exponentially; and the founders or leaders may become remote, seldom seen by the lawyers at the 'sharp end' and alienated from day-to-day operations. Such development strategies thus require the firm also to develop the managerial know-how to contain the powerful centrifugal forces endemic within the profession. The 'know-how tycoon' is perhaps only likely to survive as an important leadership role model for firms with practice areas that have a high potential for industrialisation (1987, page 97).

23.6.9 The leader as despot

This type of leader seems destined for extinction. Leaders in law firms can only lead with the consent and support of those whom they lead. Good lawyers do not want to work with despots. As Sveiby and Lloyd put it (1987, page 97): "The quickest way for a knowhow company to go bust in the information society is to be led by a despot who gets tough with the staff"!

23.6.10   Conclusions about leadership

The conclusion as expressed by Sveiby and Lloyd (1987, page 98) is, therefore, that the role of leader is never easy, least of all in a know-how business. Leaders are constantly torn between the demands of their managerial responsibilities and the need to keep their hands in professionally so that they retain the respect of the lawyers and maintain their authority over them. How they reconcile this tension, say Sveiby and Lloyd (1987, page 98), "depends on what kind of human being they are, who the others in the management group are, their relationships and the history" of the firm.

Edvinsson (1992) simplifies the dimensions neatly when he identifies the three roles of leadership as being thought leader, process leader and commercial leader. Thought leadership is about identifying, packaging and cultivating the firm's knowledge so that it is ahead of its competitors. Process leadership is concerned with "how to reach high energy and productivity in the interaction between staff and customers . . . You either create energy or steal energy from this interaction" (1992, page 34). Commercial leadership is about combining thought and process leadership to create values and to make money.

Chapter 24

INTERACTION WITHIN THE FIRM

24.1 Introduction

When we are part of an organisation, we interact with people in different ways. Each of us will probably have a different role assigned to us by the firm — as a partner, a fee-earner, a secretary, a head of department, a member of a committee, and so on. Some of our interactions with others will therefore depend on the capacity in which the interaction takes place. Simply being given a role is rarely sufficient to complete the interaction. Our ability to influence others as we interact with them will depend on the power we are able to exert over them, and the way in which we might use that power to influence them. These issues will, along with others, affect the way in which we see other people and so relate to them. Interaction involves working with others in groups, and communication, and most organisations will be able to identify many 'communication problems'.

This chapter will therefore address the concepts of roles, power and influence, relating to others, and communication. Teamwork was considered in paragraph 21.5.

24.2 Roles

Many of the concepts of role theory explored in this section are taken or adapted from Handy 1993, chapter 3. The roles of equity partners are further considered in chapter 33.

24.2.1 *The importance of roles*

All of us, in different situations, occupy a role in relation to other people (e.g., employer, teacher, wife, father, adviser). Our performance in that role depends on:

(a) ourselves — personality, skills, attributes, experience;
(b) the situation.

In fact, these two variables will also interact with each other — personality is influenced by the various situations that a person experiences, and a situation will depend on the personalities involved.

In the workplace, therefore, roles are the link between individuals and the firm. The definition of any particular role will be the result of the combined expectations of those who are affected by it (and it may thus be defined legally, occupationally or culturally). Lawyers often find it difficult to escape from the role that tradition (culture) has defined for them. The behaviour that is expected of lawyers may be constrained in such a way that, after a period of time, it becomes part of the individual, part of his or her personality. It is, then, likely that most lawyers will be alike and will behave in the same way — they are forced that way by the expectations of their role.

The roles we seek, and the way we act in them, are also the product of our 'self-concept' (see paragraph 22.5.1), that is, our assessment of our capacity, capability, potential, place in society, and of our aspirations. As we change, or develop into, roles, our self-concept may also change or develop.

24.2.2 Problems with roles

A number of difficulties arise when the nature or execution of various roles is examined. Each of these difficulties is likely to result in stress (which is considered separately in paragraph 24.2.3).

24.2.2.1 Role ambiguity
If there is any uncertainty about precisely what a role is, ambiguity and confusion will result. This ambiguity or confusion may be experienced either by the person exercising the role or by those affected by it. How often do law firms employ people to fulfil certain roles but do not define the scope of the responsibility or authority of the job, how performance will be evaluated, what the scope for advancement is, and so on? Any lack of clarity in the role may lead to insecurity, lack of confidence, irritation or anger.

Job descriptions are often thought of as a way of defining a role and reducing the ambiguities and uncertainties. However, they are rarely a complete description of the role (except, perhaps, in the case of more routine jobs). Many firms (and individuals, for that matter) want the flexibility and freedom to allow a job to develop in ways that were not originally envisaged. The duties and expectations are then left deliberately open and ambiguous — perhaps with difficulties to come later.

24.2.2.2 Incompatibility (a conflict of expectations)
Even where the definition or limits of a role are clear, a conflict in expectations can still arise. This may be caused by the role holder's

self-concept and the expectations of those affected by the role, or perhaps where ethical approaches (see paragraph 23.4) differ. The sublimation of personal goals to the firm's goals may provide another instance.

24.2.2.3 Conflicting roles

Role conflict arises when someone is expected to carry out one or more roles in the same environment — for example, a technology manager who must act as a subordinate to partners in carrying out his duties, but who may need to act as a forceful, disinterested 'consultant' in advising against buying particular hardware or software preferred by one or more of the partners. The definition and expectations of each role may be quite clear, and compatible for each role; but the roles themselves are in conflict. Many fee-earners suffer role conflict in relation to their client work and other responsibilities (such as management, training, family).

24.2.2.4 Role overload

This arises when one person has more roles to handle than he or she can cope with. This is not the same thing as *work* overload (which is too much to do in one role). Working longer hours may solve the problem of work overload, but is not usually appropriate for role overload. Many partners feel this particular problem!

24.2.2.5 Role underload

Role underload arises for most people when the reality of the role they are performing is at odds with their perception of their abilities or capabilities (their self-concept): Holzner refers to this difference as 'role distance' (1972, page 44), which seems to me a more telling description of how individuals might separate themselves from the roles they are expected to perform. For partners, delegation sometimes creates a feeling of underload — a feeling of not being needed. But underload is also often a neglected and very real problem in the 'lower' parts of the firm. Handy describes role underload as "the most insidious, but most ignored, perverter of organizational efficiency" (1993, page 68).

24.2.3 Resolving role problems

Any difficulty with a role is likely to lead to role stress. Strategies for dealing with it tend to be either unilateral or cooperative (Handy 1993, page 70). Unilateral strategies seek to redefine either the priorities or the responsibilities of the role. Cooperative strategies require close and positive interpersonal relationships with people affected by the role, but can be successful in alleviating the difficulties. Unfortunately, most instances of role stress cause personal relationships to deteriorate; unilateral strategies therefore come more naturally to people, but tend to invite retaliation and often only serve to escalate the problem. A typical unilateral response to role stress is to downgrade either the expectations of others or the importance of the role so that poor performance in that role is 'acceptable'. The problems and strategies are summarised in table 24.1.

Since role underload is so potentially harmful to someone's self-concept, it is hard for them to resist trying to enlarge their job or increase their responsibilities (that is, redefine their role). But the underload means that they can only increase their responsibilities by encroaching on those of other people — and in doing so they disrupt the natural workings of the firm.

Role problem	Unilateral strategy	Cooperative strategy
Ambiguity	Try to clarify the definition of the role by forcing the holder's expectations on those affected by the role.	Try to clarify the definition of the role by seeking clarification from key people affected by the role.
Incompatibility	Decide privately to give preference to key people and then downgrade the expectations of others.	Seek to resolve the incompatibility by asking for a solution from those people affected by the role.
Conflict	Reduce the importance of one of the roles so that poor performance in that role is no longer a problem.	An agreed compartmentalisation of life so that the roles do not overlap, and set up rules and procedures to maintain the compartments and their relative priorities.
Overload	Reduce the overload by downgrading the importance of some of the roles and turning in a low performance (which is acceptable because it is consistent with their reduced importance).	Training to deal with other/new role(s); or an agreed reassignment of the responsibilities and priorities of the roles.
Underload	Exert irritant influence (negative power) to increase visibility and 'felt' presence; or take on someone else's role as well.	Negotiate a new or expanded role.

Table 24.1: Strategies for dealing with role stress (Source: Handy 1993, pages 68–71)

24.2.4 *Practical implications of role theory*

Unfortunately (as Handy points out (1993, page 93)), role theory is much better at explaining situations than predicting them or resolving them. However, explanation and understanding can help. Law firms and partners need to do more:

(a)   to compartmentalise roles appropriately, and train partners to fulfil them; compartmentalisation between office and home may also help (including insisting that lawyers take holidays, making most weekends sacrosanct, encouraging rest after foreign trips);

(b)   to prepare people more effectively for role transition (for example, from assistant to partner): the mere act of changing is stressful — firms need to pay more attention to ways of learning a new *role* as opposed to a new set of *techniques or tasks*;

(c)   to remember that many problems in a firm arise from role stress, misconceptions about roles, underload, or poor communication because of false expectations of a role;

(d)   to encourage second or alternative careers as a way of addressing role underload problems (for example, when an individual can no longer contribute to the firm in proportion to his or her status and income expectations).

As Handy concludes (1993, page 95): ". . . roles and the perceptions of roles underlie all interactions between individuals. More understanding of role perception and of the part that roles play in interactions would surely help to reduce the misunderstandings so common with all of us."

24.3   Power and Influence

24.3.1   *The role of power and influence*

Part of our psychological contract (see paragraph 22.5.2) with a firm, or with a group within it, involves an exchange of the freedom to do what we like in order to reap the perceived rewards of being part of the firm or group. Given, then, that there has to be some encroachment on personal freedom arising from the mere fact of being part of a firm, the issues of power and influence come down to who influences you (and whom, in turn, do you influence), in respect of what activities or decisions, and in what way?

Power is the capacity to affect another's behaviour. *Influence* is the effect. Power is a resource; influence is the result of using that resource. Power is the ability to choose outcomes in the light of our own interests; influence is the actual achievement of those outcomes (see Hunt 1992, chapter 4). Power and influence are important in all organisations, and their use normally results in what is described as 'organisational politics' (see paragraph 27.6). Hunt describes politics as "power in action" (1992, page 75).

An exchange of economic resources, whether in the market or through a firm, imposes restrictions on our ability to act freely in relation to the goods or services exchanged (see chapter 6). Thus, agreeing to an exchange of labour for rewards (wages, benefits, promotion or other incentives) means that we can no longer sell the same labour to someone else, and the property rights arising from the exchange entail safeguards against opportunism and moral hazard (grabbing, leaving and shirking). The question for most people is, "How much am I prepared to give up to gain those rewards?" In making our decision, we are implicitly accepting the use of power and influence by other people in the organisation.

24.3.2   Sources of power

Power in a firm may be derived from the organisation itself (coercive or physical power; resource, reward or remunerative power; and position or legitimate power), or from the individual (expert power; personal power or charisma; and negative power). The use of this power (influence) may then be achieved through force, rules and procedures, exchanges of resources, persuasion, ecology, or personal magnetism. These facets of power and influence are all discussed in Handy 1993, chapter 5, from which the following analysis is drawn.

24.3.2.1   Power derived from the organisation or environment

(a)   *Coercive or physical power.* This form of power is both self-explanatory and unacceptable in law firms! It is the power of the tyrant or bully, and the use or threat of physical coercion should be totally out of place in a sophisticated working environment. There may, of course, be instances of the illegitimate threat of physical intimidation taking place which may undoubtedly influence others' behaviour or attitudes. There are also organisations where the ultimate threat of physical restraint is a necessary part of the environment — prisons, mental hospitals, and perhaps even schools. Coercive environments lead to coercive psychological contracts (see paragraph 22.5.2). (Intriguingly, Davidson and Rees-Mogg (1997) suggest that the declining costs of violence are altering the political and economic landscape in such a way that nation states and large organisations will disappear. On this view, increasing sophistication and technological advancement may increase the use of coercion.)

(b)   *Resource, reward or remunerative power.* This is the ability to influence decisions about such things as extra remuneration or benefits, promotion (status), or invitations to join certain committees or groups. The resources may or may not, therefore, be material resources. Whereas physical power may result in physical pain, reward power often results in psychological pain. It is prevalent in organisations where the psychological contract is calculative (see paragraph 22.5.2, that is, where there is a trade-off of actions and rewards). However, it assumes that those who are sought to be influenced perceive there to be some value or scarcity in the rewards on offer (otherwise they will not be influenced, or motivated, by them). It also assumes that they can see a necessary relationship between the desired action and the reward (or lack of it): firms that emphasise teamwork are not likely to succeed with resource or reward power. Indeed, reward power generally is not liked, since its ultimate premise is that people have a price.

(c) *Position or legitimate power.* This is the power which arises from a role that one occupies: it is the authority of the *job or position* more than the authority of the *person*. It might be described as the power of the organisation chart: one's position in the organisation is defined, and so are the power sources that go with that position. In some way, position power is underwritten by either physical or reward power, because the power of the role has to be guaranteed by the organisation. The power of the position may be invisible and deniable: for example, the ability to control information (or its availability or flow), or to control a right of access to others, may be particularly potent sources of position power available to secretaries and receptionists, the accounts department, or computer programmers. The cynics might also regard this as the exercise of *political power*! In law firms, the most frequent claims to position power are made by partners who expect others to be influenced simply because they *are* partners.

24.3.2.2 *Power derived from individuals*

(a) *Expert power.* This is the power of knowledge, of expertise and experience. Some regard it as the least objectionable form of power: it is acceptable to recognise that someone who knows more about something than you do should exercise influence over decisions within the domain of that expertise. One might readily assume that this would be the dominant source of power in law firms (if not, in fact, in all professional interactions: cf. Freidson 1986). Indeed it is — with one major caveat. Expert power can only be given by those over whom that power is to be exercised. The expertise recognised in law firms is the expertise of the *lawyer as fee-earner.* The partner who seeks to manage something outside the fee-earning arena is no more an expert than any other partner — whatever their previous training and experience. The professional manager with qualifications in finance, personnel, technology, marketing and so on, is often not acknowledged to have expert power over the owners of the law firm — the partners. Non-legal expert power in law firms may be of very limited value even though in other businesses it may be highly prized. This is why support staff often find law firms such infuriating and frustrating environments in which to work. The lawyers' cult of omniscience is at odds with claims of expert power made by others and so regularly denied to them. The management maturity of law firms (and, to be fair, of know-how businesses generally) has to improve before the dual expertise of professional (legal) and managerial know-how can be combined successfully into a rounded business enterprise (see paragraph 3.3).

(b) *Personal power or charisma.* This is the power of personality, though that may itself be enhanced by the person's office (position power) and expertise (expert power). It is not inevitably tied to any position or resources, but rather to an individual; however, an individual who ceases to occupy a certain role or control certain resources is often surprised at how quickly the personal power seems to fade. As with expert power, charisma is in the eye of the beholder and therefore will be conferred — and withdrawn — by those over whom this personal power is exercised. Thus, although personal power is valued greatly by those who have it, they nearly always seek to supplement this power source with others. In some instances, the charisma of some people is such that they become mentors, role models or heroes and in this way influence the behaviour of others (this is called *referent power*): it may be that this becomes so influential a role that the mentors/role models/heroes find themselves modifying their own behaviour in order to live up to the expectations of others — role stress, in other words, caused by role incompatibility (see paragraph 24.2).

(c) *Negative power.* This is the illegitimate use of power — use in the wrong way, at the wrong time, in respect of the wrong people — or some other exercise of power that is inconsistent with the accepted standards or expectations of the firm. Negative power is the ability to *stop things happening*. In this sense, negative power may be totally out of proportion to the position or responsibilities of the person exercising it: the ability of the mail room or courier to delay or misdeliver; the potential for a disaffected employee to disrupt the firm's technology; an irritated secretary's impression on an important client. This is not a question of what people are empowered by the firm to do, but what they can take on themselves to achieve in moments of stress, tension, frustration, irritation, anger, low morale or disappointment. Negative power is thus seen more frequently in firms that display low staff morale or role underload (leading to people wanting to make *some* sort of impression — to exercise *some* influence, *somehow*). Although derived from the individual rather than the organisation, negative power is certainly a response *to* the organisation or environment. Thus, firms that do not pay sufficient attention to giving their staff rewarding, stimulating jobs, with some degree of influence of their own (cf. paragraph 26.2.2.1(c)), will suffer from the greater exercise of negative power. Partners who try to control everything, to make all the decisions themselves, will also invite the use of negative power. Much of internal politics and resistance to change is the result of negative power.

24.3.3 *Methods of influence*

The sources of power described above allow various methods of influence to be brought to bear on people. Power can exist without being used, but power without influence will not result in any change of behaviour or attitude among those over whom the power is sought to be exercised and the influence exerted. This influence may be open and obvious, or unseen.

24.3.3.1 Force

The use of force, or the threat of force, should be rare. It is derived principally from physical power, but the use of economic force (or the threat of it) may occasionally be seen as an exercise of reward power. A partner losing his or her temper (with the consequent potential for promotion or salary to be affected) may well be seen by a fee-earner or member of staff as an instance of influence by force. As a method of influence, force is always short-lived but with longer-term effects: it may therefore be appropriate to achieve an immediate result from people with whom you do not wish to develop a long-term relationship.

24.3.3.2 Rules and procedures

No one should doubt (and certainly not lawyers) the influence of predetermined rules and procedures. They work provided that the rule-maker is perceived to have the right to make the rules (now more difficult in relation to rules, say, of office dress or personal appearance) and the power base to enforce them. So, rules and procedures often do not work with partners, because they do not acknowledge the right of others to impose them, or (even if they acknowledge that the rules may be necessary) the power to enforce them! But if partners do not acknowledge the legitimacy of rules and procedures, or the power to make them work, why should they then expect others in the firm to do otherwise? This is not providing the role model, or leading by example.

24.3.3.3 Exchange

Influence by exchange often underlies many lawyers' thoughts about motivation: what can the firm offer (or how much should the firm offer) in exchange for additional productivity, or whatever? The short answer is that the firm needs to offer something that the employee wants and that is worth the extra effort required to gain it (see the discussion on motivation in paragraph 26.2.2). In many cases, law firms offer additional rewards that are not perceived to be worth the effort, or are not what is most wanted, and then wonder why their staff do not respond positively and with motivation. Seeking to influence others' behaviour or attitudes by effectively 'bargaining' with them (a calculative psychological contract: see paragraph 22.5.2) is a difficult balance. If the influence is successful, and the exchange completed, the firm will probably be anxious to maintain the new level of commitment: the 'incentive' may become enshrined in rules and procedures (preconditions to qualifying for the benefit), or its withdrawal threatened if the new level of commitment is not maintained (i.e., economic force) — neither of which is likely to motivate or influence willingly for very long.

24.3.3.4 Persuasion

This is influence by rational argument, logic, facts, evidence — all the things that should appeal to lawyers. Like expert power or personal power — which in fact give much persuasion its ability to influence — it is perhaps the least objectionable form of influence. Persuasion is thus never pure: it is backed up by perceived expertise or charisma, or perhaps by the power of the position or the power to reward — and so perhaps by implicit force, rules or exchanges. So persuasion only works when the person to be influenced accepts and acknowledges the power source of the person seeking to persuade: the person sought to be influenced may not, in truth, be persuaded at all but instead be overwhelmed by the personality, the position, or the 'bribes'.

24.3.3.5 *Ecology*

Like negative power, organisational ecology seems to be most important when things are not going well. All behaviour (and so all workplace interactions and influence) takes place within an environment — physical, social, psychological. The firm's ecology, therefore, may help or hinder performance. To change the working environment is to influence people — though often only covertly. For example, being able to participate in something increases people's commitment (provided they regard the participation as worthwhile); small groups are easier to participate in than large groups; open-plan offices can encourage participation and communication for routine work (but conversely, noise affects concentration and performance on complicated matters); seating plans and office layout can affect the interaction and communication between various people; and so on. Environment or ecology therefore creates the conditions for people's behaviour: the management challenge is to create the physical, social and psychological environment which does not hinder or obstruct the behaviour partners would like to see. As with so many things, this starts with their own social and psychological behaviour — leading by example and consideration, again — and physical example. If the location, size and furnishings of their offices are seen to be important to them, they should not be surprised if others seek a better location, more space, or better-quality surroundings. If they show irritation rather than consideration in relation to delays or mistakes, they should not be surprised if others demonstrate the same moody, temperamental and often disproportionate reactions: could it be that competition between partners for scarce resources (people, time, money) or facilities (meeting rooms, technology, office layout) is the root cause of others' difficulties rather than their indolence or wilfulness?

24.3.3.6 *Magnetism*

This goes with personal or referent power — it is the often irrational or inexplicable pull of the charismatic. When based on expert power, the pull may have more to do with the credibility of the individual than his or her charisma, but in all cases something inspires us to trust or respect them or their ability, and so gives them the ability to shape our behaviour or responses.

24.3.4 *The effect of power and influence*

The choice of any particular method of influencing others, and the effect it has, will have as much to do with the person sought to be influenced as the person seeking to apply the influence. Nevertheless, a number of general conclusions can probably be drawn in the context of law firms:

(a)   Most law firms seek to be cooperative environments: expert or personal power tends to work best, and position power is less respected. For these reasons, expertise may be valued more than length of service. Managing partners and professional managers, who tend to have only position power to rely on (having been denied expert power by partners who value legal expertise above all other types), are rarely as effective as they could be — a self-fulfilling prophecy which partners should perhaps reflect on. Of course, according to my theory of the law firm, partnerships of integrated entrepreneurs (see paragraph 9.4) should be the most cooperative, and partnerships of individual practitioners (see paragraph 9.3) the least so. Accordingly, the former may be more prepared to give due weight to the expertise of managers, recognising this as an integral part of the firm-specific capital and giving them a competitive advantage in achieving growth and diversification.

(b)   In most situations, the ability to influence will depend on the credibility of the person seeking to exercise the influence. This credibility will arise from previous behaviour, reputation, success, and so on. A partner's stock of credibility is therefore changing all the time, and may well be different both with different groups of people, or with the same group of people at different times. Law firms can very quickly exhaust any individual's reserves of credibility, and so affect (or destroy) his or her ability to influence. This reasoning seems to underlie Nelson's attribution of power in a law firm to client following (1988, pages 5 and 19):

". . . power in the firm remains inextricably tied to 'control of clients'. The ability to plan strategically for a changing environment and to establish efficient internal administrative systems depends (1) on the political balance of power within the firm — a power alignment that is increasingly subject to rapid shifts because of the collapse of particular fields or client accounts or because of the departure of leading partners — and (2) on the ideology of the client-responsible elite. Managerial authority in the law firm can never achieve autonomy from those partners with client responsibility. . . . The power of management to control the work of professionals, for example, depends on management's position in the economic exchanges involved in the delivery of professional services. Does the organization control the flow of clients to professionals . . ., or does it primarily internalize preexisting professional–client relationships . . .?"

These are clear references both to the strength of individual capital and to contributions to firm-specific capital (see paragraph 5.2): the stronger these are, the more credibility and power a partner will have.

(c)   The more dimensions there are to a relationship, the easier it may be to influence others in that relationship (because there may well be more sources of power and influence available). For example, a lawyer who sees a client as being only in a formal solicitor–client relationship will deal with the client only within the terms of that relationship; if the client is also a friend, or a business colleague in another situation (e.g., where the solicitor sits on the board of a client company), the total relationship has different strands to it, any one of which may then be harder to sever. This total relationship will form part of the individual capital of the lawyer concerned or of the firm-specific capital of his firm (or both). Similarly, an expert who tries to persuade by sheer force of technical expertise without seeking to develop any interpersonal relationships may find the advice resisted (technical know-how will not therefore be as valuable on its own as it is when combined with other aspects of individual capital).

(d)   Individuals will respond to influence by rejecting or ignoring it, or by accepting it (cf. Handy 1993, pages 142–5). If they accept, it may be *compliance* (because they feel they have to), *acceptance* (usually because the person seeking to exercise the influence is someone the individuals admire, respect or identify with), or *adoption* (that is, the individuals adopt the proposal as their own idea). Only adoption is self-maintaining: compliance and acceptance need reinforcing, monitoring and possibly control. Adoption takes longer to achieve, but also lasts longer; acceptance is pleasant (because the individuals have submitted to personal magnetism); compliance is quickest, but is rarely based on trust, motivation or commitment, and needs enforcing. Thus, the 'agency costs' of firms (the costs of safeguarding against the risks of opportunism and moral hazard: see paragraph 6.4) can best be reduced by influence resulting in adoption of behaviour that itself reduces these risks. Partnerships of integrated entrepreneurs (see paragraph 9.4) are most likely to see investment in adoption methods of influence as an investment in firm-specific capital that will be repaid through reduced agency costs and a better return on firm-specific capital. Individualists are most likely to seek compliance from employed fee-earners and support staff, so that they can reduce their non-fee-earning input.

(e)   The alternative to rules and procedures (that is, to 'authoritarian' management — which most lawyers hate) is 'participative' management. However, this works best where resource power is evenly spread through the firm, where expert power is respected and influence is achieved through persuasion, and where there are few time pressures undermining the process through which people can react by adoption rather than compliance or acceptance (see Handy 1993, page 148). Such a description presupposes a sharing, supportive environment: participative management is therefore much more likely in a partnership of integrated entrepreneurs.

Paradoxically, therefore, the sort of environment in which most lawyers would profess they would prefer to practise law (participative management, respect for their professional expertise, ability to call on effective and efficient support staff and resources) is one that requires behaviour which some seem unable to demonstrate: sharing, respect for others' know-how, mutual support, investment, and persuasion.

Power is vital to any effective organisation, but it can also be destructive. Therefore, as Hunt (1992) suggests:

(a) Try to be honest with others (this is not a sign of weakness): try to find out what people want from the firm, highlight areas of conflict, and negotiate solutions.

(b) Avoid unnecessary power struggles by clearly defining goals and authority, rather than functions — ends rather than means.

(c) Recognise that all organisations are compromises of many needs, expectations, and attitudes, and that negotiation is essential.

(d) Understand that not only partners want power, and so involve people in decisions that affect them (that is, share power with them): the tendency of senior people in all organisations to 'hog' power — often on very trivial matters — does not improve working life for the majority.

(e) Recognise that the firm will include different groups with different expectations, and that therefore power struggles and conflicts are inevitable: organisations are pluralistic, not unitary.

24.4 Relating to Others

24.4.1 Introduction

Interpersonal relationships is a very complex subject, and this paragraph does not purport to be comprehensive or exhaustive. In essence, the way in which people relate to each other is the result of three things:

(a) their perception of themselves (the self-concept),
(b) their perceptions of others,
(c) communication.

The self-concept was discussed in paragraph 22.5.1, and will be considered further in relation to motivation (see paragraph 26.2.2.1). It will affect our attitudes about our position in the workplace and so our behaviour towards others. This chapter will primarily concentrate on perceptions of others and communication. However, relationships at work will also be affected by the prevailing organisational culture, which will also have an overarching influence on how people behave towards one another (see chapter 23).

24.4.2 Forming perceptions

Hunt describes perception as follows (1992, pages 46–7):

"Perception is that process by which the individual organizes an abundance of information (stimuli) into meaningful patterns. By this process we reduce an indigestible amount of data into meaningful lumps. . . . While we all have the same receptors our capacity to use them varies greatly, as does our capacity to process the data. . . . Unlike a computer the brain does more than receive information. It interprets and patterns it. That process is the essence of perception. Information that is not required is filtered out. Human beings do not respond to what is there (or what is real) but to their filtered version of what is there, that is, what they perceive to be the case. In this sense they are selective in their perception. . . . So we all have our own perceptual world seen through the 'eyes' of our unique self-concept. And for all of us, until contrary data are received, our perception of reality is 'true'."

Even when contrary data are received, to the extent that they do not fit our existing perceptions of reality, we may well filter them out, and thus hold a view of the world which others cannot share.

As events recur or information is repeated (that is, as our perceptions are reinforced), they lead to our formation of attitudes, values, beliefs and opinions. Like our self-concept (of which they form part), these 'patterns' start forming at a very early age. Each pattern becomes a more or less stable filtering mechanism (Hunt 1992, pages 47–8):

(a) *Attitudes*. These are statements of our position on something, and may be cognitive (what one believes), affective (what one feels), and behavioural (what one is prepared to do). Attitudes may be formed in childhood as the result of parental and educational influences (and these tend to be the more enduring attitudes), but can be adapted by peer-group influences during adolescence and by professional or organisational influences in the workplace.

(b) *Values*. These are usually deep-seated concerns about standards, and like attitudes and beliefs tend to derive from early experiences and influences within the family.

(c) *Beliefs*. Beliefs are propositions about work, or society, or people, or life in general, or whatever. Values and beliefs may well shape our attitudes.

(d) *Opinions*. These are probably the least stable and usually relate to less important — or at least more transient — issues than attitudes, values and beliefs.

24.4.3 *Perceptions of others*

When we know people very well, we can predict more accurately what their behaviour, reactions, or motivation might be in any given situation. This is because our perceptions of them have been reinforced over time, and our experience has given validity to those perceptions. When we do not know people that well, we tend to make *assumptions* about their behaviour, reactions or motivation. When there was more homogeneity among the people who became lawyers, it was therefore much easier to know instinctively how they would think and react in given situations. Now, with greater size and plurality in law firms (see paragraph 1.4.2), there will be less validity to our generic assumptions about others.

In order to make these assumptions, we have to collect information, fit it into categories that make sense to us, and then make some predictions (Handy 1993, pages 76–81).

(a) *Collecting information.* We can collect information about people from many different sources. This information may be verbal or non-verbal, public or private, first-hand or hearsay. The non-verbal clues may be gestures and body language, or physical (e.g., mode of dress).

(b) *Categorising.* Once we have information, we will begin to classify and categorise it. Indeed, there is evidence that people apply 'labels' or form a stereotype from the first available perceptual information. As a result, later information will be influenced by earlier data, and we may even filter out later information that is inconsistent with our stereotype (that is, we indulge in selective perception). This reinforces the widespread belief that 'first impressions count'.

(c) *Predicting.* When we have fixed on a stereotype that matches our initial perceptions, we can attribute to an individual all the attitudes, behaviours, reactions and motivation that experience (that is, our previous perceptions) tells us go with that stereotype. We know that, by definition, stereotypes are not in fact universal and that there are exceptions to each of them. They may be inaccurate as universal truths, but they are an easy way to think. They have the enormous benefit of making people (to us) predictable and therefore easier to work with (or harder, as the case may be).

Our perceptions of others' roles (see paragraph 24.2), and of the power that they are able to exercise (see paragraph 24.3), will help us in the process of stereotyping. Our categorising and predicting will also be conditioned by our attitudes, values, beliefs and opinions as we go about the process of forming these perceptions of others (see paragraph 24.4.2). The roles that people occupy will influence how they should behave, so again knowing their role will allow us to make predictions about them.

As if this were not complicated enough, there is also a strong tendency for people to conform to other people's expectations of them (the so-called 'halo effect'). Thus, the misinterpretation by X of the signals given by Y may result in X's (inaccurate) perceptions and expectations encouraging Y to behave differently in order to conform to X's expectations! Referring to the halo effect, Handy writes (1993, pages 81–3):

"There appear to be two reasons for this readily observable phenomenon:

1. People tend to enforce their expectations on the role occupier. . . . It is usually easier in the short-run to conform to the expectations of the role than to change the role. Not living up to role expectations is regarded either as failure or deviancy. Deviant behaviour unaccompanied by demonstrable success is regarded as failure. Only a very self-confident person will be deviant, i.e. overthrow the role expectations. . . .

2. Most individuals do not like ambiguity. . . . Explicit role
    expectations by the 'significant others' (people who matter to the
    occupant of the role) are one way of resolving the ambiguity. . . .
The implications of the halo effect are considerable. Self-fulfilling
prophecies of a positive and negative kind can readily be created by
treating people as if they already are what you want them to become."

24.5 Communication

Communication is an exchange of information or stimuli. We have five
senses that aid the reception of information — sight, hearing, touch, taste,
and smell. Most workplace communication is restricted to the first two.

To be effective, verbal communication must be delivered in the right
tone, at the correct volume and speed, and with the vocabulary and
sentence structure appropriate to the listener. It is no use saying 'I have
already told you this' if the message was not received and understood.

Verbal communication can be helped or hindered by non-verbal signals.
It helps if you 'look the part', that is, if your physical appearance is
consistent with your role and the message (see Jackson (1994) for a broad
discussion of the 'signs' of the professional). You may distract people if
you 'invade their space' by standing too close too them, or if you sit
behind an intimidating desk. Your posture may give clues about your
seriousness or intentions, as may other gestures and facial expressions,
and eye contact (or lack of it).

Effective communication is further disrupted by interpretation (or
misinterpretation) at the receiving end. Berne (1964) and Harris (1973)
both elaborate on and illustrate the principles of transactional analysis,
and in so doing show the variety and complexity of human interactions.
There may also be differences in perspective affecting the result of
interaction (see Handy 1993, page 87). There is a difference between
what I actually think (the direct perspective), what I think you think (the
metaperspective), and what I think you think I think (the metametaper-
spective). For example, A has been with a firm for the seven years since
she qualified. She is one of a group of assistants being considered for
partnership, but in fact wants to leave the firm. The firm would not
normally offer A a partnership, but her father is a valued client (the direct
perspective). A thinks that the firm is about to offer her a partnership; the
firm thinks that A is expecting to be offered a partnership (the metaperspective). A thinks that the firm thinks she would accept the offer; the firm
thinks that A thinks that they want her to stay. Neither wants to upset the
other or hurt their feelings; rather than resolve the misunderstanding, they
might well end up in partnership together!

Hunt summarises the communication issues as follows (1992, page 53):

"Usually our verbal signals are reinforced or supported by non-verbal
ones. The non-verbal signals expand or clarify the verbal. Yet in our
day-to-day lives, we are witnesses to communication breakdowns,
misinterpretations and blockages, where the transmitter's attitudes,

values, experiences, language, posture, etc. do not link together in a consistent message, or where the message itself has inaccuracies, or where the receiver's attitudes, values and perceptions cause so much filtering of the message that the intended information does not get through — what is heard is what the receiver wanted to hear, not what was said.

Communication breakdowns are the most prevalent symptom of organizational problems. However, they are usually symptomatic of something else; people don't set off for work with the intention of causing a communication breakdown. Yet, while other factors (such as structure) cause most of the breakdowns, it is undeniable that your faulty perceptions of what I am saying, and my faulty perceptions of what you are saying, can cause a whole chain of problems. Some people are just much more sensitive and perceptive in transmitting or receiving data than others."

He concludes that interpersonal communication can be improved in one or more of seven ways (1992, pages 53–4):

(a)   by continually signalling attentiveness and responsiveness to the signals of the other — it is infuriating to talk to someone who stares out of the window all the time;

(b)   by continually sharing speaking and listening — if you are trying to convey something, it is very distracting if the receiver keeps interrupting you;

(c)   by signalling attitudes and intentions towards one another — it is off-putting to try to communicate honestly with someone who remains totally bland, giving no verbal or non-verbal clues about agreement or disagreement;

(d)   by checking, over the course of time, on the assumptions about each other's signals and your mutual perceptions of them — it is confusing if I interpret your expression as annoyance when you are concentrating hard;

(e)   by using gestures which are consistent with the words — it is highly inconsistent if someone tells you to stay calm while rushing about, nervously tugging at his or her clothes, or playing with pens or paper clips;

(f)   by using gestures only to illustrate speech — it is distracting to discuss, say, marketing strategy with someone who is repeatedly combing his or her hair;

(g)   by providing continuous feedback about how the message is being received — if there is no response or feedback, a dialogue becomes a monologue.

Good communication heads off problems, allows the firm to spot issues and gives partners an opportunity to deal with those issues. Firms that have too few meetings, meetings that are scheduled and frequently called off, poor partner attendance at meetings, and few forums for open discussion, are firms with communication problems. There may be fear on the part of some partners and, understandably, the assistants, to speak their minds.

In too many firms, the 'grapevine' works far better than the formal communication system, and such firms need to find out why the grapevine is needed in the first place. Morale problems are almost always a reflection of partners' attitudes. Firms that discourage communication or do not recognise the value of good communication could be heading for trouble.

In law firms, the real problems lie in the supposed *absence* of communication and in the *method* of such communication as does take place. Unfortunately, in my experience, no matter how much or how well a firm communicates with its partners, fee-earners and staff, there will always be people who feel that it is holding something back. Given that it is impossible for anyone in an organisation to know everything about it, this criticism is a reality that leaders and managers will have to live with. As long as they are satisfied that they are doing what is right, little else can be suggested.

Hildebrandt and Kaufman make the following general observations (1988, pages 22–4):

> "*Secrecy* is the worst enemy of effective management, and it creates rumors and suspicions that are usually unfounded. This is not to say, however, that a managing partner or management committee must divulge the nature of all internal discussions. Indeed, partners who are given management responsibilities must feel they can have open and free interchanges without worrying that they will be directly quoted.
>
> The difficulty of communication is directly proportional to the size of the firm. A relatively small firm operating in one location can arrange regular partnership and firm meetings so that everyone can be kept informed and can have input into the decision-making process. . . . In large firms with multiple offices, however, communication can be, and often is, a serious problem. . . . Furthermore, the lack of dissemination of meaningful information can create an aura of a dual class of partnership and might result in a 'we and they' attitude. . . . Yet it is important that one not go too far in the dissemination of information. . . . The more that is distributed, the less that will be read and understood.
>
> The 'employee mentality' that exists among many of the partners, a very serious problem in an expanding law firm, is often brought about by the management style of older or senior partners in the firm, rather than by the younger associates. It is interesting to note how many 'seniors' criticize younger partners for their attitudes toward the management of the firm and client development efforts, while failing to recognize that *they* (i.e., the seniors) created the atmosphere for such attitudes."

These comments focus on communication between partners about partnership issues. There are, of course, many other people and issues involved and, as a consequence, no formula to be adopted.

However, it is also possible to overdo communication — particularly by internal memoranda (or the latter-day equivalents, voice-mail and electronic mail). Communication is many times more effective if targeted and done face-to-face. Regular meetings with agendas should be planned for (and see paragraph 19.4):

(a) all partners;
(b) partners in specific practice groups;
(c) all partners and lawyers in specific practice groups;
(d) all lawyers (unless the firm is so large that this has become impractical);
(e) support staff.

A certain amount of internal management and administrative material needs to be covered, but this should be kept to a minimum. Concentrate in lawyers' meetings on new clients, interesting matters, how new work was brought in (and how that process can be replicated), sharing know-how, and other issues that focus on clients rather than the firm. Do not be tempted because of pressure of client work to skip these meetings. Without them, the firm's lawyers will become sole practitioners sharing a business name and support services, and many opportunities for business development and efficiency will be missed (cf. paragraphs 9.3 and 9.4).

Finally, Hunt poses and answers a challenging question (1992, pages 54–5): Do we really want total honesty in communication?

"As we are all less than perfect, we actually need laundered messages, filtered feedback, even deliberate lies, to protect ourselves and avoid hurting others. This dilemma points to a central conflict of organizations — 'me' versus 'the system'. The system is designed for unfiltered, open communication; 'me' wants privacy, protection and some filtering in feedback. Finding the balance between me and the system is well-nigh impossible. Conducting more communication-training programmes will do little to help. Only interpersonal trust has been found to reduce the extreme forms of communication filtering arising from a defensive 'me' fighting the system, and even trust rarely reduces filtering to zero. Few marriages, even, have totally open communication. We all have our private dreams, fantasies and secrets."

Chapter 25

DEVELOPMENT AND APPRAISAL

25.1 The Context of Development and Appraisal

There are few people who now believe that our general learning and development stop as we enter adulthood. Indeed, there have always been many who believe that anything worth knowing is not really gained until we leave educational institutions and go into the 'real world' to do something. Much the same is true of development within the legal profession. There are some who appear to think that a qualified lawyer emerges fully fledged with all the knowledge and skills that he or she will ever need to practise law (though some of this may still be latent). There are others who hold the view that nothing of any value is ever learnt at law school, and that real learning begins with the experience of practice.

Whichever way you look at it, there seems little argument that practitioners become more valuable to clients (and to their firms) as their knowledge and experience increase through exposure to 'real world' events. Whether this value ever reaches a plateau may well be open to debate — though the professional life-cycle certainly appears to suggest that it does (see paragraph 3.2.2). I prefer to see professional know-how and skills developing and changing: it is not so much a matter of linear development, as the building of new know-how on the foundations and remnants of the old. To me, learning is a lifelong process, and no one can justifiably claim to know it all. This is consistent with my view that professional bodies can no longer 'certify' professionals as competent: we can no longer teach them all they need to know, but must instead facilitate their development into independent learners who will always be able to learn what they need to know (cf. paragraph 25.3.7).

In this context, some appraisal of what a professional is capable of, and some sense of continuing development, are key parts of managing the human capital in a law firm (cf. chapter 5). After all, businesses take stock of their other assets, and invest in their maintenance and improvement.

25.2 Performance Management and Evaluation

It is often assumed that people instinctively know what appraisal is, and that designing an appraisal system can follow a standard process (or, indeed, be 'borrowed' from somewhere else). In fact, the nature of any firm's appraisal scheme will reflect the different arguments about appraisal (and its objectives) that take place within that firm.

25.2.1 Types of appraisal

Fisher (1994) suggests that the types of appraisal schemes are delimited by two dimensions:

(a) whether the appraisal will be focused on accountability (results achieved or resources used) or development (behaviour);

(b) whether the appraisal will be carried out by someone hierarchically superior to the appraisee or by a peer.

The combination of these dimensions creates four possible types of appraisal: superior's review and accountability; superior's review and development; peer review and accountability; and peer review and development. A scheme must meet at least one of these purposes if it is to be described as appraisal. Each type is logically separate, though a scheme can include more than one type of appraisal (recognising that this will complicate the design of an effective scheme).

The features of each type are as follows:

(a) *Superior's review and accountability.* The focus in this type of appraisal is on setting targets for achievement. As Fisher puts it (1994, page 39): "Appraisal becomes a cascading process in which targets are set for the whole organization and are then disaggregated and allocated to people throughout the organisation". The key processes in this type of review involve assessing performance against previously agreed targets, before moving on to setting new ones.

(b) *Superior's review and development.* The purpose of this type of appraisal is focused on the appraisee's competence and development needs. Within the hierarchical context of this type of appraisal, there is an emphasis on making judgments about the appraisee's performance (and possibly rating it). The assessments are often sent up the hierarchy so that there is an organisational perspective and assessment of the skills and competences available. Such a system can then be used for identifying people with promotion potential. There is often an emphasis on integrating individuals' aspirations and abilities with organisational goals.

(c) *Peer review and accountability.* In this form of appraisal, ". . . individuals are brought to account for their actions and professional practice by their peers" (Fisher 1994, page 38). It is frequently done in the context of an external framework of professional standards, and not in terms of the firm's strategic needs, though when the firm's survival might depend on it, there may be greater emphasis on the needs of the firm. In this type of appraisal, however, ". . . there is always a default concern with protecting the professional autonomy of the person being appraised. One aspect of this concern is the emphasis given to the improvement of practice and the avoidance of any denigration or condemnation of professionals" (Fisher 1994, page 38).

(d) *Peer review and development.* The purpose of this type of appraisal is:

"to provide feedback to the appraisee and to help her or him plan their future self-development. The focus is primarily on the needs of the individual, with only broad and generalised attention being given to the needs of the firm. This type of appraisal . . . concentrates on helping the individual to make sense of his or her own practice and experience. From this perspective, the test of whether appraisal is useful is its relevance to the individual's attempts to interpret, and make sense of, future development. It does not matter if different people create different meanings from those of others in the same role" (Fisher 1994, page 37).

On this framework, law firms should be using different types of appraisal for employed fee-earners and support staff (which is likely to be a form of superior's review), and for partners (a form of peer review). Accountability is often a difficult issue with lawyers (though increasingly important: cf. paragraph 4.7.4), but continuing development is vital if the firm's stock of know-how is to increase and improve. The criteria that might be appropriate for lawyers are considered in the context of partner appraisal in paragraph 36.3.

25.2.2 Design features

In addition to choosing the type (or types) of appraisal to be delivered, Fisher also suggests that the designers of appraisal schemes should consider eight design features in framing the structure of their schemes (1994, pages 40–4).

(a) *The extent of appraisal.* In some organisations, everyone is subject to the same appraisal scheme. In others, schemes are differentiated to reflect different grades of staff or their functions. In some organisations, only some of the staff are appraised. Partners must therefore decide whether everyone in the firm (including themselves) is to be appraised. If not everyone, they must choose the categories of staff to be assessed (and perhaps be able to justify the basis of their choice). They will also need to decide whether to apply the same scheme (or fundamentally the same scheme) to the categories assessed, or whether to have significantly different approaches depending on the roles and responsibilities exercised by the different categories. Given that the people in a know-how business carry out fundamentally different roles (see paragraph 22.3), it seems to me that there should be differentiated systems.

(b) *The degree of formalisation.* This is concerned with:

> "the extent to which the scheme itself determines what is done within an appraisal interview, and the degree to which this is left to the discretion of the appraisers and appraisees. There are two elements to formalization. The first concerns *procedures* about who does appraisals, when they do them, and how the documentation is handled. Highly formalized schemes have a procedure . . . which is followed, monitored and audited" (Fisher 1994, page 43; emphasis added).

A highly formalised scheme would be illustrated by the procedures manual under an ISO 9000 accreditation. Schemes with a low degree of formalisation have general policies about the objectives of appraisal and its main functions, but do not prescribe a detailed procedure. The second element concerns whether a *standard appraisal form* is used and the extent to which it prescribes what is discussed during an appraisal interview. In some schemes, there will be no form at all, leaving complete discretion to the participants. In others, there will be detailed statements of competences and tasks, and measures of performance. In the middle ground will be forms which identify the main areas to be discussed, but which leave scope for the participants to decide how to deal with them, and whether to address other issues (Fisher 1994, page 43).

(c) *The structure of interpretation or judgment.* All appraisals involve judgments and interpretation. An important design feature is therefore the degree of structure imposed on making judgments, and this may be driven by the intention of the type of appraisal scheme being used. In peer review, judgment is an interpretative act; it may be done in a highly unstructured way with little preparation and no interpretative method, or it may be highly structured. In the superior's review and development type of appraisal, the emphasis is on assessing competence. If the scheme does not impose much structure on making judgments about levels of competence, 'ratings' would be given not as marks on a scale but as a narrative response using whatever style and vocabulary are thought appropriate. The use of rating scales, on the other hand, would imply a high degree of structure, and may appear to constrain the appraiser in making what are often fine degrees of judgment about someone's competence. In target-setting schemes (superior's review and accountability type of appraisal), targets might be expressed in terms of intent and direction or as specific outcomes of result and task. "The former are vague and it is difficult to assess whether they have been achieved; the latter are much more specific in terms of time deadlines and measurability" (Fisher 1994, page 42).

(d) *The focus of control.* This feature "concerns the relative balance of power between the appraiser and the appraisee. At the extreme of this dimension power is entirely in the hands of either the appraiser or the appraisee. The dominant partner in an appraisal is the one who sets the agenda and contributes most of the solutions, decisions and judgements" (Fisher 1994, page 41). Normally, this would be the appraiser, superior or partner. The centre point would be an interview in which the participants "jointly agree the agenda and equally negotiate the judgements and decisions that are made" (Fisher 1994, page 42), which is more likely in partner appraisal. It is important to distinguish between control of the agenda and issues, and the management of the interview. The latter role involves "making sure that the interview is focused and achieves its purpose. This customarily lies with the appraiser and can be usefully seen as a facilitating one whereby the appraiser helps the appraisee play a full part in the discussion" (Fisher 1994, page 42). This design feature is also concerned with openness and secrecy. Where the appraiser dominates the process, secrecy may be an important theme, and in an extreme case the appraisee may not even be allowed to see the completed appraisal form (though the trend in recent years has been towards increasing openness).

(e) *The frequency of appraisal.* The 'normal' frequency of appraisal interviewing is probably annual, though other longer or shorter intervals are not uncommon. In some firms, there will be formal interim meetings to review progress between the planned appraisal interviews.

(f) *The link between appraisal and pay.* This is a major consideration in the design of any appraisal scheme. A decision that it is not appropriate for information gained during appraisal to be used in making decisions about pay does not mean that a firm cannot have performance-related pay (Fisher 1994, page 40). It may, however, be very difficult to persuade appraisees that there is no link! If appraisal information is used to determine some aspect of pay, then decisions need to be made about the proportion of remuneration that should be conditional on, or influenced by, appraisal, and about the mechanisms necessary for making the appropriate link. All my observations of organisations, and of law firms in particular, have done nothing to dissuade me from the view that a firm will encourage the behaviour and performance that it is perceived to reward. In this sense, there seems to me to be an irrefutable link between performance and pay and therefore between appraisal and pay.

(g) *Appeals.* Appraisees may emerge from an appraisal interview feeling that they have been unfairly assessed or upset about the way in which the interview was conducted. At the unstructured end of the spectrum, there will be no system or process in place for resolving such grievances and ad hoc responses will be made. At the other end, there will be a formal appeal or arbitration process.

(h) *Method of involvement.* The final design feature is the extent to which staff are themselves involved in the process of design and implementation (see also Fisher 1995). Issues of consultation, committees and communication need to be considered. The degree of involvement that will be appropriate in any particular firm will depend on its previous history of consultation and communication, and the reasons for introducing an appraisal scheme.

25.2.3 *Appraisal interviews*

Like any other form of feedback, appraisal interviews require the proper degree of preparation, planning and available time. Depending on the type of appraisal (see paragraph 25.2.1), the interview will have one or more of the following aims, each of which calls for different social skills (Argyle 1989, pages 172–5):

(a) *Obtaining information for an evaluation.* Evaluation is required, for example, for performance reviews, salary increases, training and promotion, or dismissal. The purpose of the interview should be to obtain further information about someone's progress. What is being assessed (or possibly even rated) is their actual *behaviour* or the consequences of their behaviour, such as their cooperation, dependability, planning, organisation, or need for supervision. What should not be assessed or commented on is someone's *personality traits*, such as being extrovert, neurotic, or authoritarian.

(b) *Providing information on progress.* This usually amounts to feedback on performance or discussing career prospects. Feedback requires particular skills, and should be given regularly (so that fewer issues are covered on any one occasion). Ideally, the session should be seen as an opportunity for joint problem-solving to explore how performance can improve. It is important, therefore, to concentrate on what the appraisee should *do* in future, rather more than on the *results* that the appraiser wants to see. It is likely that the appraisee may be defensive, resistant, liable to quarrel, or even unwilling to accept the criteria used, so it is particularly important to adopt a structure and style of giving feedback that will be sensitive, supportive and focused.

(c) *Setting targets.* Part of the objective here is to encourage improved performance (that is, to motivate someone). The interview will therefore need to establish what might motivate a given individual, and then seek to align the individual's motivations with those of the firm (cf. paragraph 26.2). It will be necessary to demonstrate how the appraisee's goals can be satisfied by pursuing the firm's goals.

In order to achieve these various objectives, it is important for the appraisee to feel that he or she is part of the same group as the appraiser and that they are both pursuing the same goals. The appraiser's manner should therefore be pleasant, positive and sympathetic. He or she should demonstrate personal concern for the welfare of the appraisee, and show genuine interest in understanding any problems (Argyle 1989, page 173).

However, the appraiser should remain 'detached' in the sense of dealing with facts and actions, by applying the standards of assessment to the appraisee's performance, providing realistic information about career prospects, and being concerned with the effectiveness of the firm, department or group.

There is no doubt that appraisal can be an invigorating and motivating process; it can also be deflating and demotivating. Conducting effective appraisals is a management skill that requires training, practice, and preparation. Partners who see it as an interference with fee-earning, to be carried out as quickly and effortlessly as possible, and cannot be persuaded otherwise, should not bother at all: they will do more harm to the firm than good. Perhaps this should also be reflected in their own appraisal and profit-shares!

25.3 Training and Development

25.3.1 *Nature of training and development*

Training is formal, structured learning, either in knowledge or skills. It can take place on or off the job. Development can be either informal (e.g., through structured feedback from on-the-job learning), or formal and planned (e.g., through performance evaluation, job rotation or second-ment). Training and development are linked to other human resource issues (appraisal, motivation, reward), and there may well be a conflict between the firm's needs and the individual's desires.

To be effective, training and development need commitment from the top (and good role models), and a clarity of purpose. Indiscriminate use of external training courses is unproductive, as is indiscriminate use of internal resources. Further, training people without providing them with opportunities for the use and development of the knowledge or skills they acquire is a waste of time and money.

It is often said that training is an investment and not a cost. It is both. It cannot (and should not) be denied that training costs time and money. It becomes an investment when it is properly conceived, properly managed and properly used. This raises issues of the firm's culture and structure (as well as the way in which it accounts for training time and training costs). Only when the firm's approaches to all of these things are consistent will the true value of training be realised.

A training needs analysis should distinguish the needs of different categories of people in the firm, and should consider their requirements for legal, practical, and managerial training (cf. paragraph 5.2.1). For lawyers, practical skills will include such things as client interviewing, drafting, negotiating, and dictating. It should not be assumed that managerial training should be restricted to partners: all fee-earners will need some management training (for example, in time management, working with a secretary, delegation and supervision).

Training can be provided in many forms, both internally and externally: for example, long or short courses, conferences and seminars, workshops, books, videos, interactive computer systems, case studies, role play, and so on. The right form should be chosen dependent on subject matter, level of person to be trained, intended outcome, and time and money available.

25.3.2 *Continuing professional development*

Whatever might be the mandatory requirements for continuing profes-sional development, a key part of legal practice is developing every lawyer's expertise, skills and know-how. Three elements contribute to a lawyer's professional development:

(a) institutional support: efforts made by the firm to develop all lawyers' effectiveness and skills as practitioners, including induction, in-house law and skills training, external continuing legal education, and internal precedent and know-how systems;

(b) individual supervision: the development of a lawyer on-the-job, including effective work assignment, quality control, coaching, feedback, and performance appraisal;

(c) individual mentoring: efforts to integrate an individual into the firm, including socialisation, dealing with the firm's politics, and helping with personal problems.

In larger firms, such elements tend to be more formal, structured and sophisticated. This does not always add to their value. To make the most of its investment in lawyers (and tomorrow's partners), every firm should take a rounded approach to personal development. Focusing attention only on internal and external training programmes may lead to short-term and short-sighted development. It should also remember that "knowledge workers learn most when they teach" (Drucker 1991, page 78).

25.3.3 *In-house learning*

In-house training does not need to be complex or sophisticated. Simply sitting around a table with some sandwiches over a lunchtime discussing some of the firm's current cases and its approach to them can be a valuable training exercise. Reviewing standard-form documents, their use and completion, and similar 'know-how meetings', serve the same purpose. Training is not inevitably time-consuming in its preparation or expensive in its execution.

Many larger firms will think about establishing their own in-house training programmes, often in response to increasing demands from incoming trainees, to the increasing costs of external provision, and to the actions of competing firms. Bear the following points in mind:

(a) In-house programmes do not work well without commitment from the partners. They must actively encourage and participate in the training, and act as role models to other lawyers in taking the programmes seriously and attending them.

(b) Before embarking on a programme, a firm should consult widely, conduct a needs analysis, design the programmes carefully to achieve their objectives, and establish priorities. One of the best ways to do this is to form a training working party and involve them and others in the necessary work.

(c) Use in-house trainers wherever possible — but only if they have the commitment and interest to participate, the knowledge and skills to impart, and the aptitude for training. If you involve outsiders, spend some time with them to help them understand the firm's culture, standards, procedures, etc. If you put the wrong outsiders in front of busy and impatient lawyers, the cause of training may be set back considerably.

(d) Budget time as well as money for your training activities — in other words, make it a creditable way to spend time, and part of the expectations the firm has of its partners and lawyers.

(e) Training should not be restricted to trainees and recently qualified lawyers. In no other industry does training stop on qualification, or shortly afterwards. Increasing responsibilities bring new challenges, the need for greater experience and skills, and consequently the need for training.

Just as training should not be restricted to junior lawyers, so it should not be restricted only to lawyers. Secretarial and support staff also need training and development to help them do the job that is expected of them: they are all part of the economic pyramid. In many firms, high staff turnover is associated with a failure to train people to undertake what is required.

25.3.4 *Know-how collections*

In the natural course of doing their work, lawyers create or come across many types of recorded know-how (letters of advice, precedents, expert statements, damages awards, etc.). Every lawyer should keep a collection of these items. Better still, practitioners in the firm should combine their collections and make this invaluable, largely unpublished source of competitive advantage and institutional efficiency available to everyone. All it takes is a series of alphabetically arranged subject files. Larger firms invest considerable time, effort and money in the creation of know-how systems, and may even recruit dedicated 'know-how lawyers' or other information staff. Given the importance of professional expertise and know-how to the success and economics of a law firm (see chapter 5), this investment is understandable, but will be beyond the reach of many firms. Doing what is possible is better than doing nothing at all to preserve, embed and use this valuable asset.

25.3.5 *Membership of organisations*

Professional development is all about acquiring new knowledge, experience and skills, that is, to increase the volume or value of individual and firm-specific capital (see paragraph 5.2). One of the ways to do this is to meet, talk to and work with other people. Whatever type of practice a lawyer pursues, clients like to deal with people who they believe understand them — someone they would describe as 'one of us', someone with 'inside knowledge' (cf. paragraphs 18.1.2 and 18.3.1). This does not mean prejudicing the lawyer's independence and objectivity, but being able to see things almost instinctively from the clients' perspective. Moving in the same circles or being part of the same organisations as clients is part of being seen as an insider. Lawyers who belong to and participate in trade or industry organisations, or involve themselves in their local community, are almost always more successful in attracting new clients and retaining existing ones than those who do not.

Depending on the nature of an individual's or firm's practice, there may also be some benefit to belonging to lawyers' organisations (such as local law societies, or the International Bar Association).

25.3.6 *The reflective practitioner*

Lawyers become professional by learning (though rarely as the result of being taught). The whole ethos of training in law firms is on-the-job development. This means learning *by* experience, learning *from* experience, and learning *through* experience. Professional artistry does not come from advanced theoretical knowledge, but from a cumulative body of personal knowledge — gained from experience of different situations (see also Webb 1995). Most professionals know more than they can say (cf. paragraph 5.3.1), and often cannot articulate how they come to do the things that make them successful (see Schön 1991).

Learning by, from, and through experience requires reflection. This requires a *critical* look at the what and why of practice. Law schools should have taught the skills of questioning and thinking critically. But practising lawyers are *doers*: in a law firm, it is the doing that is valued, not questioning. The pressure on a new lawyer in a firm is to conform, not to question or examine critically. Indeed, those that do question are often regarded as subversive and out of place. There thus begins a cycle of doing that which reinforces existing structures and methods. This is the very antithesis of change, and can therefore make the process of change difficult in a professional environment (see chapter 27).

25.3.6.1 *The learning cycle*

The cycle of reinforcing existing practices and habits can be broken by the creation of another cycle — the learning cycle (I have borrowed this concept from Driscoll 1994). This cycle requires that actions are not simply repeated. Experience has to be examined, analysed and considered if it is to be shifted to *knowledge* or *know-how*. The cycle thus requires an *action* or experience to be *reviewed* to see what can be *learnt* from it, and to see what lessons can be *applied* to future actions (see figure 25.1). That future action may well then be modified as a result of the previous experience, or the process of learning by review may confirm that the action was correctly carried out in the first place.

For experience to be meaningful, the *review* and *learn* stages of the cycle are critical: these are the reflective parts. The elements of reflection can be described as being:

(a)   to review a situation or experience;
(b)   to understand its context; and
(c)   to modify future practice, behaviour or outcomes as a result.

More simply, these can be equated to the What? So what? Now what? sequence of questioning.

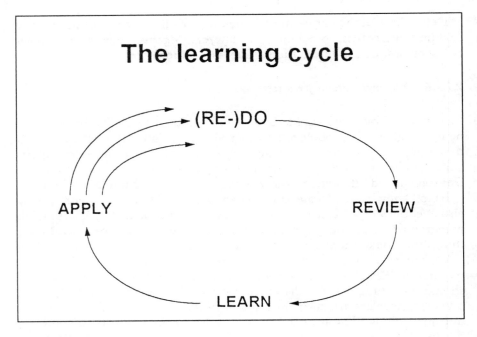

Figure 25.1

25.3.6.2 Review: What?

Reviewing a situation or experience means asking a series of 'What?' questions:

(a) What happened?
(b) What did you do (or not do)?
(c) What did others do (or not do)?
(d) What was your reaction?
(e) What was their reaction?
(f) What are the key aspects of this situation or experience?

These questions provide the basis for the reflection.

25.3.6.3 Understand: So what?

Reflection requires us to give meaning to a situation or experience. The 'So what?' questions are designed to help:

(a) So what were the effects of what you did (or did not do)?
(b) So what were your feelings at the time?
(c) So what are your feelings now?
(d) So what are the reasons for any differences in feelings then and now?
(e) So what were your experiences compared with those of others?
(f) So what are the reasons for any differences between your feelings and theirs?

Until we understand the meaning of the situation or experience, we cannot learn from it or change our actions, behaviour or attitudes in the future.

25.3.6.4 *Modify: Now what?*

The final part of reflection is to consider what might need to be done differently in the future, using 'Now what?' questions to help:

(a) Now what are the implications of what has (or has not) happened?
(b) Now what needs to change?
(c) Now what are you going to do about it?
(d) Now what happens if you do nothing?
(e) Now what might you do differently next time?

This gives a complete picture of the learning cycle and reflective process (see figure 25.2).

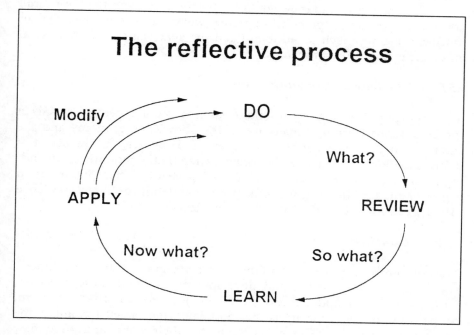

Figure 25.2

25.3.6.5 *Organisational support*

People need support from the firm if they are to develop into reflective practitioners. Reflective practice has only the *potential* for change: individuals need help from the firm if change is actually to result.

First, people need time to reflect. Learning is the transformation of experience by reflection; it is not sitting in lectures, or reading, or speaking. It is not the acquisition of knowledge. Continuing professional development time should therefore include time for reflection. Of course, the firm (and the Law Society) may well need some evidence of the *results* of the reflection (for example, an article, a presentation, an in-house practice note). But the two processes should not be confused. People need time to ask 'What?' before they can provide any proof that the question has been asked at all.

Second, people need a culture in which to reflect. This means the freedom and safety to ask 'So what?' without being criticised or judged. In most firms, this will require greater cooperation and collaboration, and is perhaps more likely in a partnership of integrated entrepreneurs (see paragraph 9.4).

Change will not take place without help and support from management. Therefore, nothing should be treated as certain or taken for granted. If clients are to be treated as individuals, the individual and the firm must be able to consider and decide 'Now what?' as part of the continuing pursuit of quality.

Experience shows that reflective practitioners do, in fact, change their ways of practising — and they would say for the better and to their overall advantage. Reflective practice therefore works. It should become an indispensable approach to flexibility and the achievement of progress in an ever-changing environment

25.3.7 *The learning organisation*

The concept of learning organisations has emerged in recent years. Given the continuous learning imperative of the knowledge economy and the Information Age, the concept is attractive. However, in practice it is difficult to define: Senge uses "an organization that is continually expanding its capacity to create its future" (1993, page 14). Those interested in exploring the idea of a learning organisation in depth could refer to Senge (1993), Pearn et al. (1995) and de Geus (1997).

25.3.8 *Conclusion*

Most businesses pay to maintain their premises and plant and machinery, and to engage in research and development. Without these expenses, business activities and success would be jeopardised. In a law firm, people's productive capacity is the most important asset: training is the maintenance cost of keeping people fit for their work, and know-how systems represent research and development.

Chapter 26

MOTIVATION AND PERFORMANCE

26.1 Understanding Differences in Performance

Our real purpose in trying to make sense of people's behaviour in the workplace is to understand how we might improve their performance and productivity. It is often all too painfully apparent that people behave differently. Some appear to be happy and committed in their work; others appear resentful. Some get on well with others; some appear to go out of their way to upset their colleagues. Some get on with their work and exercise their initiative; others will not do anything without being instructed to do so. We need to understand (so far as we are able) what leads to these differences, and how we might better manage them — or at least manage around them.

We all have different personalities, and exploring them can be endlessly fascinating. There are many 'tests' available which are designed to identify different personality traits, and so help in the process of selecting new staff. Unfortunately, personality has not yet been proved to be a reliable guide to a person's *performance* in the workplace (Hunt 1992, page 1). This is not to say that the insights gained from these tests are not worth anything: knowing whether a new person is likely to fit in with the other personalities already in the firm is useful background information.

We are on much safer ground in saying that there is a correlation between a person's ability (or abilities) and his or her performance. However, abilities are less an indicator of performance than an indicator of *potential*. Abilities can be categorised in different ways, but the classifications are often too simplistic because one 'ability' (such as the ability to type quickly and accurately) may be the result of a combination of others (such as mechanical or manual ability, as well as spatial visualisation and experience).

The only 'ability' that has been consistently associated with good managers is that known as 'helicopter vision' or being able to see the big picture (Hunt 1992, page 4). More formally, it is the capacity to conceptualise — what psychologists would call field independence. It includes collecting information, being able to identify patterns or relationships in it (inductive reasoning), and being able to convey its meaning to others through a conceptual framework.

So, although abilities are clearly important in selecting people for certain jobs, roles or tasks, there is little evidence that these abilities will necessarily result in good performance. Performance improves as a result of experience in any work that requires knowledge, skills, or practice. In this sense, an experienced member of staff will perform better than an inexperienced one. But again, a person's previous experience can only help us to predict what his or her *potential* might be: there is no guarantee that the experience will actually result in better performance.

In the context of experience, it is worth emphasising the distinction originally drawn in paragraph 3.3 between professional and managerial know-how. Professional know-how relates to the abilities and experience that people have in the technical or practical aspects of their work (for the lawyer, the ability and experience to practise law). Managerial know-how also includes experience relating to the organisational setting in which the work takes place: we might call this 'situational know-how' (see paragraph 5.2.2). Many organisations undervalue this latter experience. As Hunt puts it (1992, page 5):

> "Temporary staff suffer inordinately from a lack of experience within the organization — experience of its people, systems, structure, strategies, etc. (by experience we mean knowledge, skills and practice, and situational familiarity). . . . Performance . . . increases if an individual 'knows the scene'."

A firm will obviously run much more smoothly (and therefore cost-effectively) when staff understand how it works, how things are done. This can be procedural, but is also cultural ('This is the way we do things around here': see paragraph 23.1). The lack of situational familiarity is not restricted to temporary staff, since (as we have all experienced at some time) joining a firm as a new employee is one of the most testing times at work.

26.2   The Importance of Motivation

Personality, abilities and experience are all therefore relevant to performance in the sense that they may indicate people's potential to perform the work required of them. However, the best *predictor* of someone's performance is his or her motivation.

In my view, the best exposition of motivation is Handy's (1993, chapter 2). The exposition of motivation in this paragraph draws heavily on his thinking.

26.2.1   *Theories of motivation*

Various theories of motivation have been developed which, like the curate's egg, are good in parts!

26.2.1.1 *Satisfaction theories*

The principal foundation here is that a satisfied worker is more productive. Sadly, there is little empirical evidence to link satisfaction with productivity. However, satisfied workers do tend to stay with their employers. We may therefore conclude that conditions of work reduce staff turnover, but will not necessarily increase productivity. Given the very high costs of staff turnover in law firms (and the consequential loss of their professional, managerial and situational know-how), this result should not be downplayed.

26.2.1.2 *Incentive theories*

The basis of the incentive theories is that workers will increase their efforts to gain a reward. This is true, provided that (Handy 1993, page 32):

(a)   the reward is perceived to be worth the extra effort;
(b)   the performance can be measured and clearly attributed to the individual;
(c)   the individual wants that reward; and
(d)   the increased performance does not become a new minimum.

In firms that depend on collaboration and teamwork to achieve results, condition (b) can be difficult to satisfy, and support staff particularly will feel cheated if the rewards of good performance are appropriated by the fee-earners or partners. In general, therefore, most incentive plans fail (see Kohn 1993).

26.2.1.3 *Intrinsic theories*

The idea here is that someone's reward is the satisfaction of a worthwhile job — that the work itself is intrinsically motivating and rewarding. This form of motivation works best when people are given a worthwhile job and are allowed to get on with it. It is therefore appropriate for intelligent individuals who can work independently on challenging problems. It will not work when an individual does not have control over his or her own work. The intrinsic theories are therefore more likely to be appropriate for partners and senior fee-earning and managerial staff in law firms, but perhaps not for support staff and junior fee-earners.

26.2.2 *Handy's alternative approach*

None of the theories provides a universal analysis of motivation. Perhaps there cannot be one. But it is possible to examine the ways in which individuals respond to attempts to motivate them, and why they might react as they do.

In essence, Handy's thesis is that everyone has needs (which will inevitably differ from person to person). A person will be motivated to achieve a result if he or she perceives that that result will satisfy a need he or she has, and that the result is worth the effort required to achieve it.

26.2.2.1   Needs
There have been many different classifications of individuals' needs, perhaps the most popular being:

(a) *Maslow's hierarchy.* Maslow (1954) suggested a hierarchy of needs from the most basic to the more complex:

(i)   physiological,
(ii)   safety,
(iii)   belonging,
(iv)   esteem,
(v)   self-actualisation.

Maslow's view was that needs would only motivate to the extent that they were not satisfied, and that the higher order needs could not motivate until the lower order needs were met. This seems to be true for the lower order needs, but is less convincing for the higher order ones.

(b) *Alderfer's simplification.* Maslow's hierarchy was reduced from five categories to three by Alderfer (1972):

(i)   existence,
(ii)   relating to others,
(iii)   personal growth.

(c) *Herzberg's two-factor theory.* Whereas Maslow and Alderfer dealt with needs in relation to the totality of the human condition, Herzberg (1968) addressed workplace motivation. His two factors are:

(i)   the hygiene/maintenance factors (environment, conditions of work, money, interpersonal relationships),
(ii)   the motivators (the work, responsibility, recognition, achievement, promotion).

Herzberg thus claims that there are two dimensions to motivation at work — satisfaction and dissatisfaction. There are things which address the question 'Why work here?', and will lead to *dissatisfaction* if they are *not* in place (the hygiene issues). There are then factors which answer the questions 'Why work harder?', and will lead to *satisfaction* if they *are* in place. Some of these factors are intrinsic to the job, and some are extrinsic.

(d) *McClelland's needs.* McClelland's work (1961, 1982) identified and analysed three categories of need or motive: the need for power (perhaps a necessity in owners and managers, but as a single motivator can lead to authoritarian rule!), the need for achievement (again, perhaps a precondition for successful people, but needs to be balanced to avoid individualism), and the need for affiliation (this need for socialisation or relationships can provide a good balance to the needs for power and achievement but, like them, may not be effective on its own).

There is in these classifications a degree of commonality, and we are each likely to have our preferences (mine are for Herzberg and McClelland). They are all helpful in providing a framework for thinking about needs. Nevertheless, it is important to bear in mind that an individual's needs are likely to be many and varied, will be influenced by his or her self-concept (see paragraph 22.5.1), and will not necessarily be capable of being satisfied within or through the workplace.

26.2.2.2 *Results*

Individuals have different needs, at different times, and in different circumstances. They are not all motivated by the same things. Motivation cannot therefore be 'standardised'. Apart from specific personal differences, there may also be noticeable distinctions based on age, nationality (culture), and position (see further paragraph 26.3); there is no significant evidence that gender affects motivation. However, although there are differences, it is possible to state some 'ground rules'.

First, for any motivation to take place, the intended results must be clear. No one is motivated by uncertainty. Clarity of objective or opportunity is therefore a precondition.

Second, the result must be capable of satisfying a need of the individual to be motivated. If the intended result is not relevant to an individual's needs, it will not motivate — however valuable the offeror believes it to be. It is for this reason that a lawyer whose self-concept has him or her as a partner is likely to leave to become a partner in a smaller, lower-profile firm rather than accept an offer of more money (or other blandishments) not accompanied by an invitation to partnership.

Third, there has to be feedback: performance improves in relation to the quantity of feedback (whether good or bad) or knowledge of results. The most important factor in raising performance, therefore, is setting objectives. But setting objectives and then effectively ignoring them will lead to frustration and annoyance (Herzberg's point about hygiene or maintenance).

Finally, the results have to be pitched at the right level. Where rewards are related to performance, there is a danger that individuals will perceive that there is a greater likelihood of being rewarded for achieving a lower result. The prize of a high reward may be thought too remote or unachievable, at which point expectations (and efforts) will be reduced.

26.2.2.3 *Effort*

Whether an individual will make the necessary effort to achieve the intended result — in other words, will actually be motivated — depends on what Handy describes as 'the motivation calculus' (1993, pages 40–3). It is the calculation of whether the 'E' factors of effort, energy, excitement and expenditure (of time, money or passion) are perceived to be worthwhile. This calculation will also be affected by the nature of the psychological contract between an individual and the firm (see paragraph 22.5.2).

The calculation has three elements:

(a) the *strength* of the need that the result is intended to satisfy;
(b) the *expectancy* that the effort will yield the result; and
(c) the *likelihood* that the result will satisfy or reduce the need.

The calculation is multiplicative, that is, if any of the three elements is zero the final result is zero — that is, there is no motivation. It is also subjective: motivation is a personal assessment. Hopefully, by understanding the elements and processes of motivation, employers will be better able to assess what might motivate the individuals they employ.

26.2.3   Other issues of motivation

A number of other dimensions of motivation are worth bearing in mind:

(a) Individuals belong to more than one kind of organisation (work, family, social). It is not necessary for all needs to be met by only one of those organisations. This may explain why some people *appear* to be motivated by money — in fact, it is the only result in the workplace that can help them satisfy a *real* need that exists in another part of their lives.

(b) If the employer's and the employee's expectations about efforts and results are not mutual, there will be problems in motivation. Only when the expectations are mutual can employers predict what will motivate. Since motivation is a personal assessment, employers can only put themselves into a position to predict by treating employees as individuals, understanding them as individuals and, ultimately, motivating them as individuals.

(c) If a person's effort does not lead to the expected result, the motivation calculus is proved wrong, and can lead to dissonance (that is, a discrepancy between what is and what that person would like it to be): this can cause stress. For this reason, budgets will only raise performance if they are implemented under a certain kind of psychological contract: if they are seen as a method of control rather than of reward, individuals will lower their effort (recalculating their expectancy) or decide that they do not need the result (recalculating the likelihood that their effort will lead to the intended result).

(d) If an offered result is not needed by an individual, or is not relevant to that individual's perception of him- or herself, less or no effort will be expended by the individual to achieve it (that is, the individual is not motivated by the reward).

(e) If an organisation changes its method of control or influence (for example, by trying to change the way it motivates people), it is changing the psychological contract that it has with its employees (see paragraph 22.5.2). This contract, like others, requires at least two parties and the employer cannot assume that the change will be wanted by or attractive to the other party.

26.2.4   Money as a motivator

The following conclusions emerge from the literature (and from experience) on this thorny and contentious issue:

(a)   When money meets an individual's needs, it becomes relevant only to a comparative calculation — how that individual stands relative to other people. It is therefore possible for people to be satisfied that their level of pay allows them to do all the things that they might wish to, but to be demotivated because their level of pay is lower compared to others with whom they consider themselves equal (or better). The problem is compounded because, in the absence of knowledge, most people tend to overestimate what others earn, and are then dissatisfied! This is one reason why money is a hygiene factor rather than a motivator in Herzberg's theory — and it may be more a matter of perceived equity than of absolute amount.

(b)   Annual increments are seen as part of the conditions of work rather than as a recognition of achievement (Herzberg's hygiene again).

(c)   Bonuses are more a method of *rewarding* past effort than of *motivating* future effort.

(d)   In law firms, employed lawyers and staff often feel they have too little influence or control over those things that could lead to greater rewards. For example, hours or fees targets are often used, but junior lawyers and other staff are usually dependent on the partners to bring in enough work to keep them all busy to allow them to meet their targets.

(e)   Once you have something, it ceases to motivate (Maslow).

26.2.5   Conclusions about motivation

We are, then, left with a series of conclusions about motivation generally:

(a)   Different things motivate different people:

   (i)   lawyers and support staff are not necessarily motivated by the same rewards;
   (ii)   partners and other lawyers are not necessarily motivated by the same rewards.

(b)   Lawyers tend to be self-motivated, so it is important to avoid an environment that *demotivates* (in other words, to pay attention to Herzberg's hygiene factors):

   (i)   being given poor-quality work; being bored (particularly when the best work is perceived to be hoarded by partners);
   (ii)   being treated as subordinates;
   (iii) being expected to provide a constant level of service, attitude or behaviour: no human being is an emotionless machine;
   (iv)   being subject to 'hard managers', meaning those who manage remotely, or by numbers, by criticising and never praising, or who do not recognise the value of any contribution;
   (v)   partners and managers who stifle independence.

26.3 Patterns in Motivation

Ultimately, therefore, motivation (or the lack of it) is the result of a personal, subjective calculation that will take into account many dimensions of an individual's life. Not everyone can, necessarily, be motivated in the workplace. However, to leave the discussion of motivation at that point could lead managers to conclude that motivation is too personal, too difficult, and too time-consuming to be worth any further effort. It is clearly necessary to understand an individual's needs and motivation calculus if that person is to be motivated to the full. But are there *any* generalisations that can help us in the quest, to provide us with a framework or starting point? Hunt (1992, chapter 2) gives some help.

26.3.1 Motivation, age and career development

Although it is not possible to generalise about how to motivate any given individual or group of people, Hunt believes that it is possible to generalise about the goals that tend to be more or less relevant to people as their careers progress. Research and experience suggest that people's goals in life and work can be grouped into (Hunt 1992, pages 13–26):

(a)   a comfortable lifestyle (good health, a pleasant environment, a reasonable income);
(b)   structure (work stability, financial security): it is often difficult to separate these goals from those of a comfortable lifestyle;
(c)   relationships (personal, professional, social, etc.);
(d)   recognition/status (both by oneself and by others);
(e)   power (the opportunity to influence, control and reward the behaviour of others);
(f)   autonomy, creativity and growth (self-actualisation and self-fulfilment).

Hunt then relates these goals to career development (1992, pages 31–5).

26.3.1.1 Early career
At this stage, a person's self-concept (see paragraph 22.5.1) may still be being formed. At the same time, people also tend to be settling into personal relationships beyond the workplace. Once work and personal relationships are established, they cease to be a significant goal, and attention turns to autonomy, recognition, or power. This striving may be interrupted for young parents, when the arrival of one or more children may bring relationship goals, structure and a comfortable lifestyle to the fore. The interruption may last for as little as a year, depending on the health of the newborn and the success of the readjustment in domestic arrangements. However, the early career stage is usually characterised by high levels of energy which are channelled by firms through the carrots of promotion (bringing recognition), status (giving greater autonomy), or influence (conferring power).

26.3.1.2 Mid career

The energy burst and striving of the twenties and early thirties that the 'promotion-to-partner tournament' (see paragraph 3.6) typically encourages may give way to a sense of crisis in the late thirties. This normally stems from a realisation that one's career has, in fact, peaked. The promotions have been going to other colleagues. This realisation can cause resentment if the previous striving has been at the expense of personal, family or social relationships and the 'expenditure' is being proved fruitless. Nevertheless, the crisis or realisation leads to a reassessment of priorities, with less effort being put into work (or being transferred to a new employer), and going into activities outside the office. Work-related goals often shift from recognition, autonomy, and power, and revert to congenial working relationships and a comfortable lifestyle.

For the winners in this tournament, however, the late thirties up to the mid-to-late forties are likely to be a time of goals remaining more or less the same as they were before.

26.3.1.3 Late career and retirement

Even for the successful mid-career people who have achieved the prizes of promotion, recognition, status and autonomy (and the higher income that usually goes with them), goals may well begin to change through their forties and fifties. Indeed, for the successful, the whole range of goals tend to become *equally* important. Children are leaving home and gaining emotional and financial independence, the work-related goals have been substantially achieved, and the comfortable lifestyle has provided a measure of security and material possessions. As a result, activities and relationships outside the workplace again start taking more prominence. Personal relationships are often 'renegotiated' (or changed); leisure activities may increase; community involvement may become more important. As Hunt puts it (1992, page 34):

"Common-sense observers have long noted this 'mellowing', yet it is only recently that empirical data have demonstrated that concern for relationships does on average increase, that concern for stability and structure also increases, and that enthusiasm for the radical or the different is replaced by conservative views of the world. And this begins a shift which tends to continue until death, as comfort, structure and relationship goals become, very slowly, more and more important."

The approach of retirement may bring a period of contentment, as the level of striving and stress reduces. The achievement goals (recognition, autonomy, power) begin to decline in importance; lifestyle, security and relationships become more important. One of the trends in law firms in recent years, however, has been to place increasing emphasis on continuing performance (particularly billing achievement). For older partners, this can be contrary to their physical and psychological preferences — leading to stress and even early retirement. Age may start to bring about physiological decline as well — concerns may arise about the health of oneself, of one's family and friends. Finally, retirement itself will bring about an inevitable change in one's self-concept and in relationships with others: few people prepare adequately for it.

26.3.2 *Motivation and role*

Hunt also acknowledges that the nature of a person's work or position may also lead to generalisations about that person's goals (1992, page 38):

> "People are attracted to jobs which suit their goal priorities. However, a converse also holds. If the job fails to satisfy a goal that is important to an individual then that frustration will, over time, affect adversely the behaviour of the person, unless the job is redesigned (enriched) such that the person's goals are met. . . . Position clearly has an influence but it is probably most significant when the individual's goals are not being satisfied by the opportunities within a job. For example, . . . personnel staff positions attract individuals more concerned with structure and power. It could be frustrating to these job occupants to work in highly uncertain environments and have no power to change those environments. . . . Some of the least effective managers are those seeking autonomy, creativity and growth — all of which are highly individualistic goals whereas management concentrates on collective goals."

This serves to emphasise the point that it is often much easier to *demotivate* people than it is to motivate them. Issues of the preference of individuals for a certain type of organisational culture (see paragraph 23.2), and for the exercise of power and influence (see paragraph 24.3), are also part of this picture.

26.3.3 *Motivation and rewards*

We have already seen that, for motivation to take place, the rewards offered by the firm must meet the needs (goals) an individual has, and that the effort required to achieve those rewards is perceived by the individual to be worthwhile in satisfying the need (see paragraph 26.2). The organisational need for staff to be motivated is the need for improved performance and productivity. This is a question of behaviour. By and large, organisations encourage the sort of behaviour that they are perceived to reward: people will not expend a lot of effort in something if they feel that there is an insufficient correlation between *what they do* and *how they are rewarded*.

The challenge for a firm, therefore, is to try to match the reward system more closely with the behaviour it seeks to encourage. The questions are:

(a) What behaviour do we want (e.g., compliance, continuity of effort, performance to a required standard, cooperation with others)?

(b) How will we assess that behaviour (bearing in mind that the criteria and assessment must be relevant to the *whole* job)?

(c)   How will we reward the behaviour we want when we assess that it has taken place?

Hunt classifies rewards into six categories (1992, page 40):

(a)   *common benefits:* holiday, illness and pension arrangements;
(b)   *individual rewards:* salaries, wages, commissions, bonuses, merit awards;
(c)   *group rewards:* group bonuses, parties, outings and social events;
(d)   *compliance:* satisfying 'official' expectations, structural controls — the reward of 'doing it right';
(e)   *job satisfaction:* intrinsic satisfaction, challenge, personal development;
(f)   *goal congruence:* the firm and individual share the same goals — the reward is an emotional well-being from believing in or being committed to shared values or a superordinate goal.

He observes (1992, page 40):

"Of these possible reward systems the most potent, overall behaviours are goal congruence (sharing the same goals as the organization) and job satisfaction. But the effectiveness of rewards varies with the desired behaviour. For example, in attracting individuals to work for the firm, salary and other individual rewards are very important. Conversely, in motivating individuals to leave or withdraw, relative deprivation of individual rewards is a major influence. In retaining people in the firm, group rewards and group cohesion are powerful. In producing structured, predictable behaviour the compliance rewards are important. If the firm wishes to stimulate creativity then the compliance rewards are not effective (indeed, can be counterproductive) and the job satisfaction rewards of challenge, stretch and autonomy are important."

26.3.4   Conflict in motivation

There are thus a variety of goals, rewards and personal factors which will all enter the motivation equation. Indeed, the goals themselves are not necessarily consistent with each other (see Hunt 1992, pages 29 to 31). Personal goals may conflict (career v. family), as may personal goals and organisational goals (autonomy v. teamwork). Personal conflicts may be rationalised as the fault of the firm. For example, a spouse may blame the firm for an individual spending too much time working away from home: the individual may also blame the firm, rather than recognise that the conflict is his or her own unwillingness to recognise that relationship goals (family, social life) presently take second place to recognition, autonomy or power goals (career). Lawyers (and other professionals) often claim that there will be time later to catch up on relationships when their professional ambitions have been secured; there will not.

Chapter 27

MANAGING CHANGE

27.1 The Nature of Change

Managing change is one of the most crucial (and perhaps most difficult) aspects of managing people. Law firms are constantly interacting with a changing environment. If change is seen as the opposite of stability, then this interaction will mean that change is a constant feature of the firm — as it is for other organisations. In these circumstances, change should not be seen as unusual, and the oft-heard wish for 'a period of consolidation' is probably a vain one. In fact, it may be that it is apparent stability that should need explaining!

All change does not take place at the same pace. We must therefore consider change in relative terms — different degrees of change. And we might assume that the *process* by which change occurs will be affected by the *degree* of change. These degrees of organisational change can be categorised as (Wilson 1992):

(a) *the status quo*, meaning that no change takes place;

(b) *expanded production*, meaning that the change revolves around increasing the amount produced by the organisation — doing more;

(c) *evolutionary transition*, meaning that the organisation begins to change, but within existing parameters and substantially retaining the existing structure and systems: this might be used to describe the process by which law firms grow organically, but perhaps fragment somewhat in order to specialise and departmentalise;

(d) *revolutionary transformation*, meaning change that entails moving or redefining existing parameters, with the likelihood that structures and systems change: a law firm merger would fit into this category.

It follows that the greater the degree of change, potentially the more disruptive its effects on the firm: there are higher risks; there may be more resistance; there may be more cost; there will probably need to be better management of the process and its consequences. Anyone who has managed a law firm will realise that it can usually only cope with one major change at a time: if there are a number of issues that require action, priorities will need to be established. Too much activity will lead to 'change shock' that could well prevent anything happening at all.

27.2 The Process of Change

One of the most widely used models of change arises from the work of Kurt Lewin. He argued that change occurs through three phases (Lewin 1951):

(a)   unfreezing, when existing ways of working and values are questioned;

(b)   changing, when new forms of working are introduced;

(c)   refreezing, when the new ways of working become embedded within a new set of organisational values which support the new state of affairs.

On this basis, external factors are the most important in unfreezing the present situation (for example, economic, client-driven, governmental, professional), while internal factors are the most important in refreezing the new situation (for example, training, procedures, recognition and reward systems, communication). It is the internal area which is most often neglected, with the result that an organisation will be more likely to slip back into its old habits. It is not, therefore, just a question of going through a process of change; it is also necessary to embed that change in the new organisational structure and culture.

Lewin also developed his concept of the 'force field analysis'. The essence of this analysis is that organisations will remain in a state of equilibrium for as long as the opposing forces of drive and restraint are balanced. These driving and restraining forces constantly affect an organisation. If the status quo is to change, then it is necessary to identify what change is required, and then identify the driving and restraining forces in relation to that change. The unfreezing process begins when there is an imbalance between the driving and restraining forces.

Lewin argued that there is an optimum way to achieve this imbalance:

(a)   selectively remove the restraining forces: the driving forces should then begin to push change forward;

(b)   increase the number of driving forces, or increase the effectiveness (potency) of existing forces.

If the driving forces are strengthened before the restraining forces are dealt with (as they may be in organisations with strong, or impatient, leaders), Lewin suggests that all that happens is an equal and opposite reaction from the restraining forces. This will strengthen and entrench resistance to change.

27.3 Change in the Legal Profession

One of the distinguishing features of law firms is their 'flat' management structures — a diffuse pattern of authority. This may make it difficult for any one individual or group to have any significant effect, or at least provide a sufficient restraining force to match the power of an otherwise dominant group (cf. Nelson 1988, quoted in paragraph 24.3.4).

Machiavelli, nearly 500 years ago, could have had lawyers in mind when he wrote ([1513] 1995, page 19):

"It should be borne in mind that there is nothing more difficult to handle, more doubtful of success, and more dangerous to carry through than initiating changes. . . . The innovator makes enemies of all those who prospered under the old order, and only lukewarm support is forthcoming from those who would prosper under the new. Their support is lukewarm partly from fear of their adversaries, who have the existing laws on their side, and partly because men are generally incredulous, never really trusting new things unless they have tested them by experience."

Lawyers (like many other professionals) are notorious for defending their independence and resisting change. They often display more loyalty to the profession at large than to any one organisation (cf. paragraph 3.3). The increasing size of many law firms also makes some change more difficult to contemplate and achieve. The tendency to formalise and specialise that comes with size (cf. paragraphs 2.3.2, 8.7, 14.3.1.1 and 14.4) also begins to move towards a more hierarchical firm (if only covertly): not only does this entrench certain attitudes and procedures, it also makes the organisation as a whole become a more remote entity. Conversely, the inherently flat structure of partnership, with its consequential need for wide-ranging consultation and consensus will likewise spin out the process of change. The hypercritical environment of legal practice, which punishes (or at least looks down on) perceived failure, does not encourage risk-taking and so provides little incentive to embrace change. The culture of omniscience and the cult of the chargeable hour further reinforce the known, the comfortable, and the supremacy of individualism.

Effective change in most organisations, therefore, tends to take place during times of environmental (external) crises, combined with a change of leader — or at least with top-level support over a prolonged period of time.

27.4 Dimensions of Change

There are three different dimensions to change (Wilson 1992):

(a) *Structural.* In the 1970s, there was a tendency for structural change to be seen as the remedy for many problems. As a result, organisations, jobs, groups, rules, decision-making processes, communication arrangements, were all changed.

(b) *Cultural*. In the 1980s (largely as a result of Peters and Waterman 1982), there was a widespread belief that changing the organisational climate, values and prevailing beliefs was the key to change.

(c) *Behavioural*. Stressing the importance of interpersonal and social psychology in trying to persuade individuals to adapt to change is not going to provide the whole solution either. Behavioural concepts have not been widely used in the legal profession in order to effect change (although they are often used to explain why individuals are resisting change and refusing to adapt).

To some extent, and depending on the nature of the change, all three dimensions will come into play. The structural dimension is usually the easiest to redesign because it yields to analysis and rational decisions. But law firms, like other businesses, are organisational icebergs (cf. paragraph 2.2.1). There is the visible part (for example, organisation charts, departmentalisation, formal roles, procedures, job descriptions, communications) which are the rational, logical, and measurable elements. Then there is the (usually more substantial) invisible part (for example, the values, beliefs, and aspirations of the staff, the competition between them, the effect of the 'grapevine'). These are the cultural and behavioural aspects which affect motivation and performance.

27.5 Planning and Managing Change

The introduction of planned change involves a two-stage process of diagnosis and intervention (see Hunt 1992, chapter 11).

27.5.1 Diagnosis

Diagnosis requires management to understand *why* there is a need for change and *what sort* of change is required. Typically, diagnosis will begin with a series of questions, such as, Why are we doing this? Where do we want to get to? Where are we now? What is the gap between the two? What are the problems we need to address? Why are they problems? What are their root causes? What do we need to do to cross/reduce the gap? What solutions might be appropriate? Which are feasible? Is change welcome? Are there winners and losers? How fast can we go? Are there any cultural barriers (for example, is high fee-earning essential to esteem, or do the firm's leaders begrudge time invested in development)? Although it might be necessary or desirable to present a rational case for change, carefully analysed, these questions are not all capable of rational analysis.

27.5.2 Intervention

Intervention refers to implementing the action that is required to bring about the desired change. This action may be broken down into stages that are designed to address the three phases of unfreezing, changing and refreezing. As such, intervention will have to address the questions, What actions can we take? Do these actions need to be staged? How will we know when we have succeeded?

Hunt classifies four different types of intervention (1992, pages 272–90):

(a) *People interventions.* People need to learn if they are to change their behaviour and attitudes. The process of learning (which may go through Lewin's phases of unfreezing, changing, and refreezing) is therefore important to change, as is the creation of reflective practitioners who are better able to cope with change: see paragraph 25.3.6. The degree of change, and the process and speed of change should therefore be influenced by the degree of learning required, and the process and speed at which it can be acquired. It will also be influenced by the nature of power and influence in the firm (paragraph 24.3), and the issue of motivation (chapter 26).

(b) *Strategic interventions.* "Significant change in organizations involves an implicit or explicit change in strategy" (Hunt 1992, page 279). To be successful, strategic interventions need to be necessary, well thought through, effectively led, and properly resourced. The issue of strategic change was considered in chapter 4.

(c) *Structural interventions.* Strategic change usually also results in changes to the structure of the firm — its practice area organisation, management structure, geography, support systems and technology, and so on. These issues were addressed in chapters 14 and 19.

(d) *Cultural interventions.* Organisational culture was discussed in chapter 23. The existence of a firm-wide culture, and of subcultures in different parts of the firm, will also determine the nature, process and speed of acceptable change. To the extent that these cultural factors impede, constrain or slow the process of change, the firm's management may need to intervene to change the culture (for example, by appointing a new leader, introducing different systems of measurement, changing the motivation and reward system).

27.5.3 Cycles of diagnosis and intervention

It would be misleading to suggest that there will only ever be two stages in planned change. There may well be cycles of trial and error, of experimentation, of change followed by renewed diagnosis and intervention. Given the different dimensions of change, it would also be wrong to assume that the diagnostic process can always be rational, logical, and measurable: in other words, that with sufficient analysis, the *right* answer or the *right* approach to change will inevitably be found. Even wide-ranging consultation is not guaranteed to bring you to the right (or even a workable) approach to change. We must never underestimate the power of organisational politics.

27.6 Organisational Politics

Law firms are not organisational machines, but communities of people (cf. Handy 1993, page 291). This implies different personalities, opinions, values, priorities and goals. To reconcile these, there will be competition for power and resources. No organisation exists without internal politics: they are inevitable and in many ways necessary for change. The difference is between politics that create a force for positive change, and those that become negative or result in conflict.

Internal politics will manifest themselves in different ways. The negative type will display the following symptoms (Handy 1993, page 299):

(a) poor communication (laterally and vertically);

(b) inter-group hostility or jealousy;

(c) interpersonal friction;

(d) escalation of level of decision-making (higher levels of management and more time are taken up resolving conflicts);

(e) proliferation of rules (in order better to define the parameters and so avoid potential conflicts and the waste of management time resolving them);

(f) low morale or frustration at the inefficiency being created by the conflicts and tensions.

These conflicts will clearly be caused by different people having different goals, priorities, and standards, and so differences of opinion and approach are unavoidable. What is important then is how the disputes are handled and resolved. But they are also likely to be caused by disputes over 'territory'. These may relate to (Handy 1992, page 303):

(a) organisational territory (reflected, for example, in job descriptions, or even habit);

(b) physical territory (that is, office space — its size, location, sole or joint occupation);

(c) procedural territory (for example, committee membership, circulation lists);

(d) social territory (resulting from status, office furnishings, dining rights).

In such a context, an understanding of the use of power and influence (see paragraph 24.3) is vital. Many management writers assume that organisations can be managed on a rational, objective, consultative basis (that is, that they can indeed be *organised*). The reality is that all organisations are founded on compromise, negotiation, coalitions and bargains.

27.7 Skills of Managing Change

Managers who are responsible for change face a complex task and therefore need (or need to draw on) three different sets of skills (Buchanan and Boddy 1992):

(a)   *technical* skills relating to the substance of the change (for example, organisational design, technological expertise, personnel management);

(b)   *planning and monitoring* skills: these are typically the skills of a good 'project manager' (see chapter 21); and

(c)   *processing* skills, meaning the ability to communicate, to build and work with teams, and to influence and negotiate with others.

Which of these sets of skills is the most important will depend both on the nature of the change to be effected and the stage that the cycle of change has reached. They do not all have to be available internally, but they will have to be found from somewhere.

Kotter (1996) advocates an eight-stage process of change:

(a)   establishing a sense of urgency;

(b)   creating a guiding coalition or team with enough power to lead the change;

(c)   developing a vision and strategies for achieving it;

(d)   constantly communicating the vision, with the guiding coalition acting as role models;

(e)   empowering broad-based action to change systems and structures;

(f)   generating short-term wins, and recognising and rewarding people who are responsible for visible improvements in performance;

(g)   considering gains and producing more change through new projects, people, systems, structures and policies;

(h)   anchoring new approaches in the firm's culture with better leadership, more effective management, different behaviour, and measurement.

27.8   Helping Individuals with Change

27.8.1   *Causes of resistance*

People are all different and change will therefore affect them differently. This is true not just of the change itself, but also of the *process* by which the change is brought about. Inevitably, therefore, people will react to change differently.

Negative reactions will probably be most noticeable: they are part of the restraining forces and manifest themselves as resistance. The causes of resistance usually boil down to:

(a)   uncertainty about the intended result or the process;

(b)   lack of consultation; or

(c)   a sense of loss.

People may feel that they are losing one or more of a number of things. It is important to consider what they are since these are the *causes* of the resistance rather than its *effects*. To remove the resistance, it is important to deal with the causes. Possible sources of loss (adapted from Miller and Heiman 1987, page 141) are:

    (a)   power or control;
    (b)   leadership or status;
    (c)   authority or responsibility;
    (d)   contribution (or ability to contribute);
    (e)   recognition or potential;
    (f)   credibility or self-esteem;
    (g)   flexibility or freedom of choice;
    (h)   security;
    (i)   productivity;
    (j)   money.

If these causes are not addressed, an individual may resort to 'change terrorism'. This may be behavioural in the sense that he or she uses positive or negative power to influence the progress of change, or systematic through a resistance or refusal to acquire the new skills or knowledge that are required to effect the change.

At the end of the day, however, most organisations have some people who will never change: in the interests of the firm as a whole, it may be necessary seriously to consider their future.

27.8.2 *The transition curve*

The transition curve describes a cycle of phases which individuals experience when they undergo change. The curve describes a process, and is not therefore prescriptive. Understanding the seven phases should help to speed up the transition through change. The curve is shown in figure 27.1. The curve and the description that follows are based on Lambert (1993).

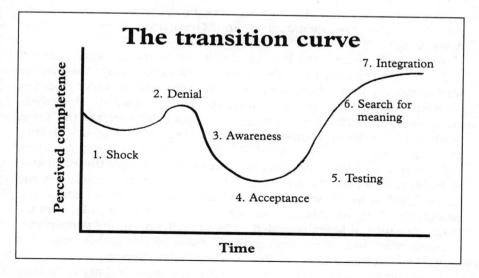

Figure 27.1 (Source: Lambert 1993)

The curve shows how someone's perception of his or her own competence in a situation or organisation will change over time in the process of coming to terms with changes.

The first reaction of people to change is often shock or immobilisation, which can be caused by the mismatch between how they see a new situation and the reality of how it is. The change causes their perception of their competence (their ability to cope) to decline — by how much depends on the extent of the mismatch of perception and reality.

After the initial shock, people will often rationalise change as really not happening, or not affecting them, or not leading to any change in their competence. There is an implicit assumption that all the individual need do is repeat previously successful behaviour. This can be particularly true for people whose 'change' is promotion. If they believe that they were promoted because of ability (rather than potential), they may not feel that there is any new learning (change) that needs to take place. An individual may never move beyond this phase. He or she may be encouraged, persuaded, cajoled or even threatened, but there is no guarantee that change will occur.

Phase 3 begins when the individual acknowledges a lack of competence in the new situation, that is, accepts the need for change in specific areas. Indeed, it is important that an individual is supported at this stage, because he or she may feel generally incompetent or worthless. This stage can be particularly frustrating for lawyers (who are used to succeeding) and to senior lawyers especially. The major cause for frustration is usually about how to manage the process of becoming 'competent'.

The lowest point on the curve comes in phase 4. There is now an acceptance of the reality of the new situation, and a recognition that it demands new skills. It also entails 'letting go' of attitudes and behaviour which have become comfortable — and which will, usually, have contributed to prior success. As such, it may be a period of uncertainty, frustration, and experimentation as an individual practises new ways of doing things.

In the testing phase, the individual will have some successes and will make some mistakes as he or she develops new skills. This is the effective way of moving from phase 4 to phase 5. However, the curve does not represent a simple (or inevitable) progression. An individual who experiences significant discomfort during phase 4 may well revert to the denial of phase 2. For the firm, therefore, phase 5 of the cycle is critical. Testing and experimentation are needed if change, new structures, new procedures, new techniques, etc. are to be introduced. People therefore need to feel that they have the opportunity to practise the new techniques and methods of working without fear of criticism or recrimination (see paragraph 27.9). In organisations where success is often judged on the 'hard' evidence of hours recorded or fees billed, and where performance is usually criticised rather than praised, where 'perfection' is prized but development often is not, this can be a particularly trying phase.

As successes and failures are experienced, the individual begins to learn the reasons for them — that is, to understand the process (phase 6).

Successful performance and behaviour can then be repeated because the process is understood. Finally, in phase 7, the individual 'internalises' the new skills and behaviour, and his or her perception of his or her own competence should now be restored to the same (or a higher) level than before the change took place.

Experience suggests that for individuals who are undergoing a significant transition in terms of their role in the workplace, the period for an effective transition can be between 18 months and two years. This does not match the most often used 'probationary period' (which is normally to be allowed 'up to a year'). However, with proper understanding and support, particularly from phase 4 to phase 5, the cycle can be shortened.

27.9 Encouraging a Climate of Change

As well as managing the process of organisational and individual change, there are a number of steps a firm can take to help create an organisational climate in which change will be encouraged. Handy suggests the following (1993, pages 310–16):

(a) Develop overarching goals: this is clearly related to developing a business strategy, theory of the business, or sense of mission, purpose or vision (see paragraphs 2.4 and 4.2). To be effective, the goals have to matter to the people involved. The firm must also provide feedback about how well the firm is achieving its intended goals.

(b) Develop a climate of experiment: teams (or individuals) should be encouraged to do all they can:

(i)   to improve what they do;
(ii)   to think of new ways of doing it;
(iii) to think of new things to do.

This requires curiosity (with the implied consequence of challenging the status quo), trust and flexibility.

(c) Encourage both sharing and privacy — meaning the sharing of information through full and frank communication (technology can help), as well as the privacy of some aspects of territory (to provide a sense of ownership, but not to the extent of losing accountability).

(d) Address internal competition: turn closed competition into open competition, and then control it through:

(i)   arbitration;
(ii)   rules and regulations;
(iii) coordination;
(iv)   open confrontation/role negotiation;
(v)   separation (if the competing roles are not interdependent);
(vi)   neglect (if all else fails).

Competition has some advantages in that it sets standards, stimulates and channels energy, and sorts out the best — but only if it is perceived to be an open competition. Unfortunately, most competition in law firms is perceived to be closed (i.e., a zero-sum game with a winner and losers), and closed competition usually results in conflict. For example, in profit-sharing, for many partners winning is more important than what is won — that is, having more than another partner is more important than the absolute amount of profit-share. The 'promotion-to-partner' tournament may also be seen as a closed competition (see paragraph 3.6). Open competition is not a zero-sum game, and usually requires collaborative competition: this requires clear, shared goals, and information on progress towards them, and no 'punishment' for failure to achieve. Surviving as a business in today's marketplace requires an internal attitude of open competition. This is most likely to be found in a partnership of integrated entrepreneurs (see paragraph 9.4).

PART VI

LAW FIRMS AS ECONOMIC ORGANISATIONS

Chapter 28

PROFITABILITY

28.1 Introduction

It would be idle to pretend that profitability is not ultimately the most important aspect of business. As Drucker puts it (1955, page 7): "Management must always, in every decision and action, put economic performance first. It can only justify its existence and its authority by the economic results it produces." Drucker was not talking only about profitability, but the maintenance or improvement of the "wealth-producing capacity of the economic resources" in the business. He was also not suggesting that maximising profits is the main goal of management: for him, profit is the result, not the cause (1955, page 44; and see paragraph 7.3). Indeed, de Geus suggests that operating with profits as a primary goal conflicts with a firm's longevity and life expectancy (1997, page 21).

At its simplest, profit is what is left over from business income after all the business expenses have been paid. What could be simpler? In order to increase profit, management's task must therefore be to maximise income or minimise expenses (or both). In accounting, a distinction is usually drawn between gross profit and net profit. Gross profit is the balance of income after the deduction of expenses directly attributable to the cost of providing goods or services (usually the cost of raw materials, but for our purposes more likely the cost of fee-earners' time, secretaries, and those other support staff costs that can be directly attributed to fee-earning activity). Net profit is the balance of gross profit after the other costs of running the business (the operating costs of premises, support staff, stationery, etc.) have been deducted. In law firm accounts, gross profit is rarely computed, although it may be used for management purposes in examining the different contributions of a firm's practice areas. For our purposes, therefore, profitability is concerned with net profits.

It is trite to suggest that profits will be increased by maximising income or minimising expenses. That is true for all businesses. But the ways in which these apparently simple results are achieved will depend on the particular circumstances of different types of businesses and (in our case) of specific firms (see also Mowbray 1997).

In essence, law firm profitability is the result of RULES:

Rates
Utilisation
Leverage
Expenses
Speed

This chapter examines each of these elements in turn.

RULES is a somewhat simpler statement of Maister's 'fundamental formula' for examining the five variables that contribute to net profit (see Maister 1984). Maister's formula does have the advantage of emphasising that, in a law firm, it is not so much the absolute level of net profit that is important as the net profit per partner (an increase in net profits will not be valued if it has to be shared among more partners, resulting in less money for any given partner). It also emphasises the multiplicative effect of each factor (1984, page 40):

"Theoretically, no one of the five is more important than any other. In practical terms, it may be much easier to effect a . . . change in [one] than in [another], but all five factors must be managed carefully. . . . I cannot count the number of times I have heard that "the key to profits is leverage" or "the key to profits is utilization". There are *five* keys. One (or more) may be chosen as the main strategic thrust for the firm, but none may be neglected."

So, for those of a more mathematical bent, Maister's formula expresses the factors of profitability as:

$$NIPP = (1 + L) \, (U) \, (BR) \, (R) \, (M)$$

where NIPP = net income per partner (i.e., average net profit per equity partner)

L = leverage (i.e., the ratio of associates/assistants/other fee-earners to equity partners)

BR = 'blended' billing rate (i.e., the average charge-out rate)

U = utilisation (i.e., chargeable hours recorded)

R = realisation (i.e., total fee income divided by the 'standard value' of the hours recorded — measured as the value of those hours at standard charge-out rates, before premiums or write-offs)

M = profit margin (i.e., net profit as a proportion of total fee income).

28.2 Rates

The obvious starting point in maximising income is to increase the fees charged for legal services. The initial reaction of many lawyers in the 1990s is to assume that this means raising charge-out rates and to conclude that it is impossible. However, what we are looking at here is the profitability of the practice as whole. The income it generates is the result of the fees charged for the *different work* of many *different people* for many *different clients*. The *nature* of the work done, the *expertise and experience* of the fee-earner(s) handling it, and the *type of client* can all therefore contribute to an assessment of the final fee.

Time sheets and time-based billing may have tempted us to believe that professional fees are capable of exact calculation. But it is important to remember that charging is an art rather than a science. In non-contentious business, the fee must be "fair and reasonable having regard to all the circumstances" (Solicitors' Remuneration Order 1972, para. 2). Even where charge-out rates have been set, therefore, it does not follow that all fee-earners — even of the same grade — have to be charged at the same hourly rate, nor even that the same fee-earner should be charged at the same rate for all the work that he or she undertakes: this is why Maister refers to the blended or averaged rate. The *cost* of each hour of a fee-earner's time may well be identical, but that does not mean that the *value* of each hour is the same (see chapter 31).

There is also the question of the client's perception. The Solicitors' Remuneration Order allows "the importance of the matter to the client" to be taken into account (paragraph 2 (viii)). This should be allied to Cobb's notion of the value curve (Cobb 1989), which may help lawyers understand clients' perceptions of the relative value of the service they are buying. Many commentators have observed that there is little fee sensitivity to those expertise or 'brains' services that require diagnosis, judgment or counselling — but there are probably few senior lawyers available to perform these services (see paragraph 2.3.3: see also Maister 1997, chapter 13). On the other hand, the increasing tendency for clients to perceive more legal services as a commodity will not help the lawyer's quest for increased profitability.

So, even in difficult economic circumstances, more flexibility on fees may be possible. Of course, I am making the dangerous and perhaps unwarranted assumption that individual firms are not already seeking to extract the highest 'fair and reasonable' fee for each matter from their clients (and I am also ignoring the constraints of legal aid rates). However, firms that are too limited in their approach to billing by time-based charging may well be missing opportunities. There are many different methods of charging for legal services (see paragraph 31.8), as well as of adding value, and this link to value must not be underestimated. Indeed, Parry's conclusion is that (1991, page 82):

"Over the long term the best way to increase the billing rate is by finding ways of providing clients with services which they find more valuable and will pay more for. Doing this will increase the overall income to the firm which will, in turn, enable the firm to reward those individuals creating these higher value products more generously. In professional firms the most direct way to increase the value of individuals' efforts is through training. . . . Services of more value can also be found by addressing issues of greater concern to clients."

Do not misunderstand me: I am not suggesting that law firms can easily increase their effective charge-out rates significantly in order to improve their profitability. As Maister points out: "Rising supply and falling demand can only mean a downward pressure on prices" (1984, page 42). If the fees charged are not competitive, a firm will lose clients to competitors and will find it very difficult to attract new clients. But it is not all a question of *increasing* rates: it is a question of increasing the *averaged realised rate* across the firm as a whole. A firm may in fact attract more business and increase its revenue by, for example, offering 'volume discounts' to clients once the amount of their business exceeds a predetermined level. It is all a question of balance, and the scope for improvement may be limited and small. However, at the end of the day, a series of limited and small improvements can collectively make a difference to the bottom line.

The concept of rates discussed here means the rates actually recovered (i.e., realised) from clients. For example, if a lawyer works 11 hours on a matter and her standard charge-out rate is £100 an hour, the value of the time is £1,100. However, when the bill is issued, the billing partner may take the view that the job is worth £1,250 (which, if paid, would raise the realised rate to £113.64 an hour). When the invoice is received, the client takes the view that the job was only worth £1,000 and after discussions with the billing partner only pays that amount. The write-off of £250 means the realised rate is £90.91 an hour. It is the average of this realised rate across all fee-earners in the firm that should be maximised. (Incidentally, the firm will not necessarily have made a loss on this transaction: only its profit will have been reduced as long as the cost of time — excluding any element of net profit — is less than £90.91 an hour.)

28.3 Utilisation

Most lawyers want to practise law, and will spend as many of their working hours doing so as they are able. Indeed, many professionals see 'admin', training and marketing as interferences with their work. Clearly, the more time that can be converted into chargeable time, in principle the more income a firm can generate. But this assumes that all the recorded hours are productive, and that the other things are interferences rather than legitimate claims for time that will, overall, improve the quality and productivity of individuals and the performance of the firm itself.

Utilisation therefore measures the extent to which *available time* is turned into *chargeable time*. Since time is being measured here, we are dealing with a finite commodity — there are only 8,760 hours in anyone's year (unless it's a leap year!). The constraints on improving utilisation are accordingly as follows:

(a)   We are assuming that there is work available to the firm's lawyers: this may depend on general economic and market circumstances, as well as a firm's (or its lawyers') ability to attract work (see paragraph 7.2).

(b)   There is a limit to the number of hours that any one person can work without affecting his or her productivity, quality or health. Maister referred even in 1984 to the "social and cultural trends" likely to affect the willingness of junior professionals to work long hours and so reduce utilisation (1984, page 42). The boom of the late 1980s may not have supported his view of the medium-term trend, but the point is nevertheless a valid one: broader economic circumstances will inevitably affect these social and cultural issues from time to time.

(c)   To remain productive, effective, busy, and profitable, a number of activities have to be carried out within a firm that are, in the pejorative terminology, 'non-chargeable'.

The key to utilisation is thus to maintain a difficult balance of generating sufficient work to keep lawyers busy, but without overburdening them to a point where quality of work or health suffers; and to invest sufficient time, energy and resources in maintaining and improving the quality and productivity of the human and other resources in the firm. As Maister states: ". . . as firms grow larger, they inevitably grow more complex (with more departments, more specialties, more offices, a wider variety of clients, etc.). Size and complexity demand management time in any business" (1984, page 42). For these reasons, chargeable time can never equate to available time.

The effective measurement of utilisation depends on up-to-date and *accurate* time records. Decisions about utilisation (which are essentially decisions about productivity) are made much more difficult without any, or reliable, time records: see chapter 31 for a fuller consideration of this issue.

28.4   Leverage

When lawyers talk of leverage (or gearing), they often refer to the ratio of fee-earners to partners, and 'partners' will include both equity and salaried partners. However, the principal importance of leverage is economic: in terms of profitability, therefore, the only partners who matter are the equity partners — those who share the net profit. Accordingly, for my purposes and in this chapter, 'partners' means the equity, or profit-sharing, partners. Leverage is the ratio of fee-earners who are not equity partners to those who are.

Perhaps more than any other factor, leverage has been pursued as the key to profitability in law firms: build a pyramid of many Indians serving a few chiefs and the profits will follow (so the theory goes). The theory is discussed and illustrated by Parry (1991, pages 37–9). His illustration of the greater leverage of a flat pyramid (more Indians) leading to markedly better profit-shares over that of the steep pyramid is dramatic. But theory and practice are quite capable of diverging, and the evidence is mixed. Figure 28.1 shows (based on figures from Legal Business 1996) the profit per partner achieved by the largest 100 British law firms plotted against their leverage. There is no necessary correlation between profit and leverage, although the highest profits *tend* to be achieved by firms with high leverage (and vice versa): these conclusions are also confirmed by Morris and Pinnington (1996a). The theory is undoubtedly correct. Unfortunately, for the theory to work in practice, the leverage must be *managed*.

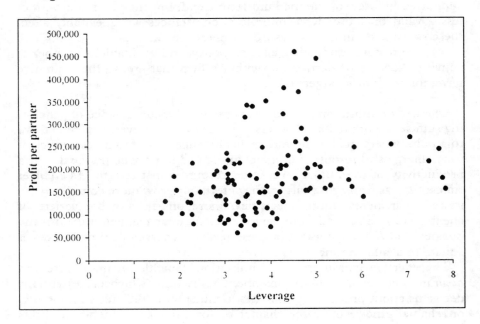

Figure 28.1 (Source: based on Legal Business 1996)

In general terms, sustainable leverage requires:

(a) *An expanding economy*. As Galanter and Palay's analysis shows, leverage creates the 'promotion-to-partner tournament' that drives exponential growth, and such growth can only be maintained in an economy that creates the additional work for exponential growth to absorb (see paragraph 3.6). Of course, even in a declining economy any given firm can continue to grow exponentially; others can maintain their leverage by taking (often difficult) measures to limit the growth in the number of partners (see paragraph 3.7).

(b) *Leverageable work*. Partners must be able to attract work that can be delegated to less experienced or more junior fee-earners (see paragraph 7.2). This depends, therefore, on:

(i)   the availability of work in the marketplace;

(ii)   the willingness of clients to allow work to be delegated to others (as the cost of junior lawyers has increased, there is evidence that clients are less willing to tolerate delegation than they used to be);

(iii)   the willingness (and ability) of partners to delegate work to others. When times are tough, there is a tendency for partners to hang on to the work they need in order to meet their own targets: other fee-earners are then told that it is part of their responsibility to start looking for their own work. When partners are busy, they may not take the time to delegate properly, so jeopardising the quality of the work being produced by others.

(c)   *A leverage structure and culture.* Part of the consequence from (b) is that the firm should have sufficient people below partner level to whom work can be delegated (and a continuing supply of such people), as well as a culture that encourages the delegation of work and the support and supervision needed to ensure its effective discharge. This is most likely in a partnership of integrated entrepreneurs (see paragraph 9.4).

Unfortunately, one of the consequences of the promotion-to-partner tournaments of the late 1980s is that many lawyers became partners simply because there was a need to go on expanding firms — to keep pace with competitors — and to prevent resources from leaving (there was a recruitment crisis in 1988). In fact, too many of those promoted were capable only of carrying out assistant-level work (which cannot now be supported at partners' charge-out rates), and were not capable of generating their own workload — let alone enough work to keep a team busy. This is the type of partner described as a 'Peter principal' in paragraph 9.5.2. Thus, while some firms appear to have good leverage, in reality they do not. Other firms stopped recruiting trainees and assistants at the beginning of the recession — as well as, in some cases, making assistants redundant: as a result, they have become 'top-heavy'. This is not necessarily all bad news, but profitability is usually affected. Mudrick and Altonji draw an important distinction in this respect between large and small firms (1993, page 4):

"For smaller firms, too many partners may not necessarily result in major problems, as long as every lawyer is pulling his or her own weight. In larger firms . . . lower net profit makes it increasingly difficult to make meaningful distinctions in [profit-shares]. As a result, the larger firms become more vulnerable to cherry-picking, which could result in further economic decline."

Maister reviews the importance of leverage in relation to the client marketplace, the people marketplace, and profitability. He describes the need to match the firm's leverage with (1993a, chapter 1):

(a)   service — that is, the skill requirements of the work that clients bring (expertise, experience, or efficiency: see paragraph 2.3.3);

(b)   satisfaction — that is, the appropriate mix of finders, minders and grinders (bearing in mind the expectations that assistants will have for promotion);

(c)   success — that is, a pyramid that yields the right charge-out rates from the best cost base to produce the highest profitability.

Parry (1991, page 158) summarises the balancing act as follows:

"The best ratio and pyramid structure is clearly that which maximizes *long-term* profits. Assuming that clients are rational and pay for what they get (in many cases a false assumption) then the best structure and ratio is that which delivers maximum client value (and therefore fee income) at the minimum internal cost to the firm. There is no simple answer to the best shape of pyramid but in moving towards a solution for any specific firm the following issues should be considered:
• Workload
• Promotion
• Client needs
• Partners' aspirations
. . . The main warning about ratios for managers is that there is a tendency for professional firms to become top-heavy over time, as a flat pyramid gives way to a steep one. This is inevitable because of the high growth rate required to sustain a flat structure."

Parry's view, therefore, is that firms are less likely to maintain their growth rate as they become larger (cf. paragraph 3.6.2), recruiting fewer new assistants than they should to maintain their historical leverage. The effects of this are to dilute leverage and, in time, net profit per partner.

28.5   Expenses

The factors so far considered have all been concerned with fee income. When profit is discussed in law firms, the first steps towards improvement are usually taken by seeking to reduce overheads. Marketing and training budgets are reduced or axed; staff are made redundant. The costs of running a business need to be controlled in any commercial environment, but the revenue line is far more important in a law firm. The reason for this is that the overhead structure of a law firm (like most professional service firms) differs from that of many other businesses. Staff costs form a major proportion of overhead (usually around 50%), with premises costs taking another significant slice (often 10 to 15%). Without long-term changes in this structure (by changing staff and moving to different premises), meaningful savings in overhead are difficult to achieve — and rarely achievable in the short term. Cost-saving thus seems to focus on those other relatively smaller or minor costs that may, in fact, jeopardise the firm's ability to go on developing a flow of business and to be able to service it at an acceptable level of quality — such as training, attending conferences to network with others, partnership retreats.

It also used to be possible to pass on some of the overhead costs to clients — for copying, couriers, telephone charges, and so on. However, there is a difference between charging these expenses on, and making a profit on them. The definition of 'cost' is therefore important: for example, does the cost of copying include the depreciation charge on the copier, and a proportion of someone's time to stand making copies, or only the direct cost of paper, toner, and perhaps some element of electricity? The profit-centre approach to support services was big business for some law firms at one time (see Beck and Orey 1991).

This is not to suggest that expenses should not be monitored or controlled, but to try to place in perspective the real scope for increasing profits by seeking to minimise expenses. Unfortunately, spending in the good times tends to be easy — and justified by rising fee income and profitability. But all this does is to create a lax institutional culture within a firm (as well as building in recurring, 'standing order' costs) that can be very difficult to change when money becomes tighter. What is needed is a cost-conscious culture.

There is also the tendency for costs to go on increasing even when revenue flattens off, or even declines. This leads to the phenomenon of 'slugflation': a constantly rising expense line will move ever closer to a flat or falling revenue line, leading to a profits squeeze (or loss). This squeezing effect can be dramatic. For example, assume that a firm has constant revenue of £1 million. In year 1, its expenses are £750,000 (giving it a profit of £250,000 and a profit margin of 25%). If expenses rise by 5% year-on-year, figure 28.2 shows how the profit is quickly eroded. After four years, profits have almost halved to £131,781. After seven years, they have disappeared. Of course, if the revenue were falling, the erosion would be very much quicker. And if costs were increasing at 10% a year, it would take only four years to wipe out the profit altogether. Finally, of course, the admission of any new equity partners during such a period would add to the financial difficulties of each partner as the value of a profit share in such reducing net profit is diluted further.

28.6 Speed

The final element in profitability is the speed with which work-in-progress is turned into revenue. There can be no fee income until a bill is rendered for work done (if the firm accounts on a bills delivered basis) or until cash is received (if the firm accounts on a cash basis — as many North American law firms do). Even if a firm accounts on a bills delivered basis, so that its revenue is increased simply by billing, there may still be a financing cost to be borne by the firm until the bill is paid and cash received (thus reducing profits) if the firm is obliged to borrow in order to continue paying its staff and other overhead expenses on a regular basis.

Proper measures for regular billing to turn work-in-progress into bills delivered, and then for credit control to ensure that bills are paid on time, are therefore very important to generating profit. This simple fact seems

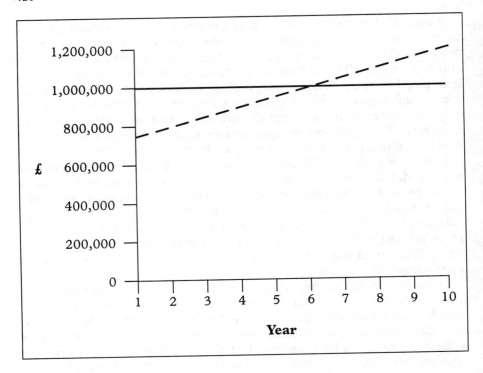

Figure 28.2

to be lost on many lawyers (including partners) who still expect to receive a regular pay cheque even though they are dilatory in sending out invoices. There is a direct correlation between preparing bills and the firm's ability to pay salaries and drawings.

However, pressures and targets to bill clients should not be so great as to encourage lawyers to invoice clients for unproductive or valueless time.

The question of improving cash flow is considered further in paragraph 29.2.

28.7   Health and Hygiene Factors

Maister (1993a, chapter 3) reviews these various drivers of profitability. Having said in relation to his fundamental formula that no one of the factors is theoretically more important in raising profits, his analysis of the health and hygiene factors of profitability does show that there are distinct differences between the short-term (hygiene) and long-term (health) factors.

In terms of RULES, the hygiene factors are expenses and speed, and the health factors are rates and leverage. Utilisation can be either: on the face of things, maximising chargeable time should lead to higher profitability. But, in principle, a 5% increase in charge-out rates will give the same boost to fee income as a 5% increase in chargeable hours recorded (assuming the hours are genuine and recoverable). However, the increased hours could have a detrimental effect on the well-being and motivation of the fee-earners: in this sense, utilisation is a hygiene factor. On the other hand, a *reduction* in chargeable time to invest in training or in a new practice area, or to target and acquire a major long-term client, will do more for the future health of the practice than short-term (and unsustainable) increases in chargeable hours. As Maister puts it: "What you do with your billable time determines your current income, but what you do with your nonbillable time determines your *future*" (1977, page 46).

Maister's point is that many of the financial controls in law firms concentrate on the short-term issues (hours recorded, fees billed and collected, expense forms), with the result that the hygiene factors are over-managed. The long-term contributors to profitability are correspondingly under-managed — and too often undervalued (developing teams, building skills and expertise through training and delegation, finding ways to add value).

28.8   Client and Matter Profitability

My description of profitability so far has assumed that it is being examined for the firm as a whole. However, as Maister (1993a, page 36) points out, it is the *nature* of work brought into the firm that contributes most to its long-term profitability (health) rather than its *volume*. In order to separate the type of work, nature of service, type of client, or location of work or client, and to explore which of these offers the best opportunity for long-term profitability, more sophisticated data collection and analysis are required. This may extend to the profit-centre analysis of different offices, departments or practice areas. For present purposes, I shall confine my observations to client and matter profitability.

28.8.1   Client profitability

There are many occasions when law firms are tempted to take on 'loss-leading' work in order to gain a foothold with a new client, or fail to take necessary actions to chase ageing invoices because someone is 'a good client'. These assessments are usually made on instinct or hunch, but without hard facts. A client may have been with the firm for a long time, and may have paid thousands of pounds in fees. But it does not follow from these mere facts that that client has been *profitable*.

Perhaps the first question to be considered is the period of time over which the assessment of any given client's profitability will be measured. At the macro level, it may take time for the firm and the client to establish a good, continuing relationship. The client may initially be 'experimenting' with low-level work to see what the firm is capable of. The firm may be putting more into the work than it normally would in order to impress the client. These issues would clearly distort 'normal' concepts of the inputs and outputs that would go into an assessment of profitability. Once this decision is made, a period should be chosen that is not too long (as a year might be) to track any changes in profitability that might suggest that remedial action should be taken, nor too short to produce any meaningful assessment. With the appropriate record-keeping and analysis, a firm should be able to see profitability on a monthly, quarterly and annual basis, as well as for the whole period of the client relationship.

The elements that make up client profitability may give rise to as much debate as those which contribute to profit-centre analyses. Again, decisions will have to be made and consistently applied. In essence the elements are the fee income and disbursements charged to (and paid by) the client, less:

(a) *Time costs*. This is the *cost of time* of the work done, derived from the time recorded by the fee-earners who have carried out any work for the client and their hourly expense rates (for a discussion of time recording and the expense of time, see chapter 31) — these costs have nothing to do with charge-out rates, or the amount eventually charged to the client. The way in which general overhead costs are allocated to client work will therefore depend on the assumptions and sophistication of the firm's expense-of-time calculation.

(b) *Matter-related overheads*. These will normally include copying, telecommunication, and postage costs that can be directly attributed to a client but which are not (deliberately or accidentally) charged to the client.

(c) *External costs*. These may include courier, travel, accommodation and subsistence, and other expenses that, again, have not been charged to the client (external costs will also include counsels', foreign lawyers' or expert witnesses' fees, search charges, stamp duty and other disbursements, but these will usually be passed on to the client).

If a client is proving profitable, well and good (unless the profitability is being achieved at the expense of quality of work or service, or by overcharging). Clients are not cash-cows to be milked for all they are worth, but assets to be nurtured (see paragraph 5.2). A profitable client is no good to a firm if he or she is also dissatisfied. Client profitability reports do not show the cost of a poor reputation, but they may highlight what is at risk, as well as the 'replacement' value of lost clients.

If a client is unprofitable, or not sufficiently profitable, the options are:

(a) to seek to increase the fee levels — which will only be fully effective if the firm's charge-out rates are out of line with the current market, if fee-earners have not been fully or accurately recording their time, or if the firm is delivering added value which the client has not previously been paying for;

(b) to seek productivity gains by improving the utilisation of fee-earners on the client's work, making sure that matters are handled at the right level, that time is not being wasted reinventing wheels, and so on: the effect will be to reduce the resource being applied to the client (as long as this can be achieved without jeopardising quality or client satisfaction);

(c)   to take a strategic decision to continue with the client at the current level of profitability because of the growth potential of the client, opportunities for better work in the future, the public profile of the client (i.e., the reputational benefit to the firm), or any pro bono or other benefit;

(d)   invite the client to seek legal advice from other sources!

As with all indicators, snapshots of client profitability can be misleading, so the firm must be sure to reach balanced conclusions on the totality of the evidence. However, the data from client profitability reports are more helpful in reaching such conclusions than the unsupported assertions of partners.

28.8.2 Matter profitability

I believe that most costs and wasted opportunities for increasing productivity and profitability arise at the level of individual matters. It is here that the scope for providing value for money is at its best. I have previously said (Mayson 1993, pages 62–3):

"It is impossible to divorce quality from value for money, and to separate value for money from the firm's cost structure. There is no disagreement about providing value for money to clients; the issue is how to calculate a fee that represents value for money in the eyes of both the client and the lawyer. It is becoming clearer that expense-of-time-plus-mark-up calculations are not adequate. Such a cost-plus calculation stops working when the overhead base of the firm is out of line with the marketplace's expectations of what it should pay for.

Investments in premises, technology and expensive young lawyers have pushed up the overhead costs of law firms in recent years. But the cost of legal services is raised far more by inefficiencies — failures in delegation and supervision, teams that are too large and don't talk to each other, young lawyers learning on-the-job, partners re-doing work that should have been better done in the first place, practitioners spinning or reinventing wheels because of inadequate know-how systems, unnecessary research, prolonged 'point-scoring' against the other side, protracted litigation, and so on. In fact, these issues are not about efficiency, but effectiveness. Clients will no longer pay for these wasted costs. And yet there are still some expenses that need to be increased: particularly training, better use of technology, and quality management. The bad news for the profession is that clients think that they are already paying for them, so they will not pay more. Without these increased expenses, law firms will be unable to remain competitive. The money will have to be found from somewhere, and there are only two solutions: the more effective delivery of legal services, or lawyers' pockets."

The proper analysis of matter profitability (together with an analysis of productivity: see paragraph 20.2) is therefore a necessary starting point in improving the delivery of legal services.

Essentially, the issues that apply to client profitability (cf. paragraph 28.8.1) apply with equal force to matter profitability. Certainly, the elements of the calculation are the same (except restricted to a particular matter), and the period of the analysis is the period it takes to complete the matter (although with longer matters, profitability may be *reviewed* on a monthly, quarterly or annual basis). See also Maister (1994).

Once matter profitability reports are produced, matter partners can be held responsible for the way in which client work is handled. They can also be rewarded for bringing in and performing profitable work rather than for simply bringing new work in or keeping themselves or a team busy. Further, by comparing the profitability analyses for the same type of matters, the firm will be able to make informed strategic judgments about the sort of work it is best able to handle profitably. This may help in decisions affecting the positioning of the firm, the allocation of resources, recruitment, and investment in fixed assets.

28.9 Predicting Profitability

If this level of analysis of profitability is possible, can profitability be predicted? Is a firm's previous track record of profitability an indicator of likely future performance? We are hampered in this country by the lack of a sufficient volume of data collected over a period of time. In the US, however, *The American Lawyer* has published the AmLaw 100 every year since 1986, showing the financial performance of the top 100 law firms in the US (measured by fee income). Maister (1993b) analyses the 1986–92 AmLaw tables and reaches the following conclusions:

(a)   Profit margins and leverage changed relatively slowly ($\pm$ 10%), whereas productivity (revenue per lawyer) can change quickly and dramatically.

(b)   Larger firms are no more profitable than smaller ones (meaning that larger firms showed as much variation in profit per partner as smaller firms), leading Maister to conclude that size is 'a zero factor'.

(c)   Location makes a difference, with New York firms consistently outperforming others (though New York firms were hurt more by the recession).

(d)   75% of a firm's profit per partner in 1992 could be predicted by its profitability in 1986 (though this declines to only 50% if only non-New York firms are considered).

(e)   Firms that increased their profitability most during the boom years were more likely to face reduced profitability during the recession than firms whose profits grew modestly.

(f)   There is no correlation between growth (the percentage change in the number of lawyers) and changes in profitability, profit margins, revenue per lawyer, or leverage.

A similar analysis was conducted using statistical regression by Chadwick and Hanna (1994). Their conclusions were similar to Maister

(1993b), but not identical. They found an advantage for New York firms (with Washington DC firms next best placed). They also found some (but a statistically weak) correlation between profitability and leverage. On the positive side, they also found that firms with higher profitability:

(a) have more minority lawyers (though again the correlation is statistically weak);

(b) have a higher proportion of lawyers from elite law schools;

(c) have a higher percentage of litigation.

Chadwick and Hanna disagreed with Maister's conclusion that size was a zero factor having no discernible effect on profits. They concluded that raw size does bring gains. What Maister had not done, they argued, was to combine his analysis of size as a variable with another variable — the number of offices. Larger firms may have branch offices (domestic or foreign). Chadwick and Hanna found that branch offices tended to reduce the profitability of firms: if this variable was separated, large firms without branches (or with fewer branches) were more profitable than those with them. Size will therefore tend to bring increased profitability provided the benefit of size is not diluted by multi-site operations. (The panel survey of solicitors in England and Wales also shows that average profit per partner increases as a firm increases in size (see Lewis 1996, paragraph 5.15).)

Another negative correlation highlighted by Chadwick and Hanna is that the link between the percentage of women lawyers in a firm and its profitability is statistically robust: ". . . it could be that hiring more women forces firms to make lifestyle changes that hurt profits; it could also be that women are attracted to firms that have already made these choices" (1994, page 65).

Chadwick and Hanna use their results to derive a model to predict profitability for 1992 based on the structure and location of any given firm. Not surprisingly, not all law firms conform to the model, but what it demonstrates is which firms have overperformed or underperformed compared to their peers. Interestingly, their overperformers are firms which would be perceived to be the best on other measures of achievement.

Chapter 29

CAPITALISATION

29.1 Introduction

Financing a business is all about introducing or generating sufficient cash to allow the business to invest in the assets it requires in order to carry on business (e.g., premises, furniture, equipment), and to cover its day-to-day operations (e.g., paying staff, buying supplies, paying telecommunications costs). Many lawyers seem to glaze over with confusion when they are asked to consider the difference between profit, cash flow, and capitalisation. They tend to assume that, because they are busy, or because the profit and loss statement shows a healthy profit, all is well. This may be a delusion. Having considered profitability in chapter 28, this chapter now examines capitalisation and cash flow.

Back in the 'good old days', little capital was needed for a law firm. The senior partners usually provided the funds that were necessary for its operations: equipment and operational costs were low, billing practices were irregular, and payments were made to partners only when funds were available. The partners truly were the owners of the firm.

During the 1970s, however, more complex equipment began to be introduced into law firms, they began to bill more often, and partners expected to earn more from their efforts. As the 1980s dawned and developed, the use of technology increased significantly, inflation took hold, many law firms experienced rapid growth and expansion, and the cost of premises, staff and insurance rose dramatically. As these pressures increased, partners found it increasingly difficult to finance their practices out of their own resources, and had to turn to the banks.

In the 1990s, the need for greater capital contributions is increasing, and it may be that partners in the largest firms face the prospect of not being able to raise or borrow sufficient money to finance their practices. At that point, the issue of third-party ownership arises (see also paragraph 8.7), and the Law Society and the profession may not be able to resist the need to change the rules to allow it — assuming, of course, that any third parties would *want* to invest in a law firm (cf. paragraphs 5.5.3 and 38.5.2)!

The following factors will all affect the pressures on law firm finances:

(a)   if clients are slow in paying invoices, and it becomes more difficult to borrow, cash flow will be a significant problem;

(b)   the costs of running a law firm continue to increase — particularly as a firm continues to grow;

(c)   the overall costs of acquiring and upgrading technology continue to increase (the unit costs of technology relative to its processing power keep reducing, but the greater number of software applications, the need to distribute and network systems, and the integration of different technologies, all add to the imperative to invest in technology to improve the quality and efficiency of work, as well as to benefit from its marketing potential);

(d)   the need to make lawyers and staff redundant ('downsizing'), or the retraining of those who remain will affect cash flow in terms of reduced fee income at a time of increased severance or retraining costs;

(e)   the lateral movement of partners will result in payments to departing partners, and to a cash flow hiatus as incoming partners establish themselves;

(f)   the expectation of equity partners that their drawings and distributions will be paid in full.

As the economics of practising law continue to change, more law firms are finding it difficult to maintain the levels of net profitability that they had become used to in the 1980s. Increasingly, they have been tempted to increase their overdrafts or other borrowings (often in order to maintain partners' drawings and distributions). The new circumstances in which law firms now find themselves have prompted many of them to re-examine their cash-flow and capital requirements.

29.2   Profit and Cash Flow

For most law firms, work-in-progress is turned into revenue as soon as it is billed (see paragraph 28.6). Net profit is then calculated on the basis of fees billed rather than fees collected. As a result, it is quite possible for a firm's profit and loss account to show a healthy net profit (and thus raise partners' expectations of good drawings and distributions), but for the collection of cash from clients to be lax — providing no cash in the bank out of which to make sufficient payments to partners. Indeed, in certain circumstances, the firm may not be generating enough cash to pay its expenses and other debts as they fall due, thus leading to insolvency. More businesses fail for lack of cash than they do for lack of profit.

29.2.1   *Meeting operational needs*

Parry points out that (1991, page 89):

"Service firms do not build stocks of finished product which must be financed prior to sale but they do have work in progress in the sense that there is a time-lag between the completion of a piece of work and getting paid for it. As the vast majority of staff (the main cost element) are paid monthly in arrears any firm which gets its money from clients more than 30 days after the work is done will need to find cash (often from reserves or borrowings) to pay its staff until the client's money is received."

The first requirement of financing the practice is therefore to ensure that sufficient cash is coming into the business to allow it to meet its operational needs. This requires that work done is turned into bills, and that bills are turned into cash in the bank. For as long as work has been done by the firm and clients have not paid for it, the firm is in effect acting as an unpaid banker for its clients. The firm's overheads have to be paid, and partners will expect drawings: money has to be found for these things from somewhere, and all sources carry a financing cost — either real (to pay for borrowings), or an opportunity cost (because partners are deprived of money for a longer period than necessary).

A key part of cash flow management is therefore to establish and implement policies and procedures for billing and collection. Along with these, control of write-offs of time and bills is also important. Such policies are often seen as bureaucratic interference by lawyers (cf. paragraph 14.2.5). Some firms therefore introduce them in stages, pinning their first introduction on the need to be more careful and systematic in avoiding conflicts of interest in taking on new matters (both from the standpoint of complying with the professional rules, but also the embarrassment to the firm that such incidents cause with clients and with other lawyers and professional advisers).

29.2.1.1 Billing cycles

A firm should examine its billing cycles, for the firm as a whole, for separate practice areas, and for individual lawyers. High levels of unbilled work-in-progress need financing (which will reduce ultimate profitability), and may be hiding problem matters or problem lawyers. Old work-in-progress also becomes harder to collect. Increasingly, clients want regular bills — quarterly or monthly — to help their own cash flow. Litigation practices typically have longer billing and collection cycles than others, and, of course, with legal aid funding, firms will be constrained in their ability to invoice and collect. Nevertheless, effective financial management still requires the monitoring of work-in-progress, billing opportunities, and cash flow (see paragraph 29.2.4) in order to assess the economic needs of the firm, and their effect on partners.

Accordingly, the firm should produce regular (probably monthly) work-in-progress reports showing the amount of unbilled time and disbursements for each fee-earner and matter. In order to make sense of the mass of figures that these reports usually produce, exception indicators should be established and used to draw attention to, for example:

(a) matters on which time or disbursements exceed previously agreed 'credit' limits for that matter (or for a client, when all matters for that client are combined);

(b) matters on which time has not been recorded for a certain length of time (indicating a problem, or the need for an invoice);

(c) matters on which time or disbursements exceed a budget agreed internally or with the client.

The purpose of work-in-progress reports is not just to prompt billing, but also to provide indicators of service delivery problems or logjams, and of staffing levels.

29.2.1.2 *Write-downs and write-offs*

The firm should also establish guidelines (or preferably rules) about writing down or writing off chargeable time or fees rendered. Unfettered discretion runs the risk of undermining the firm's budget assumptions — especially where the budget did not include any profit element. It can also be a licence to hide problems behind the façade of maintaining good client relationships. Partners should not be allowed to write off time, disbursements or unpaid bills above a previously agreed amount without the approval of the managing partner (or senior or finance partner).

29.2.1.3 *Credit control*

Similarly, firms should establish credit control procedures. Except in exceptional circumstances, it is a waste of time for lawyers to be chasing debts. They rarely have the time to do the job properly or on a timely basis, and in any event are not trained to do it. With commercial clients, the person the partner deals with may not be the one who signs the cheques or approves invoices for payment: debt-chasing also needs to take place at the right level to be effective. Partners often make the mistake of assuming that professionalism requires a kid-glove approach to chasing clients for money. Fear of losing a 'good' client can lead some partners to make extraordinary concessions, effectively allowing clients to pay their legal fees at their own convenience (if at all). Is a non-paying (or delaying) client really a 'good' client?

The responsibility for debt collection should be delegated to the firm's accounts staff: in fact, in many firms dedicated credit controllers usually pay their salaries many times over in improved cash flow. Having said that, one of the problems they experience is the prevarication of clients who claim that their work has not been completed, or that it was not up to the required standard. Clearly there has to be some liaison between credit controllers and lawyers. But equally the lawyers should have sorted out the professional and quality issues long before an invoice was issued.

Aged debt reports should be produced and monitored regularly. Statements and reminders should be issued to late-paying clients, and should be followed up with a telephone enquiry to determine if there are any outstanding issues or reasons causing the delay. Once invoices are more than 90 days old, the chances of collection fall significantly. These aged-debt reports should be monitored by the client and matter partners (and by the head of department and managing partner in larger firms).

Many collection problems are in fact a reflection of issues that arose at the time of engagement: failing to set out clearly (or, in breach of the Solicitors' Practice Rules 1990, r. 15, at all) the basis on which the client would be charged. When client dissatisfaction stems from this misunderstanding or failure to communicate, they may well 'take it out' on the firm by delaying payment. Matter acceptance guidelines, engagement letters, and clearer communication generally, are all therefore part of speeding up the process of converting work into cash.

If all else fails, legal action is possible. But as Parry rightly says (1991, page 89):

> "Although the ultimate threat of legal action is available to professional firms to enforce payment they face much greater problems than manufacturing businesses. In the event of court actions clients will often claim the quality of service was unacceptable and it is not unknown for the firm to find itself facing embarrassing criticism in open court of its professional standards when a client is forced to defend late or non-payment."

A negotiated settlement is usually much preferable to litigation and write-offs. Partners should be willing to adjust bills for clients who disagree with the amount invoiced or who are genuinely dissatisfied with the service provided (subject to limits or approval to be agreed by the managing partner).

29.2.2 Determining cash flow requirements

Many firms now prepare cash flow statements setting out anticipated cash receipts and cash outgoings on a month-by-month basis. A cash flow statement is not the same thing as taking the firm's budget entries divided by 12 because:

(a) Budgets show projected income and expenses (usually on the same basis as a profit and loss account), and may not include some cash items that will need to be paid (e.g., the acquisition of fixed assets, VAT), as well as including some deductions that do not require cash to be spent (e.g., depreciation).

(b) Clearly, receipts do not arrive in convenient one-twelfth packages, and expenses are not all incurred or paid for monthly (e.g., quarterly rents, annual insurance premiums, telephone charges, distributions to partners), although monthly standing orders may help to even out the cash flow.

A detailed attempt to predict the arrival of cash into the firm will therefore be needed. This will depend on the firm's billing and collection procedures (discussed in paragraph 29.2.1), and the firm's experience of debtor days and aged debt. For example, previous history may show that a certain percentage of invoices are paid within one, two and three months of billing. The budget may show the predicted billing pattern, and the two can then be used to predict incoming cash. The payment of expenses is usually easier to predict, although there will be some budgeted items that may be impossible to time (for example, repairs).

Cash flow histories will show that there may be peaks and troughs giving rise to cash shortages or surpluses of cash at different, though often predictable, times of the year. With planning, these peaks and troughs may be capable of being smoothed out. A bank will expect to see a cash flow forecast, too, when agreeing overdraft facilities.

29.2.3   *Cash flow and realisation*

Many law firms' budgets are deceptive because they are based on the *capacity* of the firm to produce income. The budget assumption is usually that the firm's lawyers have a certain number of hours available, and that those hours are worth so much money. There is, in fact, a process known as the 'degradation of realisation'. Of the hours available, not all will be chargeable. Of the chargeable hours recorded, not all will actually be charged to clients because of write-offs. Of the hours that are chargeable, not all will sustain the standard charge-out rate. Of the bills rendered, not all will be paid. If 10% is lost at each stage, the firm only recovers in cash about 65% of the value of its capacity. Cash flow is, therefore, the actual cash realised from the firm's business activities. Cash — as well as profit — can be maximised by improving the utilisation and realisation at each stage (that is, by improving productivity), as well as by improving and speeding up the billing and collection procedures.

If this degradation is not reflected in the valuation of work-in-progress shown in the firm's balance sheet, its current assets may be overstated and there may then be a false view of the firm's working capital (see paragraph 29.4) and cash flow.

29.2.4   *Cash flow in litigation*

A litigation practice brings its own cash flow difficulties because of the time lag between taking instructions and resolving a dispute. Appendix B of the Law Society's booklet, *Civil Litigation: A Guide to Good Practice* offers guidance on such issues as:

(a)   obtaining payments on account;
(b)   security for costs and/or lien;
(c)   agreed fees;
(d)   interim billing (drawing the important distinction between a 'statute bill' and a 'bill on account');
(e)   transfers to or payment into office account;
(f)   the VAT consequences.

It is an appropriate reminder to all practitioners of the opportunities for speeding up cash flow.

29.3   What is Capital?

Although there are many definitions of capital, it can generally be broken down into working capital and fixed capital: these categories essentially correspond to short-term and long-term requirements. Working capital is the money necessary for the daily operations of the firm; fixed capital is the money necessary to pay for the acquisition of fixed (capital) assets, such as furniture and technology.

If a firm could borrow the money it needed from a bank, it would eliminate all the unpleasantness about partners making capital contributions, buying into partnership, and paying out capital when partners die, retire or defect. Unfortunately, there are few (if any) banks who will today allow law firms to borrow for all their capital needs. Law firms were once considered one of the safest of all credit risks, but recent experience has shown that they (like all businesses) can, and do, fail. The risk is exacerbated by the tendency for partners to move between firms more than they used to. As these mobile know-how assets move on, they deprive a borrowing firm of vital sources of revenue generation but nevertheless leave the outstanding debt behind. As a result, banks want to see new borrowing structured differently (and may even want previous borrowing to be restructured). They will require more capital to be contributed by the partners themselves (to reduce the total amounts borrowed), and will want more recourse in securing the firm's debts, often in the form of personal guarantees (to reduce the risk to the bank).

It is unusual these days to find a law firm that is overcapitalised. Such a situation would be most likely to occur because partners' drawings are set at a low level relative to total net profit and the firm rarely relies on bank overdraft to fund shortfalls in working capital. These firms essentially 'capitalise' themselves by taking very low drawings during the year and only distributing large sums once or twice a year. They are using pre-tax income to fund operations and avoid bank debt except to fund the acquisition of equipment or other capital assets. However, they do incur an opportunity cost by forgoing personal cash flow throughout the year.

29.4   Working Capital

Working capital is normally defined by accountants as the excess of current assets (such as cash, debtors and work-in-progress) over current liabilities (such as creditors and borrowings): after paying all of its recurring expenses, how much money does the firm have left over? Partners who understand this concept, and have a good grasp of the firm's working capital requirements, have a much better basis for determining how much money is available to be distributed to them. Certainly, if the business is managed and operated correctly, it should be generating enough cash to pay partners on a regular basis.

Firms need to be circumspect if work-in-progress is included on the balance sheet as a current asset. It is not cash, and the billing and collection procedures in the firm may mean that it takes many months to convert work-in-progress into cash. When considering whether or not the firm's working capital is adequate (see paragraphs 29.4.2 and 30.2.7), adjustments to the value of work-in-progress may be needed.

29.4.1 *Making up the shortfall*

At some time in almost every business there will not be enough working capital to meet all the demands placed on it. Until relatively recently, fluctuations in working capital were balanced out by overdraft facilities: partners' capital was used to fund capital assets. But working capital is the result of good billing practices. For as long as the bank is effectively funding short-term needs (albeit through a discretionary facility repayable on demand) there is little incentive for partners to adopt the very best billing practices. However, if they have to make up any shortfall in working capital personally (by putting more money into the firm, or taking less out), there is a much closer correlation between behaviour and rewards. In successful firms these days, therefore, it is working capital that the firm requires to be contributed by the partners.

29.4.2 *Determining working capital requirements*

Trying to determine the firm's requirements for working capital can often be a difficult exercise. In essence, a firm should try to build a level of working capital that allows it to cover four likely needs:

(a) *The cash flow requirements of the firm's billing and collections cycle, including any disbursements (costs advanced for clients) and any write-offs.* There is often an assumption that speeding up the billing and collection process will increase working capital. It will certainly speed up the conversion of work into cash, but it will not increase working capital. The reason for this is that work-in-progress, bills delivered (debtors) and cash will normally already be included on the balance sheet as current assets. Turning work-in-progress into bills, or bills delivered into cash, may move money from one category to another but does not affect the total figure for current assets. Nor will using the cash generated by collections to reduce an overdraft affect the numbers: cash is reduced (to pay off the overdraft) so the current assets decrease, but the current liabilities are reduced by a corresponding amount (as the overdraft is reduced). The surplus of current assets over current liabilities — the working capital — remains exactly the same. The only firms for which this does not hold good is those which do not include work-in-progress on their balance sheets: turning work-in-progress into bills will then increase current assets, and so working capital. Such firms ought, however, to include an element of work-in-progress when reviewing the adequacy of the working capital disclosed by the balance sheet (cf. paragraph 30.2.7).

(b) *A cushion for normal expenses and partners' drawings during predicted cash flow cycles.* Tracking cash flow fluctuations over a sufficient length of time to see that certain times of the year are better or worse than others is therefore a necessary part of working capital management.

(c) *Any growth and expansion plans.* For example, if the firm recruits additional assistants, working capital will be needed to pay their salaries and associated overheads until they can generate sufficient cash flow to cover their own costs.

(d) *Future obligations to retired, dead or disabled partners who have a claim on future income or capital of the practice.*

Some firms use convenient rules of thumb to assess their working capital requirements, although these address only the first two of the needs identified above. One technique is to set the level equivalent to three months' expenses: some firms include partners' drawings in the calculation, others do not (in my view, drawings and anticipated distributions should be included, because partners are part of the firm's fee-earning resource and will expect some level of regular reward for their services in the same way as other fee-earners). Another is to use a percentage of gross fees (usually somewhere between 5 and 8%). However, it is more important to have the right amount than to follow slavishly someone else's formula: see also the discussion of working capital adequacy in paragraph 30.2.7.

I have already pointed out that billing and collection may not have any direct effect on the measure of working capital. They do, however, affect cash flow. And to the extent that working capital turnover is not generating sufficient cash for operations, cash will have to be found from somewhere else — the partners or the bank. Variables that affect cash flow may include:

(a) delays in collecting money from clients (i.e., an increase in debtors);

(b) increases in unbilled disbursements;

(c) investments made in recruiting additional lawyers;

(d) servicing debt.

All of these may therefore give rise to the need for additional paid-in capital from partners to fund working capital.

29.5 Fixed Capital

Traditionally, partners paid money into a law firm to cover the cost of fixed assets. This capital was, as its name suggests, fixed — it represented the permanent capital requirement of the business. As such, it was irreducible, and unrealisable (until, for whatever reason, someone ceased to be a partner). Indeed, as firms grew, and as their requirements for investment in technology increased, fixed capital also needed to increase. Even without growth and further investment, the maintenance of the stock of fixed assets requires fixed capital at least to keep in line with replacement costs and inflation.

29.5.1 *Replacing fixed assets*

Most fixed assets are wasting assets and, as such, will need replacing. Depending on the nature of the asset, this may only be a few years (e.g., computers) or several (e.g., furniture). In accounting terms, the ability to replace fixed assets is achieved through depreciation. It is not possible for a business to deduct the cost of a *capital* item when computing *income*. As a result, expenditure on fixed assets is not deductible from business income in order to calculate profit. In essence, therefore, the whole of the cost may be incurred but it is not deductible. However, the asset is being used to generate profit and in the process is wasting or deteriorating.

An accounting entry is therefore allowed to reduce income by the amount of the annual depreciation on fixed assets. Accountants will agree the appropriate period of amortisation for any given asset. Accordingly, both business income and the value of the fixed assets are reduced by the amount of the depreciation. An amount of income equal to depreciation, and which would otherwise have been distributable as net profit, is thus 'hived off' or converted into capital. On the firm's balance sheet, the overall value of the partners' capital (equity) in the business will not have been reduced, however. The net effect of these accounting entries is therefore to convert part of the value of an asset into cash that can be used to replace the asset in due course.

The position is complicated in most jurisdictions by the tax rules. These also disallow the deduction of capital expenses in computing taxes on income. They usually also disallow the accountants' entries for depreciation and substitute in their place a system of capital allowances. The effect of the tax rules on capital expenditure must also therefore be carefully considered.

Fixed capital is thus a critical element in cash flow because the purchase of a capital asset requires an outlay of cash for which there is not a corresponding deduction for tax purposes. Many firms (with strong encouragement from their bankers) now match the repayment of debt on borrowings for the purchase of assets with the depreciation of the asset over its useful life — in other words, to match a non-cash expense (depreciation) with a non-expense cash item (the repayment of principal on the asset finance). This helps to ensure that the firm has sufficient cash available to maintain drawings and distributions to partners.

Even if partners wanted to pay for the entire cost of furniture, equipment, technology, and so on at the time of purchase, there are very few firms with sufficient cash to do so. Typically, fixed assets are funded (and therefore fixed capital provided) through bank borrowings or leasing arrangements. In this way, the lender has an asset which offers some security against the borrowing, and the firm can spread the cost of an asset over its useful life. It also allows a firm effectively to spread the responsibility for paying for the asset among the present *and future* partners who will benefit from it.

29.5.2 *Determining fixed capital requirements*

To some extent, it may not be too difficult to see which assets will need replacing, and this replacement needs to be part of the firm's future plans for fixed capital expenditure. The harder task is to foresee the need to invest in new (rather than replacement) assets. There is no foolproof method, though the firm's strategy should provide a framework for anticipating future requirements. The following will be needed:

(a) longer-range forecasts for office space, technology and investments in practice areas (including the need for more lawyers and staff);

(b) an assessment of revenue and cost changes resulting from the firm's strategy;

(c) a plan for implementing changes in the firm's technology;

(d) a plan for consolidations and improvements to the firm's facilities.

29.6 Quantifying Total Capital Requirements

The total requirement for capital will therefore depend principally on:

(a) cash flow requirements (see paragraph 29.2.2);

(b) working capital requirements (see paragraph 29.4.2);

(c) fixed capital requirements (see paragraph 29.5.2).

These factors may be affected by the general economic climate (e.g., the recessionary or inflationary cycle), the interest rate environment (affecting the ability to borrow and the cost of money), and possibly the state of foreign markets. Changes in general economic conditions are usually reflected in more specific aspects of finance: for example, an economic downturn will lead to clients paying later, which will result in an increase in debtors and debtor days. They will also be affected by events which are firm-specific (such as recruitment, mergers, or office moves). Law firms should therefore re-examine their capital requirements on a regular basis (at least annually). The issue should also be considered when there are significant changes in the levels of debtors (accounts receivable), disbursements, the firm's borrowings, or in the number of the firm's lawyers, and when new partners are admitted. Changing the nature or emphasis of the firm's practice may also lead to change: for example, opening a new office, merging with or acquiring another firm, or starting or expanding a litigation practice typically lead to a need for more capital to meet cash flow needs (see paragraph 29.2.4).

Typical warning signs that capital levels are inadequate would include:

(a) the firm becoming too reliant on its bankers or other lenders to fund cash flow (for example, by having to borrow on overdraft, month after month, just to survive);

(b) increasing levels of work-in-progress and debtors without a corresponding increase in cash collected over the same period;

(c) increasing amounts of unpaid invoices that are remaining unpaid after the firm's 'normal' collection period (i.e., an increase in debtor days);

(d) inability to pay partners' drawings on a regular basis.

The division of the total capital requirement among partners will depend on how it is funded (see paragraph 29.7), and the firm's capital policy (see paragraph 29.8).

29.7 Sources of Funds

There are only two principal sources of finance for law firms — the partners themselves, or third parties. How the total capital requirement is financed will ultimately depend on the philosophy, character and culture of the firm (see paragraph 29.8).

29.7.1 Partners

As we shall see in paragraph 29.8, partners' capital was historically the basis on which law firms financed their operations, and is still a significant source of funds for most firms. It can be provided in one or both of two ways:

(a) *Paid-in capital*. Partners (or their families) actually dig into their private resources and pay money into the firm. This might be achieved by:

(i) a one-off payment;

(ii) buying in over a predetermined time by paying in so much a year;

(iii) a partner organising his or her own borrowing to cover the capital requirement (see paragraph 29.7.2(b));

(iv) the firm withholding a portion of the partner's profits over a period of time and converting the retained profit into capital: rather than require partners to find money to contribute as capital, it used to be common for firms to withhold some percentage of a partner's profit share, allowing the partner to build up his or her capital contribution over a predetermined period of time; although this method is still used, pressures on law firm finances mean that it is just as likely that an incoming partner will be required to take out a bank loan for the full amount of the capital contribution (see (iii));

(v) contributing assets with an agreed capital value (e.g., furniture, equipment, work-in-progress from a previous practice).

In all cases, the amount of paid-in capital contributed is recorded in a partner's capital account.

(b) *Undistributed profits*. In some cases, partners do not withdraw the whole of their net profit (which is recorded in their current accounts). By leaving cash in the firm, cash flow is improved. This is using current account surpluses as available cash, rather than (as in (a)) increasing paid-in capital. However, since profits are taxed when earned (rather than when distributed), the full amount of tax has to be paid whether profits are distributed or not. Many partners therefore see little incentive to leave taxed profits in the partnership. The partners may decide, however, to capitalise some of their after-tax profits by transferring money from their current accounts to their capital accounts.

Firms may consider borrowing money from partners (as opposed to seeking capital contributions). It is not a method favoured by many firms, but does represent an alternative to bank borrowings. It assumes that at least some of the partners have sufficient private wealth to be able to lend to the practice, that they are willing to do so, and that they can agree terms with the partnership. However, the result of such 'internal' borrowing may be disproportionate 'ownership' interests in the lending partners.

29.7.2 *Third parties*

The most common type of third-party funding is, of course, from the firm's bankers. Increasingly, however, law firms (like other businesses) are using other providers of finance for equipment and other fixed assets. There are essentially three forms of bank funding:

(a) *Overdraft.* In recent years, clients have been taking longer to pay their bills, and firms have been turning to bank overdraft to cover cash shortfalls. The danger, however, is that firms will become too reliant on this source of funds, which many are finding difficult to repay out of cash flow. A well-managed firm should seek not to be using its overdraft facility for at least 30 consecutive days a year. This is the indicator often needed to reassure the bank (and the partners) that the firm is not totally dependent on its bankers.

(b) *Loans to partners.* To finance a capital contribution, individual partners will borrow (usually from the firm's bankers and on more favourable terms than they might otherwise achieve). The loan is guaranteed by the firm, and is paid off in accordance with whatever terms are agreed between the partner and the bank. If the partner leaves the firm before the loan is repaid, the firm will usually pay off the loan before making any capital payments direct to the former partner.

(c) *Long-term debt.* This is perhaps now the most difficult area of borrowing for law firms, and one which has seen a complete sea change in attitude from the banks. Law firms that were once able to obtain a loan without so much as providing a profit and loss statement are finding that times have changed dramatically. Banks are now likely to examine at least three years' profit and loss accounts and balance sheets. They may prepare cash flow statements to see how the firm uses cash. They may look at many of the key financial indicators (see chapter 30), and especially look at whether partners' drawings and distributions exceed net profit — in other words, does the firm have a history of borrowing money to fund drawings? More sophisticated lenders will prepare projections to give them some sense of the firm's ability to repay debt. And increasingly, banks will require monthly or quarterly progress reports on the firm's financial position.

In addition to a financial analysis, banks often attempt to assess their risk by considering a firm's market position and internal management. For example, they will examine the types of clients a firm has, their reputation, whether there is an unusual concentration of clients in a particular industry or activity, whether there is a concentration of lawyers in a single practice area, whether the firm is too dependent on a few clients (or partners), and so on. Obviously, this is a subjective analysis, but firms that have never tried to answer such questions would be well-advised to consider them before the bank asks them. Lenders may also assess the quality of the firm's management, the cohesion of the partnership, trends and projections in the growth and demographics of the partnership, billing and write-off policies and procedures, controls on the acceptance of new clients and work, quality management and negligence claims.

I have so far assumed that third party financing is achieved by borrowing. Of course, the firm's cash flow can also be improved by delaying payments to creditors (that is, by managing its accounts payable to maintain cash in the bank), and by asking clients for payments on account of costs or disbursements (or both).

29.7.3 Sale and leaseback

There is a third option available on a one-off basis to firms that own property (usually their own offices). A sale and leaseback will put cash in the hands of the property-owning partners, but still leave the firm in its existing premises (though now paying a market rent). In the process, however, the partners may have deprived themselves of an asset that could have been used as security for the firm's borrowings. Such a sale would allow partners to contribute capital in the form of cash. The overall capital of the firm may well not change (if the premises were part of the firm's fixed assets), but its liquidity will have improved.

There are often good partnership reasons for making such a sale, in addition to the financial benefit of raising cash which can be used by the practice to fund operations rather than being tied up in an asset. When the senior or founding partners have acquired the freehold of the offices from which the firm practises, there usually comes a time when buying into this asset becomes a prohibitive cost for junior partners wishing to enter the equity partnership. One option is for the senior partners to continue to own the premises and charge the partnership a rent for their use. While undoubtedly proper, such a move may alienate the junior partners who feel that they have been excluded from an investment club (although with property prices going the way they did in the early 1990s, this became less of a problem!). They may also feel that the senior partners are holding the practice to ransom, or that they are using the property as a way of extracting more profit from the practice.

29.7.4 *Interest on capital*

Partners often wonder whether they should be paid interest on the capital they have invested in the firm. This is part of the philosophy or policy of capitalisation on which there will be different views and preferences. In terms of measuring the partners' return on their investment in the firm, one certainly ought to consider the opportunity cost of investing the same amount of money elsewhere (see paragraph 7.3). However, there is a difference between making comparisons, and actually making payments. Clearly, if the partners are making loans to the firm (see paragraph 29.7.1 above), the question of interest payments does arise — but this is a loan, not a capital contribution.

If partners share profits equally, and contribute capital equally, all are bearing the same opportunity cost, and many will argue that there is no compelling reason for paying interest on capital. Similarly, if partners contribute capital in proportion to their shares in profits, the opportunity cost-benefit falls proportionately, and so again the question of paying interest perhaps should not arise. It would therefore seem that the only situation where interest on capital ought to be paid as a matter of obligation more than of philosophy is where partners have made disproportionate contributions to capital which are not reflected in relative earnings. This may well be the case where partners have been with the firm for a long period of time and perhaps have accumulated different balances on their capital accounts as a result of undrawn profits, uneven calls for capital, and so on: some firms would take steps in these circumstances to equalise, or at least 'proportionalise', the partners' capital accounts.

For the reasons explored in paragraph 8.9, however, I believe that whether or not interest is paid, a market rate of interest on contributed capital should always be taken into account in order to assess the true return to the business risks taken by the equity partners as entrepreneurs.

29.8 Capitalisation Policies

Historically, incoming partners were required to buy a proportion of the firm. This required a valuation (usually fixed assets plus work-in-progress and debtors, less debts) on the basis of which the new partner's share would be calculated. Such a valuation combined fixed and working capital. Effectively, therefore, when a new partner was admitted, she was buying an interest from an existing (or outgoing) partner. This system of 'accrual' capitalisation is still used by some small firms, but tends to show signs of stress as a firm grows. The first sign of trouble is that the cost for new partners to buy into the partnership becomes too high (particularly if the fixed assets include freehold premises). The second sign can occur if a partner leaves the firm and either joins or sets up a competitive practice. Few continuing partners are happy to pay out money to a competitor who is taking clients and therefore a portion of their future profits! The final warning sign (and often the final straw) is that the unfunded retirement obligations to senior partners reach such a high level that the firm cannot afford to pay them or the younger partners simply refuse to honour them. Senior partners who are relying on their firms to fund their future retirement should take notice of the number of law firms that have dissolved over this issue. It is for this reason that most firms now require partners personally to make the maximum permitted contributions out of current profit-shares into personal retirement plans.

As a general rule or trend today, paid-in capital contributions are likely to be required from partners for working capital and will be fixed either equally for all partners, or in the same proportion as they share profits (fluctuations in profit-shares may mean that contributions need to be reviewed and adjusted on a regular, but not necessarily annual, basis). Fixed assets are now usually funded by third-party finance.

As well as a financial reason, there is also a philosophical reason for requiring partners to contribute capital. Some firms have been opposed to the idea of asking partners for money. Unfortunately, such an approach can easily lead to, or reinforce, an 'employee mentality' in partners (cf. paragraph 9.5.2). On this view, the firm is just a place to work and from which to derive an income, and if a better opportunity comes along — or the firm's economic performance deteriorates — it is easy enough to move on. On the other hand, partners who have put money into a firm begin to understand the risks and rewards of ownership, and develop a sense that the firm is 'our business' that depends on them rather than someone else to make it successful.

Setting a capitalisation policy (and implementing any consequential capital restructuring) can be one of the most divisive issues a law firm will face. It is not a subject that can be taken lightly, nor is it a one-off decision. Yet the failure to develop and implement a policy that will carry the firm into the future on a sound basis can have far more devastating consequences. For example, many firms are increasingly dependent on bank overdraft to pay partners' monthly drawings, especially during periods of cash shortages. In the short term, this may not pose a significant problem. But if the firm fails to move out of overdraft for at least 30 consecutive days during the year, it may effectively be mortgaging its future earnings and heading for disaster.

It may be useful to summarise the issues bearing on setting a capitalisation policy for a law firm. Most existing capital structures are the result of serendipity and historical modifications, but rarely any planning. However, these structures will have a bearing on partnership admissions and departures, as well as profit-sharing and retirement planning.

The capitalisation policy should therefore:

(a) achieve an adequate level of contributed capital;
(b) anticipate future needs for capital;
(c) meet the general criteria of banks and other lenders for a sound credit rating;

(d)   take account of the tax consequences on individual partners;

(e)   not cause problems when partners leave the firm;

(f)   be capable of being thought 'fair' by a reasonable consensus of partners;

(g)   be achievable without undue stress on individual partners;

(h)   be consistent with the firm's goals and culture;

(i)   not be unduly complex.

Perhaps the overriding criterion should be that partners must not be required to contribute more than they can reasonably afford.

Chapter 30

INDICATORS OF ECONOMIC PERFORMANCE

30.1 Introduction

A law firm should regularly monitor several key economic indicators. Partners tend to assume that if fee income, profits and profit margins are maintained or improved, all is well. If the number of lawyers or partners is increasing, then fee income and profits need to rise on a per-person basis, as well as overall, otherwise the firm's economic performance is being diluted.

In many respects, the analysis of a law firm's financial performance follows very closely the analyses of trading companies' performance. However, there are differences arising from the very different 'product' of law firms, and the raw material — people and know-how — which have implications for the assessment and analysis of law firms' figures.

30.1.1 Broader economic indicators

The indicators that I describe in paragraph 30.2 are those which are specific to a law firm's *economic* performance. In that sense, I have a very limited purpose in this chapter. However, a law firm that is worth its salt will also want to track indicators of the general performance of the economy to see if they provide any pointers to the future. For example, some of the following may help in forward planning (or thinking through how best to react to changing economic circumstances):

(a)   Gross national product (GNP) and gross domestic product (GDP) are broad indications of economic health: the range of 'normal growth' is usually taken to be 2–5%. If GNP reduces in two successive quarters of a 12-month period, the economy is in recession.

(b)   Inflation rates: when the rate of inflation rises, higher interest rates usually follow (and vice versa).

(c)   Interest rates: when interest rates are rising, it usually means that businesses are borrowing and the economy is improving. Interest is the cost of borrowing money, so rising interest rates mean rising expenses (for everyone) — and for this reason, rising interest rates often lead to falling share prices (lower profits means lower dividends, and interest-bearing investments become more attractive than shares).

(d)   Retail price index: rising expenses or a growing economy lead to producers increasing their prices. Increases in RPI are therefore likely to reinforce the need for a rise in interest rates so that the Bank of England can tighten the money supply in order to control inflation.

(e)   Retail sales: these are a sign of consumer confidence. If retail sales fall significantly — after allowing for the effects of seasonal fluctuations — it is usually because interest rates are high or a recession may be on the way (or already here). If sales fail to pick up, lower interest rates normally follow to stimulate buying. Similar indicators allow the tracking of wholesale sales, as well as industrial production and manufacturing output.

(f)   Housing starts: this is another measure of economic confidence. A falling number of housing starts is a further indicator of recession (and falling property prices) — which also creates good opportunities for those who can afford to buy. The housing market is obviously sensitive to mortgage rates (see interest rates): as they rise, house purchases, and therefore housing starts, can be expected to decline.

(g)   Employment figures: the number of registered unemployed (seasonally adjusted) and the number of unfilled vacancies are another reflection of economic health, and changes in these figures will show underlying trends.

Similar indices are prepared in other countries. Firms who themselves, or whose clients, operate in foreign or global markets will need to monitor these (and international) indicators.

For further reading on this subject, see Vaitilingam (1994).

30.1.2   Beyond the economics

This chapter is intentionally restricted to measures of economic or financial performance. However, in the overall context of a law firm it would be quite wrong to look only at these measures. Indeed, doing so can produce some distorted reactions and behaviour from partners and fee-earners. These issues were explored in paragraphs 20.2.4 and 25.2.

30.2   The Law Firm Indicators

30.2.1   Introduction

This paragraph introduces and describes more indicators than most firms will ever use or need (although it is still not an exhaustive description of the possibilities). Its purpose is to allow any given law office to pick and choose indicators which it finds useful and valuable for any part of its business at a certain time in its development. Some will be almost universally applicable; a number will not be.

As well as watching chargeable hours, billings, expenses, work-in-progress levels, aged debts, and borrowings and cash flow, certain indicators should be tracked and compared on a regular basis. Significant variations should be investigated, and the underlying causes addressed. At a time when greater efficiency and financial awareness are required, and when being lax in financial controls can significantly reduce small profit margins as a consequence of the additional financing costs, these indicators can play a vital role in assessing economic performance. The effect of inflation should also be taken into account to show real underlying differences in year-to-year performance.

The principal indicators are applied by way of illustration in the case study at the end of this chapter.

30.2.2 Fee income

Taking raw data, analysis could show the *percentage of total income derived from fees*, commission, interest, rents, and other sources, as well as the *contribution of each category of fee-earner* to the generation of fee income. Tracked over a period of time, fluctuations from year to year could be shown, together with changes relative to the rate of inflation.

The total amount of fee income is, however, in some ways misleading: it is quite possible for total income to rise but for productivity (and profitability) to be falling. For this reason, *fee income per fee-earner* is a standard measure of law firm productivity — especially when tracked over a period of time. By including other income (e.g., rental income, interest), revenue per fee-earner could also be measured; however, these additional sources of income are dependent on many factors which do not necessarily relate to productivity — which is the principal reason for measuring income on a per fee-earner basis.

If possible, fee income per fee-earner should be measured by different categories of fee-earner (e.g., partners, assistants, paralegals), by type of client and by type of work.

Fees realisation (or the collection ratio) measures fees actually collected as a proportion of fees billed (i.e., taking account of bad debts or bills subsequently written down or written off following complaints from clients). Declining realisation is indicative of clients' economic difficulties as well as a fall in productivity, quality or client satisfaction. Again, tracked on a departmental or individual basis, it can be an indicator of issues to be investigated.

30.2.3 Expenses

As with fee income, law firms often place undue emphasis on the overall level of expenses. *Expenses per fee-earner* figures give a better idea of average growth or fall in expenses. Again, it is best to break down these figures according to type of work or type of client.

Expense ratios can also be used to track the proportion of total overhead attributed to different categories of expenses, such as:

(a)   occupancy costs;
(b)   staff costs (if possible, showing benefits and training as separate items);
(c)   technology costs;
(d)   marketing costs.

The *overhead ratio* (expenses as a percentage of fee income) is often misleading because lawyers tend to focus on the numerator (expenses) rather than the denominator (fee income): see the discussion in paragraph 28.5 suggesting that attention should be paid to maximising income wherever possible rather than trying to improve profitability by reducing expenses. However, the overhead ratio can provide a useful guideline, though the trend is at least as important as the ratio itself: ratios have increased in recent years, and will also tend to increase as firms become larger. The overhead ratio is the complement of the profit margin (see paragraph 30.2.4).

30.2.4 *Profitability*

The absolute level of net profit in a firm is almost a meaningless figure in analytical terms. The *profit margin* (net profit as a percentage of fee income) is the complement of the overhead ratio: as overhead ratios rise, so profit margins fall. Nevertheless, trends in profit margins should be tracked.

Net profit per partner is the most important measure of profitability: unless it is rising in real terms, equity partners will be unhappy and restless. The *profitability index* is a measure of a firm's total effectiveness in using its fee-earners to generate fees and profit. It is calculated by dividing net profit per equity partner by fee income per fee-earner. The index is a measure of the firm's success in converting its leverage (see paragraph 28.4) into profit. Ideally, the index should not be less than 1; however, smaller firms find this difficult to achieve (and sole principals usually impossible). Further, both net profit per partner and the profitability index will be affected by the admission of new partners (or the withdrawal of others) unless there is a corresponding increase in profitability. A *dilution index* can be used to measure the actual or potential dilution of partners' incomes caused by increasing the partnership ranks (see Altonji 1991).

Partnerships must pay reasonable rewards to all partners. The *ratio of high to low profit-shares* demonstrates the egalitarian or other approach to rewards adopted by a firm. The ratio tends to increase as firms become larger and profits increase. However, when the ratio rises above 5 : 1, it is often difficult to say that partners at each end of the scale are truly partners of each other.

The *drawings ratio* (i.e., drawings as a percentage of total distributions) and the *distribution ratio* (i.e., total drawings and distributions as a percentage of net profits) are important measures, showing the extent to which partners are able to withdraw cash from the practice. Firms that cannot maintain ratios in excess of 80% (after provision for tax and agreed future investment) may have difficulty in keeping their partners happy.

30.2.5 Time

Hours recorded per fee-earner can be tracked by category of fee-earner, by department or practice area, and by office, and can show both chargeable and non-chargeable time. This information would probably provide the firm with some much-needed benchmarking to compare productivity, as well as lifestyle or work ethic.

Tracking *chargeable time written off per fee-earner*, and pro bono time, will allow the firm to develop *time utilisation measures* (i.e., the proportion of chargeable time actually billed to clients): this ratio is useful in helping firms to make more accurate assessments of the value of work-in-progress.

Lawyer (or fee-earner) utilisation shows hours recorded as a proportion of hours budgeted. Such an indicator is a preliminary measure of total fee-earning capacity, and as such raises the question of whether the firm appears to be overstaffed or understaffed.

Time realisation shows fees billed as a proportion of the value of chargeable hours recorded: as such it demonstrates how effective the firm is in turning chargeable hours into fees. It is similar to time utilisation, and the results are often similar. However, it is possible to write chargeable time off, but still recover fees through mark-ups relating to other factors.

An additional measure here is also to establish the *true charge-out rate* for the firm by dividing fees collected by the total number of chargeable hours recorded: this can be done by client, matter, fee-earner, type of fee-earner, department or practice area, office, or for the whole firm.

30.2.6 Financing

Some partners are notoriously bad at recognising that failures to bill work-in-progress and to collect invoices due carry with them a working capital or financing cost (see paragraphs 29.2 and 29.4). Most firms now track the outstanding volume of unpaid client invoices, measured either in terms of months of fee income or number of days due — *unpaid bills months* or *debtor days*.

As with unpaid bills, work-in-progress (WIP) can be measured as months of fee income or days to be carried — *WIP months* or *WIP days* — showing how long it takes to turn WIP into bills. By combining it with the unpaid bills period, the total figure (*WIP turnover period* or '*lock-up*') shows how long it usually takes to turn work done into cash: as such, it should help with improving billing and credit control as well as establishing working capital requirements. Further, by combining the time and fees realisation percentages, the firm can establish the *WIP realisation rate* (i.e., the percentage of WIP likely to be turned into cash in the bank) or the *true value of WIP* (i.e., the WIP realisation rate applied to the time-cost value of WIP).

Work-in-progress per fee-earner can be established to show whether WIP is generally increasing or decreasing (as with fee income, expenses and net profit, absolute numbers are generally unhelpful without understanding the underlying productivity).

These calculations involving WIP assume that the firm uses some systematic process of valuing WIP based on time and charge-out rates, rather than guesswork or purely nominal figures.

30.2.7 *Capitalisation*

Capitalisation is a complex subject, and very few firms have not reviewed it in recent years (see chapter 29). A number of ratios might help practitioners.

Fixed assets per fee-earner is a measure of the technological support, furniture and other tangible assets the firm uses to provide legal services to its clients. When fixed assets (net of depreciation) per fee-earner are flat or declining, partners may well be failing to replace worn equipment and may not be keeping pace with better methods of producing work.

Debt per equity partner will show levels of borrowing, and fluctuations during economic cycles. Debt is a form of financial leverage, allowing a firm to spread the cost of payments for acquisitions. Such leverage can make a poor year worse (as interest payments reduce profits, and repayment of borrowings reduces cash available for distribution), as well as a good year better (by not immediately absorbing money to pay for something outright).

Capital per equity partner can be tracked either as partners' total equity in the firm or as working capital (i.e., current assets less current liabilities). Either way, declining capital per equity partner is a sign of potential cash flow problems.

Firms should set a target working capital requirement (for example, three months of expenses and partners' drawings): the target should be set at whatever level makes the partners feel comfortable — it is as much a question of emotion as of finance. Working capital is taken to be net current assets (that is, the excess of current assets over current liabilities). *Working capital adequacy* is then measured as either the number of months for which it will cover the target (working capital months) or as a percentage of the firm's target. On this measure, working capital can only be increased by increasing current assets or decreasing current liabilities. Assuming that a firm prepares its financial statements on a 'bills delivered' basis, simply turning debtors into cash will not of itself increase current assets. This is because, as soon as a bill is issued, the debtor becomes a current asset, along with existing cash; when the client pays the bill, the debtors figure is reduced by the same amount as the cash is increased — leaving current assets at exactly the same figure. On this basis, working capital is increased either by sending out bills more quickly (i.e., reducing work-in-progress — though even this will have no effect on working capital if any element of working capital is included on the balance sheet as a current asset), or by inviting the partners to put more capital (cash) in. Borrowing on overdraft to increase cash 'availability' will increase both current assets and current liabilities, and so does not, in fact, change the level of working capital.

The purpose of calculating working capital adequacy is to assess the firm's short-term ability to finance its operational obligations to suppliers, staff and partners. As such, it is unlikely that adequacy for a period of more than three months should be measured. However, most firms will have a WIP 'lock-up' period in excess of three months; and some may have debtor days in excess of 90. Accordingly, the current asset value of WIP and debtors in the balance sheet should be adjusted. For example, if WIP lock-up is five months, only three-fifths of WIP should be included as a current asset for the purposes of computing three-month working capital adequacy.

Financial stability or solvency can be measured in the traditional ways:

(a) in the short term, by using the *current ratio* (i.e., current assets as a proportion of current liabilities): this should be greater than 1, reflecting the ability to generate sufficient cash in the short term to meet known expenses; and

(b) in the longer term, by using the *debt-to-equity ratio* (often taken as the proportion of loans and borrowings to partners' capital): this should be less than 1, reflecting sufficient ownership value to repay borrowings.

30.2.8   Personnel indicators

In addition to the financial indicators discussed above, staff ratios can also be used. These measure the leverage of fee-earners who produce work that is sold to clients, and should therefore be maximised — which requires that sufficient work is available to keep them all busy (see paragraph 28.4). They also measure the level of support necessary to help fee-earners service their clients, and these should be minimised to the greatest extent possible without jeopardising the quality or timeliness of client work, or the effective management of the firm.

30.2.8.1   Fee-earner leverage
The *ratio of non-partner fee-earners to equity partners* indicates the leverage that partners are using to produce lawyer-level work (see paragraph 28.4). A high ratio does not necessarily imply good use of others' efforts: it must also be accompanied by sound chargeable hours recorded, billed and collected. The firm can also track the *ratio of qualified to non-qualified fee-earners*: trends may help in the analysis of the firm's requirements for qualified lawyers over a period of time.

30.2.8.2   Support staff leverage
This is measured in two ways:

(a) *fee-earners per secretary*: through the use of technology, an increasing number of firms are producing work with less secretarial support;

however, too high a ratio might affect the time taken for work to be produced unless secretaries can also call on ancillary support for filing, message-taking, photocopying, and so on; and

(b)   *support staff per fee-earner*: this ratio shows the total level of support used by fee-earners; and also whether over a period of time that support is increasing or decreasing in number: by breaking down the different elements of support staff (secretaries, accounts staff, receptionists and telephonists, etc.), a more detailed assessment could be made of the changing support structure in the firm.

30.3   Inter-firm Comparisons

Conducting a financial analysis of one's own firm, and developing and tracking indicators over a period of time, will give partners a good sense of the firm's financial structure, profitability, capitalisation, productivity, and so on. It will show them how the firm is performing over the period of time they look at. It may well give them a sense of satisfaction, if the performance improves as the years go by. However, there is another dimension. The partners may think that their performance is good relative to their own previous performance. But how good, bad or indifferent is it relative to the rest of the profession (or at least those parts of it that can be regarded as comparable)? What is 'normal', 'typical', or 'acceptable' performance for a law firm, given the type of law it practises, its location, its size, its client base, and so on?

In this analysis, lawyers (and others) are hampered by the secrecy that surrounds professional partnerships. There is no requirement to file annual accounts for public scrutiny. As with all things secret, fascination follows: subterfuge, leaks, disaffection and guesswork are employed to tease out the innermost numbers of law firms. In ignorance, imagination runs wild! Recently, however, more information has been published. These include:

(a)   The Law Society's *Annual Statistical Report*: this is perhaps the most extensive and reliable (and therefore, of course, most anonymous). Each annual report provides many useful — if slightly dated — indicators, from which it is possible to assess how a firm is performing relative to the ranges and averages of similarly grouped firms. Some of this information was discussed in paragraph 1.4.

(b)   The Coopers & Lybrand survey: a useful annual review of many different aspects of law firms' financial performance, as well as thoughts from various firms about their expectations for the future.

(c)   *Legal Business 100* and the *AmLaw 100*: for the largest 100 law firms in Britain and the US, respectively, an annual review of the principal economic indicators allows some comparisons to be made between the relative performance of these large firms. Some firms included in these tables dispute the accuracy of the published data.

(d)   The Centre for Interfirm Comparison: this organisation conducts financial analyses of the results of similar firms, and produces a tailor-made report (available only to the firms that participated). Such an approach produces reliable data and comparisons, but is, of course, restricted to self-selecting firms who are prepared to disclose their innermost financial secrets and pay for such a service.

30.4 Case study: Allwright & Co.

In order to demonstrate the use of some of the indicators described in this chapter, the following pages show the profit and loss account, balance sheet, and supplementary information for a hypothetical firm. Various indicators are then calculated based on the accounts and information supplied.

ALLWRIGHT & CO.
PROFIT AND LOSS ACCOUNT FOR THE YEAR ENDED
30 APRIL

	Year 2 £	Year 2 £	Year 1 £	Year 1 £
FEE INCOME		4,377,278		3,793,829
EXPENSES				
Wages and related costs	1,562,868		1,432,629	
Rent	337,798		337,798	
Rates and water	35,429		32,411	
Light, heat and cleaning	31,556		29,121	
Telephone	141,011		126,765	
Insurance	149,569		138,360	
Motor and travelling	54,402		41,487	
Repairs and renewals	30,420		21,562	
Printing, postage and stationery	81,800		62,415	
Equipment leasing	40,356		38,237	
Accountancy and professional	6,237		6,686	
Training, library and subscriptions	7,287		6,154	
Loan interest, bank charges and interest	55,097		81,925	
Bad debts	70,048		91,096	
Sundries	7,182		7,293	
Depreciation	42,414		35,137	
		2,653,474		2,489,076
PROFIT		1,723,804		1,304,753

BALANCE SHEET AS AT 30 APRIL

	Year 2			Year 1
	£	£	£	£
CAPITAL ACCOUNTS		1,155,424		935,515
FIXED ASSETS		531,495		468,485
Current assets				
Debtors and				
prepayments	1,425,623		1,489,054	
Cash in hand	831		457	
	1,426,454		1,489,511	
Current liabilities				
Creditors and				
accruals	325,641		369,068	
Loan	200,000		200,000	
Overdraft	276,884		453,413	
	802,525		1,022,481	
NET CURRENT ASSETS		623,929		467,030
NET ASSETS		1,155,424		935,515

STAFFING

	Year 1	Year 2
Equity partners	9	10
Salaried partners	7	6
Assistants	13	15
Total lawyers	29	31
Trainees and paralegals	5	5
Secretaries	24	25
Administrative staff	19	19
Total staff	77	80

STAFFING RATIOS

	Year 1	Year 2
Other fee-earners to equity partners (note 1)	2.5	2.35
Support staff to fee-earners (note 2)	1.37	1.31
Fee-earners to secretaries (note 3)	1.31	1.34

Notes:
1. Assumes trainees and paralegals are treated as 0.5 fee-earners: other
   fee-earners for year 1 (7 + 13 + 2.5 = 22.5) ÷ 9 equity partners
   = 2.5.

2. Secretaries and administrative staff (24 + 19 = 43) ÷ fee-earners
    (9 equity partners + 22.5 other fee-earners = 31.5) = 1.37.
3. Fee-earners (31.5) ÷ secretaries (24) = 1.31.

PROFITABILITY

(Assume that the solicitors' index of inflation April year 1 to April year 2
= 2.3%: the inflation-adjusted figures* revise the year 2 figures to show
them in year 1 'real terms')

	Year 1	Year 2	Inflation adjusted*
Fee income	£3,793,829	£4,377,278	£4,276,601
Expenses	£2,489,076	£2,653,474	£2,592,444
Net Profit	£1,304,753	£1,723,804	£1,684,157
Profit Margin (note 4)	34.4%	39.4%	
Fee income per fee-earner (note 5)	£120,439	£130,665	£127,660
Expenses per fee-earner (note 6)	£79,018	£79,208	£77,386
Expense ratios:			
(a) occupancy costs (note 7)	16.9%	16.4%	
(b) wages and related costs (note 8)	57.6%	58.9%	
Wages and related costs per employee (note 9)	£21,068	£22,327	£21,813
Net profit per equity partner (note 10)	£144,973	£172,380	£168,415
Profitability index (note 11)	1.20	1.32	

Notes:

4. Net profit (£1,304,753) ÷ fee income (£3,793,829) = 34.4%.
5. Fee income £3,793,829) ÷ fee-earners (31.5: see note 2) =
    £120,439.
6. Expenses (£2,489,076) ÷ fee-earners (31.5) = £79,018).
7. Occupancy costs (rent, rates and water, light, heat and cleaning, and
    repairs and renewals = £420,892) ÷ expenses (£2,489,076) =
    16.9%.
8. Wages and related costs (£1,432,629) ÷ expenses (£2,489,076) =
    57.6%.
9. Wages and related costs (£1,432,629) ÷ employees (total staff (77)
    − equity partners (9) = 68) = £21,068).
10. Net profit (£1,304,753) ÷ equity partners (9) = £144,973.
11. Net profit per equity partner (£144,973: see note 10) ÷ fee income
    per fee-earner (£120,439: see note 5) = 1.20.

CAPITALISATION AND FINANCING

	Year 1	Year 2	Inflation adjusted
Capital per equity partner (note 12)	£103,946	£115,542	£112,884
Fixed assets per fee-earner (note 13)	£14,873	£15,866	£15,501
Creditors per equity partner (note 14)	£41,008	£32,564	£31,815
Debt per equity partner (note 15)	£72,601	£47,688	£46,591
Work-in-progress (note 16)	£1,876,507	£2,092,593	£2,044,463
WIP per fee-earner (note 17)	£59,572	£62,465	£61,029
Months of revenue (note 18)	5.94	5.74	
Debtors	£1,489,054	£1,425,623	£1,392,834
Debtors per fee-earner (note 19)	£47,272	£42,556	£41,577
Months of revenue (note 20)	4.71	3.91	
Total months of revenue in WIP and debtors (lock-up)	(note 21)	10.65	9.65
Short-term solvency: current ratio (note 22)	146%	178%	
Long-term solvency: debt-to-equity (note 23)	70%	41%	
Working capital adequacy (note 24)	172%	251%	

Notes:
12. Capital (£935,515) ÷ equity partners (9) = £103,946.
13. Fixed assets (£468,485) ÷ fee-earners (31.5: see note 2) = £14,873.
14. Creditors (£369,068) ÷ equity partners (9) = £41,008.
15. Debt (loan and overdraft = £653,413) ÷ equity partners (9) = £72,601.
16. Work-in-progress is not included on the firm's balance sheet: this figure is taken from the firm's management accounts, and represents unbilled time at standard charge-out rates.
17. WIP (£1,876,507) ÷ fee-earners (31.5: see note 2) = £59,572.
18. Revenue per month is fee income (£3,793,829) ÷ 12 = £316,152; WIP expressed as months of revenue is WIP (£1,876,507) ÷ revenue per month (£316,512) = 5.94.
19. Debtors (£1,489,054: technically, one should take out prepayments and other non-client debtors) ÷ fee-earners (31.5: see note 2) = £47,272.
20. Debtors (£1,489,054: cf. note 19) ÷ revenue per month (£316,152: see note 18) = 4.71.

21. WIP months (5.94: see note 18) + debtor months (4.71: see note 20) = 10.65.
22. Current assets £1,489,511) ÷ current liabilities (£1,022,481) × 100 = 146%.
23. Debt (loan and overdraft = £653,413) ÷ equity (capital accounts = £935,515) × 100 = 70%.
24. Working capital adequacy is a matter of comfort rather than of accounting principles, and each firm should make its own judgment: see paragraph 30.2.7. The partners in Allwright & Co. have determined that they would like the firm's working capital to cover three months' expenses and three months' drawings for equity partners (they draw at £7,500 a month each). They therefore require expenses cover of £2,489,076 ÷ 4 = £622,269, and drawings cover of 9 × £7,500 × 3 = £202,500, giving a total of £824,769. Working capital is £467,030 (net current assets): however, WIP is not included on the balance sheet, and it would be reasonable to assume that some amount of this would be billed during the next three months. If three months' worth of the WIP is treated as a current asset ((3/5.94 × £1,876,507 = £947,731), this would increase the net current assets to £1,414,761 (£467,030 + £947,731). This would give working capital adequacy of £1,414,761 ÷ £824,769 = 172%. This suggests that the equity partners can feel very comfortable about the level of working capital, but it does assume that WIP will be turned into bills: financial management will therefore be crucial.

Chapter 31

THE COST AND VALUE OF TIME

31.1 Introduction

For many lawyers, time recording is a burden — a type of 'spy in the cab' mechanism that they would prefer to do without. In order to understand the proper role of time recording, we must look at its development and wider benefits.

Time recording was first 'sold' to the legal profession as a way of measuring the cost of providing legal services. By comparing the hours spent on various aspects of client work with the overhead cost of running the practice, the hourly cost rate (or expense of time) can be calculated. For many lawyers, these calculations were a revelation. They had no idea how much it actually cost them to serve clients (except by referring to the total cost of overheads); they had only a 'feeling' that their charges were rendering a profit; and they consistently underestimated the time they spent on client work. Time recording was, then, a major contributor to greater financial awareness within many law firms and for some of them resulted in increased billings.

Unfortunately, however, time recording was then hijacked. From knowing the hourly cost of providing legal services, it is but a short step to adding on a profit element and coming out with an hourly charge-out rate — a charge that can be used for calculating fees based on the amount of time spent on a client's matter. On the face of it, this is a fair way of charging clients for legal services (at least compared with the old method of weighing the file and guessing at what the client could afford). But subsequent experience has shown that the ability to record time shows nothing more than the ability to record time. If clients are charged by the hour, there is little incentive for lawyers to carry out their work quickly and efficiently, for the longer they work on a matter the more a client will have to pay.

Such a system has no intrinsic merit. It overlooks the value of a matter (and of the advice given), and bears no necessary relation to the expertise brought to bear by the lawyer involved. We all know that a piece of advice that may save the client many hundreds or thousands of pounds can be given in a very short space of time; conversely, relatively simple advice may take longer to produce and have less value to the client. So we have been hooked on a system designed for one purpose being used for a different purpose for which it was not designed and is ill-equipped. Time-based billing rewards the inefficient and even the incompetent, and may not reward the truly high-value advice. Of course, lawyers have tried to overcome this unfairness by adding on a further profit element (permitted by the Law Society's professional rules) when the value of the transaction or advice reflects complexity, speed, value or various other factors. Clients do not particularly object to this, but they are never too happy to receive low-value advice for which the lawyer insists on a minimum time-based fee.

This confusion of time with billing has had many unfortunate side-effects. The performance of lawyers, or even whole departments, has been assessed on their ability to record time and turn that time into fees billed. Whole appraisal and reward or bonus schemes have been built around the fallacy of the results of time-recording. Promotion, career development and even redundancy have been decided on the mirage of these figures.

Client surveys show that clients distinguish between effort and results when they assess whether they receive value for money from their lawyers, and their principal (or only) focus is on results. Time-recording at best can only measure a lawyer's effort: it bears no relation to the results perceived by clients. It is therefore a very crude approximation to assessing the value of legal services to clients.

31.2 The Real Purpose of Time-recording

The only real value and purpose of time-recording are to provide management information on the basis of which partners can make sensible and informed decisions about their firm. The information can be used for billing purposes, but only to determine the real cost of providing advice: the challenge being offered by clients now is to find a method of billing that reflects the value of the advice given and is fair to both lawyer and client (rather than just to the lawyer). Without some measure of the 'baseline' of the cost of providing a service, it may be very difficult to assess value added.

The information that the firm can glean from its time-recording system includes the following:

(a)   The way in which time is spent by various lawyers or departments: this will typically include both chargeable and non-chargeable time. From this information, the firm can determine the average time spent on chargeable work, how long certain matters usually take to handle, where there are peaks and troughs within departments and between departments, how much time to budget in the forthcoming year for various levels of lawyer in the firm (or even for specific lawyers), how much time is spent on research, training, marketing, management, and so on.

(b)   On the basis of recorded hours, the firm can create income budgets (subject to the usual caveat about not equating the value of time recorded with fees to be billed), and establish financial standards against which to monitor work-in-progress levels, financial performance and profitability.

(c)   Variations in workload can be used to establish staffing and recruitment needs.

Time-recording can also be used as the basis for setting productivity standards for routine work.

These are all vital management activities which, without time-recording, would be difficult and in some cases impossible. The partners do not in fact need a time-recording system to allow them to assess fees (although it may provide useful additional information), and they should not need it to know whether their lawyers are working hard or hard enough.

The popular misconceptions about the role of time-recording continue to lead many lawyers astray. They also result in the imaginative and creative recording of time: lawyers whose performance will be measured against targets based on time recorded will do all they can to ensure that they meet their target. This may mean over-recording time on certain matters, keeping work to themselves that they should hand over to someone more senior, more junior, or more specialised, and generally stacking the numbers in their own favour. Once this happens, the value of the information recorded becomes negligible — even for the purpose of assessing individual performance.

31.3   Accuracy and Consistency of Time-recording

Time-recording must be done as accurately as possible if the information is to have any value. Above all, therefore, fee-earners must be encouraged (or required) not to make performance or billing decisions at the time they fill in their time sheets. They should faithfully record the time they have actually spent on their various activities. It is someone else's decision to decide how much of that time is to be billed to a client.

There are some grey areas where different firms have different policies or, indeed, no policies at all. Take the following situations:

(a)   A lawyer is asked to research a particular point on behalf of client A. It takes five hours. The next day, someone else asks the same lawyer to prepare a memorandum on exactly the same point for client B. It takes one hour. Does the lawyer record five hours, one hour, or three hours for each client? The answer is to record the actual time spent: the billing partner is the person who decides how much the firm wishes to charge the client for the advice or memorandum (and should take the client's concept of the value of the advice or memorandum into account in doing so). Even if the point researched is something that the lawyer felt he or she should have known anyway, the actual time spent should still be recorded. The lawyer may, of course, want to put a note on the relevant client file to remind the billing partner of the issue when she reviews it for billing purposes.

(b)   During the course of a matter, a fee-earner spends several hours with a more senior lawyer not producing anything of value to the client but in being trained or supervised. It may not be clear when the time sheet is completed whether or not the client should be charged for this time, so the firm should establish how the time should be recorded — as chargeable time (that may subsequently be written down or written off), or as non-chargeable training time.

(c)   There are other grey areas. For example, the time that a lawyer spends supervising other fee-earners involved in a matter; the time a specialist spends answering detailed questions on points of law or practice arising from matters being handled by other lawyers in the firm; the time spent being 'entertained' by clients looking for some free or cheap advice. In each case, the principle should remain: record accurately the time actually spent on each activity. If it relates to client work, record the time against that matter: the appropriate billing partner will make the charging decision at some subsequent time. Subjective judgments about the value of the time to the client should be discouraged. Be sure that fee-earners understand whatever time-recording policies your firm has.

Training may well be needed: workshops based on hypotheticals are often best. You might be surprised that, although you might think the time-recording issues are simple and unambiguous, others will record the same events and elapsed times in any number of idiosyncratic (or creative) ways!

31.4   Recording Non-chargeable Time

If the real purpose of time-recording is to provide an accurate picture of how lawyers spend their time so that management and strategic decisions can be made, then it must follow that non-chargeable time should be recorded as well. The categories should be limited and well-defined, and there should be as little temptation as possible for fee-earners to use them as a 'dumping ground' for otherwise chargeable time for which they cannot find a suitable home.

The appropriate categories might include:

(a)   non-chargeable client work (e.g., pro bono);
(b)   travel (distinguishing client-related and firm-related travel);
(c)   invoicing;
(d)   client development and entertainment;
(e)   marketing and prospecting for new business;
(f)   marketing research/preparing marketing materials/newsletters, etc.;
(g)   departmental and other internal meetings;

(h)   writing books or articles;
(i)   continuing education/attending seminars, etc.;
(j)   training or supervising others;
(k)   management (as, for example, head of department, managing
partner, training partner, member of committee).

Just as many firms set targets for chargeable work, so they may choose
to set them for different non-chargeable activities. This information can
be used in performance assessments, and can allow the firm to begin to
manage expectations about what is a 'respectable' use of time within
the firm. In this way, it can improve (but still manage and monitor) the
amount of time spent on the range of activities that is required in a
balanced and successful law firm.

31.5   Time-recording and Budgeting

Provided recorded chargeable time is not equated with invoices to be
issued, fee income projections can become more realistic with accurate
time-recording. As long as fee-earners are not making billing decisions at
the point of time-recording, a more realistic picture of the firm's fee
potential can be built up. If the time-recording is not accurate, fee-earners
will distort the firm's financial information, and make it impossible to
assess the true productivity and profitability of lawyers, departments or
areas of practice, different offices, types of work, types of clients, specific
matters and specific clients. The other dimension to profitability —
overheads — may also need allocating, and in many firms some of the
allocation is made on a time basis. Again, without accurate records,
the allocation is distorted.

Many firms with fixed-fee practices or rates set externally still consider
budgeting and time-recording a waste of time. But without them, it is
impossible to monitor the firm's financial performance effectively, or to
examine the profitability of various types of work or individuals in the
firm.

31.6   The Expense of Time

The economic rationale of a law firm is to make a profit. For this purpose,
profit is the excess of the firm's fees and other income over its expenses,
bad debts, notional salaries (market 'wage') for partners, and interest on
capital (see paragraphs 8.9 and 28.1). In order to create and sustain this
excess, therefore, a firm's approach to the efficient delivery of legal
services and their competitive pricing must have a keen appreciation of
the unit cost of providing those services. The usual way of calculating this
is, of course, on an hourly time-costing basis, and this requires accurate
time records.

31.6.1 General principles

The calculation often follows the Law Society's *Expense of Time* guidance. The calculation separates salaries for non-partner lawyers (salary overhead) from the other expenses, including interest on capital (general overhead). At its simplest, it then proceeds:

(a) apportion half of the general overhead to individual fee-earners on a per capita basis (treating part-time fee-earners as an appropriate percentage of a full-time one);

(b) apportion the other half of the general overhead to individual fee-earners in proportion to their share of the fee-earners' salary costs (including notional salaries for partners);

(c) for each fee-earner, add the results of (a) and (b) to his or her salary costs; and

(d) for each fee-earner, divide the result of (c) by the number of chargeable hours that he or she can reasonably be expected to record.

The nature of these calculations serves to emphasise the importance of accurate time-recording. If hours are understated or overstated, they will distort the calculation of the cost of time, and induce the firm to make wrong judgments about the cost, pricing and profitability of the services it provides.

It is possible for firms to be more sophisticated in their approach to these apportionments, for example, by separating out the costs of different departments or practice areas, offices, or types of work. Unless there is a good business reason for doing so (e.g., a legal aid or private client practice conducted from a separate building), the result may not be worth the effort.

31.6.2 Example

Assume:

(a) A regional firm with three equity partners (notional salaries of £26,250 each), a full-time assistant solicitor earning £25,000, a three-quarters-time assistant solicitor earning £15,000, and a full-time legal executive earning £14,500.

(b) Projected expenses for the next 12 months of £340,000 (including inflation and employee salaries).

1. Total expenses   £340,000
   Salary overhead   £54,500
   General overhead   £285,500

2. 50% of general overhead apportioned on a per capita basis:

   £142,750 ÷ 5.75 = £24,826 per full-time fee-earner

3. 50% of general overhead apportioned pro rata to salary:

Partner 1	26,250 ÷ 133,250 × 142,750 =	28,122
Partner 2	26,250 ÷ 133,250 × 142,750 =	28,122
Partner 3	26,250 ÷ 133,250 × 142,750 =	28,122
Solicitor 1	25,000 ÷ 133,250 × 142,750 =	26,782
Solicitor 2	15,000 ÷ 133,250 × 142,750 =	16,069
Legal Executive	14,500 ÷ 133,250 × 142,750 =	15,533
	133,250	142,750

4. Individual expense of time:

	Overhead per capita	Overhead pro rata	Salary	Total	Anticipated chargeable hours	Hourly expense of time
	£	£	£	£		£
Partner 1	24,826	28,122	26,250	79,198	1,000	79.20
Partner 2	24,826	28,122	26,250	79,198	1,200	66.00
Partner 3	24,826	28,122	26,250	79,198	1,200	66.00
Solicitor 1	24,826	26,782	25,000	76,608	1,200	63.84
Solicitor 2	18,620	16,069	15,000	49,689	750	66.25
Legal Executive	24,826	15,533	14,500	54,859	1,200	45.72

This form of allocation will work for most practices most of the time. However, it should not be followed slavishly in circumstances where more sophistication may be required. When a firm is trying to establish the relative profitability of different practice areas, more consideration will need to be given to overhead allocation in order to establish the costs of each practice area. For example, non-litigators might argue that a litigation practice makes disproportionate claims on the firm's resources (e.g., technology for litigation support, paralegals, or meeting rooms for housing and sorting documents during discovery). Unfortunately, trying to draw such fine distinctions may be more trouble than it is worth (and is more likely in a partnership of individual practitioners than of integrated entrepreneurs: cf. paragraphs 9.3 to 9.5).

31.7 Conclusion

So much of the economics of law firms is dependent on turning the capacity of lawyers into fees. In many ways, the only way to measure and manage this productive capacity is by time. The thrust of this book is that *measuring and managing* by time does not necessarily equate to *charging* by time or for time. Nevertheless, effective financial management of the income-generating capacity of a law firm is all but impossible without comprehensive and consistent time-recording.

31.8 Charging for Legal Services

31.8.1 *The role of market forces*

In a market economy, the price of economic resources is a function of supply and demand. In this sense, lawyers' fees may well reflect the industry life cycle (see paragraph 2.3.1) and the services life cycle (see paragraph 2.3.3); they will depend on what clients perceive their providers to be selling (cf. Maister 1997, chapter 13). However, it would be a rare occurrence for any jurisdiction to leave the marketplace entirely to its own devices to determine the level of all lawyers' fees. There is, in fact, usually a continuum from strictly regulated fees to unregulated fees (see Skordaki and Walker 1994, paragraph 2.5.4).

As a generalisation, strict regulation is more common in civil law jurisdictions and there is less regulation in common law jurisdictions. Nevertheless, even in common law countries, one frequently finds control of fees charged for contentious matters exercised by the courts, as well as control of publicly funded legal aid by the government (see Skordaki and Walker 1994, paragraphs 2.5.4 and 2.7.1). In some jurisdictions, the legal profession's regulatory body will also exercise control, either generally (see, for example, the Solicitors' Remuneration Order 1972) or through the use of scale fees. Given the nature of legal services, and the difficulty clients have prospectively in assessing quality (cf. paragraphs 17.1.2, 17.1.3 and 20.3.3.4), control of fees by the government, the courts, or professional bodies can offer clients greater predictability and uniformity of legal costs, and provides some assurance of 'reasonableness'. But even then, it may not be clear to the client how the amount charged by the lawyer (for example, as a predetermined scale fee) relates to the work actually done (Skordaki and Walker 1994, paragraph 2.10.4).

31.8.2 *'Alternative' billing*

The very use of the expression 'alternative' presupposes that something is 'the norm'. In jurisdictions where the expression is used (principally in the US and, to a lesser extent, the UK), the norm is time-based billing or hourly rates. Time-based billing assumes that a firm has some form of time-costing process. But this is the fundamental dilemma: the cost of time is the *cost* of the lawyer's input, but the bill to the client should represent the *value* of the output or outcome. The cost of inputs and the value of outputs bear no necessary relation to each other.

Time-based billing makes sense if you sell time — but not if you sell know-how (cf. paragraphs 3.1 and 5.1). Although the *cost* of each hour may be constant, the *value* of each hour is not. Time-based billing runs a serious risk of turning an art (or craft) into a science. The question is not — or should not be — what mark-up should be applied to the cost of time; it is what are you selling, and what is it worth?

31.8.3   *The value of legal services*

The value of the know-how sold by a lawyer will usually depend on:

(a)   the size, importance and novelty of the matter;
(b)   the range and complexity of the know-how brought to bear (cf. paragraph 2.3.3);
(c)   the time taken and the nature of the outcome.

These are, in fact, broadly the elements in paragraph 2 of the Solicitors' Remuneration Order 1972. Assessing value is therefore a judgmental exercise, which can be done from a variety of standpoints.

One of the difficulties of charging by the hour is that too many lawyers are perceived by too many clients to be poor time managers and to have a vested interest in 'stacking the hours' or 'churning the file'. Clients doubt the control and accountability of lawyers, and as such feel that they are bearing all the risk.

A way of sharing the risk is for lawyers to undertake work on a fixed-fee basis or subject to a cap on their normal time charges. For this to be effective, lawyers need to be able to 'scope' a matter before they take it on, and be able to 'project manage' the work they do (cf. chapter 21). This in turn requires clarity of objectives, instructions and assumptions on which the lawyer's work is to be based, and unambiguous communication with the client and all the other fee-earners in the firm who may be involved. Unfortunately, not all clients are able to express their objectives and instructions clearly — they may not even know what they really want — and not all matter partners are able or willing to communicate clearly, sufficiently or at all with their team members. Fixed or capped fees may therefore prove more successful (if judged by client satisfaction) where the client is a sophisticated buyer of legal services, and the fee-earners are used to a communicative, integrated environment (cf. paragraph 9.4).

Retainers for legal services are generally less popular than they used to be. The idea of paying a lawyer or law firm a given amount of money a year in return for legal advice and services is predicated on a continuing relationship and a certain degree of predictability in the range and type of the client's legal needs. With more transactional buying and shopping around by clients, the element of 'swings and roundabouts' in the lawyer–client relationship is often less evident than it used to be, but is a necessary consequence of a retainer arrangement — even where (as is common) the retainer is reviewable either annually or on an interim basis.

Conditional (and especially full contingency) fees are anathema to many practitioners, who do not want to feel that their professional objectivity or independence of advice is — or is suspected to be — compromised by their financial interest in the outcome.

Whatever the regulatory or professional issues involved, firms, practice areas or individual lawyers who undertake work on a conditional or contingent basis need an excellent understanding of the economics of legal practice generally, and of the specific services or transactions in particular. They also need excellent project management and communication skills. Whereas time-based billing might be thought to put all the risk of legal services on to the client, conditional fees can be said to put all the risk on to the lawyer. For some clients, and for some types of legal representation, this may be appropriate: it does not mean that conditional or contingent fees should become the profession's universal standard.

31.8.4 Conclusions

Lawyers exist in a more competitive marketplace than ever before, and the fees charged are an element of that competition. The truth is that there is no one best method of pricing legal services. Some clients will need a conditional or contingent fee arrangement if they are to be able even to contemplate engaging a lawyer's services. Hourly rates may be seen by some as a licence to print money, but some clients still prefer them as a way of paying for legal services. The issue is, first, the *appropriateness* of the method of charging to the client's circumstances, the issues involved, and the lawyer's input; and second, the *proportionality* of the fee to the outcome.

Contrary to popular belief, not all clients are looking for certainty of fees in their dealings with lawyers, because they understand that there are uncertainties and variables involved. Understandably, they want as good an idea as the lawyer can give them, and an intelligent and rational discussion about the nature, extent and likely effect of the variables that might affect the final fee. What they dislike intensely is complete uncertainty, surprises along the way, and a lawyer's indifference to the issue. The 1990s and beyond require greater transparency, greater risk-sharing and accountability, and better communication (Skordaki and Walker 1994, paragraph 2.11).

PART VII

OWNERSHIP OF LAW FIRMS

Chapter 32

NATURE OF OWNERSHIP

32.1 Introduction

Having established the underlying theory of law firms in general (chapter 8) and applied it to different types of law firm in particular (chapter 9), it should now be possible to deal more systematically and analytically with some of the fundamental issues facing partnerships today. The principal conclusions from part II are that fully effective partnerships will put a premium on the development of individual and firm-specific capital (the continuous development of professional and managerial know-how), on the existence or cultivation of *shareable* surpluses of capital (business development and cross-fertilisation), on the reality of sharing (horizontal or vertical delegation), and on monitoring the performance consequent on sharing (supervision and management).

The types of law firm analysed in chapter 9 show that there is a spectrum of practice, from sole practitioners (and partnerships of individual practitioners) to a partnership of integrated entrepreneurs: it is, if you like, a spectrum from *individualism* to *integration*. It is important to recognise, however, that, because there is a spectrum, it is not necessarily a question of making a choice between the two. Individuals may have a preference, but any combination of individuals is unlikely to be totally at one end of the spectrum.

On the basis that equity partnership is often seen as equivalent to ownership, it might be appropriate to begin the discussion of partnership with a review of the theory of the law firm as it relates to ownership.

32.2 The Mirage of Ownership

I have often before described ownership in a law firm as a mirage. By 'ownership', in this context, I mean equity partnership. By 'mirage', I intend to refer to ownership both as being increasingly elusive to those who seek it, and as not being what it was thought to be to those who attain it.

In founder-led firms, ownership might be thought to have real meaning and value. The founders are responsible for developing clients, running the business, and doing the work at a profit. They create a firm, and acquire property rights in the exchanges of assets that create it (cf. paragraph 6.5). But what are the assets subject to their 'ownership'? They may be premises, furniture, equipment and fittings. For the most part, premises are taken on lease and are therefore more of a continuing liability than an asset; and the furniture and equipment are a depreciating asset at best. There is, of course, the value of work-in-progress and accounts receivable, but they represent work already done — the past, not the future. Ownership of a share in the past is certainly a questionable asset in the context of earning a living. Further, none of the assets so far discussed is a mainstream money-earner for the firm.

The thesis of this book has been that the principal asset of a law office is human capital — its collective individual and firm-specific know-how. Know-how is, therefore, the only asset worth anything to partners as the owners of the business. *But except to the extent of their own individual capital, it is not owned by them* (see paragraph 9.8).

If knowledgeable and experienced people determine the ability of a firm to survive, develop and prosper, and know-how is not owned by the partners, we might expect the profit-takers to show respect and concern for those people. Unfortunately, what we too often see is an environment lacking in mutual respect — an environment of hypercriticism and hypersensitivity, where support staff are given low status and where they (and, indeed, some of the fee-earners) resent their imposed sense of inferiority (cf. paragraph 23.3). Ownership in these circumstances is worth nothing; it is a mirage.

32.3 Beyond the Founders

Founder-led businesses tend to be better at valuing all contributions than more established businesses. They usually respect the role everyone plays in building a new business, and they present an exciting, challenging and motivating environment. However, a start-up cannot last forever, and the founders will begin to consider the future of the firm. This, of course, means admitting new partners. In the early days of a firm, the new partners may well have been trained by the founders, and they will owe a lot to their mentors. But, as firms develop, this link with the founders (and therefore with the business idea and culture they promoted) becomes more tenuous. Analytically (as discussed in chapter 9), the first partners are dependent on the founders' individual capital; but as increased sharing creates more extensive and valuable firm-specific capital, this dependence on (and the domination of) the founders and their individual capital becomes weaker.

The result of this process of development is the Anglo-American 'model' of law firm partnership that has evolved (discussed in paragraph

3.6). In the traditional form of the model, an assistant (or associate) becomes a partner as a reward for being a good lawyer who has endured the firm for so many years. Under this model, a career track of sorts is clearly identified and understood: every good lawyer who sticks around and does a good job can expect to become a partner (someone who is no good as a lawyer will be got rid of anyway). So *everyone* begins with partnership expectations; not to be offered partnership is interpreted as failure, and the unfortunate passed-over tend to seek new pastures. Thus, the 'up-or-out' system in theory perpetuates itself, leading to exponential growth (see paragraph 3.6.2). The 'jam tomorrow' approach of keeping assistants working hard in the expectation of the large profit share, status and involvement of a partner has been the foundation of many British and American firms. In its supposed quest for the elite, it can in fact engender mediocrity: in this model, insufficient attention is often paid to the need for business management and client development — indeed, in many firms, non-partners are positively discouraged from both — and inadvertently creates employee-minded partners. Thus, the elite partnership of integrated entrepreneurs is declining (see Morris and Pinnington 1996b), and more mixed partnerships are emerging (cf. paragraphs 9.4 and 9.5).

32.4 An Ownership Mentality?

Perhaps it is not therefore surprising that many law firms today are having to cope with weak, employee-minded partners who do not understand the nature of entrepreneurial (or ownership) risk, and whose expectation of a continuing high and increasing income is at odds with the economic reality of practising law in the 1990s and with their own contribution to the firm's development.

In these mixed partnerships (see paragraph 9.5), one increasingly finds:

(a) the belief that clients are personal property, resulting in a failure to cross-sell and develop existing clients to the benefit of both the firm and the clients;

(b) a lack of mutual respect and a failure to conform, with individual partners 'doing their own thing';

(c) no interest in being accountable to fellow partners;

(d) a lack of a strong leader or culture — or, paradoxically, the existence of a strong leader and culture but a naive refusal of partners to accept that both are prerequisites to continued prosperity;

(e) partners' frustration that their status brings no real involvement in the firm; and

(f) a disregard of the needs of fee-earners and support staff for training and development, feedback and appreciation.

Further, with increasing numbers of assistants and pressures on economic performance, law firms simply cannot afford to maintain this traditional approach towards partnership elevations. Sadly, increasing media attention on the legal profession may encourage the belief that success can only be measured by the number of partners, number of fee-earners, size of fee income, fee income per lawyer, profit per partner, or profit margins. This is nonsense.

32.5 The Challenge

The successful law firm of the 1990s will restore real value to the notion of partnership. The 'reward' of equity partnership should be restricted to those who demonstrate not only legal ability, but who — as entrepreneurs or managers — secure the future of the business by playing a major role in client development or the effective management of the firm (cf. paragraph 7.2). There may be some individual 'sole practitioners' who can be fairly said to own the individual capital which gives them the opportunity to practise law on their own account. And there will be others who, while they undoubtedly have individual capital, find more benefit from sharing it along with firm-specific capital. The latter cannot 'own' the firm-specific capital on which they rely to make a living. But they can regard themselves as *custodians* of it. Their role as custodians is to preserve and enhance the assets within their custodianship — not with any thought of acquiring part of that capital value when they leave the firm, but with the objective of leaving those assets in better shape than they found them. Their financial contributions to capital then become, not so much the purchase of an 'ownership interest', but more like a subscription paid to a club. For as long as they are members, they have certain membership rights — to exploit the firm-specific capital, and to receive certain benefits. When they stop paying their subscription, their entitlements cease.

The challenge for custodians, therefore, lies in being entrepreneurial with firm-specific capital in addressing surplus client needs and surplus opportunities (cf. paragraphs 8.4 and 8.5). This means creating a flexible know-how environment that encourages, motivates and challenges lawyers, that establishes known standards of quality, that demonstrates strong leadership and culture, that succeeds in transferring and sharing know-how among senior and junior fee-earners, and is able to change both its leaders and staff without compromising the quality or continuity of the firm. They effectively become 'multipliers' or net contributors, adding more to the business than they take out of it.

The mirage therefore continues: the choice is between the 'reality' of custodian equity in an institution, where firm-specific capital is the continuing bedrock of future growth and development, or the 'ownership' of individual capital in a firm that may well be successful for its immediate owners but which is just as likely to destroy itself by its own inherent weakness or lack of cohesion.

Chapter 33

ROLES AND RIGHTS OF EQUITY PARTNERS

33.1 Introduction

Having developed a theory of the law firm (in chapters 7, 8 and 9, and summarised in chapter 10), we can now begin to analyse the roles that partners in law firms should be expected to carry out. It might be tempting to think that the roles are simply those of entrepreneur, worker, and financier. But although these descriptions could be described as roles, I prefer to think of them as *functions*, and these functions are too broad to provide a sufficient articulation of the *roles*. We have already seen that not every person identified as a partner will necessarily be an entrepreneur, worker and financier. Similarly, not every partner will necessarily carry out the same roles.

33.2 An Analysis of Roles

In my view, all equity partners should be expected to carry out one or more of the entrepreneurial activities identified in paragraph 7.2. Activities (a)(i) to (iv) and (vi) involve introducing new services, opening a new office, or selling. They cover what might be described as 'generating new business'. From these entrepreneurial activities, it is likely that a firm will develop through the internalisation (cf. paragraphs 6.1 and 10.1) of various people's individual human capital, that is, through employment relationships being established. These, in turn, will give rise to the existence of property rights (cf. paragraphs 6.5 and 9.8) and the need for financial capital. It is in this sense that partners might be said to own something. Activities (a)(v) and (vii) cover introducing new methods of working, and combining resources in different ways. These activities might be regarded as more 'managerial'. Activities (b) and (c) are about ensuring maximum benefit, both currently and prospectively, from the development of existing client relationships and of the individual capital of the fee-earners. As such, they could rightly be attached to the *delivery* of legal services, and thus considered a part of the fee-earning role. However, these activities are not simply responding to current legal needs but represent an investment in individual and firm-specific capital. To this extent, they are entrepreneurial and therefore properly part of a partner's role.

In many of these activities, partners will also be expected to display leadership qualities to ensure that what they want doing by and through others will actually be achieved. As Gilson and Mnookin (1985, pages 388 and 389) write in the context of trying to develop firm-specific capital:

> "Several of the new firms that have experienced substantial growth over the last decade have succeeded largely because of the leadership and drive of a small number of entrepreneurial lawyers in the firm. In many of these instances, it appears that a dominant figure helped develop a firm culture based on sharing principles. . . . it appears that these leaders in essence created the firm-specific capital that helped glue the new firm together by declining to claim as much income as they might have. . . . We suspect that those newer firms that have developed along the lines of the sharing model were able to do so because dominant lawyers both set an example and in essence transformed what could have been their individual capital into firm-specific capital."

In these senses, therefore, we can identify a number of roles for partners, reflecting the broad definitions of entrepreneurialism in paragraph 7.2:

(a)   Generating new business:

    (i)   partners as business developers;
    (ii)   partners as lawyers;
    (iii)   partners as client managers;
    (iv)   partners as networkers;
    (v)   partners as writers and speakers.

(b)   Combining resources:

    (i)   partners as case and project managers;
    (ii)   partners as delegators;
    (iii)   partners as fee-earners;
    (iv)   partners as trainers and mentors;
    (v)   partners as team players.

(c)   Ensuring achievement:

    (i)   partners as supervisors;

(ii)   partners as employers;
(iii)   partners as business managers;
(iv)   partners as leaders;
(v)   partners as owners.

Some partners find it difficult to 'let go' of some roles, and do not delegate (or recruit) when they should. Others often have problems with a wide range of roles, and may tend to stick with those that they find comfortable. But as Bhide points out: "Entrepreneurs who aspire to operate small enterprises in which they perform all crucial tasks never have to change their roles. In personal service companies, for instance, the founding partners often perform client work from the time they start the company until they retire. Transforming a fledgling enterprise into an entity capable of an independent existence, however, requires founders to undertake new roles" (1996, page 129; and cf. paragraph 9.4).

33.3 Problems with Partners' Roles

None of the identified roles is necessarily 'pure': there may be overlaps. It is often difficult for partners themselves (let alone those around them) to know which role they are exercising at any given moment. This can give rise to a number of role problems (discussed in paragraph 24.2.2).

How often are partners clear about their role (because they are exercising it in a manner with which they are comfortable), but others around them are not? This lack of clarity (role ambiguity) often creates confusion, resentment and duplication of effort.

Even where the nature of a role is clear, a conflict in expectations (role incompatibility) can still arise. For example, the expectations of partners in their role as business developers are usually well known. But some partners may feel that they are required to act in a way which they regard as unprofessional or which is 'just not me'. Which is the real problem: the role, the expectations, or the individual? The answer may depend on which type of practice one is examining. Partnerships of integrated entrepreneurs (see paragraph 9.4) will probably find less incompatibility than a partnership of individual practitioners (see paragraph 9.3) because roles in the former tend to be better understood and defined, expectations are mutual, and partners have ideas and abilities that are consistent with their environment. Sole principals (see paragraph 9.2) will probably not articulate any roles very well (because they will know what they expect of themselves and will not be too concerned with others' roles), and are not likely to have many mutual or common expectations.

The most serious incompatibility problems probably arise in mixed partnerships (see paragraph 9.5), where individualist practitioners, employee-minded partners, or lateral partners, are more likely to experience a conflict of expectations.

Role conflict arises when a partner is expected to carry out one or more roles in the same environment (for example, as head of department and as a member of the firm's management committee, where she may have to make firm-wide decisions which are antithetical to the interests of her department). The definition and expectations of each role may be quite clear, and compatible for each role; but the roles themselves are in conflict. Many partners seem to find themselves in this situation, with their role as fee-earner usually taking precedence over all others. This will be acceptable in a partnership of individual practitioners; but it could lead to problems in partnerships of integrated entrepreneurs or mixed partnerships (where typically more roles are recognised), although the integrated entrepreneurs of the former may be better suited to resolving the conflicts.

Given the variety of roles identified in paragraph 33.2, it would not be surprising if most partners feel the problem of role overload! It could be that overload will be less of a problem in a partnership of integrated entrepreneurs because a sharing practice is also likely to be more careful about delegation, sharing out roles, and in developing and supporting those whom it expects to carry them out.

For some partners, however, delegation can create a feeling of underload — a feeling of not being needed. Role underload could potentially arise in any type of practice, but is perhaps again less likely in the supportive and developmental environment of the partnership of integrated entrepreneurs.

With such a potential for role problems, the existence of role stress (cf. paragraph 24.2.3) among partners should not be a surprise. Again, it may be that the sharing environment of the partnership of integrated entrepreneurs would be most likely to encourage cooperative responses to role stress; conversely, partnerships of individual practitioners and, to some extent, mixed partnerships would be more likely to experience unilateral strategies.

It is well known that, in law firms, client work takes priority. It is superficially easy to justify this as an economic issue. But to do so is short-termist. No multimillion-pound business can run and develop itself. Indeed, in an industry built so much on geographical and service fragmentation, and on personal service (see paragraph 4.7.3), success requires a variety of input from the same individuals — hence the multiplicity of roles for partners identified in paragraph 33.2.

Lawyers have traditionally been trained only for their fee-earning role (and then not necessarily for their client or case management activities). Tradition has also defined a certain behaviour which may not be consistent with the perceived needs for business development or managing a business. If partners do not understand their other roles, and have not been trained for them, it is not surprising that they should rationalise their behaviour by emphasising the importance and credibility of fee-earning and by downgrading the importance and priority of other things. Fee-earning is where they feel comfortable and where direct contributions to profitability can be noticed.

In short, I believe that many partners in law firms suffer from role stress, caused principally by ambiguity, conflict and overload. This stress is usually resolved unilaterally in such a way that, collectively, partners set up self-fulfilling expectations of poor performance in non-fee-earning roles that conspire against constructive change. Role conflict and overload

(which most partners experience) is dealt with by reducing the importance and priority of the non-fee-earning roles; role ambiguity is dealt with
by reducing the importance of the other fee-earners and support staff (by
adopting a 'mill-owner' property rights approach to leadership and
ownership, and forcing their narrow concept of the role of partner on
others: see paragraph 9.8). Finally, some instances of the apparently
increasing problem of 'unproductive partners' could be seen as an
instance of role underload: see further paragraph 36.5).

33.4 Power and Influence

As we have already seen (chapters 6 and 8), a law firm is an organisational
response to the need to allocate economic resources — particularly human
capital and labour. Becoming part of an organisation means accepting that
there will be internal governance mechanisms to guard against opportunistic behaviour, in return for which certain rewards and benefits will be
offered (see paragraphs 3.6 and 6.4). The question for any individual is,
"How much am I prepared to give up to gain those rewards?"

There are some partners in law firms who prefer to behave as complete
individualists: unfortunately, any organisation, and particularly a partnership, is not the place for anyone who wishes to remain the complete
master of his or her own destiny. Sole practitioners who buy office space
and services from others in the market may come closest, but all other
forms of law firm organisation necessarily entail internalisation of resources and people — and therefore co-operation, direction and control.

In these circumstances, the exercise of power and influence by partners
may well be constrained. The most successful and effective partners will
understand this (more often than not only instinctively). For the analysts,
the discussion of power and influence will be found in paragraph 24.3.

33.5 Decision-making

The exercise of power and influence is perhaps most noticeable in the
context of partnership decisions. There may well be formal mechanisms
set out in partnership agreements specifying the circumstances in which
votes are required, and the degree of support required. These mechanisms
will include a right of veto, or a need for unanimity, special majority
(usually 90% or 75%), simple majority (more than 50%), or weighted
voting (where certain partners or partnership interests are given more
than their proportionate vote in specified circumstances). Nevertheless,
influence may be brought to bear — it is often called 'consensus-seeking'
in law firms! — by those with power in order to persuade other partners
to exercise their votes in a certain way. A genuine consensus is more likely
to arise in a firm that is built on sharing principles — the partnership of
integrated entrepreneurs (see paragraph 9.4).

On voting, Hildebrandt and Kaufman write (1988, pages 117 and 119):

"Some firms give young partners a lesser vote than partners who have
been with the firm for a longer period of time. This practice is

objectionable because it flies in the face of the basis of partnership. If the seniors in the firm cannot obtain the support of the young partners by leadership example, arbitrary attempts to control their voice treat symptoms rather than problems. If voting rights is a real issue, the firm should seriously consider a two-tier partnership. The voting arrangements in a law firm reflect to a large degree the heart of the relationship of the partners and often tell a good deal about the management philosophy in the firm. . . .

Those firms in which partners have to worry extensively about the voting criteria are usually firms in which problems exist. A need for carefully-defined voting generally reflects a lack of trust among the partners and in the leaders of the firm.''

The authors are, of course, implying that the partnership of integrated entrepreneurs is the 'best' or 'right' model of practice, but in that context their comments are valid. In other types of law firm, where partners are driven by individualism and self-seeking behaviour, provisions in a partnership agreement covering the exercise of voting rights may well be needed as part of the firm's governance structure in order to reduce some of the risks of such behaviour.

33.6   Capitalisation

I have dealt elsewhere with the subject of capitalisation and financing a law firm (see chapter 29). The issues to emphasise in the context of this discussion of the roles and rights of equity partners are:

(a)   Contributed capital should be expected from those who are prepared to take risks, that is, from entrepreneurs. Such a contribution is required to encourage a sharing of the risks of entrepreneurship (and thus reducing some of the risks of opportunism and moral hazard that other financiers might feel if only they were taking the financial risks): see paragraph 8.8.

(b)   Partners who contribute financial capital should regard part of their share of net profits as an interest payment if they are not otherwise paid market-rate interest on capital (see paragraph 8.9.1).

(c)   Contributed capital (part of the partner's capital account) should be returned to the partner on retirement, withdrawal or death. Any surplus over and above the amount originally contributed, after allowing for any capitalised interest or undrawn profit-share, may be regarded as part of the return to individual or firm-specific capital (a form of capital appreciation). Any decrease would similarly represent depreciation in the human capital.

33.7   A Statement of Roles and Rights

The nature of equity partnership is multidimensional. It can only be described, therefore, from a number of different standpoints. There is a danger that the resulting list of attributes, attitudes and qualities looks formidable, unreasonable or unrealistic. However, some attempt must be made, bearing in mind that it is for any given partnership to decide which of the dimensions are most, more, or not, important to it. The following description first appeared in Mayson 1992, appendix 3: the emphasis is on the aspects of partners' roles that might be expected in a partnership of integrated entrepreneurs. Though comprehensive, it does not claim to be exhaustive. For those firms that distinguish between equity and salaried partners (and, arguably, through lock-step profit-sharing, between full equity and other partners), the difference usually is the sustained and consistent ability of full equity partners demonstrated in more of the roles than is demonstrated by others.

33.7.1 *General*

Equity ownership in a law firm should be offered to a lawyer who meets the necessary business and professional criteria identified by the firm as important to it in maintaining a viable business responsive to clients' needs. Equity partnership is a position of trust — trust in the legal and business ability of other partners, and trust that partners will be given equitable treatment. While admission to partnership gives partners certain rights, it also imposes important responsibilities.

33.7.2 *Accountability*

Perhaps the most important element of trust amongst partners is their willingness to place the interests of the firm ahead of their individual interests, and to be accountable to other partners for both their professional and business conduct.

A partner's willingness to be accountable is evidenced in day-to-day behaviour. It includes:

(a) Accepting work for which there is the likelihood that the firm will be paid at or above the normal rates (unless any other arrangement has been approved beforehand).

(b) Delegating wherever appropriate.

(c) Complying with the firm's billing procedures.

(d) Chasing aged debts with the same energy used to represent clients.

(e) Submitting time sheets on time.

(f) Subscribing to and implementing the team approach to practice.

(g) Earning her keep — not just for a few years, but until retirement, departure or otherwise altering the relationship with the firm.

33.7.3 *Expectations*

When a lawyer is invited to become a partner, it means that the other partners are demonstrating their trust in her, and that the new partner is not only a good lawyer but has many other qualities that are important to building a law firm. These qualities and characteristics are difficult to define. Further, not every partner has every characteristic, and each partner will have these qualities in varying degrees.

Partners should be expected:

(a)   To develop clients:

(i)   Be effective in developing new business from existing clients and prospects.
(ii)   Contribute to the business development efforts of others.
(iii)   Develop and maintain positive relationships with clients.
(iv)   Be available and attentive to clients.
(v)   Have the client's confidence in their abilities and satisfaction with their work.
(vi)   Be willing to transfer the responsibility for clients to others when appropriate.
(vii)   Handle client complaints or other quality control problems as they arise.
(viii) Promote and cross-sell the firm's other services.

(b)   To manage their practice as a team player:

(i)   Introduce clients to other lawyers to ensure continuity.
(ii)   Contribute to the efficient distribution of work and client contacts.
(iii)   Specialise and develop expertise in particular areas to complement other abilities in the firm.

(c)   To be a dependable team player:

(i)   Be willing to put in extra hours to handle surges in workload.
(ii)   Exhibit stability and maturity.
(iii)   Be dependable and handle referred matters diligently.
(iv)   Work well under pressure.
(v)   Maintain good working relationships with partners and staff.
(vi)   Respect each partner's professional and managerial judgment.
(vii)   Comply with management procedures.
(viii) Support the firm's objectives and treat clients as assets of the firm rather than as personal possessions.
(ix)   Attend the firm's meetings diligently.

(d)   To work productively:

(i)   Work efficiently and effectively.
(ii)   Work at their level of competence, demonstrating a willingness and ability to delegate work both to the lowest competent level and to a higher level when appropriate.
(iii)   Supervise the work they delegate.

    (iv) Manage a reasonable workload, working independently and producing work in a timely fashion.

(e) To produce quality work:

    (i)   Know the applicable law within their own specialised area (including current developments).
    (ii)   Handle complex client matters.
    (iii)   Analyse a situation quickly and accurately.
    (iv)   Be creative and innovative in solving client problems.
    (v)   Be able to plan and implement legal strategies.
    (vi)   Work accurately and thoroughly.
    (vii) Write clearly and persuasively.
    (viii) Negotiate skilfully in a client's best interests.
    (ix)   Be able to handle the unexpected.
    (x)   Exercise good judgment, differentiating between when to decide and when to consult with others.
    (xi)   Continue to develop professionally.

(f) To be involved in professional and community activities:

    (i)   Participate in professional bodies and activities.
    (ii)   Hold positions of leadership in community organisations.
    (iii)   Maintain good relationships with other lawyers and professionals in the community.

33.7.4 Rights

Ownership in a law firm typically brings with it the right to participate in the firm's business affairs, and in its success or failure. These rights are usually set out in the partnership agreement, and typically include:

(a) Voting on various issues.
(b) Sharing in profits and other benefits.
(c) Receiving benefits for building the firm (on death, disability, or retirement).
(d) Participating in management if elected or appointed.
(e) Sharing in the obligations for the firm's debts.
(f) Sharing in the remaining funds (if any) if the firm dissolves.

Chapter 34

PARTNERSHIP TIERING

34.1 Background

In many English law firms, there is only one type of partner — the full equity partner, who shares in the 'ownership' of the firm and is rewarded by a share of the net profit. This structure is particularly entrenched in the largest London and New York firms, where assistants tend either to be promoted or asked to leave — the so-called 'up-or-out' system (this is confirmed by Morris and Pinnington 1996b, page 8).

Other firms have the concept of the 'salaried' partner, a lawyer whose name appears on the notepaper as a partner but who does not share in net profits (and in many firms does not participate in certain aspects of partners' meetings or decision-making). Historically, salaried partnerships were introduced either to delay the admission of further equity partners (which would dilute profit-shares or voting rights), or as a 'staging post' to allow the equity partners to assess more closely someone who was thought to have equity potential.

Many firms with salaried partners find the concept difficult to operate in practice, and have created serious morale problems both among existing salaried partners who saw their eventual promotion to equity as inevitable, and among assistants who feel cheated by another hurdle on the way to (supposedly) more power and money.

It is not surprising that firms should be sceptical about the concept of salaried partnership. But the changes taking place in the profession, and the need to maintain the fee-earning pyramid, may mean that the imperative for some firms to introduce such two-tiered partnership structures is unavoidable. Provided the change in structure is handled and implemented properly, there is no reason why it cannot work to everyone's benefit. It does seem, though, that firms with a strong sense of sharing and shared values are least likely to introduce a two-tier system, essentially because of their adherence to up-or-out policies (see Morris and Pinnington 1996b, page 18). In some firms, although all partners are called equity partners, there is a level of 'junior' or 'fixed income' partners who should more properly be regarded as salaried partners for the purposes of this chapter (even if they hold a nominal equity points allocation that gives them a variable bonus every year dependent on the firm's profits).

34.2 Virtues of Two Tiers

As we have seen (paragraph 8.9), it is possible to distinguish the various contributions that 'partners' make to the firm. Law firms are increasingly having to recognise that some of their lawyers are not able to handle all of the responsibilities expected of an equity partner (cf. paragraph 33.7), even though they can still make a significant contribution. Historically, firms dealt with this situation in one of two ways:

(a) by adopting the 'up-or-out' approach under which every assistant either became a partner or left (cf. Baden-Fuller and Bateson 1990, and Malos and Campion 1995); or

(b) by promoting to the partnership lawyers who really did not meet the criteria.

As a result, the notion took hold within the profession that partnership was *the* career goal for a qualified lawyer, and that not becoming a partner was professional failure. It has to be time to rethink this particular waste of human capital. Two-tier partnerships, properly handled, provide an option; and it does seem that up-or-out is becoming rarer, even in the City of London (see Morris and Pinnington 1996b).

Adopting a two-tier structure does not mean lowering the standards of partnership. If anything, it will *raise* standards and redefine what it means to be an equity partner. The main difference between the criteria for becoming an equity partner and for becoming a salaried partner should lie in the separation of the functions of equity partners (and in particular the requirement for them to be entrepreneurs, as defined in paragraph 7.2), and in the *consistent* ability of equity partners to satisfy the criteria for entrepreneurial activity and contributions as workers. While salaried partners must demonstrate some of the same abilities, the firm should not expect the same degree of consistency. So any firm that lowers its standards for admission to partnership when it introduces salaried partners misunderstands the true reason for the two-tier structure.

34.3 Not a Solution for 'Problem' Partners

The increasing focus on 'unproductive partners' (see further paragraph 36.5) and the realisation that a firm may have made some mistakes in its previous elevations to equity partnership, may tempt the firm's powerful equity partners into thinking that the introduction of a two-tier structure would be an ideal opportunity to correct past mistakes by demoting one or more of the current equity partners. Forget it! Most firms will have one or more equity partners who would oppose the new structure if they suspect that they might be a 'victim' of it. Problem partners certainly have to be dealt with, but using salaried partnership as a dumping ground for them will devalue that tier. It is conceivable that, at some time in the future, equity partners will become salaried partners: they may even choose to make that move themselves. But if the possibility is raised at the time of the proposed restructuring, the odds are that the new structure will not win sufficient partner support to implement it at all.

Having said all this, it is also important to bear in mind that if salaried partnership is introduced as a way of accommodating lawyers who do not currently have all the qualities and consistency required for equity involvement, some salaried partners may never become equity partners because they will never have or will not develop the requisite characteristics. In other words, salaried partnership is not inevitably just one step on the ladder to eventual equity: it is a tier of partnership for lawyers who demonstrate certain characteristics, *some* of whom may improve their net contribution to the business to a point where equity partnership is offered. Partners should therefore be valued for what they are and what they contribute, not looked down on or devalued for what they did not become or could not sustain.

34.4   More Fundamental than Profit-sharing Differentials

Some partners believe that their firms can achieve many of the same results of two-tier partnerships by maintaining broader differentials between the profit-shares of the partners. By bringing all new partners into the equity, but rewarding the junior partners at much lower levels than the seniors, the concept of salaried partnership, they argue, becomes unnecessary. Such an approach overemphasises remuneration, which is not the only feature of salaried partnership, nor the only reason to consider a two-tier structure. Indeed, payment of a 'wage' for labour is not properly in my view a dimension of partnership at all (as discussed in paragraphs 8.9.2 and 8.9.4). We are addressing what the firm expects from its partners, and what a partner actually contributes to the firm.

Often, such an implicit two-tier system also causes more problems than it solves. There is no clear definition of roles or expectations; and many new partners soon feel that, as equity partners, their incomes should be more comparable with those of the senior partners because they genuinely believe that they make as valuable a contribution and could undoubtedly make a better job of running the firm! When all partners are structurally part of the same tier, it can be more difficult to manage this mismatch of perception and expectation.

The best professional, personal and economic reasons for introducing a two-tier structure are never achieved simply by income differentials between partners.

34.5   Dealing with Assistants' Reactions

It would be naive to believe that a two-tier structure can be introduced without any adverse reaction from the current assistants. Equally, though, such a reaction is not inevitable if the process is handled carefully. These days, assistants often read the same legal press as partners, and talk to their friends in other firms. They see the fundamental changes taking place in law firms. They are beginning to understand the economics of practising law. Most recognise that the criteria for partnership have changed.

The two-tier partnership can therefore offer them a career track that they appreciate, and the ultimate goal of equity partnership will still be there and respected for the right people. If salaried partnership is presented to them as an attractive alternative to an 'up-or-out' policy, becoming a permanent assistant, or leaving the firm, adverse reaction can be minimised. Assistants (especially the most senior) should be involved in the discussions, and invited to give their views. They may also need educating about the benefits to the firm as well as to themselves. More than ever, they must understand that it takes more than being a good lawyer and working so many hours in order to become a partner. When lawyers reach the point where they are being paid more than their net economic contribution resulting from charging for their own time, something more has to happen.

For some partners, adopting a new approach to equity partnership amounts to 'moving the goalposts' and perhaps going back on the firm's explicit or implicit recruitment promise about the prospects of partnership.

There are few firms left that still tell new recruits that if they do a good job and serve their time they will become partners (and if there are any firms still doing this, they should stop immediately). The business and economic climate for providing legal services has changed, and delaying the restructuring will benefit no one. It is reality now that not all assistants will have the opportunity to become a partner in their early thirties and aspire to the highest levels of income within the firm.

The introduction of a two-tier system is not likely to make recruiting new assistants more difficult, either. Young lawyers recognise the changing legal environment, and many no longer expect to stay with their first choice of firm for the rest of their professional lives. Partnership as a professional carrot is increasingly less valuable as it becomes more remote, more expensive and attracts greater responsibility and obligation. Indeed, salaried partnership may represent an attractive career alternative or lifestyle choice. Far from hindering recruitment, a two-tier partnership can help — provided it is properly sold and implemented.

34.6 Involve the Salaried Partners

Part of the proper selling of salaried partnership is to be careful not to devalue it or create the notion of second-class partners. With some exceptions, therefore, salaried partners should be treated identically to equity partners.

In firms that regard salaried partnership as a testing ground, or form of elevated employment, equity partners are often reluctant to share information about the firm. Yet they still claim to be testing and assessing the salaried partners' performance. Equity partners want the salaried partners to participate and take on more responsibility to demonstrate their abilities, but do not provide the support to encourage success. The only time that anyone actually behaves as an equity partner is when they *are* an equity partner. Salaried partnership as a testing ground therefore has some self-limiting goals.

Often, there is a concern about diluting voting control by allowing salaried partners to participate more fully in partners' meetings — especially where voting is by show of hands rather than by reference to partnership share. These are legitimate concerns, but redefining the role of equity partners does not mean that a firm has to discriminate against salaried partners. There are specific decisions that should be identified and reserved to equity partners in all firms: examples would be those entrepreneurial issues (and their consequences) that should be reserved to entrepreneurs such as introducing new services, opening new offices, mergers, capital and debt issues (salaried partners do not typically make capital contributions, or guarantee debt, leases or similar long-term commitments), division of the residual (net profit), admitting new partners, exceptional expenditure, and dissolution. Salaried partners should therefore attend partners' meetings, receive financial and other information, and vote on decisions — except to the extent that entrepreneurial decisions are being taken.

Treating salaried partners as lesser beings will quickly lead to resentment. Living in the expectation that the cherished goal of equity may only be two or three years away may be sufficient for some salaried partners to grin and bear it. But as the second tier becomes more of a permanent career track for some salaried partners, these issues cannot be ignored. In my view, the market reacts far better to a firm that loses an assistant who did not make it to partnership than it does to one which loses a 'partner' who is discontented because of the way equity partners behave.

Over time, an effective two-tier structure can help the firm identify the true entrepreneurs, meet varying career expectations, reward top fee-earning lawyers, and secure a healthy future.

34.7 Consultants

In the same way that firms may choose through the medium of salaried partnership to structure the admission of partners without immediately (or ever) offering full equity participation, so they may choose to structure differently at the 'outgoing' end. The position of 'consultant' is often occupied by partners who have retired from the firm: they are no longer equity partners, but they may continue to serve in some way. Such a position may also be used to accommodate an equity partner who would not today be offered equity partnership in her own firm because her abilities, performance or contribution would not merit such promotion, but whose current position as an equity partner makes it impossible to 'demote' her to salaried partnership; it is also an alternative to 'early retirement'.

As with salaried partnership, provided the criteria are established, understood, and consistently and fairly applied, there is no reason why the position of consultant should not be effective and successful. Such a person should not normally be expected to be either an entrepreneur or a financier. Their return would therefore be a 'wage' for services provided; the label of 'consultant' is incidental (or even irrelevant) in economic terms, but may be important from a professional, reputational and emotional standpoint.

Chapter 35

CHANGES IN EQUITY PARTNERS

Against the background so far discussed, it is now possible to examine issues surrounding the admission and departure of partners.

35.1 Admission

35.1.1 Admission criteria

The question of who is admitted into partnership, when, and at what level can be considered by responding to the issues raised in part II. Thus, a sole principal may consider admitting a partner based on the entrepreneurial qualities of a new recruit and the degree of that person's continuing dependence on the principal's individual capital (see paragraphs 8.4.4 and 9.2). Partnerships of individual practitioners will not be too concerned with someone's entrepreneurial activities, but partnerships of integrated entrepreneurs will. In my conception of equity partnership (and therefore of law firm ownership), the issue of entrepreneurial behaviour is all-important. But running through these economic and structural preferences, there will also be issues of attitudes, beliefs and socialisation which will provide indications (or contraindications) of suitability for partnership: see paragraphs 14.2.5, 22.5 and 23.4.

Based on these preferences, firms can thus identify the qualities and roles (see paragraph 33.2) that will be required of equity partners in their firms. They can also use this analysis to decide when the most appropriate time for admission would be, based on the demonstration of these qualities and the actual or potential development of an individual into the required roles. In practice, it would seem that fee-earning ability and bringing in new business are still paramount, and that management ability is of little significance (see Morris and Pinnington 1996b, table 1).

If an individual has not shown sufficient development or consistent demonstration of the attributes required for admission as an equity partner, that person could be admitted as a salaried partner (see chapter

34). Whether that person will then advance to equity partnership should depend on the further demonstration or development of the entrepreneurial and other qualities that should be necessary for admission to that tier.

In other words, it is not possible (and may be dangerously misleading) to produce a statement of standard admission criteria purportedly appropriate to all partnership positions in all law firms — except perhaps as a checklist of the range of possibilities.

35.1.2 *Lateral admission*

Admission of partners laterally raises many of the same issues. The timing of an immediate decision is necessarily predetermined. But the consistent demonstration and development of the necessary performance and qualities can be dealt with in the same way as with the 'vertical promotion' of assistants. If the requirements are met, admission could be to equity partnership (although for reasons that will be suggested in paragraph 36.5.4, this may not be wise); if not, the further conditions can be specified and the lawyer admitted to salaried partnership in the meantime.

35.1.3 *Mergers*

Mass lateral recruitment — in the form of merger or acquisition — poses much greater problems. It is usually the case that the constituent firms will have equity (and salaried) partners already, and none of them will choose voluntarily to change their status — except upwards — in deciding whether or not to support the merger. As a result, the merged firm may find itself forced into a type of mixed partnership (see paragraph 9.5). If partners on both 'sides' wish to avoid this result, careful investigation and discussions must take place before the merger is approved and implemented: see chapter 12.

35.1.4 *Incorporated law firms*

In principle, the question of who to admit to 'partnership' should be no different simply because the practice is incorporated, though the admission will involve the formal issue of shares. The difference with incorporated practices, however, is that lawyers can be admitted to an ownership interest in the firm (by the issue of shares) even though they may not be considered 'partners' on the traditional definition. Nevertheless, it seems to me that, although these share-owning lawyers may be entrepreneurs in the sense that they are investing in the practice, it is still necessary to separate them from those who engage in entrepreneurial activities as defined in paragraph 7.2. If so, it is still necessary to apply 'admission criteria' stringently to these individuals (who will probably, as a result, acquire more shares than the other share-owning lawyers).

35.1.5 New partner induction

Just as people coming into the firm need induction and socialisation (see paragraph 22.4.2), so I believe that new partners need to receive some induction and socialisation into the partnership. The promotion is part of their personal development, and represents a significant change of role (cf. paragraph 24.2). They need the firm's support. For this reason, an induction programme should be set up to give the new partners background information about the partnership, to establish the expectations that the partners have of them, and to provide skills training in some of the new roles that they are now expected to perform.

35.2 Retirement

The retirement of a partner gives rise to two related questions: when and how should the retirement take place; and what are the financial consequences of retirement?

35.2.1 Sole practitioners and sole principals

For a sole practitioner, the retirement issue is usually straightforward: she stops practising, realises any surplus cash from the business by settling any liabilities, collecting outstanding debts and selling assets. For a sole principal, the position is much the same (subject perhaps to finding alternative employment for staff). Both might, of course, want to sell the practice as a going concern. It is unlikely, however, that there will be any question of continuing income from the practice, and so a sole practitioner or principal will need to have made suitable 'funded' arrangements out of current income during her working years.

35.2.2 Partnerships of individual practitioners

In partnerships of individual practitioners, again, the position may be little different from that of truly sole practitioners. There may be issues of dealing with continuing obligations on the shared premises and services — which the continuing partners, being individualists, may not be willing to pick up. But the outgoing partner may be able to sell her practice as a going concern, or alternatively she or the firm may be able to find a new individualist to bring in.

The retiring partner may have made some financial contribution to the firm, and the return of this capital can be expected after retirement. It is, of course, highly unlikely that there will be any continuing income being paid from the firm after retirement — other than fees collected after the retirement date for work done by the retired partner before it.

35.2.3 *Partnerships of integrated entrepreneurs or mixed partnerships*

Whereas sole practitioners and sole principals will often retire with relative ease (and possibly enthusiasm), in partnerships retirement is usually particularly difficult for founders and other entrepreneurs. They will have invested a good deal of themselves — financially, professionally, physically, and emotionally — in building the firm. They may not willingly want to leave. A fundamental issue for a firm, therefore, is whether it will require a partner to retire at a certain age (or to begin a 'phase-down' at a certain age with a view to retirement at a later age). If the founder or entrepreneur is genuinely concerned to see the firm continue beyond her retirement, forced retirement at a known time will focus her mind on transferring and securing the individual and firm-specific capital on which her practice depends. A phase-down is a useful method for planning this process. However, people approach retirement differently and it is questionable whether an automatic, enforced phase-down is always in an individual's or the firm's best interests.

A retiring partner can expect her financial capital to be returned, and her current account (reflecting undrawn profit-share) to be paid out. It may not be possible for the firm to repay it all in one sum. If so, a repayment process will need to be set out in the partnership agreement (or negotiated at the time) which meets the legitimate expectations and economic circumstances of both parties. Subject to the firm's balance sheet at the retirement date including a valuation of work-in-progress, the total of a partner's capital and current accounts shown in the balance sheet would represent her full entitlement. The work-in-progress element represents the payment of a surplus return on individual and firm-specific capital (since the partner will have received her market 'wage' in the current year up to the retirement date — usually as part of her profit-share for that year). In a partnership of integrated entrepreneurs where, on joining the partnership, the incoming partner receives a profit-share for the year of admission based on work-in-progress billed in that year but arising in years before admission, there may be no entitlement to a share of work-in-progress on retirement.

Beyond this, it used to be common for retired partners to receive retirement annuities from their former firms at a rate and for a period agreed beforehand. Such arrangements are less common today, and may be difficult to justify economically or philosophically. Unless these annuities are demonstrably part of the partner's 'deferred compensation' for the use of her individual capital or contribution to firm-specific capital, it is difficult to see that a retired partner should have any continuing claim. It is certainly unlikely that present partners will feel comfortable with the notion that part of their current residual gain will have to paid to someone to recompense her for past contributions. Thus, unless the retired partner becomes a consultant (see paragraph 34.7), so that continuing rewards represent the 'wage' for continuing labour, she should ensure that her retirement is fully funded out of current income during her working life.

Indeed, many partnership agreements now require partners to cover their retirement in this way so that there is no question of future partners feeling morally or otherwise obliged to support retired partners or their families.

35.2.4 *Incorporated law firms*

This may be a situation where retirement is a smoother process. The shares held by the retiring partners can be acquired by continuing shareholders or by new ones: the retiring partners might therefore expect a quicker settlement than in the case of a partnership. However, for as long as the retiring partner remains a solicitor, there is no reason in principle why she should dispose of her shares. Any undrawn income should be paid out. The partner might remain as a salaried employee of the company, in which case she would be paid a wage for that continuing supply of labour. Apart from this, no other payments can be expected.

35.3 Withdrawal

This situation assumes that a partner chooses to leave before retirement (or, perhaps, is asked to leave because of chronic underperformance — expulsion perhaps dressed up as 'early retirement'). Given the increasing lateral movement of partners, this situation is becoming more important. The purpose of this discussion is to consider the position of the individual partner and the firm that she leaves. Thus, although a sole practitioner or sole principal can join another firm laterally, by definition she will take her practice into the new firm and will not therefore leave a firm behind: it is not a withdrawal, but a merger or acquisition. This paragraph accordingly applies only to partnerships.

For most financial purposes, withdrawal is very similar to retirement (see therefore paragraphs 35.2.2 and 35.2.3 for the discussion of the financial consequences) — except, of course, that there will be no question of any continuing income, annuity or involvement. Capital and current accounts will be paid out (possibly more quickly where the withdrawal has been instigated by the firm).

The principal point of difference may relate to shares in work-in-progress, where that work is billed after the withdrawing partner's departure. In the individualist practices (which may, for these purposes, have to include a mixed partnership), partners may expect to receive payment of this 'deferred compensation' after they have left; in integrated partnerships, this is less likely, subject to the partner being paid her appropriate 'wage' up to the date of withdrawal.

35.4 Illness or Disability

As with retirement, the circumstances and time at which partners might be able to withdraw from the partnership (whether voluntarily or compulsorily) because of prolonged illness or a disability should be spelt out before the situation actually arises. Just as retirement can now be funded outside the firm, so can permanent health insurance: the risk can, in other words, be diversified from the individual or the firm to the insurance market (cf. paragraph 8.1.2).

The rationale of an integrated partnership may be (at least in part) the ability of partners to be mutually supportive when illness or disability demonstrates the reality of the unsystematic risk borne by lawyers in private practice (see paragraph 8.1). But there are few firms that are either able or willing to diversify this risk internally for an indefinite period.

Once the circumstances have been determined in which a partner suffering from long-term illness or disability might leave the partnership, the financial issues again become very similar to retirement (see paragraphs 35.2.2 and 35.2.3).

35.5 Death

Although far more "traumatic and emotional" (Hildebrandt and Kaufman 1988, page 126) than other departures, the financial consequences of a partner's death-in-harness present few issues that have not been addressed in relation to retirement, withdrawal or disability. Capital and current accounts will be repaid, as will an appropriate 'wage' (and, if appropriate, a share of work-in-progress) to the date of death.

Unlike the other situations, however, the time of death will be unpredictable (except, to some extent, where it is the result of long-term illness). This may present funding difficulties in paying out capital and current accounts, as well as interrupting current income generation through the unexpected loss of a productive member of the firm. As a matter of the firm's philosophy, it should previously have decided whether to take out any 'key-man' insurance to protect revenue flows; it should also have considered whether the firm will assume any moral or other one-off or continuing obligations towards the deceased partner's family.

35.6 Timing of Payments to Former Partners

When partners have retired or died, they or their estates will most probably want to receive any money owing to them as quickly as possible. The firm may not be able to fund any significant payments in the short term. It is therefore important that the partnership agreement should set out the period over which former partners or their estates will be entitled to receive payments, and what proportion of the total outstanding will be paid over at each stage. The firm may also wish to protect its continuing partners' incomes and capital by placing a cap on the total amount of payments that the firm will be required to make to all former partners or their estates in any one financial year. If there is a 'bulge' of retirements, therefore, the continuing partners will not be faced with unmanageable obligations to former partners.

Chapter 36

PARTNER APPRAISAL

36.1 The Issues

Why does the mere mention of 'partner appraisal' turn otherwise rational and intelligent beings into quivering wrecks or belligerent bullies? In most working environments, it would be bizarre to suggest that all learning and personal development stops somewhere around the age of 30, or when one is otherwise elevated into a management or leadership position, but this is frequently the case in professional service firms (cf. Morris and Pinnington 1996c).

The 'up-or-out' system of promotion to partnership (discussed in paragraph 3.6) is an extreme form of appraisal. With its use declining, it may be that an alternative form of assessment and recognition is needed. Indeed, if the incentive of promotion was part of the governance mechanism of the firm, designed to guard against opportunism and moral hazard (see paragraph 6.4), then the withdrawal or reduction in its frequency of use would suggest that an alternative form of monitoring and incentive is required. Appraisal could be seen as the response (see Morris and Pinnington 1996b, page 15).

Nevertheless, partner appraisal is rarely welcomed in law firms. Perhaps the reason has to do either with a misunderstanding of the purpose or process of appraisal, or with the method of execution and subsequent use of information gained. Developing measures of performance in any professional service environment is notoriously difficult, and law firms are no exception. The issues of appraisal then become, What are we trying to appraise? and Why?. In this sense, paragraph 25.2 should be regarded as providing a framework for partner appraisal as it does for those who are not partners.

In an ideal world, appraisal is an opportunity to review a partner's personal and professional contribution and development, not with a view to penalising her in some way for what she may not have done or achieved, but with the intention of helping her to develop yet further. Like any other business, a law firm should assess the state of its principal asset (its human capital) annually and decide what further investment is required. Partners usually represent the 'cream' of this asset. Why, then, should it be immune from assessment with a view to further investment? There is some evidence that this 'developmental' aspect of appraisal does motivate its introduction (see Morris and Pinnington 1996b, page 16).

36.2 Partner Appraisal and Business Strategy

Partners will also be responsible for the success or failure of the firm's strategic objectives. Any appraisal process must therefore ensure that it enhances these objectives. And here lies the first problem. Most assessment of human endeavour in law firms is based on hard facts that are readily available (chargeable hours recorded, fees billed, write-offs, the number of clients or the volume of new business brought in, and so on). These are all measures of 'input'. If the firm's strategic objectives are to retain existing clients, to serve them well, to be recognised for specialist expertise, and other such 'soft' measures of client satisfaction or market position, the normal input measures do not help. These soft criteria are important, but not readily measurable. Partners will then assume that any appraisal of their effort will be too subjective (or misinformed) and so not valuable. After all, who else can understand precisely what they have been doing for the past 12 months? Even to think this (let alone suggest it) is to advance the existence of moral hazard as a reason for not conducting appraisals: any theory of the firm would seek to find ways of *reducing* the risks of moral hazard, not recognising and then ignoring them.

It is possible, then, that the way in which a firm assesses partners' performance (both formally and informally) makes it less likely that it will achieve its strategic objectives because its measurement of performance is perceived not to relate to the achievement of those objectives. Unfortunately, like it or not, any organisation will see the behaviour that it is perceived to encourage, assess and reward. That is why so many law firms are hotbeds of individual competition. The only things they are perceived to measure and reward are individual inputs: they concentrate on the returns to individual capital, often ignoring its development as well as the use and development of firm-specific capital.

36.3 Choosing the Criteria

The key to effective partner appraisal, therefore, is to encourage partners to agree to a wide range of performance goals. These goals must reflect the combination of entrepreneurial activity, fee-earning and other labour contributions, and should therefore reflect the particular roles that it wishes each partner to perform (see paragraph 33.2). The distinction between 'hard', measurable, objective criteria based on hours and fees performance, and 'soft', subjective factors representing a broader contribution is as valid here as it is in relation to profit-sharing systems (see paragraph 37.4). However, consistent with their findings on criteria for partnership admission (see paragraph 35.1.1) and performance-related profit-sharing (see paragraph 37.4), Morris and Pinnington's research shows that fee generation ranks highly in partner appraisal criteria and management ability does not (1996c, page 11).

A broader range of criteria might cover, perhaps, the following areas:

(a)   hours worked (chargeable and non-chargeable, including time spent on training and development, marketing and management); fees billed, collected, written off; contribution to profit; value of client work managed; value of new work brought in; number of files opened, closed, managed;

(b)   contribution to quality of service as well as to quality of work (the two are not viewed as the same thing by clients: see paragraph 20.3.3);

(c)   the willingness and ability to develop a specialisation;

(d)   the multiplier effect — being the ability and willingness to make a net contribution to the firm through business development, delegation and supervision, and effective management;

(e)   being a team player, working with others, developing work for others, and not hoarding work or practising alone;

(f)   contribution as a leader or manager to firm-wide and practice area management;

(g)   work ethic, including both how hard and how smart the partner works;

(h)   accountability — meaning a willingness to follow the firm's precepts and to be held responsible for one's actions and inactions.

Not all of these categories will be appropriate for every partner, and others could be mentioned (for example, playing a part in the local or professional community). But goals should be developed — personally for each partner rather than generically for all partners — and they should be recorded in writing (for an example, see Hildebrandt and Kaufman 1988, appendix D; see also Maister 1993a, chapter 22). As such, they should be regarded as a 'model' or 'contract' between a partner and the firm of what will be regarded as an acceptable contribution. This contract could be seen as part of the monitoring arrangements consequent on the exchange transaction of labour for 'wages' (see paragraphs 6.4 and 8.9.2); it could also be seen as a prospective business and risk assessment of the partner's entrepreneurial activities (see paragraphs 7.2 and 8.9.3).

36.4   The Benefits

Firms that are willing to spend the time required to use these performance models or contracts effectively experience a number of benefits. First, the efforts of each partner are focused on activities that both the partner and the firm perceive to be in their mutual interests, and each partner has a vested interest in her own plan. Second, communication is improved because each partner knows what is expected and on what basis her performance is to be assessed: it is hard to accuse any other partners involved in the appraisal of making up the rules as they go along when each partner has contributed to her own model. Third, for the same reason, the model removes suggestions of subjectivity. Finally, perhaps the greatest benefit is that partners are likely to accept more accountability when they have been involved in defining their own expected contribution.

Objections to appraisal systems are often founded on the assertion that 'The partners won't like the idea', or that 'It won't work on Mary'. Under any system, some partners will hoard work, take on work outside their area of expertise, not function as team players, upset long-standing clients, treat staff badly, and so on, if the structure and ethos of the partnership encourages and accepts such behaviour. If firms do not want this, it is the responsibility of the firm's management to spot these problems and deal with them. The problems are not created by appraisal (or the lack of it); but their solution may be easier and more palatable if everyone's contribution is defined and agreed and the collective expectation brought into the open.

If a firm decides to go down the appraisal path, then there is one final piece of advice: it is better to do too much than too little. Success lies in involving all partners in the process, and so eliminating surprises and unarticulated expectations. If the partners are not prepared to take the time to make the process work properly, they should not be allowed to start the journey.

36.5 Underperforming Partners

Once appraisal is introduced, it may become clear that some partners do not perform at the same level as others. A partnership needs to think through how it proposes to deal with these situations *before* they happen.

36.5.1 What is 'underperformance'?

How many partners do you know whose productivity is impaired by dependency on drink or drugs? Or by physical or mental illness? You would be unfortunate indeed if you know too many. Perhaps you know a handful more whose productivity is impaired by family difficulties, mid-life or other personal crisis, other distractions or downright laziness? You probably know others whose contribution to the firm is affected by the loss of a client, or a decline in their area of practice. Some also no doubt lack judgment in accepting new clients or in billing existing ones. Do you know some who face an ethical or legal problem that diminishes the reputation of the firm? And how many who are content to record chargeable hours, but do not want to go out marketing or contribute to the successful running of the firm?

The point here is that there are many factors — professional, personal, environmental, ethical, emotional — that affect a partner's performance. At some stage of a career spanning decades, just about *every* partner will be perceived by someone to be underperforming. The hawks who would like to fire *every* partner who is unproductive or underperforming on the broadest definition would most likely end up as sole practitioners! The problem lies not in dealing with a lack of productivity, but in being clear about the *nature and degree* of failures to perform, and the firm's response to them.

36.5.2 *Dealing with performance problems*

Truly unproductive partners (meaning chronic underperformers) can have a debilitating influence on a firm, and every partnership should, in advance, develop reasonable provisions for dealing objectively and fairly with these sensitive situations. Ad hoc, 'let's-wait-and-see' reactions do not usually solve the problems or address the real issues, and often work to the firm's detriment because they set up tensions and uncertainty in those whose futures should not be in doubt. Of course, it matters what type of firm the partner belongs to — individual practitioners, integrated entrepreneurs, or mixed. A partner who is an individualist practitioner, or who is employee-minded, cannot expect the same level of support that she would find forthcoming from integrated entrepreneurs, since the rationale of a sharing partnership is as fully as possible to diversify the unsystematic risk arising from the unexpected ups and downs of professional practice (see paragraph 8.1).

The most difficult issue in the 1990s has been dealing with partners whose client base or practice area has shrunk, or whose specialisation is no longer needed. No one wants to be hard on a person who is capable but less than fully productive primarily because of external circumstances. In such a case, difficult questions need to be answered, including: Should the decline have been foreseen? Was management made aware of the extent of the problem soon enough to plan for its consequences? Should the partner concerned have worked harder at replacing lost business? Partners in partnerships of integrated entrepreneurs or mixed partnerships have to be accountable to each other. But if they came together in partnership in order to diversify the unsystematic risk associated with any individual's practice, throwing out an underperforming partner at the first sign of difficulty would completely undermine the rationale for the firm.

Options for dealing with an underperforming partner include renewing business development efforts, training the partner in new areas, or reassigning her to a new practice group. The partner's income (the 'wage' element of profit) may need to be reduced. Nevertheless, a firm wishing to maintain its economic health cannot be expected to sustain such a partner indefinitely. If, after a mutually agreed period, there has not been the level of expected progress, the firm should 'bite the bullet' and consider out-placement or early retirement. For smaller firms, the need for a turnaround is all the greater. In all of this, however, I am assuming that the firm has done its very best to support the partner concerned and has not simply left them alone to 'work out their own problem'.

Some firms are overloaded with partners who wish to do no more than the work assigned to them. These partners see no value in business development and management: produce quality legal work and all will be right with the world. As I stated earlier (paragraphs 8.9.2 and 8.9.4), firms do not need to share residual gains to entrepreneurial risk with legal 'grinders' who play such a limited role and add no value to the firm; they do not even need to make them salaried partners unless they are beginning to undertake *some* entrepreneurial activities. There is an abundance of good assistants who can be appointed or recruited to fulfil a fee-earning role. Firms that want to develop to their full potential, taking advantage of opportunities to diversify, need partners who are willing to make significant non-chargeable contributions. Partners who do not contribute in this way need help to see the light or should perhaps be moved on.

36.5.3 *Marginal productivity*

Firms that are heavily populated with marginally productive partners (say, more than one in five) have a major problem. Such firms are generally over-partnered, but are prevented by culture, or the partnership agreement, from taking difficult decisions. Their choices are:

(a) finding the will-power to reduce the number of partners (almost impossible to achieve);

(b) reducing the partners' profit-shares in accordance with the firm's productivity and profitability (which many partners, in defiance of economic reality, seem unwilling to accept);

(c) making assistants or support staff redundant (which might work in the short term, but sets up longer-term economic and productivity problems); or

(d) orderly dissolution.

Merger with a firm in a better position or condition is often thought of, but this is usually out of the question (see paragraph 12.2.3). No healthy firm is likely to want to take on these problems (though it might, of course, want to 'cherry-pick' the best and most productive fee-earners — which may precipitate a disorderly dissolution).

36.5.4 *Preventive measures*

There are ways that firms can avoid 'underperforming partner' crises. Effective long-term solutions are, first, to evaluate assistants more openly, honestly and stringently; and to be more selective and careful with partner admissions. Second, have clear and mandatory disability and retirement policies. Third, give a senior or managing partner, or management team, the authority to deal with underperforming partner problems without also subjecting them to an undue amount of carping and second-guessing. Fourth, have a written partnership agreement that provides a fair and objective way of dealing with various difficult productivity issues. Finally, if a firm brings in partners laterally, it should phase them in to equity over at least a two-year period so that any productivity issues or differences of expectation can be addressed before they are given 'tenure'. Guaranteed drawings plus a discretionary bonus are preferable in the short term to an equity interest and a percentage of profits. If the title 'partner' is important to the lateral on entry (as it may well be — particularly if she is a partner in her existing firm), then salaried partnership with a bonus or a fixed-income equity share and bonus can be negotiated (see chapter 34).

Partnerships that do not deal effectively with productivity issues are foolish because the potential consequences for the firm are enormous. Quality of service, continuing client relationships, professional competence, and the firm's standing and reputation are all at risk. No firm today can afford this gamble with its collective individual and firm-specific capital.

Chapter 37

PROFIT-SHARING

37.1 General

Profit-sharing should be seen as part of a wider picture of providing incentives to entrepreneurial partners. To many people, however, the question has more to do with providing *financial* incentives rather than taking any broader view of partner motivation. Unfortunately, law firms often create environments in which performance is either criticised or taken for granted. Career development is represented by admission to partnership; there may be few other positive opportunities for encouragement or motivation. Even firms which introduce appraisal systems usually do not give them sufficient time or attention for them to play a meaningful role in motivation. For partners (where formal appraisal is a rarity but backbiting often too apparent), the opportunities for motivation are probably even more scarce.

Fortunately, most lawyers are self-motivated and will derive much of their satisfaction from the client work they do. Such motivation is possible and tends to work well when people have control over the work they do — and the way they do it — and have strong needs to develop the quality of the clients they deal with or of the work they handle (see paragraph 26.2.1). This should be most true of partners (and would-be partners), but may not be true for all fee-earners. As with others, incentives for partners should not be confined to financial incentives offered through the profit-sharing system.

37.2 The Role of Profit-sharing

There are many different ways of sharing profits among equity partners. The system used may be capable of motivating or demotivating the partners. For most partners, their profit-share will be part of a broader picture of rewards and benefits they derive from their firm — association with a good 'name', quality clients, quality work, collegiality, and the like. Any discussion of profit-sharing should be seen in that broader context.

In any firm, the net profit for distribution will be a finite amount of money. For any partner to receive a greater share of the profits, one or more other partners must necessarily receive less. Once a lawyer decides to practise in partnership with others, rather than as a sole practitioner or sole principal, there is no certain way of knowing that he or she has received an objectively 'fair' share of the profits as compared with another or others. Equal profit-sharing presupposes equality of effort, performance, results, and risk. But who is to say that there is such equality if the partners cannot agree between themselves?

At the end of the day, therefore, the ever-present difficulties of profit-sharing assessments relate to perceptions of relative rewards and the acceptance that someone (or some group) has to make a decision about the allocation of available profit. The relativities may relate to the internal 'pecking order' created by different profit-shares, or to knowledge or perceptions that supposedly equivalent partners in other firms are earning more. In other words, they may concern the relative rewards of individuals within the firm, or the relative profitability of the firm as against competitors. Internally, the important issues here are believing that the system is as fair as it can be, that it is fairly applied, and that partners trust those who make the decisions about profit allocation. Without perceived fairness and trust, no profit-sharing system can work. In this sense, profit-sharing is as much an emotional and cultural issue as a rational one.

Profit-sharing is, I think, ultimately about values and value judgments. Where partners share the same values, the system used is more likely to be perceived as right and fair, and as producing acceptable results. Where they do not share the same values, then value judgments of relative contribution and worth are less likely to match, and profit-sharing disputes will arise.

37.3 Equality and Seniority Systems

In the 'purest' partnership, where all partners are presumed equal, profits will be shared equally. It is unlikely that a partnership of any significant size will adhere to this method. Indeed, it can only be sustained where partners are perceived by each other to be making broadly equal contributions in terms of effort, productivity and results (in whatever role or roles those contributions are made). This degree of perception is usually based on close working relationships and day-to-day contact.

The nearest variation is probably the 'lock-step', or seniority, system. New partners are admitted at the bottom of a profit-sharing scale. The scale is usually based on a percentage or a number of points. After a period of time, the percentage or number of points is increased according to the next step on the predetermined scale. This 'stepping' process is repeated until the partner is at the top of the scale where all partners share at the same rate (parity or plateau partners). Equality and seniority systems still appear to be the most common forms of profit-sharing in the UK (see Morris and Pinnington 1996a).

Initial decisions have to be made about the number of steps to parity (usually between five and ten), the timing of moves to the next step (usually annual), and the relative value of each step (usually resulting in a differential between the value of top and bottom shares of about 2 : 1 or 3 : 1). And a firm must decide whether there are to be steps down from parity towards retirement (cf. paragraph 35.2.3), and if so over what period of time and at what rate. Annual decisions about individual profit-shares are then predetermined by someone's position on the scale and the amount of net profit for distribution. One of the great benefits of the lock-step system is that, once the structure is agreed, it is easy and cost-less to apply. Although there may not be certainty about the amount in advance, there is certainty about the process.

Equal profit-sharing and seniority systems are ultimately based on mutual trust, which requires personal knowledge: that is why they can be so difficult to sustain as a firm grows or after a merger, when a significant number of partners have been brought in from other firms, or when a firm is made up of 'mavericks' who tend to act as sole practitioners (partnerships of individual practitioners or mixed partnerships: see paragraphs 9.3 and 9.5). Once equality or relativity of contribution is no longer perceived — if only through ignorance of others' contributions — mutual trust is usually broken and the perceived fairness of the system comes under increasing doubt. The next 'logical' step then appears to be some notion of performance-related pay. Interestingly, when there are perceived differences of contribution, most firms are ready to divert more profit to overachievers, but are very reluctant to deal with the underlying causes of underperformance (see paragraph 36.5). In many cases, problems of lock-step profit-sharing have more to do with the lack of appraisal and no (or ineffective) correction of underperformance than with the system itself.

One possible way of correcting perceived unfairness in the automatic progression (or maintenance of parity) is the 'intolerant lock-step', where a partner may not automatically be advanced up the steps (or be maintained at parity), but can be 'held' on the current step or even 'demoted'. In this event, however, the issue of who is entitled to make the decision to hold or demote, and on what evidence, is as acute for a lock-step system as it is for a performance-related system.

37.4 Performance-related Profit-sharing

At its simplest, performance-related profit means that firms pay bonuses to partners: a certain amount of money or percentage of profits is retained from the normal process of allocation and is awarded to 'overachievers'. To be worthwhile, the bonus award to individual recipients should be a meaningful sum of money because small differentials of income can be divisive. A firm with a lock-step system could therefore 'hive off' a certain proportion of total net profit for distribution in some way other than in accordance with the predetermined lock-step.

More often than not, though, this creates another problem: how does a firm recognise and measure the degree of overachievement? Who makes the assessment, and on what evidence? How can performance be accurately measured and results attributed to the efforts of one individual? When credits are given, for example, for new client origination or client billing, think of all the possible claims that will emerge for who introduced, courted, nurtured and worked on a client!

A performance-related assessment can be either objective (looking at 'hard', measurable data such as hours worked, fees billed, number of new clients, etc.) or subjective (looking at 'soft', qualitative assessments such as entrepreneurial efforts, or contributions to management, training, the community, reputation, and so on). Objective assessments tend to focus on a relatively narrow range of factors capable of measurement and usually ignore the much broader contributions that law firms need from their partners if they are to be successful (cf. paragraphs 33.2 and 33.7). The narrow focus can also give way to manipulation as partners 'massage' the numbers to give the result they want.

In addition, in most of its forms, performance-related pay rewards individual performance. If a firm is a collection of individual practitioners, an 'eat-what-you-kill' philosophy might be acceptable. But in other law-firm cultures, it can be the negation of the firm, and can leave partners feeling uncomfortable and demotivated. Internal competition motivates only those who are motivated by internal competition: it may not promote inter-partner harmony or good client service. It is less likely to be found in a partnership of integrated entrepreneurs — except, perhaps, where distinctions are drawn between effort and results, those distinctions are recognised and accepted, and the decision-makers are seen to act fairly and impartially in the best interests of the firm as a whole.

Effective subjective performance-related profit-sharing is only possible with a sophisticated approach to partner appraisal (see chapter 36) that seeks to assess the total contribution of effort, performance and results, and the assumption of risk. In practice, firms with performance-related profit-sharing are (as one would expect) significantly more likely to have an appraisal process for partners (see Morris and Pinnington 1996a, page 12). However, whatever the profit-sharing system, and whether partners are formally appraised or not, fee-earning productivity and the generation of new business predominate in the assessment of a partner's performance, and management ability does not (1996a, page 13).

Like all forms of management, performance-related profit-sharing is an art, not a science. Its application cannot be reduced to a simple set of criteria, effortlessly applied and resulting in universally happy partners. The quality and acceptability of the result is directly proportional to the effort that goes into its design, implementation and application. For certain types of firm (such as a mixed partnership), it may be the right system. But, like lock-step, the right performance-related system badly applied will still be a disaster. Performance-related profit-sharing is not an alternative to management — it is part of effective management. Firms must spend time gathering appropriate data and opinions, deciding from where to collect them, how, how often, for what period of time, what analysis should be carried out, and who should do it. They must deal with the underachievers (and not just by paying them less). They must spend time discussing contributions and performance with individuals in order to help everyone benefit from the process and make them think that it is worthwhile. And (perhaps most difficult of all) they must identify an individual or group of partners with the authority, credibility and respect necessary to make decisions or recommendations about relative performance and therefore about relative rewards. These activities all have a cost: collection, analysis, assessment, discussion, and allocation, will take time. The value of the process must exceed the opportunity cost of partners' and management's time in doing it. If a firm is not willing to invest, it should not expect to reap any of the rewards; it should not expect its partners to feel motivated, or its performance and reward problems to slip quietly away.

For a personal approach to performance and incentives to work, the firm must adopt an open, supportive management style that provides positive and constructive feedback. At the end of the day, a firm will see the behaviour that its culture is perceived to encourage and recognise (in the widest context, not just financially). As the 'owners' and leaders of the business, equity partners *can* choose what that culture should be and take the appropriate steps to reinforce it. A well-designed approach to defining the expected contributions of partners and for reviewing their performance is needed.

37.5 Hybrid Systems

It is, of course, possible for a firm to go beyond a simple modified lock-step (which remains a fundamentally seniority-based system with a small element of performance-related bonus) without moving totally to a performance-related system: this is the most likely scenario in a move away from pure lock-step (see Morris and Pinnington 1996a, page 16). It can combine a substantial lock-step (to, say, 40% to 70%) with a performance-related system (applying to the remaining 30% to 60%). Alternatively, it can have 'bands' of profit-sharing approaches, under which, for example, all partners receive a minimum profit-share (based either on a fixed amount of money each or of profits, or a certain percentage of profits), together with another band which is lock-stepped, and a further band which is performance-related.

The combinations are almost endless, but the underlying principles of each part of the system remain as discussed in paragraphs 37.3 and 37.4.

37.6 Is There a Right Way to Share Profits?

Gilson and Mnookin (1985) explore the relationship between profit-sharing and productivity. They do so by reference to two extreme methods of profit-sharing: one is lock-step and they call it 'the sharing model'; the other is a performance-related method which they call 'the marginal product approach'. Their analysis is detailed, and is worth reading in full.

The sharing model exemplifies the approach of firms following an 'integrative' rather than 'individualist' approach. Partnerships of integrated entrepreneurs (see paragraph 9.4) are often best placed to seek and benefit from diversification — because of their inclination and ability to share clients, work, opportunities and risks, as well as their ability to create a structure of monitoring and incentives that minimises the risks associated with the agency problems of grabbing, leaving and shirking. The variety of effort required to make a diversified (or diversifying) practice successful is difficult to measure — much has to be taken on trust. In this sense, by fostering a sense of collegiality and sharing the risk–reward equation across the partnership, the sharing model of the seniority or lock-step system should, in principle, be best placed to support a firm in its strategic aims. Accordingly, we should expect to find partnerships of integrated entrepreneurs using the sharing model of profit-sharing. However, to the extent that the profit-sharing method is part of the incentive structure designed to encourage the development of a sharing or integrated firm in the first place, the argument may be circular.

Of the sharing method, Gilson and Mnookin write (1985, pages 342 to 346):

"Under a lockstep seniority system, an individual lawyer, upon being admitted to the partnership, is quite literally exchanging his human capital for participation in a portfolio of human capital diversified both with respect to the personal characteristics of the lawyers and with respect to specialty. Indeed, it is striking just how well diversified the portfolios of established firms are. New partners in such firms in essence 'buy into' mutual funds through which they are able to share not only in the future income of their contemporaries, but also in the future income of lawyers who offer differing levels of expertise and experience and who span two or even three generations. . . . In theory, the ratio between the income of the most senior partners and that of the least senior partners, and, within reason, the length of the road to a full share, are *not* central, so long as the terms of the bargain are known in advance and not subject to change. . . . In the real world, however, the ratio matters a great deal. A high ratio and a long road to parity mean that the partnership payoff is heavily weighted towards a lawyer's later years. An entering lawyer faces the risk that the firm may suffer a decline or even break up before he or she reaches the top. And this only exacerbates a highly productive lawyer's incentives to grab or leave: a young partner may believe he is worth more now; having to wait increases the risk, and therefore decreases the value, of his interest in the partnership. At the other extreme, were a firm to pay its lawyers almost all of their expected lifetime incomes in the early years, there would be an enormous incentive either to shirk or to leave (depending upon each lawyer's preference between leisure and the income he could earn by joining another firm) after receiving the bulk of his expected future earnings from this firm. Nonetheless, a lockstep seniority system, which implements a progression that minimizes these problems, can provide individual lawyers with the opportunity to capture the gains from diversifying their human capital. . . . The challenge of the sharing model is thus to provide diversification without giving rise to shirking, grabbing, or leaving.''

The point Gilson and Mnookin make about the ratio is, I believe, an important one. If the ratio between the highest and lowest profit-shares exceeds 5 : 1, it becomes very difficult to say that the individuals involved are really *in partnership* with each other.

Conversely, partnerships of individual practitioners (see paragraph 9.3) might be expected to emphasise individual productivity in their intra-firm structure and relationships, and so to prefer the marginal product approach to profit-sharing. Because these systems reward individual productivity and contribution, there should be a closer correlation between what the individual puts into the firm (hours worked, fees billed, new clients generated, etc.) and what he or she takes out. For this reason, there should be fewer incentives to grab, leave or shirk. But in practice, the difficulty with marginal productivity systems is the basis on which productivity is measured: indeed, because they usually incorporate a formula that acts as a proxy for actual productivity, these systems are also known as 'formula systems'. If the system tracks measurable factors, the danger is that an individual lawyer will seek to 'grab' or 'shirk' by playing a numbers game to ensure that his performance maximises the numbers that are measured. A further consequence of the marginal product approach would then be, in theory, to jeopardise attempts at diversification by the firm (because of the lack of any significant firm-specific capital on which to build and of incentives to work together — in fact, there are incentives to compete against each other).

Of the marginal product approach, Gilson and Mnookin write (1985, pages 346, 351 and 352):

"As an abstract proposition, paying each partner in proportion to his contribution to firm profitability sounds straightforward enough, albeit coming at the expense of diversification. In actual operation, however, it is a very complicated task that is impossible to accomplish with complete accuracy. Not only is there likely to be a gap between actual productivity and the firm's approximation of productivity, but the use of some formula to make this approximation also leaves the firm vulnerable to a new set of agency problems: Partners are given an incentive to maximize their own income by maximizing the factors measured by the formula, rather than by actually maximizing their productivity. . . . A formula thus does not prevent the interests of the individual lawyer and those of the firm from diverging. . . . That lawyer is then in the same position as a more productive lawyer in a sharing firm — his income does not reflect his actual productivity — and he has the same incentives to grab and leave.''

37.7 Making a Choice

So which profit-sharing system is best? For present purposes, Gilson and
Mnookin's conclusions can be summarised (1985, pages 352–3, and
380–1):

"Our examination of the two paradigmatic methods of dividing the pie
demonstrates that, in the absence of agency costs, a sharing model has
the advantage of capturing the gains from diversification. Once agency
costs are introduced, however, there is, in the abstract, no easy basis on
which to prefer one model to the other. A sharing model captures the
gains from diversification and avoids the divergence between profit
maximization for the firm and profit maximization for the individual
partner that accompanies, to a greater or lesser extent, any productivity
formula. A sharing model, however, creates a greater incentive to shirk,
grab, or leave than does a marginal product approach. A marginal
product approach, in contrast, will reduce shirking, but eliminate
diversification. And to complete the terms of the necessary balancing,
a marginal product approach creates its own set of perverse incentives
and may also be subject to the shirking, grabbing, and leaving problems
that are generally associated with the sharing model.

The choice between a sharing model and a marginal product approach thus turns on the ability of a law firm to devise a structure that
most effectively reduces the agency costs associated with cooperation.
If the agency costs associated with a sharing model cannot be overcome, a marginal product approach rather than an ineffective sharing
model, becomes the second best alternative. . . .

A partnership in which lawyers share income provides the possibility
for individual lawyers to diversify their human capital. Indeed, a
seniority-based system of dividing the partnership pie is an outstanding
way to diversify. We have seen that shirking, grabbing, and leaving pose
threats to a sharing firm's stability and profitability. Nonetheless,
productivity-based divisions of partnership income are not superior to
a division based on sharing principles. Sharing firms can minimize
shirking problems by a variety of monitoring techniques and by developing a supportive firm culture. Moreover, the concept of 'firm-specific
capital' explains why some sharing firms achieve substantial efficiencies,
tend to be among the most profitable law firms, and avoid the risks of
grabbing and leaving. We have seen that the absence of firm-specific
capital contributes to instability. In a sense, then, our analysis suggests
a paradox: 'Sharing' enhances the success of successful firms with
substantial firm-specific capital while contributing to the instability of
less successful firms without much firm-specific capital."

Gilson and Mnookin's conclusions, and my application of the theory of
the law firm (chapter 9) would perhaps therefore suggest that partnerships
of individual practitioners should adopt a marginal product approach
(performance-related systems), and that partnerships of integrated

entrepreneurs should use the sharing model (equality or seniority systems). In fact, it may be that the existence of significant firm-specific capital is a precondition to the success of the sharing model. It may certainly be the case that effective leadership is (see the extract from Gilson and Mnookin 1985 at paragraph 33.2). Mixed partnerships perhaps present the greatest difficulty, and the choice of profit-sharing system may well depend on the balance of power within them. If the sharing entrepreneurs hold that balance, a sharing model could be used because the reliance on firm-specific capital will be significant; if not, the firm may be forced into the marginal product approach as a 'second best alternative'. Where the power is finely balanced and the reliance on firm-specific capital not so marked, a modified lock-step may be adopted (under which a proportion of net profit is held aside from the lock-step distribution and divided according to marginal productivity principles).

Nelson (1988), however, suggests that Gilson and Mnookin's analysis is flawed. He assumes that the sharing model encourages diversification on an equal basis — that is, that new partners will be admitted to take advantage of opportunities for diversification and will then share on equal terms. He writes (1988, page 65):

"Firms do not have unlimited possibilities for diversification and indeed often face serious constraints on expansion. While Gilson and Mnookin tend to conceive of specialty groups as equal parties to a contract, typically there is a hierarchy of specialties within a firm. The fields bringing in the largest clients get the largest share of the profits. Central to Gilson and Mnookin's model of sharing among specialties is the argument that the best means to maximize diversification is a system of compensation based on lockstep seniority in which lawyers of equal seniority receive equal financial rewards. But the clear trend in compensation systems in law firms is away from pure seniority systems. Strict lockstep income systems are now limited to a small set of exceptional law firms. Moreover, there is no evidence that seniority-based profit sharing has led to enhanced diversification or improved economic performance. . . . If Gilson and Mnookin's thesis were correct, we would expect lockstep firms to diversify more rapidly than others."

I believe that Nelson distorts the analysis. His point about rewarding partners at the same level is valid, and I shall deal with this in paragraph 37.9. The constraints on diversification are acknowledged (see paragraph 8.5). Further, a conclusion that the sharing method would be the most appropriate profit-sharing system for partnerships of integrated entrepreneurs shows that such a system *would* only be for a small set of exceptional firms, since partnerships of integrated entrepreneurs are themselves exceptional. The fact that other partnerships might have tried to use (and moved away from) a system of profit-sharing that was inappropriate to their structure, expectations and needs is hardly evidence that the sharing method is wrong in principle as a support for diversification. Finally, even though partnerships of integrated entrepreneurs, using a sharing method of profit-sharing, might be better placed to take full advantage of diversification, this does not mean that they must inevitably do so: whether they do or not will depend on the aspirations and priorities of the entrepreneurs themselves and their assessment of the risks involved. Equally, such a conclusion cannot prevent *other* types of partnership from seeking to diversify.

In short, Nelson seems to attribute to the entirety of law firm partners knowledge of the theory of the law firm and of its application that the vast majority of them would never have considered and still less would have applied to their businesses. To suggest (as he does at pages 64 and 65) that because partners do not explain their motivating factors in language identical to Gilson and Mnookin's, the latter's argument is "fundamentally wrong" seems grossly unfair to those authors. To the extent that partners express those motivating factors as "the opportunities for tapping new client sources and providing additional services to existing clients" (1988, page 65), Nelson's exposition seems identical to mine in identifying surplus client needs and surplus opportunities (see chapter 8): these are entirely consistent with the foundations of Gilson and Mnookin's analysis.

37.8 Conclusions

There is, then, no easy basis on which to prefer one system to another. I have seen both lock-step and performance-related systems be successful, and I have seen both fail; I have seen each of them encourage precisely the sort of behaviour and attitudes that are supposed to be encouraged by the other. At the end of the day, a firm will see the behaviour that its culture is perceived to encourage and recognise (in the widest context, not just financially). As the 'owners' and leaders of the business, equity partners *can* choose what that culture should be and take the appropriate steps to reinforce it (Maister's view is that this is an issue of what the firm is prepared to tolerate, and intolerant firms are more successful than tolerant ones: 1997, chapter 9). A well-designed approach to defining the expected contributions of partners and for reviewing their performance is needed. A lock-step system is perhaps better at encouraging collegiality and allowing a firm to diversify its practice; it also reduces the potential discrepancy between maximising profits for the firm and for the individual partner. However, it creates a greater risk of partners coasting or leaving the firm if they feel that the relative rewards are distorted. A performance-related system, on the other hand, reduces the risks of partners shirking, but may compromise the firm's attempts to diversify (particularly where this involves investment, risk-taking, teamwork and cross-selling). A performance-related system may introduce its own set of distortions as partners seek to 'play the numbers' to ensure a favourable individual result.

The choice between a lock-step and performance-related system may therefore turn on a firm's ability to devise a structure that most effectively encourages inter-partner cooperation. If the lock-step system is not achieving this because of the distortion and suspicion created by perceived inequality of contribution, then a performance-related system becomes the best alternative to an ineffective lock-step.

The experience of law firms (particularly those in the US), however, is that once a firm moves away from lock-step to some form of performance-related division of profit, it is all but impossible for it to move back to lock-step if the move proves unsuccessful. Making the move is therefore a significant decision, not to be taken lightly.

One factor in the equation may be the extent of the firm's reputation, continuing client relationships and goodwill (that is, on its firm-specific capital: see paragraph 5.2). If a firm relies on its collective reputation and established client base for its flow of future work and profits, there is some evidence that the lock-step system helps to consolidate the firm's position (this appears to be borne out by Morris and Pinnington's research: 1996a, page 11). Partners are equally reliant on established work flows. However, if the firm is dependent on the 'rainmaking' abilities (the individual human capital) of some of the partners to generate significant new business (particularly in a transactional market), the lock-step system can make the firm unstable: the individuals who take the risks of client development and use their own reputations to bring work in expect a greater share of the rewards, and a seniority system may not deliver them.

But few firms will be entirely at either end of this spectrum. Where a firm has a mixture of continuing business from established client relationships and a need for rainmaking and entrepreneurialism, the choice of an acceptable profit-sharing system may well depend on the balance of power. If the custodians of continuing business hold that balance, a lock-step system may be preferable because the reliance on collective reputation and contribution, and on mutual support, will usually be significant; if not, the firm may need a performance-related approach. Where the power is finely balanced and the reliance on collective reputation and goodwill not so marked, a modified lock-step may be adopted (under which a proportion of net profit is held aside from the lock-step distribution and divided according to performance-related principles).

There is a final point about profit-sharing. It seems that, whatever the chosen method, "the overwhelmingly powerful predictors of income differences are seniority and client responsibility. . . . Regardless of managerial ideology, the law firm is, and is likely to remain, an age-graded pyramid in which older lawyers control the clients and make the most money" (Nelson 1988, page 191; and see Maister 1993a, chapter 25 and Morris and Pinnington 1996a).

Whatever the theory, it seems that in practice a variety of profit-sharing arrangements exist in large UK law firms, and that there is still a greater following today for the lock-step system than there is in the large US firms — which have largely switched to some form of performance-related system (Griffiths 1996).

37.9   An Entrepreneurial Division of the Spoils

None of the analyses of profit-sharing arrangements discussed in paragraphs 37.3 to 37.5 draw the distinctions I suggested in paragraph 8.9. Because of this, I depart from the logic of both the sharing model and the marginal product approach, and therefore instinctively prefer neither approach — even for the extremes of partnerships of integrated entrepreneurs and partnerships of individual practitioners. The profit-sharing systems discussed by almost all commentators relate to the *totality* of the net profit. The sharing method emphasises the importance of firm-specific capital and seems to assume that the partners' profit-shares are returns for broadly equivalent exploitation of this capital. The marginal product approach emphasises individual capital, and therefore sees profit-shares as individual returns to the use of that capital, with little concession to the existence or value of firm-specific capital.

My preferred analysis assumes that in all firms there can be returns to both individual *and* firm-specific capital. I would not therefore expect to find broadly equivalent profit-shares, even in sharing, integrated firms. Partners may have contributed different amounts of financial capital; their expertise may attract a different level of market 'wage'. It may be that their surplus returns for the exploitation of firm-specific capital are (and should be) equal because as entrepreneurs their risk is identical. But the aggregation of these components, separately computed on different assumptions, is by no means the same exercise as dividing total profit according to a lock-step system.

Using my apportionments, one should expect a senior lawyer to earn more (because his market 'wage' should be higher — but will not *inevitably* be higher — to reflect greater expertise and experience). In addition, those individuals who control client relationships will accordingly have valuable *individual* capital: there should again therefore be some *surplus* return to individual capital as well (if it is not against the partnership ethos to compute it).

I would take exactly the same approach to partnerships of individual practitioners (and mixed partnerships). The relative underdevelopment and under-exploitation of firm-specific capital will reduce the returns to that capital — perhaps even to zero — as compared with the partnerships of integrated entrepreneurs. Thus, different market 'wages' for fee-earning and other expertise, and differences in surplus returns to individual capital, would again account for conceivably significant differences in levels of total remuneration. But, as before, one would expect this to result in senior practitioners with substantial client following receiving more total remuneration than others.

This just leaves the method of calculating the different elements. The return to financial capital (interest) can be fixed relative to base rates in the money market. This is perhaps the easiest of the elements to deal with. In some firms (especially where partners contribute financial capital equally, or at least broadly in proportion to their profit-shares), the partnership takes a deliberate decision not to pay interest on capital. The rationale is usually expressed to be either that they all have the same amount (or proportionate amount) at risk, and that their profit-shares represent adequate recompense, or that the contribution is in a sense a 'subscription' that entitles a partner to participate in the firm and to share its profits. The issue I am seeking to analyse here, though, is not whether interest on capital is *actually* paid, but at least to examine the distribution of the residual profit on the basis that it is, so that each firm (and equity partner) can determine the *true* return to the entrepreneurial risk that they are taking. If they lent or invested the same amount of financial capital somewhere else, they would expect a return for its use (cf. paragraph 7.3).

The 'wage' for services might lead to some individualism (the 'perversity' which distorts the marginal product approach to profit-sharing by encouraging grabbing, leaving or shirking). But it would be possible to introduce some objectivity here by consulting independent recruitment specialists (or they could be used as final arbiters in negotiations): they would have to be instructed, of course, that the rate to be fixed is not the equivalent total profit-share that one would normally associate with partnership, but only the 'wage' element. The figure to be arrived at is the wage that would be need to be paid for a qualified lawyer performing the same sort of fee-earning work as the partner concerned and should therefore include benefits, pensions contributions and other elements that a senior employee would receive from the firm at that level of reward.

The difficulty here is that wages are subject to market fluctuations depending on general economic conditions, the availability of suitable fee-earners in the marketplace, or the relative buying power of clients in setting the fee levels for the area of expertise in question. In partnerships of individual practitioners (see paragraph 9.3), the partners necessarily bear the full force of these fluctuations. However, a partnership of integrated entrepreneurs (see paragraph 9.4), being based on sharing and the diversification of risk, would probably not want to expose individual partners to these fluctuations in 'wage' — otherwise the individual's unsystematic risk would *not* be diversified (cf. paragraph 8.1.2) to the extent expected by participating in such a partnership. In these firms, then, we might find a 'base wage' being fixed for all partners (which may well be close to that paid in the firm to salaried partners or the most senior assistants). Mixed partnerships face the same dilemma, and the resolution will probably depend on the balance of view within the firm (cf. paragraph 9.5.4).

The division of surplus residual gains to individual and firm-specific capital would then fall to be determined by whatever profit-sharing system the partners agreed on. An individual with extensive and successful networking and client development skills should be 'worth' more than the 'wage' that is fixed for her fee-earning work: this is the surplus return to individual capital. The internal appraisal of that partner would need to determine the extent to which she is relying entirely on her own individual capital or is relying on the firm's human capital for a continuing flow of work. This will be a difficult (subjective) decision to make — but is one that is implicitly made in most partnerships anyway. A partner who relies entirely on her own capital without calling on others to help in business development or delivery is, to my mind, an individual practitioner. Her market worth may be high, but will be limited by her own capacity to network and carry out client work. One is most likely to find this situation in a partnership of individual practitioners, and the return will probably equate quite closely to the gross profit from the fee income she generates (less the interest and 'wage' elements already agreed). As soon as she begins to rely on the firm's infrastructure and others in the firm, she uses firm-specific capital: she is dependent on sharing and integration, and any surplus over and above the 'wage' is then a return to firm-specific capital. In most firms, however, there will be partners who have a significant 'personal' following which they can only turn into a serious flow of business when they can combine it with an expertise or resource base (that is, with a credible law firm). Here, the partner's return should be higher than that for another who simply relies on the firm's reputation (firm-specific capital) to produce a flow of work. The former should be rewarded with some surplus return to her individual capital as well as from the return to firm-specific capital which her individual following has allowed the firm to exploit. These are precisely the issues with which, it seems to me, many partnerships are grappling in their performance-related profit-sharing assessments. I believe that they are only possible with some form of sophisticated partner appraisal (see chapter 36).

In my system of dividing the spoils, therefore, it would only be in relation to this surplus over and above interest and wages 'payments' to partners (the 'true' residual) that the usual methods of profit-sharing become relevant, rather than in relation to the entire net profit. At this point, *and in relation to this surplus only*, I would support Gilson and Mnookin's conclusions about the effects of the sharing method and marginal product approach. In practice, of course, a firm of integrated entrepreneurs with a preference for a pure equality or lock-step system will probably not want to make the distinctions between financing, wages and entrepreneurial risk that I am suggesting. But unless firms make these distinctions, I do not believe that they are truly able to distinguish one firm's performance with another's, or even to compare their own performance year-on-year.

PART VIII

THE WAY AHEAD

Chapter 38

THE FUTURE OF LEGAL PRACTICE

38.1   The Shape of the Future

It is both difficult and dangerous to forecast the future. We can be sure that legal practice at the end of the next millennium will be very different from legal practice at its beginning. But we cannot be entirely sure what it will be like by the year 2005, or 2010, and certainly not by 2040 (which is roughly when someone qualifying in 1997 would be thinking about retiring!). Nevertheless, on the basis of the messages in this book, I believe that certain of the foundations are already laid and that it might be possible to engage in some reasonable speculation about the next 10 to 15 years. I must emphasise — if any emphasis were needed in these circumstances — that these are personal, and necessarily idiosyncratic, views.

If law firms are know-how businesses, then the economics of know-how requires that lawyers will be paid for their expertise, experience or efficiency (see paragraph 2.3.3 and chapter 5). If lawyers are to survive in business (and want to remain in business) — as opposed to becoming a nationalised public service, for example — then as entrepreneurs they will seek opportunities for above-average returns on their know-how. This in turn seems to suggest one or more of four things:

(a)   developing a high level of specialisation: all specialisation is founded on individual ability and experience, and such individuals continue to bear the unsystematic risk that such personal dependency brings (see paragraph 8.1.2), although a specialist may consider practising alone or with others;

(b)   providing multiple services to the same clients, that is, adding value to any one service by combining it (in a meaningful way to clients) with other services: this will require diversification (to provide breadth of service and, if combined with (a), depth) and cooperation between practitioners as they each provide their services to a common client, though not necessarily at the same time;

(c)   providing joint services to the same clients, that is, being able to provide simultaneous services that individual practitioners (or smaller firms) cannot because they do not have the depth of expertise, resources or geography to meet a large or complex client need: this may or may not require diversification (the work may require a team whose members each have the same know-how rather than a multidisciplinary approach), but it will require collaboration and a high degree of teamwork and 'project management' among practitioners; or

(d)   repackaging know-how and becoming a provider of legal information of use to many clients rather than specific advice for just one client at a time (this is the 'legal information engineer' concept of Susskind 1996).

Whichever of these options is chosen, entrepreneurialism will be needed to turn them into reality (see chapter 7).

It is not enough just to have 'legal' knowledge: the characterisation of know-how suggests that many other dimensions are now required (see paragraph 5.2), and they may 'encroach' on areas traditionally regarded as the territory of other professions (see paragraphs 17.1.1 and 38.4).

38.2   Choices for the Future

Each fee-earner therefore has a basic choice to make: whether to practise as a sole practitioner, or join a firm — to choose a point on the spectrum from individualism to integration (cf. paragraph 32.1). A sole practitioner carries undiversified risks, and is dependent on a personal client following; but he or she will usually have little need for the infrastructure costs of a firm (and the economics of the client work undertaken may not be able to sustain them). Someone who is a sole practitioner in work, attitude and economics should not join a firm — and probably should not even create one by becoming a sole principal. Even so, a sole practitioner will not survive without entrepreneurialism: most sole practitioners carry risks that many law firm partners would find unbearable.

Those who join law firms should be aware of the consequences. It seems to me that law *firms* are built on sharing (clients, work, opportunities, resources, risks, and rewards). Individualism is the antithesis of sharing, and puts a firm's success at risk. In these environments, a different type of entrepreneurialism is required, and delegation, teamwork and coordination are at a premium: this is my partnership of integrated entrepreneurs (see paragraph 9.4).

Lawyers who combine in partnership must agree if they are together simply to share overheads and resources, but otherwise to practise as sole practitioners (the chambers concept that has served the Bar so well). This is the partnership of individual practitioners (see paragraph 9.3). Such a partnership is not, to my mind, a true law firm. Equally, they must agree if they are in business to share clients, work, opportunities, resources, risks, and rewards. I am not claiming that one of these types of partnership is inherently better or more likely to be successful: they are completely different and have different measures of success. Both can be successful in their own terms, and no one can suggest that a particular approach is best. But I can (and do) assert that the partners should know *which* type of partnership they wanted to be in, and are in fact in; and I can (and do) assert that a firm which has a mixture of the two approaches (see paragraph 9.5) is more likely to find business life difficult and frustrating.

It might have been possible in a different, more relaxed environment for legal services for these differences of approach to coexist. But the marketplace is now much more mature and competitive, and there is less room for economic and organisational 'slack' (see paragraph 4.7.4). A partnership needs to understand the basis on which it is in business.

38.3 Challenges of a Mature Marketplace

In a mature marketplace, buyers have more choices (and are better placed to exercise them), and providers do not. Sophisticated buyers make informed choices among alternative credible suppliers. Seeking to meet all the legal needs of all-comers is not a credible approach to informed, sophisticated clients. Lawyers, as the providers of legal services, therefore have to decide what their core business is — what combination of clients, services, and geography is their practice going to focus on? To what extent can they diversify their practices and remain credible with clients? And in what ways and to what extent can they appear unique or different to potential clients so that the client will choose them rather than a rival? These are the strategic challenges discussed in chapter 4.

Clients' choices are influenced not only by the legal know-how of lawyers, but also by the way in which they deliver their services. Relative quality and cost-effectiveness are assessments that clients can, and will, make. Uniqueness and differentiation in a mature marketplace are more likely to be drawn from differences in, or the breadth and depth of individual and firm-specific know-how, than from other resources (most of which can be replicated). Increasingly, therefore, law firms must invest in strengthening their 'invisible' balance sheets: they must develop and strengthen both their professional and managerial know-how.

One of the key challenges for a law firm, now and for the future, is managing the productivity of its fee-earners. Partners must be aware that any fee-earning leverage they create will not result in profitability unless they are able to: sustain that leverage by maintaining a flow of appropriate work (marketing and selling); 'feed' it by sharing work with fee-earners through effective delegation; manage it through supervision, matter management and other appropriate monitoring of performance; and to preserve it by the appropriate combination of promotion and recruitment: see paragraphs 3.6, 7.2, 20.2.1, and 28.4.

38.4 The Fall of Professional Boundaries

38.4.1 The decline of former certainties

I have already said that it is no longer sufficient simply to have legal knowledge (see paragraph 38.1). The shift towards (or, some would say, back to) greater attention to clients' business and personal needs rather than pure law begins to blur the boundaries between different areas of legal expertise. The increasing globalisation of the movement of goods, services, technology and people, and the development of free trade areas, is blurring the boundaries between national legal systems and may lead to the collapse of nation states and 'superstates' (cf. Davidson and Rees-Mogg 1997). The removal of professional monopolies and broader deregulation is blurring the boundaries between different professional disciplines. Specialisation is blurring the work of a professional. The very notion of a 'profession' is based on a body of defined knowledge, the certification of certain individuals as having that knowledge, and the maintenance of standards of the performance and behaviour of those individuals (see also Freidson 1986). But it is now impossible to define what this certifiable knowledge is, and for any one professional to know it. The idea of a profession is under threat, and the increasing polarisation of professional services hastens its transformation (cf. paragraph 1.4.2 and Paterson 1996).

All of these developments are removing the former certainties of the boundaries and limits of professional services, within law firms, across national boundaries, and between professions (see paragraph 17.1.1). The emergence of greater interdisciplinary work, multinational practice, and multidisciplinary practice is apparent for all to see, and is probably unstoppable — whatever practitioners and professional bodies might wish.

It is in this sense that perhaps we cannot talk about the future of the legal *profession*. However, I believe that there will continue to be a need for law and lawyers, and there is therefore a future for legal *practice*. We just may not recognise its form and players from the Industrial Age model that we are familiar with.

38.4.2 *Multinational and multidisciplinary practices*

Multinational and multidisciplinary practices are a form of business enterprise. Like any other, they will succeed and survive to the extent that they accurately and effectively identify and meet market needs. Clients will ultimately decide whether or not these new forms of business organisation survive or not. I think that there is, and will continue to be, a need for these types of practice. Inevitably, they will change the definition of 'legal' services, perhaps even more fundamentally than the removal of the conveyancing monopoly, the introduction of extended rights of audience, legal aid franchising, or 'Big Bang'. Perhaps. But the reality that *some* clients will use such practices does not mean that *every* law firm should now be thinking about becoming a multinational or multidisciplinary practice. Nor does it mean that all those who have made steps in these directions were all correct in doing so, or that all of them will be successful (cf. paragraph 4.4.3).

Like the incorporation of law firms, multinational and multidisciplinary practices are a means to an end, not an end in themselves. Some firms will make them work; some will not. It seems to me that there will be three major constraints on their success (even assuming that the client need exists):

(a)   the increased diversity that these practices necessarily entail may not be credible to clients, and in particular, these types of 'know-how conglomerates' may not be able to maintain the quality of their services at a sufficiently high and consistent level across a greater variety of services (cf. Sveiby and Lloyd 1987, page 102);

(b)   increased size and diversity bring a greater likelihood of client conflicts;

(c)   professional, service or geographical diversity brings a need for managerial know-how and maturity that allows the development of appropriate structures, attitudes, management, accounting and accountability that have hitherto been rare in professional service firms.

Even if multinational and multidisciplinary practices are successful, it will not follow that other types of law firm will disappear: what matters is what the market needs are, and whether partners will be able to structure and manage a firm to meet them. Provided the clients, partners and staff are satisfied with the results, *what* is done and *how* it is done will be for the personal preference of those involved: the important thing will be for people to be in the right environment for them.

38.4.3   *Multitalented practices*

What may be more widespread, however, is the development of what I would call 'multi-talented' practices. The normal idea (or fear) behind multinational and multidisciplinary practices has been that there will be a merging — whether legally or pragmatically — of two more or less equivalent firms of professionals (although the reality has so far been different). As a law firm responds more to clients' wider needs, there is room for the recruitment of people whose know-how is not predominantly legal: it might be accounting, banking, insurance, medical, construction, engineering, project management, scientific, and so on, depending on the nature of the firm's practice. The influx of this know-how will not be such as to change the fundamental character of the firm, but to add value through combining legal know-how with other relevant knowledge and experience. To be sustainable, this might well require changes in the professional rules to allow people with this valuable expertise to progress to partnership in the firm. Indeed, given that the survival of a law firm as a know-how business will depend on managerial as well as professional know-how, the broadening of the 'professional' dimension to include non-legal know-how and a track to partnership should be recognised as a parallel development equivalent to the acquisition of managerial know-how which should also be recognised through a path to partnership.

38.5   The New Partnership

38.5.1   *Entrepreneurial custodians*

A growing recognition that law firms are built on various dimensions of know-how, and on sharing, coordination, collaboration, teamwork and other descriptions of integration, should shift partners' conceptions of their position away from ownership and rights, and more towards custodianship, stewardship, responsibility, and accountability. This is not to say that tomorrow's partners will be little more than glorified employees. The roles and duties of partners will remain onerous, and should not be taken lightly. The business of law will still require entrepreneurship, and investment.

The new partnership will therefore require entrepreneurial custodians who are prepared to invest their time, energy, money, and — above all — know-how, in creating, developing and maintaining their business. Financial contributions will not represent the acquisition of an ownership interest, but more a 'club subscription' that offers certain privileges during membership, but gives rise to no lasting capital asset that can be sold. Their objective will be to leave the firm in better shape than they found it — in terms of the quality of its know-how, client base, reputation and economics (cf. paragraph 32.5).

38.5.2 Incorporation and selling out

So what of incorporation, being bought out by accountants or other third-party investors, and the floating of law firms on a stock exchange? I have already argued that incorporation will become more appropriate for larger, integrated firms (see paragraph 8.7). But the idea of 'selling out' and flotation does not appeal to me. The successful practice of law requires a continuing flow of business, and the constant application of professional know-how to client work. Without that know-how, there is no client work, and without both there is no business. The valuation of law firms has to assume a continuing flow of business (see paragraph 5.5.3). For the partners to sell up and move on would remove a significant part of the know-how on which the business relies, disrupt the future flow of business, and reduce the firm's value. For the partners to sell up and remain while someone else took part of the profits from the exploitation of their individual and collective know-how seems implausible. To assume that non-owning fee-earners would stay is a significant assumption that may not be justified (see paragraph 3.2 for a reminder of the BZW experience). Know-how businesses have a fundamental fragility, a dependence on key people, and comparatively little need for financial capital that makes the idea of third-party investment problematic — even if the professional rules ever allowed it.

Goodwill (which is what many lawyers would see themselves as ultimately being able to sell — to their continuing partners or to new ones) is based on firm-specific capital. Firm-specific capital is rarely worth anything on its own because it needs to be combined with individual know-how to maximise its productivity and value (cf. paragraph 5.2.3). If the real value of goodwill lies in the individual know-how of the lawyer who leaves, or in the combination of that know-how with others in the firm, it may be worth very little when that lawyer has died, retired or moved on. Buying it represents a considerable risk. The future value of goodwill lies in a continuing flow of client work: the clients will determine this, not the lawyer who seeks to sell the 'following'. Perhaps the only time goodwill (and firm-specific capital) is worth anything independent of a lawyer's continuing involvement is when the firm's know-how processes have been proceduralised and internalised to such a degree that clients are buying a 'branded', commodity service that will survive the departure of individuals. But whether that value would be sustained if all the partners sold up and left could be a moot point.

Incorporation is already a reality — and I anticipate that its popularity will increase. But I also believe that it needs to be combined with limited liability (in fact, I believe that professional *partnerships* should now be allowed limited liability). Clients increasingly treat law firms as merely another supplier, and lawyers are in danger of being disadvantaged. Potential liabilities in legal practice are huge: if there is no limit on joint and several unlimited liability, there is an increasing risk that good people will not enter — or stay in — law firms. There is no longer any broad equivalence between a lawyer's personal wealth and the likely liability to clients; and the increasing size of law firms makes it much harder to be aware of — still less to control and be responsible for — everyone else's actions and advice. And perhaps most important of all, the falling boundaries that I have referred to are destroying the fundamental premise of a profession — defined, certified knowledge (see paragraph 38.4). This greater fluidity creates greater professional risk. However, I would also wish that limited liability for professional acts and advice would not imply any lesser degree of professionalism.

38.6   The Virtual Law Firm?

38.6.1 *Dimensions of virtuality*

The business world generally is exploring the concept of 'the virtual office'. Will it extend to law firms? The discussions often confuse two types of virtuality — physical and organisational, which I think we should do well to separate.

38.6.1.1 *Physical virtuality*
Physical virtuality means that one or more people formally belong to an organisation, but are not always — or possibly ever — physically present in its offices. This is the idea of a serviced office or business centre (which principally provides communication facilities, but not necessarily permanent office space), and home-working. Physical virtuality is made much more feasible by advances in technology. For some time, technology (telephones, fax machines, computers) belonged to a place, and could not be moved: as the technology has become mobile, it no longer belongs to a single, fixed location. Work is now what we do, rather than where we go.

Physical virtuality results in the creation of a virtual office in the sense in which that expression is most often used. A firm will usually shift people from the real world of premises and equipment to the firm's virtual world. The shift to physical virtuality is not entirely a product of technology, but it is certainly a lot easier to achieve and sustain with it.

38.6.1.2   Organisational virtuality

Organisational virtuality means that people do not formally belong to an organisation, but appear to. This is the idea of shared facilities and resources, networking, and outsourcing. A firm can appear to be bigger, and to have more breadth and depth, and resources, than its real size would normally suggest, because it has acquired rights of access to know-how and other resources without having to acquire them permanently and 'internalise' them within the firm.

Organisational virtuality results in the creation of a virtual organisation. Whereas physical virtuality is usually the result of a shift from the real world to the virtual, organisational virtuality can result from a shift in either direction. A 'real' organisation could outsource many of its internal functions and become more virtual (it externalises the people or resources that it presently relies on). Conversely, a business that has been operating within a network relationship could decide to become one business, moving from the virtual to the real (it internalises the people or resources that it presently relies on). If physical virtuality is principally about empowerment through technology, organisational virtuality can be created through human beings or technology (or both). Virtuality is therefore an issue of setting the boundaries of the firm (see paragraph 10.1); it is about the allocation of economic resources (discussed fully in chapter 6).

38.6.2   Implications of virtuality

Virtuality creates a need for some new thinking about the firm (and I am grateful to Charles Handy (1995) for prompting mine). First, it causes a rethink of 'the organisation'. The centre of the organisation becomes more of an administrative hub, the office more like a clubhouse where people meet from time to time. The space requirements of firms will change: a decreased need for fully equipped offices, but more space required for business meetings with clients, and with colleagues, and perhaps more space for socialising.

Virtuality will cause a rethink of 'ownership'. A virtual organisation will provide fewer opportunities for people to meet 'by accident', and its members may well experience a stronger sense of needing to feel that they belong to an organisational community. Again, the concepts of 'membership' and 'custodianship' come to the fore.

Virtuality also causes a rethink of 'management'. Managers become responsible for people they cannot see — they may not know where these people are, or what they are doing.

To Handy, trust is the key to virtuality (1995, page 41). The difficulty is that firms generally are an organisational response to a *lack* of trust — the risks of grabbing, shirking, and leaving (see paragraphs 6.3 and 6.4). And the management paradigm of the structural creation of hierarchies and the style of command and control also assumes that people cannot be trusted (although we might wonder to what extent this creates a self-fulfilling prophecy: Handy 1995, page 44).

At first blush, virtuality looks impersonal: it reduces the scope for interaction between people in person; it keeps them away from the office or at arm's length. But if trust is the key to making virtuality effective, it will be *very* personal. You cannot trust someone you do not know or understand. Trust requires knowledge of and about people. There will be a greater need for people to meet (both to work and to know each other better), and these meetings will have to be scheduled — because the people who will need to attend will not necessarily be 'in the office' already. Trust also has to be mutual and reciprocated: it cannot be a one-way street. At this point, virtuality may pose the greatest practical difficulties for larger firms. There are more people to know, and therefore more who need to be trusted. This implies a greater need for meetings and coordination among people who are probably more organisationally fragmented already. This may lead to increasing differentiation in the functions of the firm, and more distinctions between those at the 'core' of the organisation, and those on its 'periphery'.

38.6.3 Complications of virtuality

In the context of legal practice, the idea of virtuality seems to me to present a number of challenges. Typically, law firms are not naturally trusting organisations. Typically, law firms prefer 'command and control' management for support staff (if not for employed fee-earners as well). Typically, law firms are not very good at holding scheduled meetings (they are cancelled, postponed, or key people turn up late or not at all). And typically, law firm partners are wedded to proprietorship rather than custodianship, to rights rather than accountability.

I hope this characterisation is unfair, because the challenges of virtuality are there to be grasped. As more commercial clients embrace these new approaches to the organisation, to ownership, and to management, law firms again run the risk of being left behind in a world that clients no longer understand.

38.7 Conclusion

I cannot know precisely what the future will bring, but the thrust seems to be:

(a) different business boundaries, caused by the breaking down of the traditional territories of professional practice resulting from increasing client sophistication, globalisation, and professional competition;

(b) different organisations, caused by the adoption of new structures (incorporation, multinational and multidisciplinary practices, and virtuality), and new approaches to ownership (entrepreneurial custodianship and — though less likely — third-party investment);

(c) different economics, caused by a continuing profit squeeze and focus on productivity, quality and value for money; and

(d)   different forms of management, caused by differences in organisational structures (see (b)), greater sophistication and maturity, and the professionalisation of management.

The important issue here is not the accuracy of the predictions, but the ability of any given firm to react and adapt to those changes that do occur (cf. Maister 1997, chapter 16).

The responses of individual firms to the challenges ahead cannot conceivably be the same: different markets impose different requirements, and different lawyers have different preferences. Strategies, structures and ownership will be different, and will necessarily change over time. This leaves me with the conclusion that legal practice will continue its march towards greater diversity, polarisation, and fragmentation. My fervent hope is that it will not also lose its integrity and professionalism.

Chapter 39

A PHILOSOPHY OF LAW FIRM MANAGEMENT

39.1 The Emergence of a Philosophy

The word 'philosophy' means different things in different circumstances, and to different people. My own use of it here is similarly varied. At one level, philosophy is "investigating the intelligibility of concepts by means of rational argument concerning their presuppositions, implications and interrelationships", and "the critical study of the basic principles and concepts of a discipline" (*Collins English Dictionary*). This book is my attempt at such an investigation and critical study of law firm management.

At another level, *a* philosophy is "any system of belief, values, or tenets", or "a personal outlook or viewpoint" (also from *Collins English Dictionary*). This book has identified a number of fundamental issues and themes, and the purpose of this chapter is therefore to bring them together as a personal statement of my beliefs and outlook on law firm management. This philosophy is the result partly of the investigation and critical study presented in this book, partly of my experience as a consultant to the legal profession, and partly of my experience of working in a law firm.

As in chapter 10 with the summary of my theory of the law firm, I shall state my philosophy of law firm management as a series of propositions.

39.2 The Propositions

39.2.1 Businesses are responses to their environment

Proposition 1. All businesses are an organisational response to their environment, and law firms are no exception.

Proposition 2. The environment is made up of socio-political, economic, and professional dimensions (see chapter 1).

Proposition 3. The response that any particular business makes will be limited by its interpretation of the environment, by its resources and ability, and by its attitude (to the environment, to its resources, to cooperation, to appropriate behaviour and ethics, and to risk).

39.2.2 A changing environment requires changes in organisations

Proposition 4. A changing environment means that organisations must change.

Proposition 5. A firm's strategy must represent a match between its constantly changing environment and its resources and competencies (see paragraph 2.4 and chapter 4).

Proposition 6. The ability to recognise changes in the environment, and the opportunities that they present, and to organise an appropriate matching response, requires entrepreneurialism (see chapter 7).

Proposition 7. Environments and organisations experience evolution and life cycles (see paragraph 2.3), and they are subject to different types of risk (see paragraph 8.1.1). As a result of evolution and risk, they must expect and be able to manage change, internal politics, and projects (see chapters 21 and 27).

39.2.3 Law firms are business organisations

Proposition 8. Law firms are business organisations. As such, there is no necessary conflict between being business-like and being professional. A professional organisation can be business-like, client-driven, financially well-managed and successful, a caring community, and ethical.

Proposition 9. Law firms can be analysed in the same way as other business organisations (see chapter 2).

Proposition 10. As with other businesses, a law firm's structure must combine sufficient and appropriate autonomy and specialisation of its various fee-earning and support functions with the requisite degree of management and coordination (see chapters 14 and 19).

39.2.4 Law firms are client-driven organisations

Proposition 11. To satisfy the entrepreneurial requirement on them (Proposition 6), law firms must also be able to provide effective marketing and selling of legal services to actual and potential clients, and be able to manage the firm's reputation and referral relationships (see chapter 18).

Proposition 12. To meet the expectations and needs of clients, law firms must develop and maintain appropriate structures and processes for the delivery of cost-effective legal services to an appropriate standard of quality (see chapters 19 to 21).

39.2.5 Law firms are economic organisations

Proposition 13. The economic rationale for the formation of a law firm is to diversify risk, and to share surpluses of client work and market opportunities. A firm will emerge when the cost-benefit of organising and coordinating know-how and resources through the firm exceeds the cost-benefit of using independent suppliers or networks (see chapter 8).

Proposition 14. The boundaries of the firm will be determined by the extent to which the firm chooses to 'internalise' suppliers and resources that would otherwise be accessed through arm's-length contracts or affiliations (see paragraph 10.1).

Proposition 15. The successful financial performance of a law firm is dependent on the proper management of its realised average charge-out rates, the effective utilisation of its fee-earners' capacity for chargeable work, the creation of an appropriate 'pyramid' of equity partners and other fee-earners, the proper control of overheads, and the effective management of work-in-progress, billing, and credit control (see chapters 28 and 29).

39.2.6 Law firms are social organisations

Proposition 16. Like any grouping of people, a law firm is a social organisation in which members will seek a sense of community, a sense of belonging, and a sense of support.

Proposition 17. People's response to an organisation will be shaped by their perception of themselves, their perceptions of others, their roles, the way in which power and influence are used, and its culture (see chapters 22 to 24).

Proposition 18. A person's performance in a business will depend predominantly on motivation, but he or she will also respond to effective leadership, appraisal, and training and development (see chapters 23, 25 and 26).

Proposition 19. A law firm should also be an ethical and trusting organisation, balancing client satisfaction, partner satisfaction, and staff satisfaction while remaining true to its culture, values and beliefs, and managing cultural diversity within the firm (see paragraph 23.4).

39.2.7 Law firms are know-how organisations

Proposition 20. A law firm is a know-how business and, as such, requires a balance of professional and managerial know-how (dual expertise): see paragraph 3.3.

Proposition 21. As a know-how business, a law firm must develop and exploit both individual and firm-specific human capital, and make investments in that capital (see chapter 5).

Proposition 22. Law firms must respect professional autonomy and encourage self-management; but individual professionals must also respect the need for responsibility and accountability (see paragraph 14.2).

Proposition 23. Because partners in law firms do not own the know-how of other partners, or of employees, the principal assets on which their business and profitability is based are not owned by them. In this sense, 'ownership' in a law firm is a mirage, and the concept of custodianship or stewardship is more appropriate. On this basis, the principal role of partners is to leave the business in better shape than they found it (see chapter 32 and paragraph 38.5.1).

39.2.8 Conclusions

Proposition 24. The variety of factors that affect law firms is so great, and the interplay of many variables so significant, that merely mimetic behaviour (the 'herd instinct', or doing something simply because other firms are doing it) is an irrational response by a law firm to its environment.

Proposition 25. If a law firm is to make any business sense, it must be built on certain fundamental preconditions (see chapter 8):

(a) Partners must identify, acquire or develop surplus client work or surplus market opportunities.

(b) Those surpluses must be both shareable and actually shared by partners (whether horizontally with other partners, or vertically with employed fee-earners).

(c) The firm's partners and managers must make effective use of its resources, and effectively monitor that use to minimise the risks inherent in sharing surpluses with others.

(d) The firm must deliver the rewards and promotion to employed fee-earners and staff that are required to secure their effective longer-term motivation and performance.

However, these are necessary, but not sufficient, conditions. If the firm is to be successful, it must also be founded on a common purpose that will create a framework for the work and actions of individual partners and staff, and on common values that will provide a framework and basis for their behaviour.

Proposition 26. There are three principal structural types of law firm (see chapter 9):

   (a)   a sole practitioner who works without any other fee-earners and who relies entirely on his or her own individual know-how;
   (b)   a sole principal who works with other employed fee-earners, but who relies principally on his or her own individual know-how;
   (c)   a partnership, which in turn can be found on a spectrum between:

      (i)   a partnership of individual practitioners who do not routinely share surpluses with each other, and whose practice is built on the exploitation by each partner of his or her individual know-how, and
      (ii)   a partnership of integrated entrepreneurs who routinely share surpluses with each other and with other employed fee-earners, and whose firm is built on the collective exploitation of the individual know-how of the partners and fee-earners and of firm-specific capital, with
      (iii)   somewhere in the middle, a mixed partnership made up of a mixture of sharing entrepreneurs with either individual practitioners, employee-minded partners, or unintegrated laterals (or a combination of them).

Proposition 27. An incorporated law firm, and an in-house legal department, can be based on the same principles as the law firm structures in Proposition 26 (see paragraphs 9.6 and 9.7).

Proposition 28. An individual's choice of practice for the future lies on a spectrum from individualism to integration, but becoming a partner (particularly in an integrated firm) carries significant roles, responsibilities and accountability (see chapters 33 to 37).

Proposition 29. Like all businesses, law firms need entrepreneurs and all equity partners should be entrepreneurial (as defined in paragraph 7.2).

Proposition 30. A law firm's profits should be seen as a combination of interest on contributed financial capital (the return to financiers), a 'wage' for the use of individual labour and know-how (the reward for working), and a 'true profit' as a return for the business risks and uncertainties borne by entrepreneurs (the residual gains to entrepreneurs): see paragraphs 8.9 and 37.9.

39.3   A Summary

Pulling these propositions together, the 'philosophical' threads that emerge can be succinctly stated. In summary, my philosophy would be for a law office:

(a)   to recognise socio-economic, professional, organisational and personal evolution;

(b)   to invest in and value both individual and firm-specific know-how, and both professional and managerial know-how;

(c)   to encourage and reward entrepreneurialism, sharing and integration;

(d)   to develop as many shared values (or as much 'glue': see paragraph 40.2) as it can; and

(e)   to balance intuitive 'feel' with rationality and reflection: this is the true value of managerial know-how.

Chapter 40

SO WHAT IS A LAW FIRM, AND WHAT HOLDS IT TOGETHER?

40.1 A Definition

At the end of this exposition of the principles of law firm strategy and management, I cannot resist the temptation to try to pull it all together. It may seem odd to try to define a law firm, but the very act of defining forces us to package in concise form a variety of otherwise complex and diverse issues and, perhaps, to recognise some home truths. In fact, we should be able to see the differences between what law firms *are* and what they *should be*. What follows is a narrative definition with pointers to more detailed elements discussed afterwards:

A law firm is a business unit wholly owned by lawyers (1) comprising lawyers of varying degrees of expertise and experience (2), together with support staff (3). By cooperating with each other (4) and with clients (5), these people must achieve the firm's business objectives (6). Those objectives are to match (7) the legal (8) and managerial (9) know-how within the firm to clients' needs for legal services (10), and to deliver those services (11), in such a way that economic and other benefits (12) result both to clients and to the law firm. Decisions about the business objectives to be followed, and the way in which they are realised, will together create and reflect the firm's mission, culture and values (13).

1   *A business unit.* Like any other form of business enterprise, a law firm will have owners who will cooperate together through some form of business entity. This will usually be a partnership, but in some jurisdictions it can now be an incorporated practice. In the UK, all of the partners (or all of the shareholders and directors of an incorporated practice) must be solicitors. This imposed requirement of owner-investors, and usually owner-managers, leads directly to many of the challenges of law firm

management. The firm will need appropriate and adequate capitalisation, and may grow organically, or through mergers and acquisitions. (The recent trend of international affiliations and joint ventures between law firms is not regarded for the purposes of this definition as resulting in new business units but rather a collection of business units.) In making business assessments, however, lawyers must not forget that they are not *just* a business: they still have professional and ethical responsibilities, in particular as officers of the court. The discharge of these responsibilities often emphasises the individualism and independence of lawyers. However, in my view, there is a difference between a law *office* which is a collection of individual practitioners essentially pursuing independent practices sharing little more than a common trading name, premises and administrative support, and a law *firm* where the whole represents more than the sum of its parts as a result of common objectives, cooperation, and the sharing of clients, client work, and the development and management of the business (see note 2).

2   *Lawyers of varying degrees of expertise and experience.* It is a characteristic of law firms that there are usually lawyers of different ages and at different stages of their careers. Some will be partners (whether equity or salaried), and some will participate in management; others will be assistants (or associates), legal executives or paralegals, and trainees. These varying degrees of expertise and experience allow a firm to 'leverage' its legal talent to provide a cost-efficient pool of legal advisers consistent with giving best advice to clients. The existence of such leverage implies a different basis (and lower levels) of remuneration for those who are less experienced. It also imposes on the firm a requirement to train other people over a period of time to assume more complex matters and so eventually to succeed the more senior and experienced lawyers. By so doing, the firm can ensure continuity of client service, as well as the opportunity for its lawyers to develop professionally and fulfil their personal ambitions. Although a firm may begin with lawyers of equal status whose clients and practice areas may be mutually complementary, a *firm* does not truly develop until these 'founders' begin to leverage their excess capacity to others. Effectively, therefore, a law firm is an organisational framework that allows the lending of 'surplus' client work from one lawyer (usually an established practitioner with a client following, whom we can describe as a principal) to another lawyer (usually less experienced without a client following, whom we can describe as an assistant) who has — or who can develop — some expertise and time to handle that surplus. This 'surplus' need not, of course, be partner-level work: it may be incidental but necessary work arising from the partner's own involvement with a client transaction or matter, or it may be non-partner work specifically developed by the partner for the benefit of the assistant.

3   *Support staff.* This expression describes all staff who support the lawyers in the provision of legal services to clients, but who do not usually have direct fee-earning contact with clients. As such, it includes

professional managers (e.g., partnership secretaries, practice managers, directors of administration, finance, personnel, marketing) and other administrative staff, secretaries, receptionists, telephonists, messengers, librarians, etc. The extent of a firm's investment in support staff and services usually depends on its size (see note 9).

4 *Cooperating with each other.* Unfortunately, in many firms there is a divide between the fee-earning and support staff resulting from professionals who adopt a lofty, 'I am better than you' attitude towards support staff. This master and servant mentality in working relations has virtually disappeared in other businesses and is a relic of a bygone era; it is indefensible and inexcusable in a modern business. Support staff may be as highly trained in their area as lawyers are in theirs. The business cannot function without commitment and professionalism from everyone, and cooperation between them. Sadly, many law firms are also characterised by competition between the lawyers themselves — competition for clients, for client work, for billings, for profit shares, for promotion. Such behaviour is the antithesis of cooperation, and will prevent any business from reaching its full potential (and therefore full profitability).

5 *Clients.* Many firms enjoy a plurality of clients, ranging from private clients to business clients. Even firms that have shed their private client base normally have commercial clients across a wide spectrum. Some will be 'institutional' clients who use the firm for all of their legal advice; others will be 'transactional' (and some may even shop around). Some will be legal aid or even pro bono clients. This diversity in the client base requires different approaches to be taken, as well as sensitivity to the needs and requirements of the various categories of clients (and these days even to individual clients).

6 *Business objectives.* Many firms gave up their strategic plans when the recession of the early 1990s rendered their recent business plans useless. However, all businesses need a strategic focus to their activities. They cannot be all things to all customers or clients. Law firms are no different: the owners need to agree, articulate and understand *why* they are in business together — to know what is the glue that holds them together. Decisions have to be made about whether to be local, regional, national or international; whether to be a niche practice or multi-service; whether to stay as a strictly 'legal' practice or to move into related activities such as property selling or financial services; whether to act for all types of clients or those of a specific type or belonging to a particular industry or business activity; whether to grow; what professional and personal style is appropriate; and so on (see note 13).

7 *Match . . . know-how . . . to . . . clients' needs.* This matching operation is the essence of strategy and marketing or business development. Having decided *which* business(es) or practice areas to be in (see note 6), a firm must decide *how* to compete for business. It requires the firm's lawyers to

consider the specific needs of clients. Attention to client relationships is vital, and requires considerable investment of time. At one time, clients would have conducted this matching operation by themselves on the basis of the perceived quality of a firm's advice and service (that is, its reputation). Since the advent of 'promotion', the marketplace has become competitive, more comparative information is available, and clients have to be targeted and persuaded. The geography of the firm's offices in relation to its client base is important, as is the organisation of the firm into fee-earning and management units (see notes 8 and 9).

8 *Legal . . . know-how*. The legal know-how of a firm's lawyers is the firm's ability to practise law and to service clients. It is what differentiates one lawyer from another and one firm from another. In this sense, law firms are 'know-how businesses'. The technical legal expertise of lawyers must therefore be constantly updated, improved and extended. The development and maintenance of specialisation is a key part of practice area management, as is the organisation of the lawyers into fee-earning groups to maximise the opportunities for sharing their know-how. The most enlightened firms today invest significant resources in developing and sharing individual and collective know-how and in creating know-how systems. They also ensure that their lawyers are continuously trained — not just in legal knowledge and skills, but also in *business* knowledge and skills. Individual lawyers will go to great lengths to understand their clients' businesses and industries.

9 *Managerial know-how*. These days, even a modestly-sized law firm can be a multimillion-pound business. Increasingly, lawyers are recognising that such businesses do not run themselves, and cannot be run effectively by committees of the whole partnership. Business management has become respectable at last. Proper management structures are being introduced, and partners with management responsibilities are being trained to fulfil them (and also being held accountable to their fellow partners for their performance). Professional managers are being brought in to firms in key management roles to support (but not usually to take over) the proper running of the firm. This is the investment that firms must make in their managerial know-how. In addition, as partners, assistants and other staff become familiar with the way a particular firm operates, they develop what might be described as 'situational know-how'. It is this know-how that allows the firm to operate more efficiently as people come to understand 'how we do things around here'. Law firms thus need a combination of legal and managerial expertise to be a fully fledged 'professional' business.

10 *Clients' needs for legal services*. These needs are many and varied; some are common to all clients, and others are exclusive to particular clients. The successful practice of law in a competitive environment requires them all to be met. Again, strategic and managerial decisions have to made: client focus is essential. Practice area organisation has to be considered;

so does geography, and the need for multitalented, multidisciplinary and multinational practices (see note 6).

11 *To deliver those services.* It is not sufficient merely to know what clients' needs are: the firm must be capable of delivering legal services that will meet those needs. A vital part of the management of a law firm is therefore to address the organisation and delivery of legal services. Practice area organisation, the productivity of lawyers and support staff, the use of information technology, training and know-how, and quality management are core elements in meeting the needs of sophisticated, discerning and demanding clients.

12 *Economic and other benefits.* The benefits being looked for by clients usually encompass the resolution of problems (contentious or otherwise), the achievement of some result, or the transfer, protection or restoration of some property. In assessing the value of that benefit, economic considerations such as the level of the lawyers' fees and value for money will be important. Professional empathy with a client is therefore import- ant in achieving the substantive legal benefit required. But so too is business empathy — incorporating the billing arrangements and wider aspects of the lawyer–client relationship. For the lawyer, the economics and profitability of legal practice are important (and increasingly difficult to sustain). Career advancement cannot be ignored — or assumed. However, intellectual stimulation and satisfaction, as well as public and community involvement, are also key motivating factors. Balancing the personal objectives of individuals and the overall business objectives of the firm is one of the major business challenges of the 1990s. It is only just beginning to dawn on partners that their money-making asset (human capital or know-how) ultimately resides in the minds of mobile, tempera- mental and vulnerable people — in other words, that they do not really *own* anything of value. How these human assets are managed, motivated, developed, and rewarded is fundamental to the sustained performance and success of a law firm.

13 *Create and reflect the firm's mission, culture and values.* Like any other business or organisation, a law firm *lives*. It is not (or should not be) a bland, uninspiring object to be shaped; it will change over time. Like other organisms, therefore, it needs guiding principles, beliefs, excitement and development. What the people in it do and say will create an atmosphere, a structure, a culture; and what is achieved as a result may be at odds with those structures and objectives formally set by the firm's owners and managers. A firm must therefore understand its culture, and the values that underlie the actions of its partners and staff. The desired objectives will only be met, and the desired structure and culture will only be created, if the objectives, structure and culture are consistent with the firm's underlying values. It is up to the owners to shape and breathe life into their creation. The intangibles in a law firm are far more valuable than the tangibles — a fact that financial statements ignore. Know-how,

goodwill, reputation, image, motivation, culture and values are more important to long-term success in a law firm than premises, equipment, technology, books and cash.

The richness and complexity of this definition should convince anyone (reinforced, I hope, by the earlier content of this book) that law firms are not simple businesses that will develop and run themselves. Those who step up to the podium to be an owner and manager assume a significant responsibility for their firms. It is an honour; it should be well rewarded; but the status and rewards will come from performing these ownership and management roles well — not simply from occupying them.

40.2 The Idea of Glue

With all this diversity and complexity, the final question therefore is: What holds a firm together? What is it that brings people into the office, day after day, week after week, year after year? Cynics might say that it is the money; but that does not hold true for all people in a law firm, not all of whom are well-paid.

Let me introduce you to 'Mayson's glue'. A number of people can practise together in partnership. Whether they will survive together and be successful over a period of time depends on whether there is the 'glue' that is necessary to hold them together. This bond can come from a variety of sources. Interviews and conversations with hundreds of partners in law firms over the years lead me to suggest that these sources may relate to the reasons why the practice was formed, the person or people around whom it was formed (or who now lead it), the type of clients the firm serves or the law it practises, and so on.

With some tinkering, the glue can be described as one or more of five Ms: mission (the vision or purpose of the firm), mates or mentors (the people in it), matters (the work it does), method (the structure, systems and procedures for doing the work), and money (the rewards of doing it). The full picture is shown in figure 40.1.

For each source of glue, there is a set of issues framed by an appropriate question; and for each of the issues, there is a range of topics (which, broadly, reflect the parts of this book in dealing with a law firm as a business organisation (strategy and management), a client-driven organisation (delivery), a social organisation (people), and an economic organisation (economics).

The following conclusions might be worth bearing in mind:

(a) Firms may draw their glue from different sources at different times, and it is not necessarily a bad thing for the source to change.

(b) The clearer the agreement between partners about what the glue is, the stronger the partnership.

(c) The more glue there is (and the more sources of it) the better. The firm will inevitably be stronger for it.

Mayson's Glue

ISSUES	WHAT ARE YOU IN BUSINESS FOR?	WHO ARE YOU IN BUSINESS WITH?	WHAT DO YOU DO?	HOW ARE YOU DOING IT?	WHAT ARE YOU GETTING OUT OF IT?
CONTENT	Strategy Environment A mix of: clients services geography style	People Leader(s) Partners Fee-earners Support staff Culture	Delivery Specialisation Marketing Training Quality	Management Structure Offices Priorities Systems Human resources Finance Premises Technology	Economics Charging Leverage Profits
GLUE	MISSION	MENTORS & MATES	MATTERS	METHOD	MONEY

Figure 40.1

(d)   If no glue can be found, the firm may be destined for trouble — because there is nothing, literally, to hold it together.

(e)   If the only glue is money, the firm may not hold together for long, because there are very few firms that can make enough money over a sufficient length of time to satisfy the expectations of a sufficient number of partners.

(f)   A partnership of individual practitioners (see paragraph 9.3) is more likely to draw its glue — if it has any — predominantly from matters and money, since mission, mates and management require sharing and coordination.

(g)   A partnership of integrated entrepreneurs (see paragraph 9.4) is more likely to draw its glue predominantly from mission, and mates and mentors (though it will also respect the need for management and coordination), since matters and money tend to emphasise individualism: this is not to suggest, however, that a partnership of integrated entrepreneurs cannot draw its strength from matters, because it may well enjoy working on matters in specialist teams.

(h)   A mixed partnership (see paragraph 9.5) might draw its glue from any of the sources but, because it is mixed, different partners may seek it from different sources with the result that there is no predominant source of glue. This will lead to differences of approach, and possibly tensions and conflict.

Is anything holding your firm together?

BIBLIOGRAPHY

Alderfer, C. (1972) *Existence, Relatedness and Growth* (The Free Press, New York).

Altonji, J. (1991) 'How many slices of the pie?' *Hildebrandt Report*, Vol. 5, No. 4, page 1.

Argyle, M. (1989) *The Social Psychology of Work*, 2nd ed. (Penguin, London).

Badaracco, J.L. (1991) *The Knowledge Link* (Harvard Business School Press, Boston MA).

Baden-Fuller, C. and Bateson, J. (1990) 'Promotion strategies for hierarchically organised professional service firms: is "up or out" always the best?', *International Journal of Service Industry Management*, Vol. 1, No. 3, page 62.

Baden-Fuller, C. and Stopford, J.M. (1992) *Rejuvenating the Mature Business* (Routledge, London and New York).

Barnes, J. (1984) *Flaubert's Parrot* (Picador, London).

Barney, J. (1991) 'Firm resources and sustained competitive advantage', *Journal of Management*, Vol. 17, page 99.

Bartlett, C.A. and Ghoshal, S. (1994) 'Changing the role of top management: Beyond strategy to purpose', *Harvard Business Review*, November–December, page 79.

Bartlett, C.A. and Ghosal, S. (1995a) 'Changing the role of tope management: Beyond structure to processes', *Harvard Business Review*, January–February, page 86.

Bartlett, C.A. and Ghosal, S. (1995b) 'Changing the role of top management: Beyond systems to people', *Harvard Business Review*, May–June, page 132.

Barwise, P., Marsh, P.R. and Wensley, R. (1989) 'Must finance and strategy clash?', *Harvard Business Review*, September–October, page 85.

Beck, S. and Orey, M. (1991) 'Skaddenomics: the ludicrous world of law firm billing', *The American Lawyer*, September 1991, page 3.

Becker, G.S. (1993) *Human Capital*, 3rd ed. (The University of Chicago Press, Chicago and London).

Belbin, R.M. (1981) *Management Teams* (Butterworth-Heinemann, Oxford).

Benson, S. (1991) 'Managing litigation', *Practical Law for Companies*, Vol. II, No. 5, page 3.

Berne, E. (1964) *Games People Play* (Penguin, London).

Bhide, A. (1996) 'The questions every entrepreneur must answer', *Harvard Business Review*, November–December, page 120.

Blackler, F. (1995) 'Knowledge, knowledge work and organizations', *Organization Studies*, Vol. 16, page 1021.

Blau, P.M. (1967-68) 'The hierarchy of authority in organizations', *American Journal of Sociology*, page 453.

Briner, W., Geddes, M. and Hastings, C. (1993) *Project Leadership* (Gower, Aldershot).

Buchanan, D. and Boddy, D. (1992) *The Expertise of the Change Agent* (Prentice Hall).

Chadwick, K. and Hanna, R. (1994) 'Predicting profitability', *The American Lawyer*, July/August, page 63.

Chambers, M. (1996) 'Networks and alliances: strategies of the international law firms', *Commercial Lawyer*, Vol. 1, No. 7, page 17.

Chryssides, G.D. and Kaler, J.H. (1993) *An Introduction to Business Ethics* (Chapman & Hall, London).

Coase, R.H. (1937) 'The nature of the firm', *Economica new series*, Vol. 4, page 386 (reproduced in Williamson & Winter (1993), pages 18–33).

Cobb, W.C. (1989) 'The value curve and the folly of billing-rate pricing', in Reed, R.C. (ed.) *Beyond the Billable Hour* (American Bar Association, Chicago).

Crawford, R. (1991) *In the Era of Human Capital* (HarperCollins, New York).

Cyert, R.M. and March, J.G. (1963) *A Behavioural Theory of the Firm* (Prentice Hall, New York).

Davidow, W.H. and Uttal, B. (1989) 'Service companies: focus or falter', *Harvard Business Review*, July-August, page 77.

Davidson, J.D. and Rees-Mogg, W. (1997) *The Sovereign Individual* (Macmillan, London).

de Geus, A. (1997) *The Living Company* (Nicholas Brealey, London).

Demsetz, H. (1967) 'Toward a theory of property rights', *American Economic Review*, Vol. 57, page 347.

de Oliveira, E.T.V.D. (1996) *The Development and Inter-relations of Organisational and Professional Commitment* (unpublished PhD thesis, The University of Liverpool).

Dietrich, M. (1994) *Transaction Cost Economics and Beyond: towards a New Economics of the Firm* (Routledge, London and New York).

Driscoll, J. (1994) 'Reflective practice for practise', *Senior Nurse* Vol. 13, No. 7, January/February, page 47.

Drucker, P.F. (1955) *The Practice of Management* (1996 reprint; Butterworth-Heinemann, Oxford).

Drucker, P.F. (1991) 'The new productivity challenge', *Harvard Business Review*, November-December, page 69.

Drucker, P.F. (1993) *Post-capitalist Society* (Butterworth-Heinemann, Oxford).

Drucker, P.F. (1994) 'The theory of the business', *Harvard Business Review*, September-October, page 95.

Edvinsson, L. (1992) 'Service leadership — some critical roles', *International Journal of Service Industry Management*, Vol. 3, No. 2, page 33.

Esland, G.M. (1971) 'Teaching and learning as the organization of knowledge', in Young, M.F.D. (ed.) *Knowledge and Control* (Collier Macmillan, London).

Fisher, C.M. (1994) 'The differences between appraisal schemes: variation and acceptability - part I', *Personnel Review*, Vol. 23, No. 8, page 33.

Fisher, C.M. (1995) 'The differences between appraisal schemes: variation and acceptability - part II', *Personnel Review*, Vol. 24, No. 1, page 51.

Flood, J. (1996) 'Megalawyering in the global order', *International Journal of the Legal Profession*, Vol. 3, page 169.

Freidson, E. (1986) *Professional Powers* (University of Chicago Press, Chicago).

Galanter, M. and Palay, T. (1991) *Tournament of Lawyers* (University of Chicago Press, Chicago).

Gilson, R. and Mnookin, R. (1985) 'Sharing among the human capitalists: an economic inquiry into the corporate law firm and how partners split profits', *Stanford Law Review*, Vol. 37, page 313.

Grant, R.M. (1995) *Contemporary Strategy Analysis*, 2nd ed. (Oxford, Blackwell).

Greiner, L.E. (1972) 'Evolution and revolution as organizations grow', *Harvard Business Review*, July-August, page 37.

Griffiths, C. (1996) 'Balance of payments', *Legal Business*, September, page 14.

Gummesson, E. (1992) 'Quality dimensions: what to measure in service organizations', in Swartz, T.A., Bowen, D.E. and Brown, S.W. (eds.) *Advances in Services Marketing and Management*, Vol. 1 (JAI Press, Greenwich CO and London).

Hamel, G. and Heene, A. (eds) (1994) *Competence-based Competition* (John Wiley, Chichester).

Hamel, G. and Prahalad, C.K. (1990) 'The core competence of the corporation', *Harvard Business Review*, May–June, page 79.

Hamel, G. and Prahalad, C.K. (1994) *Competing for the Future* (Harvard Business School Press, Boston MA).

Handy, C.B. (1989) *The Age of Unreason* (Arrow Books, London).

Handy, C.B. (1991) *Gods of Management*, 3rd ed. (Century Business, London).

Handy, C.B. (1993) *Understanding Organizations*, 4th ed. (Penguin, Harmondsworth).

Handy, C.B. (1994) *The Empty Raincoat* (Hutchinson, London): published in the US as *The Age of Paradox*.

Handy, C.B. (1995) 'Trust and the virtual organization', *Harvard Business Review*, May-June, page 40.

Harris, T.A. (1973) *I'm OK - You're OK* (Pan, London).

Harwood-Richardson, S. (1991) *Annual Statistical Report 1991* (The Law Society, London).

Heinz, J.P. and Laumann, E. (1982) *Chicago Lawyers: The Social Structure of the Bar* (American Bar Foundation, Chicago).

Hendry, (1995) *Human Resource Management* (Butterworths, London).

Herzberg, F. (1968) 'One more time: how do you motivate employees?' *Harvard Business Review*, January-February.

Heskett, J.L., Jones, T.O., Loveman, G.W., Sasser, W.E. Jr and Schlesinger, L.A. (1994) 'Putting the service–profit chain to work', *Harvard Business Review*, March–April, page 164.

Hildebrandt, B.W. and Kaufman, J. (1988) *The Successful Law Firm: New Approaches to Structure and Management*, 2nd ed. (Prentice Hall, Clifton NJ).

Holzner, B. (1972) *Reality Construction in Society* (Schenkman, Cambridge MA).

Howard, J.H. (1991) 'Leadership, management and change in the professional service firm', *Business Quarterly*, Spring, page 111.

Hunt, J.W. (1992) *Managing People at Work*, 3rd ed. (McGraw-Hill, London).

Itami, H. (1987) *Mobilizing Invisible Assets* (Harvard University Press, Cambridge MA and London).

Jackson, B.S. (1994) 'Towards a semiotic model of professional practice, with some narrative reflections on the criminal process', *International Journal of the Legal Profession*, Vol. 1, page 55.

Jenkins, J. (1992) *Annual Statistical Report 1992* (The Law Society, London).

Jenkins, J. and Lewis, V. (1995) *Trends in the Solicitors' Profession: Annual Statistical Report 1995* (The Law Society, London).

Jones, T.O. and Sasser, W.E. Jr (1995) 'Why satisfied customers defect', *Harvard Business Review*, November–December, page 88.

Kaplan, R.S. and Norton, D.P. (1996) *The Balanced Scorecard* (Harvard Business School Press, Boston MA).

Kohn, A. (1993) 'Why incentive plans cannot work', *Harvard Business Review*, September–October, page 54.

Kotter, J.P. (1996) *Leading Change* (Harvard Business School Press, Boston MA).

Lambert, R. (1993) A Cycle of Change: the Transition Curve, unpublished paper, Cranfield School of Management.

Legal Business (1996) *Legal Business 100* (Legal Business Ltd, London).

Lewin, K. (1951) *Field Theory in Social Science* (Harper Row, London).

Lewis, V. (1996) *Trends in the Solicitors' Profession: Annual Statistical Report 1996* (The Law Society, London).

Lovelock, C.H. (1983) 'Classifying services to gain strategic marketing insights', *Journal of Marketing*, Vol. 47, Summer, page 9.

Lovelock, C.H. (1992) 'A basic toolkit for service managers', in Lovelock, C.H. (ed.) (1992) *Managing Services* (Prentice Hall, Englewood Cliffs NJ).

Machiavelli, N. (1995) *The Prince*, translated by George Bull (Penguin Books, London) (written 1513, first published 1532).

Maister, D.H. (1984) 'Profitability: beating the downward trend', *The American Lawyer, Journal of Management Consulting*, Vol. 1, No. 4, page 39.

Maister, D.H. (1993a) *Managing the Professional Service Firm* (The Free Press, New York).

Maister, D.H. (1993b) 'Where the profits come from', *Legal Business*, October, page 69.

Maister, D.H. (1994) 'Measuring profitability matter by matter', *The American Lawyer*, July/August, page 38.

Maister, D.H. (1997) *True Professionalism* (The Free Press, New York).

Malone, G. and Mudrick, H. (1992) *Anatomy of a Law Firm Merger* (American Bar Association, Chicago IL).

Malos, S.B. and Campion, M.A. (1995) 'An options-based model of career mobility in professional service firms', *Academy of Management Review*, Vol. 20, No. 3, page 611.

Maslow, A.H. (1954) *Motivation and Personality* (Harper, New York).

Mayson, S.W. (1992) *Personal Management Skills* (Blackstone Press, London).

Mayson, S.W. (1993) 'The client-driven lawyer', in Shapland & Le Grys (eds.) *The Changing Shape of the Legal Profession* (Institute for the Study of the Legal Profession, Sheffield).

McCall, S., Andrews, C. and Gormley, P. (1996) *Fit for the Future* (The Law Society, London).

McClelland, D.C. (1961) *The Achieving Society* (Van Nostrand, New York).

McClelland, D.C. and Boyatzis, R.E. (1982) 'Leadership motive pattern and long-term success in management', *Journal of Applied Psychology* Vol. 67, page 737.

McGregor, D. (1960) *The Human Side of Enterprise* (McGraw-Hill, London).

Mill, R.C. (1989) 'Productivity in service organisations', in Jones, P. (ed.) *Management in Service Industries* (Pitman, London).

Miller, R.B. and Heiman, S.E. (1987) *Conceptual Selling* (Warner Books, New York).

Mintzberg, H. (1987) 'Crafting strategy', *Harvard Business Review*, July-August, page 66.

Mintzberg, H. (1993) *Structure in Fives: Designing Effective Organizations* (Prentice Hall, Englewood Cliffs NJ).

Mintzberg, H. (1994) *The Rise and Fall of Strategic Planning* (Prentice Hall, Hemel Hempstead).

Morris, T. and Empson, L. (1996) 'Organisation and expertise: knowledge bases and the management of the professional service firm', paper for BAM Conference, Aston University, 17 September.

Morris, T. and Pinnington, A. (1996a) *Patterns of Profit Sharing in Professional Partnership Firms*, Centre for Organisational Research Working Paper Series No. 41, London Business School.

Morris, T. and Pinnington, A. (1996b) *Promotion to Partner and the Reform of Professional Firms*, Centre for Organisational Research Working Paper Series No. 42, London Business School.

Morris, T. and Pinnington, A. (1996c) *Evaluating expert labour: An empirical analysis of the adoption and use of formal appraisal in professional firms*, Centre for Organisational Research Working Paper Series No. 48, London Business School.

Mowbray, R. (1997) *Maximising the Profitability of Law Firms* (Blackstone Press, London).

Mudrick, H. and Altonji, J. (1993) 'Leverage: looking beyond the partner/associate ratio', *Hildebrandt Report*, Vol. 7, No. 4, page 1.

Nelson, R.L. (1988) *Partners with Power* (University of California Press, Berkeley).

Nelson, R.R. and Winter, S.G. (1982) *An Evolutionary Theory of Economic Change* (Belknap Press, Cambridge MA).

Nonaka, I. and Takeuchi, H. (1995) *The Knowledge-creating Company* (Oxford University Press, New York and Oxford).

Office for National Statistics (1996) *Key Data* (HMSO, London).

Office for National Statistics (1997) *Labour Market Trends*, Vol. 105, No. 1 (The Stationery Office, London).

Orey, M. (1991) 'Take me to your leader', *American Lawyer*, December, page 3.

Paine, L.S. (1994) 'Managing for organizational integrity', *Harvard Business Review*, March–April, page 106.

Parasuraman, A., Zeithaml, V.A. and Berry, L.L. (1985) 'A conceptual model of service quality and its implications for future research', *Journal of Marketing*, Fall, page 41.

Parry, R. (1991) *People Businesses* (Business Books, London).

Paterson, A.A. (1996) 'Professionalism and the legal services market', *International Journal of the Legal Profession*, Vol. 3, page 137.

Payne, A. (1993) *The Essence of Services Marketing* (Prentice Hall, Hemel Hempstead).

Pearn, M., Roderick, C. and Mulrooney, C. (1995) *Learning Organizations in Practice* (McGraw Hill, London).

Peters, T.J. (1992) *Liberation Management* (Pan Macmillan, London).

Peters, T.J. and Waterman, R.H. (1982) *In Search of Excellence* (Harper-Collins, New York).

Polanyi, M. (1966) *The Tacit Dimension* (Peter Smith, Gloucester MA).

Porter, M.E. (1980) *Competitive Strategy* (The Free Press, New York).

Porter, M.E. (1985) *Competitive Advantage* (The Free Press, New York).

Porter, M.E. (1996) 'What is strategy?', *Harvard Business Review*, November–December, page 61.

Quinn, J.B. (1992) *Intelligent Enterprise* (The Free Press, New York).

Raelin, J.A. (1989) 'An anatomy of autonomy: managing professionals', *The Academy of Management Executive*, Vol. III, No. 3, page 216.

Rayport, J.F. and Sviokla, J.J. (1994) 'Managing in the marketspace', *Harvard Business Review*, November-December, page 141.

Reed, R. and DeFillippi, R. (1990) 'Causal ambiguity, barriers to imitation, and sustainable competitive advantage', *Academy of Management Review*, Vol. 15, page 88.

Reich, R.B. (1991) *The Work of Nations* (Simon & Schuster, London).

Reiss, G. (1992) *Project Management Demystified* (E & FN Spon, London).
Ricketts, M. (1994) *The Economics of Business Enterprise*, 2nd. ed. (Harvester Wheatsheaf, Hemel Hempstead).
Roach, S.S. (1991) 'Services under siege — the restructuring imperative', *Harvard Business Review*, September–October, page 82.
Roach, S.S. (1996) 'The hollow ring of the productivity revival', *Harvard Business Review*, November–December, page 81.
Salter, M. (1994) 'On the idea of a legal world', *International Journal of the Legal Profession*, Vol. 1, page 283.
Scarbrough, H. (ed.) (1996) *The Management of Expertise* (Macmillan, Basingstoke).
Schein, E.H. (1983) 'The role of the founder in creating organizational culture', *Organizational Dynamics*, Summer, page 13.
Schneider, B. (1994) 'HRM — a service perspective', *International Journal of Service Industry Management*, Vol. 5, No. 1, page 64.
Schön, D.A. (1991) *The Reflective Practitioner* (Ashgate Publishing, Aldershot).
Schultz, T.W. (1971) *Investment in Human Capital* (The Free Press, New York).
Secretan, L.H.K. (1997) *Reclaiming Higher Ground* (McGraw Hill, New York).
Sells, B. (1994) *The Soul of the Law* (Element Books, Shaftesbury).
Senge, P.M. (1993) *The Fifth Discipline* (Century Business, London).
Shostack, G.L. (1992) 'Understanding services through blueprinting', *Advances in Services Marketing and Management*, Vol. 1, page 75.
Skordaki, E. (1996) 'Glass slippers and glass ceilings: women in the legal profession', *International Journal of the Legal Profession*, Vol. 3, page 7.
Skordaki, E. and Walker, D. (1994) *Regulating and Charging for Legal Services: An International Comparison*, Research Study No. 12 (The Law Society, London).
Stewart, T.A. (1997) *Intellectual Capital* (Nicholas Brealey, London).
Stoakes, C. (1994) 'Law firm marketing: turning the tanker', *International Law Firm Management*, February/March, page 26.
Strong, T. (1914) *Landmarks of a Lawyer's Lifetime* (Dodd Mead, New York).
Sull, D. (1997) 'Blinded by science', *Financial Times*, 3 February, page 13.
Susskind, R. (1996) *The Future of Law* (Clarendon Press, Oxford).
Sveiby, K.-E. and Lloyd, T. (1987) *Managing Know-how* (Bloomsbury Press, London).
Tannenbaum, R. and Schmidt, W.H. (1973) 'How to choose a leadership pattern', *Harvard Business Review*, May–June.
Toffler, A. & H. (1994) *Creating a New Civilization* (Turner Publishing, Atlanta GA).
Vaitilingam, R. (1994) *The Financial Times Guide to Using Economics and Economic Indicators* (Pitman, London).
von Krogh, G. and Roos, J. (eds) (1996) *Managing Knowledge* (Sage, London).

Webb, J. (1995) 'Where the action is: developing artistry in legal education', *International Journal of the Legal Profession*, Vol. 2, page 187.

Willet, S. (1966) *The Mortgage* (Mandarin, London).

Williamson, O.E. (1975) *Markets and Hierarchies: Analysis and Antitrust
Implications*, (Collier Macmillan, London).

Williamson, O.E. (1985) *The Economic Institutions of Capitalism: Firms,
Markets, Relational Contracting* (Collier Macmillan, London).

Williamson, O.E. and Winter, S.G. (eds) (1993) *The Nature of the Firm:
Origins, Evolution, and Development* (Oxford University Press, Oxford).

Wilson, D.A. (1996) *Managing Knowledge* (Butterworth-Heinemann, Oxford).

Wilson, D.C. (1992) *A Strategy of Change: Concepts and Controversies in
the Management of Change* (Routledge, London).

INDEX